DRAWING SCHOOL

FUNDAMENTALS

FOR THE BEGINNER

A COMPREHENSIVE DRAWING COURSE

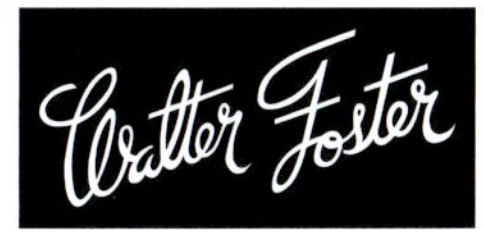

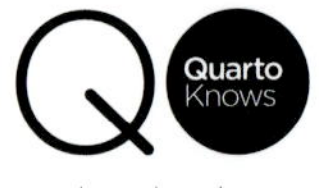

Brimming with creative inspiration, how-to projects, and useful information to enrich your everyday life, Quarto Knows is a favorite destination for those pursuing their interests and passions. Visit our site and dig deeper with our books into your area of interest: Quarto Creates, Quarto Cooks, Quarto Homes, Quarto Lives, Quarto Drives, Quarto Explores, Quarto Gifts, or Quarto Kids.

First Published in 2018 by Walter Foster Publishing, an imprint of The Quarto Group.
6 Orchard Road, Suite 100, Lake Forest, CA 92630, USA.
T (949) 380-7510 **F** (949) 380-7575 **www.QuartoKnows.com**

ISBN: 978-1-63322-486-5

Digital edition published in 2018
eISBN: 978-1-63322-487-2

Printed in China
10 9 8 7 6 5 4 3 2

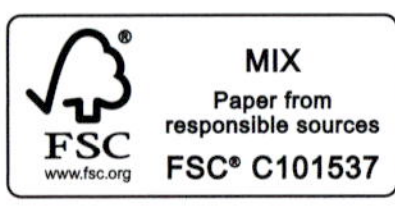

DRAWING SCHOOL

FUNDAMENTALS

FOR THE BEGINNER

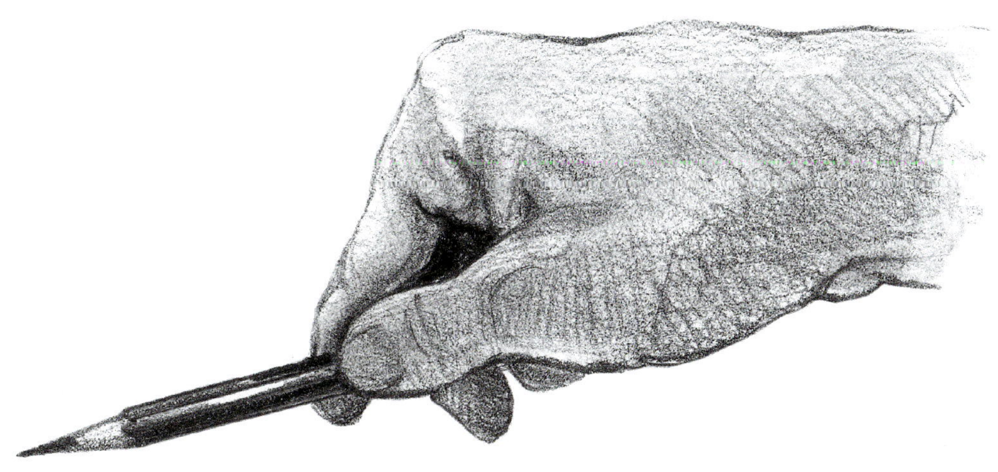

TABLE OF CONTENTS

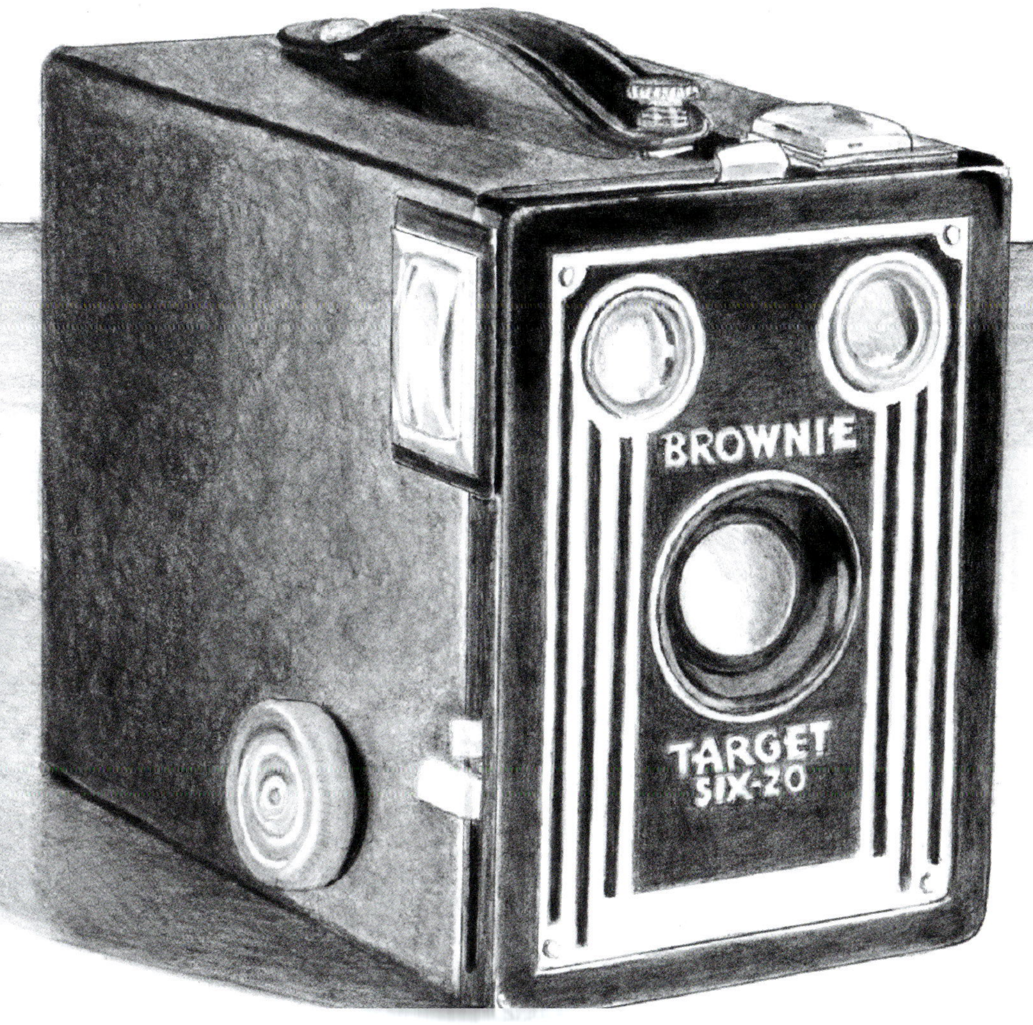
BROWNIE
TARGET
SIX-20

Introduction

The ideas, concepts, and techniques in this book are based on an academic model of drawing instruction developed over the last 500 years, first taught in Europe and now worldwide. These traditional principles are alive and well wherever there is a desire to impart formal fundamental and foundational instruction in realistic, accurate artistic interpretation.

This book seeks to impart to the serious, but beginning, drawing student a solid foundation that leads to the creation of artwork that combines strong draftsmanship, spatial comprehension, and an overall energetic drawing experience.

The most important aspects of successful drawing are sensitivity, focus, and passion. We are all born with the ability to create; in some children this ability is nurtured, while in others it may be repressed. As adults, we still have the ability to "tap into" our creative side, but it takes practice, patience, and guidance.

Sensitivity

Sensitivity in drawing refers to the handling of tools, as well as the ability to use visual sense to isolate the structure, organization, and mood of a subject. By manipulating the pressure of a drawing tool on paper, the artist can create multitudes of variable line weights: long lines; short, choppy strokes; bold calligraphic marks; and nuanced, subtle tonalities. This is called "mark-making," and most of us have been doing it since before we could talk or walk. With direction, mark-making can be refined to the point where recognizable subject matter can be created. But it is important to note that all marks are not created equal! One of the most important attributes of a successful drawing is a sensitive application of varied line weight.

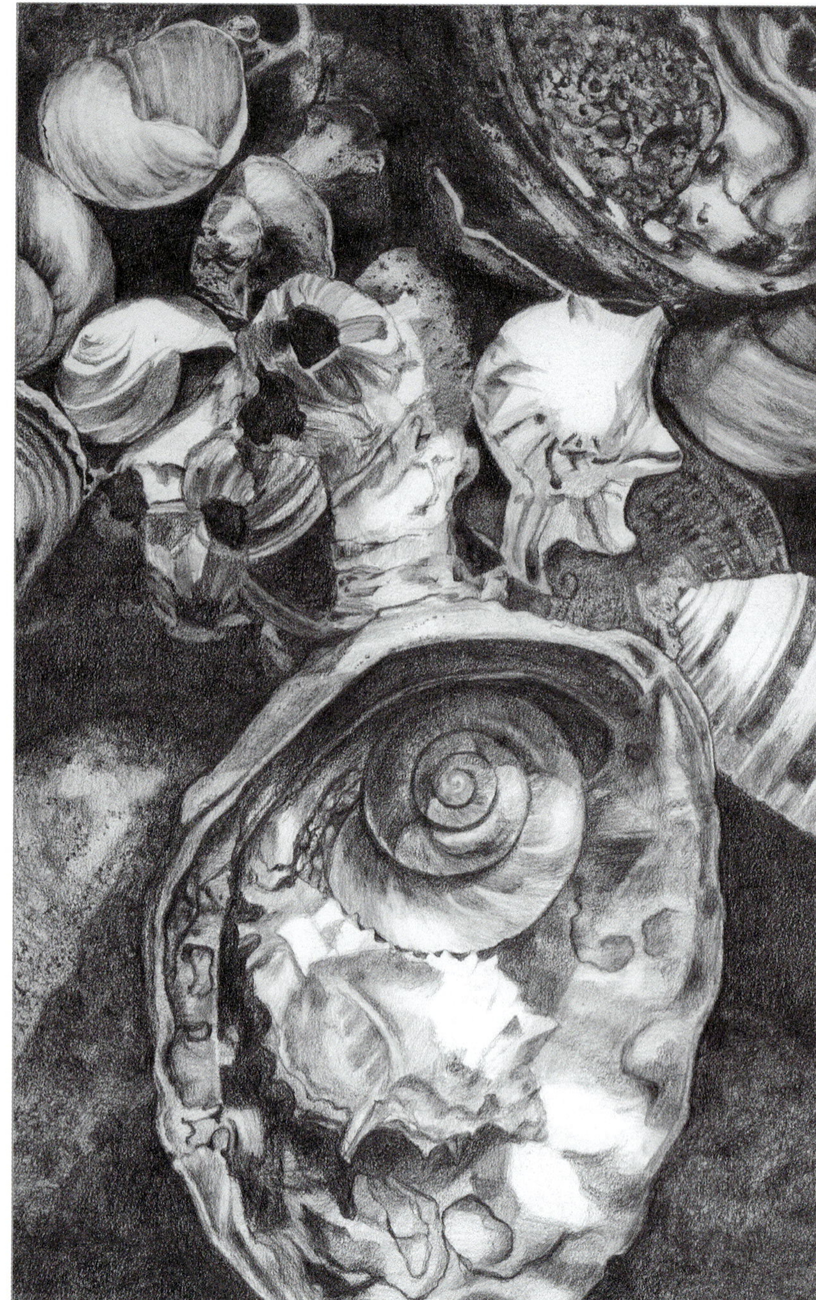

STUDENT DRAWING by Joanna Mendoza.

Focus

In drawing, focus refers to the ability to concentrate on and develop a clear image of the subject. In this book, the emphasis is on drawing a realistic, or representational, interpretation of the subject from observation. It is about attempting to depict a three-dimensional form on a two-dimensional surface. This is a visual alchemy that artists have struggled to achieve since the days of the first cave paintings. Focus is an essential skill that can be achieved with patience, practice, and the right environment. For some, it is the right combination of silence and/or background music that can help create this focused environment. Most importantly, try to clear your mind of clutter and negative thoughts, and avoid undue visual or aural distractions.

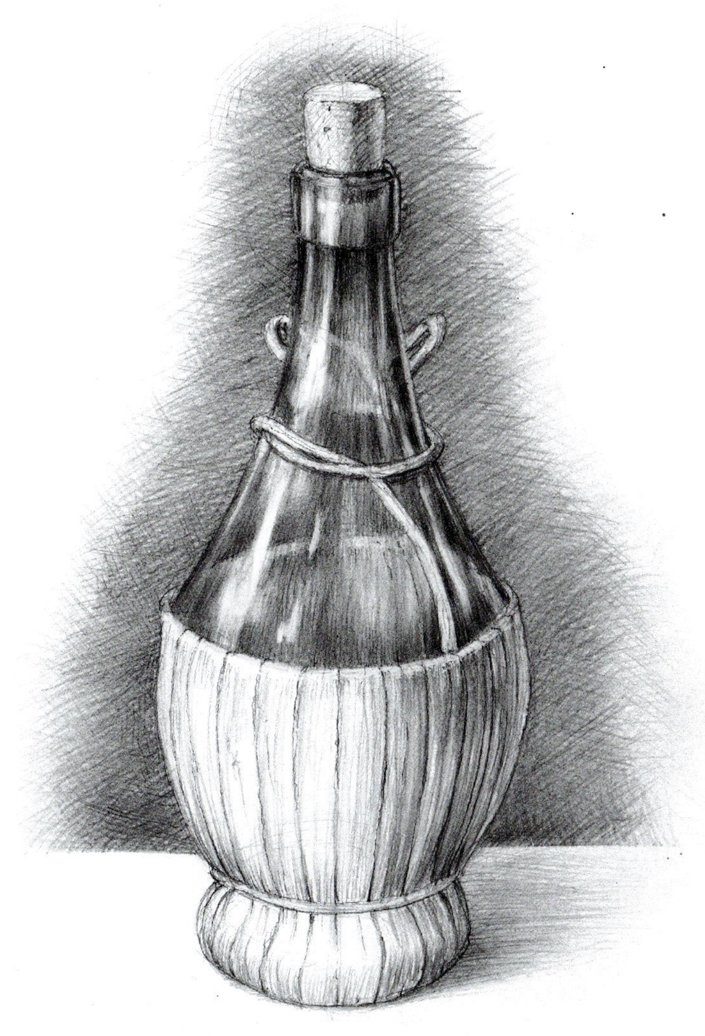

Passion

Passion in drawing, as in life, is the desire for something meaningful that can fulfill, entertain, heal, and ultimately satisfy the creative impulse. You can attain sensitivity and focus, but without the third leg of the stool—passion—you won't have the desire to draw all the time. And that is what makes a successful artist—drawing tirelessly, constantly, and happily, over and over again.

Getting Started

In this book, I will take you through a journey of many steps, some easy and some challenging, as we continue along a path that will establish a strong foundation for the fundamentals of drawing. It is my goal to inform, motivate, and inspire you every step of the way along this new creative journey.

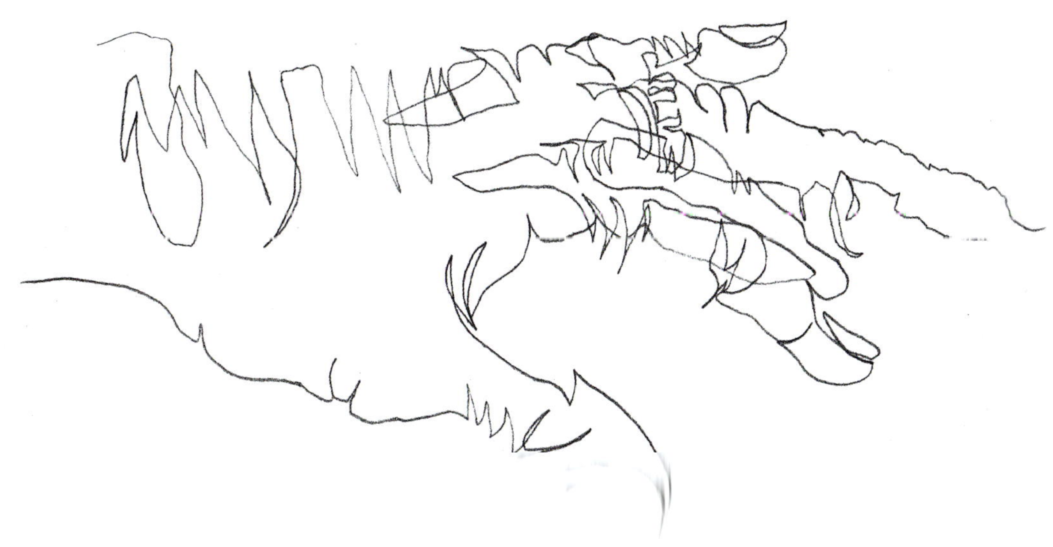

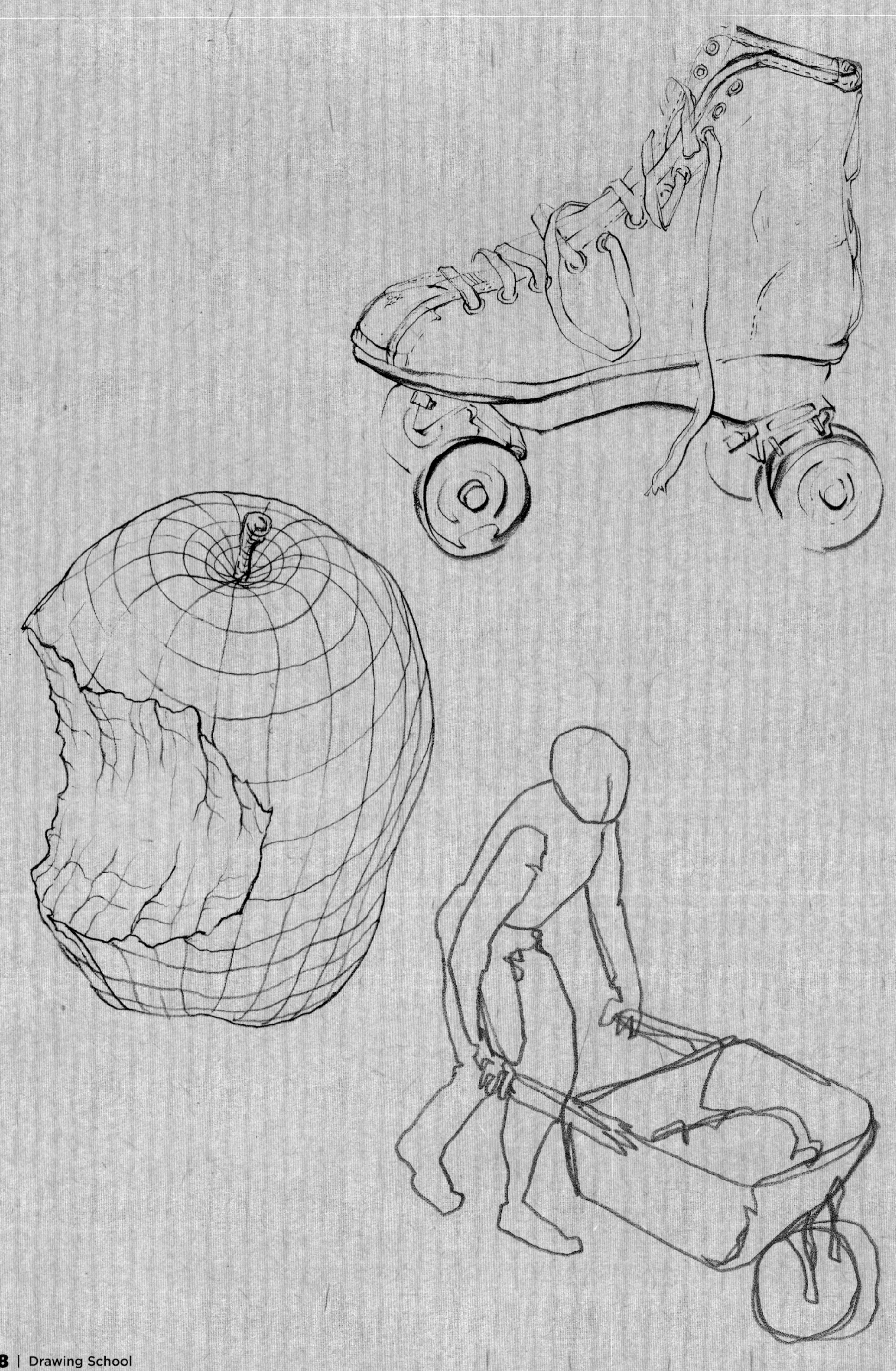

PROCESS & PROCEDURE

In this initial chapter, we will explore the arrangement of the drawing surface for maximum effectiveness, how holding a pencil can make a difference in the way a drawing looks, how making marks on a drawing surface can represent a dimensional reality, and how to successfully build a drawing from the understanding and use of a few key fundamental steps. Remember: A long journey begins with small steps.

Getting Started

Drawing & Viewing Arrangement

The ideal way to see a subject and the drawing surface simultaneously is to elevate the drawing surface as vertically as possible, while maintaining a comfortable and accessible drawing position. The artist's eyes should be the only things that move, back and forth or up and down, from the subject to the paper. The more a drawing surface is angled away from the artist's line of sight, the less the artist will be able to comfortably view the subject. Working at an easel is an advantageous position for a variety of reasons. Most importantly, the less the artist has to move his or her head the better.

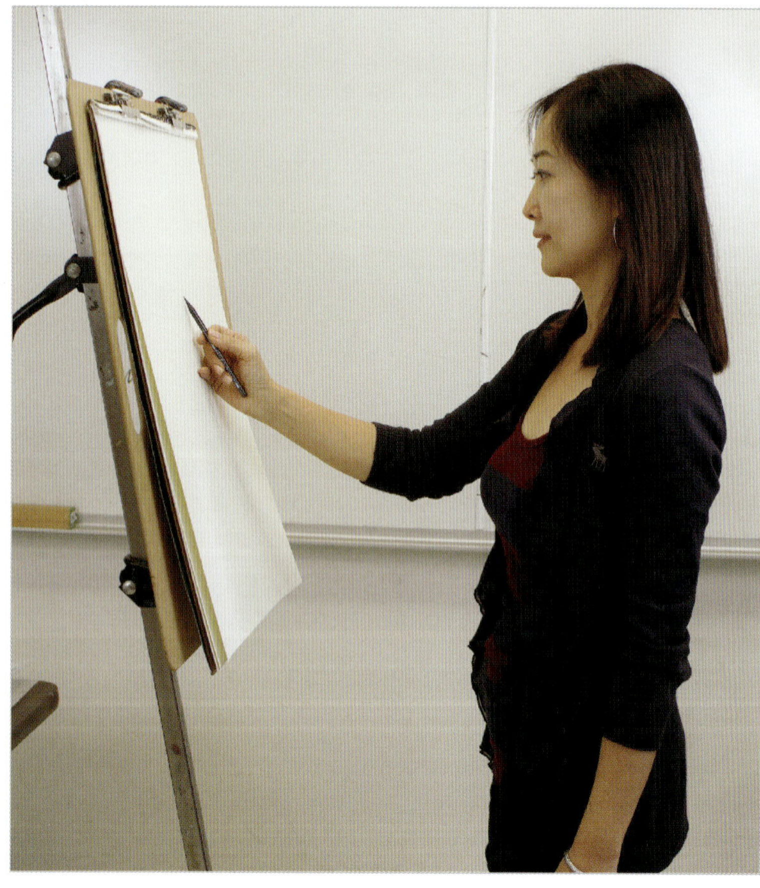

An easel allows the artist to simultaneously face the paper and the subject while drawing. Set up the easel slightly to one side of the subject so that you can see it as well as the paper with a slight back-and-forth motion of the eyes. Another advantage is the ability to more easily step back from the easel to critically evaluate the process.

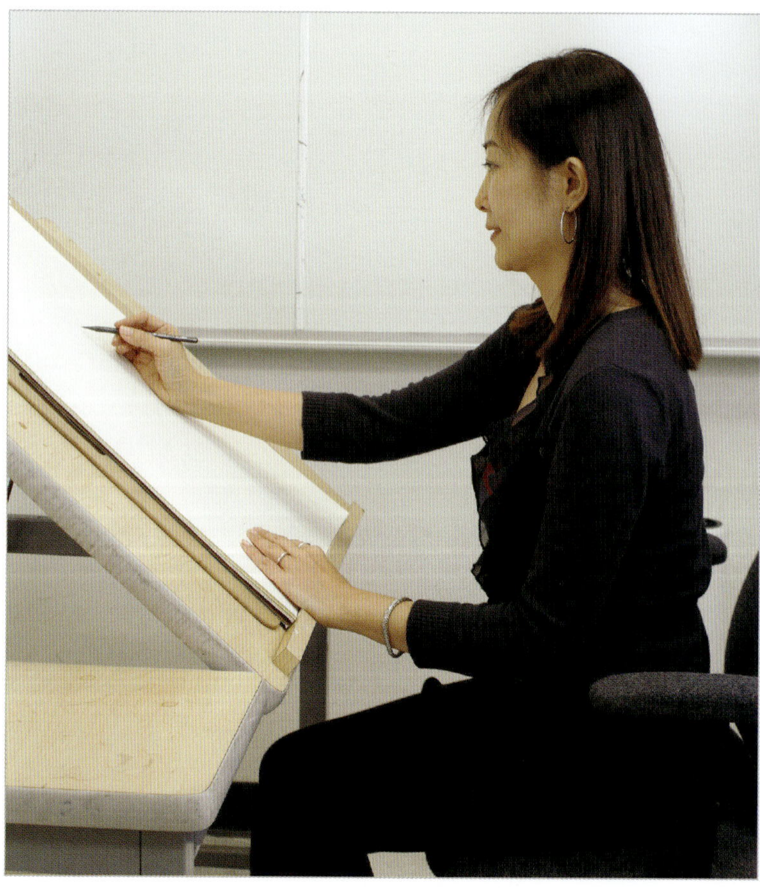

You may also choose to use a drawing table, which can be elevated to a height similar to the viewing situation an easel would provide. Elevate the table as close to a 90-degree viewing angle as possible, while still being able to see the subject over the elevated table edge.

Holding the Pencil

There are two ways to hold a pencil while drawing. The first is the basic overhand, or "handwriting," position. The pencil sits in the crook between the thumb and first finger, with the palm of the hand parallel to the paper. Most people instinctively hold a pencil this way because it is comfortable and how we are typically taught to write. This is a good way to hold the pencil if you are working on detail and want more control.

The second way to hold a pencil is in the "underhand" position. The pencil sits comfortably in the palm of the hand, with the barrel balanced and supported by the thumb and the first and second fingers. There are several variations of this position. The palm may be placed parallel to the paper or at a right angle to the paper's surface. The pencil may be gripped at the point for more control or further up the pencil barrel for more expressive mark-making.

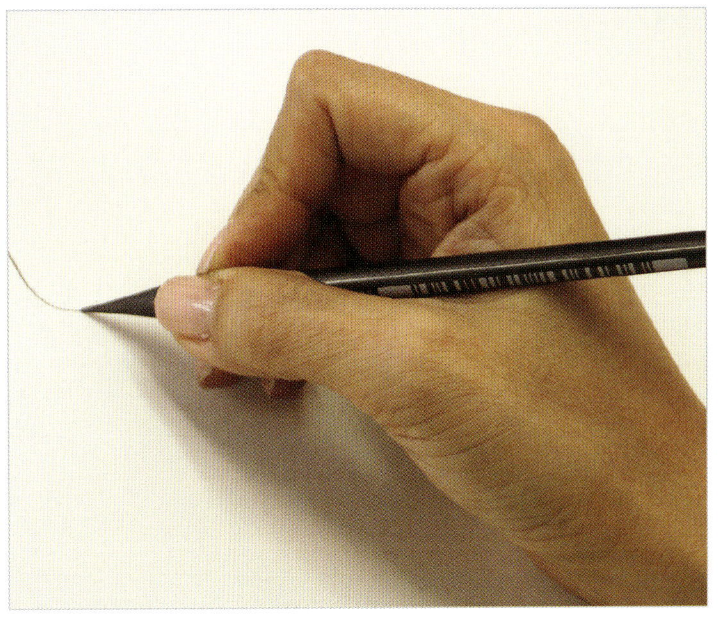

Overhand

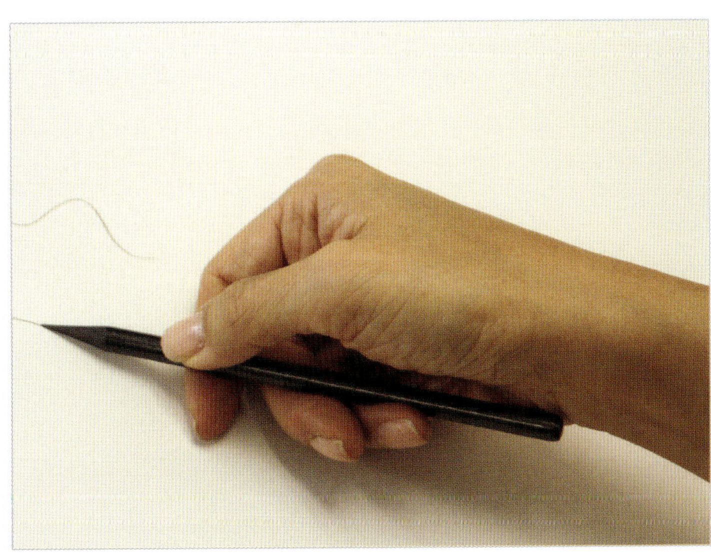

Underhand

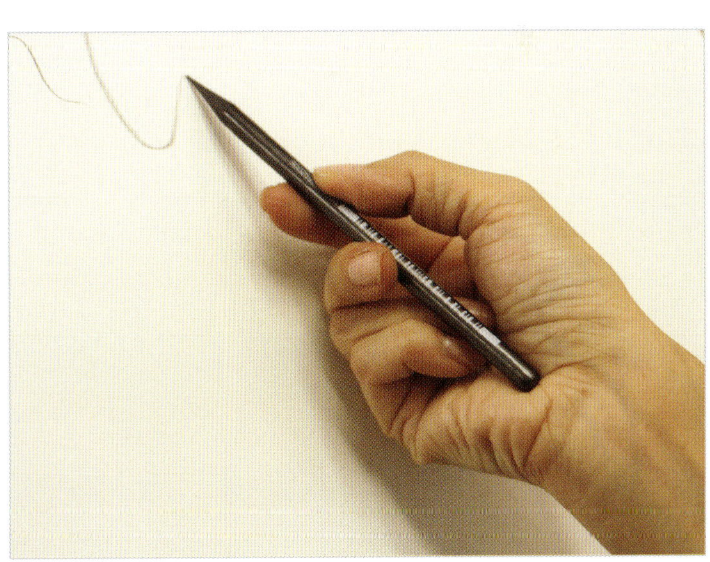

Mark-Making

The idea of making a mark to record an interpretation of an object is, and has always been, a primary goal of humanity across all cultures. All representational drawing is based on this abstract concept: the accumulation of marks or lines meant to represent reality. Marks can also be purely ornamental or nonrepresentational, but here we refer to mark-making as a method that leads to a perception of reality and an understanding of a subject. Mark-making can be as varied as the tools used to make it.

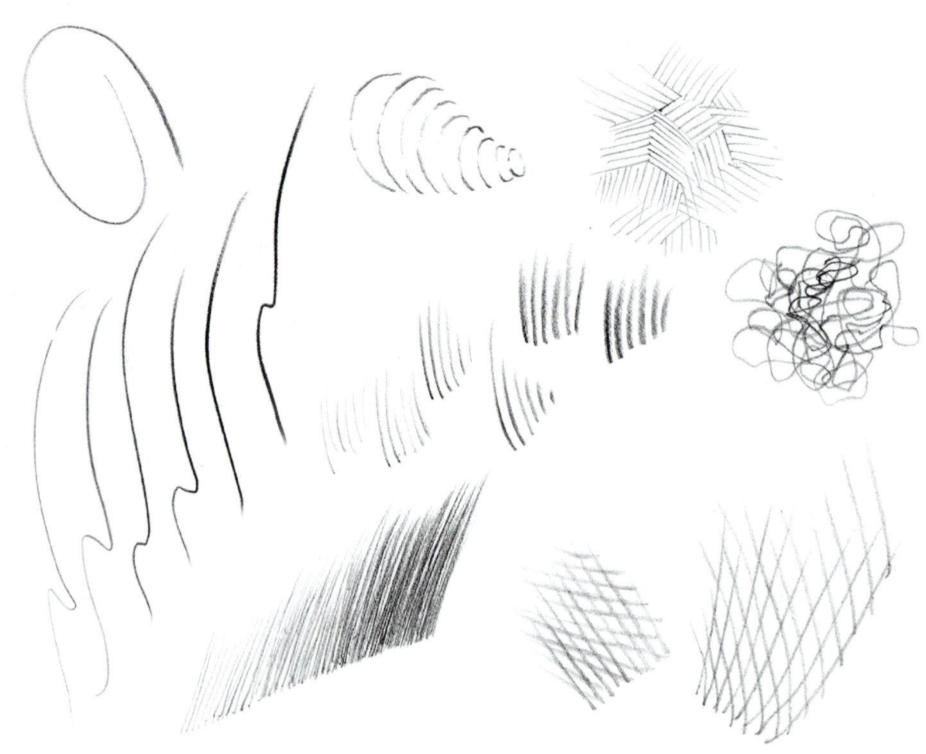

Line Weight

The weight of a line refers to the lightness or darkness of the line based on how much pressure the artist chooses to apply with his or her pencil. A weighted, or variable, line weight is much livelier and more interesting than a line that remains consistently the same. Imagine a lilting delivery of a Shakespeare soliloquy by an accomplished actor, and then compare it with a flat, monotone approach.

Line weight and variety in a drawing can convey texture, weight, and lighting on the surface of a form. It can also serve to focus the viewer's eye on a certain part of the drawing—strong line weight draws the eye more than weak line weight. This is helpful in demonstrating visual hierarchy, when one object is in front of another.

Variable line weight can be used to lead a viewer through the journey of a drawing, creating a dialogue between the artist and the viewer.

Gesture Drawing & Contour Line Drawing

Gesture drawing and contour line drawing are two opposite approaches to the drawing process; however, they can be used together. Gesture drawing is a very quick, all-encompassing glimpse of the subject. Contour line drawing is a slow, methodical, detailed observation of the subject. When used together, these two differing approaches to drawing the subject can become the foundation for a successful drawing.

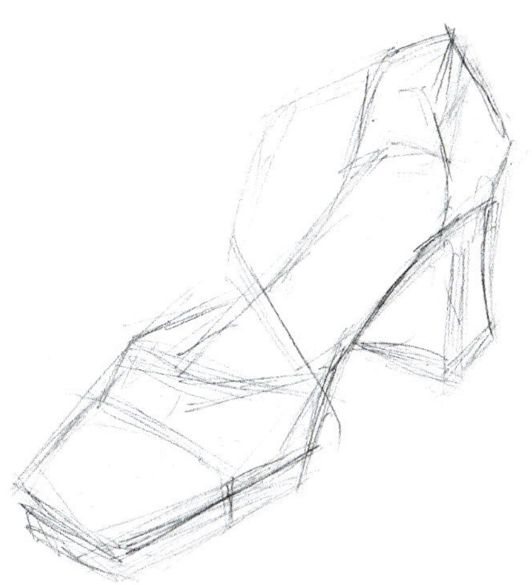

Gesture Drawing

A gesture drawing conveys an interpretation of the subject through continuously flowing, rhythmic line, without any sense of detail or refinement. Drawing in this manner can be used to warm up your hand, like exercising. A gesture drawing can also act as a preliminary sketch for a more detailed drawing. This method employs continuous movement of the arm and hand without lifting the pencil off the paper or using short, choppy lines or strokes. Imagine that the pencil is actually on the form itself and not merely touching the paper. This takes practice and patience to do well, but it is very much worth the effort.

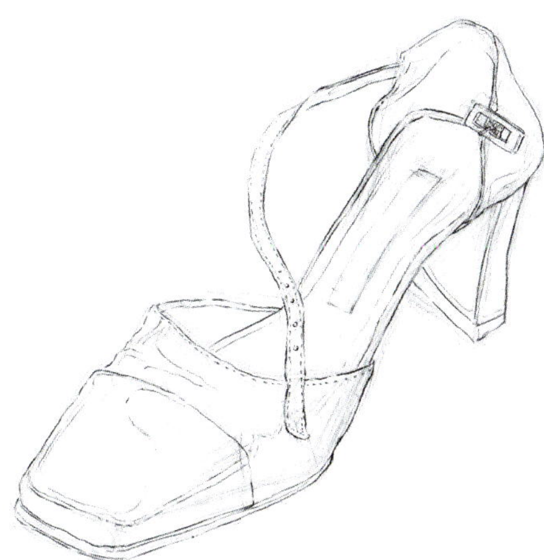

Contour Line Drawing

Contour line drawing is a detailed interpretation of the subject matter, without employing tone or shading. This type of drawing is not just a simple outline of the outer edges of a subject, however, which would give the impression only of a flat shape or silhouette. Dimensionality is achieved through a careful investigation of all inner and outer "touchable" edges. To develop and implement the sensitivity and skill that this type of drawing requires, the eye and the drawing hand should travel around the form of the subject at a slow, searching pace, without hurried sketching.

Blind Contour Line Drawing

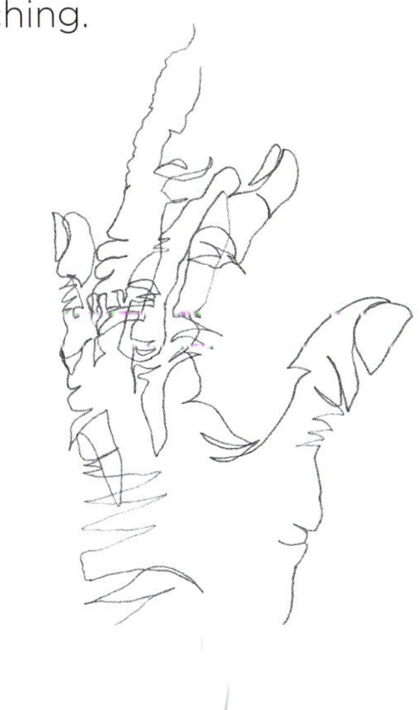

Blind contour line drawing is a valuable exercise in learning and refining your observational skills. Drawing a subject on paper without looking at the paper while you draw involves a careful approach to observation and good hand-eye coordination. Start drawing anywhere on the form, and imagine that the tip of the pencil is touching the actual form. As you move the pencil slowly around the form in a continuous line, only look at the subject, not the paper. You may stop at any time and glance at the paper to relocate your pencil on the form, but don't start drawing again until you [illegible]

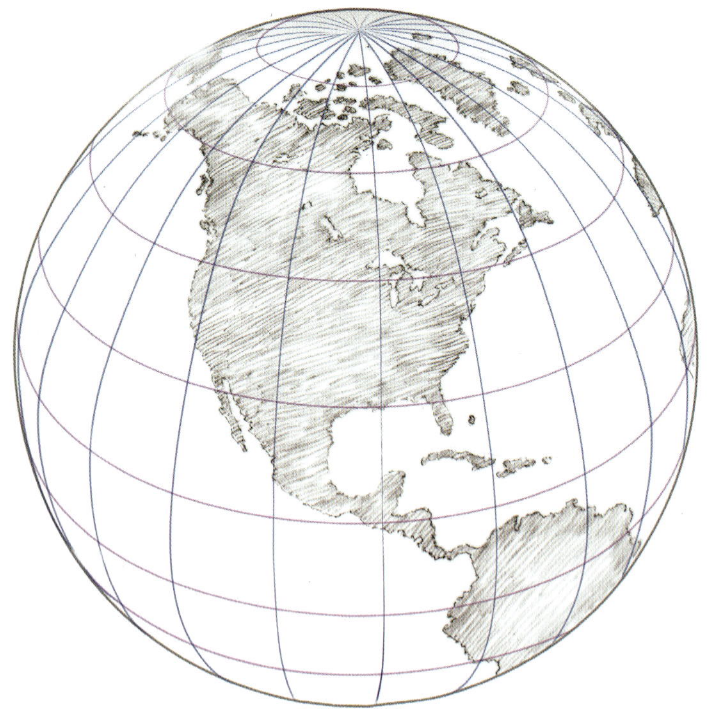

Cross-Contour Drawing

Cross-contour drawing is an effective technique that conveys the feeling of a three-dimensional form on a two-dimensional surface. This technique builds on contour drawing by describing the mass and volume of an object, in addition to its shape.

This technique employs sensitive line application, including variable weight lines across the entire surface of a subject, not just the touchable edges. This continuous line application is ideal for conveying the variations inherent in natural, organic forms.

To understand how to start this type of drawing, think of a basic three-dimensional geometric form, such as a sphere, and understand how horizontal and vertical lines would look across it's surface. As these parallel lines move toward the tops and sides of the sphere, notice how they appear closer together until they almost converge. This is known as *foreshortening*.

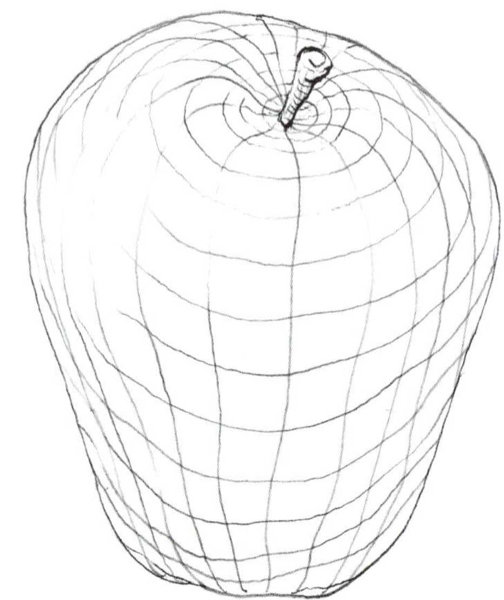

Applying this technique to a more organic shape, such as an apple, demonstrates how this type of mark-making shows the exterior shape of an apple as well as the subtle variations within the form. Imagine wrapping a string or wire around the form to represent drawn lines as they would appear on the object's surface.

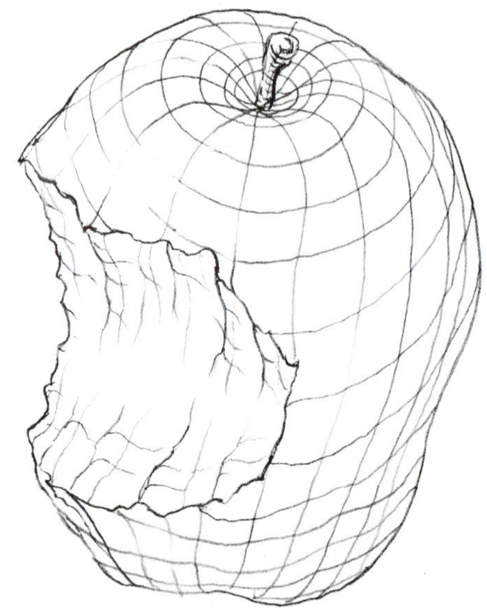

To create even more three-dimensionality and a sense of volume, use a variable weight line across the form's surface, which can elicit a feeling of depth (nearness or distance from the viewer), as darker lines tend to come forward and lighter lines tend to recede. This is also an effective way to show the effects of light on the form, as lighter lines suggest areas facing a light source and darker lines suggest those in shadow.

Additional Considerations

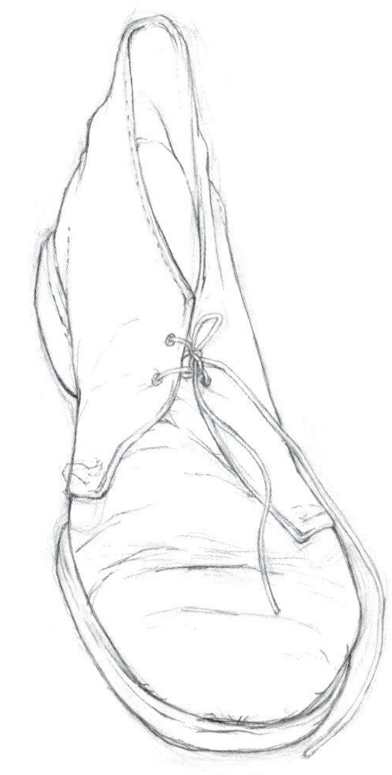

Foreshortened Forms

When an elongated subject, such as a shoe, is viewed at a certain angle (sometimes called "straight on"), the overall length of the subject seems much smaller, or shorter in length, than we actually know it to be. This is the result of compression of space within the form. This compression is best explained by the overlapping of forms in a "foreshortened" manner. We will discuss this more thoroughly in the chapter on how we see and interpret our subjects.

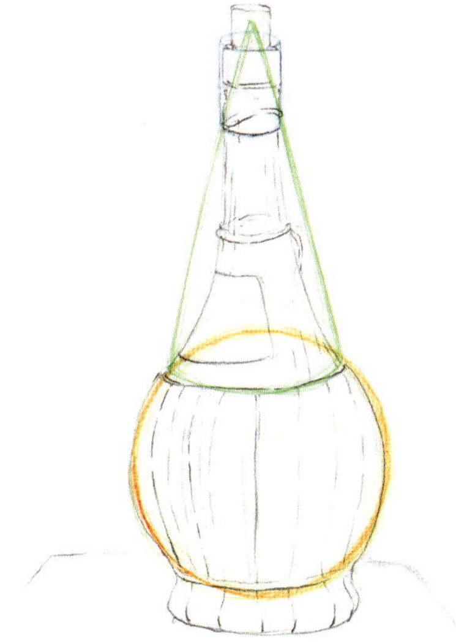

Shapes

An important aspect of the initial gesture block-in sketch is to always start with the basic geometric shapes that most resemble the form or forms you see. The most common shapes found within most forms, either organic or man-made, are the square, sphere, cylinder, and cone.

Overlapping Objects

When combining multiple objects in a small composition, start with a gesture drawing of the furthermost object. As the objects advance toward you and overlap each other, sketch them in loosely and lightly over the object behind it. If you sketch each object's initial shape, each object retains its own three-dimensional space or volume (also called its "footprint").

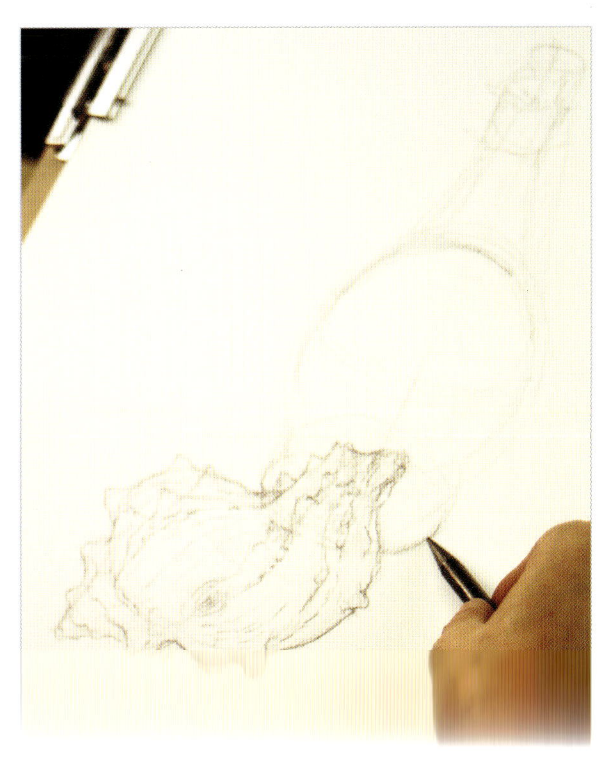

When you are finished with the blocked-in gesture sketch, complete a contour line drawing over the light gesture sketch of the object that is closest to you in the foreground. This method allows you to maintain control over overlapping shapes. Finish the contour line drawing for the nearest object before you start on the object behind it [illegible]

Transferring an Image

A quick way to achieve an accurate drawing, without the initial stages of sketching, is to transfer the main lines of a photographic reference onto your drawing paper. First, print out your reference at the size you plan to draw it. Then place a sheet of tracing paper over the printout and trace the outlines. Coat the back of the tracing paper with an even layer of graphite and place it over a clean sheet of drawing paper, graphite-side down. (Instead of coating the back of the tracing paper, you might choose to purchase and use transfer paper, which already has one side coated with graphite.) Tape or hold the papers together and lightly trace your outlines with a ballpoint pen or stylus. The lines of your tracing paper will transfer to the drawing paper below.

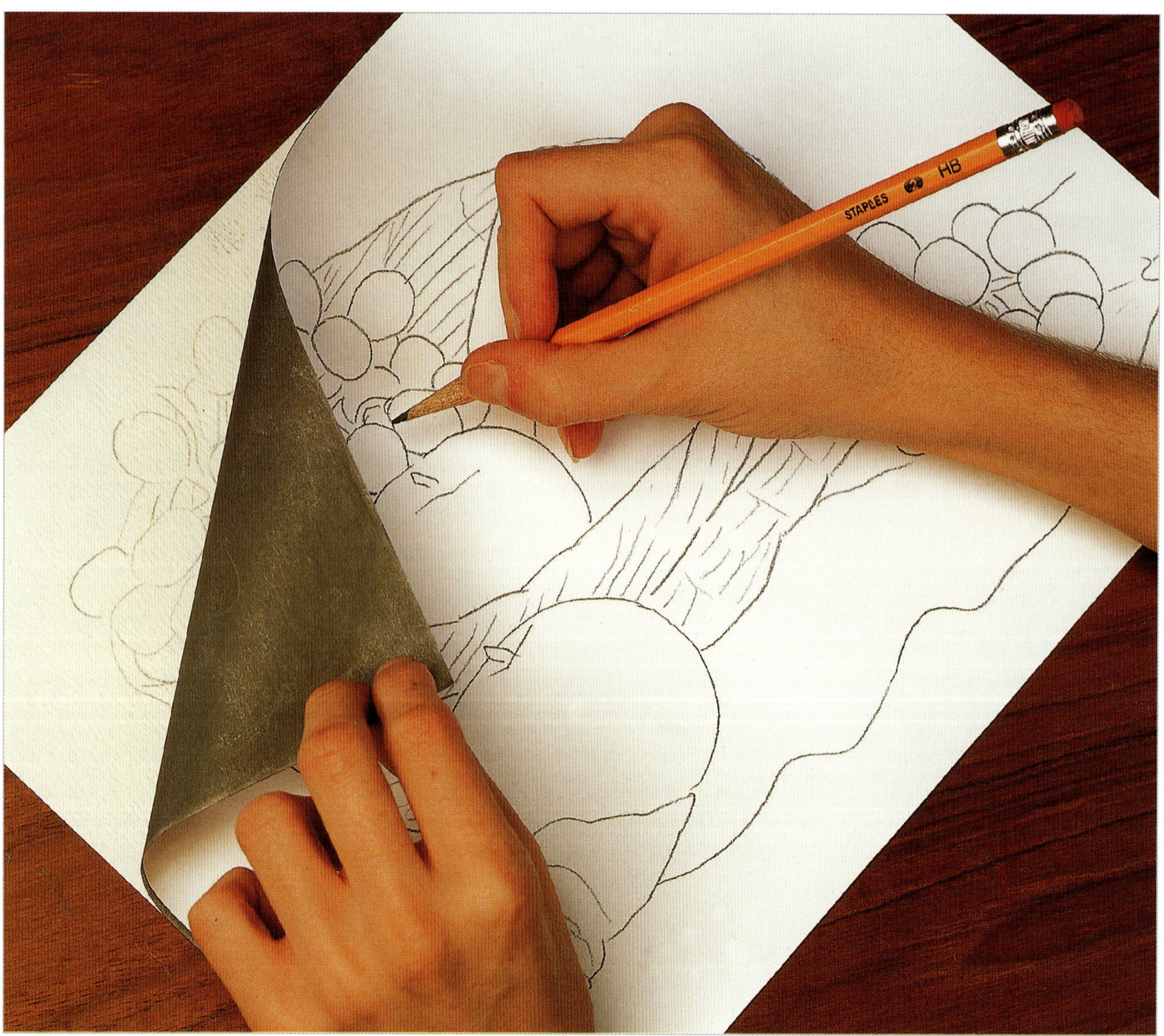

While tracing the lines, occasionally lift the corner of the sketch (and the transfer paper, if present) to make sure the lines that have transferred aren't too light or too dark.

Learning to "See"

Many beginners draw without really looking carefully at their subject; instead of drawing what they actually see, they draw what they think they see. Try drawing something you know well, such as your hand, without looking at it. Chances are your finished drawing won't look as realistic as you expected. That's because you drew what you think your hand looks like. Instead, you need to forget about all your preconceptions and learn to draw only what you really see. The following contour drawing exercises are great for training your eye and hand to work together to represent what is truly in front of you.

Contour Drawing

In contour drawing, you pick a starting point on your subject and then draw only the contours—or outlines—of the shapes you see. Because you're not looking at your paper, you're training your hand to draw the lines exactly as your eye sees them. Try doing some contour drawings of your own; you'll be surprised at how well you're able to capture the subjects.

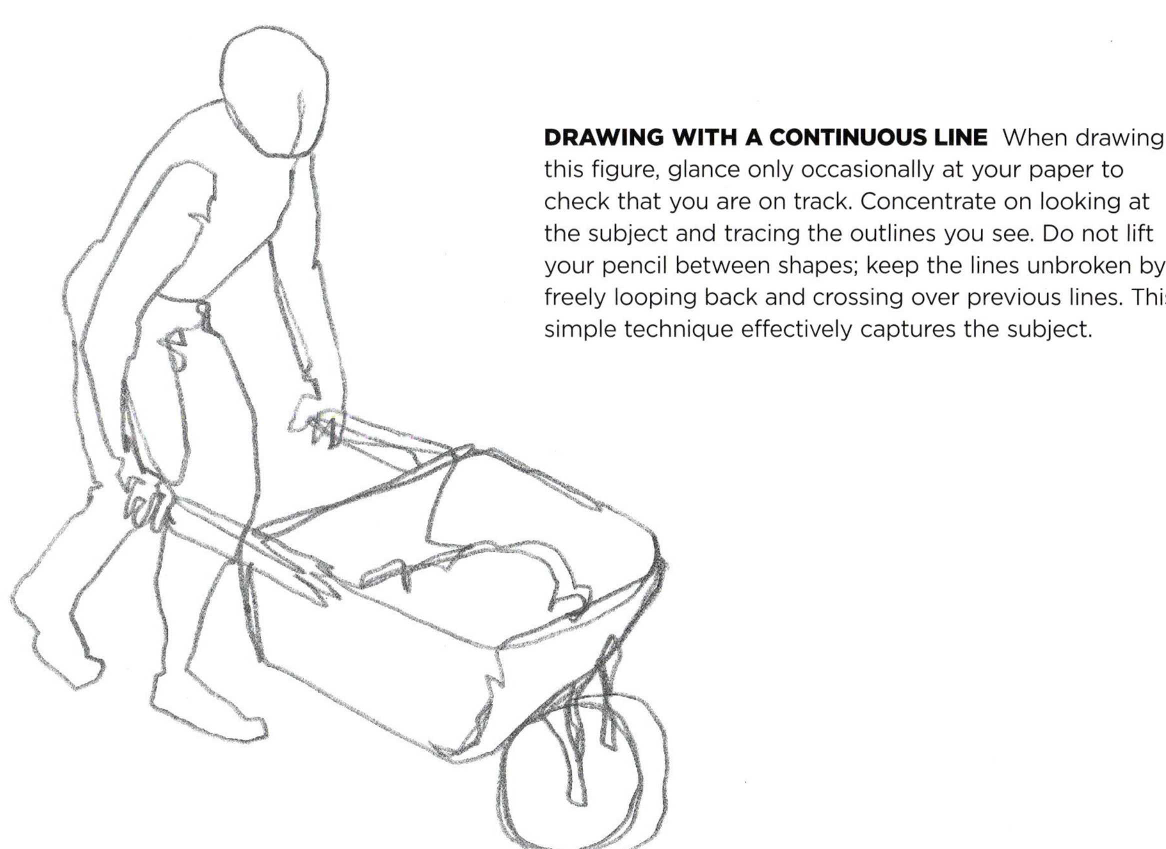

DRAWING WITH A CONTINUOUS LINE When drawing this figure, glance only occasionally at your paper to check that you are on track. Concentrate on looking at the subject and tracing the outlines you see. Do not lift your pencil between shapes; keep the lines unbroken by freely looping back and crossing over previous lines. This simple technique effectively captures the subject.

To test your observation skills, study an object very closely for a few minutes, and then close your eyes and try drawing it from memory, letting your hand follow the mental image.

DRAWING "BLIND" For the contour drawing on the left, the artist occasionally looked down at the paper. The drawing on the right is an example of a blind contour drawing, where the artist drew without looking at his paper even once. It's a little distorted, but it's clearly a hand. Blind contour drawing is one of the best ways of making sure you're truly drawing only what you see.

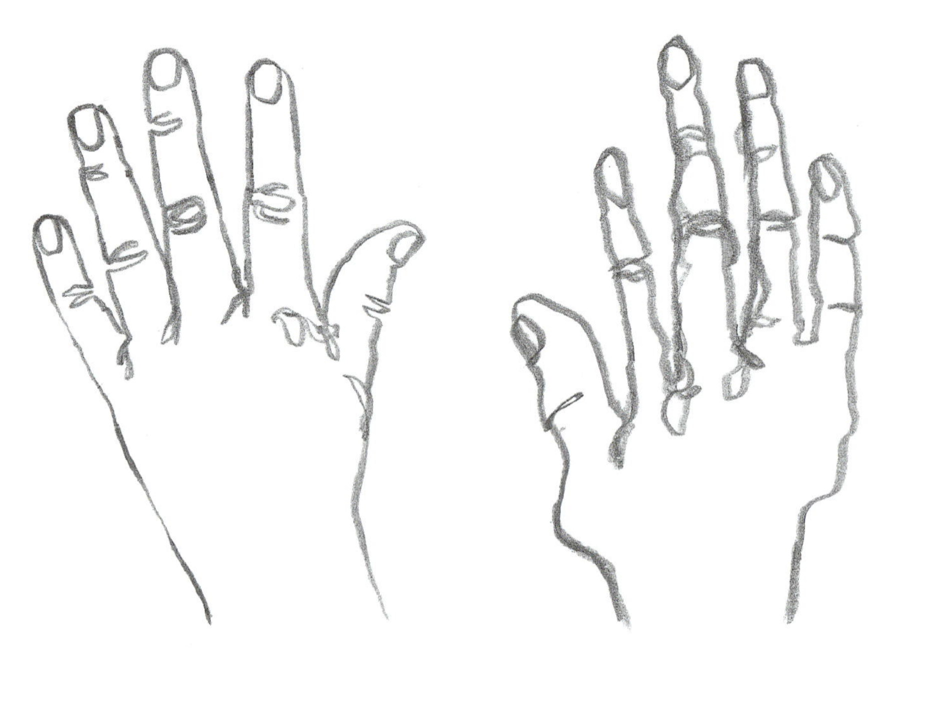

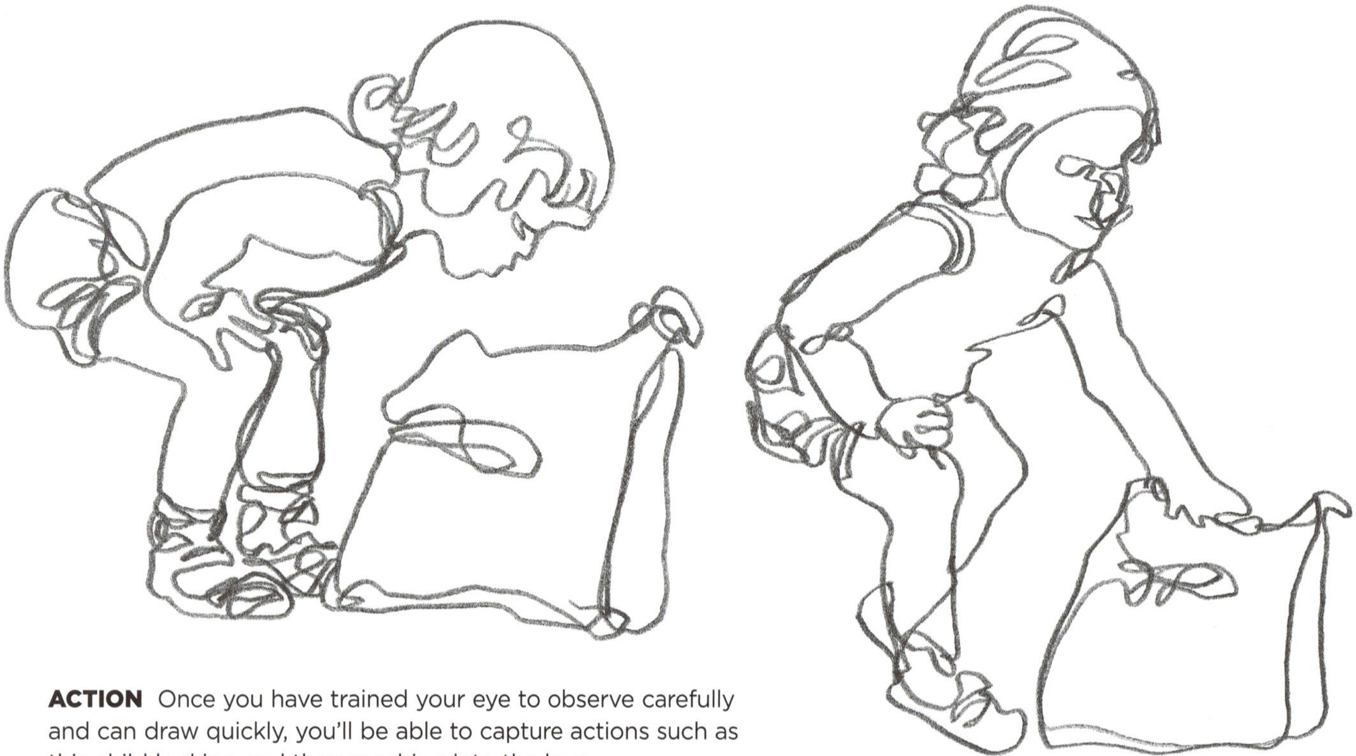

ACTION Once you have trained your eye to observe carefully and can draw quickly, you'll be able to capture actions such as this child looking and then reaching into the bag.

Putting It All Together

By using all of these techniques in one form or another, you will see a marked improvement in your drawings, both in appearance and accuracy. In order to combine gesture and contour line effectively, follow these quick tips:

- Start with a quick, light gesture sketch that provides the correct size, proportion, structure, and placement on the page. Remember, if the underlying gesture sketch is too detailed or dark, the subsequent contour line drawing will appear redundant and self-conscious.
- Next apply a "finishing" layer of contour line that is more detailed and that engages the viewer with interesting and expressive line quality and variety.
- Use a light graphite pencil, such as an H or F, for the initial gesture sketch and a darker graphite pencil, such as a B, 2B, or 4B, for the contour line. (See the following chapter for more details about pencil grades.)

YOUR HOMEWORK

For your first homework assignment, we will focus on some of the most important areas of study in this chapter. Pick subject matter that interests you, but is organic in nature—inherently simple in shape and form—and presents an opportunity to draw contours inside the form, as well as outer contour edges. This type of seashell is a perfect example.

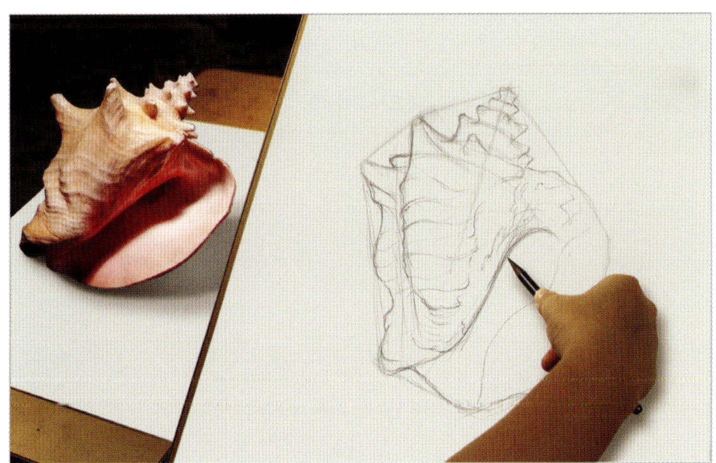

STEP 1 Use an H or HB pencil to develop a quick gesture sketch of the object, taking no more than 2 to 3 minutes to block in the entire structure. Don't worry about details or dark lines.

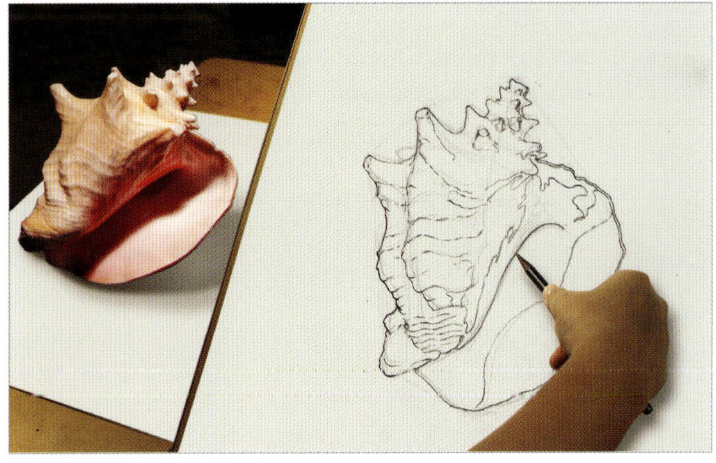

STEP 2 Slow down, and draw a weighted contour line drawing over the gesture. Take your time; spend 20 to 30 minutes on this part of the exercise. Remember to contour draw all of the touchable edges of the form, not just the outside contours.

EXERCISES FOR PRACTICE

You can create a variety of effects, lines, and strokes with pencil simply by alternating hand positions and shading techniques. Many artists use two main hand positions for drawing. The writing position is good for detailed work that requires hand control. The underhand position allows for a freer stroke with arm movement and motion that is similar to painting.

Shading Techniques

The shading techniques below can help you learn to render everything from a smooth complexion and straight hair to shadowed features and simple backgrounds. Whatever techniques you use, always remember to shade evenly.

HATCHING This basic method of shading involves filling an area with a series of parallel strokes. The closer the strokes, the darker the tone.

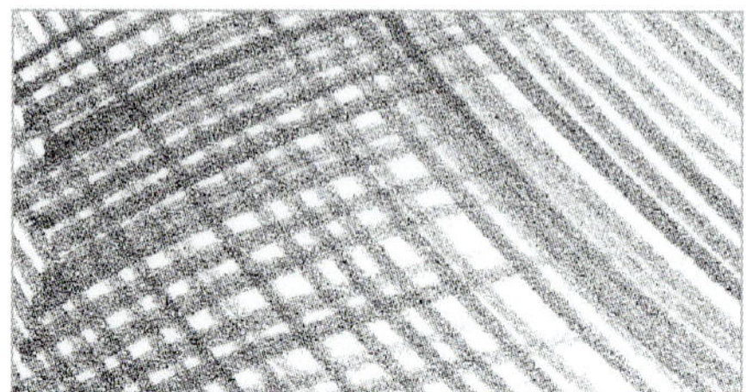

CROSSHATCHING For darker shading, place layers of parallel strokes on top of one another at varying angles. Make darker values by placing the strokes closer together.

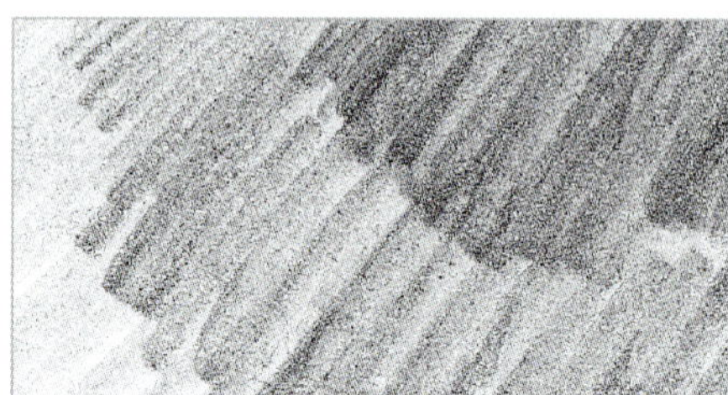

GRADATING To create graduated values (from dark to light), apply heavy pressure with the side of your pencil.

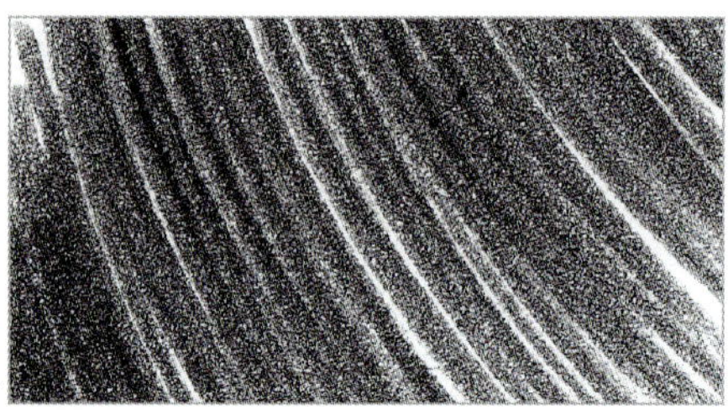

SHADING DARKLY By applying heavy pressure to the pencil, you can create dark, linear areas of shading.

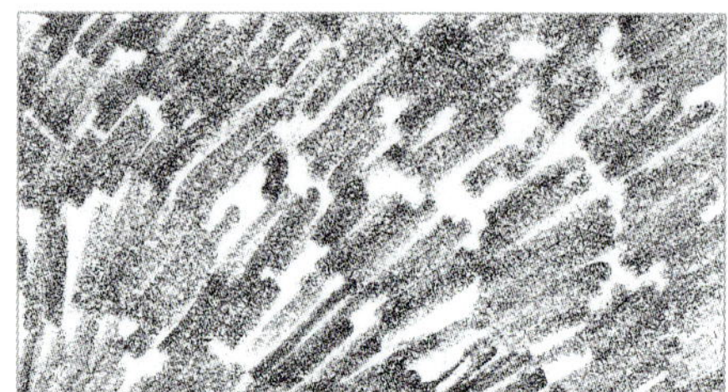

SHADING WITH TEXTURE For a mottled texture, use the side of the pencil tip to apply small, uneven strokes.

BLENDING To smooth out the transitions between strokes, gently rub the lines with a tortillon or tissue.

Other Pencil Techniques

Below are a few more techniques for experimenting in graphite. For these exercises, you will need hard and soft pencils, as well as a water-soluble pencil.

CREATING A GRAPHITE WASH
Shade an area with water-soluble pencil and blend the strokes with a wet brush. Always use water-soluble pencil on thick paper, such as vellum board, and avoid using too much water on the brush.

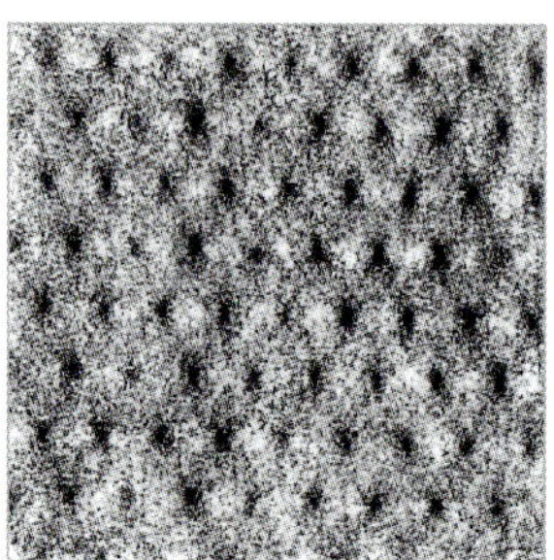

RUBBING Place paper over an object and rub the side of your pencil lead over the paper. The strokes of your pencil will pick up the pattern underneath and replicate it on the paper. Choose an object with a strong textural pattern, such as a wire grid, as shown at left.

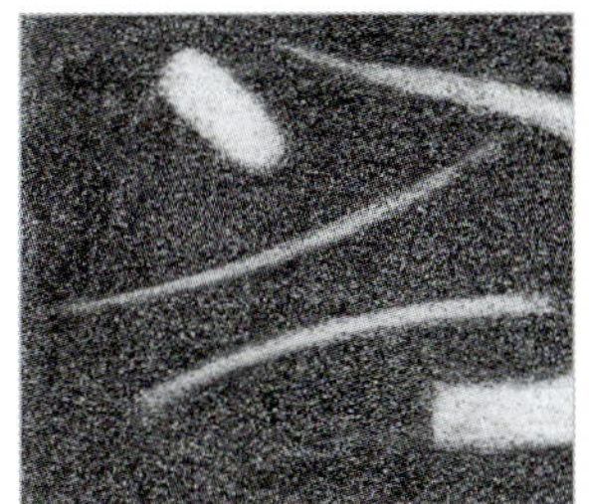

LIFTING OUT Blend a soft pencil on smooth paper, and then lift out the desired area with a kneaded eraser. You can create highlights and other interesting effects with this technique.

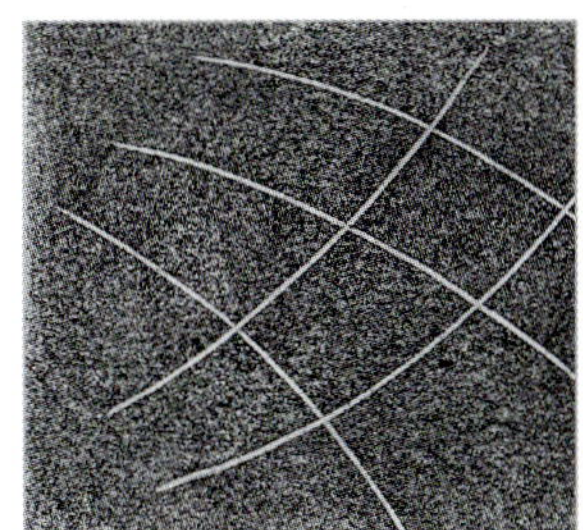

PRODUCING INDENTED LINES "Draw" a pattern or design with a sharp, non-marking object such as a knitting needle or stylus. Next, shade over the area with the side of your pencil to reveal the pattern.

Practicing Lines

When drawing lines, it is not always necessary to use a sharp point. In fact, sometimes a blunt point may create a more desirable effect. When using larger lead diameters, the effect of a blunt point is even more evident. Play around with your pencils to familiarize yourself with the different types of lines they can create.

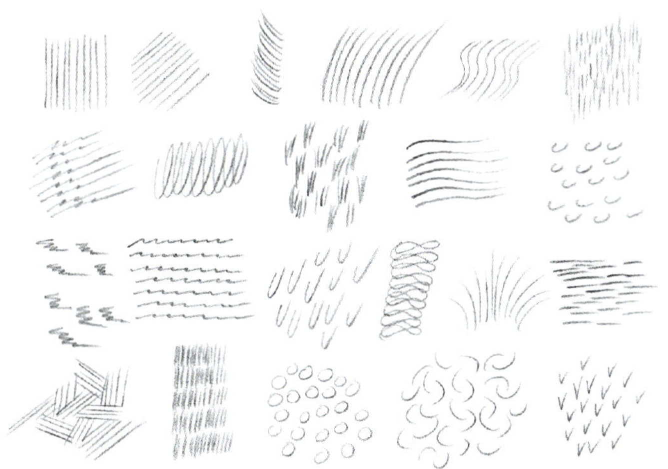

DRAWING WITH A SHARP POINT The lines above were drawn with a sharp point. Draw parallel, curved, wavy, and spiral lines; then practice varying the weight of the lines as you draw. Os, Vs, and Us are some of the most common alphabet shapes used in drawing.

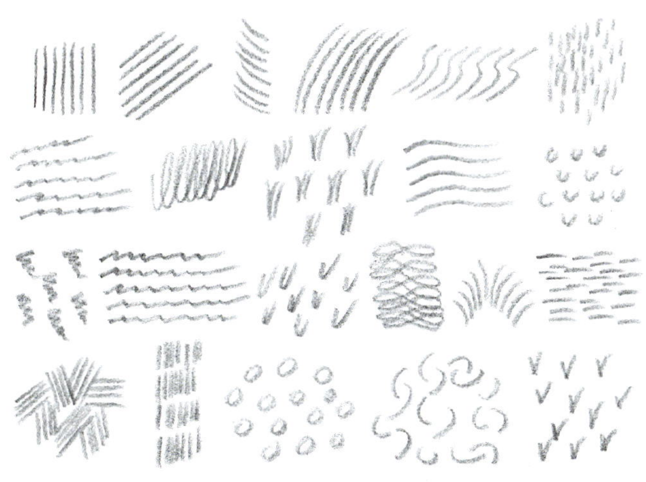

DRAWING WITH A BLUNT POINT The shapes above were drawn using a blunt point. Note how the blunt point produced different images. You can create a blunt point by rubbing the tip of the pencil on a sandpaper block or on a rough piece of paper.

Smudging

Smudging is an important technique for creating shading and gradients. Use a tortillon or chamois cloth to blend your strokes. It is important that you do not use your finger; your hands produce natural oils that can damage your artwork.

SMUDGING ON ROUGH SURFACES

SMUDGING ON SMOOTH SURFACES

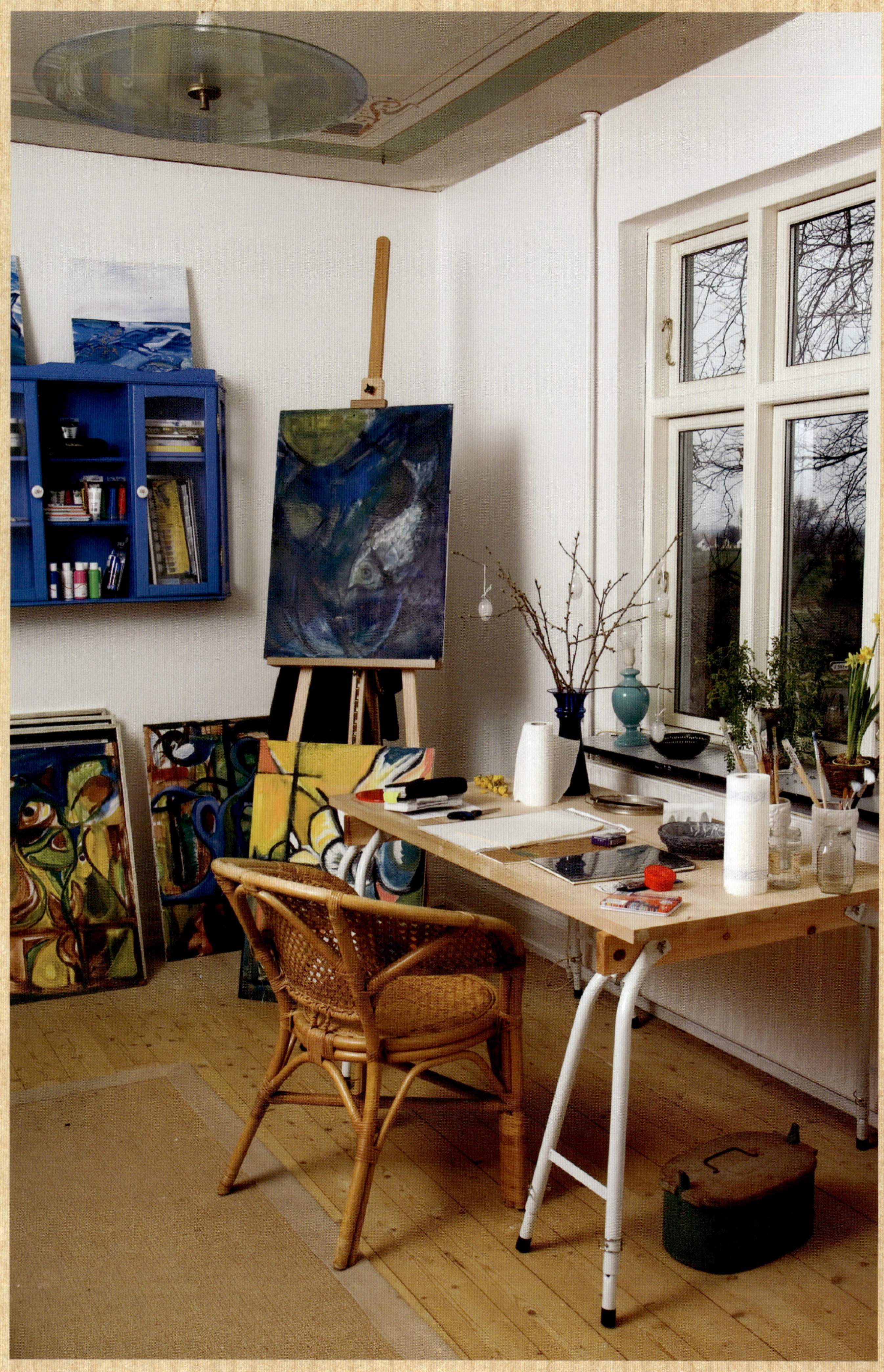

MATERIALS

There is a whole host of drawing media available, from graphite and colored pencils to charcoal, crayon, and pastel. The myriad tools can yield smooth tones, expressive strokes, dramatic monochromatic palettes, and richly colorful pieces. This chapter covers a variety of drawing materials available to artists, arming you with the information you need to get started in using and mastering the tools. There is a wide range of high-quality materials available at art & craft stores or other art suppliers, and each artist has his or her own preferences. Experiment with different brands and types of materials to discover which ones you prefer.

Graphite Pencils

Graphite pencils come in a range of values, starting with 9H lead as the lightest (or hardest) and graduating through a succession of pencils to 9B, which is usually considered the darkest (or softest). Some manufacturers carry grade EB and EEB for "extra black" and "extra extra black." HB and F graphite pencils are positioned as the middle-range value.

Leads can also be purchased without a protective wood or plastic cover; these leads can be used with a separate holder, usually retractable, that is made of metal or plastic. They can be sharpened with their own "lead pointer" or on a sandpaper pad.

A carpenter's pencil is a flat and wide variation on the graphite pencil. They are available in a limited range of values.

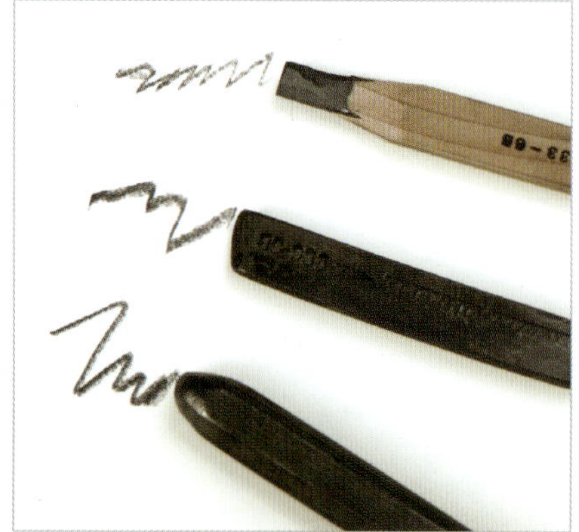

Graphite sticks are available in a narrow range of values (usually only B and 2B), but can be very useful for large, loose, expressive applications of graphite; these sticks are usually sharpened or chiseled with a sandpaper pad or block.

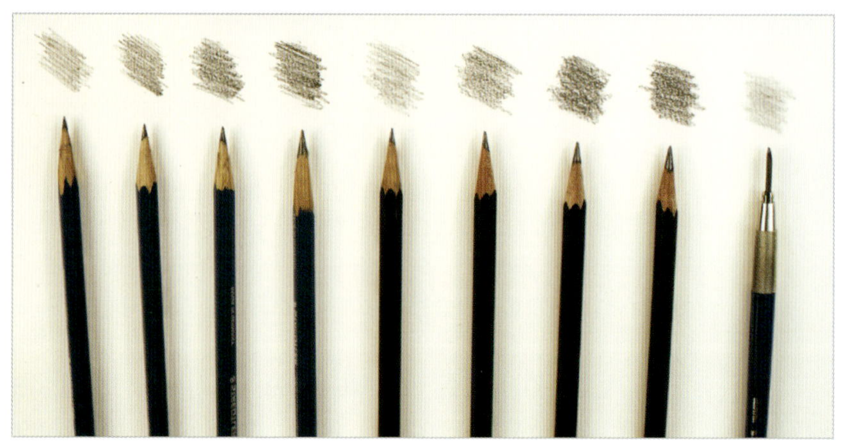

These graphite pencils represent two different manufacturers' ranges of graphite pencils, including an HB, 2B, 4B, and 6B, from lightest to darkest. The lead holder at the end contains an H grade graphite lead.

Sharpeners

There is a wide range of pencil sharpeners available for graphite pencils, from the small plastic sharpener most people are familiar with from grade school to a high-end electric motor that gives pencils a beautifully long and tapered point.

Mat knives or hobby knives can also be used to cut away the wooden cover of the pencil, as well as to sharpen the lead's point.

Many artists use sandpaper pads to sharpen various types of art media, including graphite pencils. Sandpaper pads are useful for creating a chiseled tip, which gives an artist the ability to create soft, wide strokes.

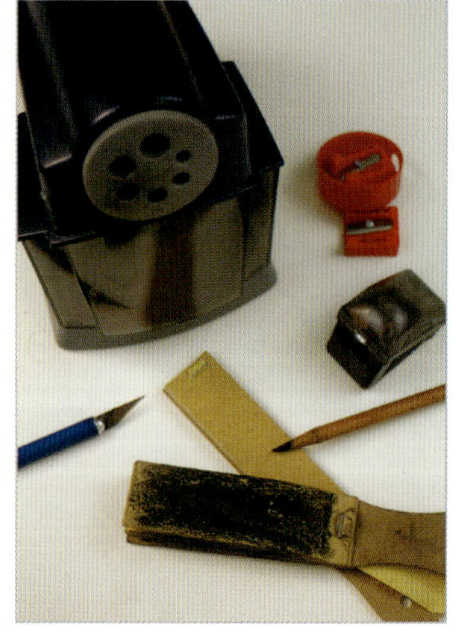

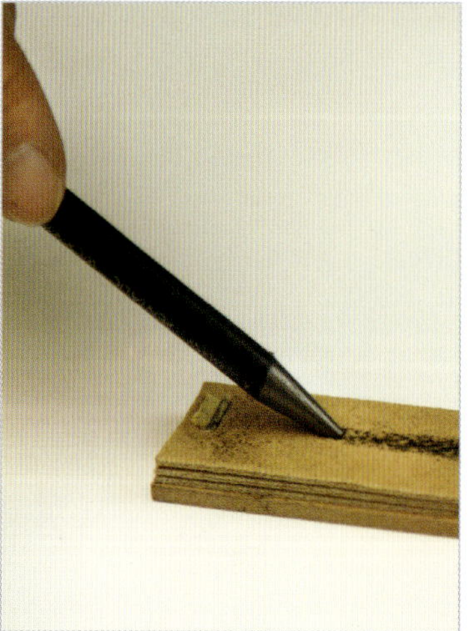

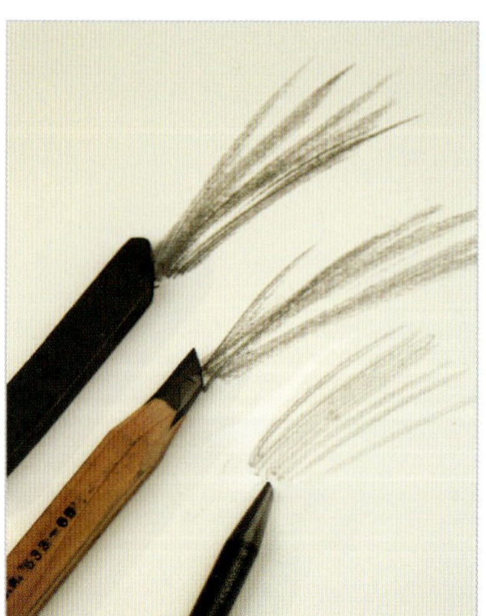

Erasers

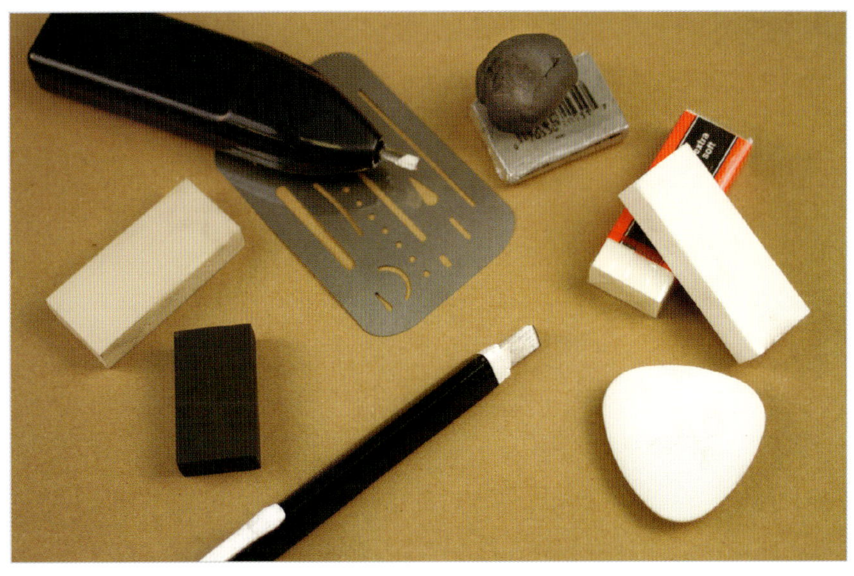

Erasers should be considered effective drawing tools, not just something to remove mistakes. They can be used to create light areas and sharp highlights and to subtly alter and vary the value of a flat graphite application.

Good options for erasers include white plastic or vinyl erasers and the kneaded eraser, a personal favorite for its ability to be "kneaded" into any shape, even a point. This eraser does not leave residue or crumbs behind.

Stick erasers are functional for erasing small, precise areas of graphite and can be chiseled with a knife for even more accurate erasing.

Electric erasers are another option for removing small areas of graphite, particularly in the creation of highly-lit sharp edges on a form, as well as small highlights on reflective surfaces.

Charcoal

Charcoal is created by slow-burning wood in the absence of oxygen in order to create carbon. This carbon residue is mixed with binders to create sticks and pencils. There are many varieties of charcoal media, but they can usually be separated into these categories: *vine charcoal, compressed charcoal,* and *charcoal pencils.*

Vine charcoal is typically made from burned grapevine and tree branches, usually willow. Willow charcoal and vine charcoal have very similar qualities; they are usually very soft and light when applied to paper and can easily be blended and lightened with a kneaded eraser or chamois. Both come in hard, medium, or soft grades.

Compressed charcoal is charcoal or carbon mixed with a gum binder that makes it darker and more permanent than vine or willow charcoal. Compressed charcoal tends to have a velvety matte-black appearance that is much richer than vine or willow.

A charcoal pencil contains a "lead" of compressed charcoal, covered with a wood or plastic sleeve. Some charcoal pencils have a paper outer coating that allows the tip of the pencil to be exposed to

Conté Crayons

Conté crayons are available as sticks and pencils. Made of a mixture of graphite and clay, in differing amounts for variations in softness and color, Conté is usually available in black, white, and several varieties of red and brown tones.

There are also several alternatives to Conté pencils, available from different manufacturers, that have similar clay-to-graphite ratios and are either encased in wood barrels or sold in long crayons that fit into specially designed plastic or steel holders.

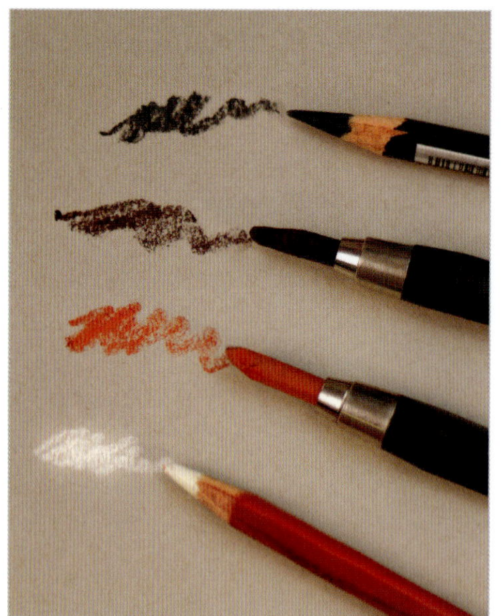

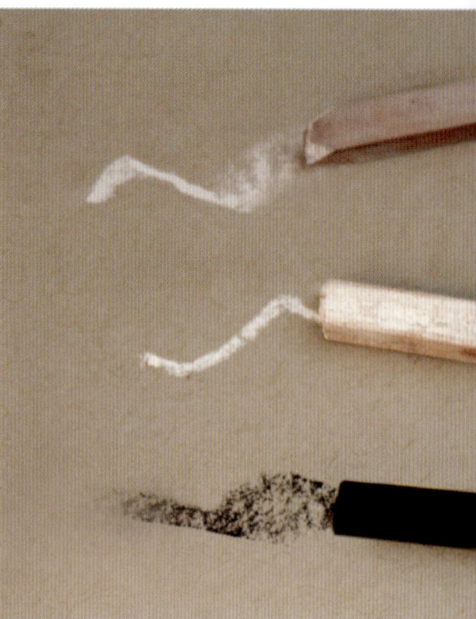

Dipping Pens

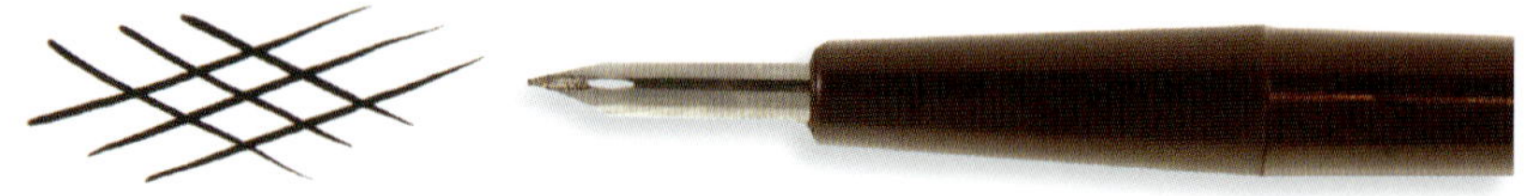

Pens are a very traditional way to work with ink; steel and copper pen points are repeatedly dipped into an ink bottle, or other liquid reservoir, to refill the pen. The amount of ink collected on the nib depends on the size of the nib. The thickness of the drawn line depends on the amount of pressure applied, as well as the size of the nib. The smallest pen points carry only as much ink as their surface area allows and must be repeatedly dipped into the ink.

Larger nibs have a two-tiered ink collection system that holds an amount of ink directly above the point; the ink is released as pressure is placed on the paper with the nib. There are different types of large nib tips: flat, round, and square. Each type has several different sizes. A favorite for all-purpose drawing is the B (round tip) 5½. These types of drawing nibs allow for a wide range of expressive line weights, along with expressive flourishes similar to what a brush can do.

Ink

Inks have been used for thousands of years, for both written documents and art. Today, inks consist of soluble dyes in a shellac solution and are either water-soluble or waterproof. They are available in a variety of colors, including black. Inks may be mixed with water to create washes with a variety of different values.

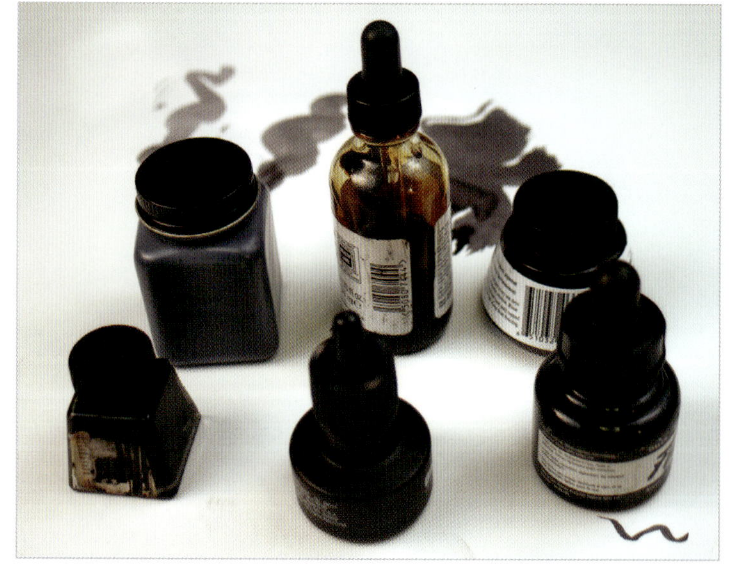

Drawing Pens

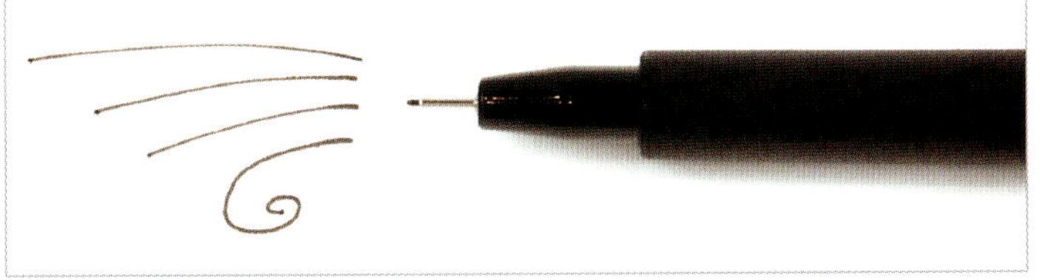

Drawing pens provide rich black ink flow in various sizes and widths, but without the variation in line weight that dipping pens allow. They are a clean and simple alternative for sketching and drawing, without the cleanup associated with dipping pens, which must be washed after each use. These pens can be purchased individually or in sets of differing point sizes.

Ink Brushes

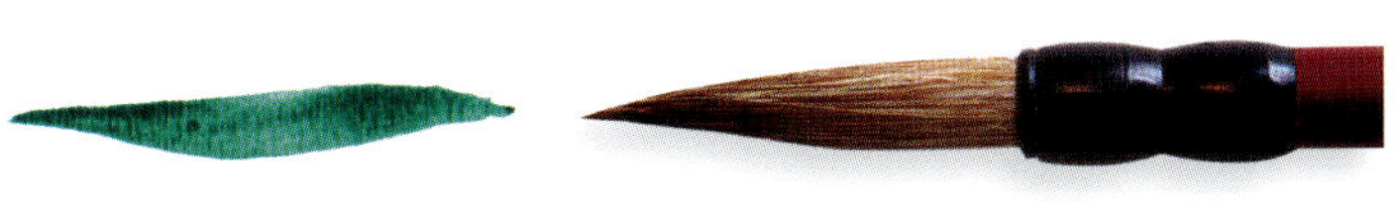

Bamboo brushes are the most common type of brush used with ink and ink washes. The shellac in ink can degrade an expensive brush, and bamboo brush fibers are usually blends of inexpensive goat, sheep, or badger hair. These hair fibers can be easily molded into a fine point, and their absorbent nature means they hold a lot of liquid. They come in many sizes, from very small to very wide.

Ink Brush Pens

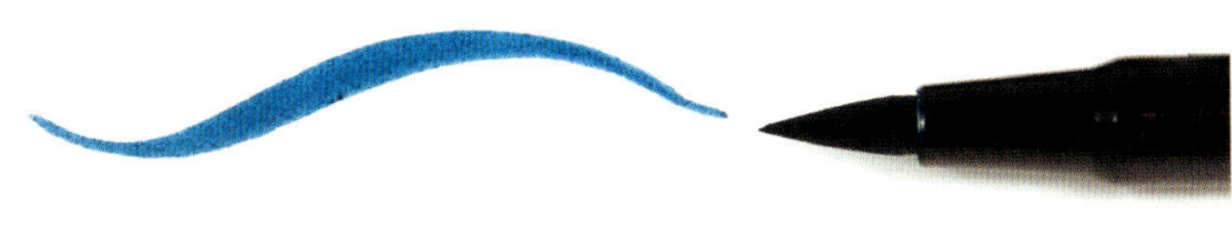

Ink brush pens are an expressive type of disposable ink pen that come in many different sizes and colors, as well as sets, including black and shades of gray. They are great for more expressive mark-making than a regular ink pen, as well as practical, since they don't need to be cleaned after each use.

Markers

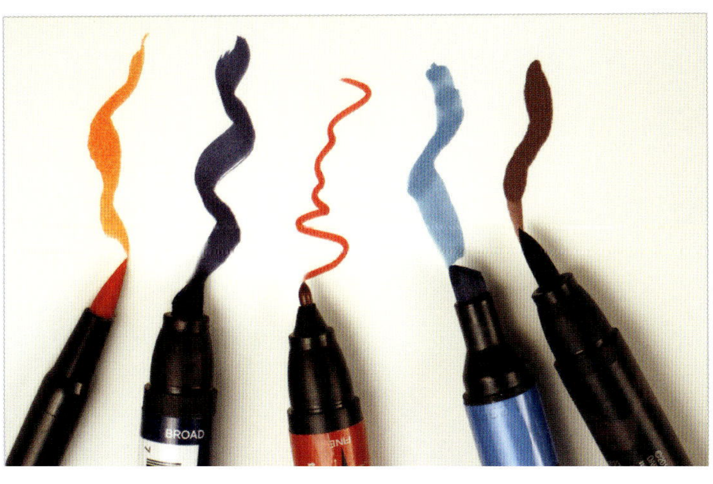

Felt-tip markers come in a variety of colors, sizes, and shapes, including flat, chisel, point, and brush. Most markers are either water- or alcohol-based; markers that contain other types of solvent base should be avoided for health reasons. Markers are versatile for sketching and adding quick tone or color. They are considered a "dry" medium, as they dry quickly upon application. However, markers are not used much in fine art, as their color is fugitive and tends to fade over time. Instead, they are used extensively in commercial art applications, for product and

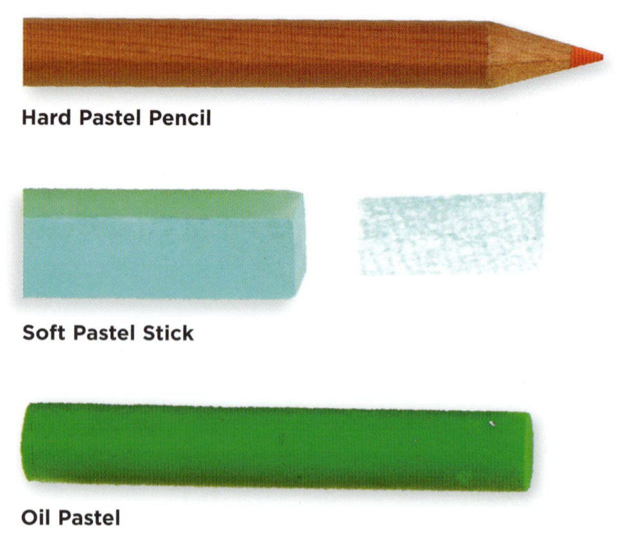

Pastel

Pastels are powdered pigment compressed into sticks with a gum arabic binder.

Pastel sticks and pencils come in varying degrees of hardness and softness, depending on the proportion of binder to pigment. Softer pastel sticks usually come with a paper wrapper for protection. The most inexpensive "pastels" are usually made of chalk, similar to what is used in a grade-school classroom or on the sidewalk. The pigments are generally weaker and the binders are inferior for good paper-surface adhesion.

Oil pastels have pigment and an oil or wax binder. They feel sticky or waxy to the touch, as opposed to the dryness of a soft pastel. The look of an oil pastel drawing can be similar to that of a soft pastel drawing, but it can also be more layered and less blended. Generally, the more expensive the oil pastel, the more vibrant the color and softer the texture. However, an inexpensive oil pastel set is suitable and affordable for beginners, as the quality does not suffer as much as in soft pastels.

Colored Pencils

Colored pencils consist of wax-based pigments encased in a protective wood cover. They are available in sets from 12 up to 150, depending on the manufacturer. They also vary in hardness and color intensity, depending on the cost, as well as their intended use. Some very hard colored pencils are used primarily for sketching and detail use; therefore they lack the color intensity of a fine-art type of colored pencil. Generally, the softer and more expensive the colored pencil, the more lightfast and brilliant the color.

Papers

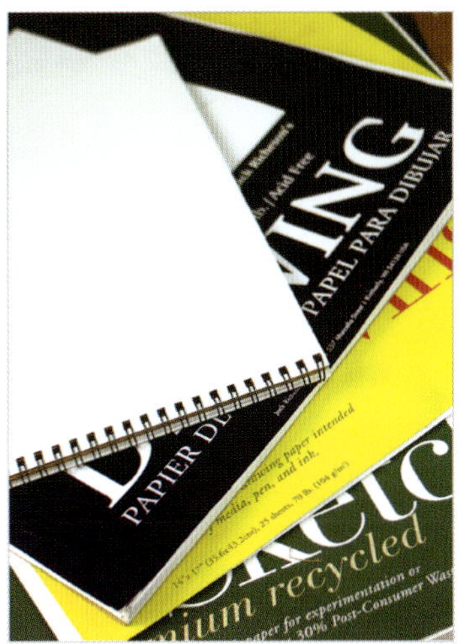

Art papers are classified in many different ways depending on their use, surface texture, weight, and other characteristics.

Generally, papers are split into two categories: *cold-pressed* and *hot-pressed*. Hot-pressed paper, also called "plate surface," is the paper of choice for pen and ink drawing, as well as some graphite techniques that call for precise rendering. Cold-pressed paper, which has more surface texture, comes in different grades, including smooth, vellum, and rough. Cold-pressed paper is usually the overall choice for most techniques involving graphite and charcoal.

Drawing papers come in pads of varying sizes, starting around 9" x 12" up to 18" x 24" and are usually labeled as either "sketch" or "drawing" pads. Sketch pads are usually inferior in quality to drawing pads but can be more economical, especially for beginning artists. The least expensive alternative is "newsprint," which I do not recommend, as graphite application on this paper tends to look weaker; these papers are also prone to yellowing and brittleness.

The gold standard for drawing paper is acid-free, 100 percent cotton rag paper, but there are some good alternatives on the market, especially some of the "recycled" cotton drawing pads.

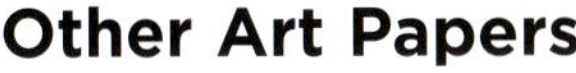

Other Art Papers

Laid papers are quality white or toned papers that have a grid pattern embedded into their surface texture. This texture holds medium well, making the surface very good for soft media, such as charcoal and pastel. There are also many types of printmaking and pastel papers that are quite conducive to all dry media. Pastel papers are usually thicker ply and have a rougher textured surface than traditional drawing papers in order to retain the soft strokes of pastel on the surface.

Tracing Paper

Tracing paper, sometimes called "sketch paper" when it comes in a roll, is a translucent lightweight paper used in situations where layers of refined drawings are desirable. Vellum is a thicker-weight translucent tracing paper, which has a surface similar to drawing paper. Most commercial artists use tracing paper and sketch paper, due to their economical and translucent qualities.

Other Helpful Materials

- Drawing board (wood or Masonite and large enough to accommodate at least 18" x 24" paper)
- Large brushes for sweeping away eraser crumbs
- Utility knife for sharpening pencils
- Rulers, a T-square, and triangle
- Artist tape to hold drawings or create borders
- A viewfinder for proportions

Working Surfaces & Easels

Your working surface should depend largely on the medium you use most often. For artists who draw and work with dry media, a flat or slightly tilted surface is best; for artists who paint with oil or acrylic, an easel is the traditional choice.

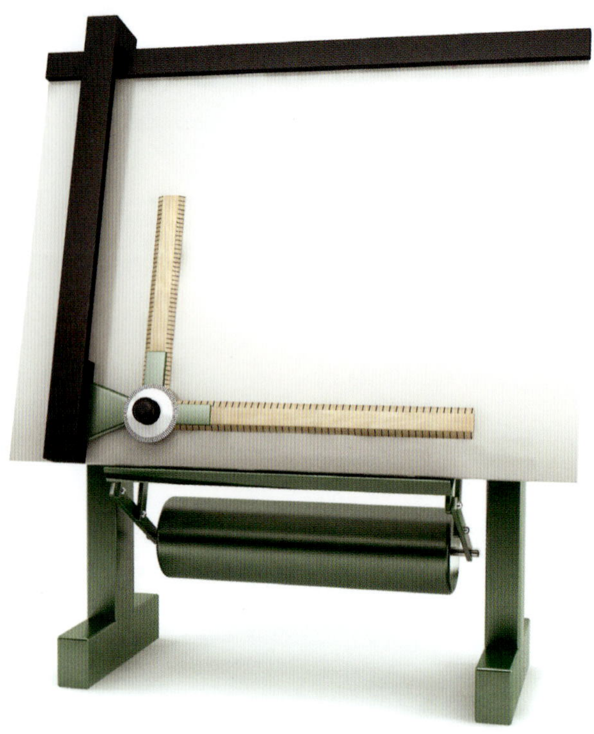

Drawing & Drafting Tables

Drawing and drafting tables feature large, smooth surfaces that tilt to varying degrees. Often made of wood, composite wood, or tempered glass, these desks sometimes feature ledges or compartments along the side for holding pencils, erasers, or other drawing materials. Some even include straightedges on the surface, wheeled legs, and drawers for storing materials.

A simple sheet of composite wood can serve as an inexpensive drawing surface. However, you might find the sharp corners and edges less desirable than a drawing board designed for comfort.

Drawing Boards

A drawing board offers a sturdy, smooth, and portable surface for supporting your paper as you draw or paint. You can use it in your lap and rest it against the edge of a table; and, if you wish, you can secure your paper to the board with clips or artist tape. Many wood-surfaced drawing boards feature a honeycombed core to reduce weight; others are made of composite wood or plastic. Drawing boards are available in a range of sizes, but an 18" x 18" board is a great size for beginners.

Studio Easels

Studio easels are sturdy, freestanding canvas supports. Traditionally they are made of wood, but you can also find lighter-weight metal varieties. Studio easels often fold flat, so you can tuck them away into a corner of the studio if needed; however, they are more cumbersome than portable easels (such as box easels, page 32). Below are two common studio easel formats.

Drawing boards may include:

- Rounded corners and edges
- Handle
- Clamps
- Rubber band around body
- Adjustable straightedge
- Stand for tilting on a flat surface

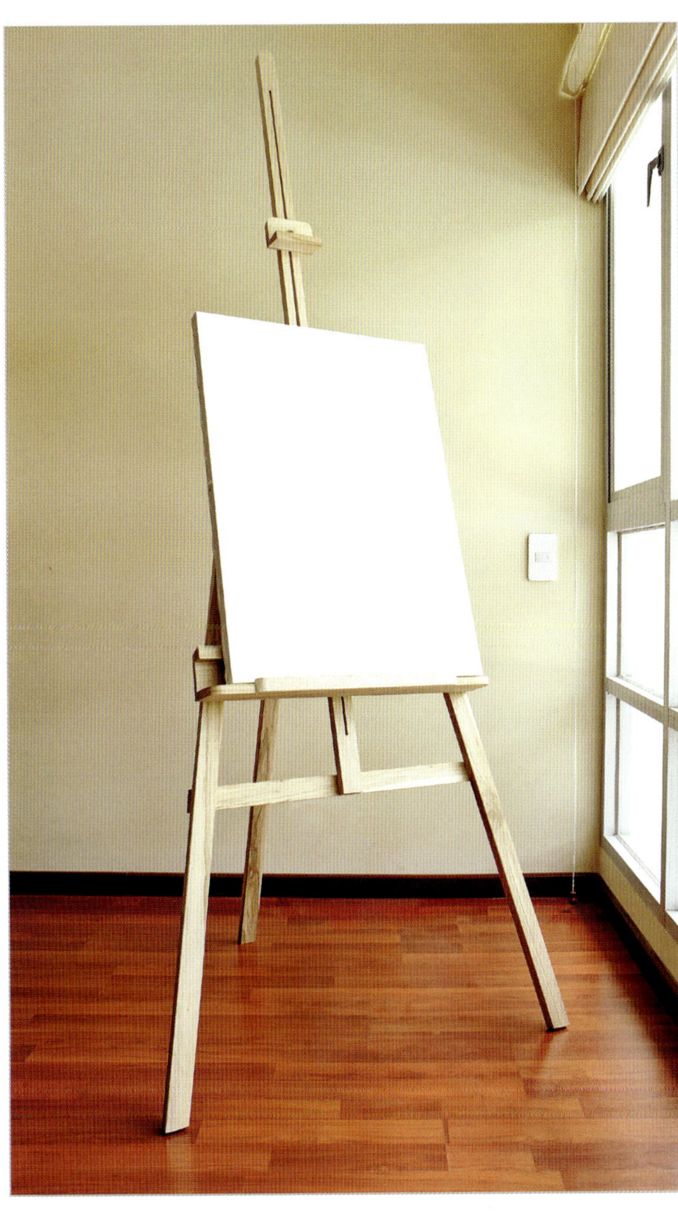

An A-frame easel is perhaps the most common format. The main frame, which is shaped loosely like an "A," is supported by a third leg. This easel requires a good amount of floor space, and the legs are vulnerable to accidental kicks.

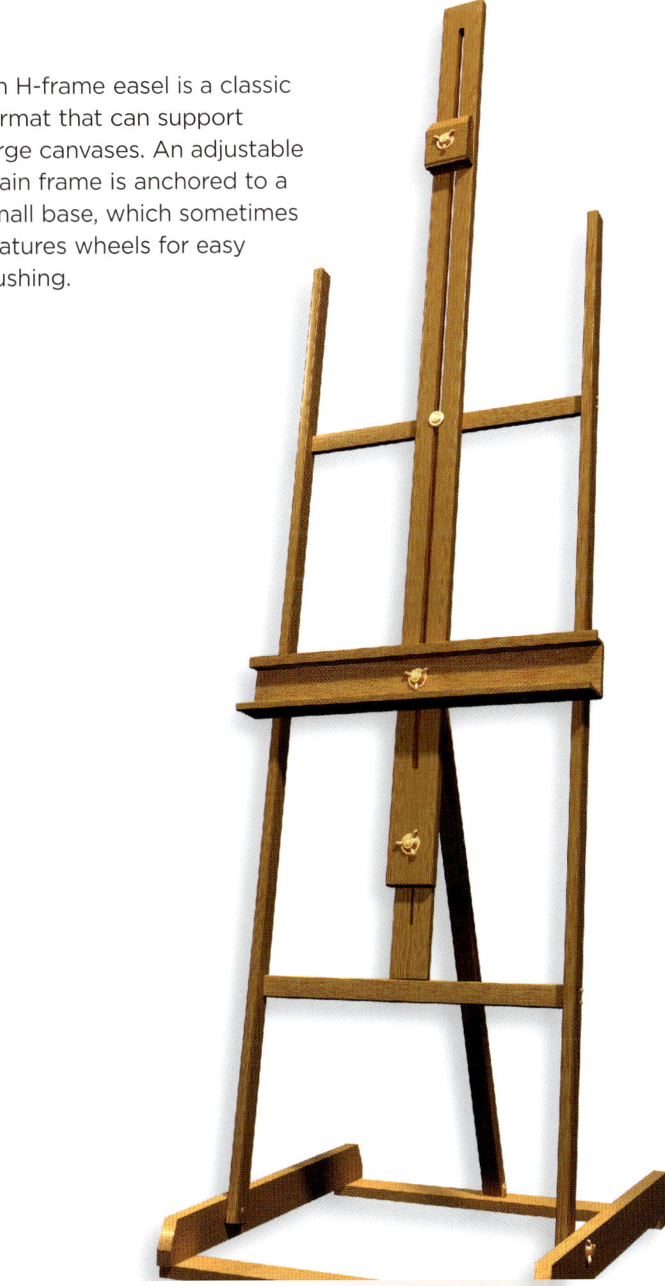

An H-frame easel is a classic format that can support large canvases. An adjustable main frame is anchored to a small base, which sometimes features wheels for easy pushing.

Portable Easels

Also called a French easel, a box easel is a great option for artists who work outdoors. This portable unit collapses into a compact box and features a handle for easy toting. The easel has three adjustable legs that support a wooden box; the lid serves as a canvas support with a ledge, and the box acts as a drawer holding materials.

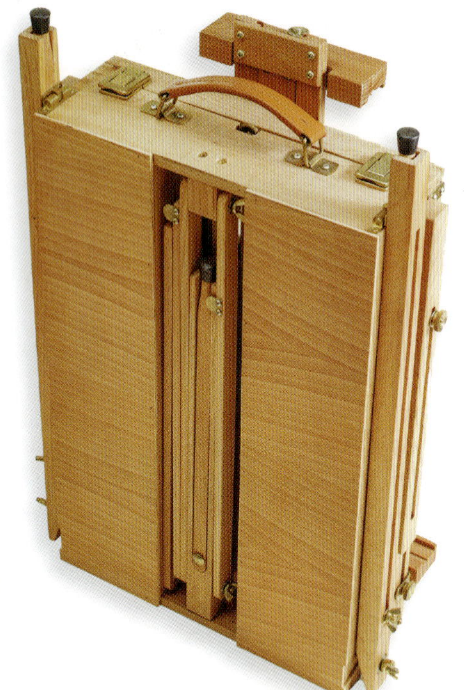

Box easel, closed and ready for traveling

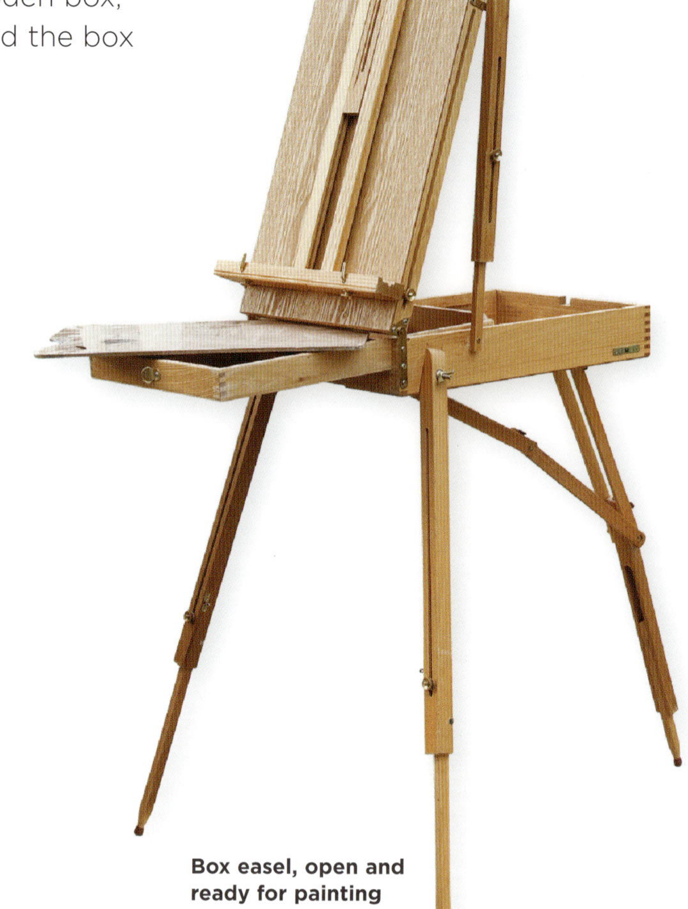

Box easel, open and ready for painting

Aluminum watercolor easel

Image courtesy of Alvin & Co. www.alvinco.com

Watercolorists who paint on site often choose to work on pads or spiral sketchbooks, while others stick to single sheets attached to a hard board with clips or artist tape. To support your paper while painting, consider a watercolor easel that allows for a slightly tilted surface. Many are available in collapsible, lightweight metal formats, making them easy to carry on-site.

Tabletop Easels

This type of easel sits atop any flat surface and holds your work upright as you paint. They are usually mini H-frames or mini A-frames in format. Tabletop easels are sometimes used to display finished artwork on desks or countertops.

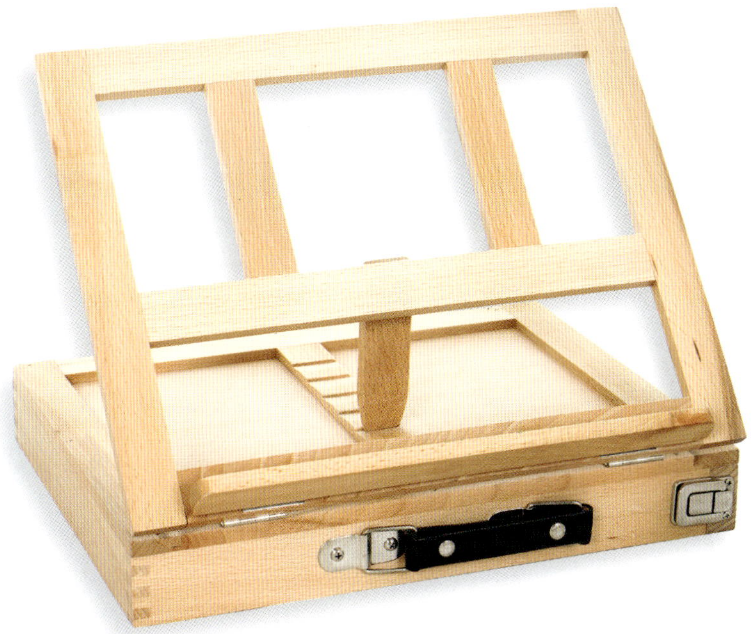

Box-style tabletop easel

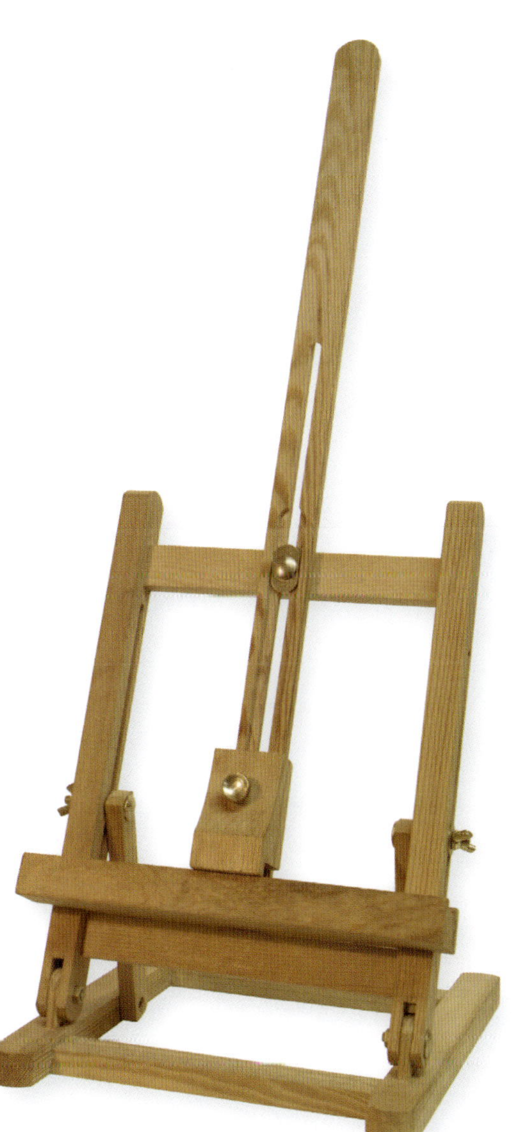

Standard H-frame

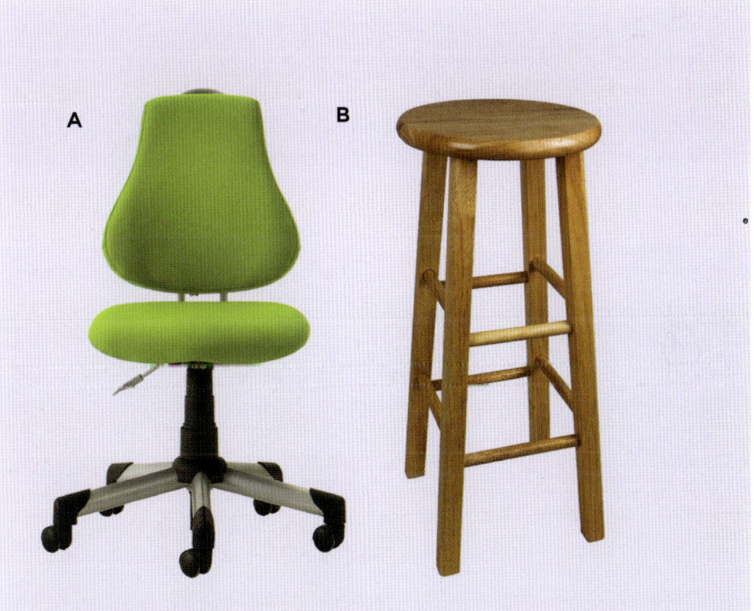

A comfortable chair is an important aspect of an artist's studio. A chair with a padded seat, back support, adjustable height, and wheels is ideal and can help prolong your studio sessions (A). For painters who like to stand frequently at the easel and enjoy freedom of movement, a simple elevated stool is a great choice (B).

Setting Up a Studio

Every artist's dream is to have a large, airy studio with a north-facing window. But the reality is that any place you find to paint—a spare bedroom, a basement corner, or the kitchen table—is suitable. Choose your workspace to match your style. Some people like to stand to allow free arm movement; others sit at a table for more precise work; and some prefer to sit in an oversized chair. Select an easel, table, or lap desk to hold your paper while you work. And wherever you do work, you will need good lighting, such as a floor lamp, desk light, or clamp-on light. As an artist, you may prefer to use a "natural" or "daylight" bulb, which mimics sunlight and is easy on your eyes.

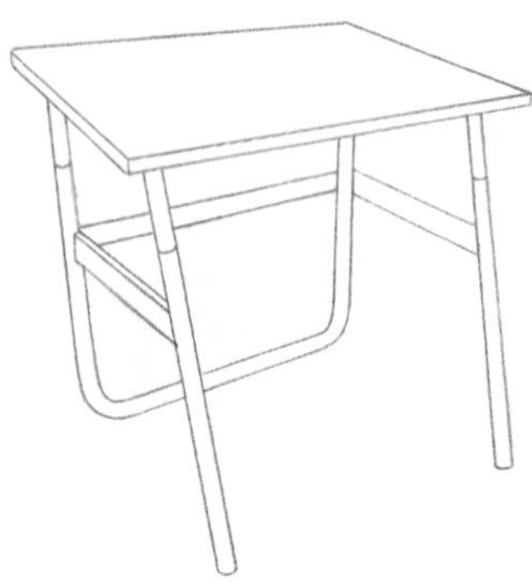

DRAFTING OR DRAWING TABLE You can angle these tabletops for comfort. If space is short, get a folding table.

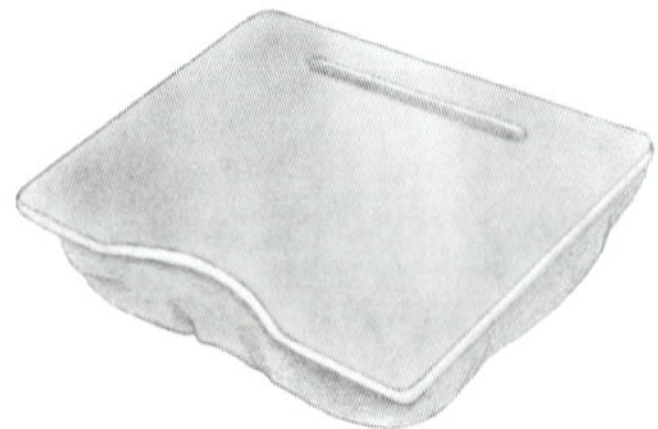

LAP DESK A laptop board with an attached pillow allows you to put your feet up, lean back, and draw.

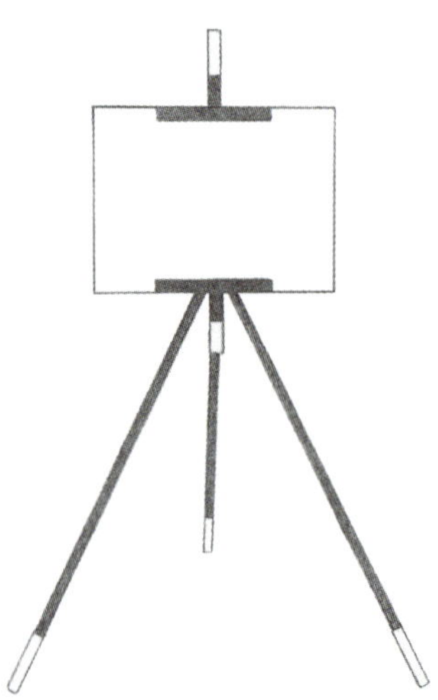

EASEL An easel will hold your work upright, so you can work standing or sitting.

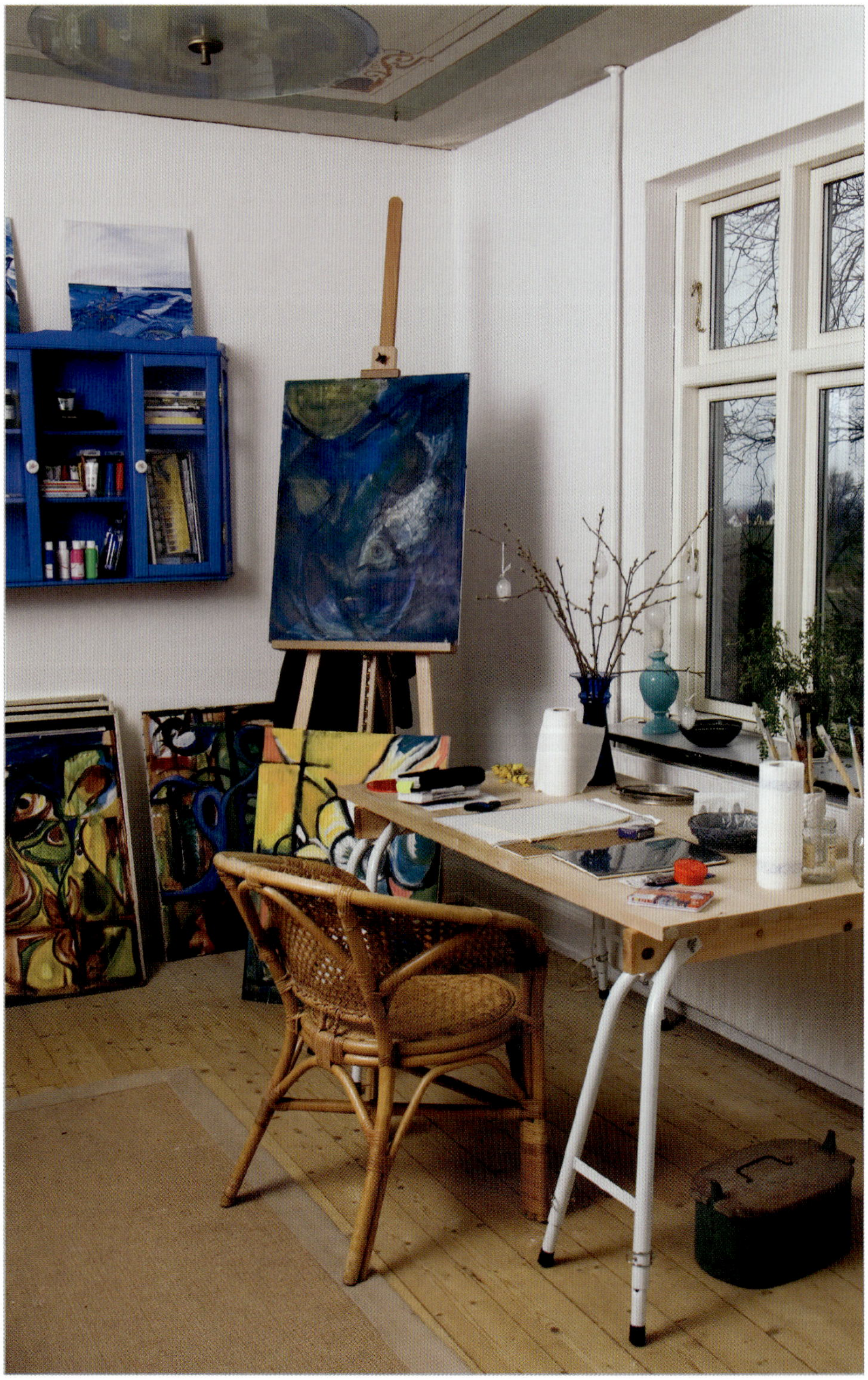

Lighting

Traditionally, the best lighting for artwork is plentiful natural light coming from the north. This shows color and values in their truest forms, prevents rays of light from falling directly on the work, and reduces eyestrain for the artist. An ideal studio features large, high north-facing windows. Artists who don't have the luxury of north light or who work at night must use artificial lighting to illuminate their work spaces. There are myriad possibilities for lighting a studio; ultimately, personal preference will guide the way.

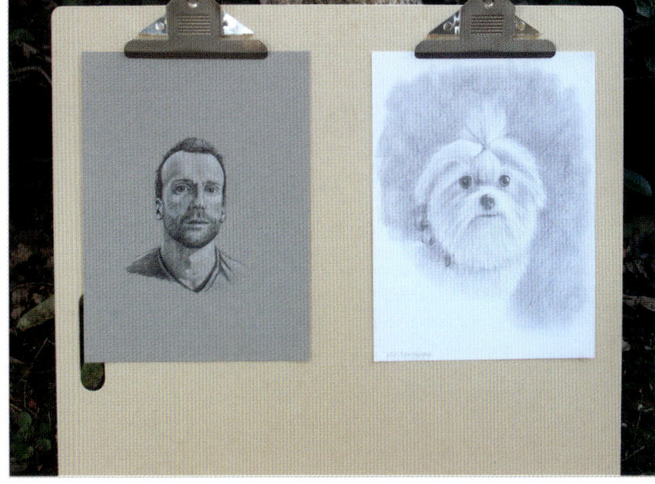

A

Studio Lighting Considerations

Temperature	The light in your studio should be neutral in color, so avoid a setup that leans too cool or too warm. Some artists use a combination of incandescent and fluorescent bulbs, while others rely solely on daylight simulation bulbs.
Direction	Most professional studios feature both general overhead lighting as well as task lighting, which focuses light on a smaller workspace. Both overhead and task lighting should be positioned so as not to create shadows of your hand across your work. For example, if you are right-handed, light should come from above and from the left; if you are left-handed, light should come from above and from the right.
Presentation	Artists can often find out how commissioned artwork will be displayed and lit. Many find it beneficial to paint their work in the same lighting conditions to help control how the viewer will see the colors and values.

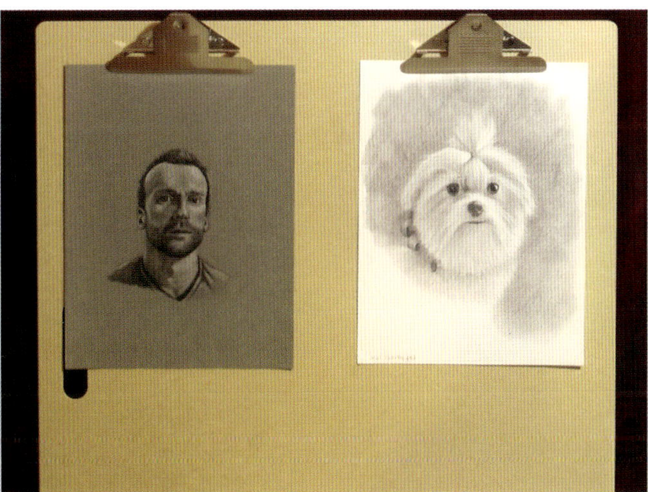

B

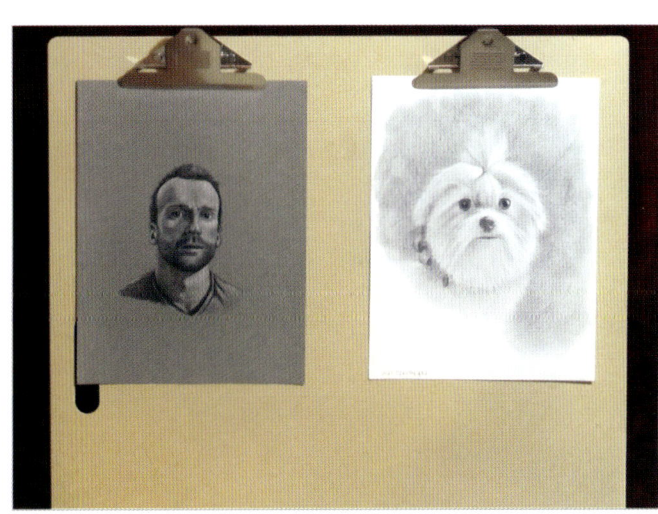

Shown is the same drawing board under three different types of light: cool light from the shadows of late afternoon (A), a warm incandescent bulb (B), and a full-spectrum daylight bulb (C). If natural northern light is not available, full-spectrum daylight bulbs (or a combination of warm and cool lighting) bring out the truest colors and values.

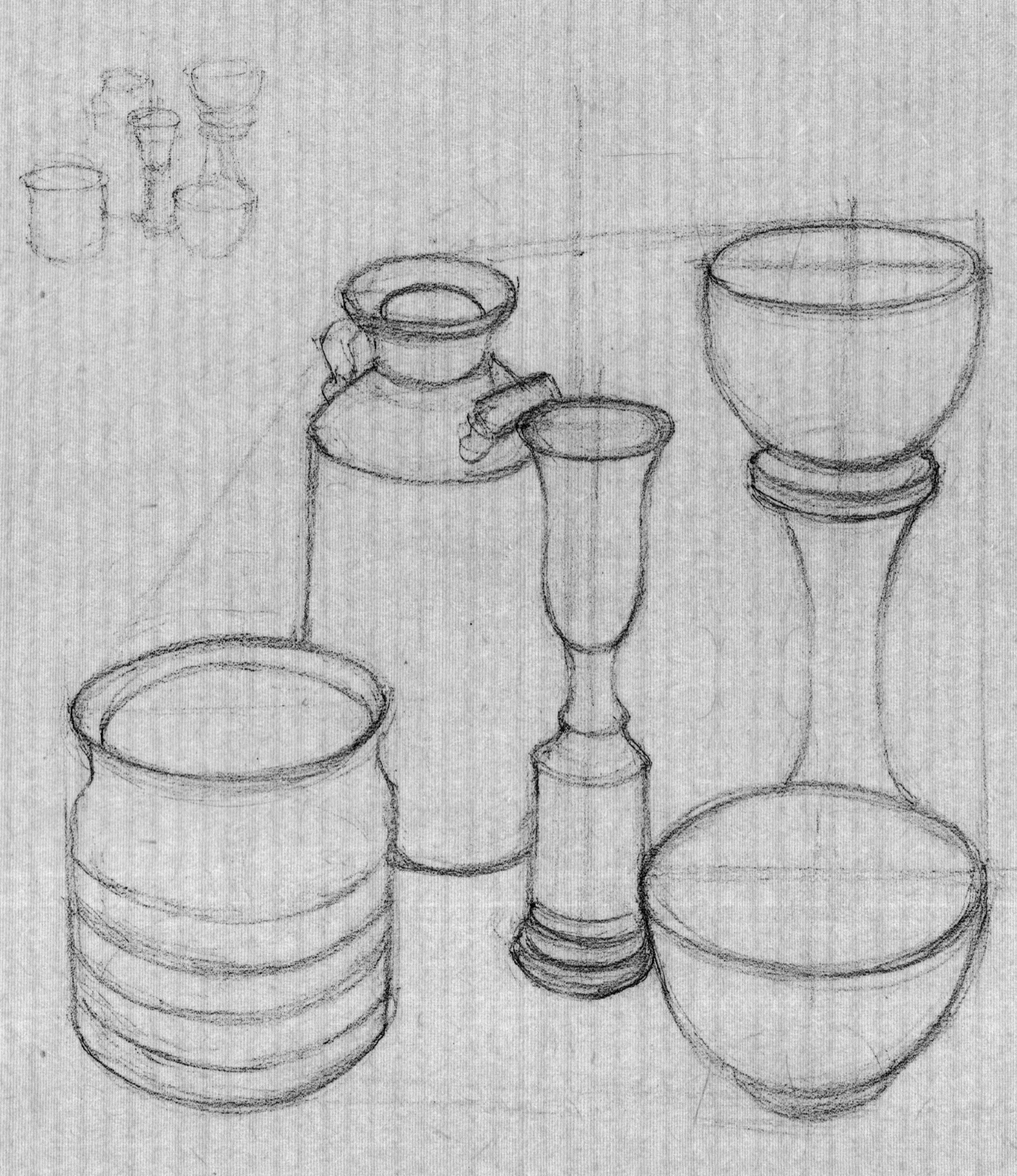

HOW WE SEE & INTERPRET

In the first chapter we concentrated on the simple act of making marks on the page—marks that are intended to represent three-dimensional objects on a flat piece of paper. As we prepare to transition to more difficult and complex subjects, such as still life and architecture, we need to understand and analyze what exactly we see, and how best to apply that scene to the drawing surface. This chapter will demonstrate some simple, yet effective, techniques that artists have employed for hundreds of years that can help the artist organize and understand a complex scene in a logical way. The information on the picture plane—measuring, eye level, and visual spatial interpretation—will be discussed at length throughout the chapters in this book.

Proportion & Size Relationships

The Picture Plane

In considering the way we see and re-interpret objects in space, the first concept to understand involves the *picture plane*. The picture plane is an imaginary glass window that stands parallel to the viewer (the artist) and between the viewer and the subject. This imaginary plane is meant to represent the flat surface that the artist is drawing on (the paper surface). In an ideal theoretical situation, the artist would be able to trace the subject directly onto the glass window. In reality, there are ways for the artist to make use of this imaginary window to transfer the subjects seen through it onto the paper surface.

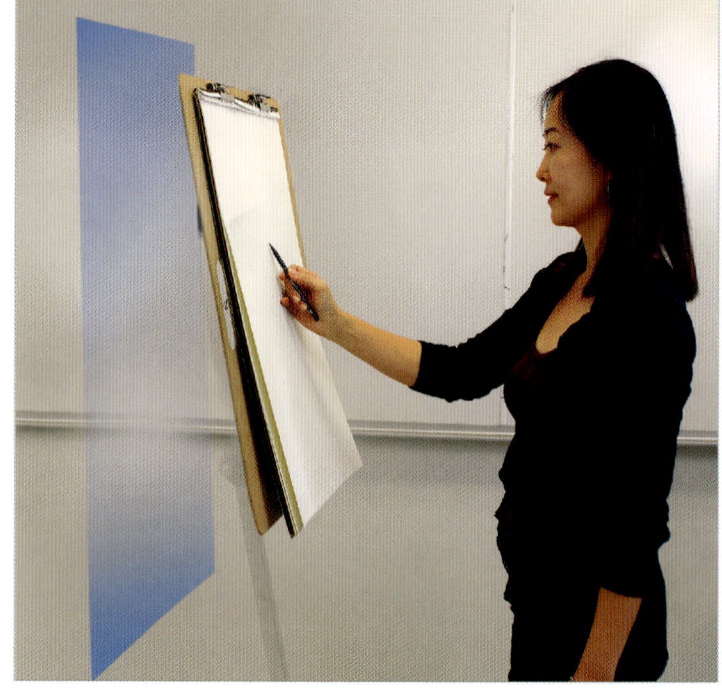

Consider the picture plane (blue rectangle) as an imaginary "window" parallel to the drawing surface. We see what we are drawing through this imaginary window.

Space and Depth

When viewing objects sitting on a flat ground plane in close proximity to each other, such as the coffeepots below left, we can easily see that the objects are of similar size. When the far left pot is moved toward the picture plane and the center pot is moved toward the back of the ground plane, there is the illusion of a change in the size of the pots (below right).

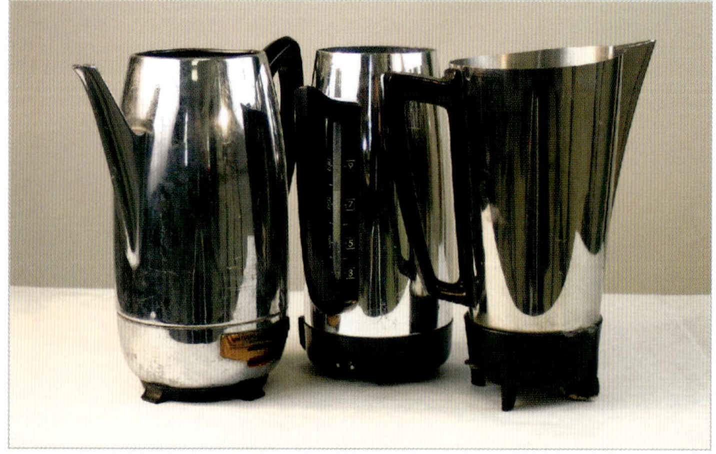

These coffeepots are very close to each other, sitting on the ground plane at about the same horizontal depth, approximately midway from the picture plane to the back of the ground plane.

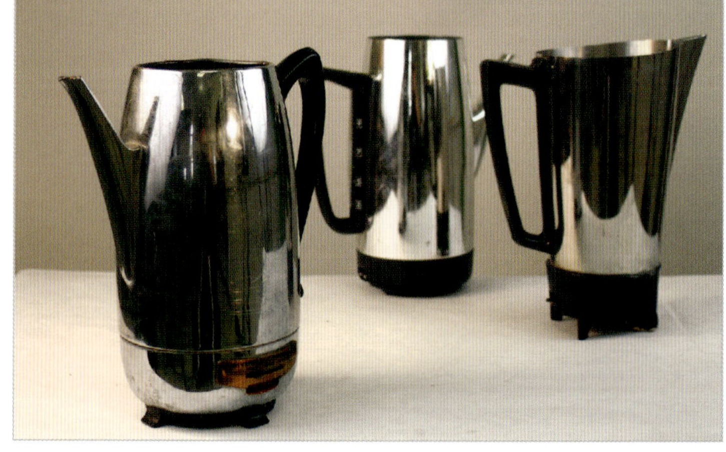

The left pot is now the largest in relation to the other two and is near the bottom of the picture plane. The center pot's base is now the highest of all three within the picture plane. The top rims of all three pots are still relatively level with each other, when viewed horizontally across the picture plane. This relates to how we perceive cylindrical tops that are close to eye level.

As we move the objects around the ground plane, we can see the "changes" that occur in their relative size—though we know that the objects are all physically the same size. This illusion is the result of a visual interpretation called *diminution*, a hierarchy or size relationship caused by an increase in space between the objects, making objects of similar size look smaller as they move away from the picture plane.

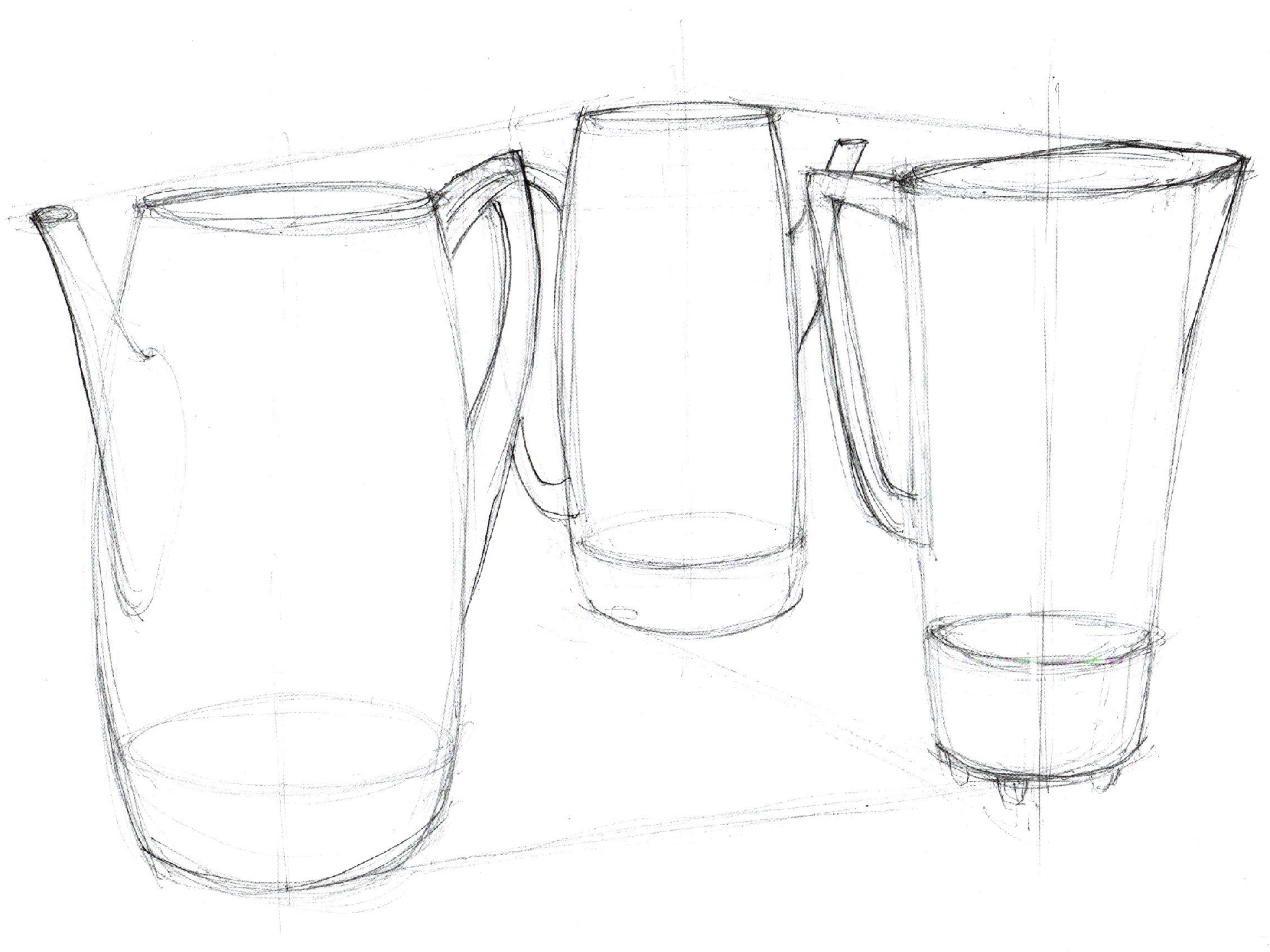

Most people recognize this intuitively, but it is important to note how size diminution appears to the artist through the picture plane. The three coffeepots above are at the artist's eye level. We know this because we can still see the tops of the pots, and even just a bit down into them. As the pots advance toward the viewer, the tops appear lower on the picture plane, but the overall heights appear taller, and the widths seem wider. The pot closest to the viewer is the largest, and its base is the lowest on the picture plane. This consistently happens when objects are viewed from above or below eye level.

Eye Level

Eye level, also called the "horizon line," is an imaginary horizontal line that corresponds to the precise location of the viewer's eyes and what is seen when the viewer looks directly ahead, without tilting the head up or down. It's important to realize that the artist may move their head up or down to view an object or objects; this is called "line of vision." Even as the artist's head moves up and down, however, the eye level stays the same.

Imagine being at the ocean, where the horizon line (eye level) is easily seen. If there is an airplane traveling from the horizon toward us, we watch it get closer by raising our line of vision until it is directly above us. We have not brought the ocean edge (horizon line) up to where the plane is flying—it stays at the eye level, where it belongs. This is how the eye level and picture plane work together.

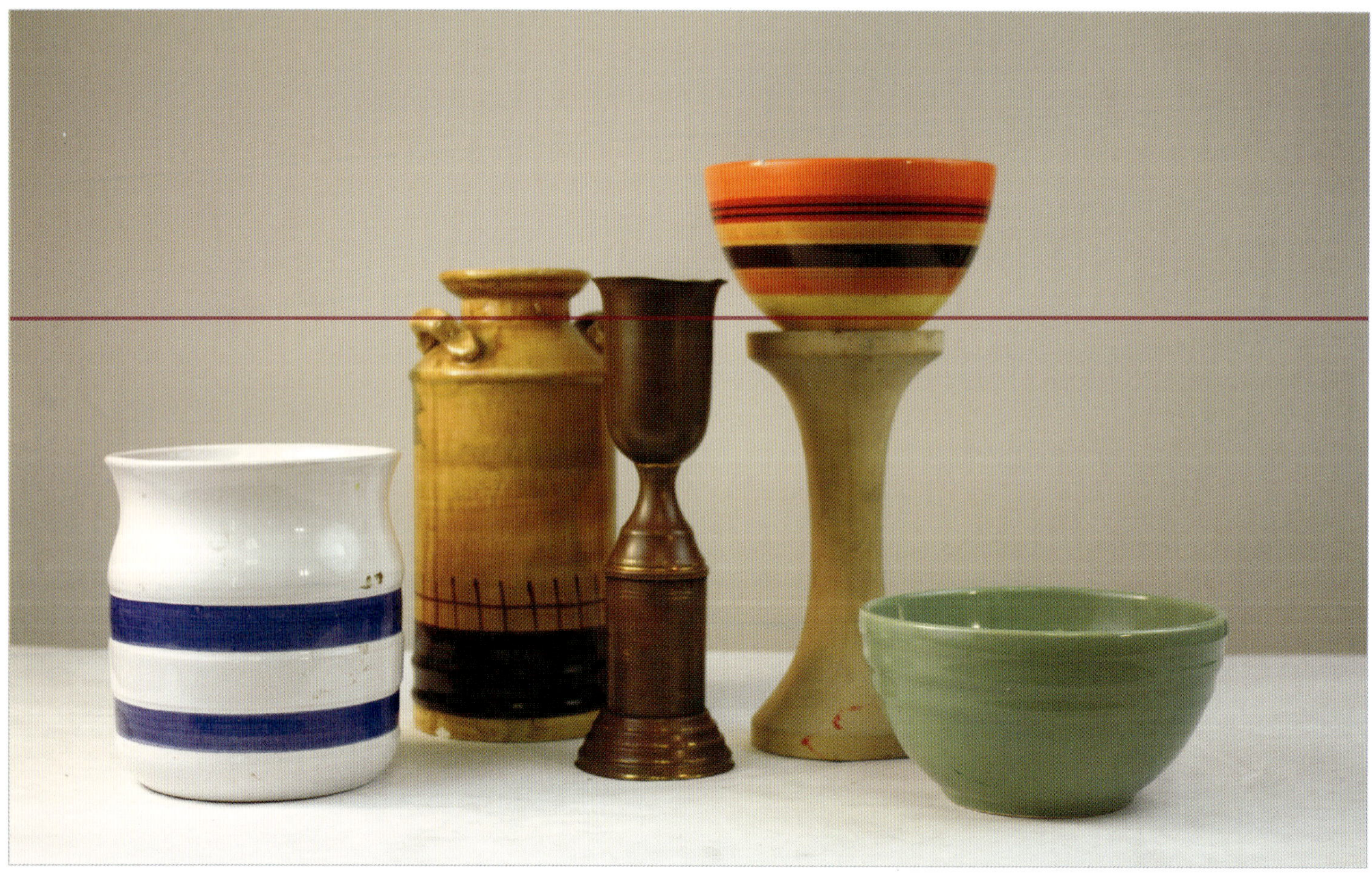

For a visual explanation of eye level we'll use this set of pots, of different shapes and sizes. Eye level is located somewhere between and within the height range of the objects, as the viewer is able to see the inside top of the objects that are below eye level, but not of those above eye level. Notice that the bases of all the objects seem to be in similar locations across the ground plane.

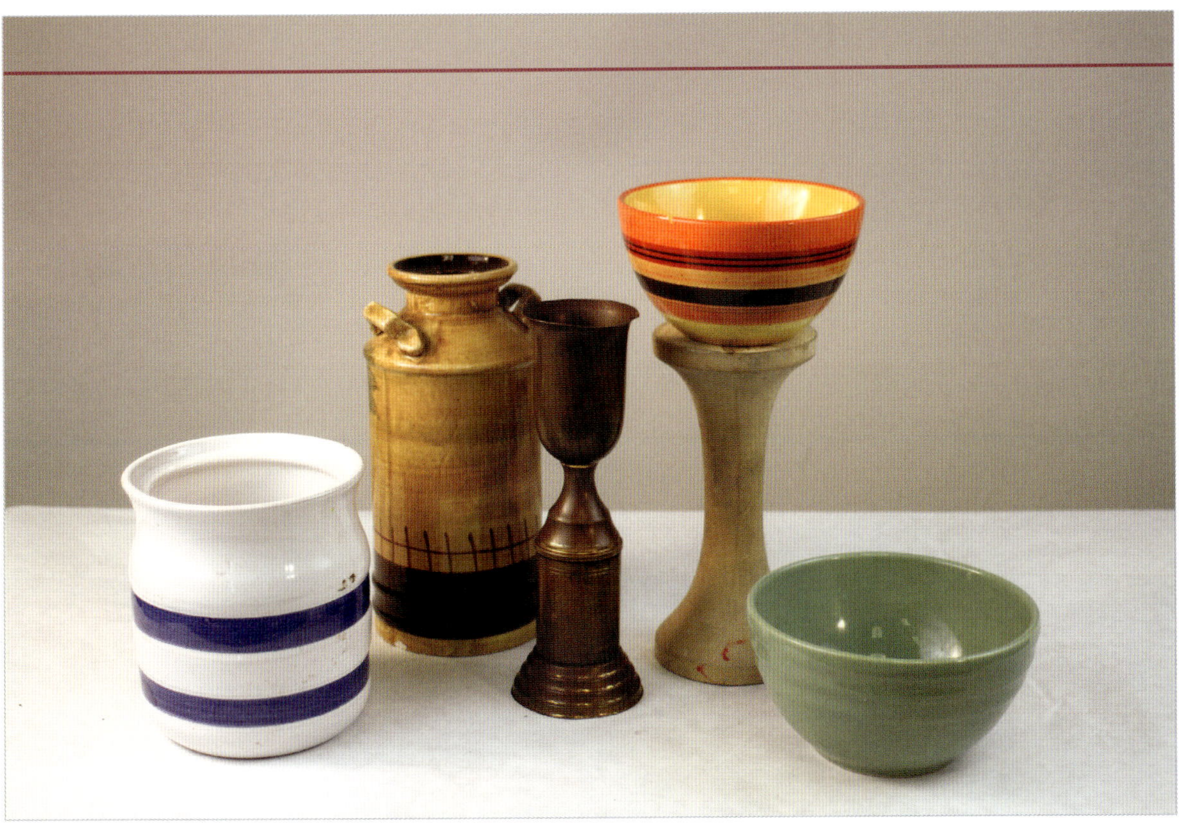

Now the viewer's eye level is above the level of the pots, and it is much easier to see inside all of them. The differences in orientation across the ground plane are more apparent, as is the space that each pot's "footprint" occupies.

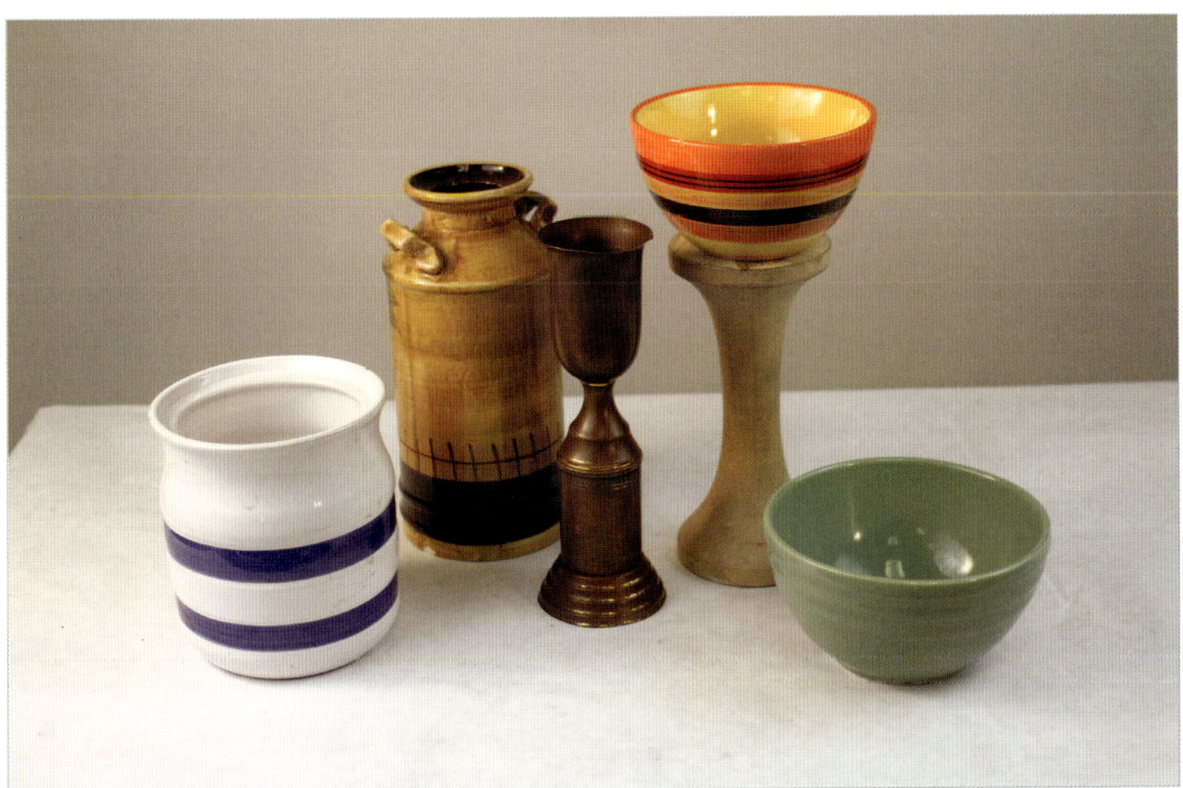

In this third picture, the eye level is higher and completely out of the image. The given space between each object is more apparent. Note that the objects nearest to the bottom of the picture plane are the closest to the viewer. This type of overhead view for a group of objects makes it easier to understand

Other Uses for the Picture Plane

When attempting to compose a still life on the drawing surface, it is helpful to use a straight tool, such as another pencil or, in this case, a long chopstick. A good starting point is to use the chopstick to gauge overall implied angles that the objects present to each other within the context of the composition.

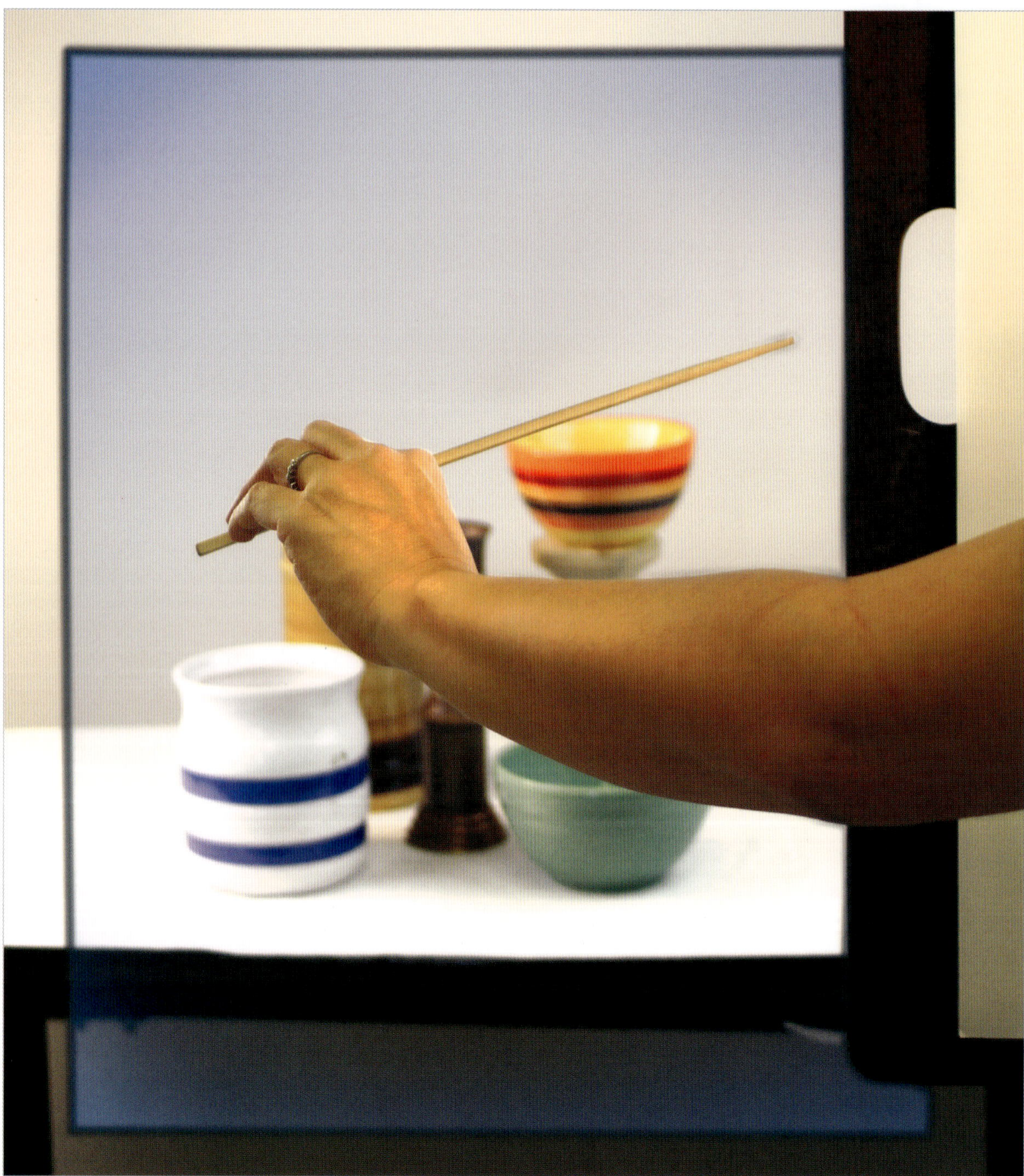

A chopstick is helpful, when used as a viewing tool against the picture plane, in understanding how objects are perceived in relation to one another. Remember to keep the chopstick parallel to the imaginary picture plane.

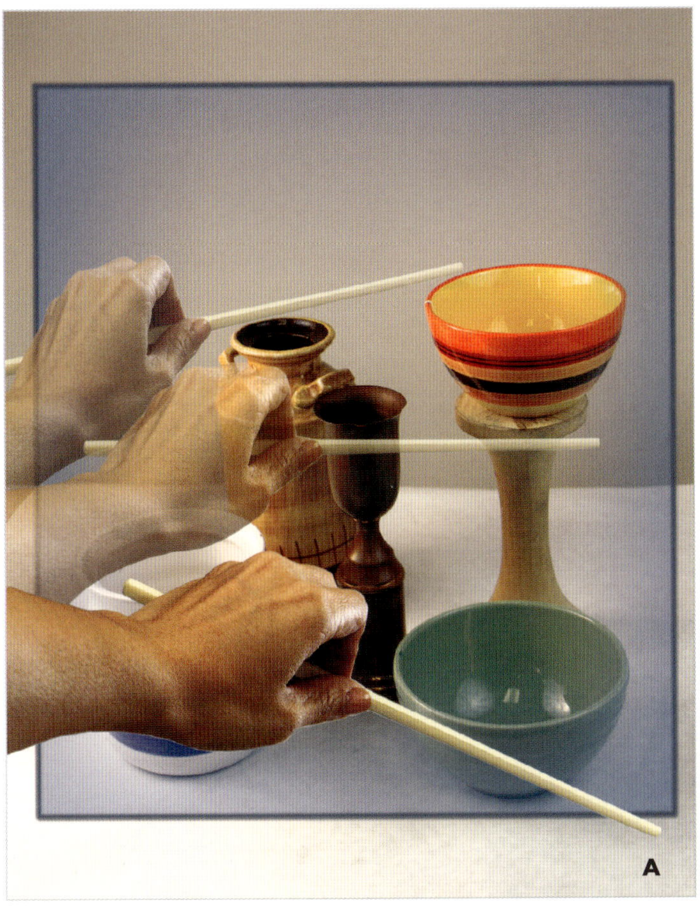

Rotate the chopstick to observe the imaginary angles that objects have in relation to each other when viewed through the picture plane.

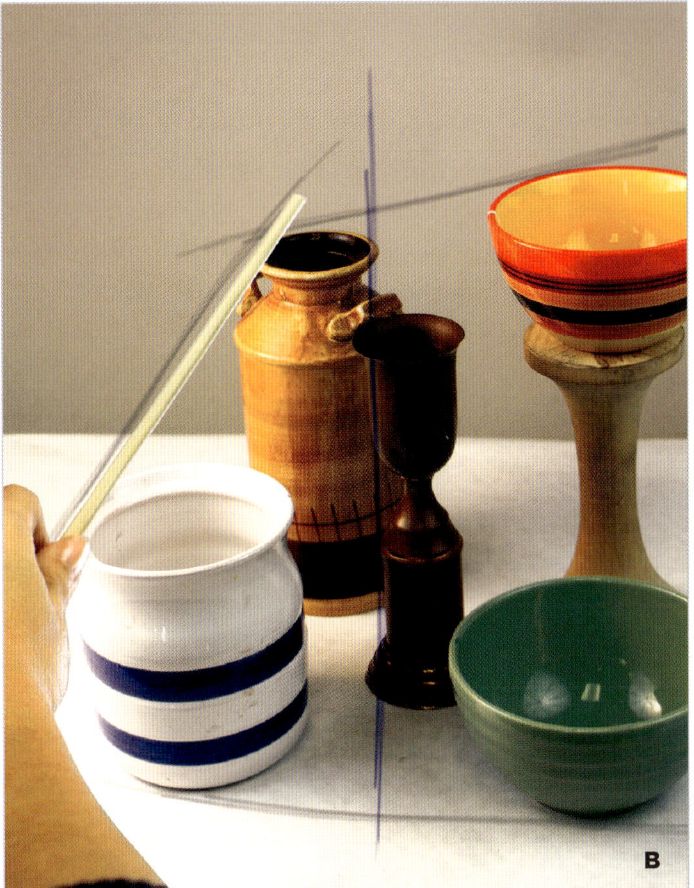

These imaginary angular relationships can be recorded as lightly sketched lines in an overall preliminary, gestural blocked-in sketch.

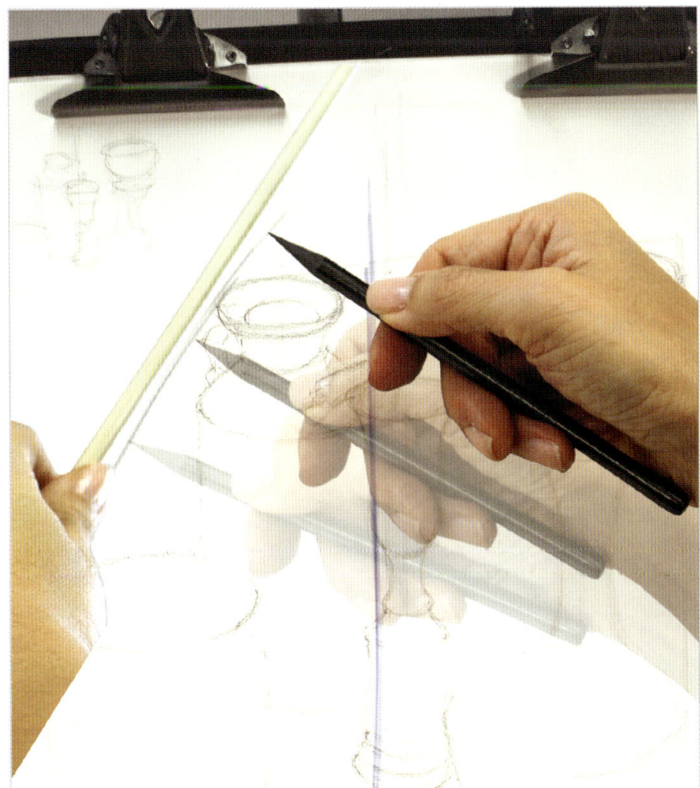

As you view these angles, it's imperative to keep the chopstick parallel with the picture plane (A). The chopstick can be easily rotated around the imaginary plane, as long as this rule is followed. This way any angles of coincidence can be seen in the still life and applied to the drawing surface, as long as that surface is parallel with the picture plane (B, C).

Symmetry of Form

Symmetry refers to the similarity of form across a midline, also called an "axis." In a symmetrical object like this bottle, this means that each side of the bottle is the same, separated by a common midline (the axis), here called a *major axis.*

The axis is an invisible vertical line that runs directly through the object from top to base. Seeing the axis makes it much easier to draw any kind of symmetrical object.

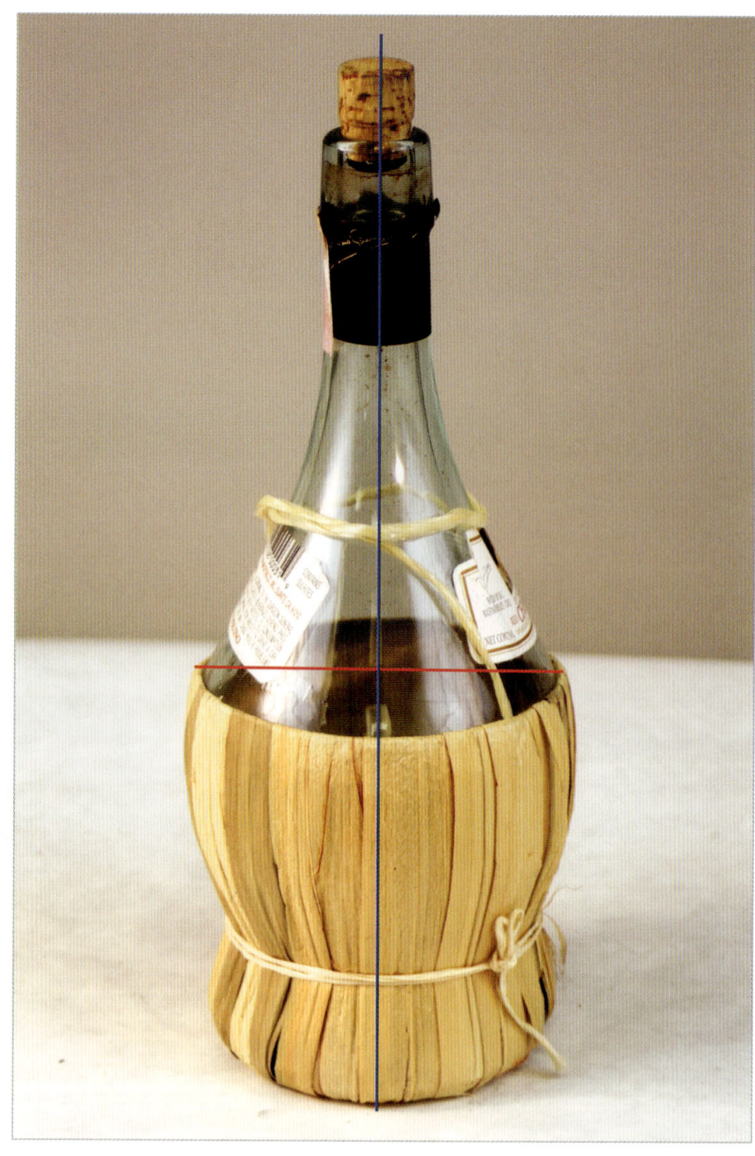

This bottle has an identical structure on both sides of its midline (blue), and is therefore a symmetrical object. The red line representing the width of the bottle is equal on both sides of the midline.

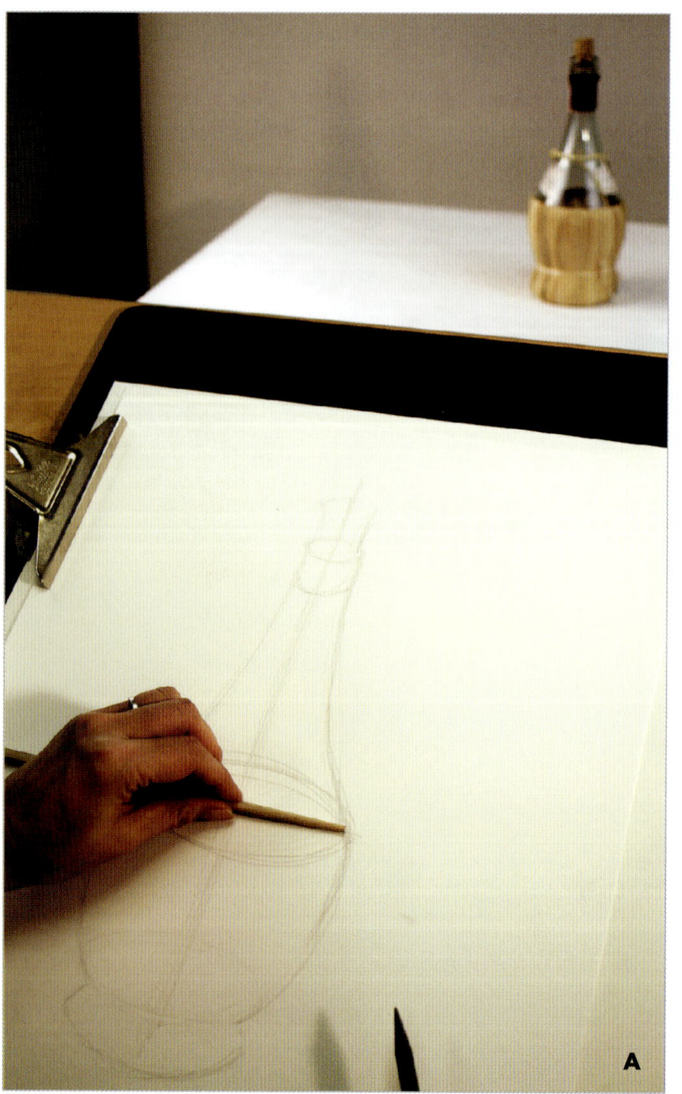

After finishing the light gesture drawing, and before moving on to a stronger, more refined drawing, use the chopstick to gauge accuracy and spacing on both sides of the midline axis (A).

Use a chopstick to check the accuracy of the drawing on both sides of the midline.

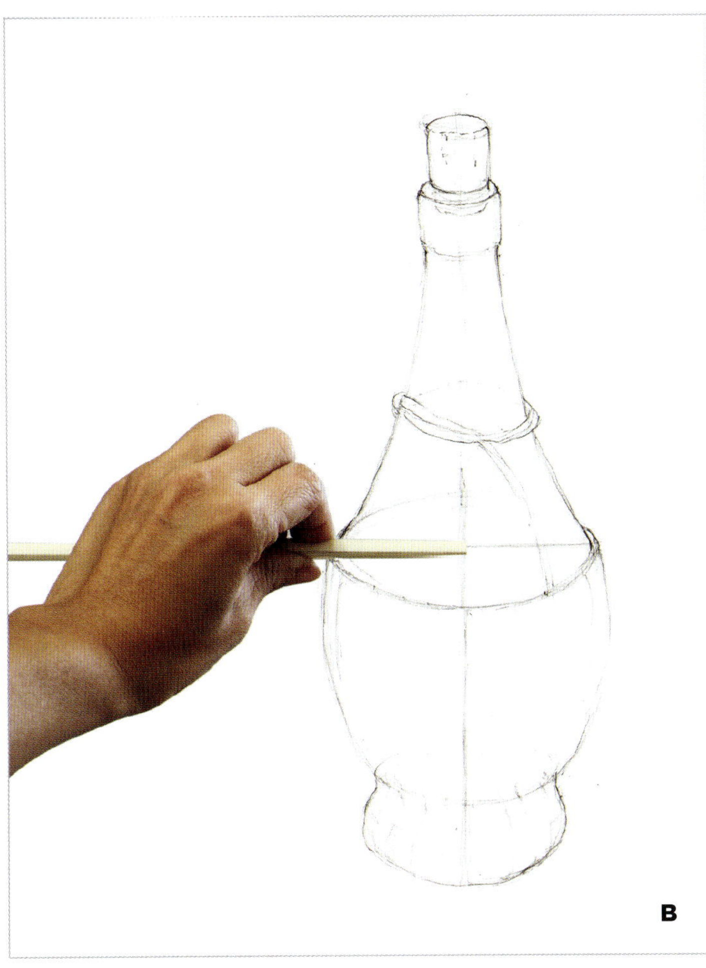

B

Do this at several points along the vertical length of the axis until you are satisfied that the entire object is symmetrical (B, C). If there are any instances where the symmetry is wrong, it's easy make corrections to the light drawing.

To measure the object, place the end of the chopstick at the object's midline axis and hold the chopstick with thumb and forefinger placed at the left edge of the object. This constitutes one unit of measurement.

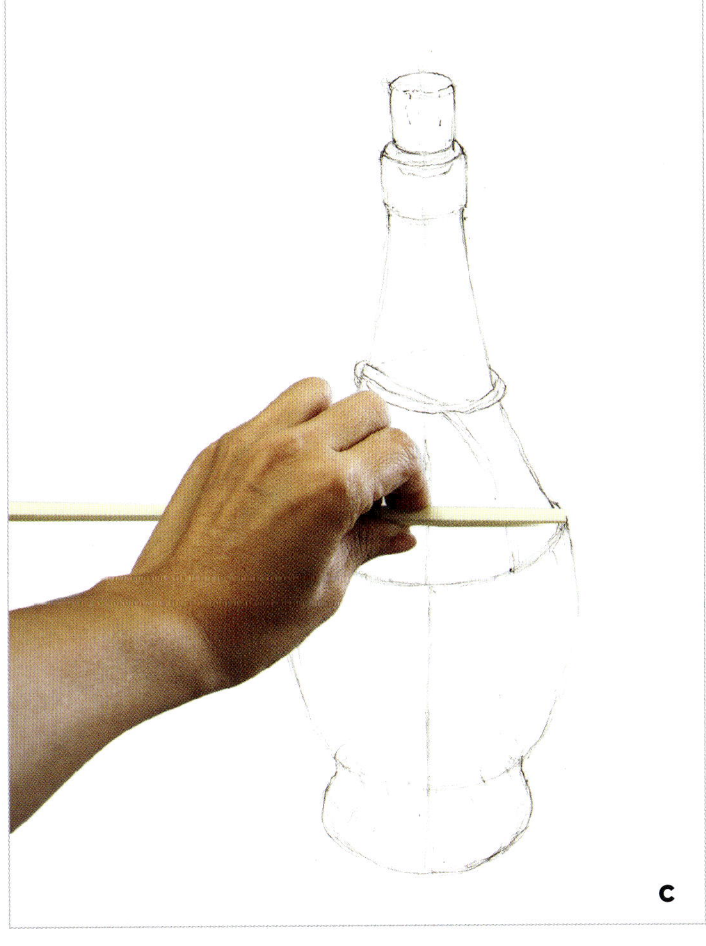

C

Without changing your finger placement, move the chopstick laterally so that your thumb and forefinger are at the midline; the end of the chopstick is now on the object's right side. If both measurements are the same, the object is symmetrical across this dimension.

Units of Measurement

The chopstick can be very useful in finding accurate measurements of objects and proportional relationships between objects in a still life. It's important to remember that the arm must always be straight and parallel to the picture plane when measuring an object. This way any object's height or width can be used in comparison to any other height, width, or distance in the still life.

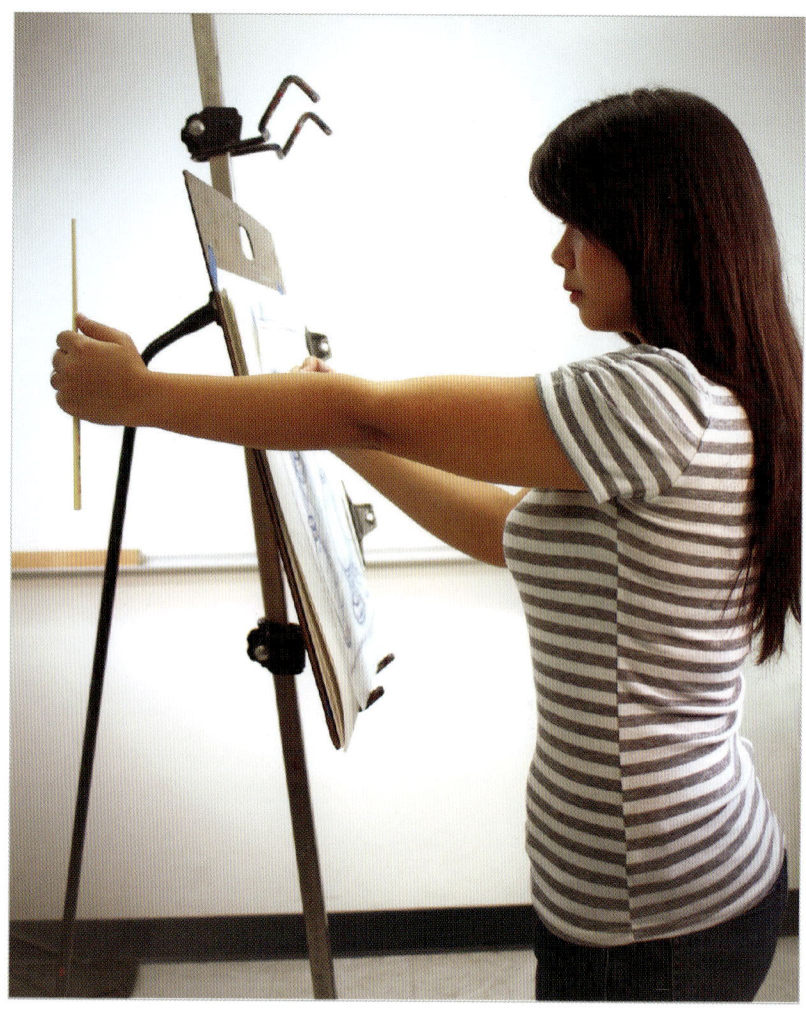

In this still life, we're focusing on the pot with the blue stripes in order to find a unit of measurement to use as a baseline proportion. The thumb and forefinger are placed on the chopstick at the base of the object, while the tip of the chopstick is placed at top of the object (A, B). This is the unit of measurement that can be used to ascertain the objects' relative sizes or the relative distance from one object to another (C). This should be done after the objects are lightly blocked in during the overall gesture sketch, before any refinement or detail is added. At this stage, any necessary corrections to size and placement can still be easily made.

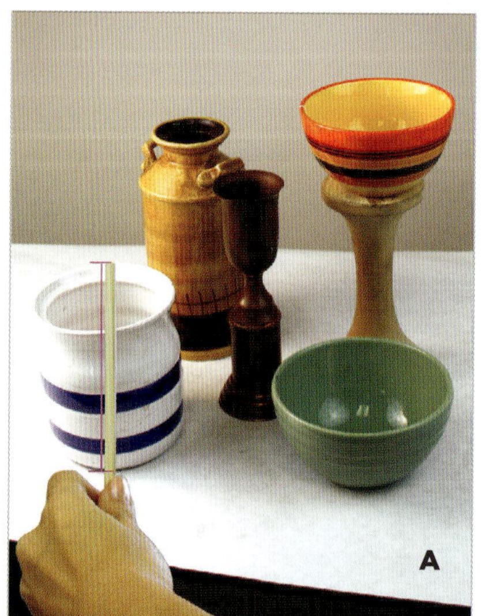

The chopstick can be used to obtain a unit of measurement that the artist can use against other objects and spaces between objects. A good object to use for this unit of measurement is something simple and close to a squared form.

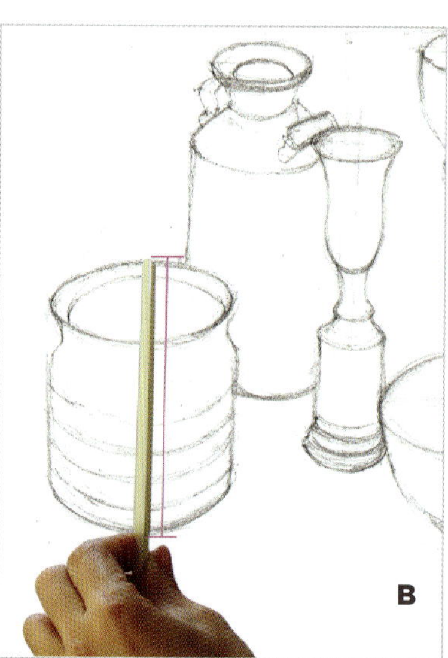

After an initial, light blocked-in gesture sketch of the entire still life, the artist uses the chopstick to find the unit of measurement.

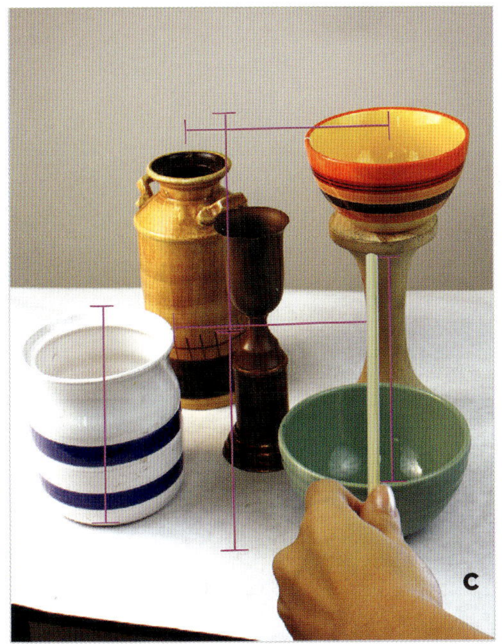

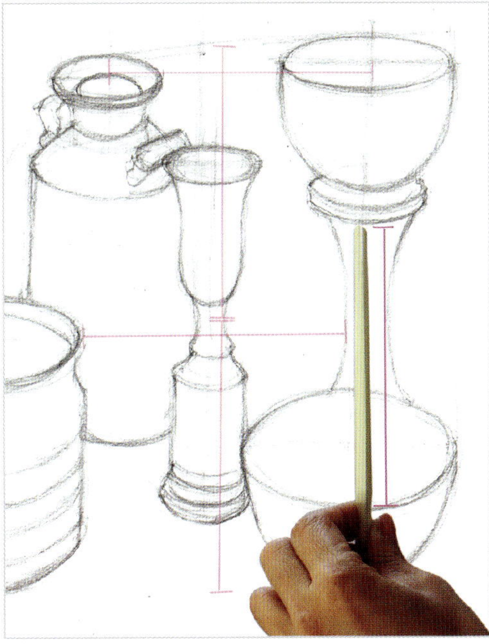

Within this still life there are several objects that are similar to the basic unit of measurement and some that are double the unit of measurement. The same can be said for the spaces between objects.

Bringing It All Together

In this still life, the angles corresponding to the heights and locations of each object are determined with the aid of a chopstick kept parallel to the picture plane. The angles are then sketched onto the light, blocked-in gesture drawing of the still life.

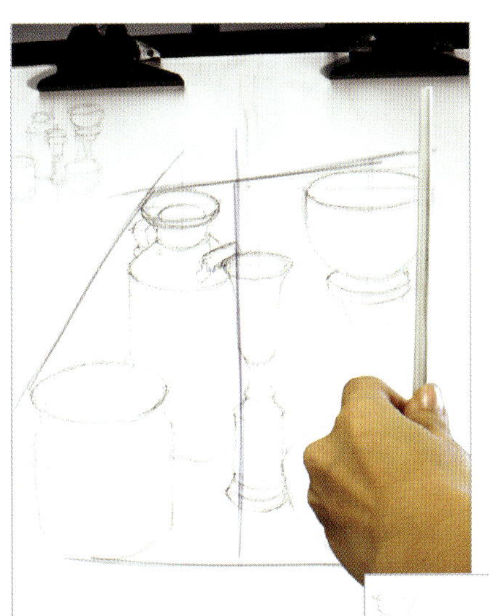

The unit of measurement for the striped pot is applied to several objects and distances for comparison, and the midline of each symmetrical object is sketched and used to verify the accuracy.

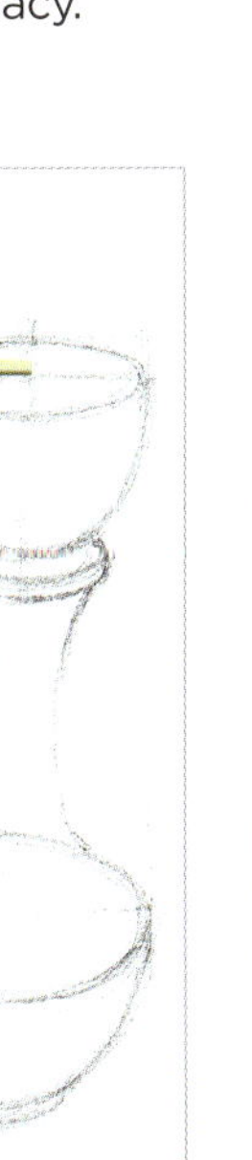

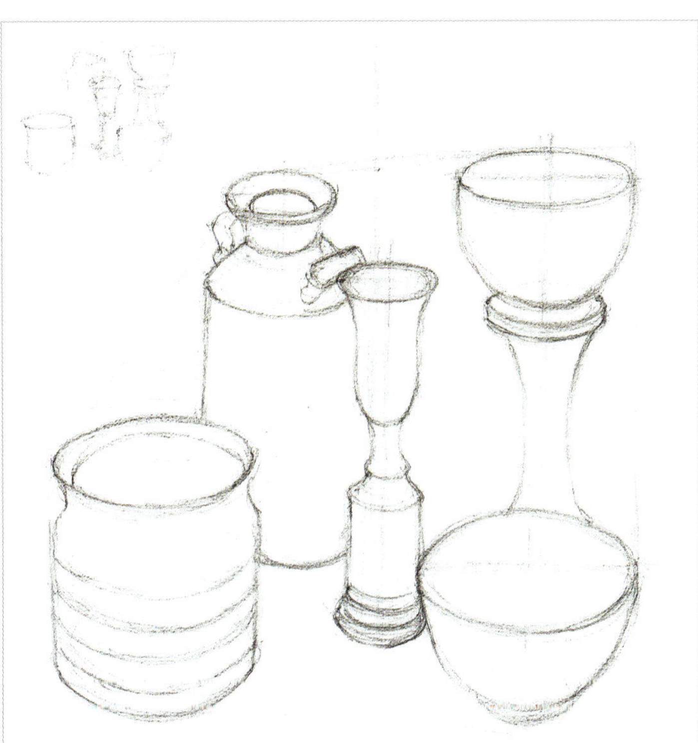

The final sketch is shown here with a small initial thumbnail sketch at top left that can be created prior to starting the large sketch. The thumbnail sketch is normally accomplished in 5 to 10 minutes and can aid in the initial placement of objects within the still life in the larger drawing.

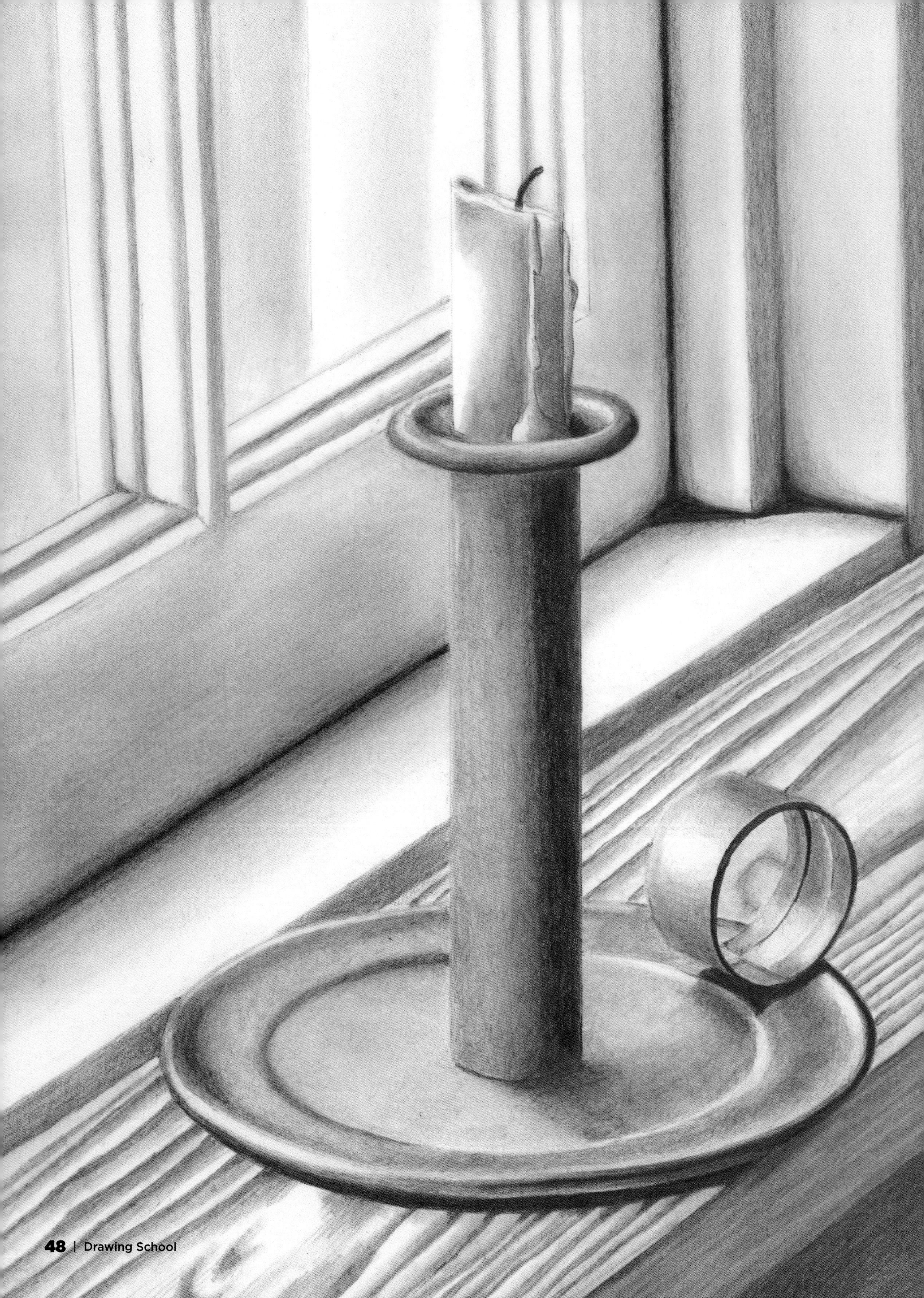

DRAWING CIRCLES IN PERSPECTIVE

In this chapter, we will discuss the nature and drawing of circles in perspective, called ellipses. We will discuss practical techniques that are intended to aid the beginning drawing student in a fairly straightforward and accurate discussion and demonstration. Remember: Good drawing comes with a lot of practice, so once you understand what ellipses are—and how to draw them—practice whenever you are able. Nothing gives away an artist's deficiencies more quickly than a drawing with poorly constructed ellipses; even to the untrained eye, lack of accuracy in drawn ellipses can usually be spotted, although the viewer may not quite understand what is wrong with the picture or how to fix the problem.

Ellipses: Foreshortened Circles

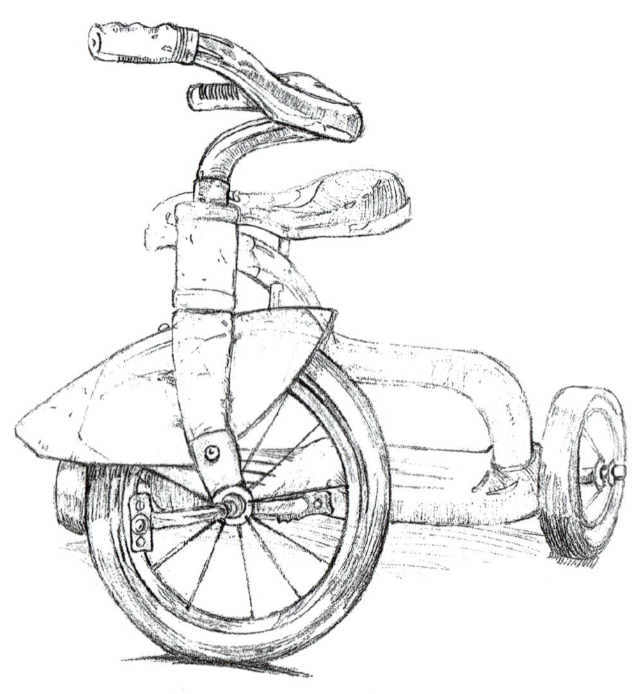

An *ellipse* is a circle in perspective. It sounds simple, yet many artists find it challenging to accurately draw them. Once you learn some simple rules and properties of ellipses, the mysteries will be revealed, and you can successfully and easily render them.

We see ellipses in objects all around us—rims of cups, bowls, and other cylindrical objects; wheels on cars, bicycles, and roller skates, etc. Observed straight on, these forms are circular, but it is much more common to see them at angles. Therefore, it is in the artist's best interest to learn as much as possible about ellipses.

One of the most important elements that dictates how we see the shape of an ellipse is its relationship to eye level. Knowledge of eye level and its location is a key component in almost every drawing, but especially in regard to ellipses.

Wrong Ways to Draw Ellipses

Demonstrated at right are a few illustrations of the wrong ways to draw ellipses. The first example shows the classic "football" shape of an incorrectly drawn ellipse; the edges of an ellipse should always be rounded and never pointed.

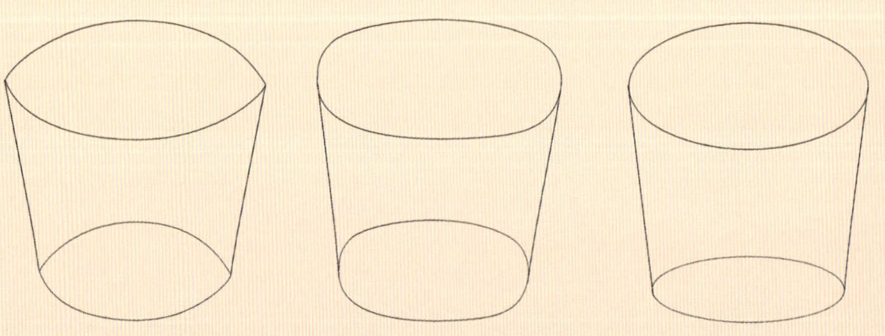

In the second example, the edges of the ellipse are too rounded, with the top and bottom edges too straight across their length. Ellipses should always curve continuously and have no straight edges.

In the third example, the ratio of closed-to-open ellipses is wrong. The nearer the ellipse is to the viewer's eye level, the tighter that ellipse appears; conversely, the farther from eye level, the more rounded the ellipse appears.

Attributes of Ellipses

All circles fit into a square. When drawing an ellipse, first visualize a circle within a square and then project it into perspective to observe the foreshortening that occurs. The circle is divided into equal quadrants by a horizontal axis and vertical axis. Notice what happens when the square and circle are projected into perspective space: The horizontal axis shortens in width, and the vertical axis shortens in height.

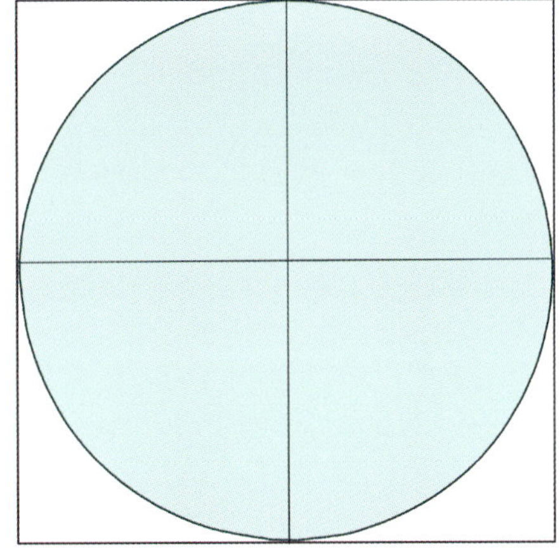

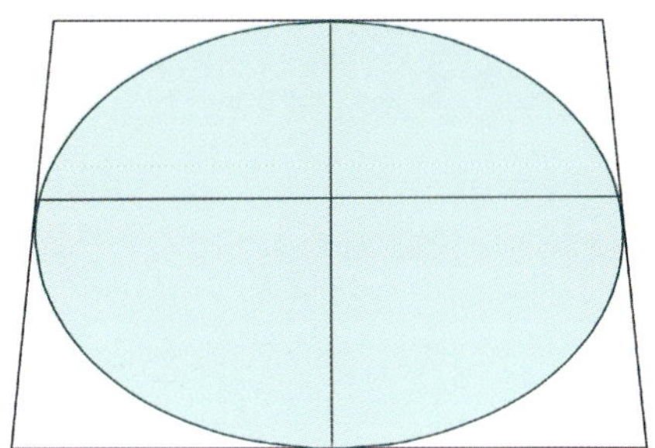

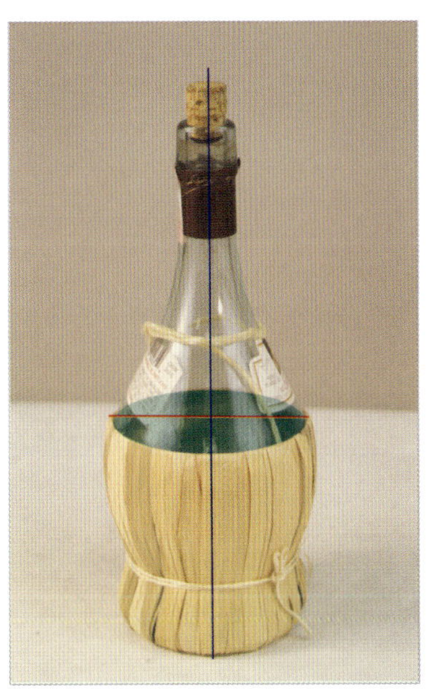

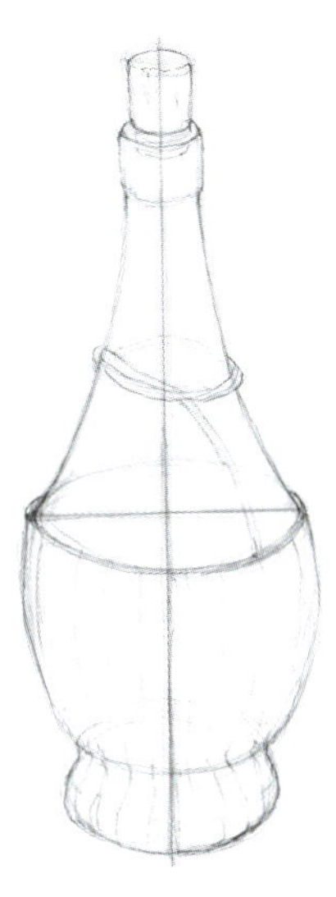

On this bottle, the horizontal axis is the major axis of the ellipse (red line). The vertical axis is the major axis of the bottle, but it is the minor axis of the ellipse (blue line). These axes are always at right angles to each other when a symmetrical object stands up straight on the ground plane. The major axis, or midline, of the bottle coincides with the ellipse's minor axis and is perpendicular to the ellipse's major axis. This is the rule when any symmetrical object's base rests on the ground plane, such as the still-life objects in the image below.

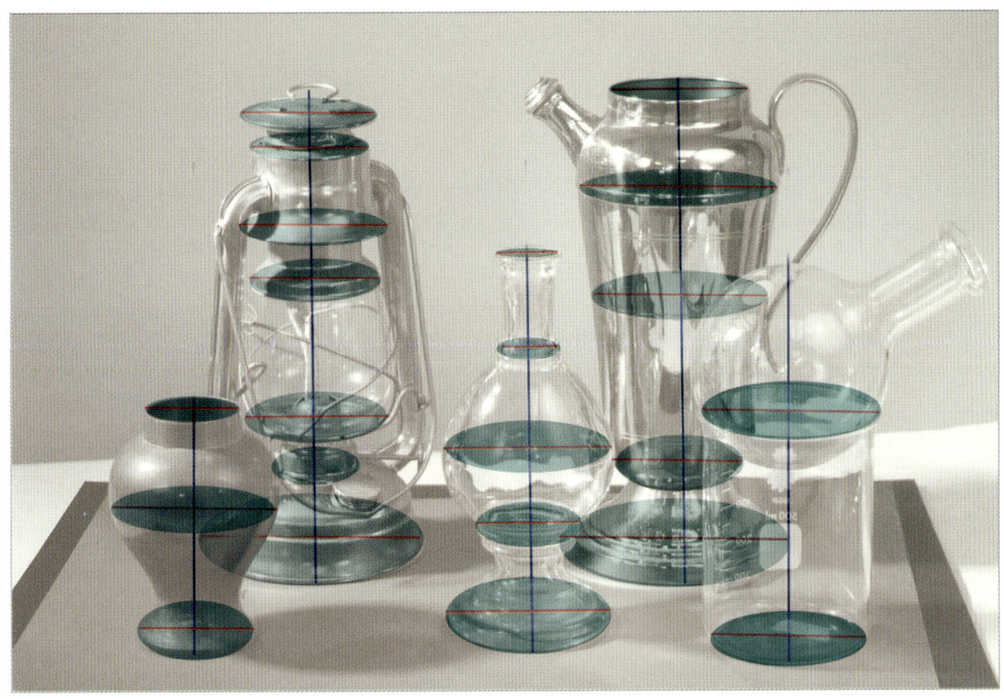

In this still life, notice the gradual change in length of the blue minor axes of the ellipses as they rise toward eye level. The relative width of the major axes (red) stays the same, however.

Size Ratio of Ellipses

Ellipses can be explained in degrees of angle to the viewer's eye level, with 90° equal to a true circle and 0° when the ellipse is viewed at eye level. As an ellipse moves toward eye level, the length of the minor (vertical) axis is reduced. As an ellipse moves away from eye level, the length of the minor axis increases. Ellipses that are parallel to each other, or in similar locations horizontally, will have very similar size ratios (see image below).

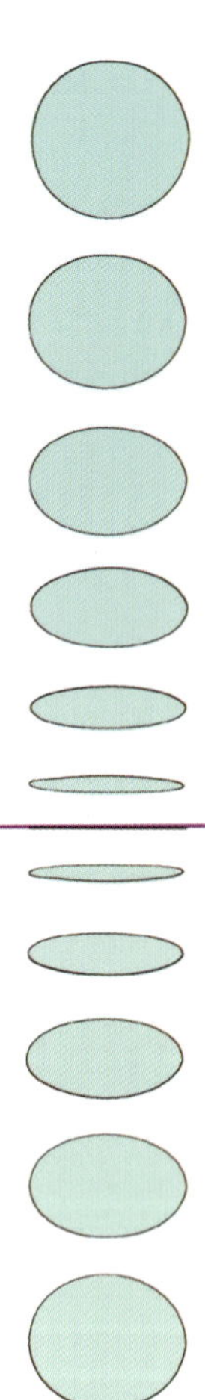

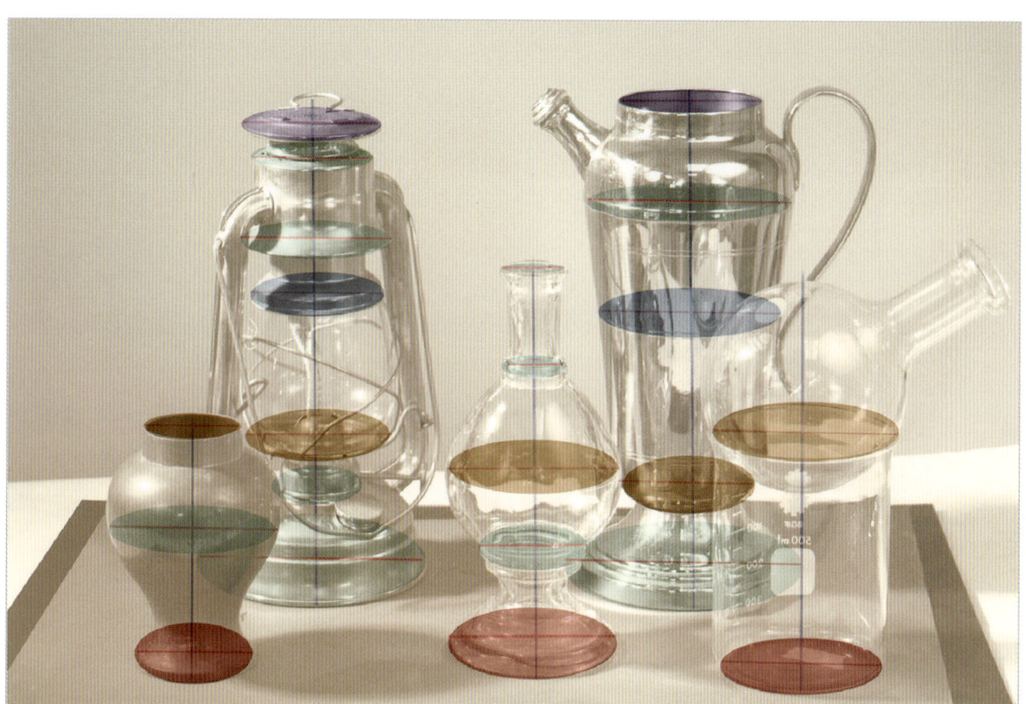

THIS PHOTOGRAPH illustrates how ellipses relatively close to each other across a horizontal location are similar in their ratio of roundness. For instance, all of the ellipses at the objects' bases (magenta) have similar ratios of roundness; let's say 50°. The middle, tan-colored ellipses are all around 30° to 35°, and the very tops of the objects (purple) are about 10° to 15°, as they are the closest to eye level.

Ellipses Not Parallel to the Ground Plane

As a circular object moves away from standing vertically on the ground plane, there are similarities and differences to the ellipses that we have already discussed.

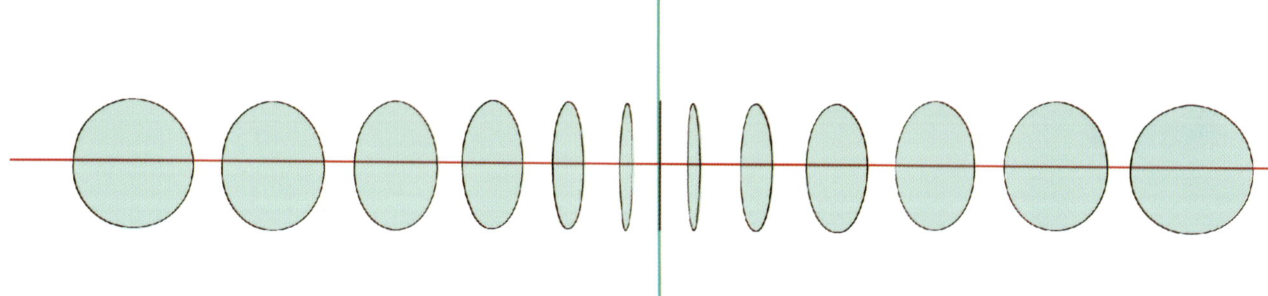

Study this photograph of four pots resting horizontally on the ground. Notice that the pot farthest from the viewer has an ellipse for its rim that is almost a straight line; as the pots rotate around the ground plane toward the viewer, the ellipse of the rim rounds out more with each successive rotation toward the viewer.

Also note that the pots tend to shift away from eye level and farther down on the picture plane. The center midline axes of the pots also present more of a perspective angle to the viewer. These midline axes are directly related to the perspective angle of the side of each pot, bisecting its symmetry.

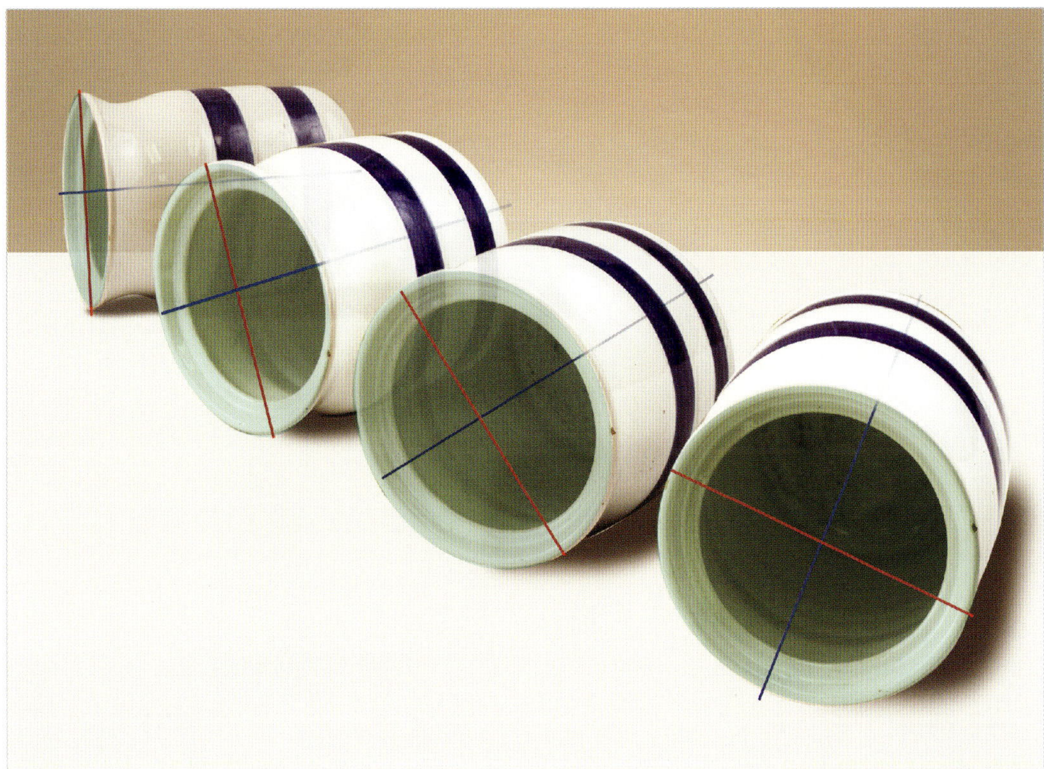

As the pots rotate toward the viewer from left to right, the ellipses become rounder, the blue midline (minor axis) becomes more of an acute angle to the picture plane, and the red major axis always stays at a right angle to the minor axis. The angle of the major axis of the pot (the minor axis of the ellipse) is dictated by the perspective construction angles of the sides of the pot.

Here is what the sketch of these pots would look like, with the major axis of the pot (also the minor axis of the ellipse) and the major axis of the ellipse sketched in lightly.

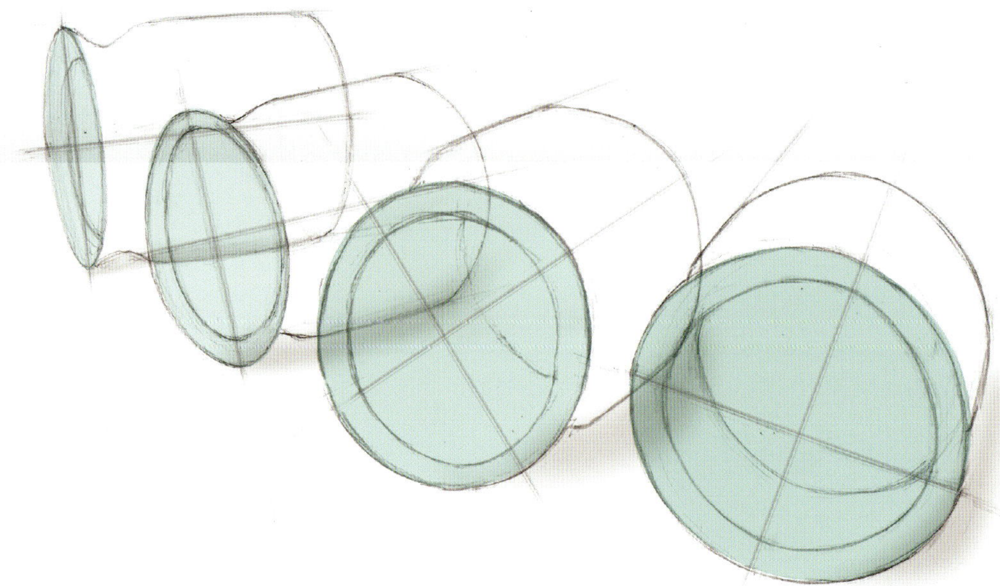

Drawing Ellipses in a Still Life

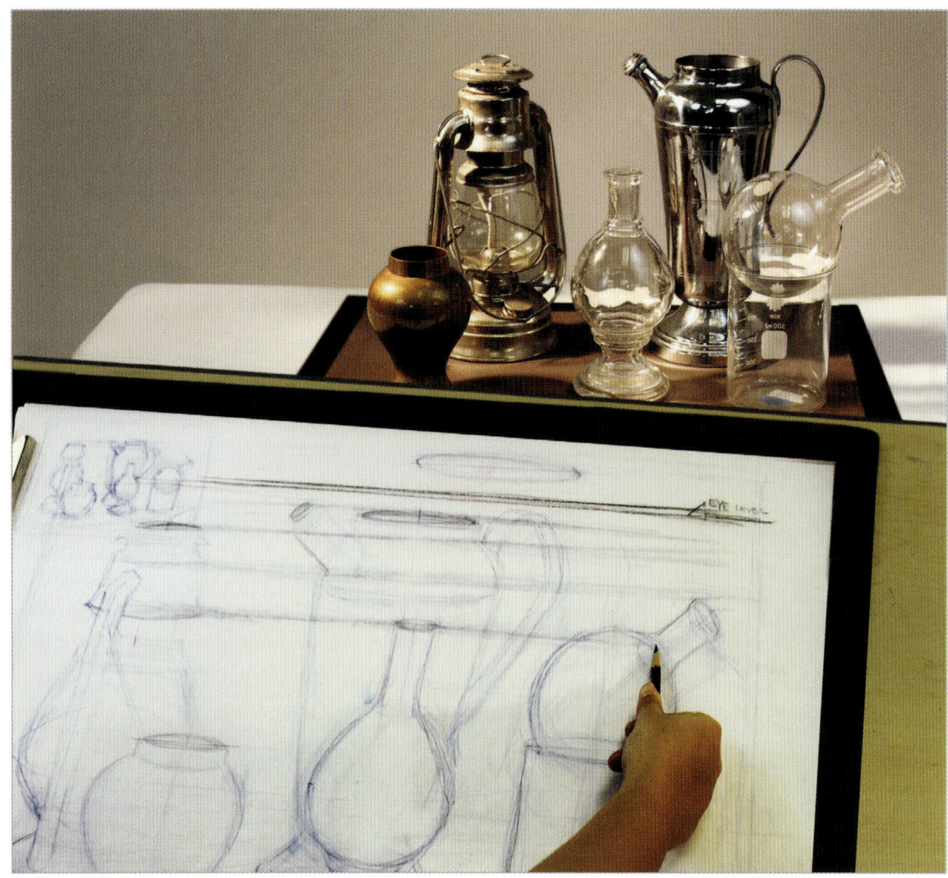

STEP 1 Make a quick thumbnail sketch in the corner to establish the objects. Then use a chopstick to see and apply visual relationships as you lightly sketch. To ensure height accuracy in each object, sketch light horizontal lines across the tops of objects and the ellipses of objects. This enables you to see which ellipses are on the same horizontal plane or on similar planes. You can then ensure that the ellipses are consistent within each plane.

STEP 2 Draw the major axis of each object freehand, remembering that the midline axes of symmetrical objects are exactly vertical.

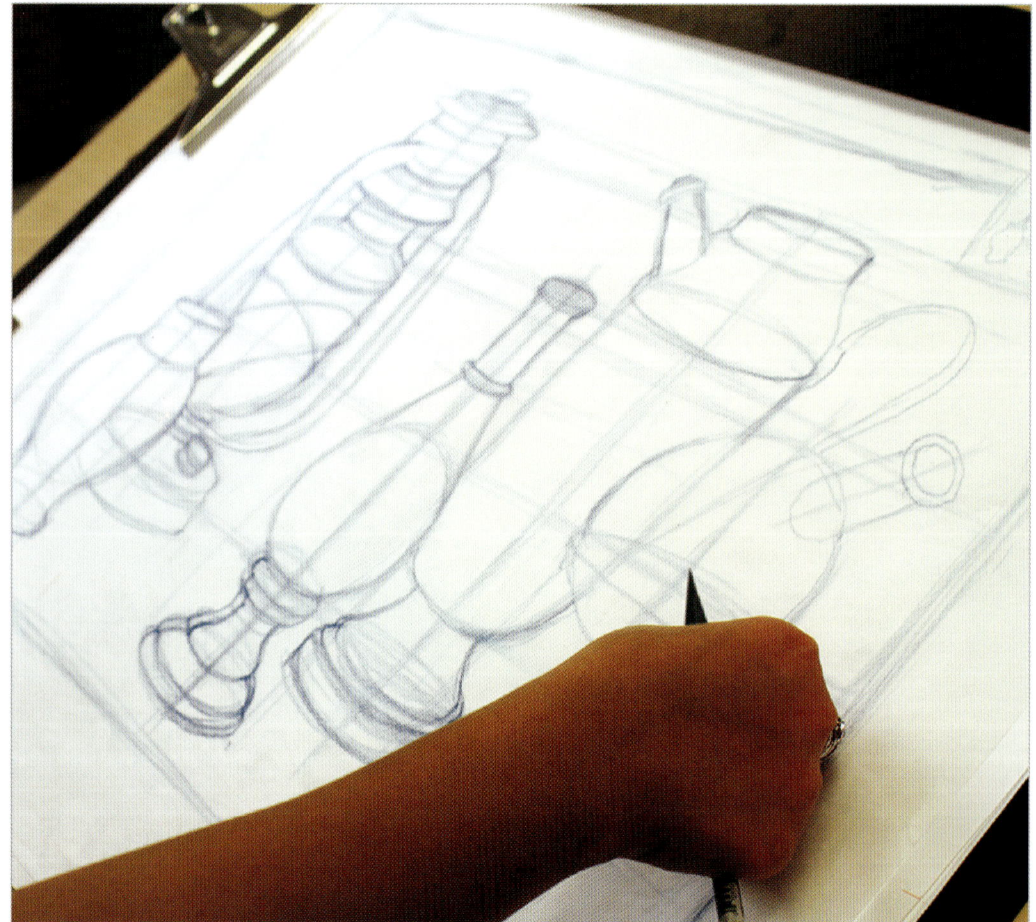

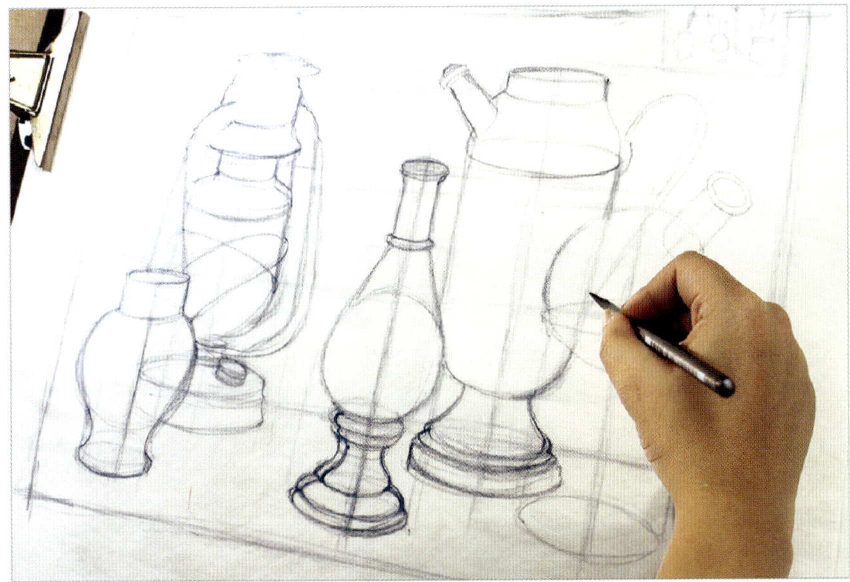

STEP 3 Check the integrity of the symmetry by using a chopstick to measure at several points along the length of each object. When all is accurate, strengthen the sketch with a contour line drawing over the light lines, using a darker graphite.

Using a Triangle

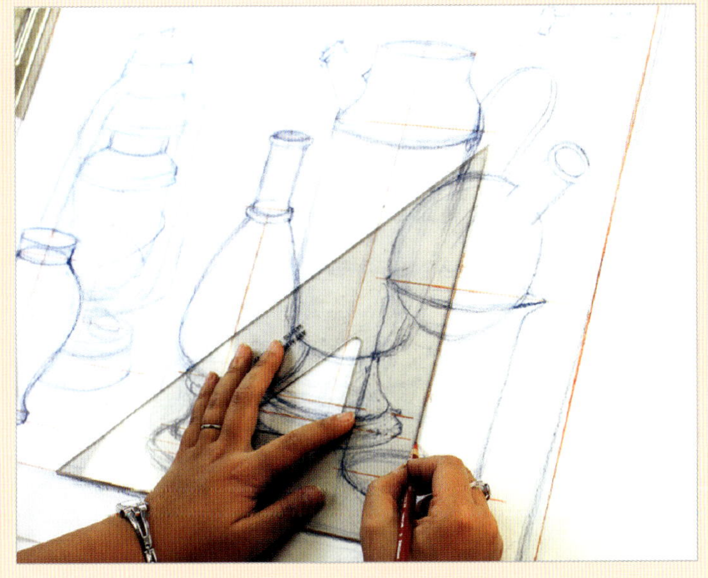

When a project calls for more refined accuracy, I recommend using a triangle to confirm the verticality of the true midline. Place the bottom of the triangle on a true horizontal line drawn below the still life. The 90° right-angle edge gives a true vertical line. You can also use a triangle to check the horizontality of the major axis of each ellipse, which should either be a right angle or perpendicular to the object's vertical midline.

Transfer the Drawing

There are many ways to transfer a preliminary drawing to art paper for the final rendering. The method you choose depends on what type of paper is used, the value of the paper, and what type of final media will be used for rendering. Here is a technique for this type of project, which will be black-and-white colored pencil on dark gray toned art paper.

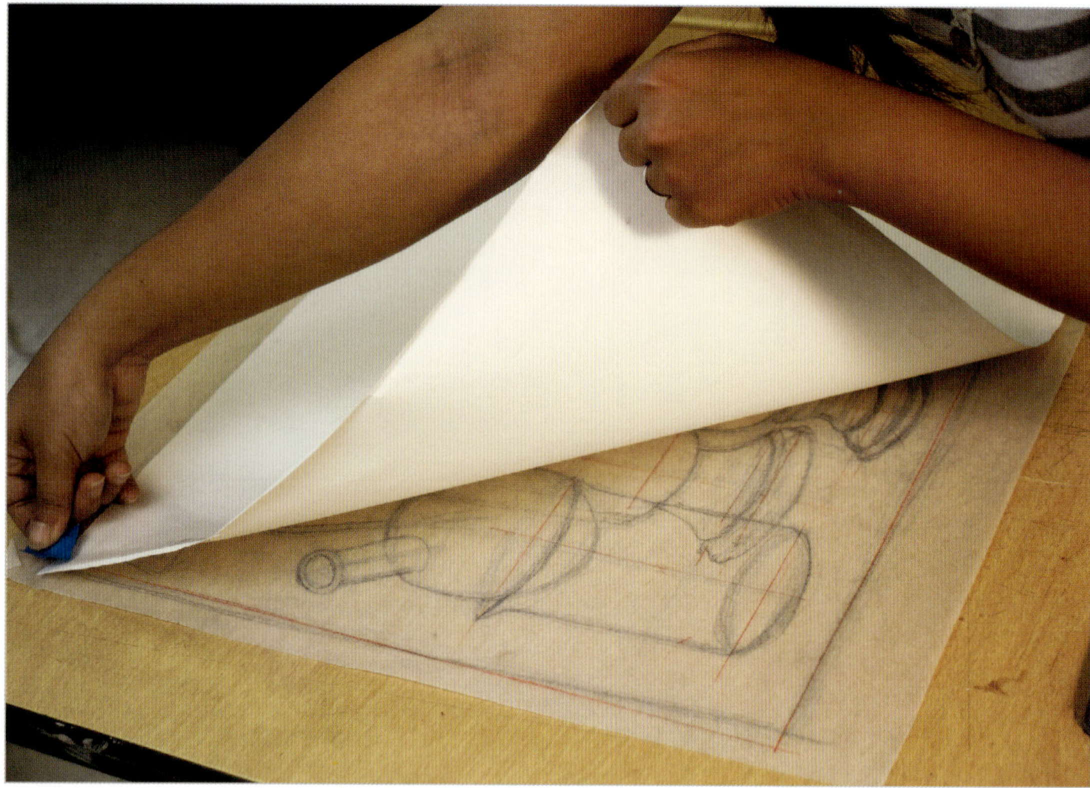

STEP 1 First tape a separate piece of white or tracing paper to the back of the drawing. This white sheet will enable you to see the line drawing when you apply dark pastel on the back of the tracing paper sketch after it is turned right-side up.

STEP 2 Use a dark coat of pastel, typically a combination of dark brown and black. Dark Conté crayons work equally well, as they have a waxy quality that makes for a nice, easy transfer. Liberally apply pastel to the back of the drawing and rub it in with your finger or a paper towel.

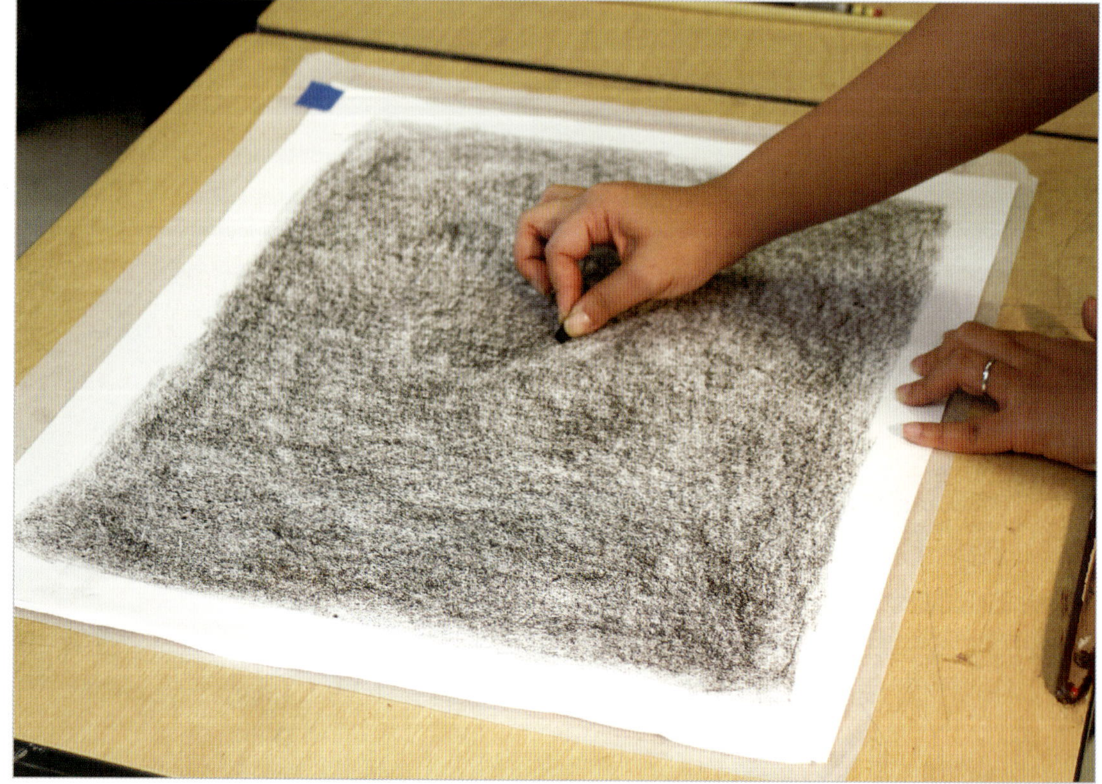

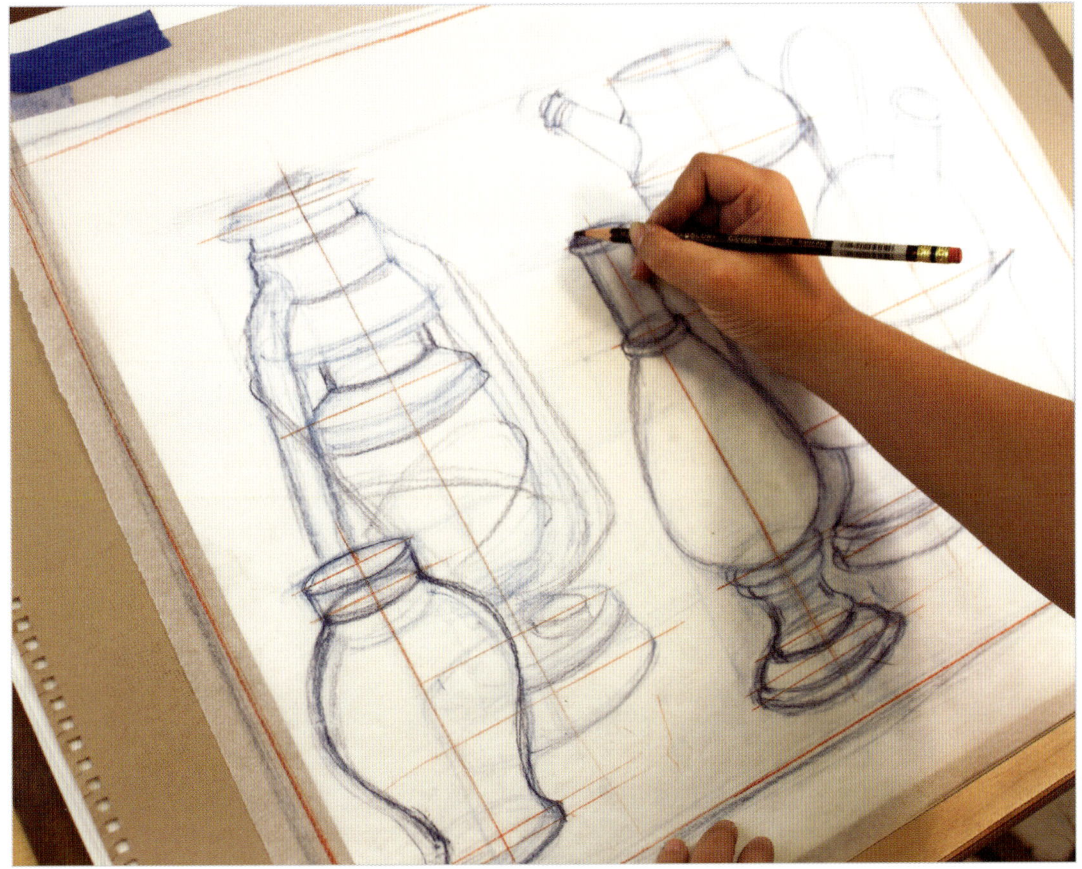

STEP 3 Turn the paper right-side up, with the sketch facing you, and tape it securely in place to the toned art paper. Then trace over your sketch. Use a different colored pencil for re-drawing/transferring so that you can clearly see what has already transferred.

STEP 4 With the initial sketch transferred to the toned drawing paper, you can develop the drawing to a full rendering. (Final tonal drawing by student Polly Hung.)

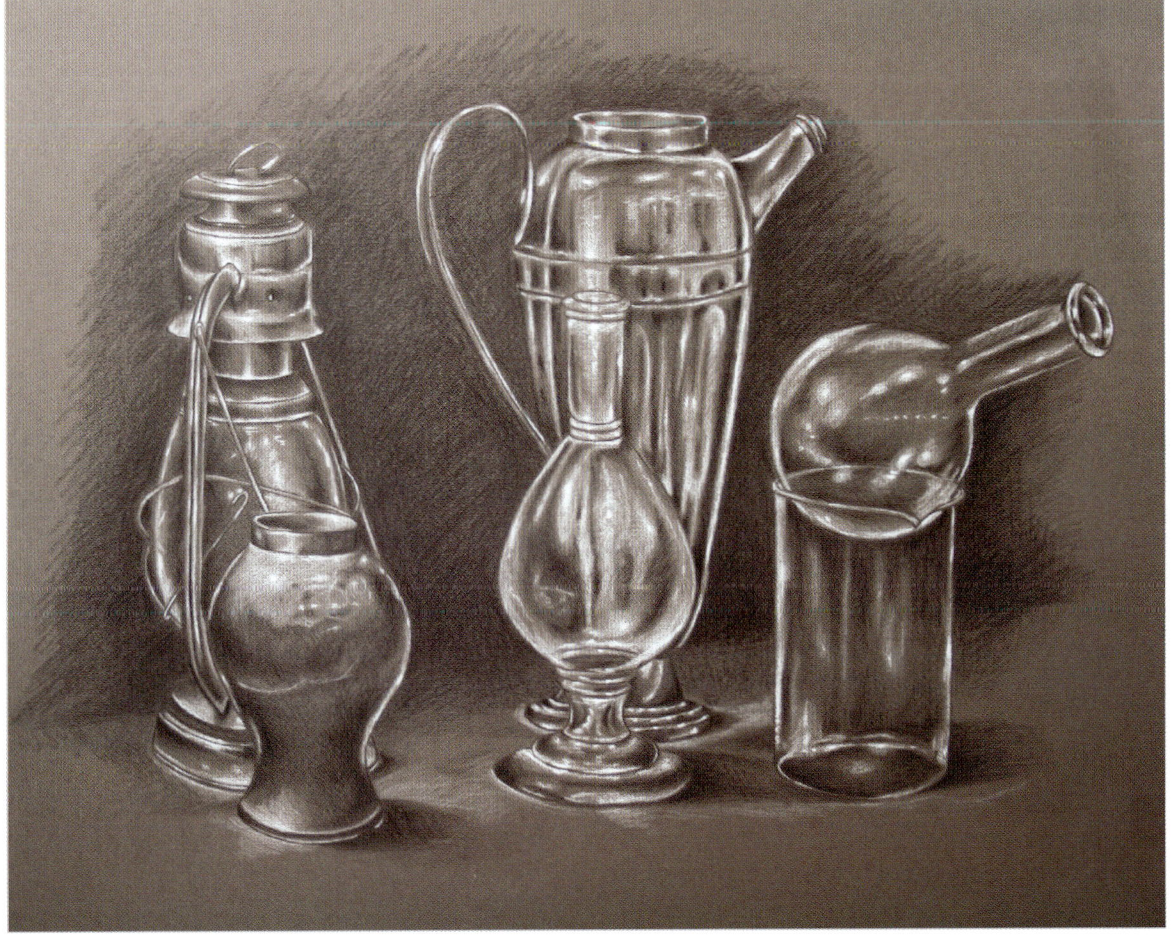

YOUR HOMEWORK

For your homework assignment, set up a simple still life (two or three objects), using glass and reflective-surface subjects. Create a line drawing using all the techniques for measuring and symmetry you've learned in this chapter. You'll find it helpful to use objects of differing sizes and shapes.

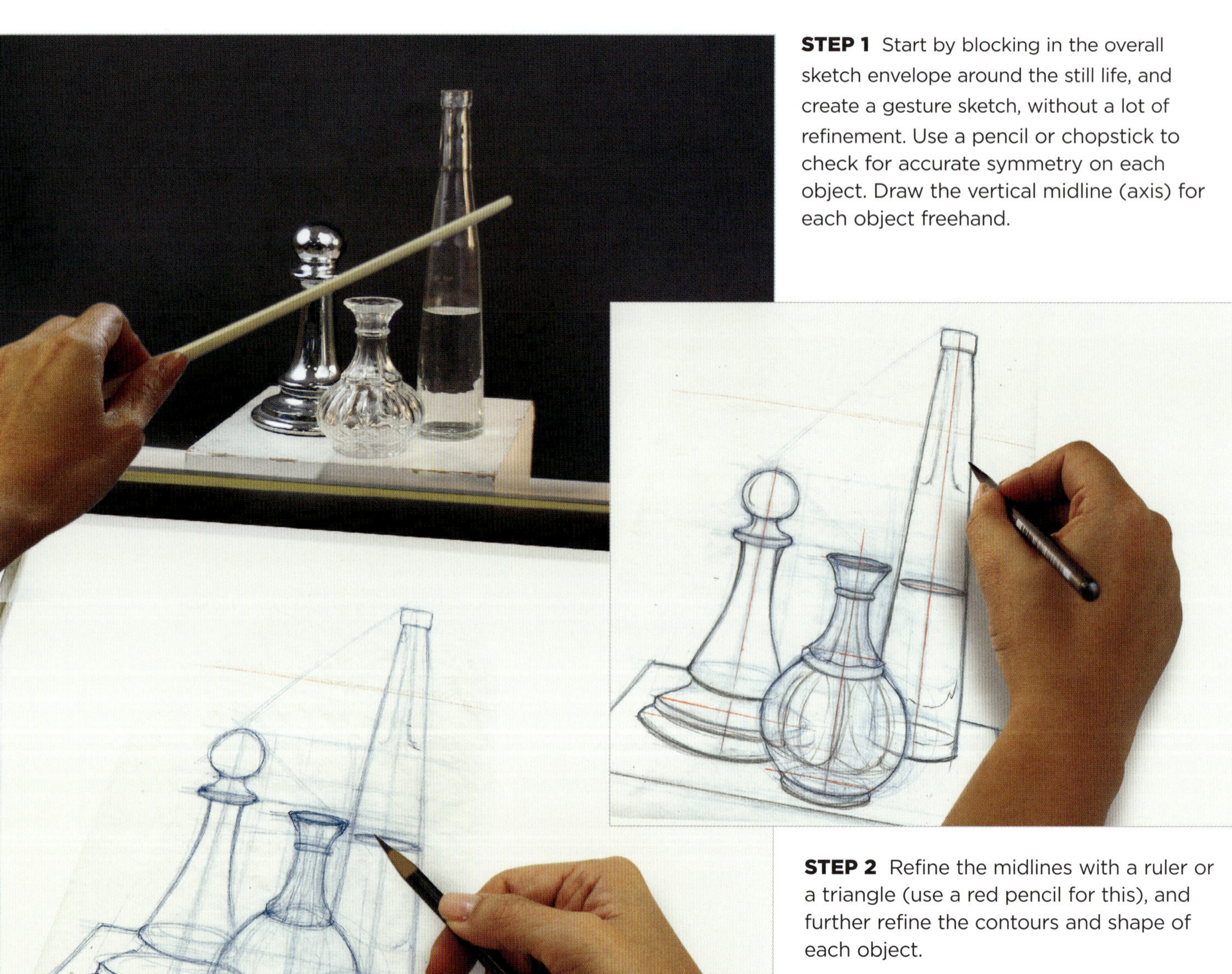

STEP 1 Start by blocking in the overall sketch envelope around the still life, and create a gesture sketch, without a lot of refinement. Use a pencil or chopstick to check for accurate symmetry on each object. Draw the vertical midline (axis) for each object freehand.

STEP 2 Refine the midlines with a ruler or a triangle (use a red pencil for this), and further refine the contours and shape of each object.

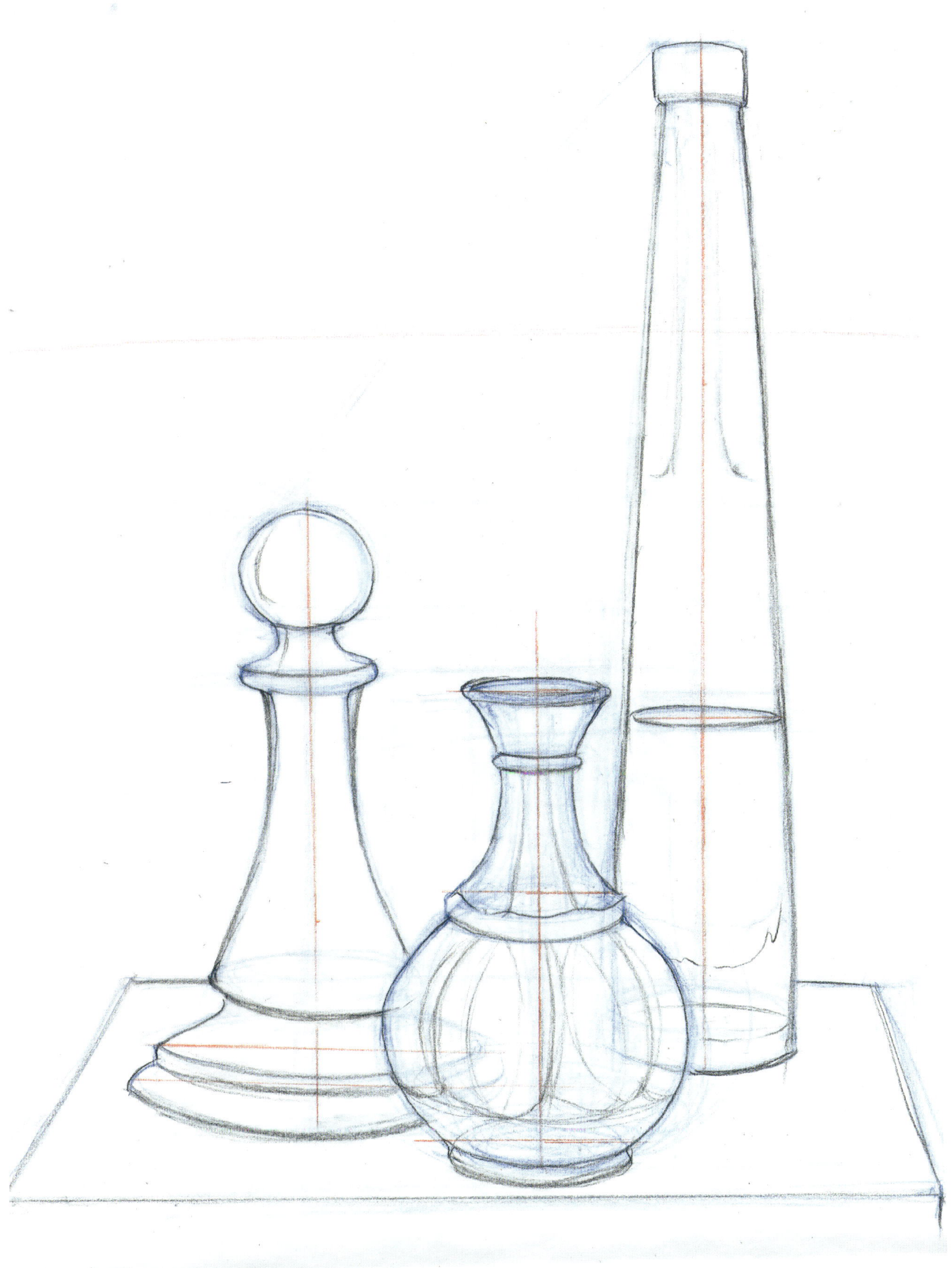

STEP 3 Here is the finished contour line still life, with an indication of the ground plane.

EXERCISES FOR PRACTICE

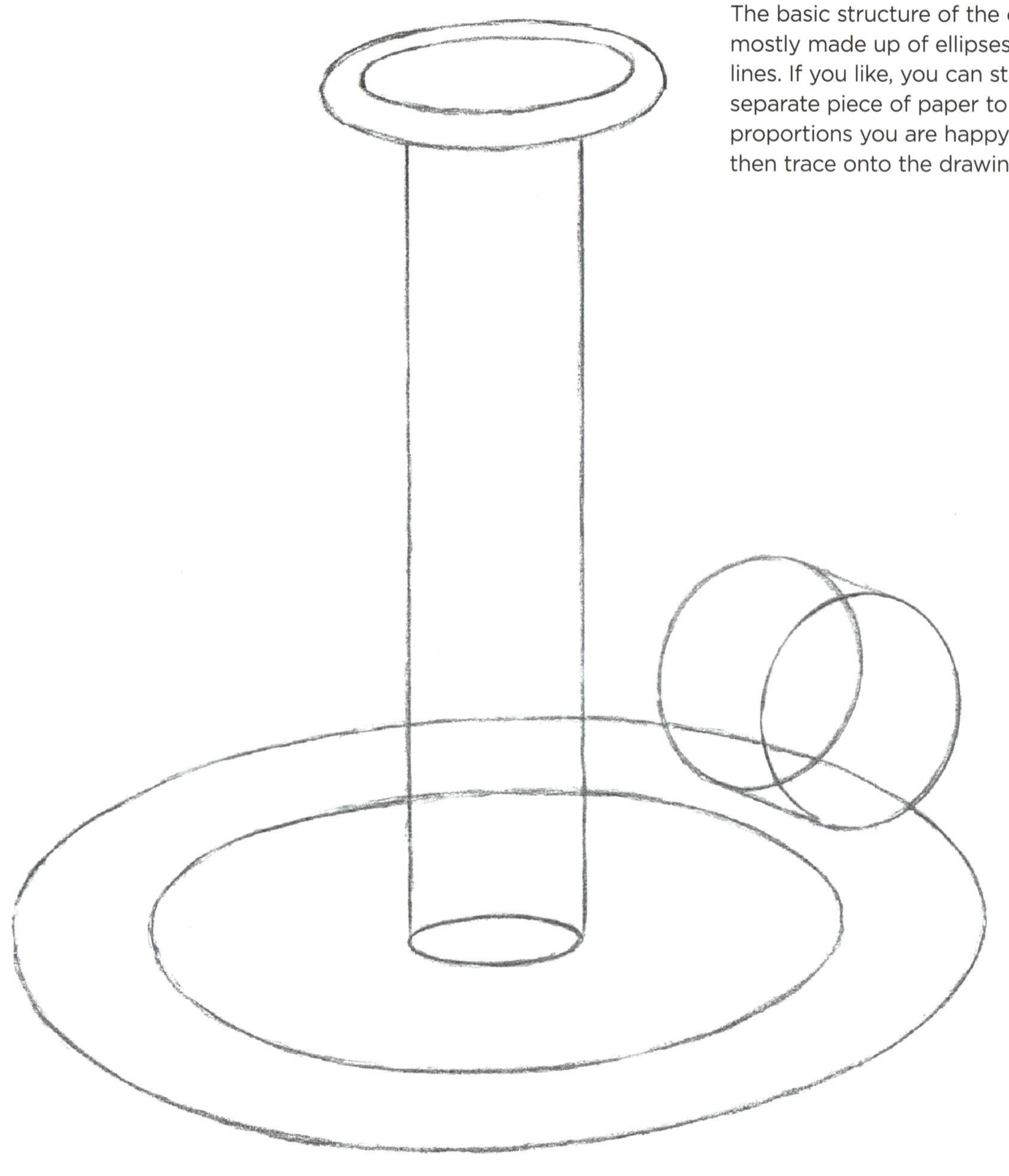

The basic structure of the candlestick is mostly made up of ellipses and straight lines. If you like, you can start on a separate piece of paper to achieve the proportions you are happy with, and then trace onto the drawing paper.

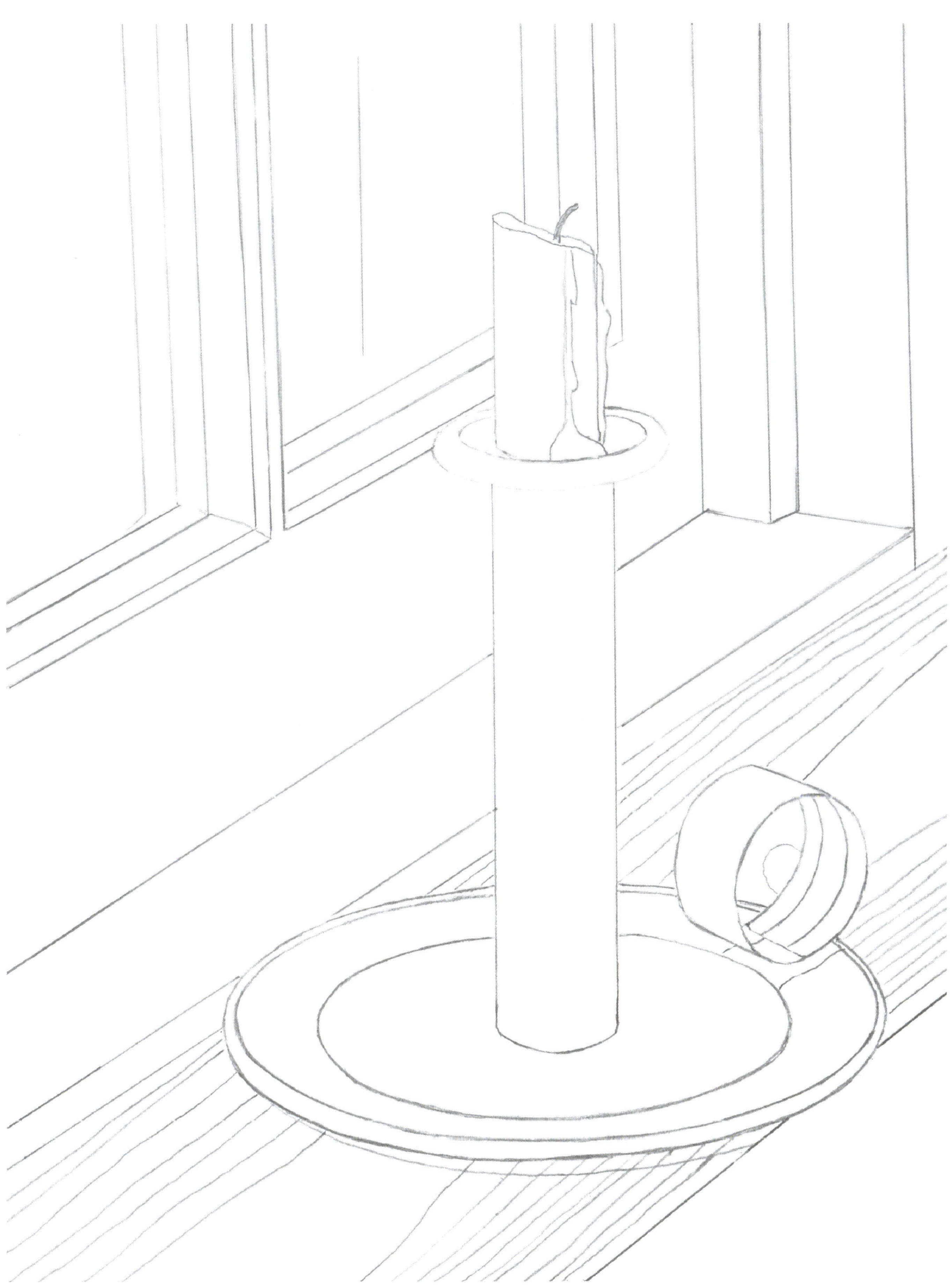

Add the candle, wood grain, and window details using very light lines. An HB or 2B pencil with light pressure works best because the lines are easy to erase later if necessary. You can use a ruler to get the lines straight where needed.

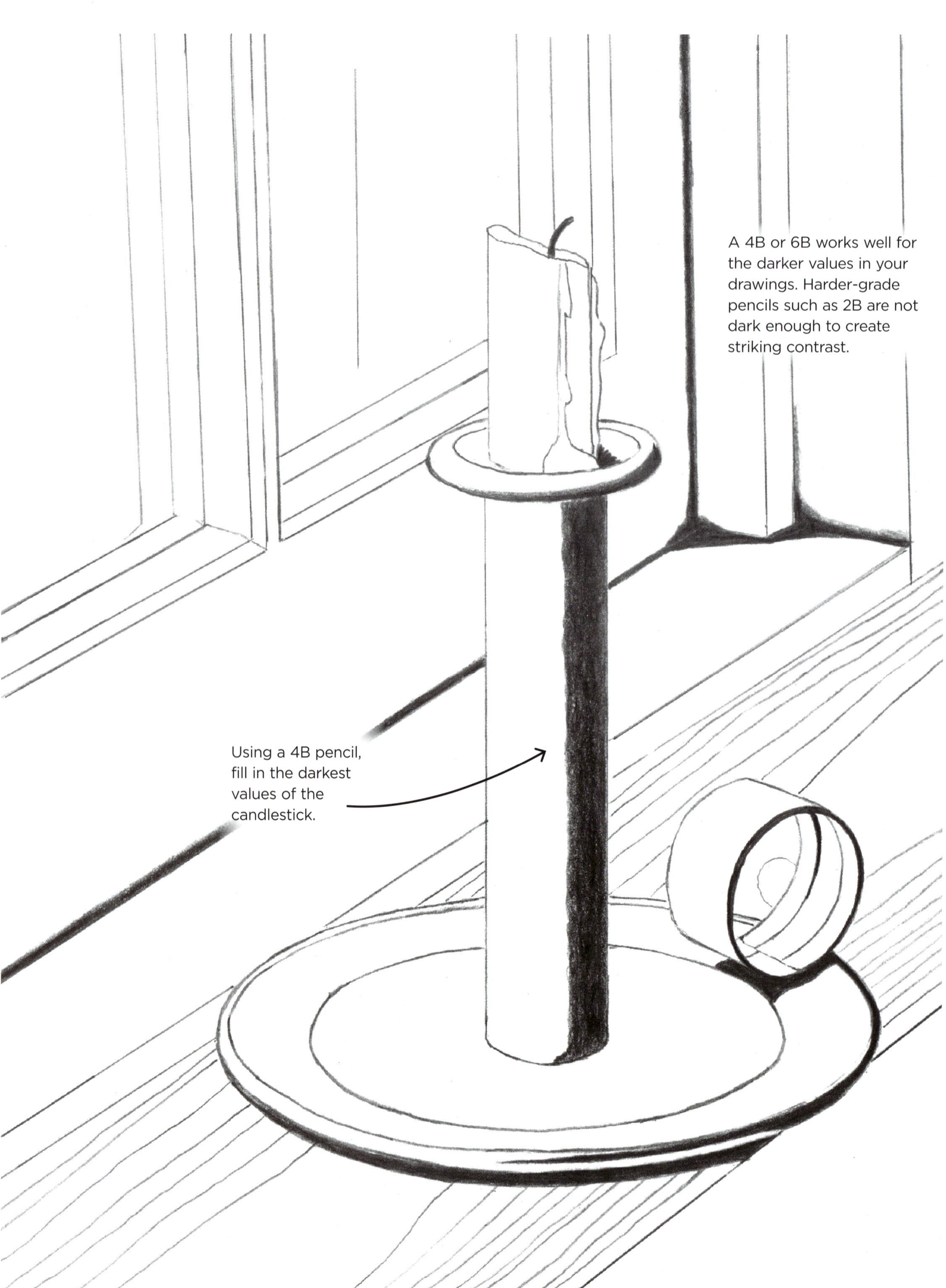
A 4B or 6B works well for the darker values in your drawings. Harder-grade pencils such as 2B are not dark enough to create striking contrast.
Using a 4B pencil, fill in the darkest values of the candlestick.

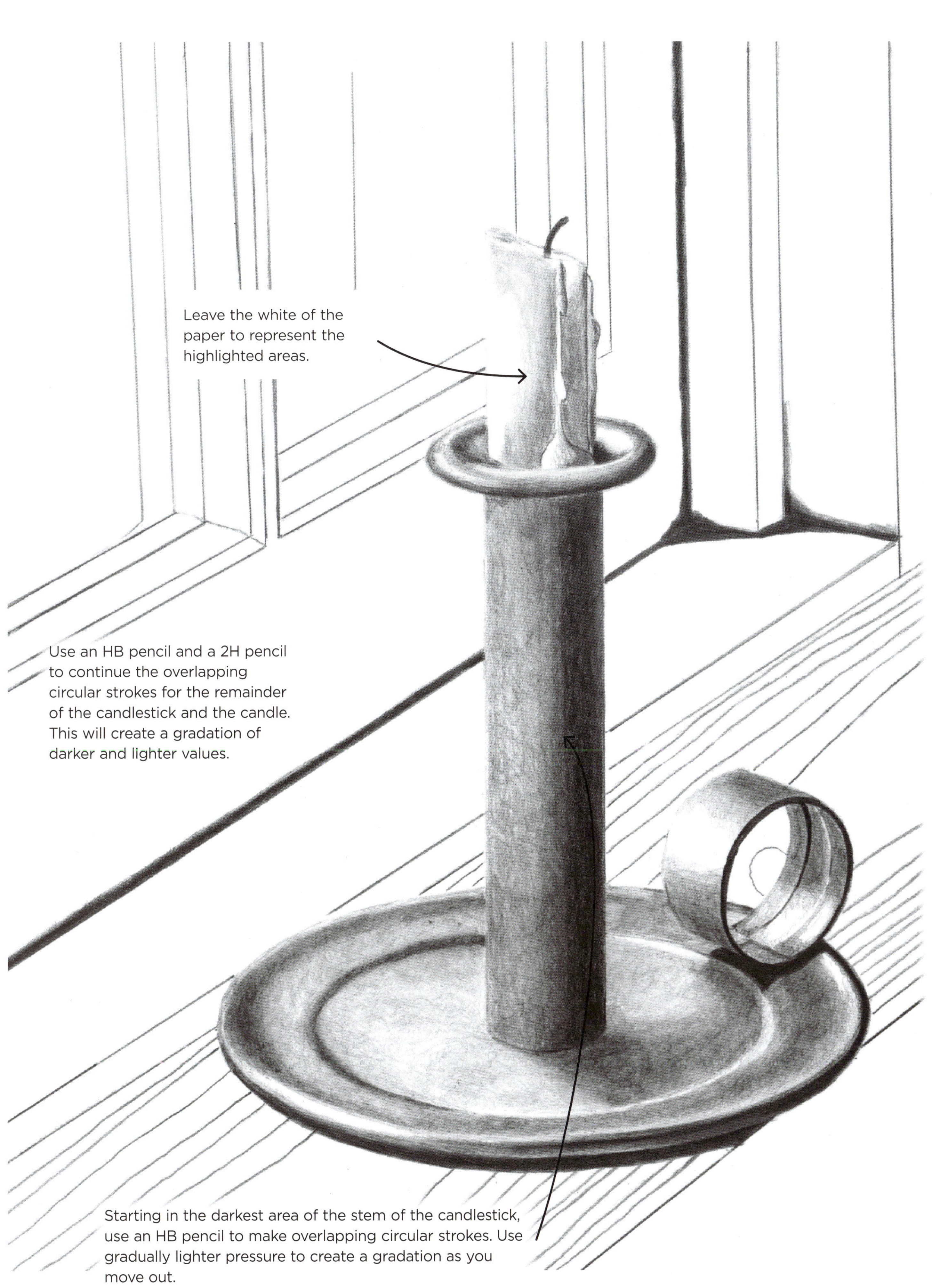
Leave the white of the paper to represent the highlighted areas.
Use an HB pencil and a 2H pencil to continue the overlapping circular strokes for the remainder of the candlestick and the candle. This will create a gradation of darker and lighter values.
Starting in the darkest area of the stem of the candlestick, use an HB pencil to make overlapping circular strokes. Use gradually lighter pressure to create a gradation as you move out.

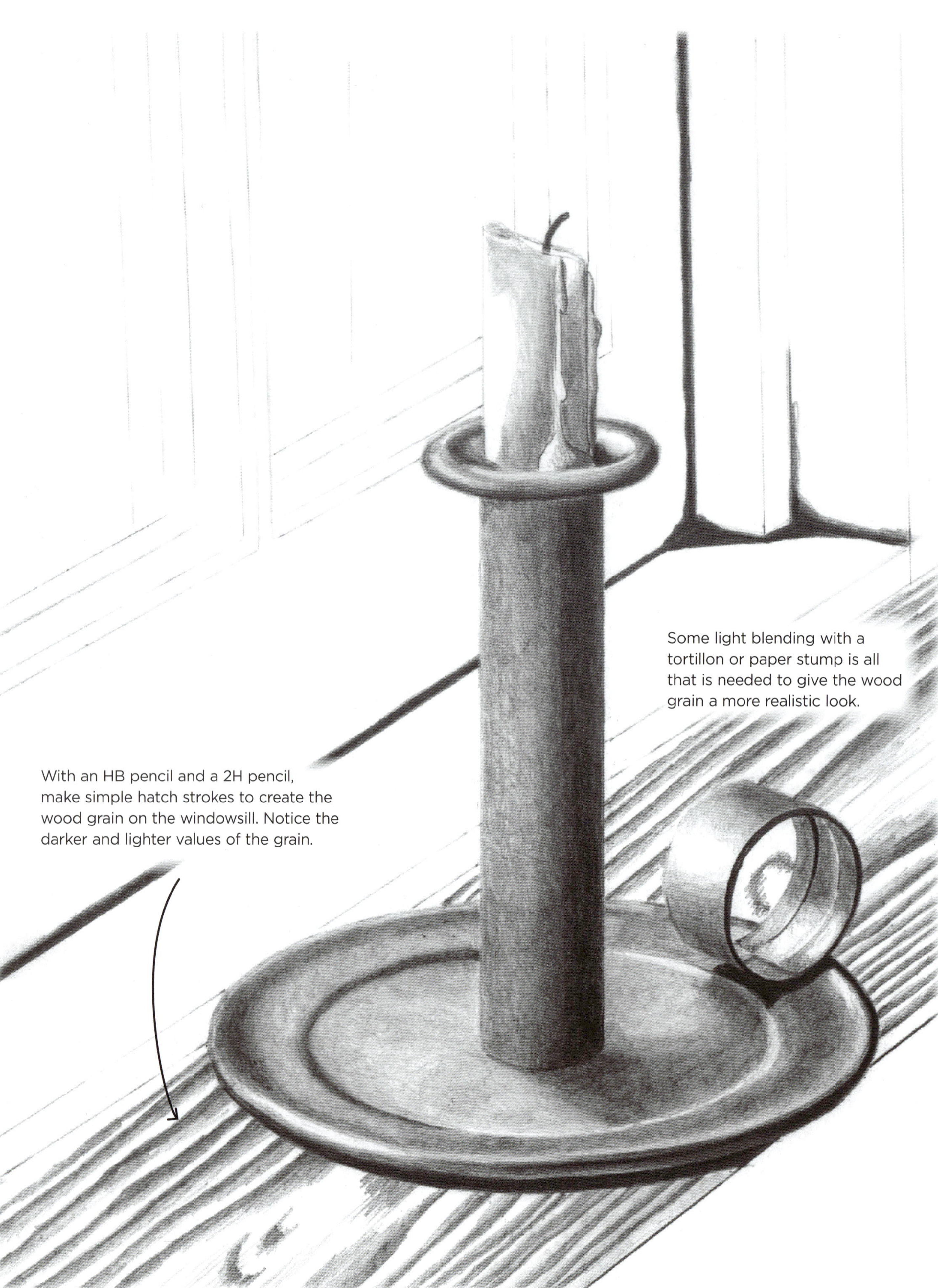
Some light blending with a tortillon or paper stump is all that is needed to give the wood grain a more realistic look.
With an HB pencil and a 2H pencil, make simple hatch strokes to create the wood grain on the windowsill. Notice the darker and lighter values of the grain.

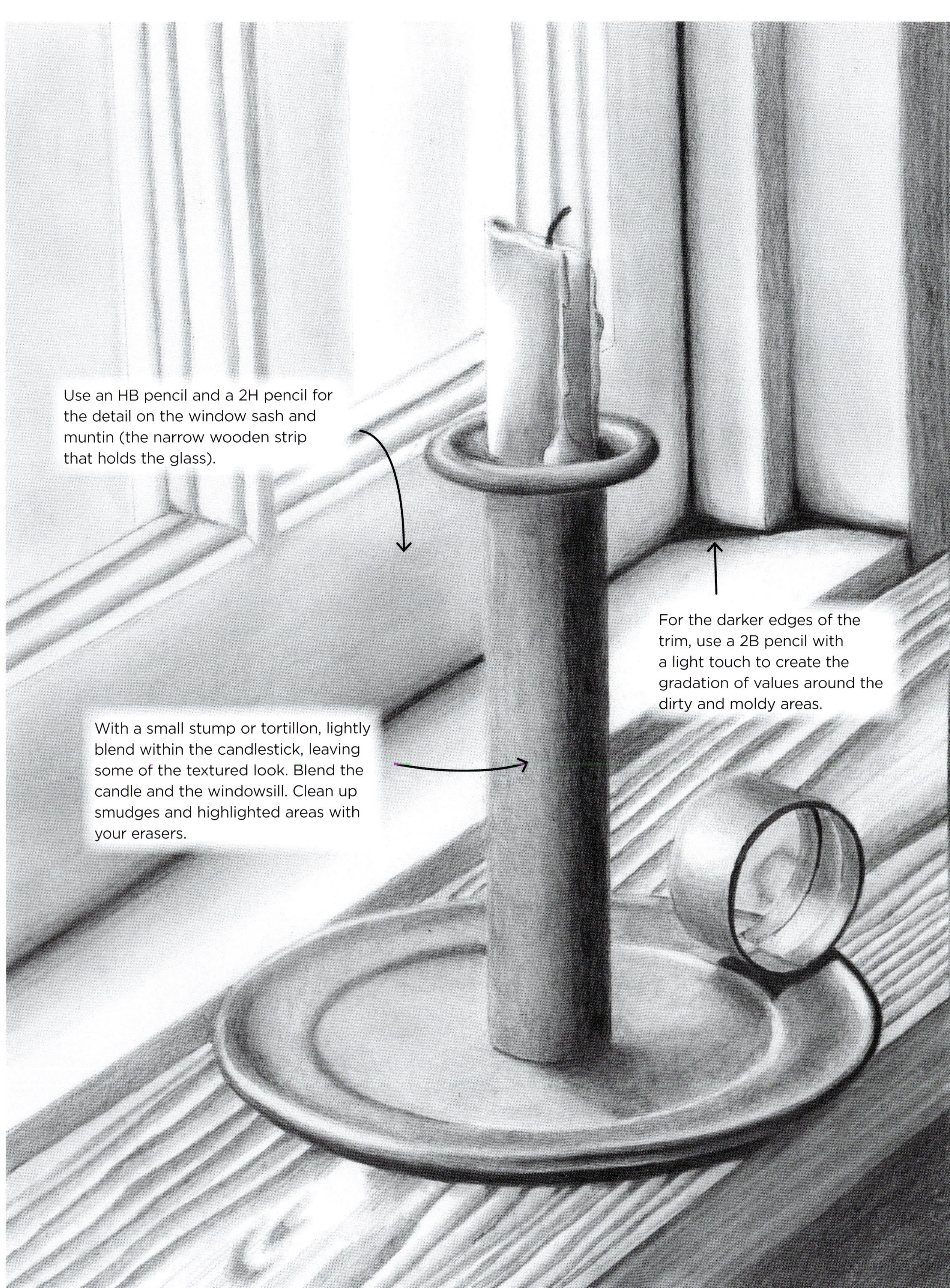
Use an HB pencil and a 2H pencil for the detail on the window sash and muntin (the narrow wooden strip that holds the glass).
For the darker edges of the trim, use a 2B pencil with a light touch to create the gradation of values around the dirty and moldy areas.
With a small stump or tortillon, lightly blend within the candlestick, leaving some of the textured look. Blend the candle and the windowsill. Clean up smudges and highlighted areas with your erasers.

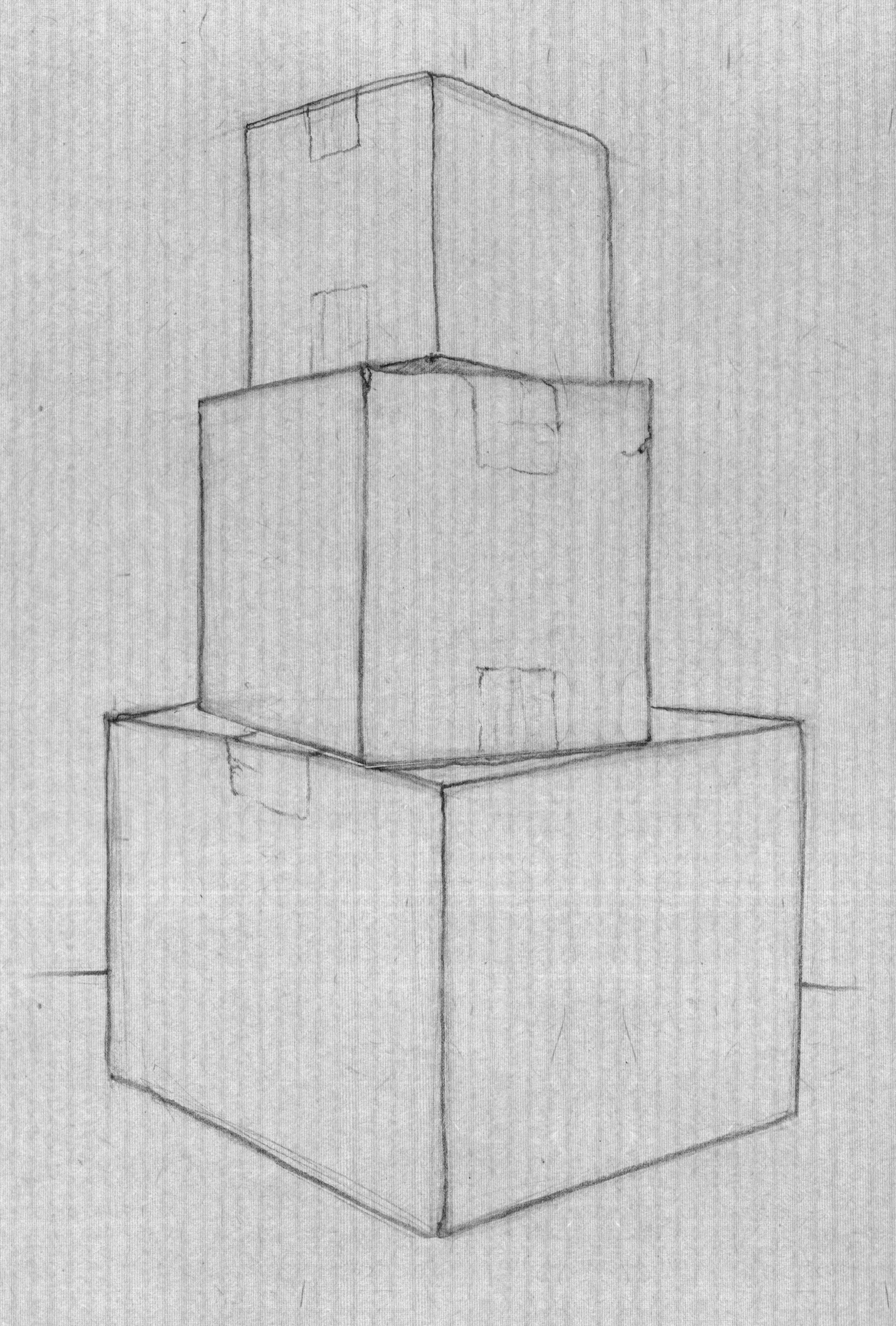

PERSPECTIVE & THE PICTURE PLANE

In the previous chapter, we discussed how to draw circles in perspective. In this chapter, we will focus on accurately drawing non-circular, hard-edged objects—boxes—in perspective. We will also discuss further uses of the picture plane, new information on applying accurate object dimensions and sizes in a complex still-life arrangement, and the best way to simplify a complex arrangement at the onset in order to more easily and successfully block in the subject matter.

Part I: Perspective

Perspective is essentially your viewpoint. When someone asks you how you "feel" about a subject, the person wants to know your point of view, or your perspective. In drawing, we relate perspective to how the subject is viewed by the artist. For example, when you stand at an easel and draw a subject, you see the subject from a different viewpoint, or perspective, than you would if you were sitting in a chair and drawing the same subject.

Perspective Terminology

Perspective Drawing When we draw from observation, we are depicting three-dimensional objects in front of us onto a flat surface—the drawing paper. We are attempting to give these objects dimension, depth, and an impression of reality.

Line of Vision Also called the "line of sight," line of vision is the direction in which the viewer is looking.

Picture Plane As discussed previously, the picture plane is an imagined, transparent sheet of glass between the viewer and the subject. The picture plane is perpendicular to the ground plane.

Vanishing Point The vanishing point is the point where retreating parallel construction lines converge. Vanishing points are usually on eye level. (Exceptions include three-point perspective and inclined planes, which will be discussed in a later chapter.)

Horizon Line Also called "eye level," the horizon line is an imaginary line consistent with our eye level. It stretches horizontally across our view and is the location of all of the vanishing points in a drawing.

Ground Plane The ground plane is the plane on which the drawing subject sits. For objects resting on a table, the ground plane is the tabletop. In architectural structures, the ground plane is literally the ground. Eye level is always parallel to the ground plane; however, eye level and the ground plane are rarely the same.

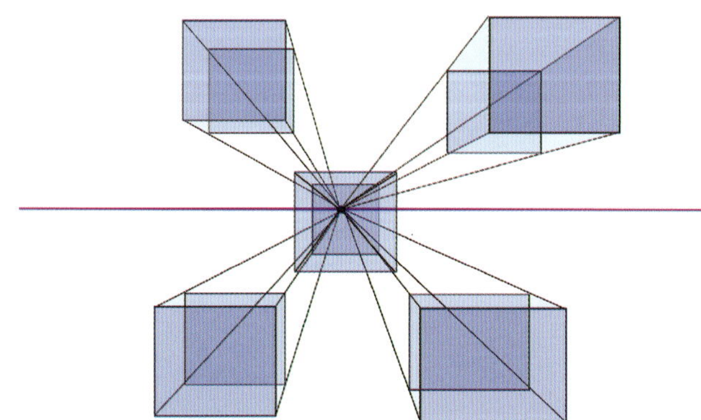

One-Point Perspective

In relation to box-like constructions like the examples here, or in the case of interior or exterior architecture, one-point perspective is indicated by a front plane and back plane, each parallel to the picture plane, with two side planes that converge toward a common vanishing point within the picture plane. The vanishing point is always on eye level.

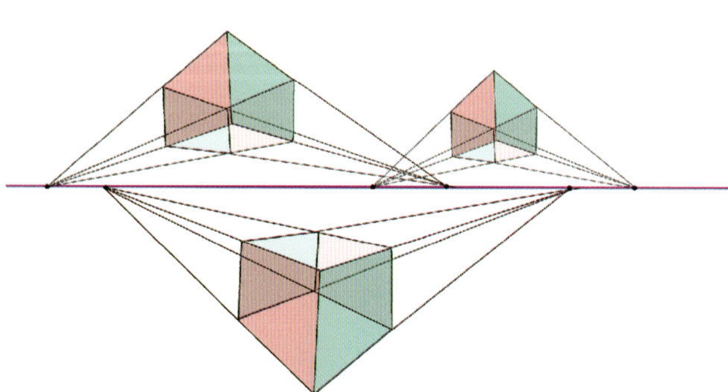

Two-Point Perspective

In situations similar to the box-like constructions shown, only the vertical edges of the boxes are parallel to the picture plane in two-point perspective. The parallel sets of sides converge diagonally toward common vanishing points, one on the right side of the picture plane and one on the left. Both of these vanishing points are always on eye level.

Eye Level

Now that you have some familiarity with perspective terminology, let's put these terms to use in tangible situations. Drawing boxes is a very good way to understand the principles of still life, or "tabletop," perspective.

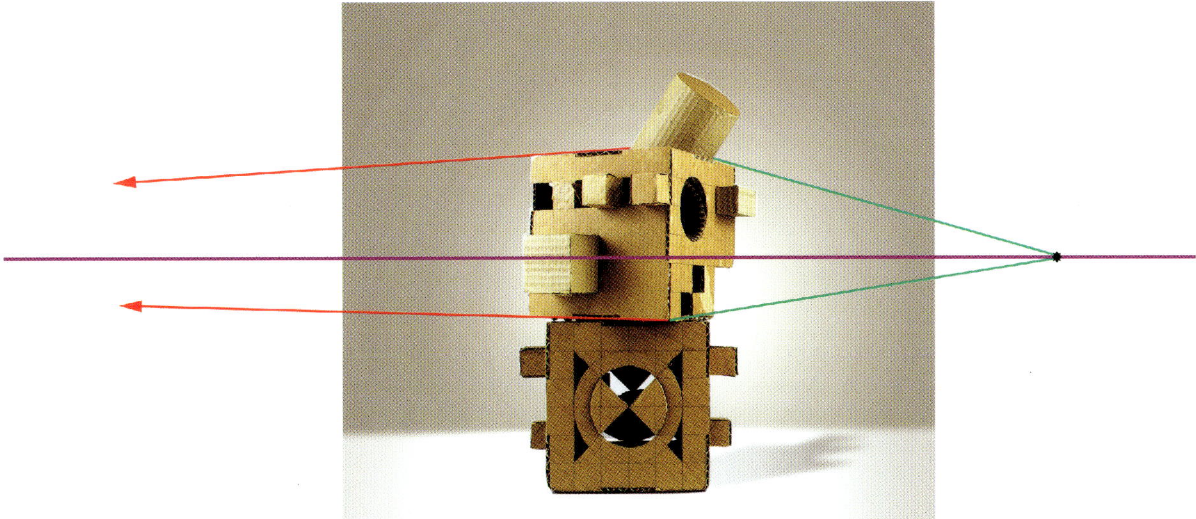

In one-point perspective, the front and back of the boxes are parallel to the picture plane, and the vanishing point for the perpendicular sides is within the picture plane.

Imagining that the picture plane is located vertically between the boxes and ourselves, we'll start by viewing a two-point box on top of a one-point box, with eye level within the picture plane. For the two-point box on top, the convergence of its edges is toward eye level, and the subsequent vanishing points are on eye level, one on the left and one on the right. Because the one-point box on the bottom shows only its front face, we know that it is parallel to the picture plane and that its vanishing point is directly behind it, also on eye level.

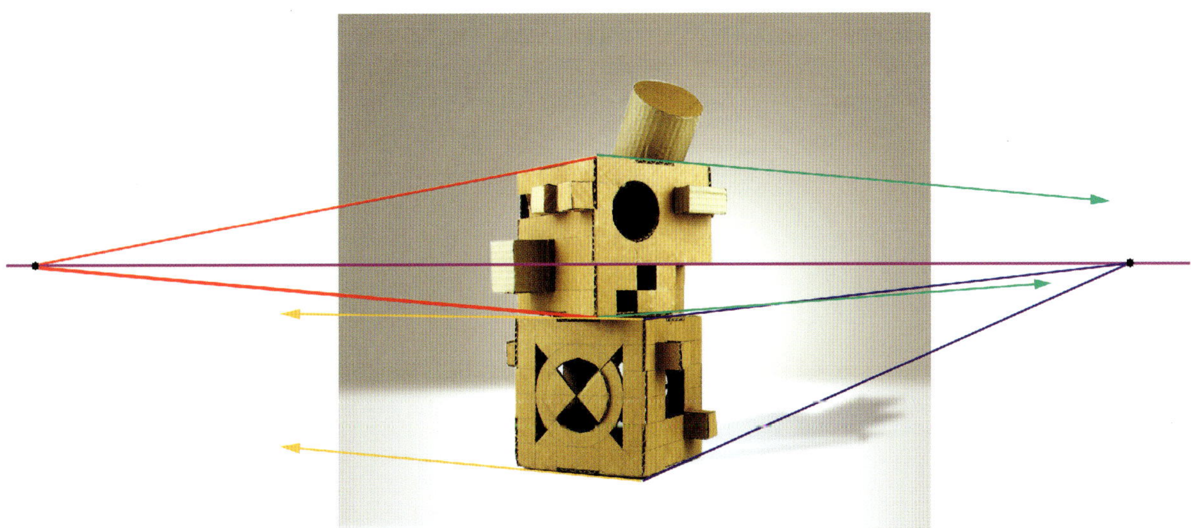

From this angle, both boxes are now considered two-point boxes. The parallel faces of each box converge to common vanishing points on eye level.

As we rotate the box construction slightly, we can now see that both boxes are in a two-point perspective situation, but each box has it's own left and right vanishing points, still on the horizon line.

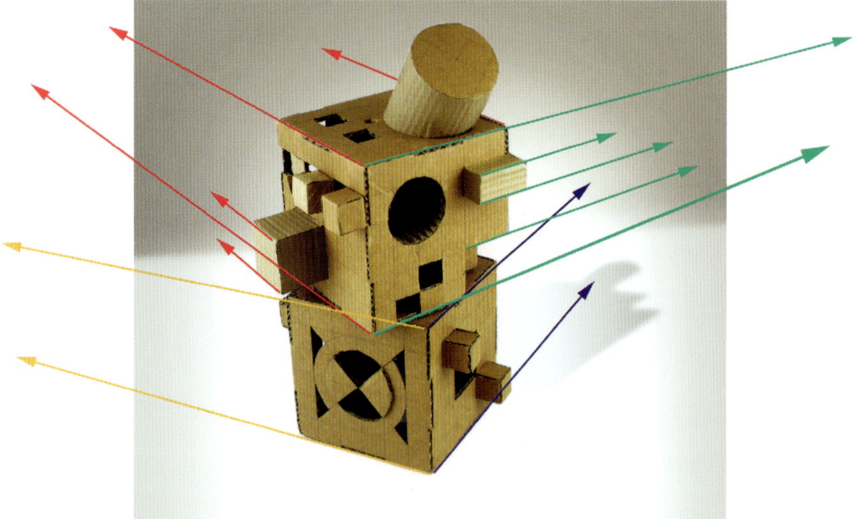

The boxes are still two-point boxes, but now the eye level is above the level of the boxes. The viewer can see the tops of the boxes easily, and the angles of convergence are more acute.

In this third view, the eye level has risen above the picture plane, and the line of vision is looking down onto the tops of the boxes. These new angles of edges, especially on the bottom of the lower box, are particularly acute, with vanishing points now much closer to both boxes than they were at previous locations on eye level.

Drawing the Two-Point Perspective Setup

As you can see from several different viewing angles, the vanishing points for one side or the other can be fairly distant from the box, many times off the edge of the paper. If the front face of a box is slightly turned from a one-point perspective, the diagonals of the face converge to a vanishing point far from the box. In order to draw the boxes accurately, we need a way to illustrate the angles of the boxes' edges without the vanishing points, which are sometimes (or usually) outside of the picture plane. The way to achieve accuracy is with an angle tool—in this case, a chopstick—which can help us see any angle that the boxes present, as long as we keep it parallel to the picture plane.

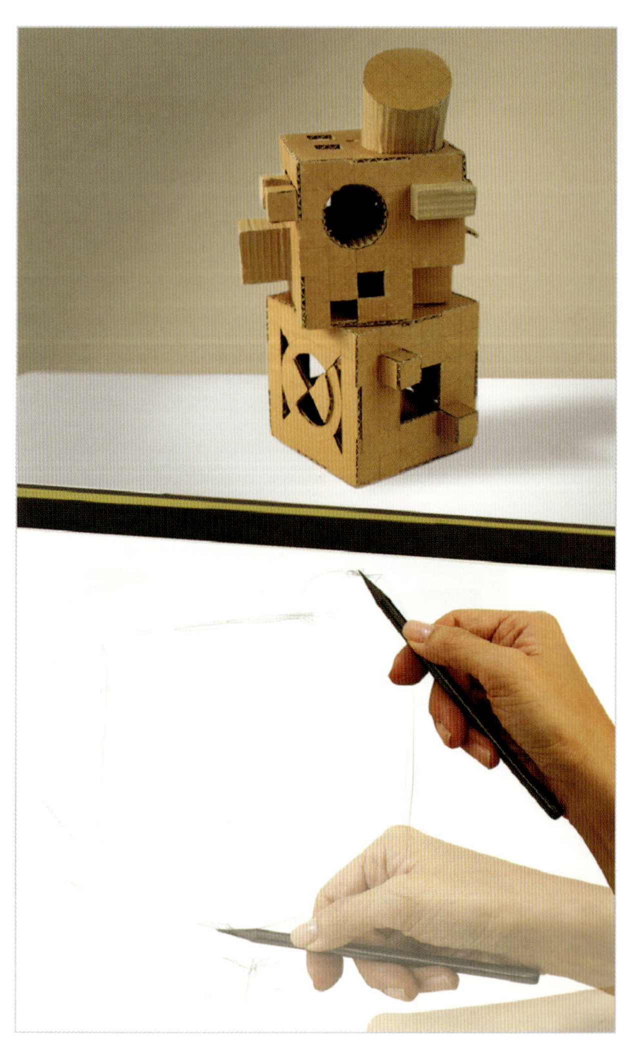

STEP 1 Check the angles with a chopstick, and then mark the top and bottom of each box to establish proportions and composition. Sketch lightly and loosely.

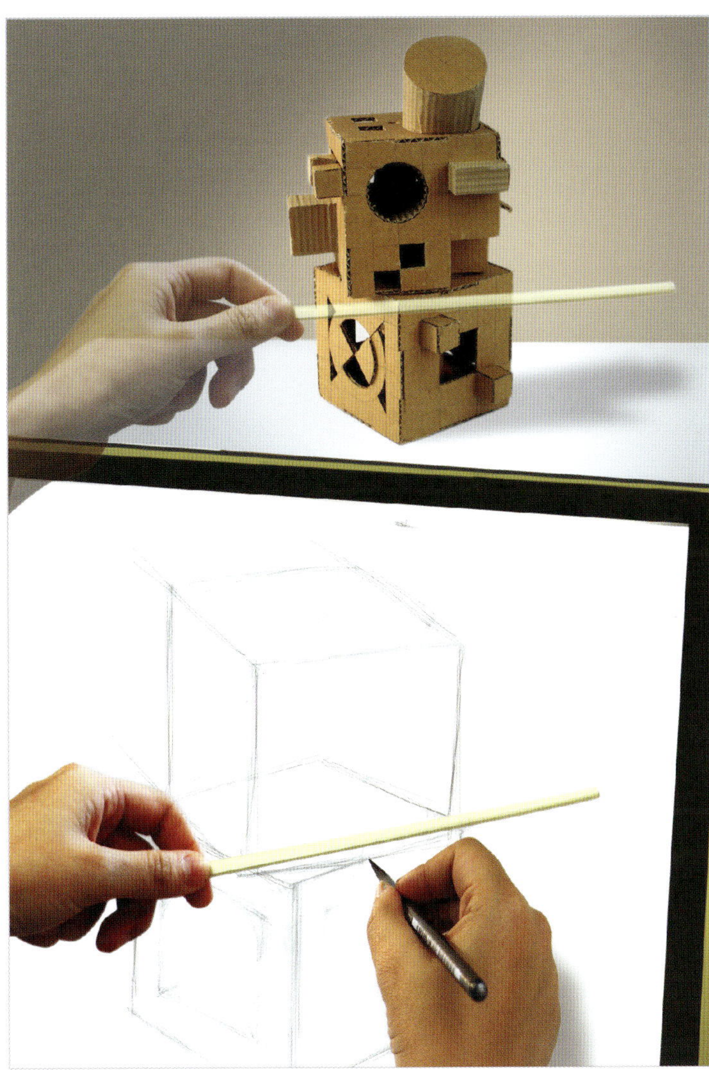

STEP 2 Once the boxes are lightly sketched, start to establish the accuracy of all the angles, in this case starting with the bottom box and moving on to the top.

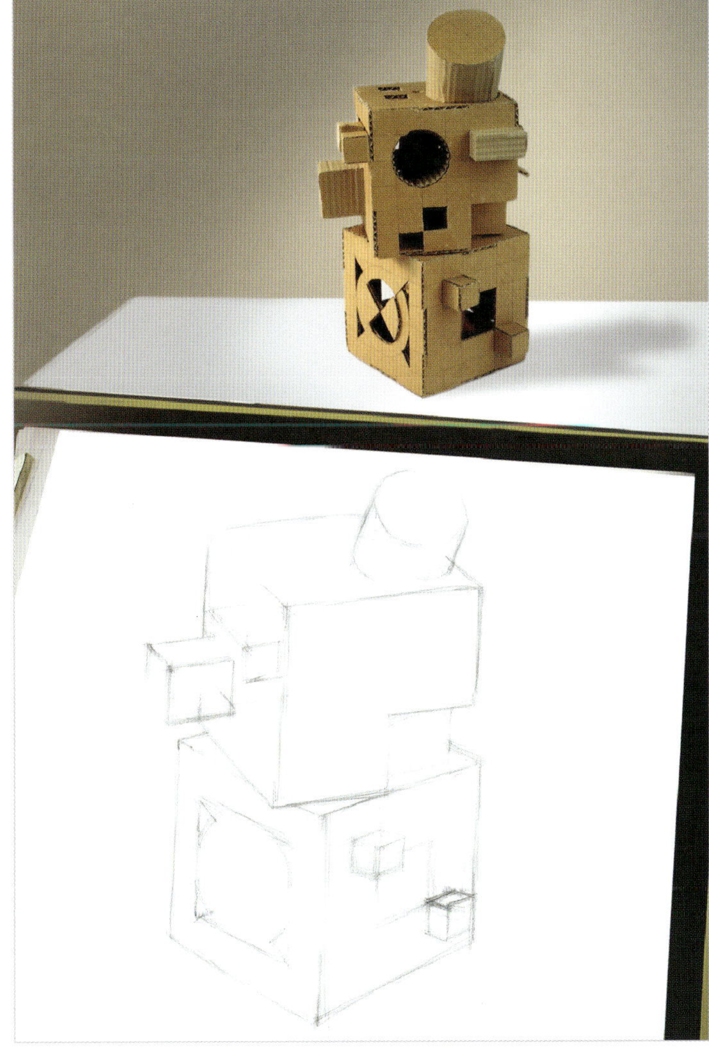

STEP 3 When you are certain of the accuracy of the converging lines, strengthen and refine your drawing. All of this is accomplished without rulers! A ruler may give you a straight line, but it does not necessarily give you an accurate line. Your eye and a good freehand sketch can do a better job.

Part II: The Picture Plane & the XY Grid

Now we will use the picture plane in front of a more complex set of objects that make up a large still life. We will again use a chopstick as a tool for angles and relative sizes, but also for accurate locations. A chopstick is helpful in finding angles on the picture plane when held diagonally, but it can also be used horizontally and vertically to help us line up the subject matter in a simple, straightforward way.

By using the chopstick horizontally and vertically at various points of intersection in the still life, we can superimpose an imaginary grid over our drawing of the still life. The horizontal lines are called "X-axis" lines, and the vertical lines are called "Y-axis" lines. The imaginary grid is called the "XY grid."

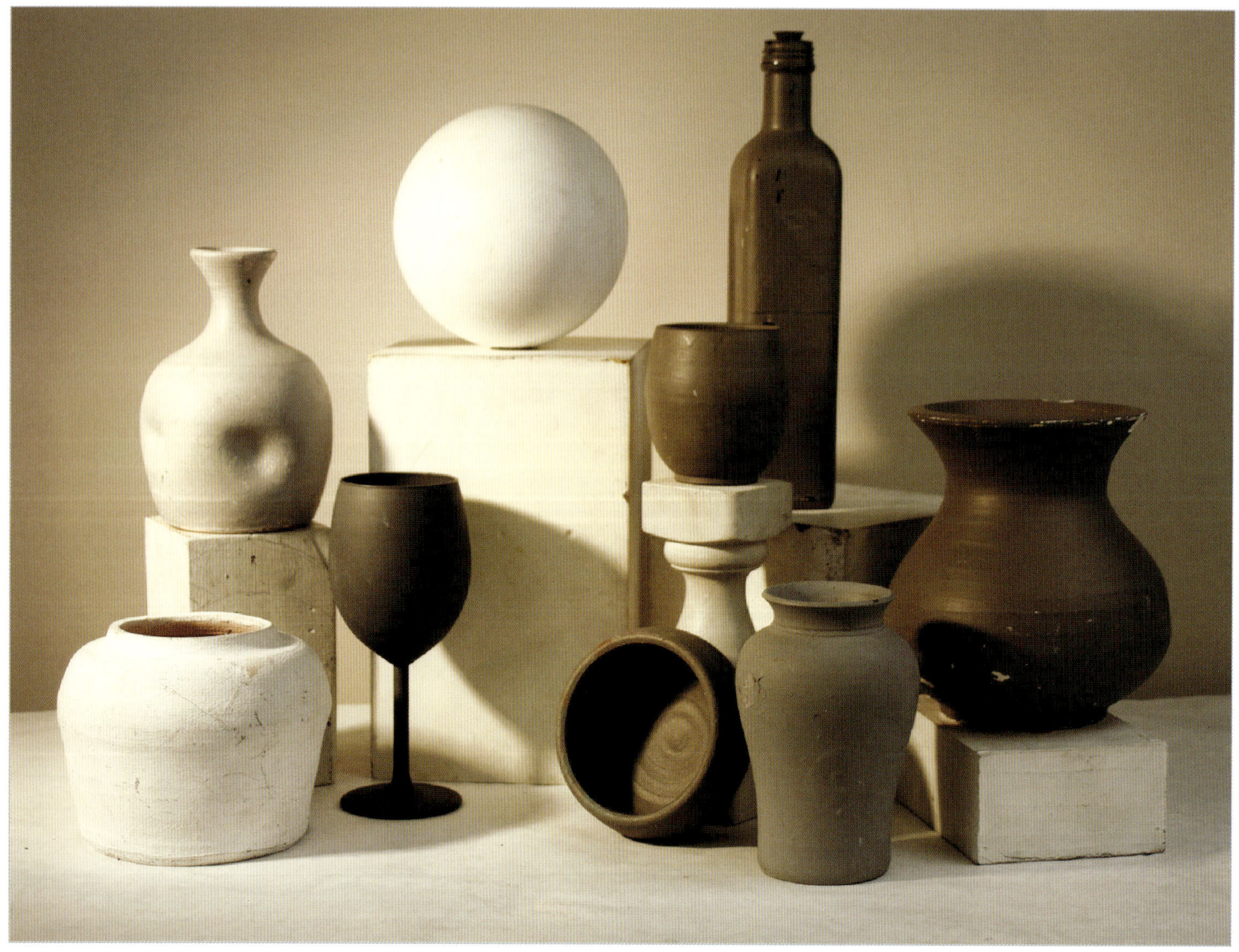

We will use this complex still life setup to demonstrate the use of the XY-grid construction method.

Using a Viewfinder

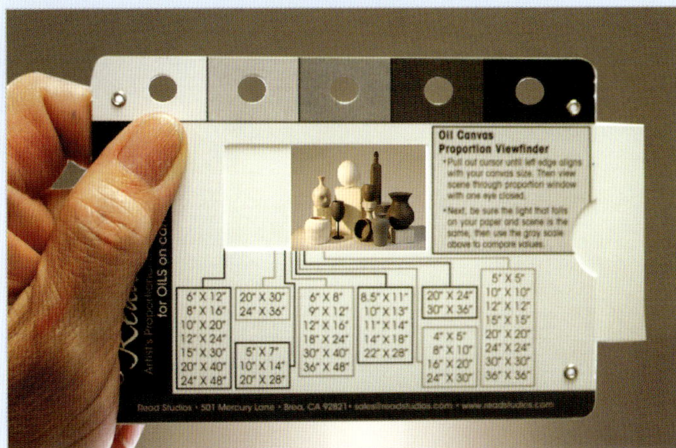

You can purchase a viewfinder at an art supply store. Viewfinders help the artist pre-visualize what their composition will look like on the page. The format (size) of the paper can be adjusted with a movable interior slider.

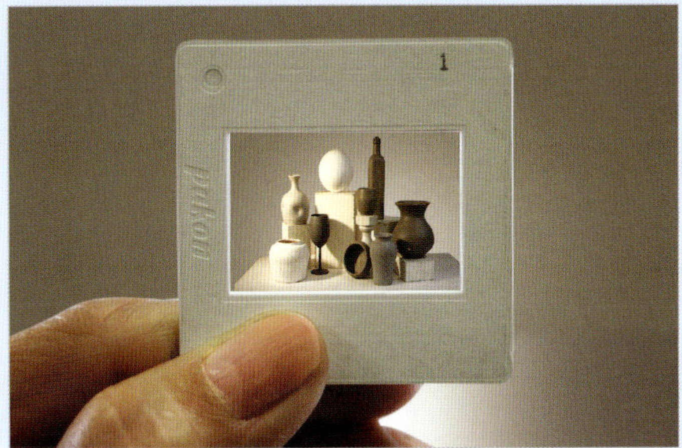

I find that a simple plastic slide frame does a similar job of framing the composition. The proportion of the slide opening is similar to most standard art paper sizes. Try blocking in the overall composition with quick marks that reflect the top, bottom, and sides of the composition while looking through the slide.

The Drawing Process

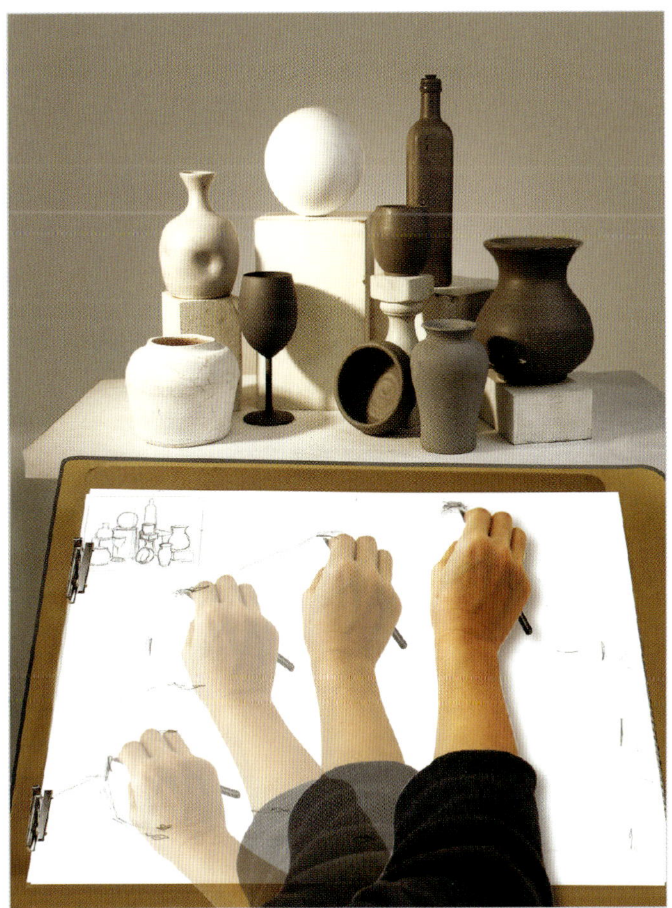

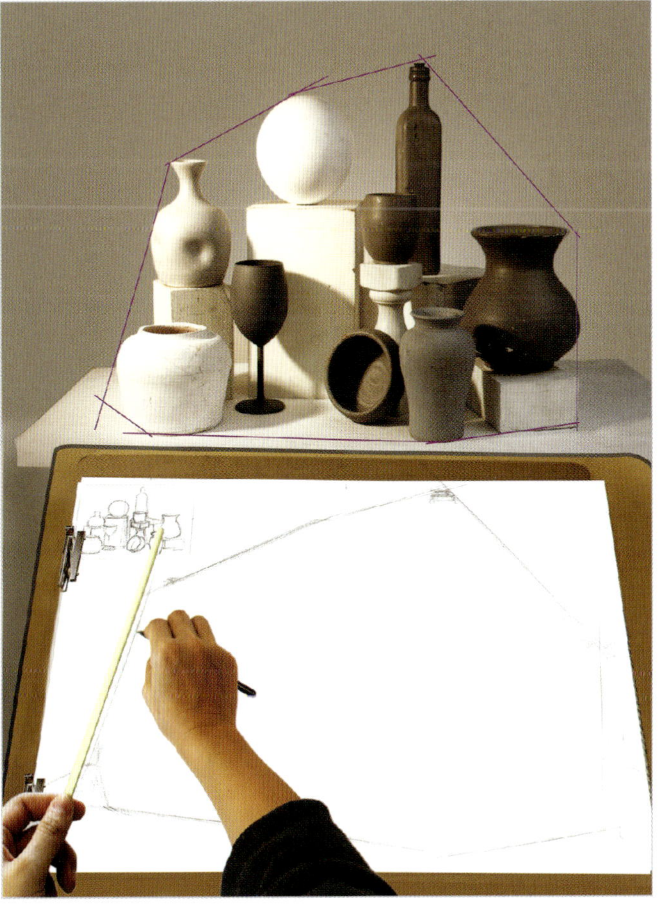

STEP 1 After making a thumbnail sketch, start by marking very generalized locations of the tallest, lowest, and widest form edges of the still life. Don't worry about detail; just concentrate on the top, bottom, and general location of each object. Then use the chopstick to create an "envelope" around the entire still life.

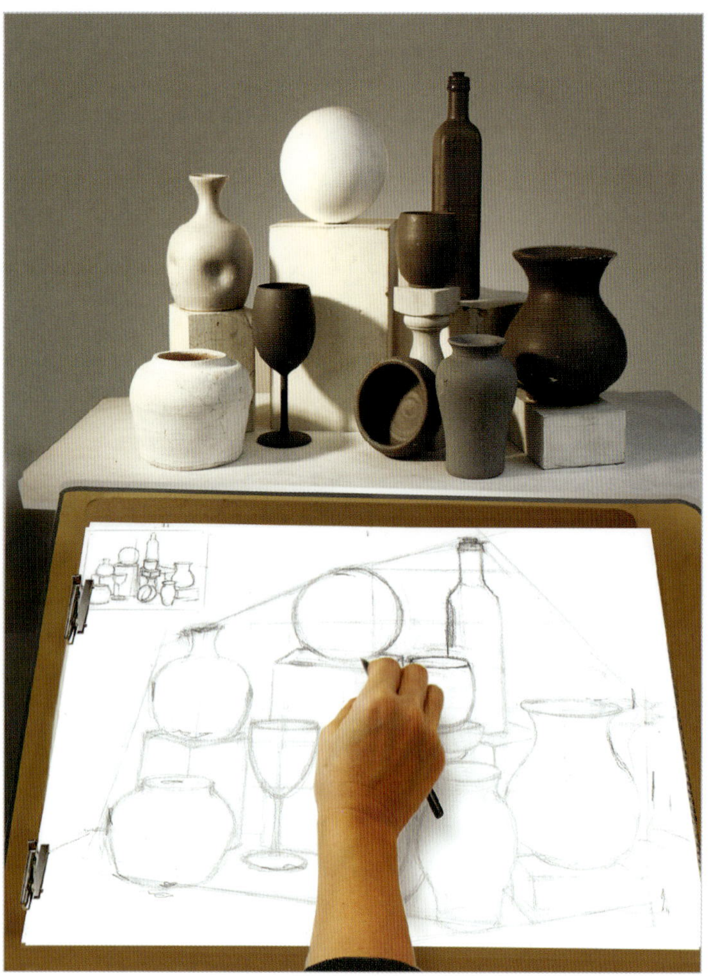

STEP 2 Next is the initial block-in stage. This stage is not about detail or refinement, but only general scale, proportion, and placement. Make use of the chopstick as a proportional measuring tool by selecting one object in the still life to use as the base unit of measurement for all the other forms.

STEP 3 Once most or all of the objects have been blocked in lightly (light forms are key; they are easier to refine and adjust), the XY grid can be initiated. As you check the first horizontal X-axis on the still life, notice which other objects' heights fall across this line, and apply that information to your drawing with a light horizontal line. If you need to make an adjustment to a form or its location, make a mark for that change. If you have sketched accurately, you won't need to make many adjustments; move down to the next point of intersection on the still life and create another X-axis on the grid; sketch this on your drawing as another light horizontal line.

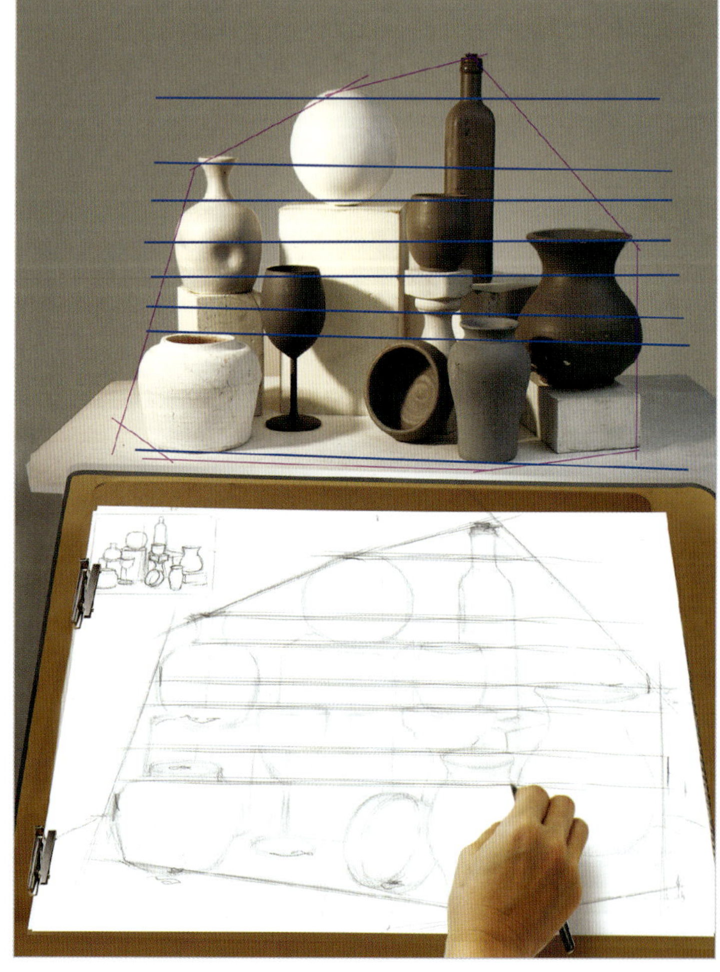

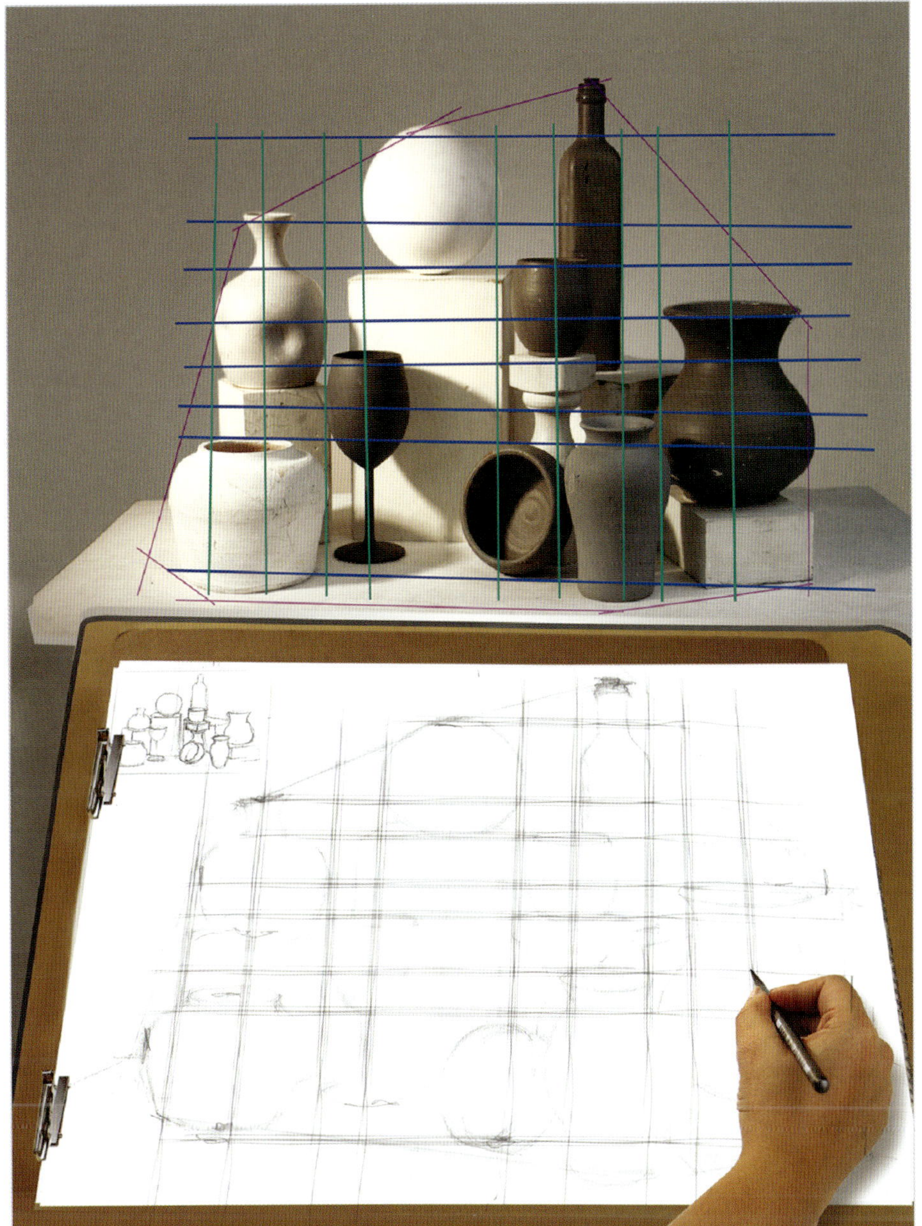

STEP 4 As you move down the still life, you should be able to adjust most or all of the height locations of the objects. Then it's time to check the width and horizontal locations of objects with the Y-axis lines, making sure that all objects are properly aligned with one another. Transfer the imaginary Y-axis lines on the still life as light vertical lines on your drawing, so it resembles a horizontal and vertical grid.

YOUR HOMEWORK

Based on the first demonstration in this chapter on page 70, create a still life of stacked boxes (at least three), with your eye level somewhere between the top of the highest box and the base of the lowest box; turn the boxes at different angles to one another.

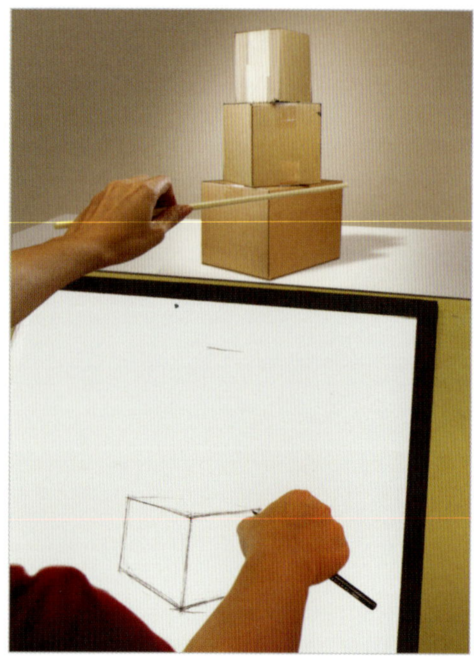

STEP 1 Mark the top and bottom of the composition based on the highest point of the top box and the lowest corner of the bottom box, respectively. These are "guesstimates" only and may be adjusted during the course of the drawing. Start with the bottom box sketch, checking angles of edges with your chopstick or pencil.

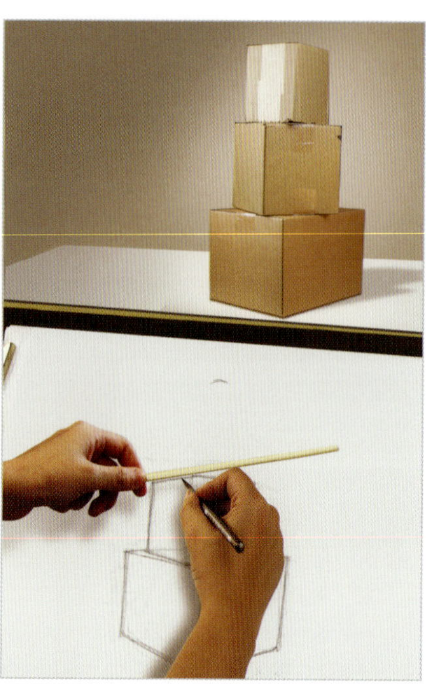

STEP 2 Use a pencil or chopstick to gauge angles on the still life, and then apply the angles to the second box.

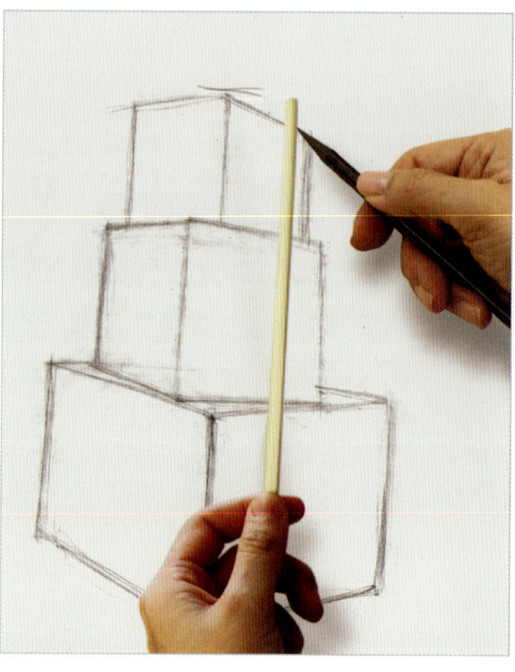

STEP 3 Check for vertical edges on all corners of all of the boxes; refine if needed.

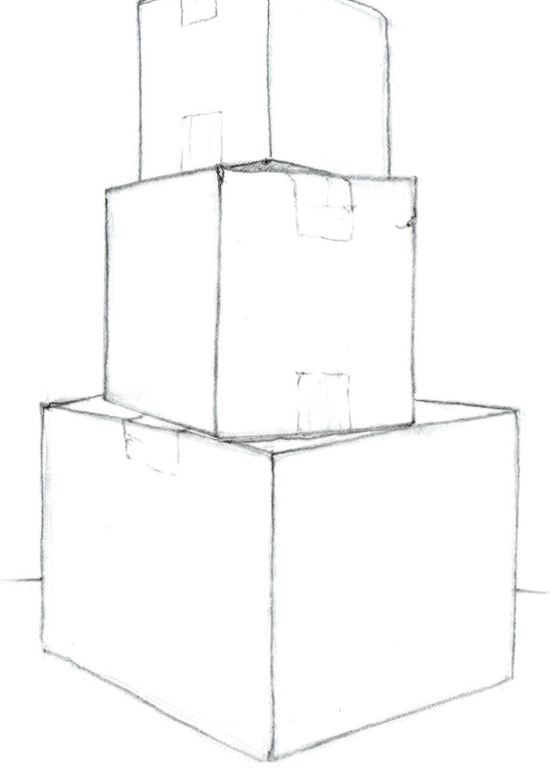

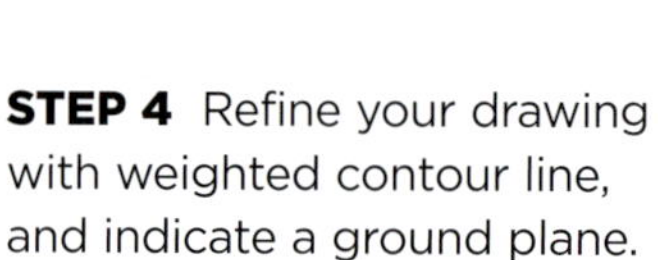

STEP 4 Refine your drawing with weighted contour line, and indicate a ground plane.

EXERCISES FOR PRACTICE

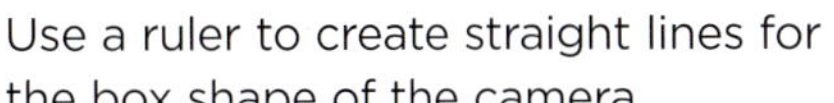

Use a ruler to create straight lines for the box shape of the camera.

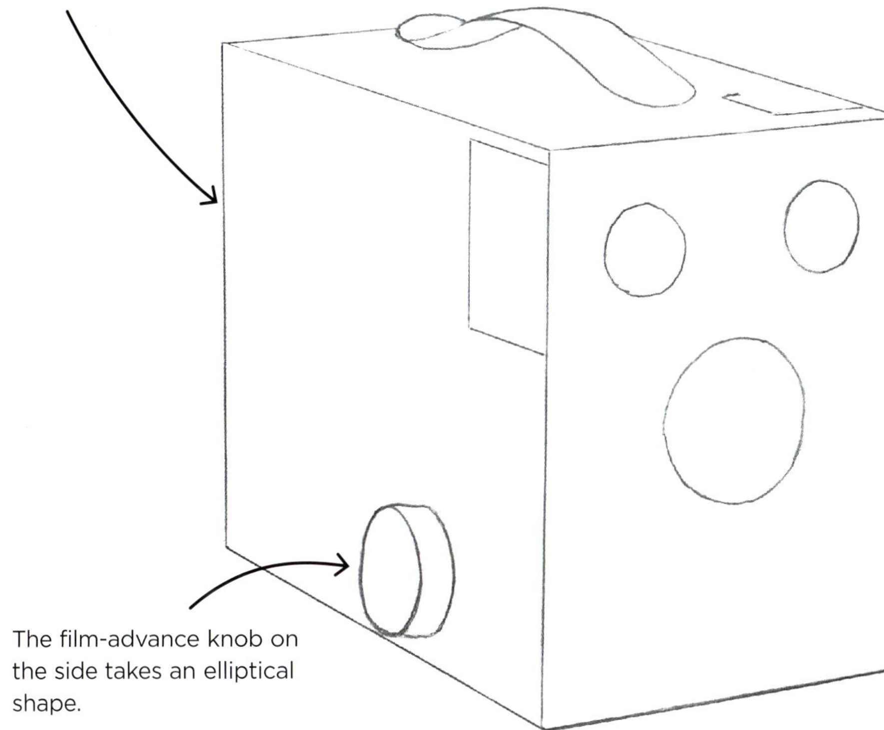

Sketch the three lenses on the front, which have a slight elliptical shape due to the position of the subject and the perspective of the viewer.

The film-advance knob on the side takes an elliptical shape.

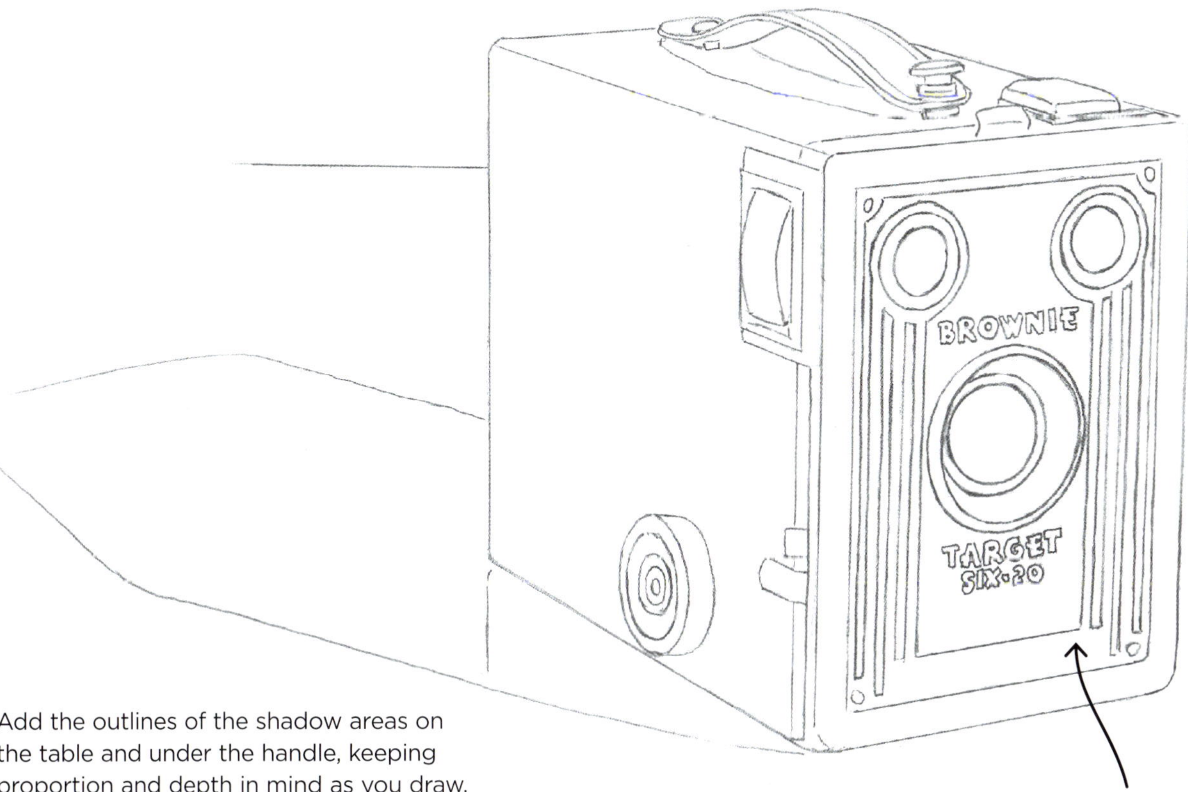

Add more detail to the lenses, handle, and shutter release.

Add the outlines of the shadow areas on the table and under the handle, keeping proportion and depth in mind as you draw.

Use the ruler again for the Art Deco detail on the front of the camera, and then draw in the block lettering.

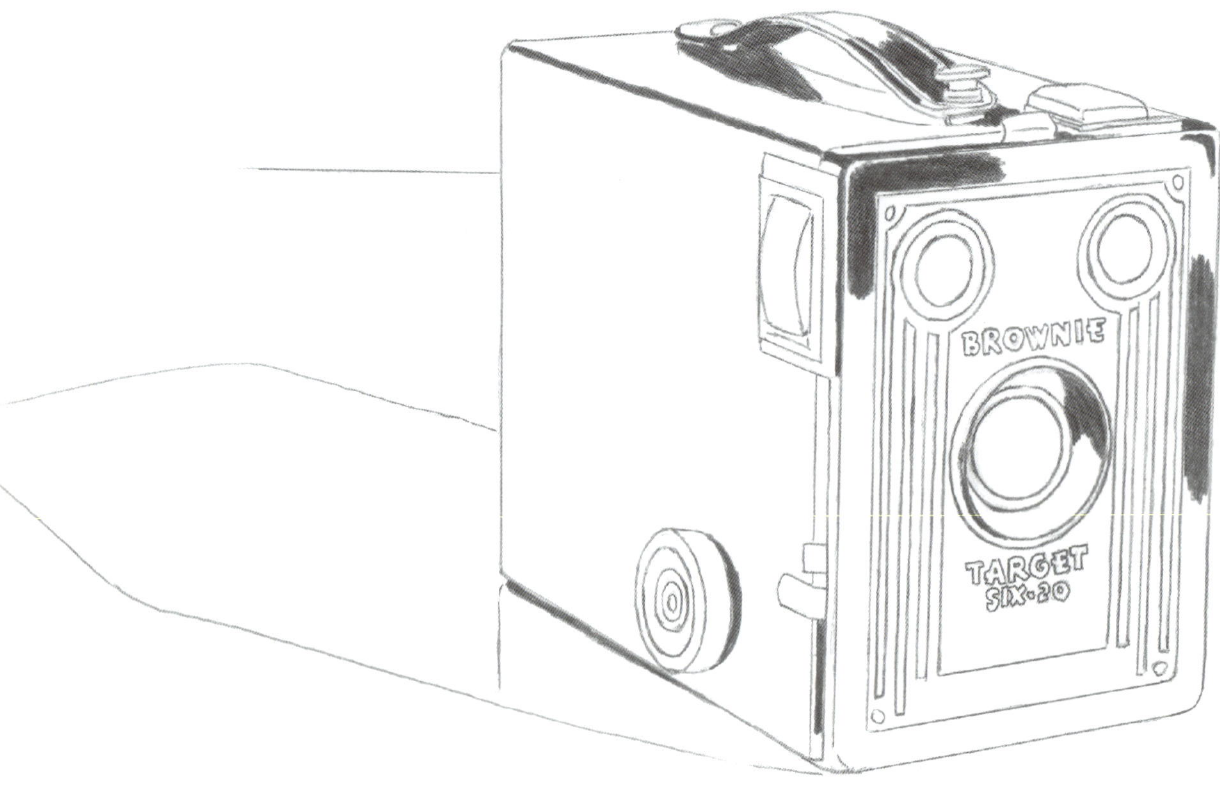

Using a 4B pencil, start shading in the darkest values of the drawing. The subject is very dark in color, but it contains a subtle assortment of values around its face and edges. Really study the camera to discern the different areas of shading and value.

Using a technique called "negative drawing," fill in the areas around the lettering and the design using a 2B pencil. This emphasizes the lettering and lines on the front of the camera.

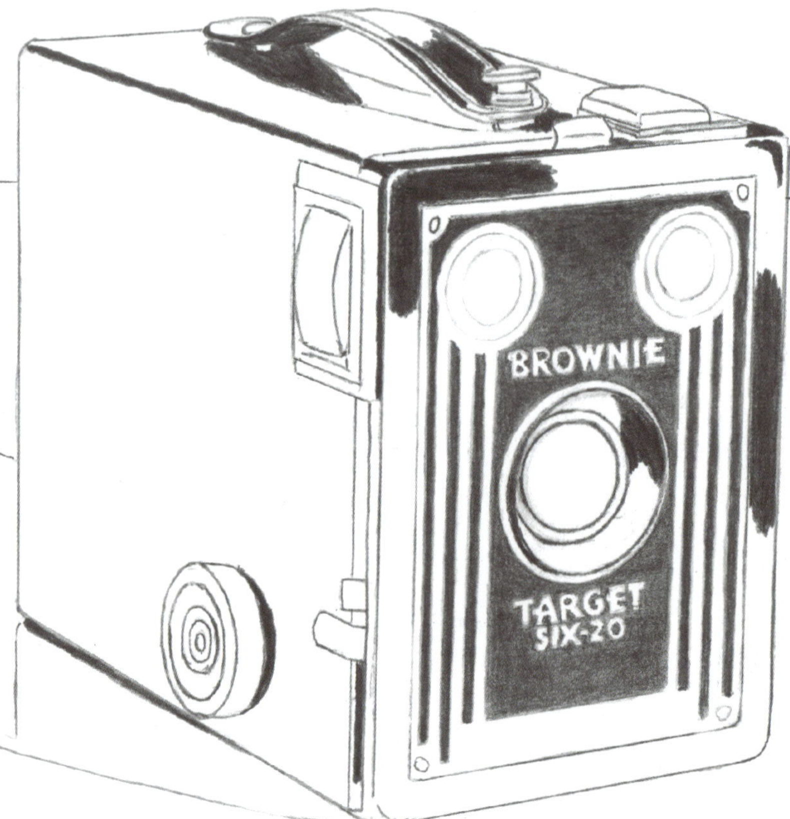

To finish the face of the camera, use a 2B pencil to add value with linear hatching, leaving the edges lighter.

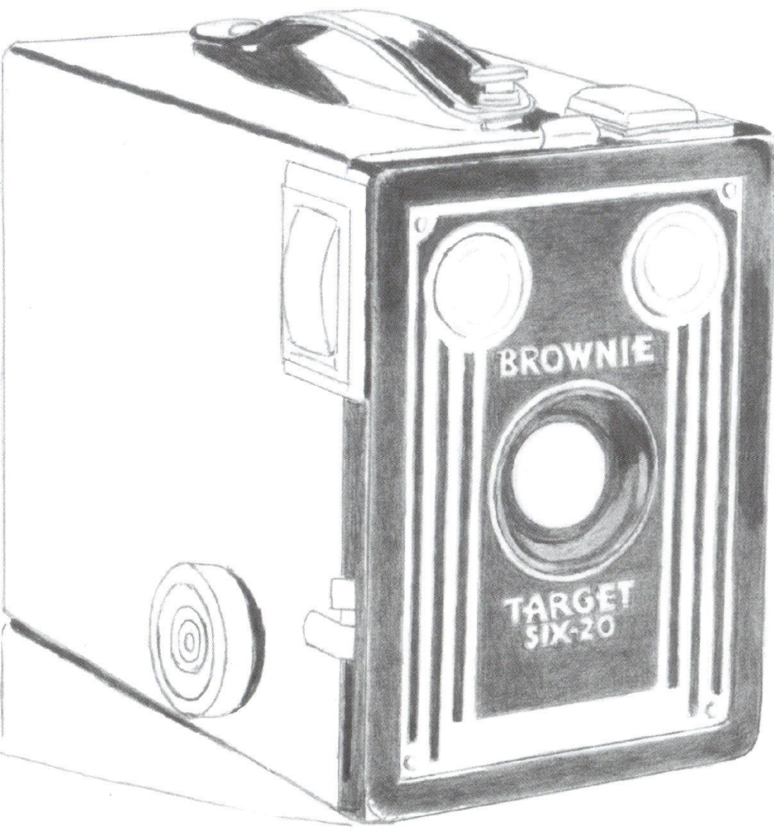

Finishing Techniques

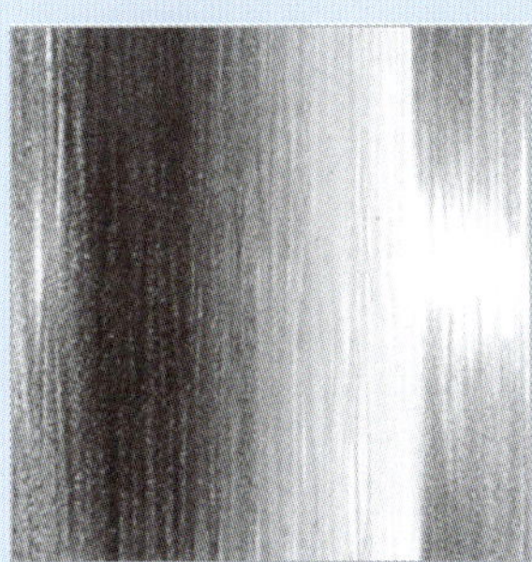

LINEAR HATCHING In linear hatching, use closely drawn parallel lines for tone or shading. You can gradually make the lines darker or lighter to suggest shadow or light. Draw varying lengths of lines very close and blend for a smooth finish. You can also curve your lines to follow the contour of an object, such as a vase.

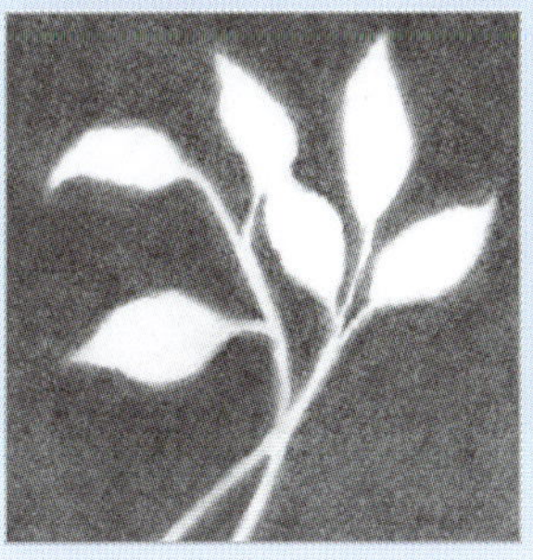

NEGATIVE DRAWING Use your pencil to draw in the negative space—the area around the desired shape—to create the object, leaving the white of the paper—the positive space—as desired shapes.

On the camera body, use a 2B pencil for the darker areas and an HB for the lighter areas.

The leather handle on top has stitching around the edge and should be left a little lighter in value.

Use overlapping circular strokes to render the camera's textured, leatherlike outer covering, which should give it a more realistic look.

Keep your pencil very sharp for the finer details.

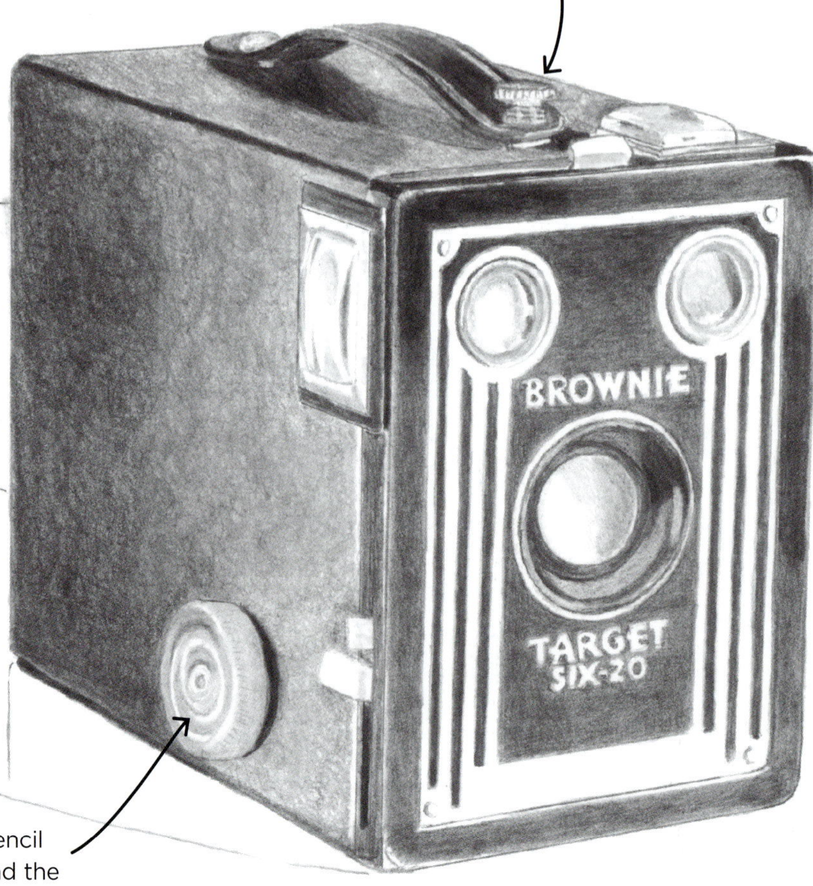

Use an HB pencil and a 2H pencil to give detail to the lenses and the knob. Lightly blend these areas using a tortillon.

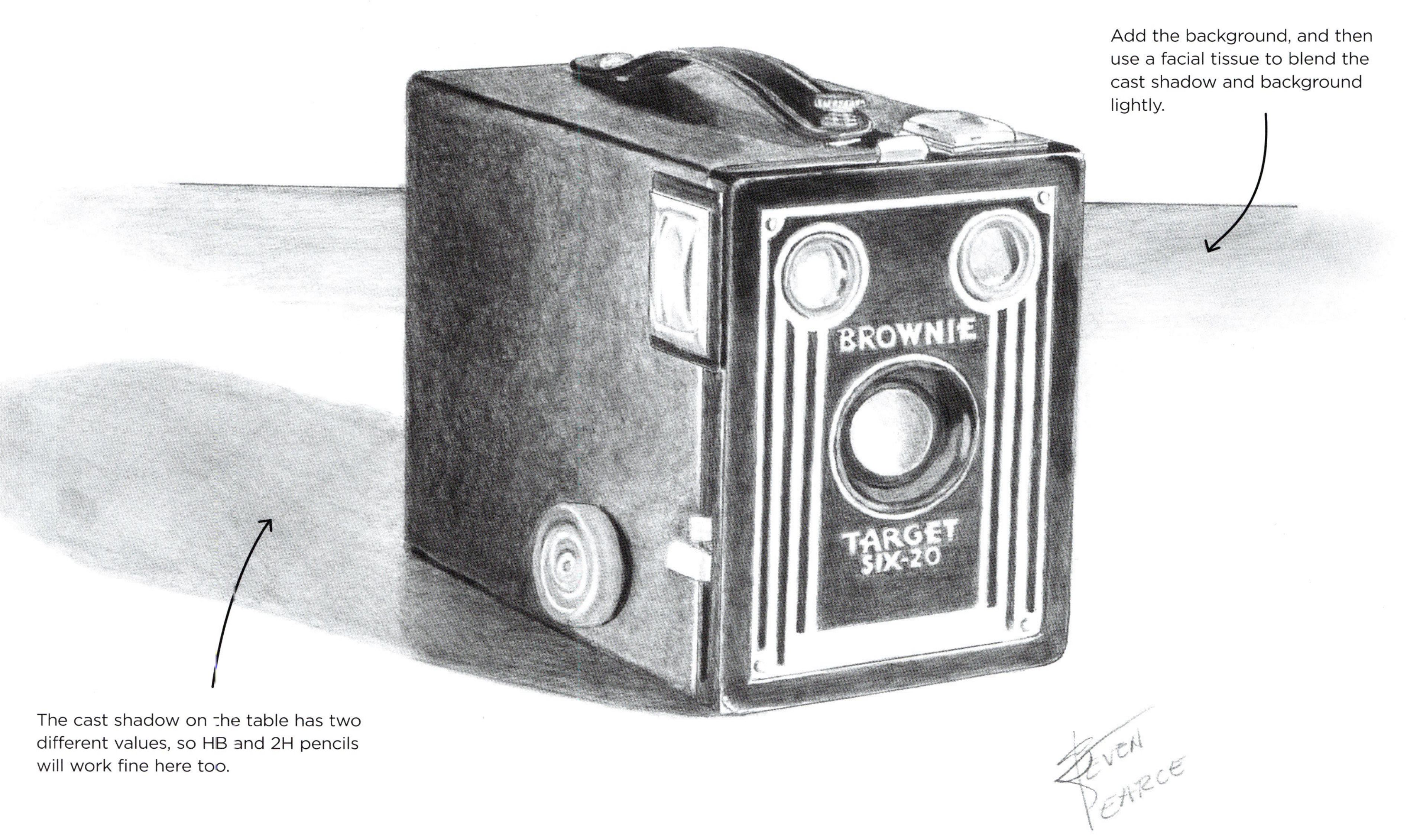

Add the background, and then use a facial tissue to blend the cast shadow and background lightly.

The cast shadow on the table has two different values, so HB and 2H pencils will work fine here too.

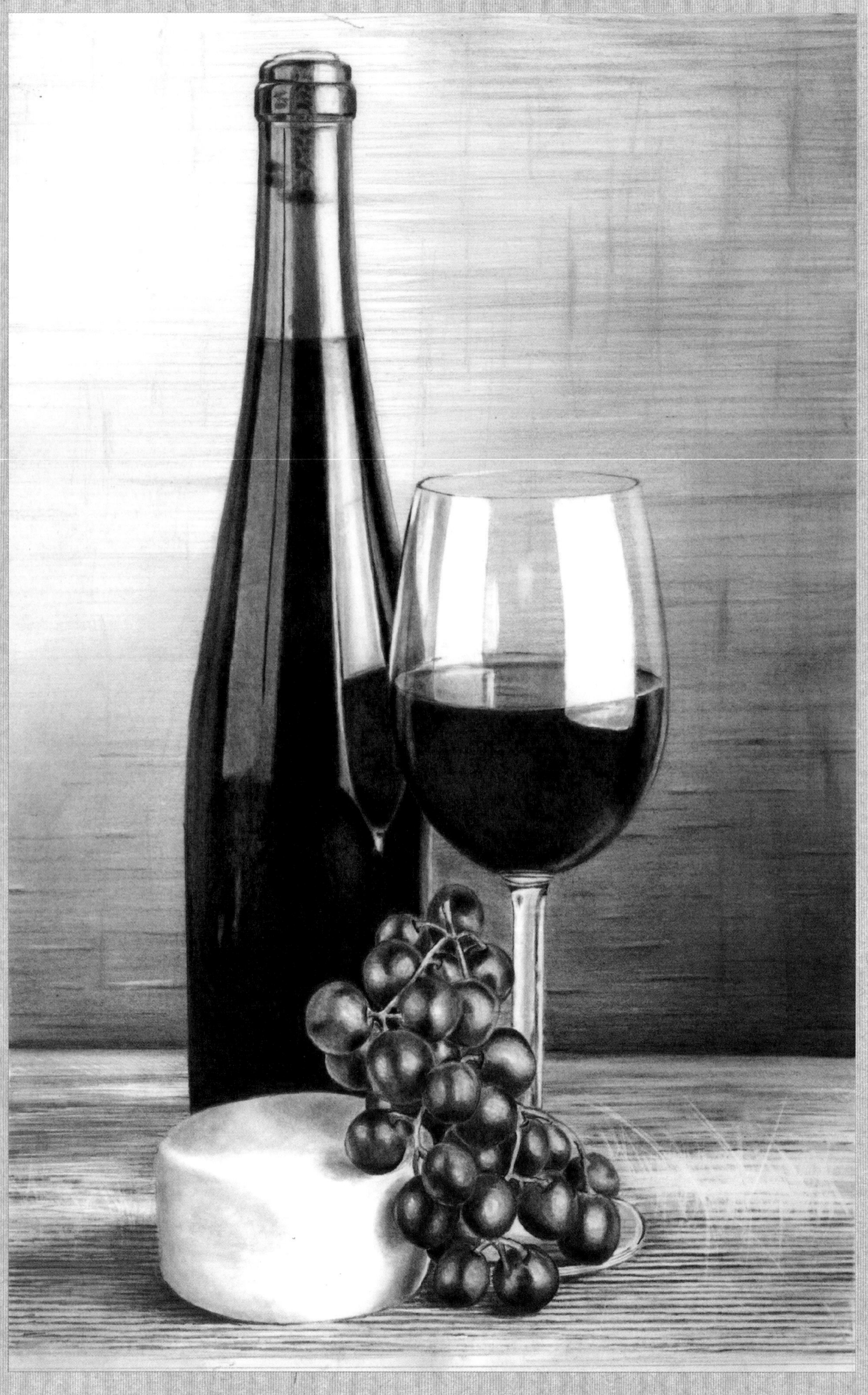

COMPOSITION

A composition is a visual organization of forms into a unified, balanced, harmonious arrangement. Many artists and art instructors rely on intuitive skills to attain successful compositions, and this is fine. However, it is also a good idea to know and review some of the tenets of what really constitutes a successful composition.

Ask yourself: Is there balance in the forms or subject matter within the composition? Do your eyes move freely around the composition? Are there focal points to pull your interest to the composition or to individual objects? Is there a variety of shapes and forms for interest? These are just a few of the questions that will be discussed in this chapter to help you employ successful composition design.

Elements of Composition

The elements of composition are point, shape, mass, volume, texture, value, and color. Let's talk about them one by one.

Point

A point is a single mark on a page without depth, height, or length. A group of points in a row or an arc can create a line—or at least imply a line. Points used closely together can suggest a three-dimensional object.

Line

Geometry defines a line as an infinite number of points. A line is the earliest tool that most children use intuitively to visualize and represent the world around them. A line represents the building-block foundation of most drawings. Lines can be bold, weak, varied, geometric, organic, energetic, or calm. We discussed gesture and contour line extensively in Chapter 1 (see page 13).

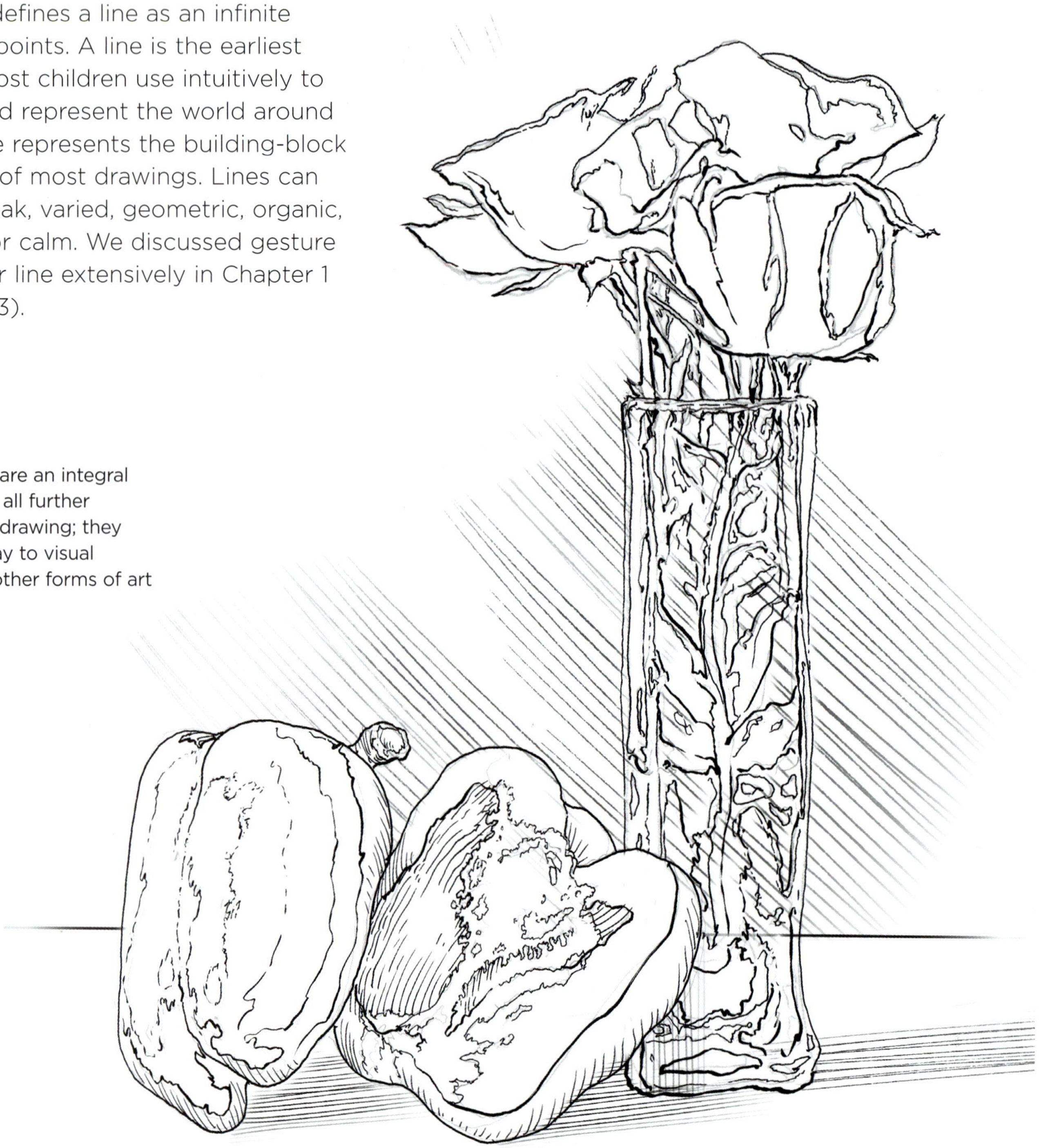

Line drawings are an integral foundation for all further exploration of drawing; they are the gateway to visual expression in other forms of art as well.

Shape

A shape can also be called a "form." A shape is usually considered to be an area or object that is either: (a) completely enclosed by lines or (b) perceived as a separate entity through isolation of shape (through contrast of value or color). In the example of positive and negative space, the recognizable shape is the positive shape while the area around the form is the negative shape. This is also called the "figure and ground" relationship. Negative shapes can be just as interesting as positive shapes.

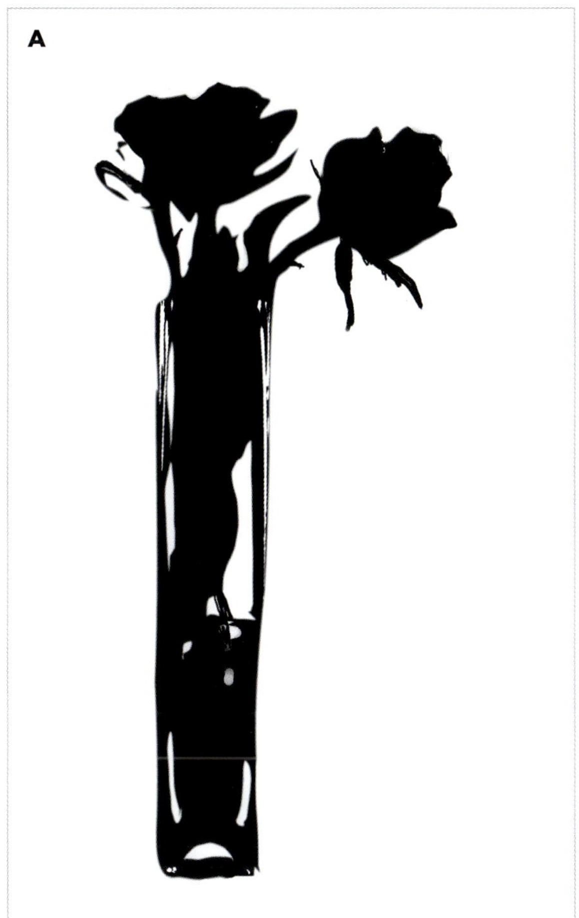

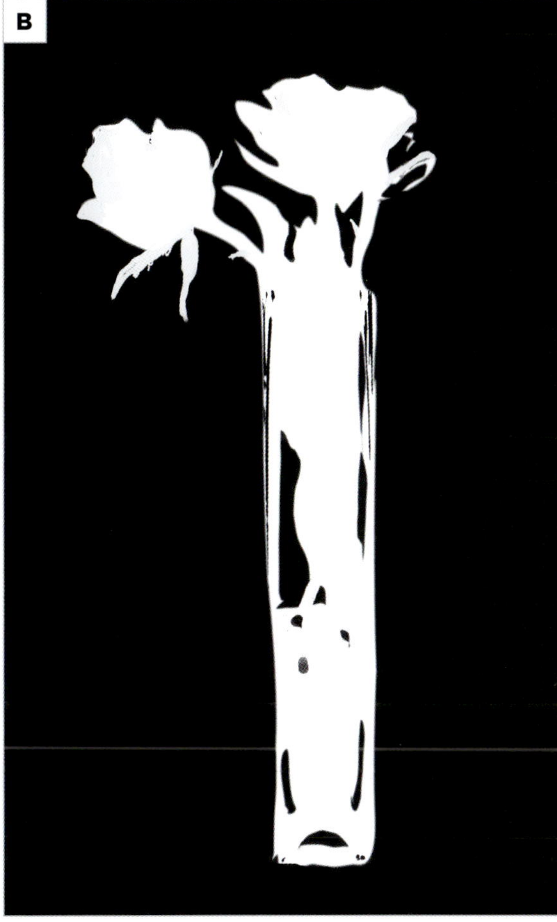

Also called the "figure/ground relationship," the recognizable shape of the subject becomes the positive shape or form, and the space around it becomes the negative shape (A). Shape can be bold and dramatic, with the negative area around the shape becoming just as interesting as the positive shape (B).

Volume and Mass

While shape usually defines a flat form or area, "volume" or "mass" is the terminology used to describe a form with three-dimensional qualities. Architecture and sculpture are associated more with mass and volume than drawing or painting. However, mass and volume can be inferred on a flat, two-dimensional surface through strong contrasts in value—light and dark—within a drawn object.

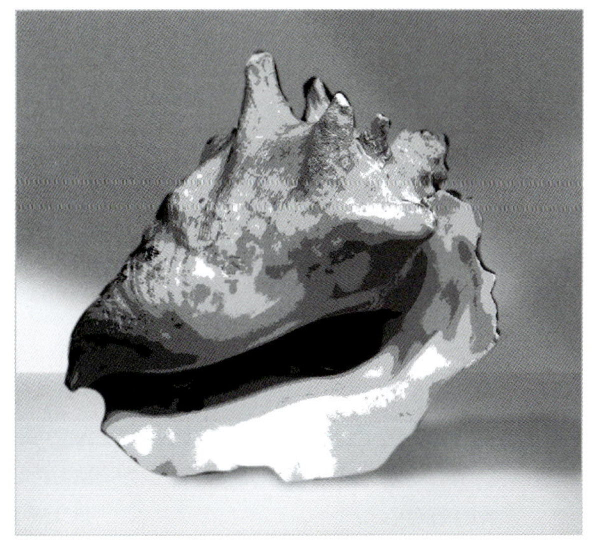

The close cropping of the format, along with the high contrast across the form, gives this shell solidity and weight, or mass.

Texture

Texture refers to the tactile quality, actual or rendered, of an object. In a drawing, texture isn't so much the surface on which we work, but rather the way the artist manipulates the drawing materials to evoke a textural feeling. We work to create a visual depiction of a texture. However, there are certain textural qualities inherent in various paper surfaces that can help facilitate a smooth surface, a mottled surface, a rough surface, or even a wet surface. This is part of the magic that an artist can bring to a drawing for the viewer.

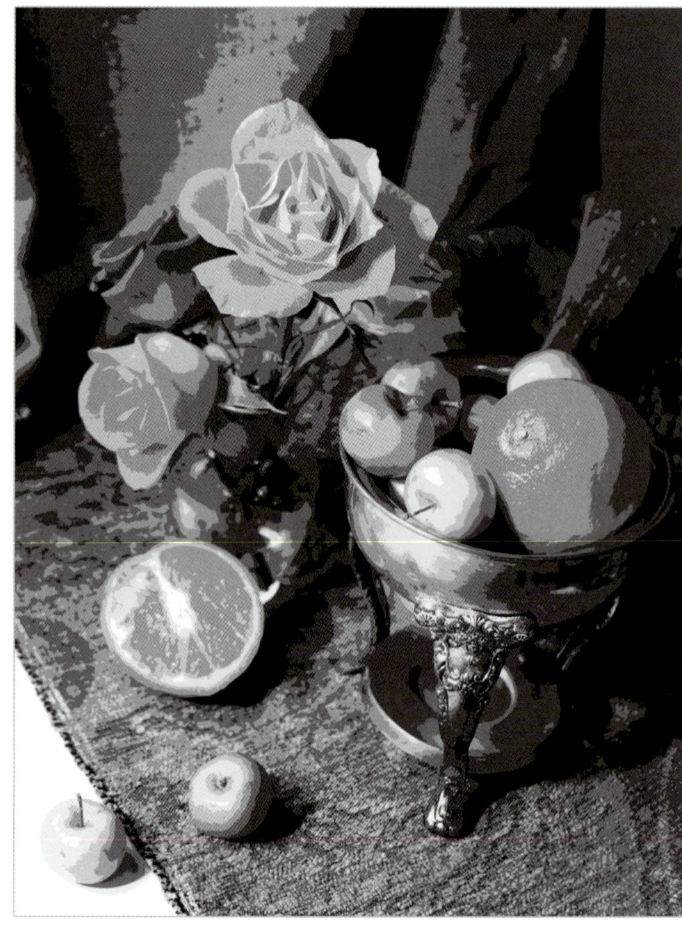

Texture takes on many examples here, ranging from the rough quality of the fabric and the pebbly surface of orange skin to the slick, metallic quality of the vase and the wetness of the sliced orange.

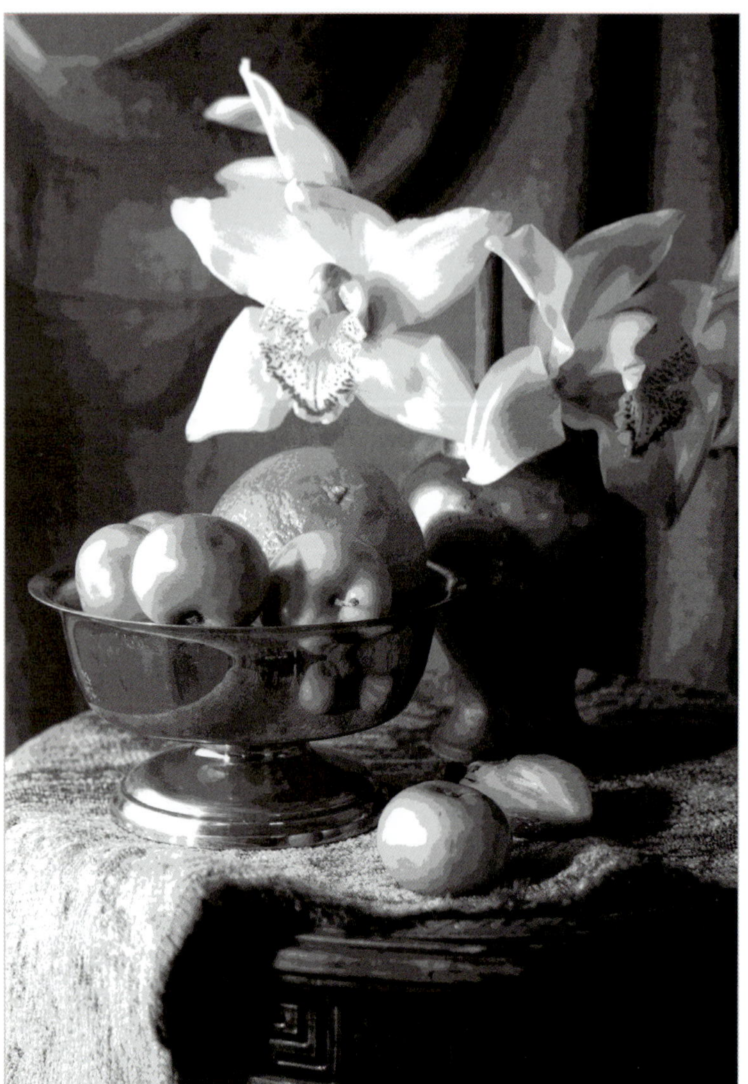

Value

Value is the range of light from white to black, or very light to very dark. Values in a drawing help us determine the direction of the light source and the shapes and structure within a form. Value also helps explain and portray depth in a drawing; dark values appear to advance toward the viewer, while lighter values tend to recede into the background. Additionally, high-value contrast within a form can bring the object closer to the viewer, while low-value contrast makes the object move away from the viewer. This phenomenon is also known as "atmospheric perspective."

This is an example of high-contrast value, with a range of values from very dark to very light.

Value Scale

A value scale is a helpful tool to use when trying to decide what values are inherent in the subject matter. For ease of explanation, value scales are typically broken down into 10 value gradients, from black (10) to white (0).

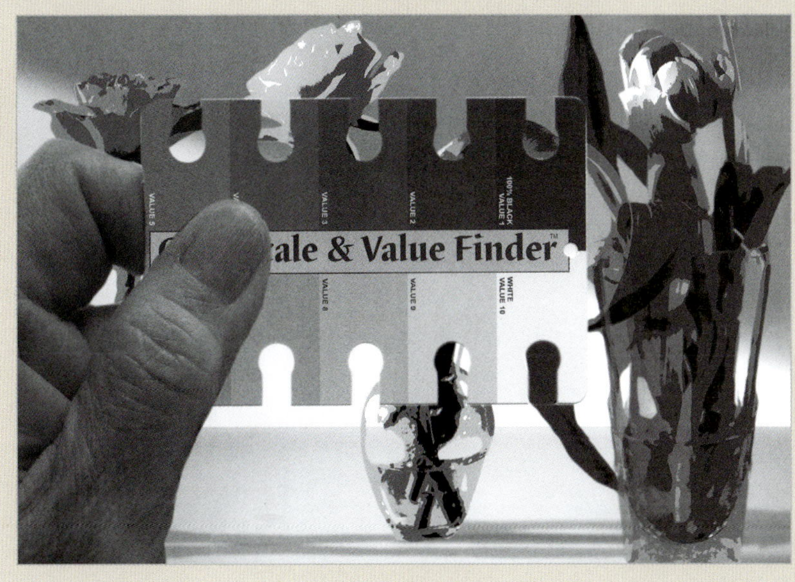

Color

An entire book could be written just about color, and many have been! There are a few important basics to know about color. Color is all about light and the way it affects our perception of an object. In two-dimensional artwork, we attempt to portray the effects of light on a form or object through the color mixing of pigments and dyes.

Color has three important characteristics: *hue, saturation,* and *value.* Hue is the actual name or family of color, such as "blue," "red," or "green." Saturation, or "intensity," refers to the brightness or dullness of a color. A pure blue pigment has a much higher intensity, sometimes called "chroma," than a blue that is mixed with its complement on the color wheel (orange). Value refers to the darkness or lightness of the color. Color is discussed more comprehensively on page 159.

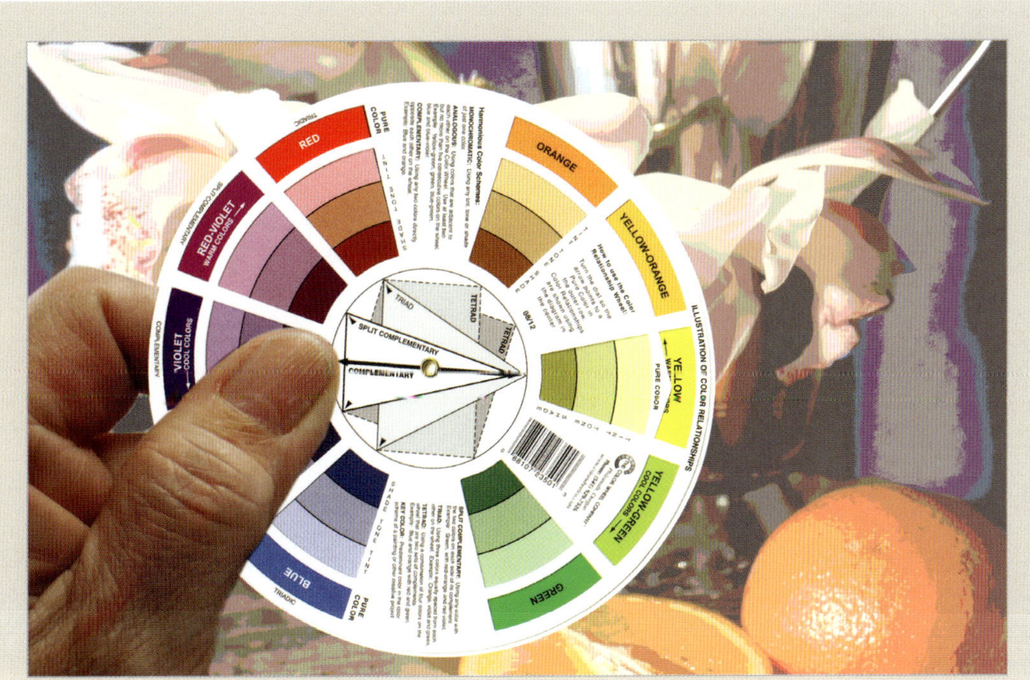

Color Wheel

A color wheel is a helpful tool that not only describes the color, but also gives information on harmonious color combination and mixtures.

Principles of Composition

A pleasing composition appears balanced and harmonious, with the various elements working together to create an eye-catching scene. There are a variety of ways to achieve a good composition. Over the next couple of pages we'll discuss several principles of composition and how to use them to achieve a well-balanced drawing.

Unity

Unity is the overarching dynamic that integrates and connects visual imagery into a cohesive and successful composition. The path to unity starts with understanding how different principles of design can help the artist attain unity in a composition. In good composition there should be a feeling of a plan, not a random arrangement of forms.

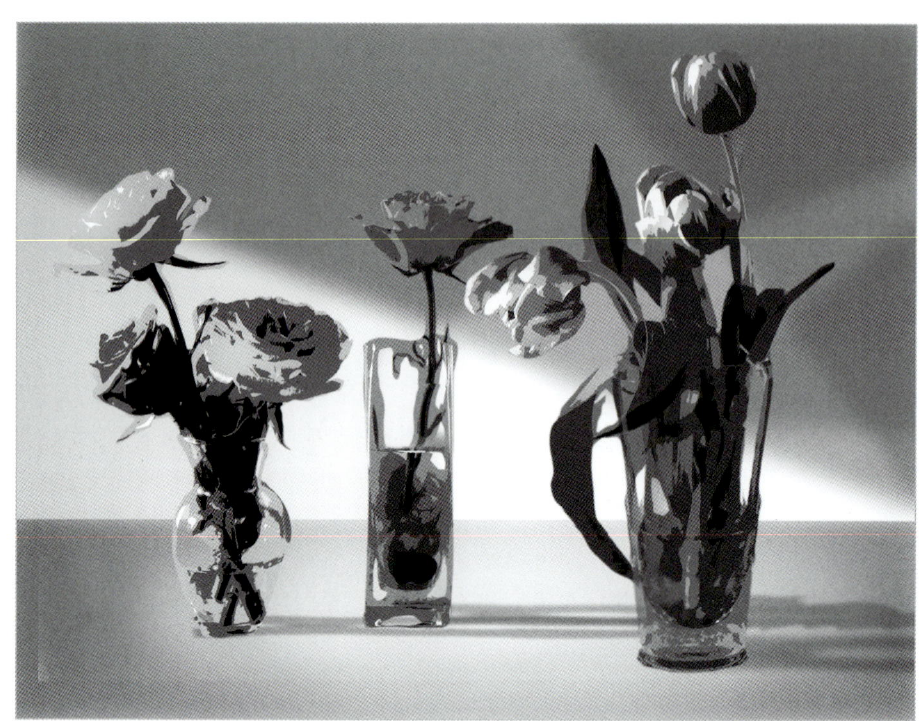

There is a structured feeling in this photograph due to the combination of flowers, which unify the composition with recognition; however, the variety of shapes, heights, and values add interest to the composition.

Variety

A composition that includes variety is typically more interesting than a rigid repetition of similar shapes. Different sizes, shapes, and values add variety to a composition.

You can also achieve unity with repetition. In this image, note how the repetition of shells promotes unity with recognition, yet the different types and sizes add just enough variety to keep the composition from being static.

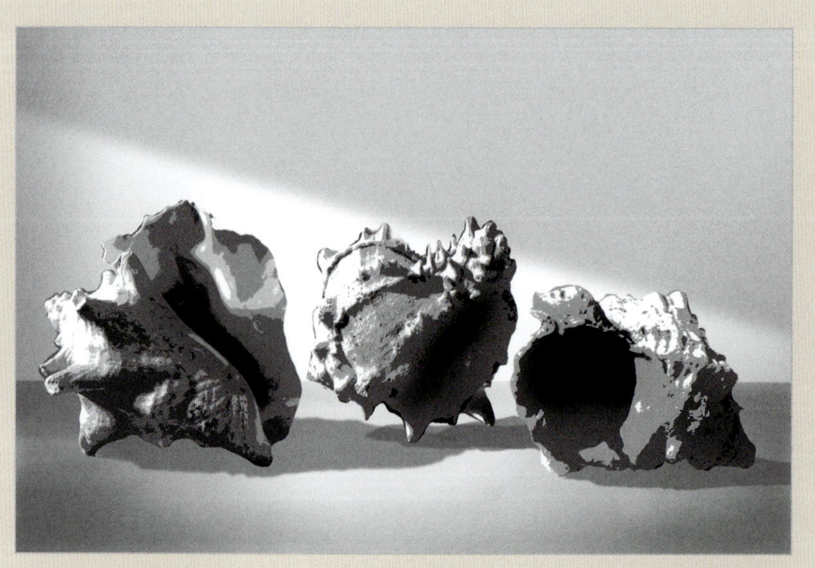

Emphasis

Emphasis in a composition will help lead the viewer's eye to a *focal point*, or area of interest. This can be achieved through contrasting values, particularly high contrast (A). You can also achieve emphasis in a composition by using contrasting colors or a combination of hard and soft edges. The focal point of a composition is the best area to use a combination of hard edges, high value or color contrast, and lines or edges that direct toward the focal point. These diagonals or curves are called "directional forces" (B). Emphasis may also be achieved by isolating the focal point from the rest of the composition (C).

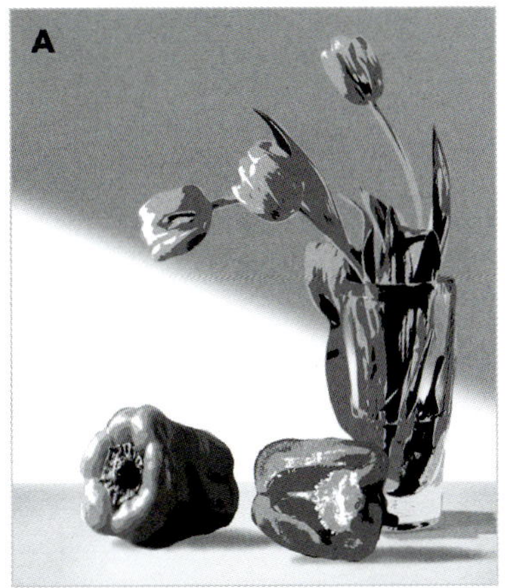

A

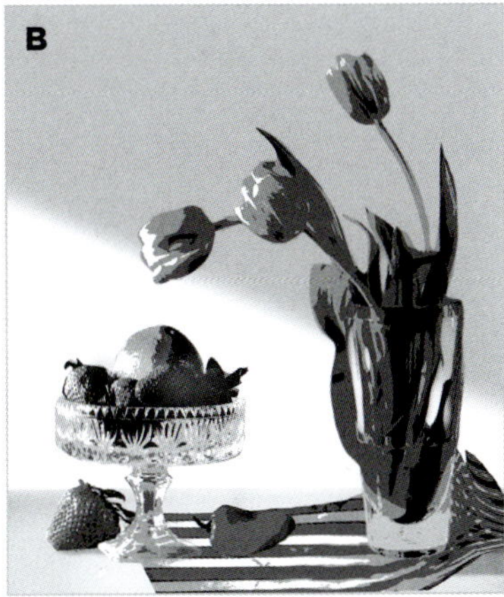

B

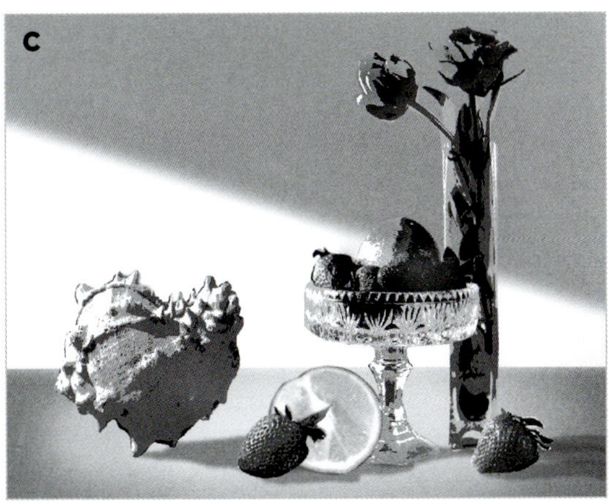

C

Harmony

Harmony is achieved through the orderly arrangement of elements that creates a unified composition. There are various ways to achieve harmony, including the repetition of shapes, values, or colors, which creates patterns for the eye to follow. The term "harmony" is more closely associated with music, but harmony and rhythm in a drawing composition bear similar characteristics: an orderly repetition of elements in a flowing and pleasing pattern.

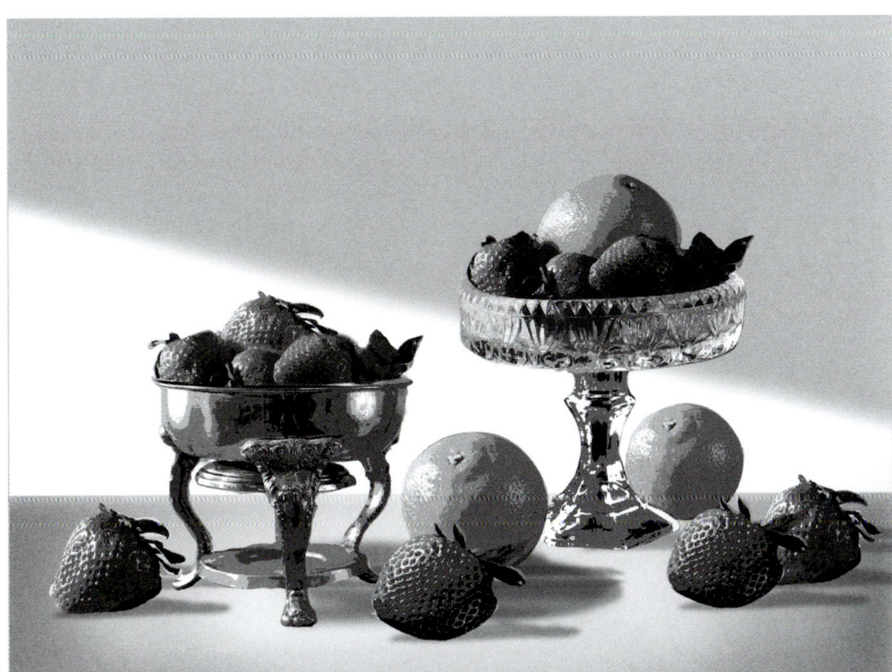

Harmony in a composition can be achieved with the repetition of similar shapes throughout, such as the strawberries in this image, to tie different elements together into a unified design.

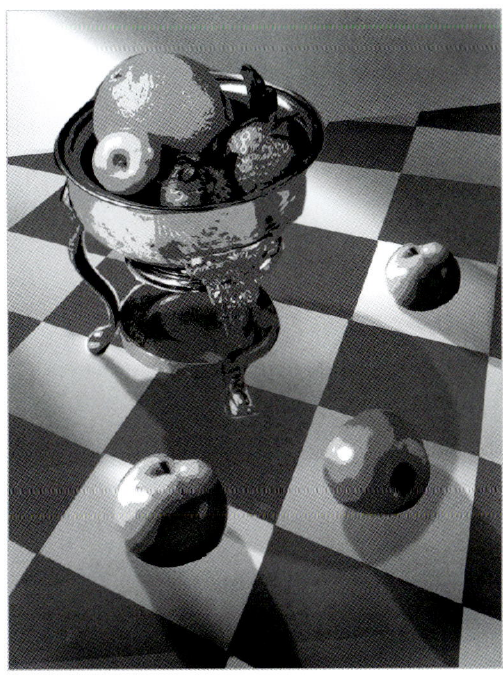

The pattern on the ground plane in this image is accentuated by the placement and repetition of similar shapes around the vase. Pattern can also add to the feeling of harmony in a composition.

Balance

Balance in a composition generates a feeling of equilibrium in the emphasis or weight of objects in relation to one another. Symmetrical compositions are the same on both sides, practically mirror images. Symmetrical balance is also called "formal balance." In asymmetrical balance, the two sides appear to have the same visual weight, though the arrangement may consist of objects of unequal sizes or weights. Asymmetrical balance is also called "informal balance."

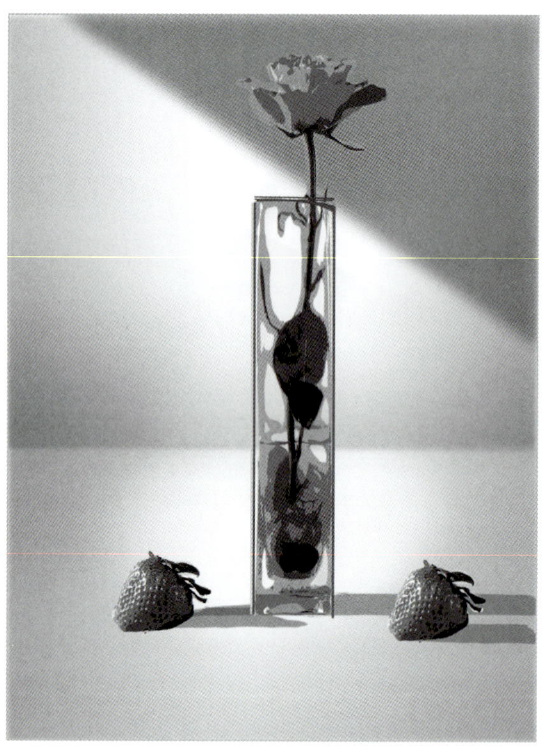

SYMMETRY Symmetry is the same arrangement on both sides of a strong central form. This formal balance in a composition can sometimes be visually unexciting and seem static.

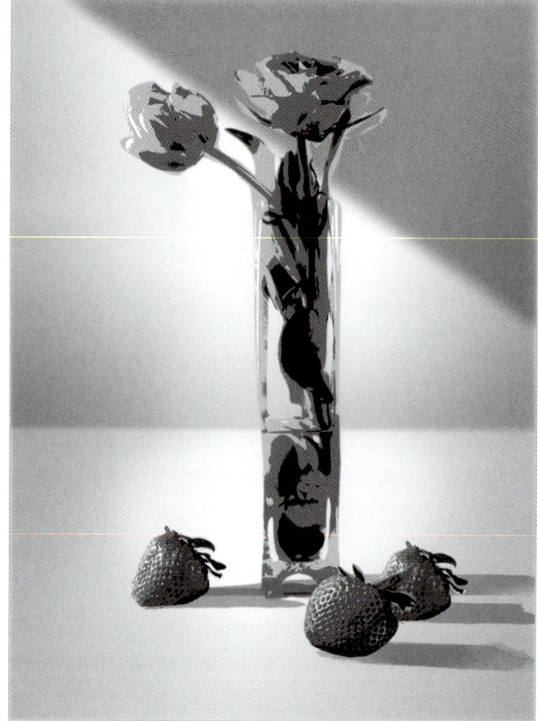

NEAR SYMMETRY
This is a more pleasing arrangement of forms that is still very symmetrically balanced.

Proportion and Scale

In design, proportion refers to the relative size of objects to each other. Scale is another word for size. Scale and proportion are closely related to emphasis and focal point.

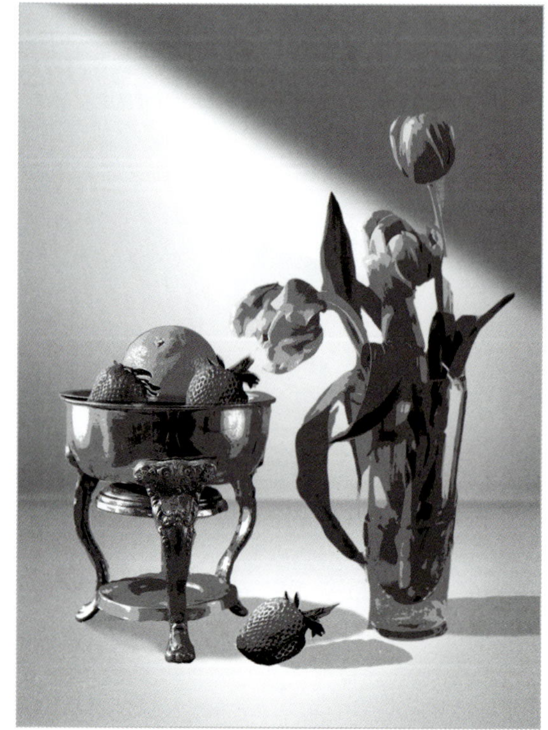

ASYMMETRY In general, asymmetry is achieved through equilibrium of objects that, even though they may be different in scale and proportion, are equal in weight.

The Golden Ratio

Also called the "golden rectangle," this mathematical construction was developed by the ancient Greeks to represent the perfect ratios and proportions on which to base their architecture and design. These proportions have influenced art and design throughout the centuries ever since. The golden ratio is: width is to length as length is to length plus width.

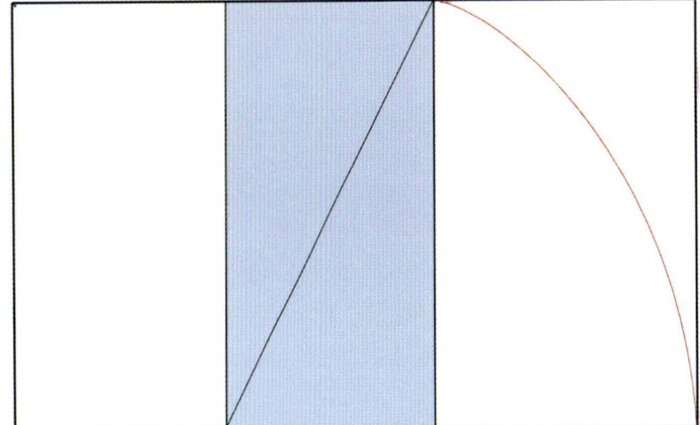

The golden rectangle can be created by rotating the diagonal of the half square (blue).

A variation on this becomes the "true golden mean." By adding a square to the long rectangle, another smaller—but proportional—rectangle is created. This process can be continued infinitely, if desired, and the resulting smaller perfect proportion will always be the same.

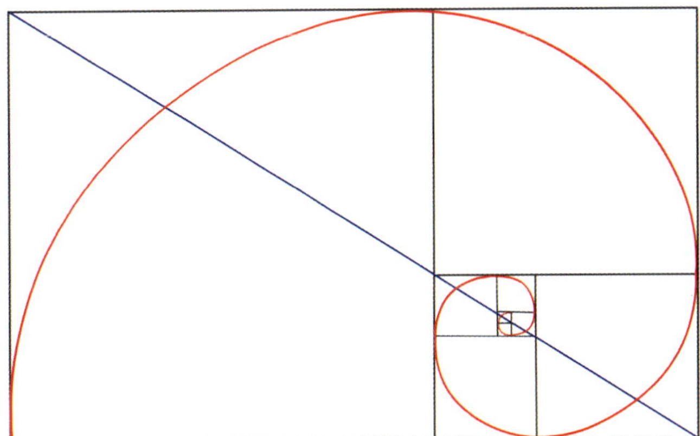

Many artists, designers, and architects believe that the convergence of increasingly smaller squares in this variation of the golden ratio creates the most desirable area of focus in a composition.

Rule of Thirds

A simplified and equally effective mathematical formula for locating focal points is called the "rule of thirds." This rule divides the format into nine equal divisions with two equally spaced horizontal lines and two equally spaced vertical lines. The points at the convergence of these lines, as well as the lines themselves, are effective locations for guiding the eye successfully around the composition. Aligning a subject along these lines creates more interest, balance, and energy than simply centering the subject or randomly placing it in the composition.

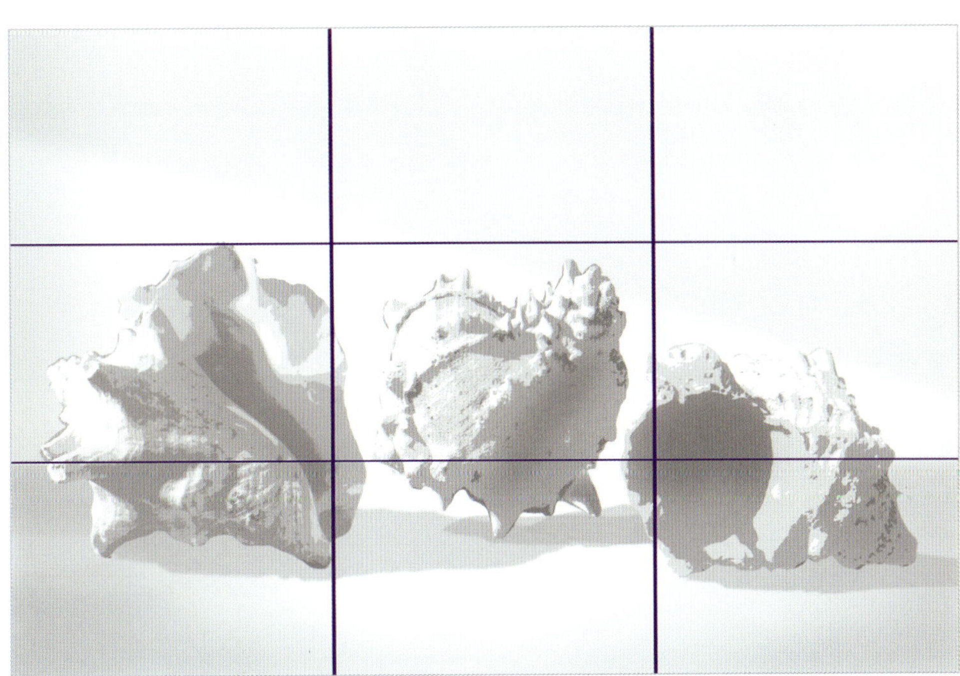

Many artists and photographers use the rule of thirds, an effective and simplified formula for successful focal-point placement. The rule of thirds divides an image or subject into nine proportional segments. The points at which the lines converge are effective focal points.

YOUR HOMEWORK

Your homework for this chapter is to create a flower arrangement—using either real flowers or synthetic—and place them in a vase or hang them from a string or wire on the wall in front of your drawing board.

Start with an overall gesture drawing quickly executed with light line (preferably using an H or HB pencil).

Block in the entire still life in 15–20 minutes as you continually move around the gesture drawing, defining the forms with a line that is still lightly drawn, but a bit more refined.

Finish the drawing with a weighted contour line using a darker graphite pencil, such as a B or 2B, or both.

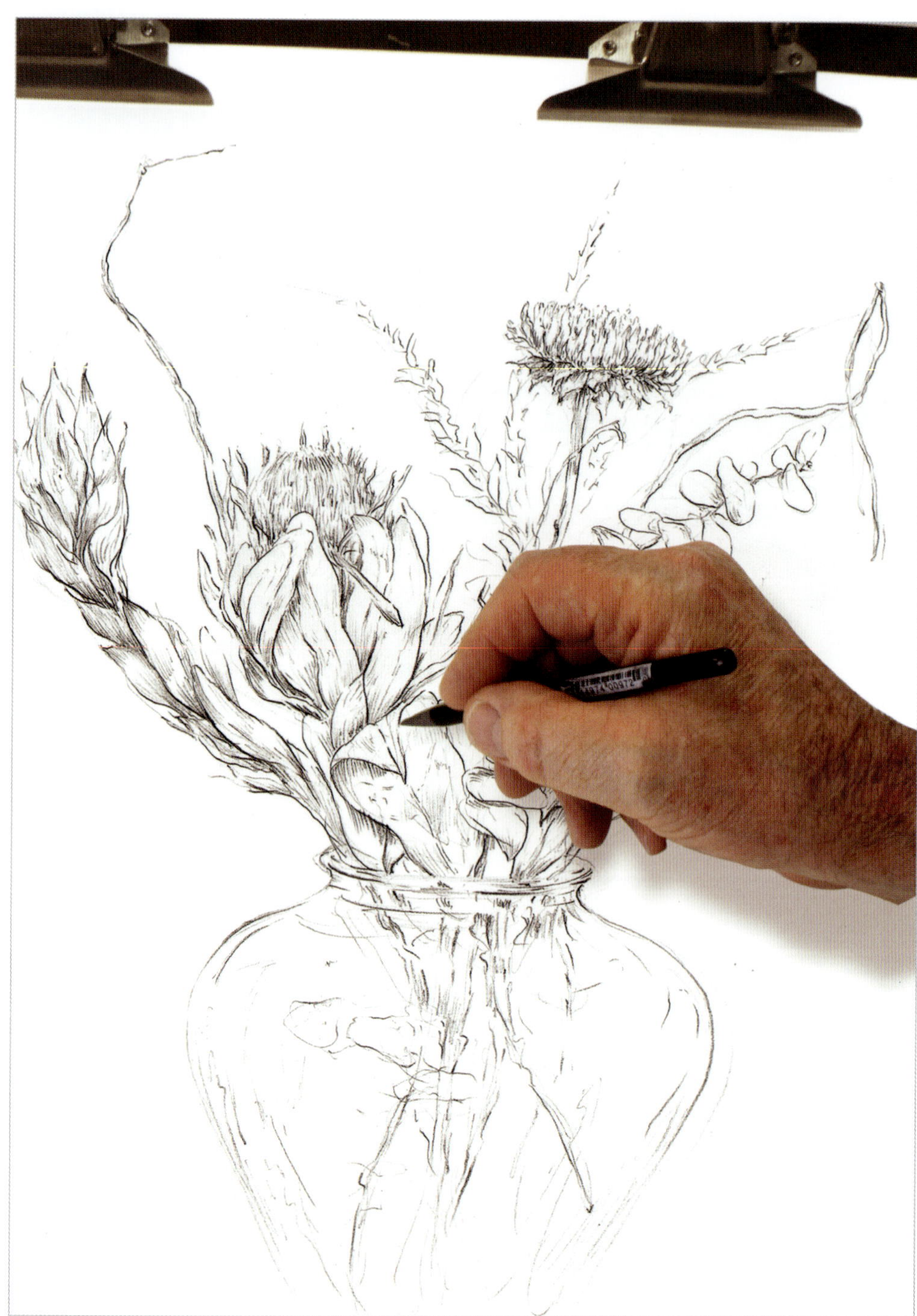

EXERCISES FOR PRACTICE

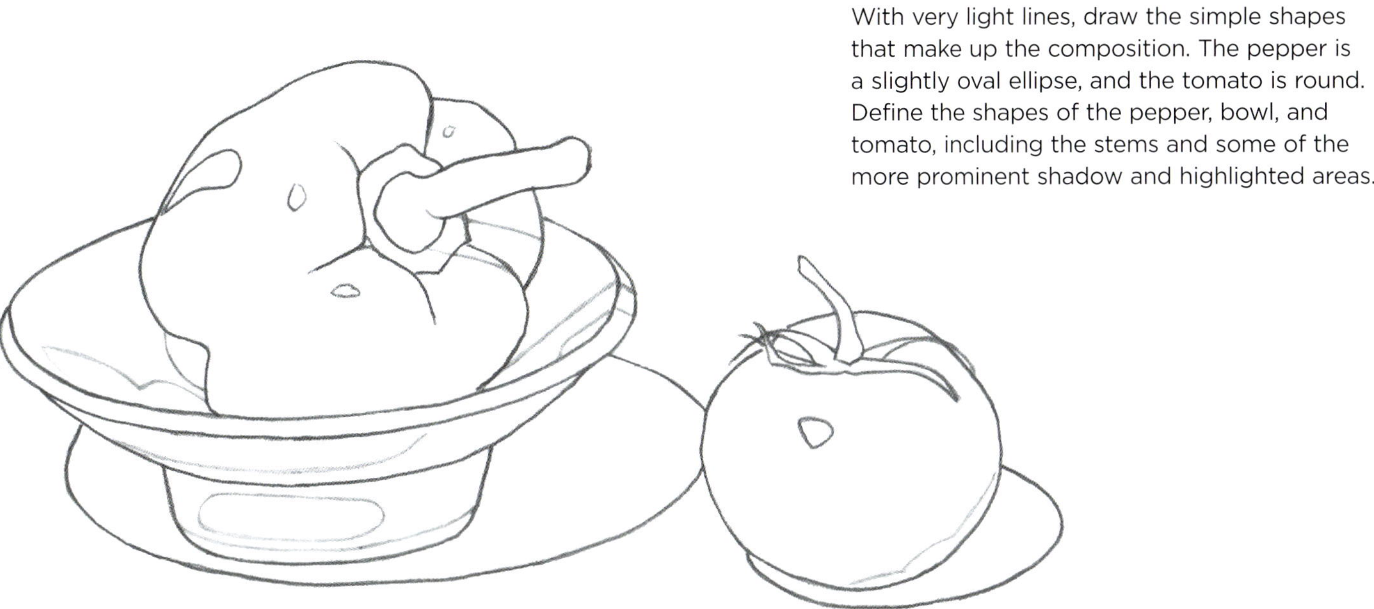

With very light lines, draw the simple shapes that make up the composition. The pepper is a slightly oval ellipse, and the tomato is round. Define the shapes of the pepper, bowl, and tomato, including the stems and some of the more prominent shadow and highlighted areas.

Identify and draw in the darkest-value areas of the composition using a 4B or 6B pencil.

Using a 2B pencil and an HB pencil, mostly with hatch strokes, follow the curvature of the stem of the pepper and the stem and leaves of the tomato.

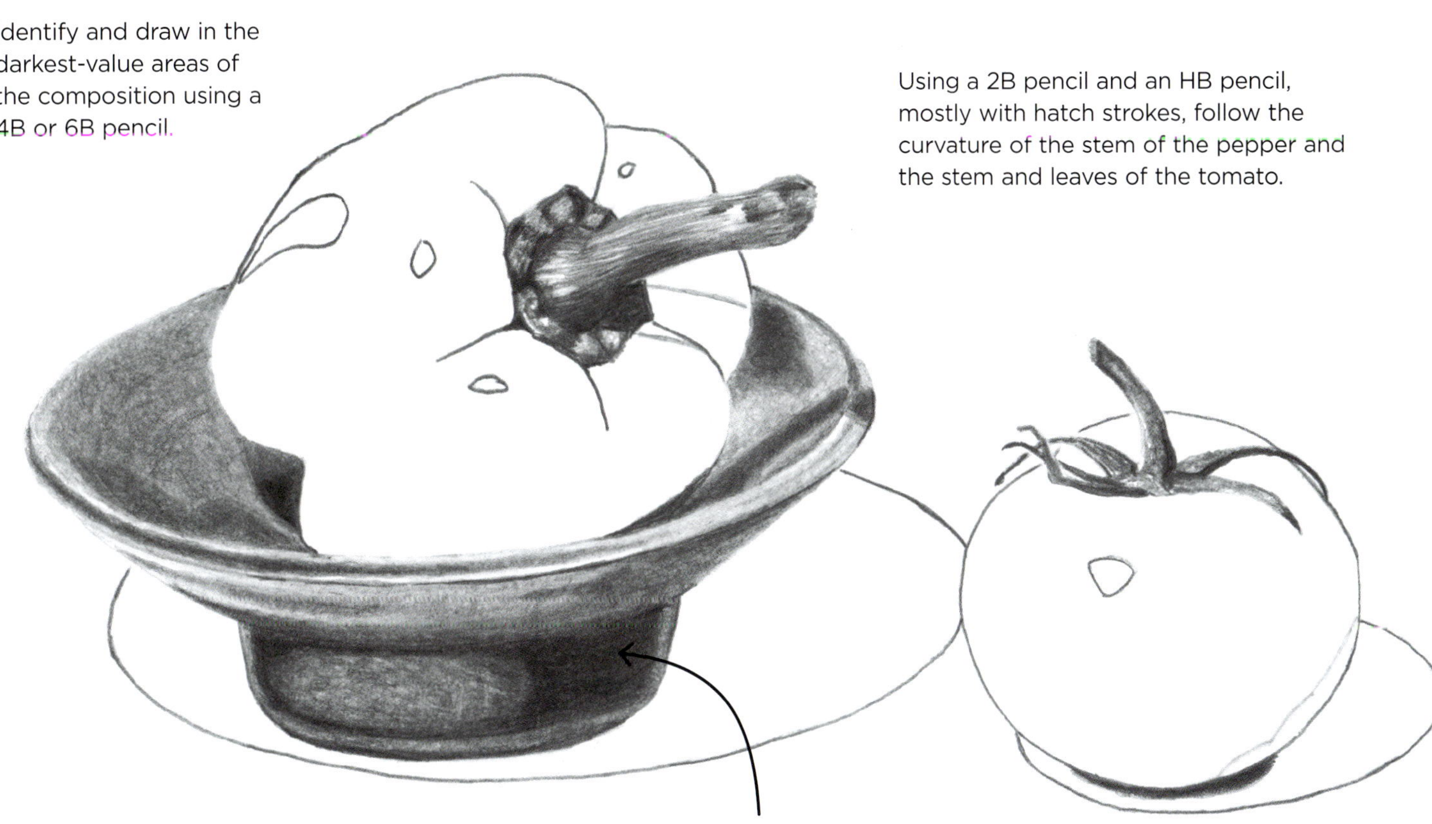

Use a 2B pencil with circular overlapping strokes for the cast shadow and darker areas of the bowl. For the lighter areas, use an HB pencil and a 2H pencil.

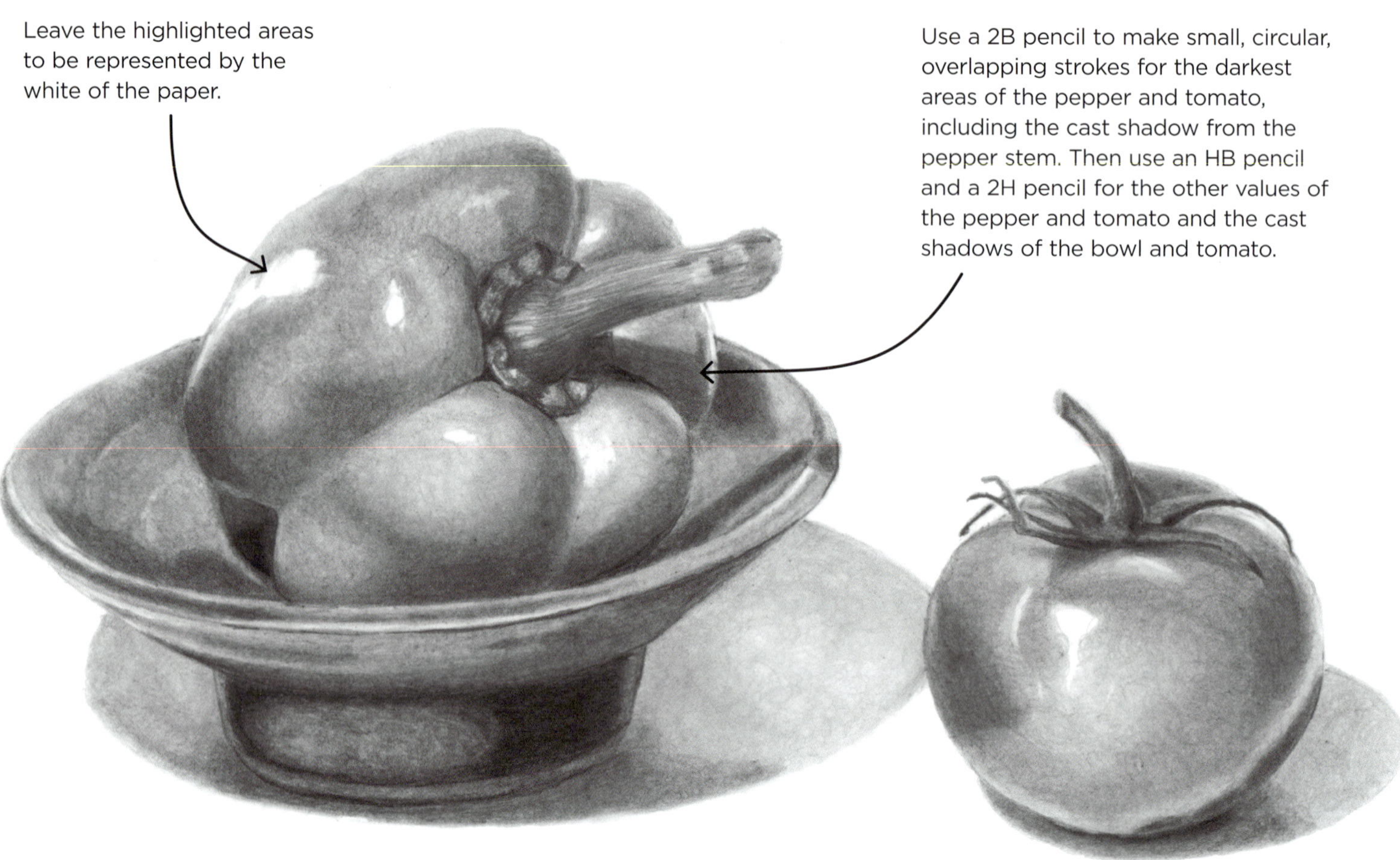
Leave the highlighted areas to be represented by the white of the paper.
Use a 2B pencil to make small, circular, overlapping strokes for the darkest areas of the pepper and tomato, including the cast shadow from the pepper stem. Then use an HB pencil and a 2H pencil for the other values of the pepper and tomato and the cast shadows of the bowl and tomato.

Apply some stippling to match the look of the bowl, and then do some light blending.

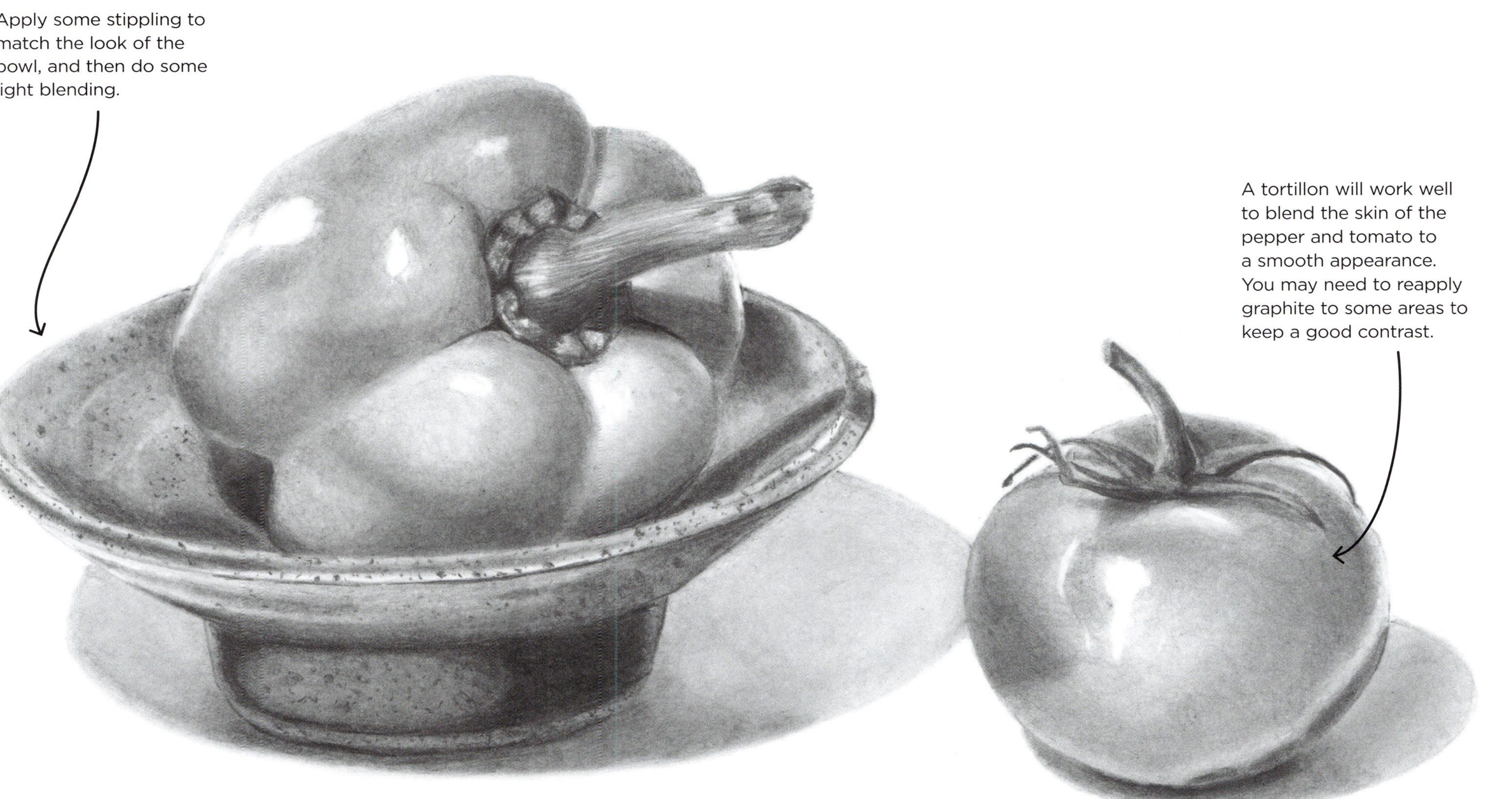

A tortillon will work well to blend the skin of the pepper and tomato to a smooth appearance. You may need to reapply graphite to some areas to keep a good contrast.

Using a pencil and a kneaded eraser, clean up some of the highlighted areas and bring out some of the other lighter areas as needed throughout the drawing.

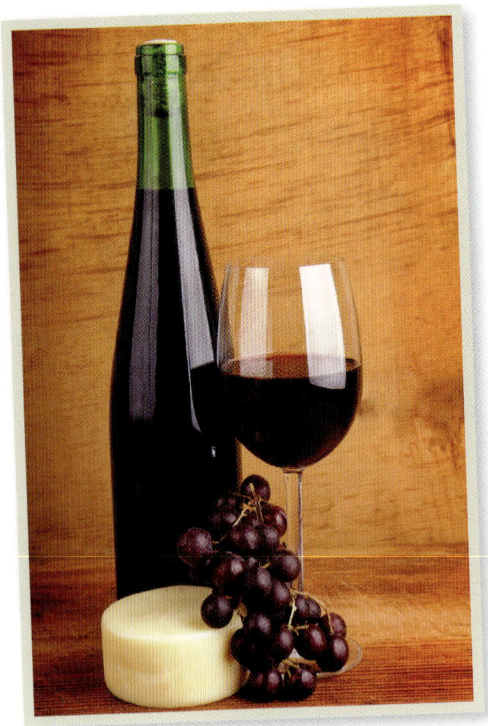

Wine & Cheese

This classic still life setup is great practice for drawing a variety of textures, including glass, wood, and the smooth skins of grapes and cheese. In this lesson, we'll also learn how to bring out reflections and shade evenly.

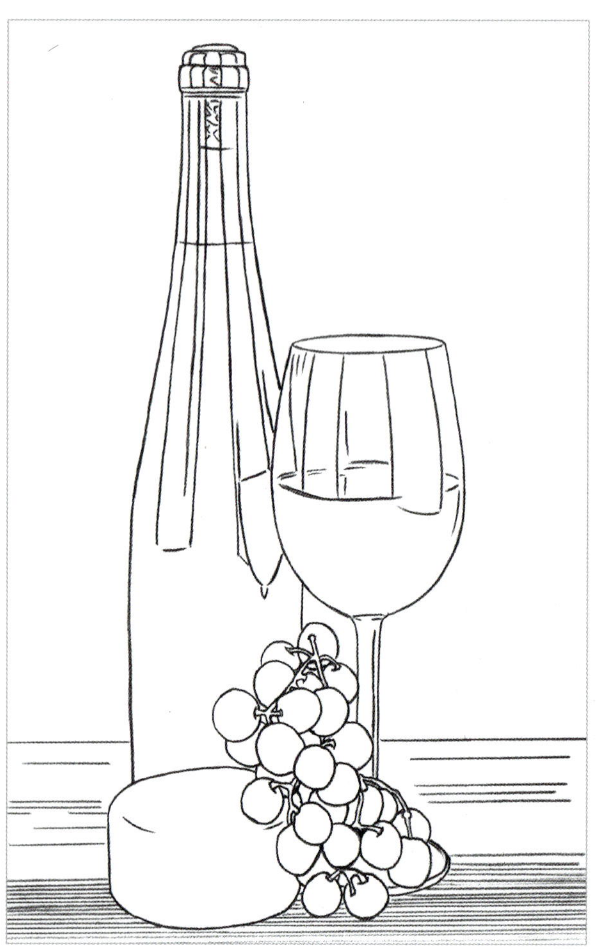

STEP 1 Begin by drawing an outline. The drawings that follow have much darker lines for demonstration purposes; draw your outline very lightly. It is easier to darken the lines later in the drawing where needed than to erase to make them lighter.

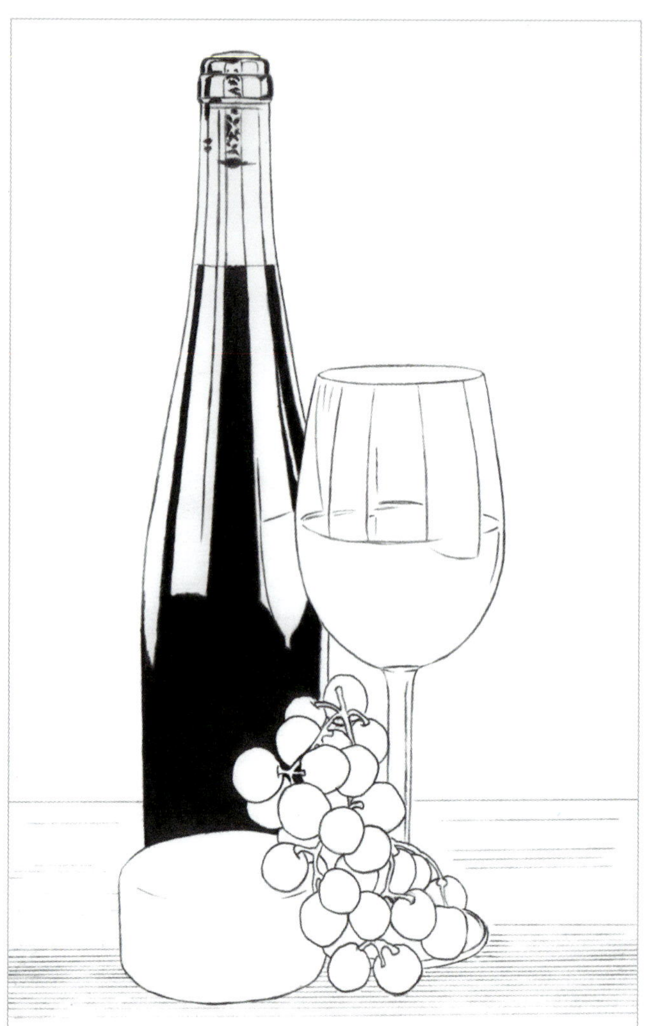

STEP 2 Start on the wine bottle using a 4B pencil to establish the darkest values of the drawing. Use a circular motion and then burnish over it with a 2B, which gives a rich, dark tone. When drawing a large area like this, be very patient to create an even tone. You may need to reapply the 4B in some places.

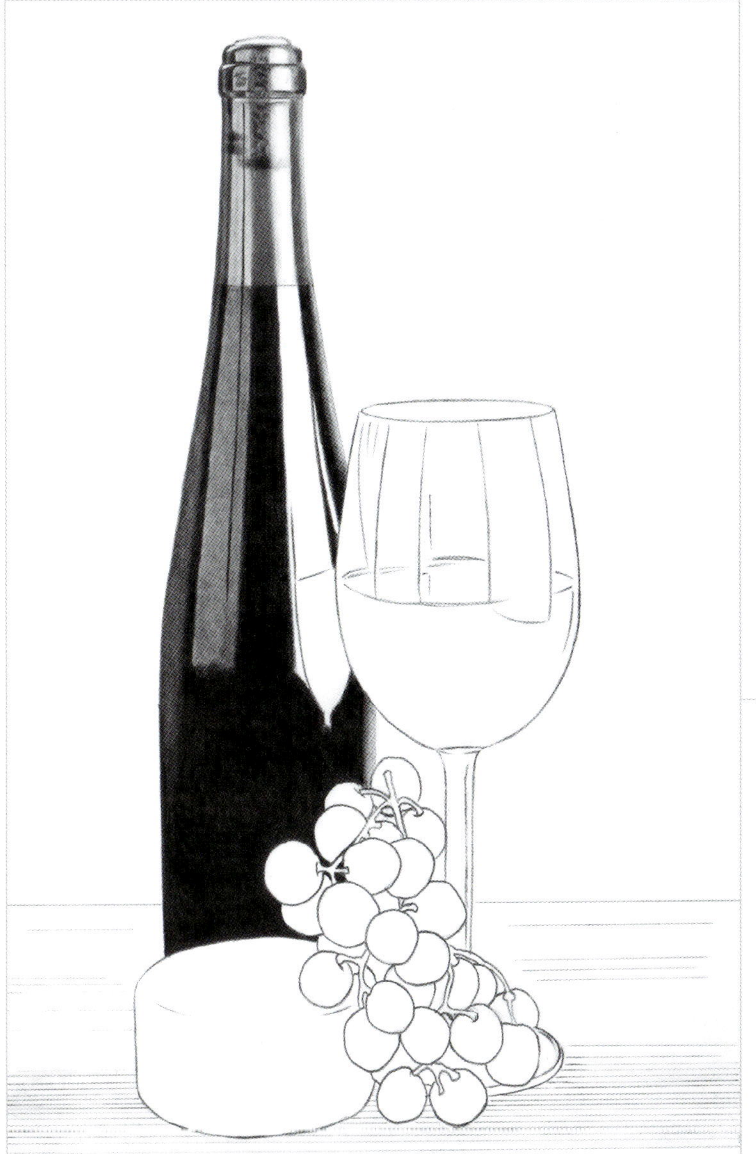

When burnishing over graphite, use a pencil that is one or two grades harder than the one used initially. Make sure the point is a little dull rather than too sharp.

A used tortillon or stump works well for "drawing" in some shaded areas. You can also dip it in graphite shavings to shade darker areas.

STEP 3 Now work on a couple areas below the fill line of the bottle. On the far left edge, use a 2B pencil to create a slightly lighter tone, followed by light blending with a tortillon. The reflection just to the right is lighter, so use an HB followed by light blending with a tortillon. On the far right edge of the bottle, use an F and blend the same way. For the top of the bottle, above the fill line, use F and HB pencils for the darker and lighter tones, lightly blending with a tortillon. Leave the white of the paper for the highlighted area.

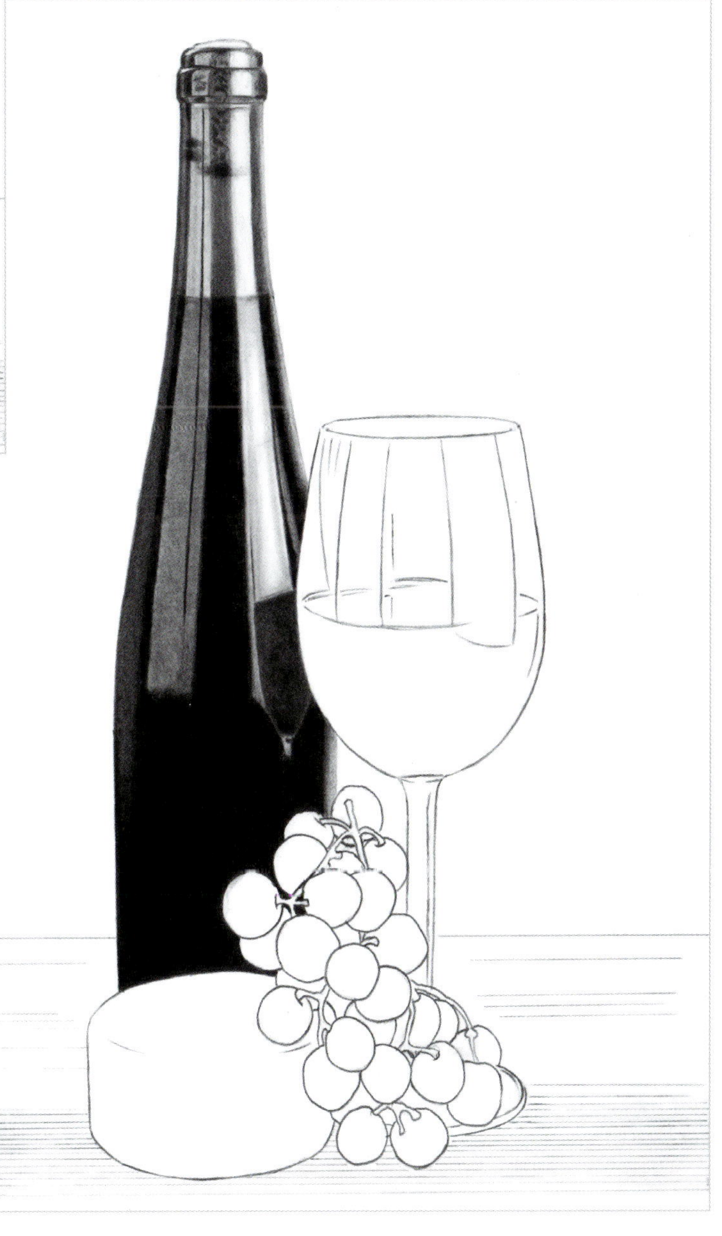

STEP 4 For the small reflection of the wine glass on the bottle, use a 2B and burnish with an HB. Above this area, use a 2H and blend lightly with a tortillon. For the two slightly darker vertical lines in the reflection, simply draw them using the graphite on the tortillon.

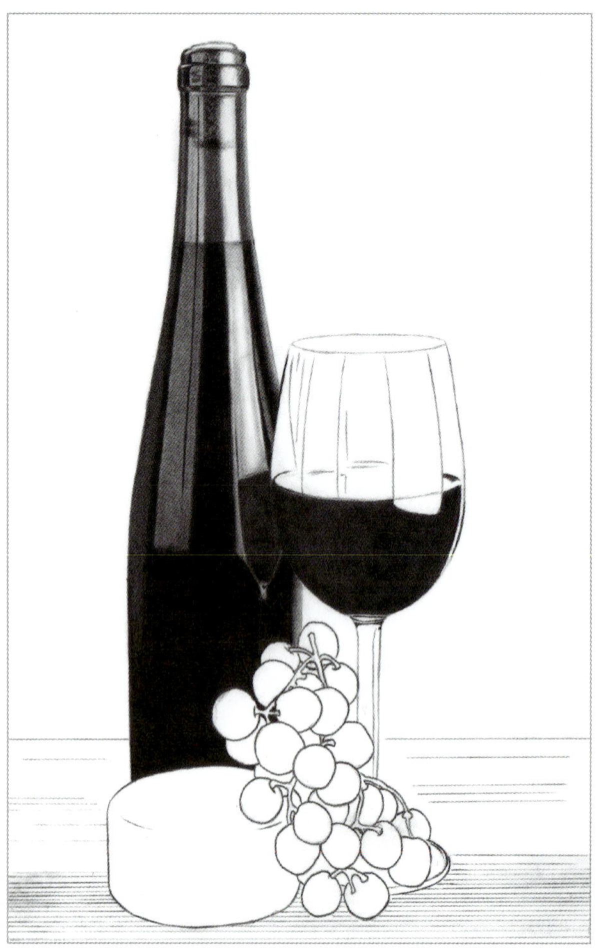

STEP 5 Use a 2B pencil on the wine glass because you want it to be slightly lighter in tone than the bottle. Then burnish using an HB. Use the 2B as well for the small dark areas where the stem connects to the glass.

STEP 6 Use F and HB pencils for the lighter details of the upper glass, over the surface of the liquid in the glass, and on the stem. Then blend lightly with the tortillon.

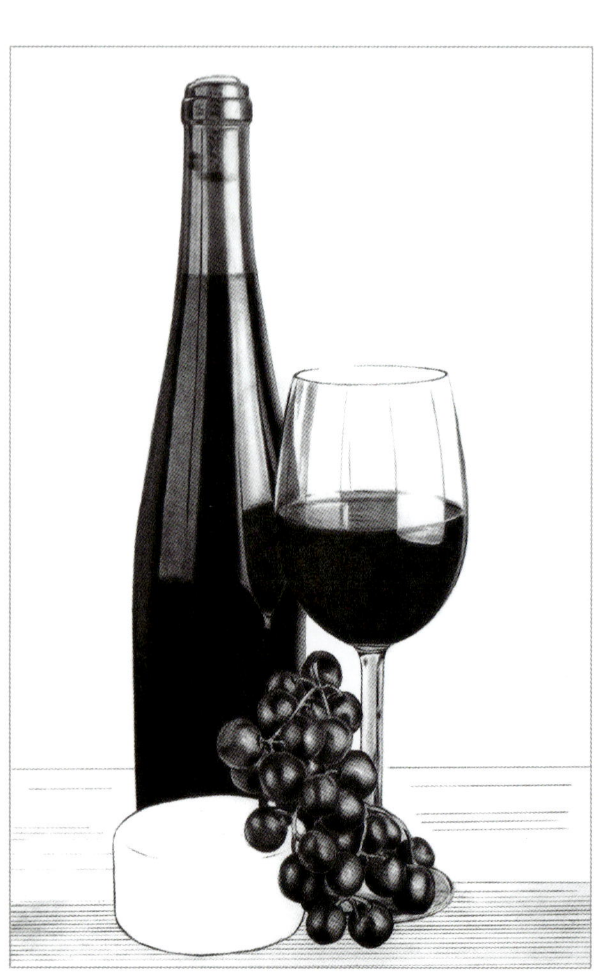

STEP 7 For the grapes, use 2B and F pencils to create the light and dark areas on the fruit and stems. Use a circular motion, keeping it loose in areas where you see interesting texture. Lightly blend with a tortillon, trying to save some of the delicate texture on the grapes. Notice that a few of the grapes around and above the cheese show some slight reflected light from the cheese.

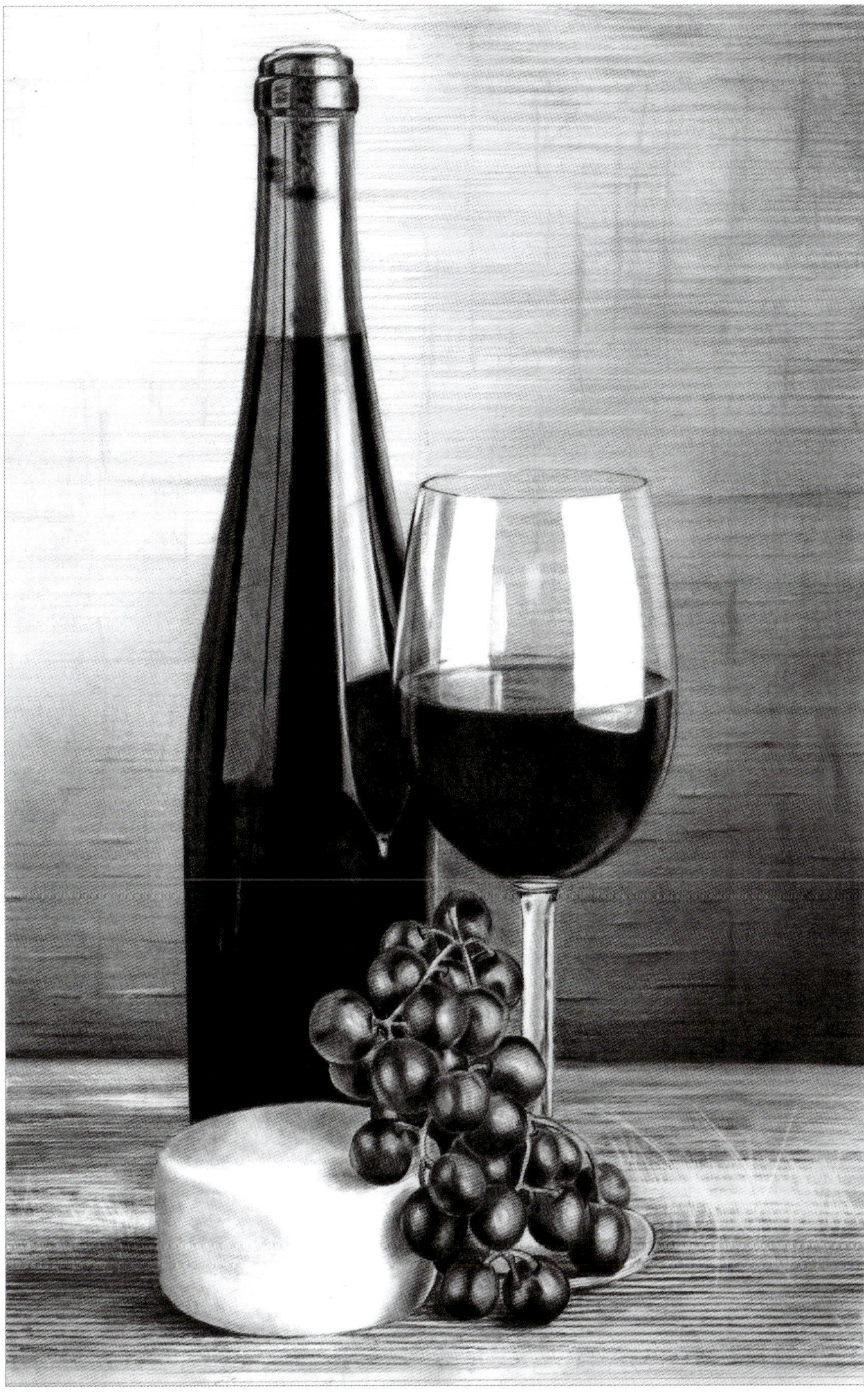

STEP 8 Darken and thicken the wood grain on the table with a 2B pencil and lightly blend with a tortillon. Use a pencil eraser to lighten areas in the wood grain and create the appearance of knife cuts in the wood. Also using the 2B, add shadows on the table from the cheese and grapes. Lightly shade the cheese with an F and blend with a stump in the shadow areas. You can also use a stump with graphite to achieve a similar result. For the background, use 2B, F, and 2H pencils to shade. Then use a stump and facial tissue to blend. Using my kneaded and pencil erasers, bring out a few subtle areas of reflection on the bottle and glass.

Cut the tip of your pencil eraser at an angle and use it to create fine white lines in your drawing.

Onions

This simple setup against a clean, crisp background is perfect for beginning still life drawing. These onions are very basic in shape, and their smooth, subtly grained skin is ideal for practicing both hatching and blending.

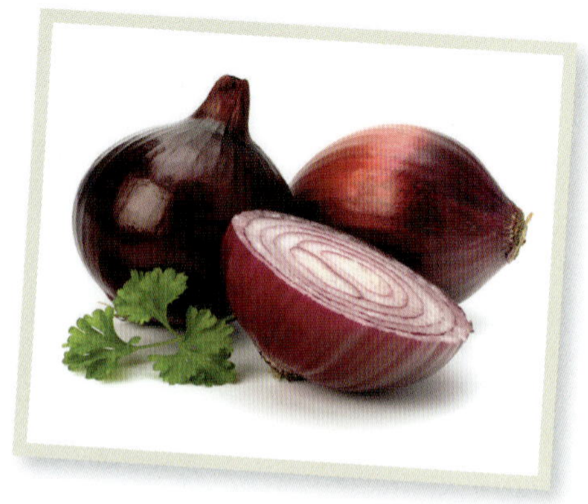

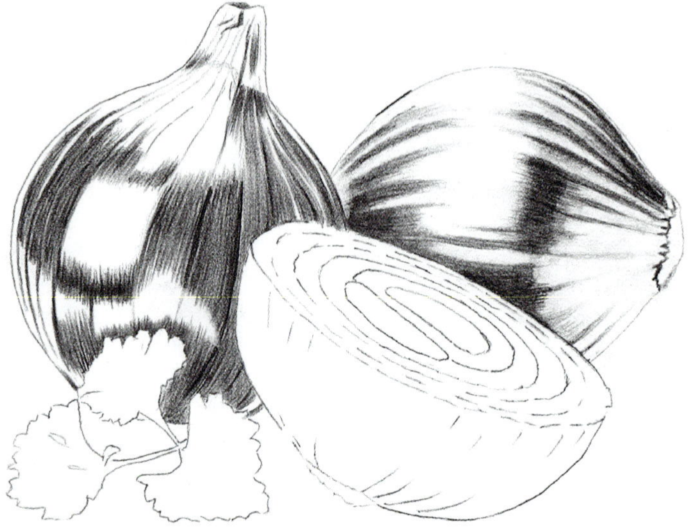

STEP 1 First sketch an initial outline. When you're happy with it, transfer the outline onto the drawing paper. Next establish the darkest areas on the two whole onions. Use a 2B pencil with the linear hatching technique, lifting the pencil at the end of each stroke and tapering toward the lighter areas. This will make for smooth transitions of hatch marks when using a harder pencil for the lighter areas. Follow the shape of the onion with your lines.

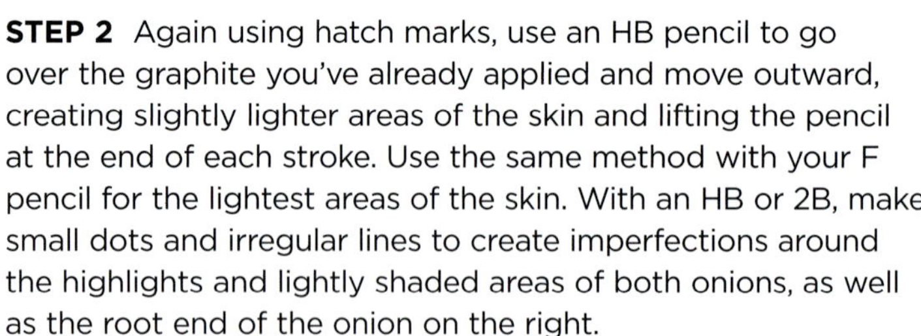

STEP 2 Again using hatch marks, use an HB pencil to go over the graphite you've already applied and move outward, creating slightly lighter areas of the skin and lifting the pencil at the end of each stroke. Use the same method with your F pencil for the lightest areas of the skin. With an HB or 2B, make small dots and irregular lines to create imperfections around the highlights and lightly shaded areas of both onions, as well as the root end of the onion on the right.

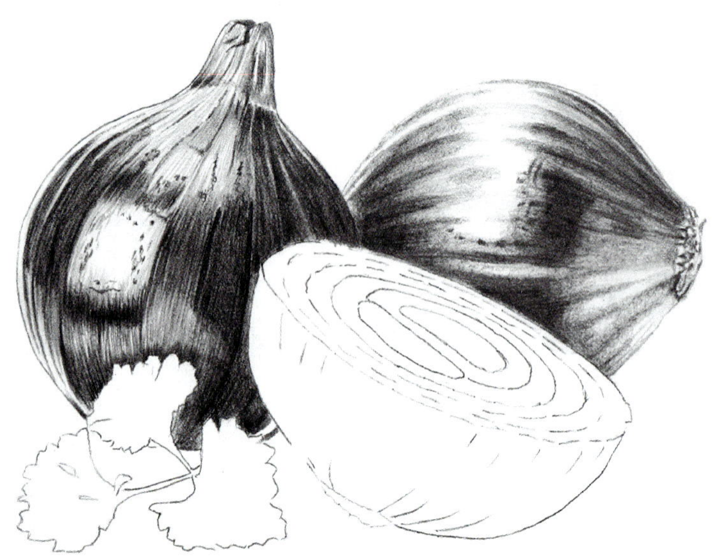

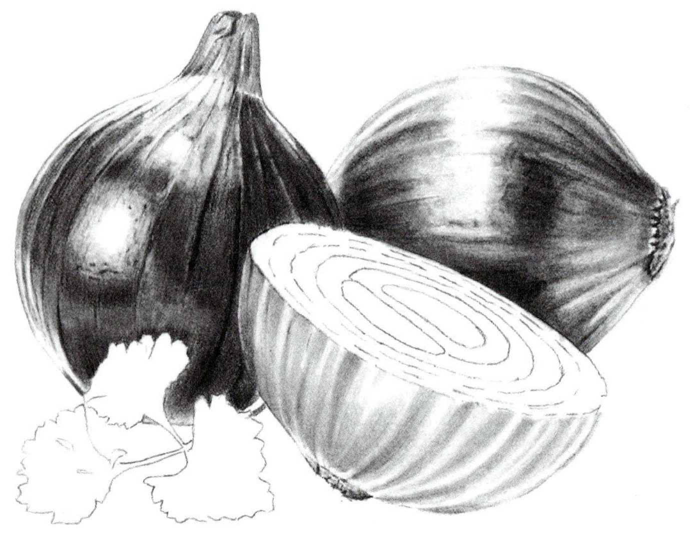

STEP 3 The skin on the cut onion appears much smoother and lighter in value. Use an F pencil and hatching strokes to follow the curves. For the slightly darker areas, use a light touch with an HB. Use the HB or 2B to work on the root end. Use a tortillon with a light, circular motion to blend the two back onions. Use the same light, circular motion to blend the skin of the cut onion. Pay close attention to the gradual transition of tone toward the highlighted areas or white of the paper. Use your kneaded eraser and the sharp edge of a cut pencil eraser to lighten these areas as needed.

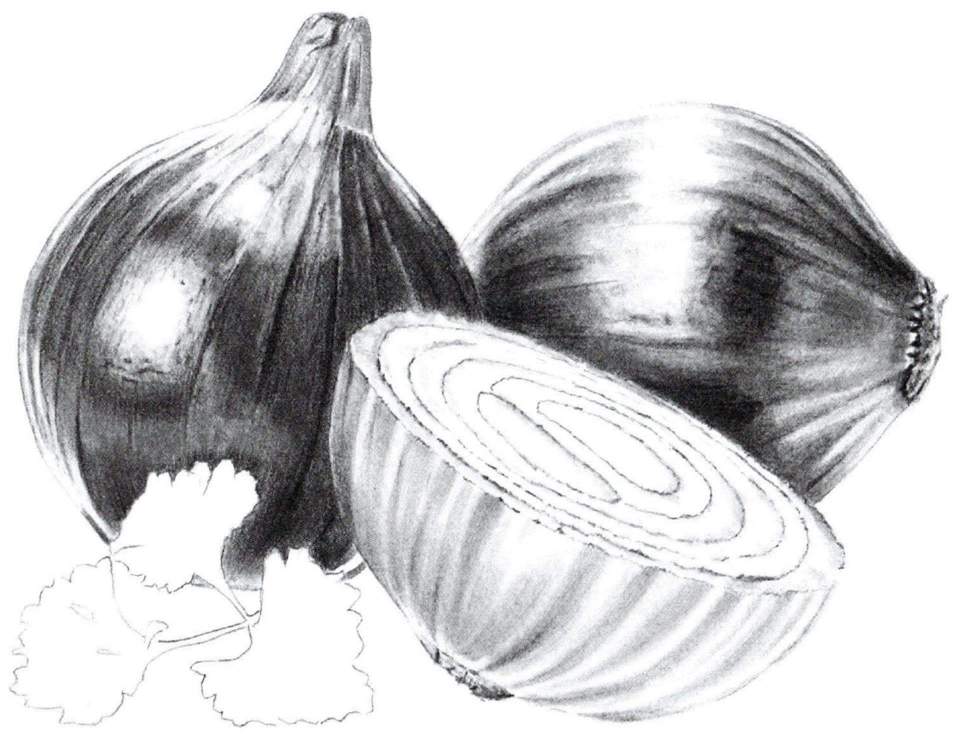

STEP 4 Re-draw the rings of the cut onion using an HB pencil and lightly blend them with a tortillon. You can also use the graphite on the tortillon, or apply graphite to the tip, to create the light shading around the rings.

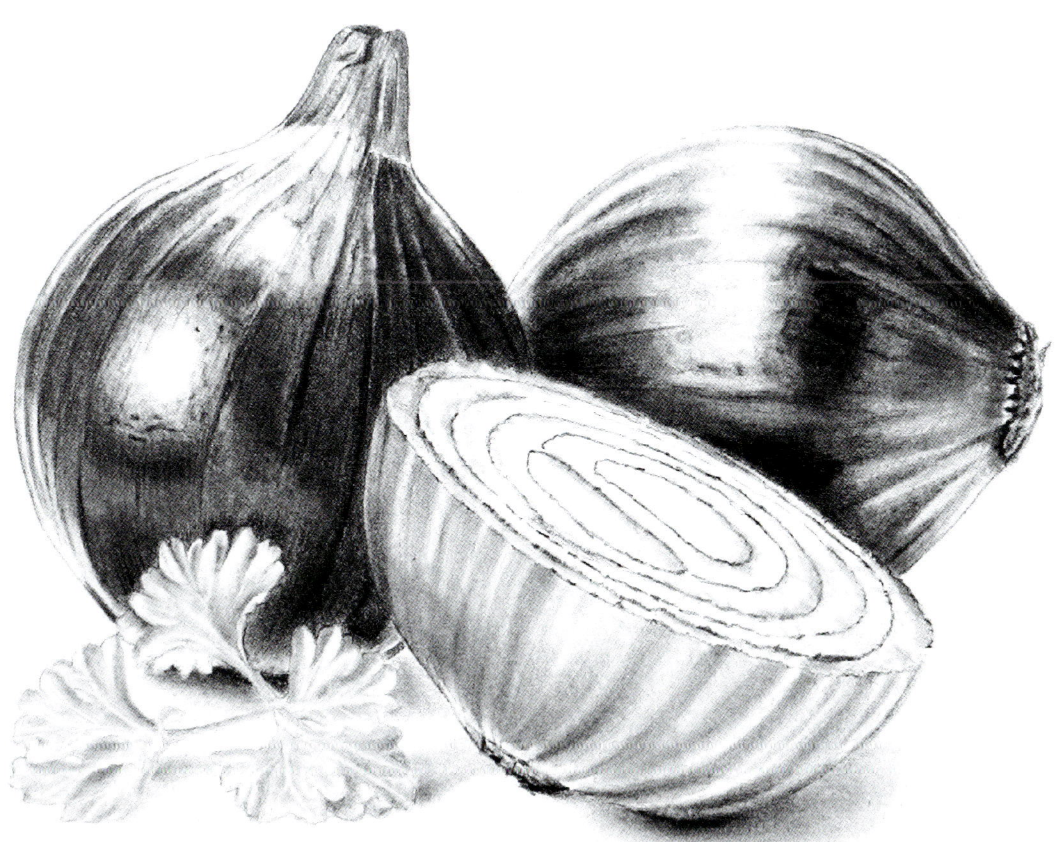

STEP 5 Create the light and dark areas on the parsley leaves using 2H and F pencils. Use the sharp edge of a cut pencil eraser to make the veins of the leaves. Then add the shadows with a 2B for the darkest areas, fading them out with my tortillon. You can also use the graphite on the tortillon to create the shadows around the leaves. Finish by cleaning up smudges around a drawing with a kneaded or block eraser.

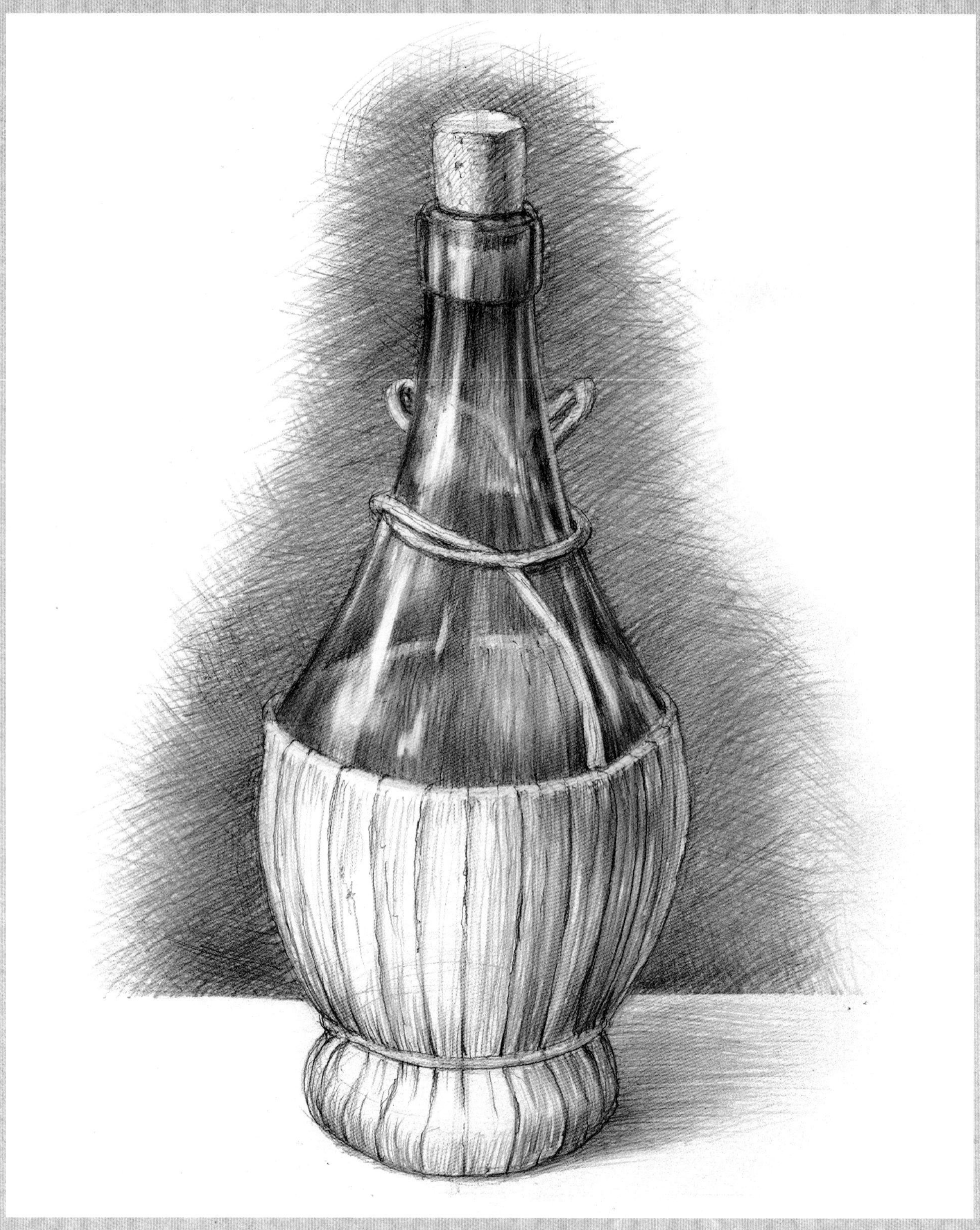

GRAPHITE TONAL APPLICATION

In this chapter, we will discuss the qualities and perception of value—gradations of illumination from very light to very dark—and how to portray the value range accurately in graphite. Graphite is a great medium with which to learn the process of value application, as graphite lead is manufactured in a wide tonal range, from very light (hard leads) to very dark (soft leads). The process of applying graphite gradations, combined with extra time in making sensitively applied pencil strokes, can be effective and logical and, ultimately, give the viewer an accurate account of the subject's value structure.

Value & Light Logic

We perceive the visible world around us because of light on form, or *illumination*. When the artist adds value, or tone, to an object in a line drawing, its volume, texture, surface, direction, and depth become more apparent, and the object takes on a reality that is immediately apparent to the viewer.

Value Scale

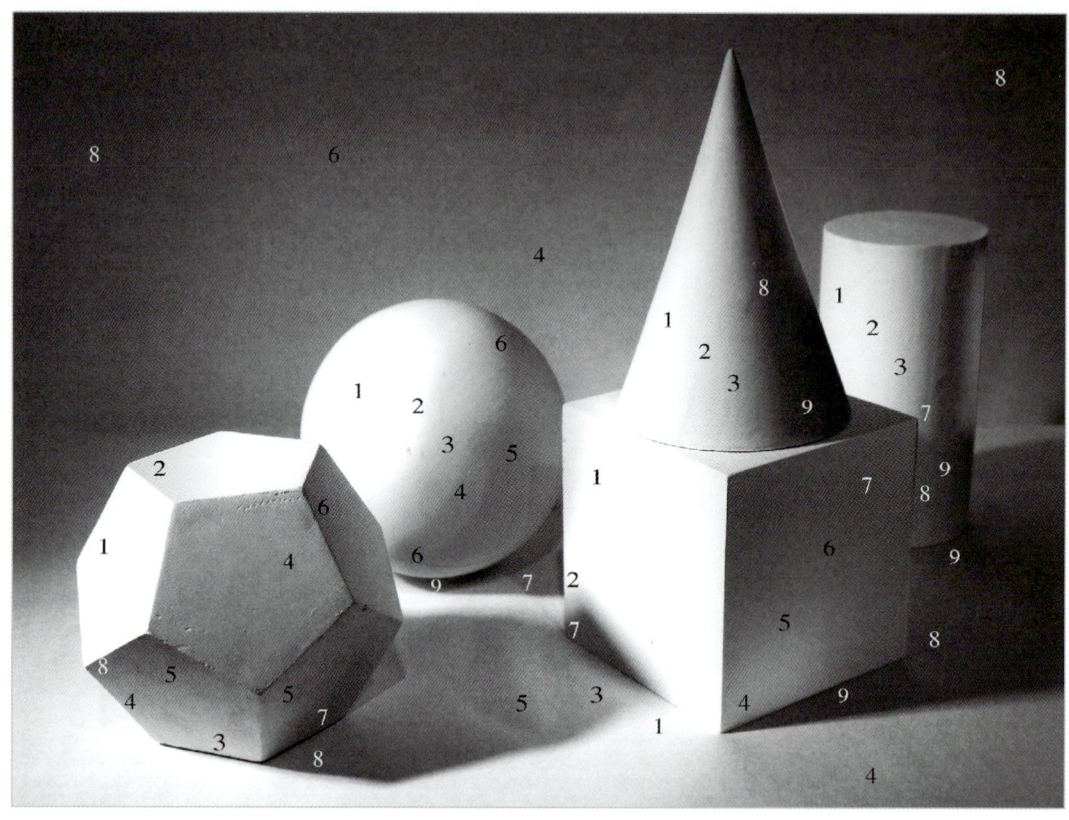

As explained on page 86, value represents the visual range of light to dark, with successive gradients of gray between. Creating a value scale is a great exercise to help the beginning artist understand value perception. A value scale typically includes less than 10 gradients, from white to black.

This still life drawing, identifies a nine-value range, with a true 50 percent gray at the center of the scale and four light values and four dark values on either side of it. These basic forms are a helpful example of how light affects the surfaces and forms without influences of texture, surface irregularity, or surface complexity. There is a certain predictability to this type of lighting situation, which we call *light logic.*

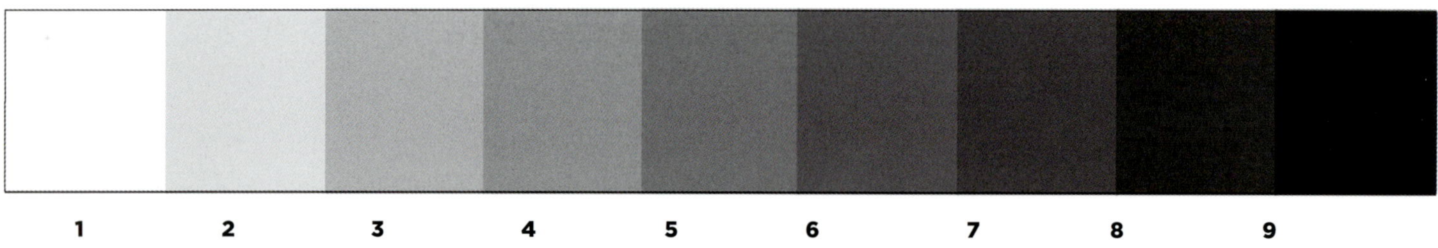

These simple geometric shapes (with a strong single illumination source) present a good example of the range of values inherent in a still life. Each form presents generalized rules of light logic, as well as specific light characterizations. Notice how the numbers in different areas correspond to the numerical value range.

Light Logic

In the drawings here, the effect of the light on the forms is called *chiaroscuro*—an Italian word that essentially means "light and shade." This type of lighting situation uses a full tonal range and gradual transitions from very light to very dark. It produces dramatic value changes and promotes strong three-dimensionality. Just as we tend to simplify a value scale into gradual but understandable units, there is a system of terminology that describes the effects of light on a form (see below).

1. Highlight
2. Light
3. Shadow
4. Core Shadow
5. Reflected Light
6. Cast Shadow

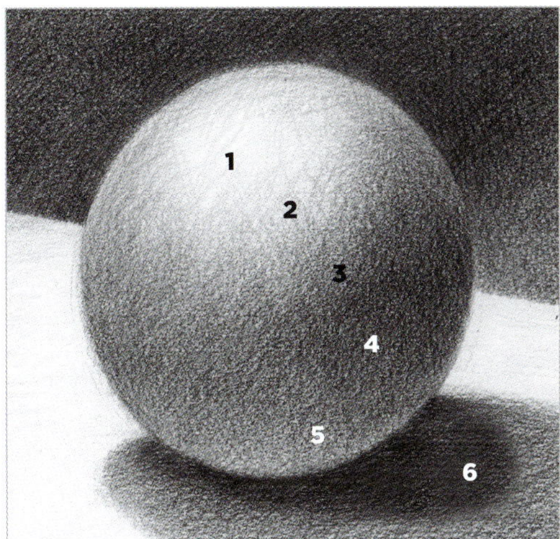

Light Direction/Light Source It is vital to understand where the light that shines on an object is coming from, as well as the importance of keeping that light source separate and singular. The artist should understand how the light source direction, proximity, height, and intensity affect the appearance of the objects.

Highlight is the area of a form that receives the most direct effect of the singular light source.

Light describes the overall area of a form that receives generalized directional lighting from a single light source. On flat planes, the light is uniform; on curved surfaces, the light diffuses as the rounded form curves away from the light source. These subtle differences are evident in value transitions on spheres, cones, and cylinders.

Shadow describes the area of a form that does not receive any light. On rounded forms, the transitional change that separates light from shadow is very soft and gradual. On a hard-edged surface, such as a square, the definition is sharp and clear.

Core Shadow is the darkest area of the shadow; it receives no effects of light from the transition zone between light and shadow or from reflected light on the side of the form that faces away from the light source.

Reflected Light bounces off another lit form or surface into the form's shadow area. On a curved surface, reflected light usually appears on the shadowed edge of the form—the side opposite the form's lit side.

Cast Shadow is the shadow an object casts onto the surrounding surface, ground plane, or other object. Cast shadow is diffused, and it softens as it moves away from the form.

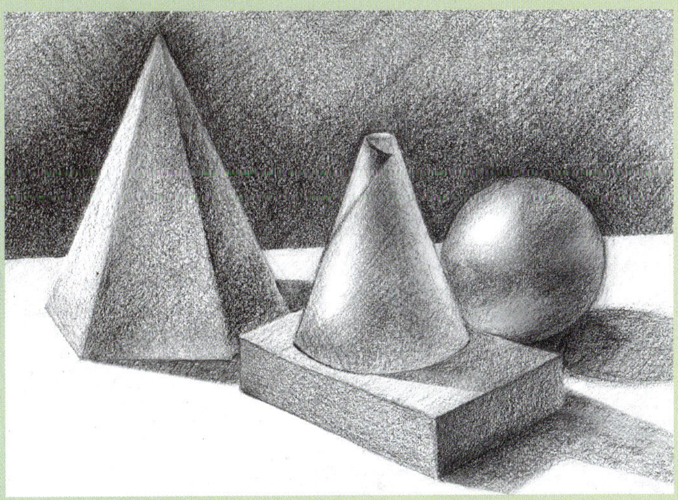

Student example of this value exercise, with simple forms in strong, single-light illumination.

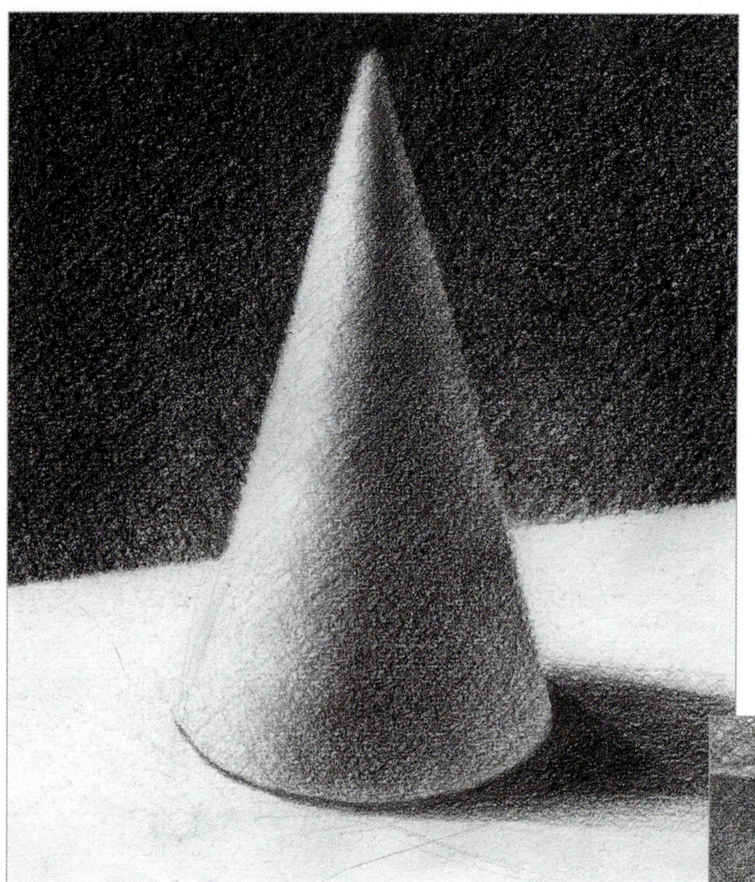

Cones and cylinders share similarities to the light logic inherent in spheres, but the core shadows and reflected light correspond to the length of the object, with subtle variations across its entire length. Consider how the reflected light on the shadowed side of a cone subtly transcends from light to dark as the dark background changes to the lighted surface of the ground plane.

Hard-edge forms like these boxes present high-contrast lights and darks, unlike the soft light-to-dark transitions of spherical and conical forms. Notice how the value on a plane in shadow can vary depending on the amount of light that is reflected onto it. Note also how the edge of a plane in shadow that abuts the lit edge of another plane can look much darker.

Graphite Value Scale

Graphite is a good medium to use to simulate subtle value changes from very light to very dark. Graphite pencil grades range from 9H (lightest) to 9B (darkest), but it's best to create a value scale with no more than six to eight pencils.

The value scale shown below was completed with six pencils. Hatching was used to create tone, simply drawing lines across the paper. For darker tones, crosshatching was used, drawing lines in the opposite direction of the hatched lines. The more you crosshatch in multiple directions, the darker the surface will appear.

The value scale above was created on paper with a vellum surface, which has slightly more tooth, or texture, than smooth drawing paper. The pencil tips were chiseled to a 45° angle with a sandpaper pad. The resulting softer pencil tip creates wider and lighter pencil marks. For a darker surface or a more pronounced mark, keep the pencil point long and sharp.

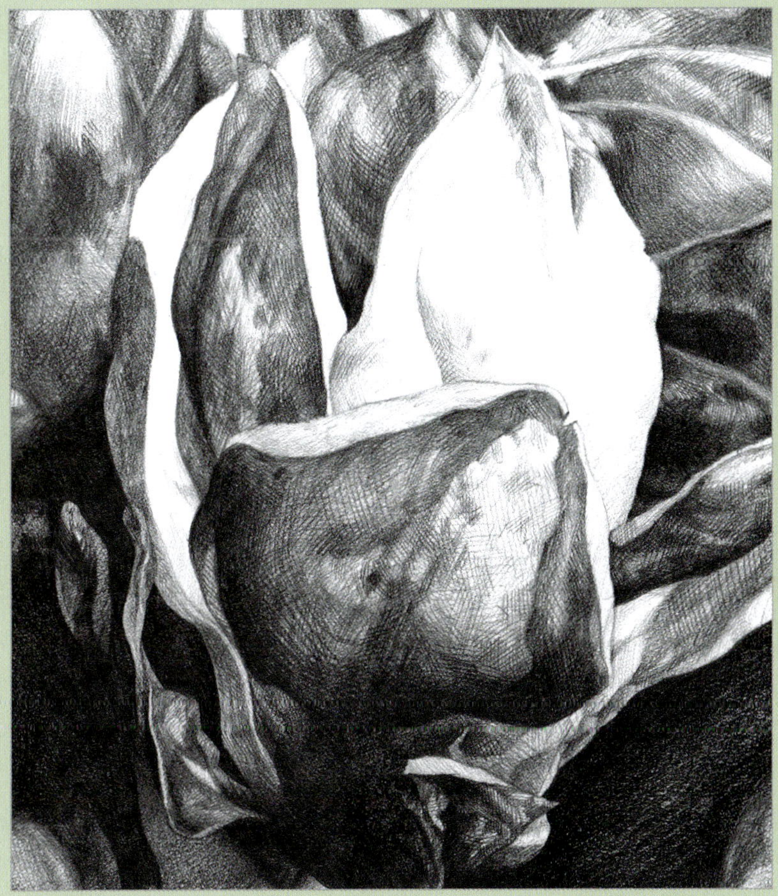

Detail of a drawing by student Yea Jin Shin. Note the application of crosshatching in order to achieve value variations on the shadow surfaces of the flower petals.

Tonal Application Exercises

Shell

Follow along in your sketchbook with this shell demonstration drawing. This project layers, or *glazes*, one pencil grade over another, from lightest to darkest, with hatching and crosshatching. Never purposely smear or blend the graphite layers with a stump, cloth, or finger, as blending tends to give the drawing a muddy or dirty look. While this method can be more time consuming, the process is more logical and produces tangible, visible results.

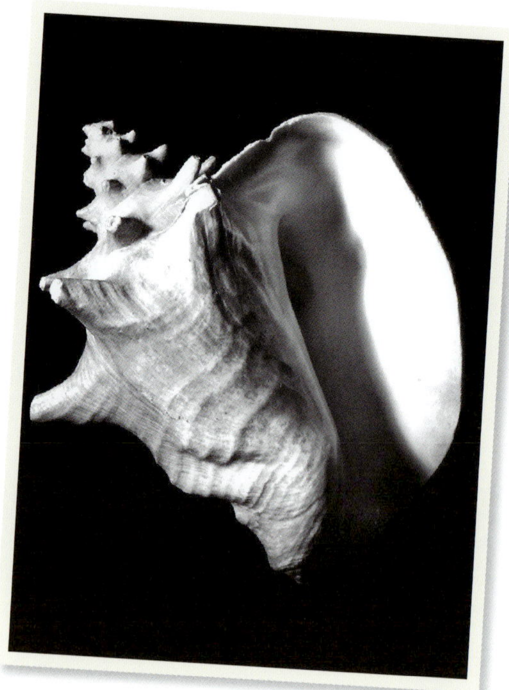

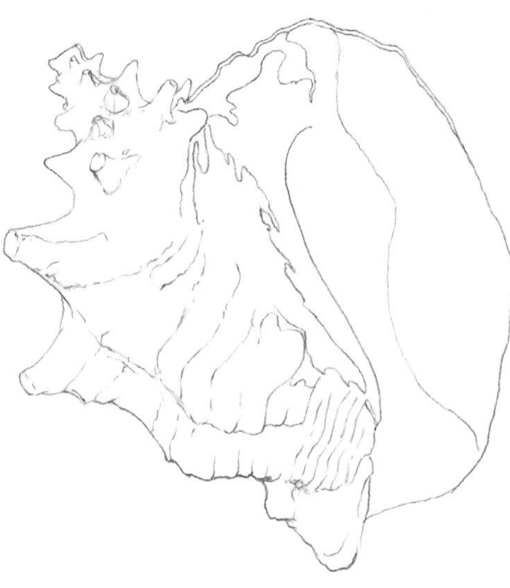

After making an overall gesture drawing of the shell, refine your sketch to a contour line drawing.

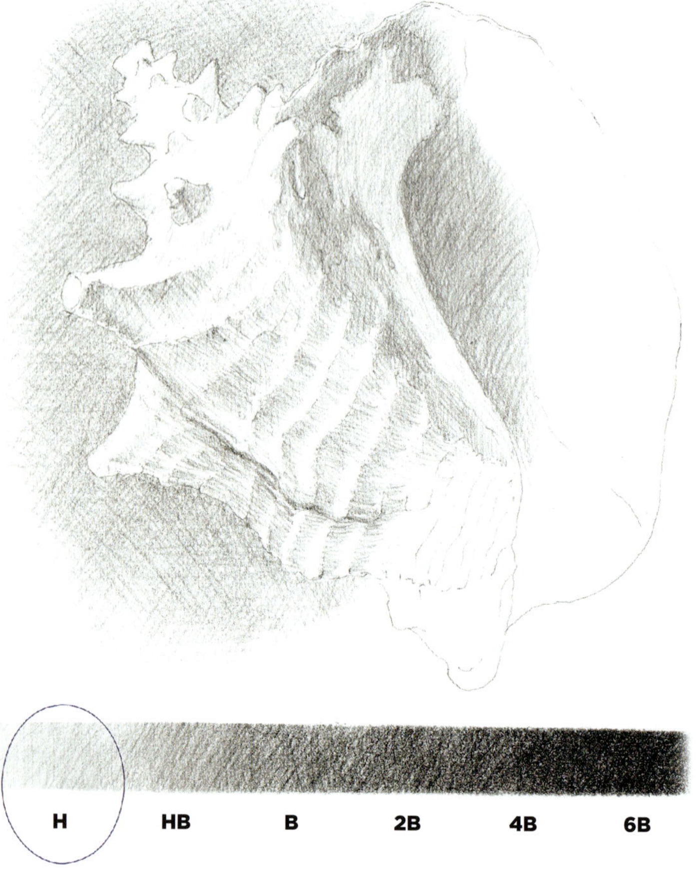

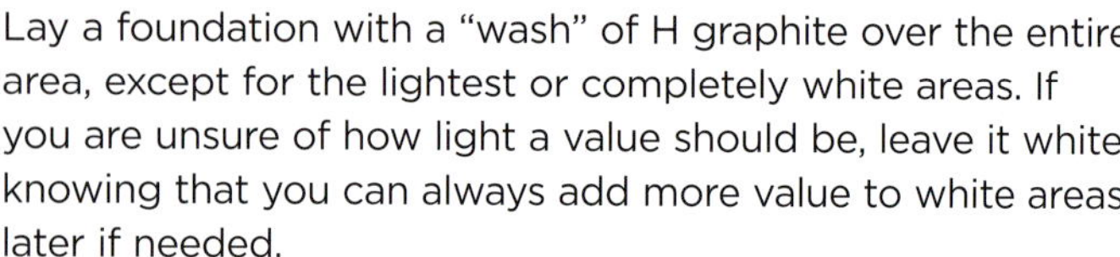

Lay a foundation with a "wash" of H graphite over the entire area, except for the lightest or completely white areas. If you are unsure of how light a value should be, leave it white, knowing that you can always add more value to white areas later if needed.

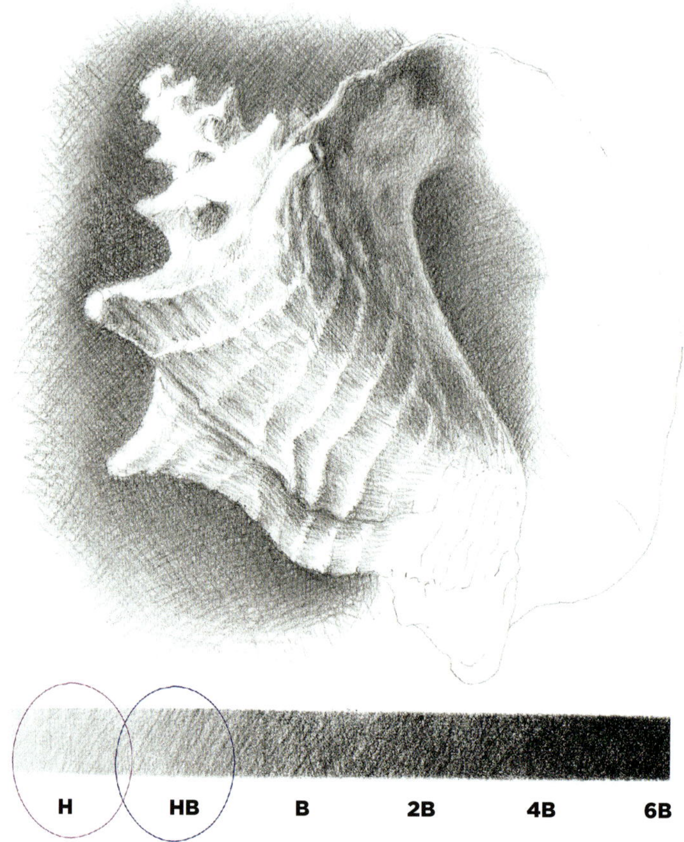

Next develop value with a specific application of the next darkest pencil—an HB.

It's best not to blend because the process of layering graphite—light to dark—involves little guesswork as to what grade (or darkness) of pencil should be used. It also doesn't require excessive pressure on the pencil point to attain the appropriate tonal range. Switch to the next darkest pencil when the tone of the current pencil does not get appreciably darker without applying lots of pressure.

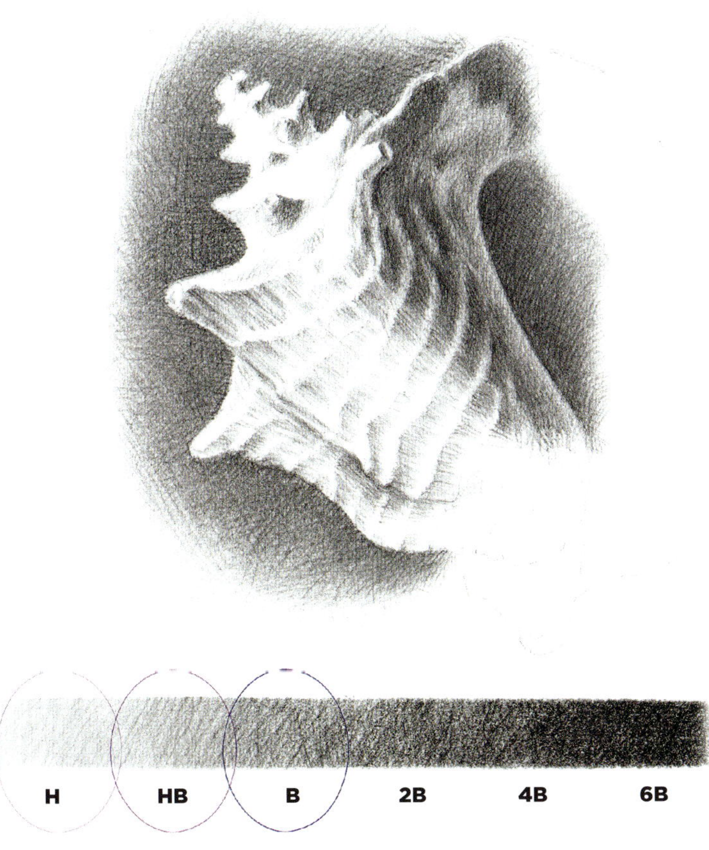

Next apply a layer of B pencil over the two previous tonal applications. It's important to note that a large portion of the overall time spent on this type of drawing is in laying a foundation of tone with the lightest pencils. As you progress through the range of light to dark pencils, you'll spend a significantly smaller portion of time on each successive darker layer.

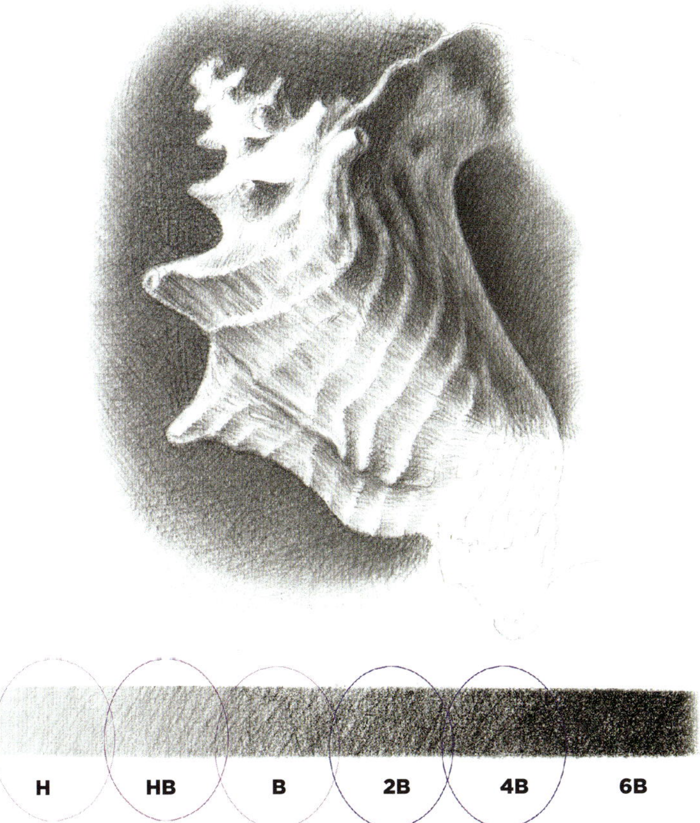

Add darker values of 2B and 4B pencil over the deeper areas of shadow and the background. Use a 6B pencil to accent a few of the deepest darks.

There is usually a distinct difference between H pencils (hard) and B pencils (black)—you can also use an F pencil, instead of an HB, between the hard and soft pencils.

Reflective Surfaces

Light has various effects on different types of surfaces—something the artist needs to keep in mind in representational drawing. Reflective metal surfaces tend to have much stronger value contrasts than their surrounding environment. These strong reflections can become abstract in regard to recognition, but they always follow certain rules of lighting and contour over the form. Glass has certain consistent qualities of reflection and transparency that demand keen and careful observation. The demonstrations that follow offer an overview of some of these challenging situations.

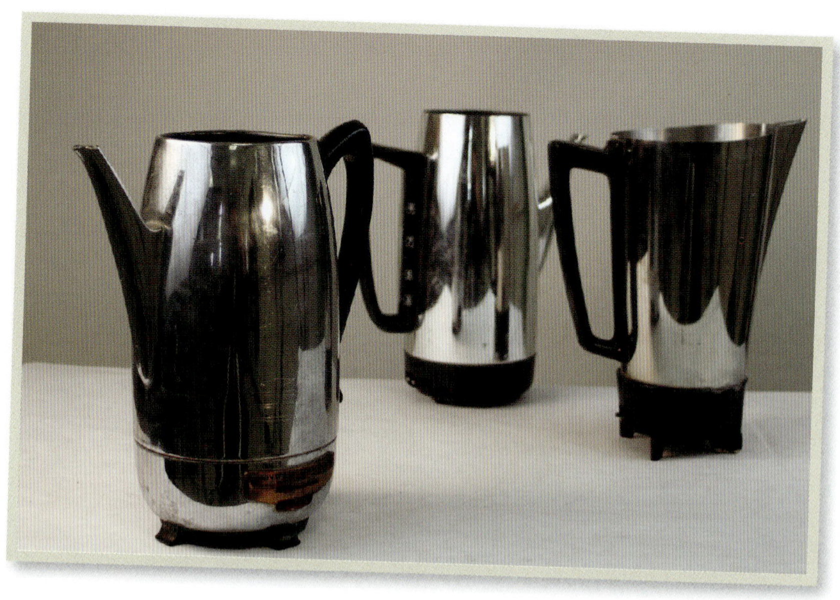

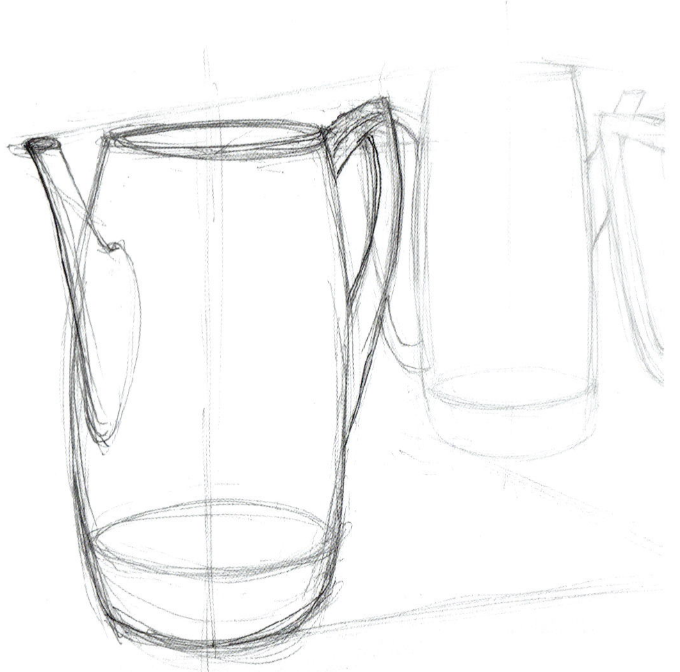

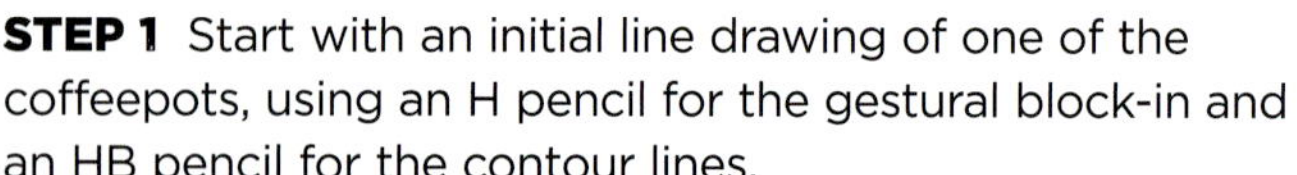

STEP 1 Start with an initial line drawing of one of the coffeepots, using an H pencil for the gestural block-in and an HB pencil for the contour lines.

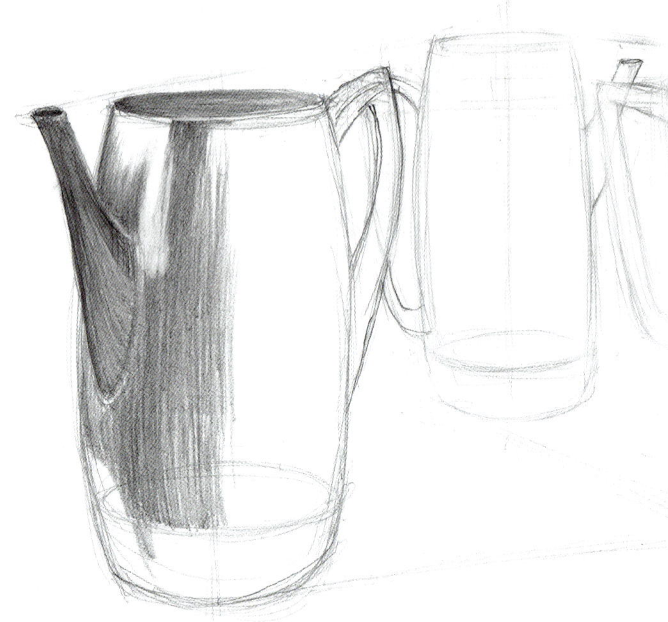

STEP 2 Apply an initial layer of H and HB graphite over the entire surface of the pot, except for the highlights. Highlights on chrome or reflective metal tend to be hard-edged and strong, as do all reflecting values from the surrounding environment.

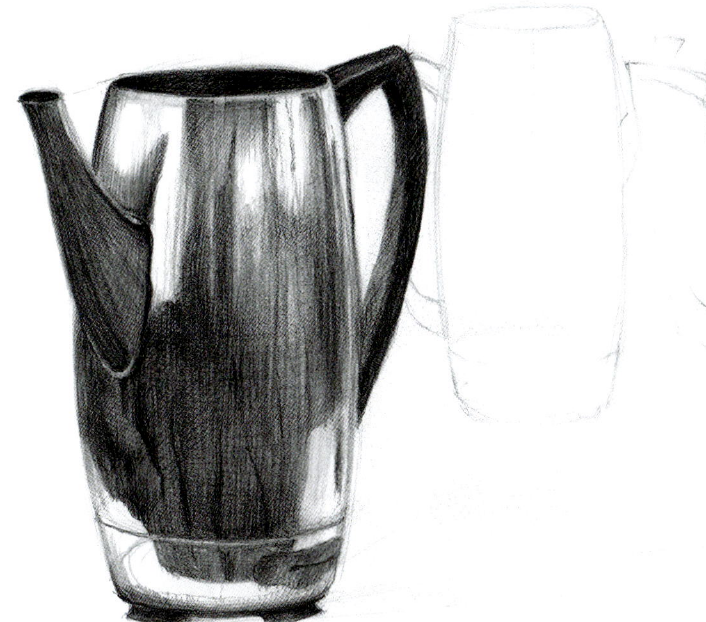

STEP 3 Apply successive layers with B and 2B pencils to bring out the highly reflective appearance.

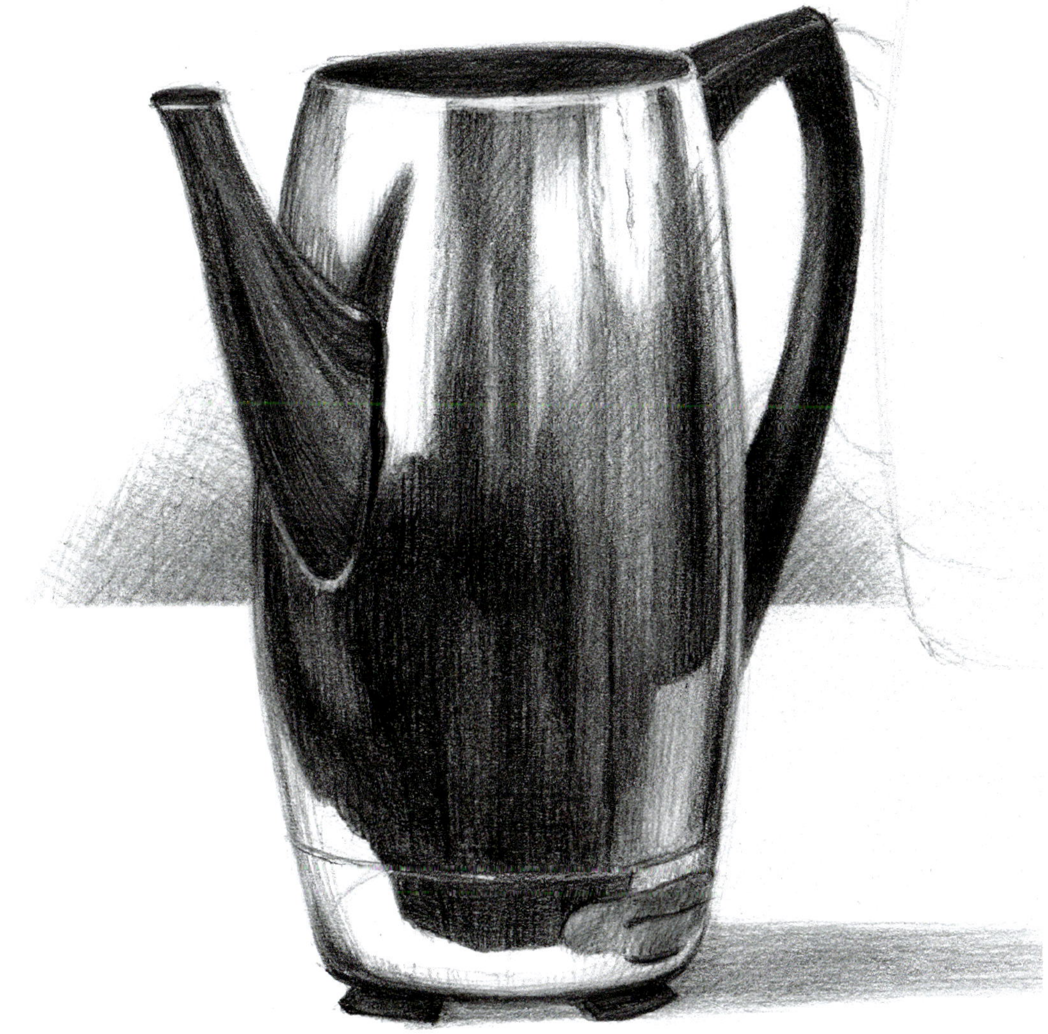

STEP 4 Apply a final layer of 4B and 6B graphite in the darkest areas of the pot and add background value and cast shadow to bring depth and solidity to the scene.

STEP 1 This underlying gesture drawing and contour line drawing took about 30 minutes to complete.

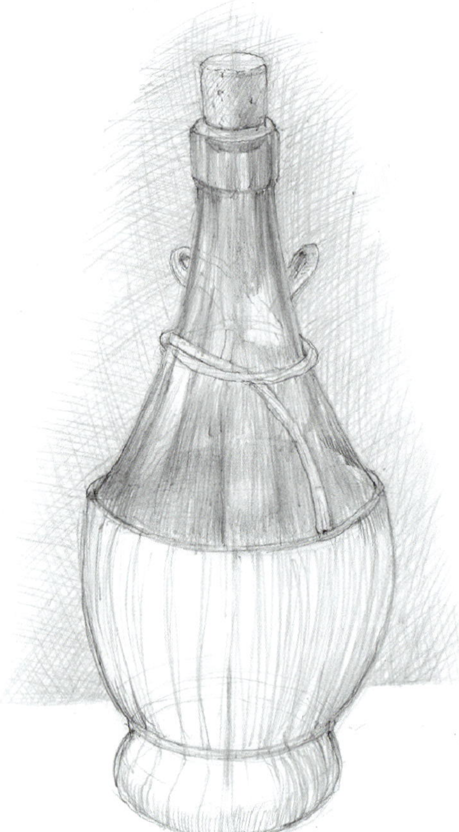

STEP 2 Use an H pencil to establish the transparency and overall pattern and direction of the reflections, as well as the background.

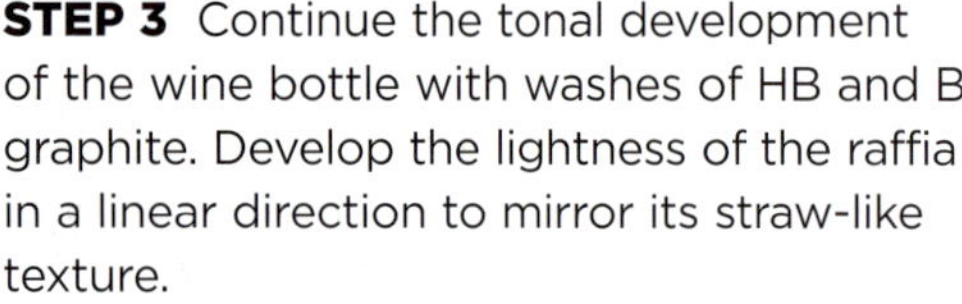

STEP 3 Continue the tonal development of the wine bottle with washes of HB and B graphite. Develop the lightness of the raffia in a linear direction to mirror its straw-like texture.

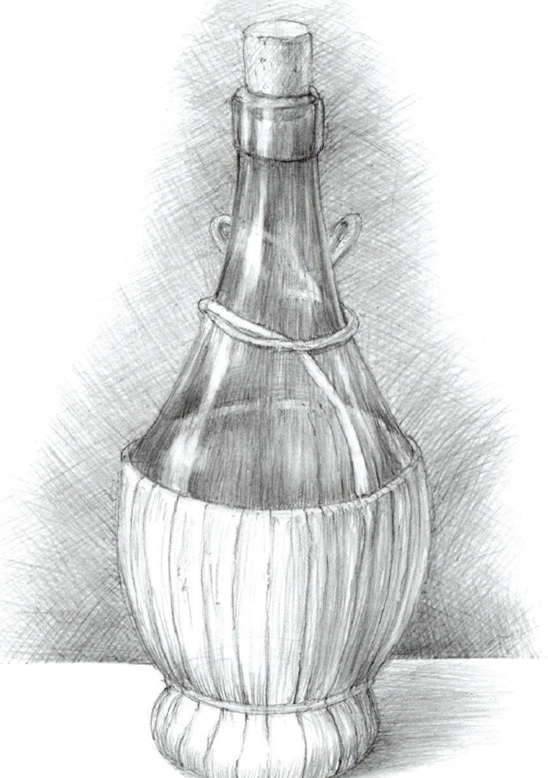

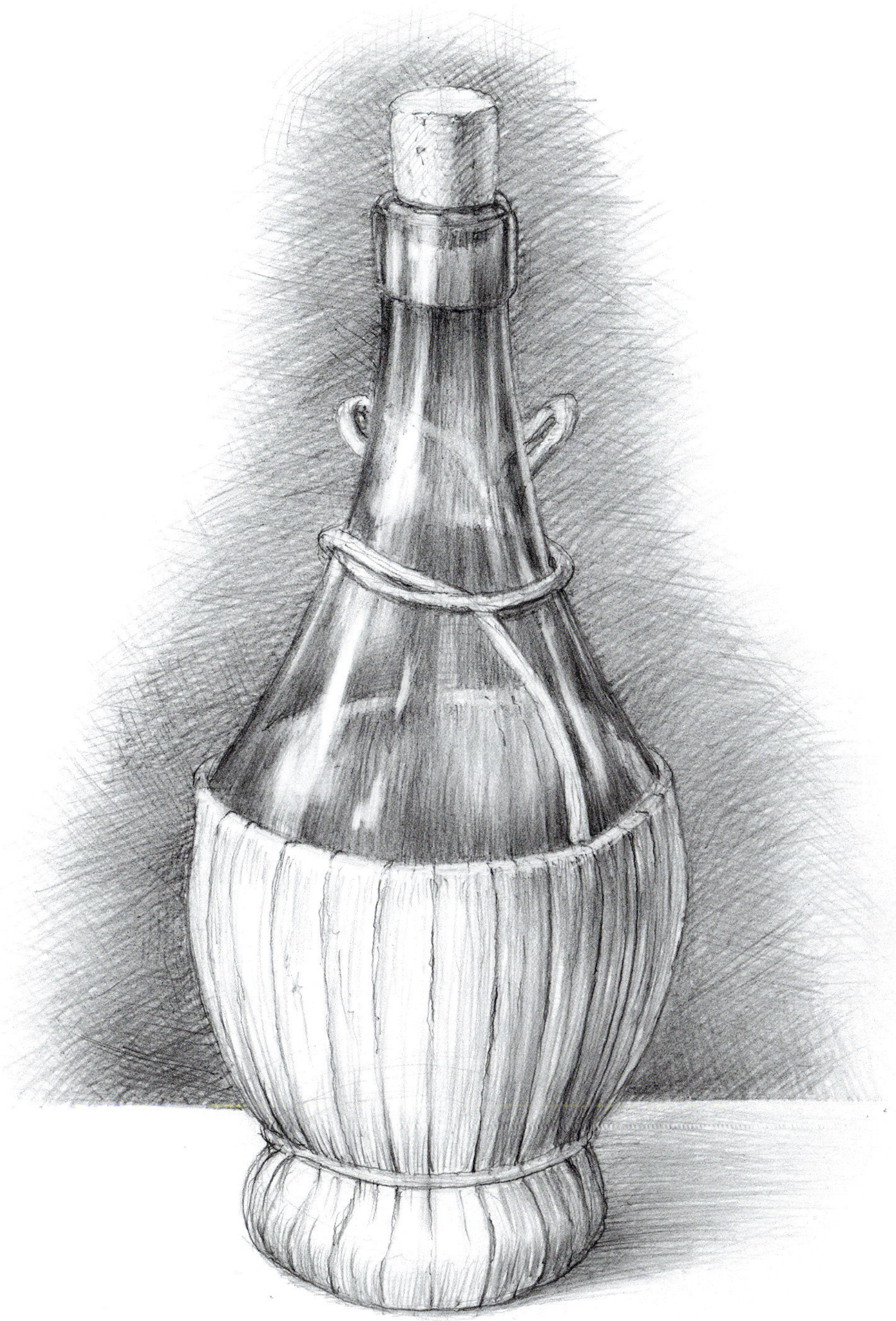

STEP 4 Use a 2B graphite pencil extensively, mostly on the background and darker reflections in the glass. Since the background is viewed through the glass, the reflections need to be darker than the background and lightened where appropriate with a kneaded eraser. Apply the last layers of 4B graphite and use a 6B pencil in the darkest shadows.

When rendering glass, the background and glass object should have similar tonal consistencies for believable transparent quality. Overall, the glass should be slightly darker in value (not including dark and light reflections) than the background that is viewed through it, which is essentially seen through two layers of glass!

How to Construct a Grid

When working from a photograph as a reference, it's important to be able to enlarge the drawing based on the photo and maintain accurate proportions. One of the best ways to achieve this is to use a grid; one grid is the same size as the photo, and the other grid is an enlarged proportional copy for the drawing. The size that you wish to enlarge the new grid copy to has no limits. It can be as large as you want it to be.

There are several variations on a grid system. Most grids involve the use of squares covering the surface of the reference, and then enlarging each square proportionally for the drawing. This type of grid is accurate, but can be tedious to construct and to draw from. This variation is simpler and based on geometry, bringing sketching back into the process in a much more fluid and organic way.

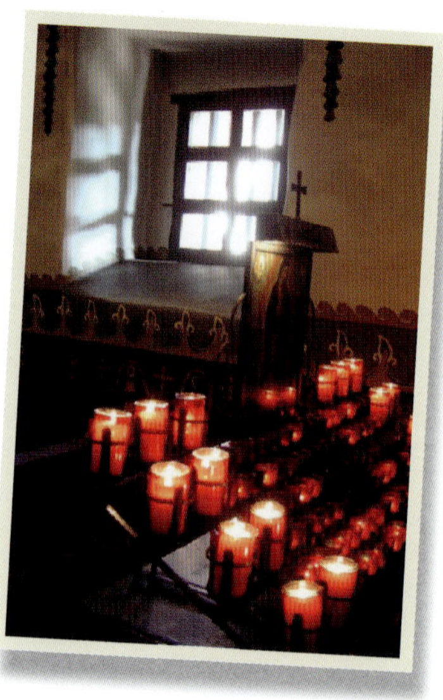

Here is the photograph that was used as a reference for an extended graphite drawing.

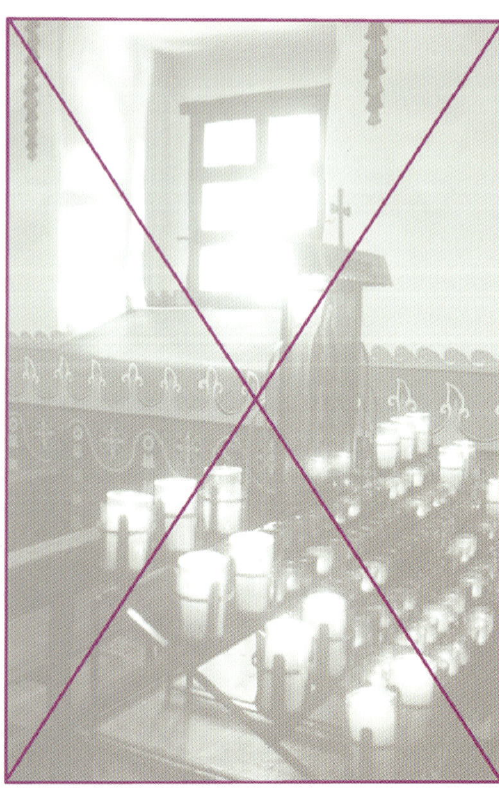

STEP 1 First make an enlarged, black-and-white photocopy of the reference, on which the grid can be drawn. To begin the grid, start with marking a big "X" from corner to corner. It's helpful to use a colored pencil for the grid instead of graphite, which is difficult to see on a photocopy.

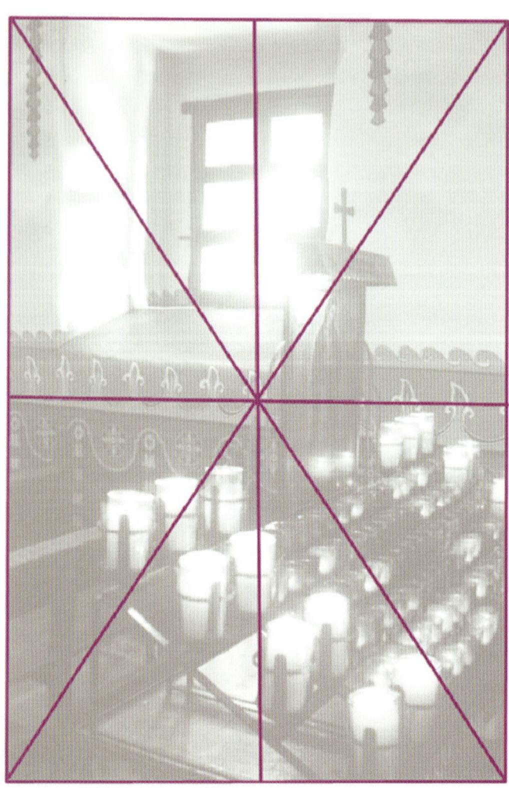

STEP 2 Next add the horizontal and vertical lines through the midline of the "X." Now the original size is divided into proportional fourths.

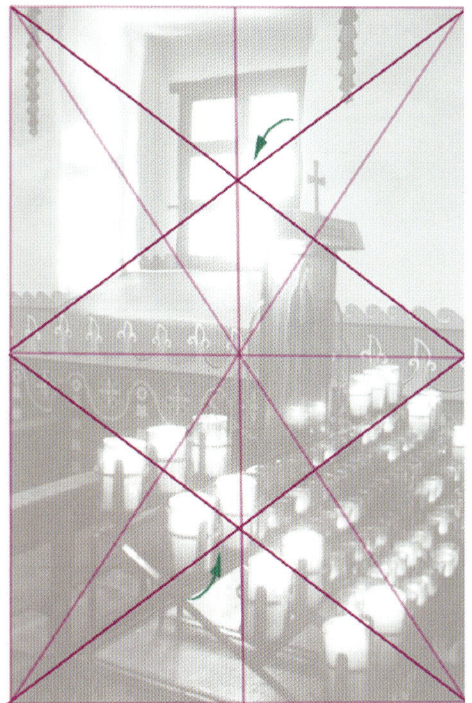

STEP 3 Now add smaller "Xs" to the upper and lower halves from the midline.

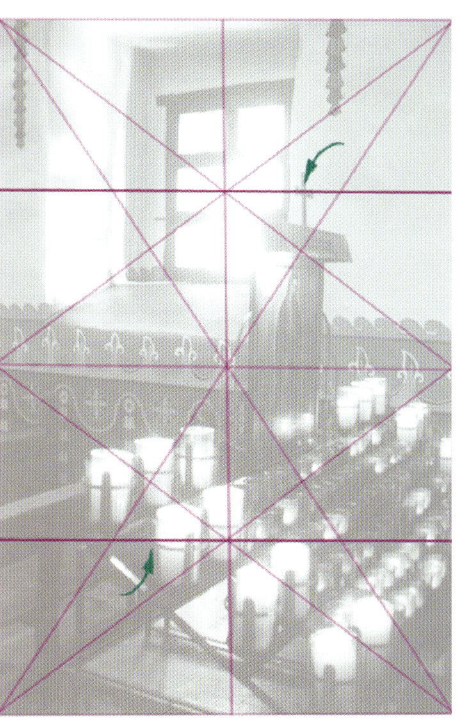

STEP 4 Add horizontal lines through the mid-point of the halved "Xs."

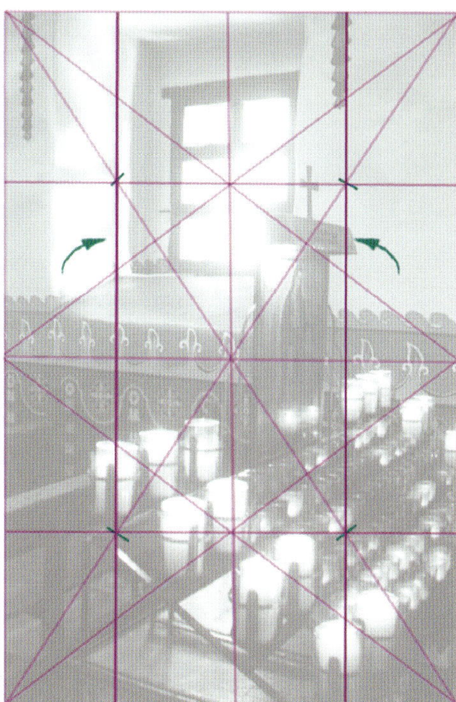

STEP 5 The last two lines are vertical and bisect either vertical half of the grid. The points of intersection from the previous drawn lines are shown here in green.

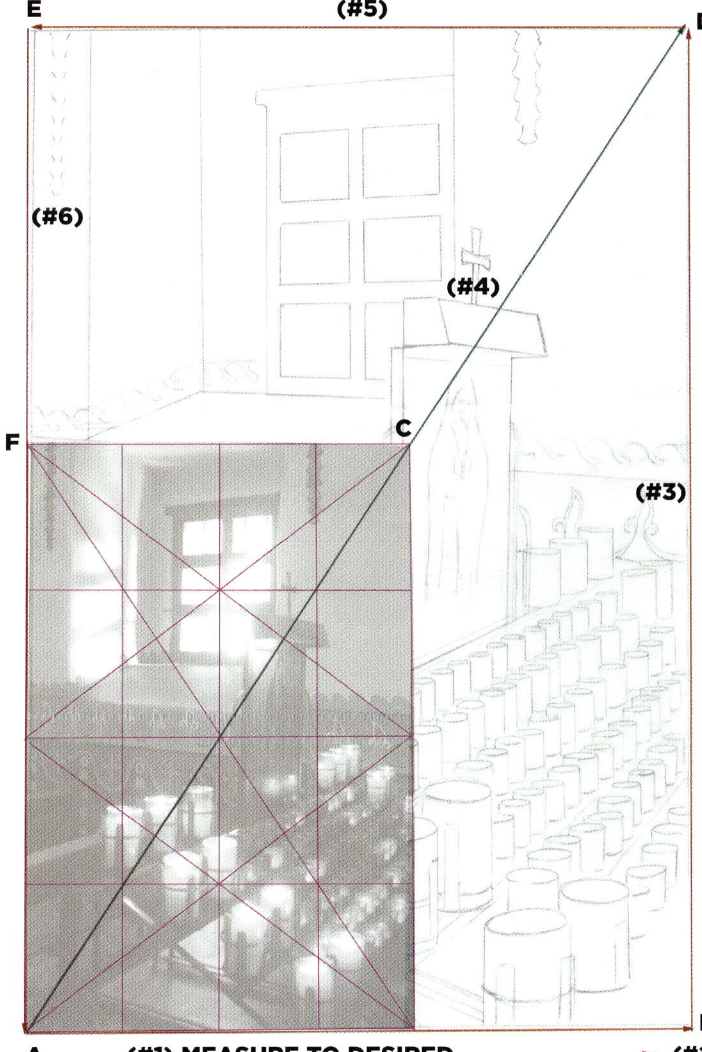

STEP 6 Tape the grid onto your drawing paper (or a large piece of tracing paper to transfer to art paper later). From point A at the bottom left corner of the photocopy, draw a continuous line to whatever width you wish the drawing to be (point B). Then, from point B, draw a vertical line almost to the top of your paper. Now draw a diagonal line from point A through point C, extending the vertical line from point B. The point where the diagonal line from points A to C intersects the vertical line from point B is the proportional height for your drawing (point D). From point D, draw a horizontal line across to point E, and then draw a vertical line from E back to point A (#6). Now you have an enlarged proportional format for your drawing.

There are photomechanical devices on the market specifically for artists that can enlarge photos very easily. The camera-like device is called a lucigraph—most artists in the know call it a "lazy Luci" because it does all the work for you. It's important to know the grid method, because whenever given the chance, you should draw! The Masters used grids to enlarge their drawing for paintings, and if it was good enough for them, it should be good enough for us!

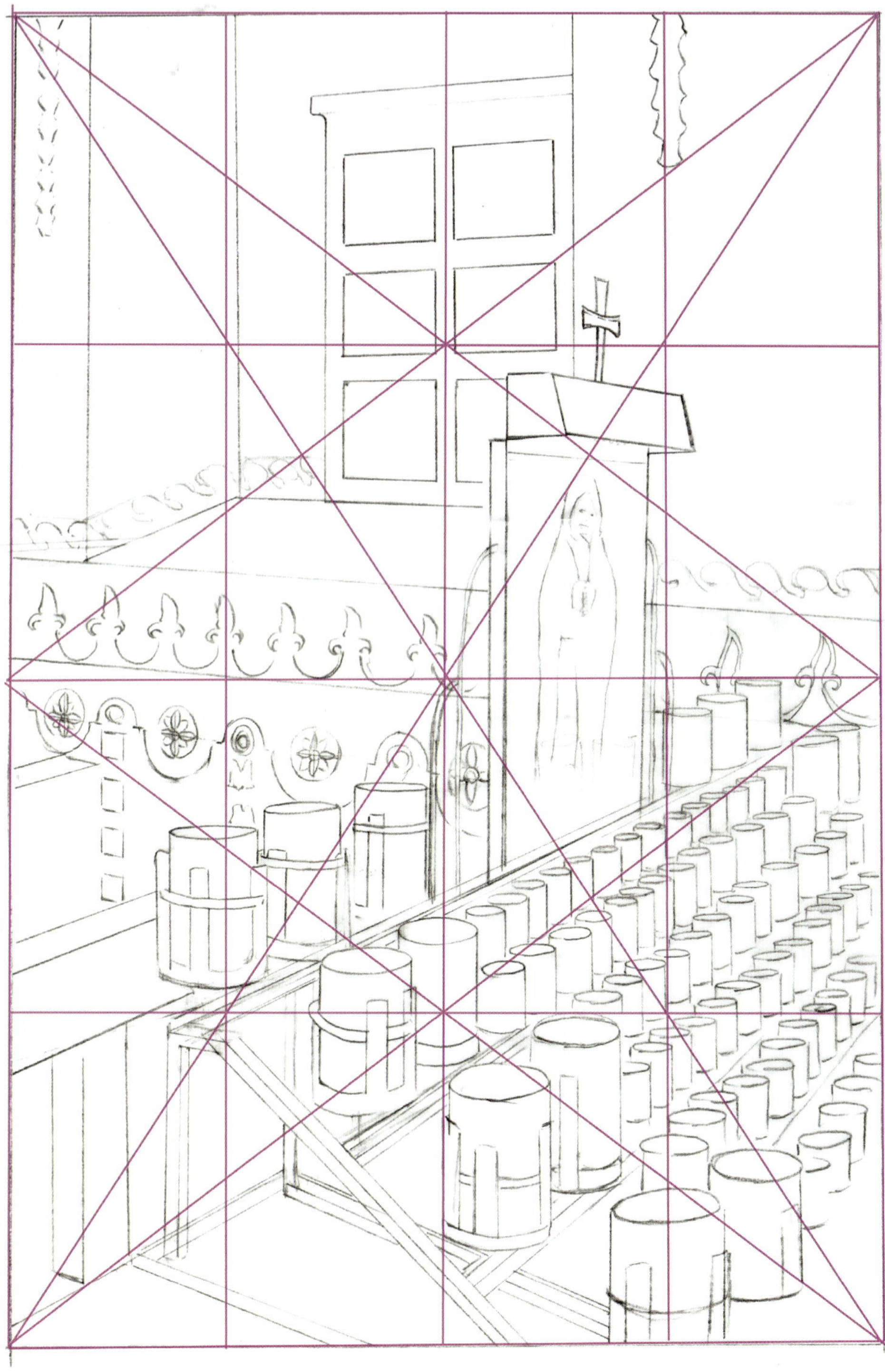

Here is the enlarged grid with the finished contour line drawing. (Preliminary drawing by student Jarek Creason.)

YOUR HOMEWORK

Your homework for this chapter is an exercise in value development, with a range of at least five different grades of graphite pencils that will create value gradients from very light to very dark. A brown paper bag may seem like a fairly easy and simple subject, but it lends itself very well to tonal development.

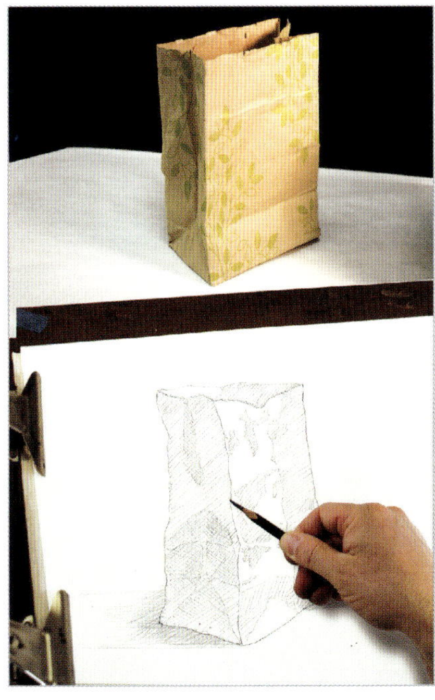

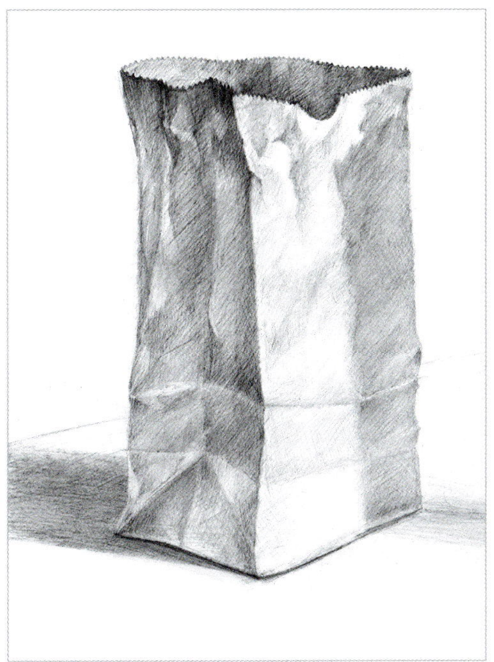

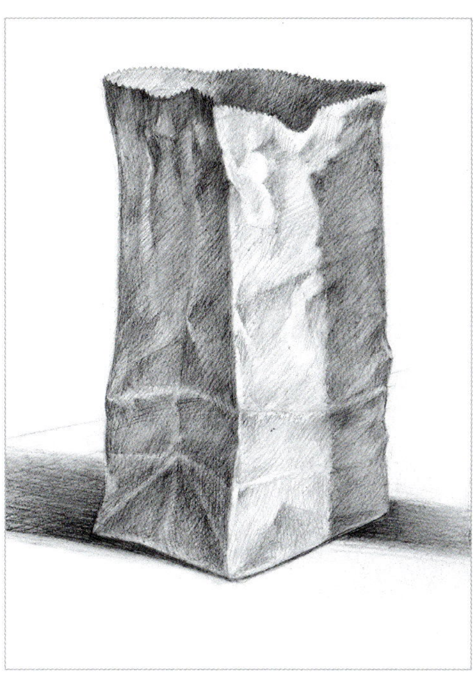

STEP 1 Find and set up a brown paper bag—the older and more used, the better! This subject contains interesting facets and folds, with a wide range of values and value changes, both subtle and sharp. Start with a gesture drawing. Then map out the overall shadow changes in light contour line.

STEP 2 This drawing casts the shadow from another bag (outside of the picture plane) onto the lit surface of the bag, for more value variety and interest. Use a single light source to illuminate your bag, creating the highest contrast possible with the placement of the light source. Begin to create value with washes of H and HB over all the shaded and shadowed surfaces, leaving the white of the paper for the lightest areas.

STEP 3 Continue to develop values with your chosen range of graphite pencil gradations, from light to dark. Add subtle washes of the lightest grades of graphite to any white areas of the bag as needed. Don't forget to add the cast shadow and, if desired, background value.

Whenever possible, develop your tonal drawings with a combination of hatched and crosshatched line work. This technique provides more energy and a higher level of sophistication in the work than blending with a stump or other method. Blending is easier to accomplish, but it does not bear the same craft-like quality. It is important to remember that these are drawings—and they are meant to look like drawings, not photographs! So, even when copying references from photographs, remember that the work is created by the artist's hand—your hand—not a machine.

EXERCISES FOR PRACTICE

Sketch three slightly different-sized circles, and block in the top of the pear shape.

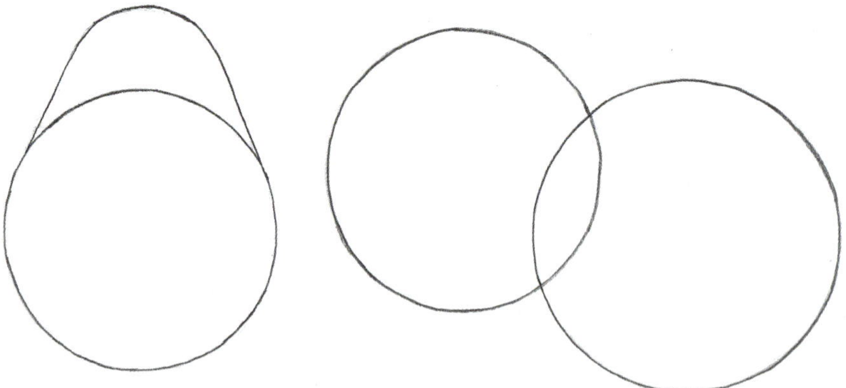

The apples and pear are not perfectly formed, so you will need to reshape some areas. The apple in the middle is slightly wider at the sides, and the contours of the pear are not perfectly rounded.

Add the stems, and lightly draw in the areas where the shadows, highlights, and reflections will be.

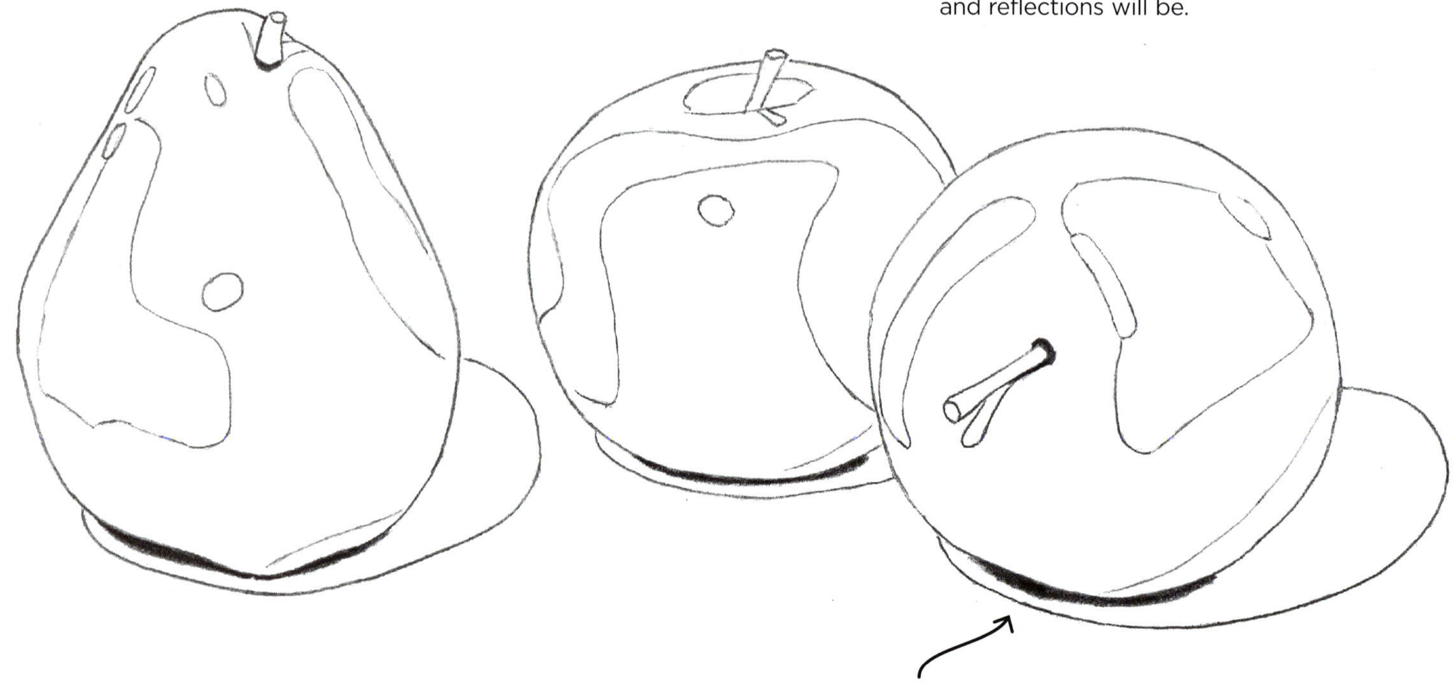

Using a 4B pencil, draw in the darkest values first in the cast shadows and at the base of the two outer fruits' stems.

Using small, circular, overlapping strokes, fill in the darker-value areas on the pear and the apple on the right. Use slightly lighter pressure around the edges of these areas, creating a gradation.

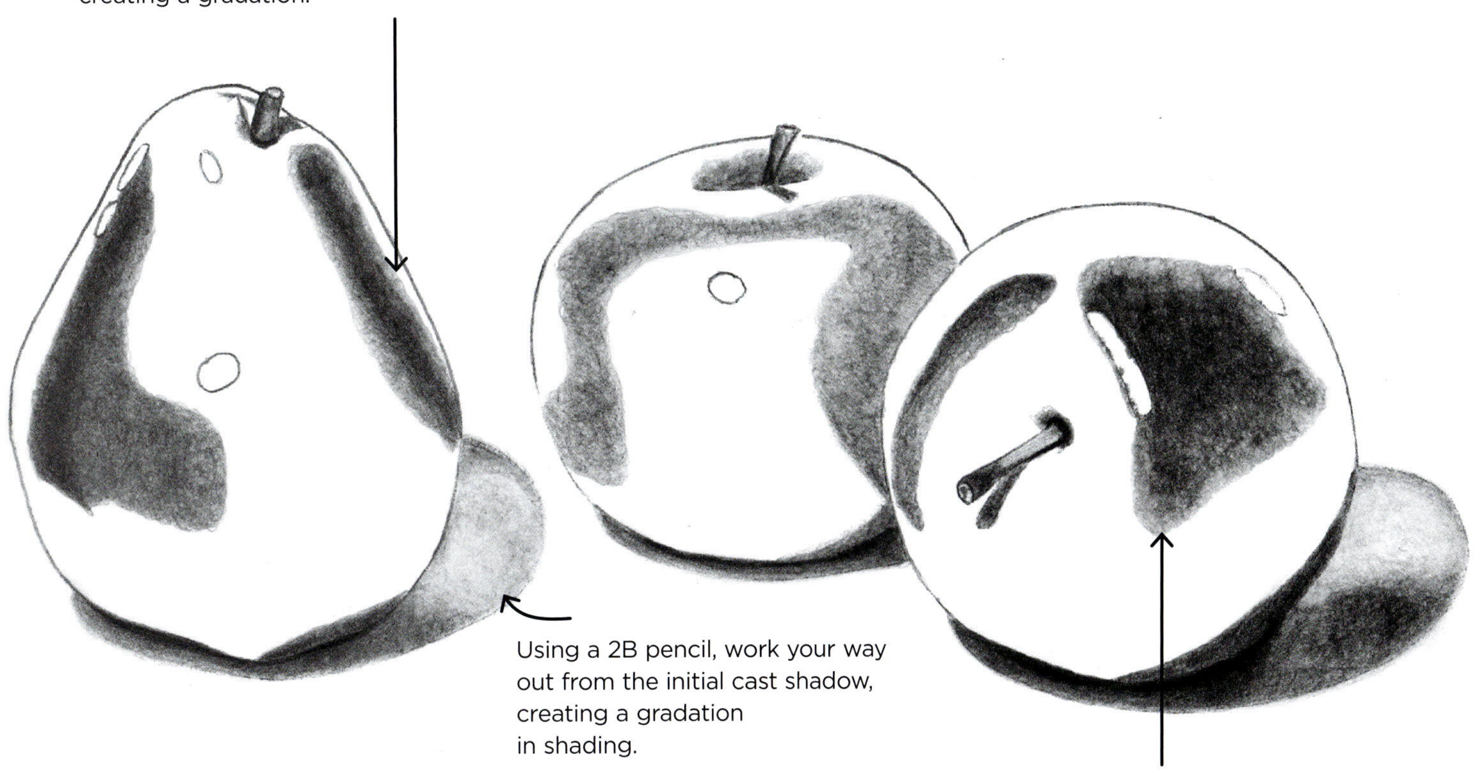

Using a 2B pencil, work your way out from the initial cast shadow, creating a gradation in shading.

Switch to an HB pencil or use less pressure to finish the lighter areas. Use a 2B and an HB pencil to create the different values on and around the stems.

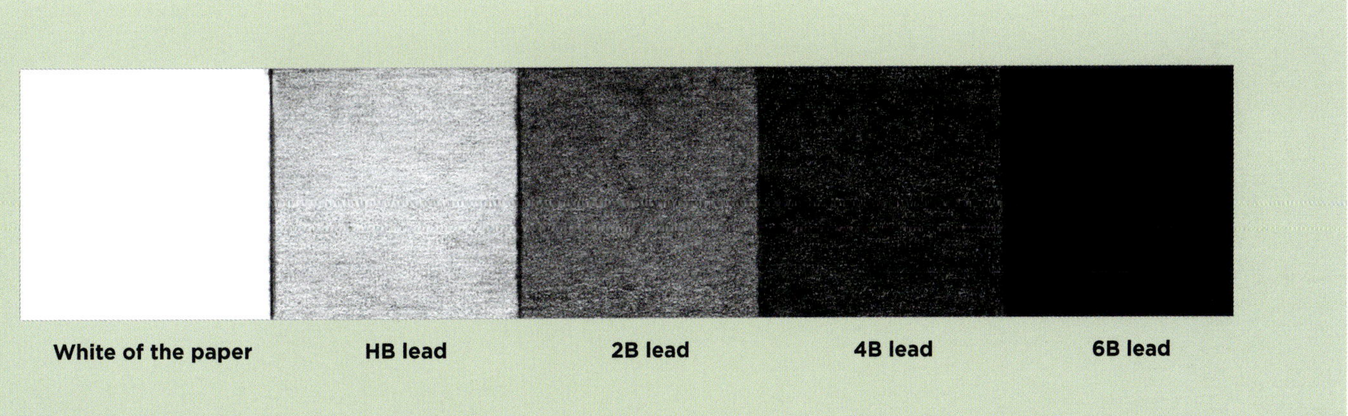

Graphite can produce every value from light gray to black, depending on the pencil choice and the amount of pressure applied. A value scale helps us choose the right pencils and pressure to use in a drawing.

Continue with overlapping circular strokes on the lighter areas using an HB pencil. Leave some white of the paper to show the highlighted areas on the fruit.

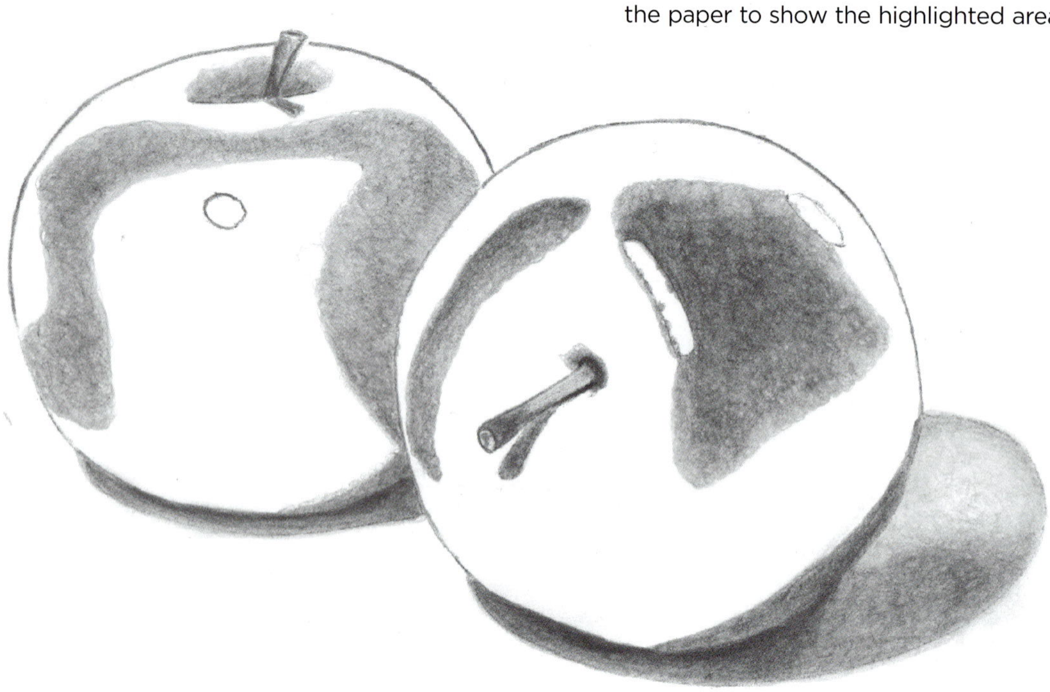

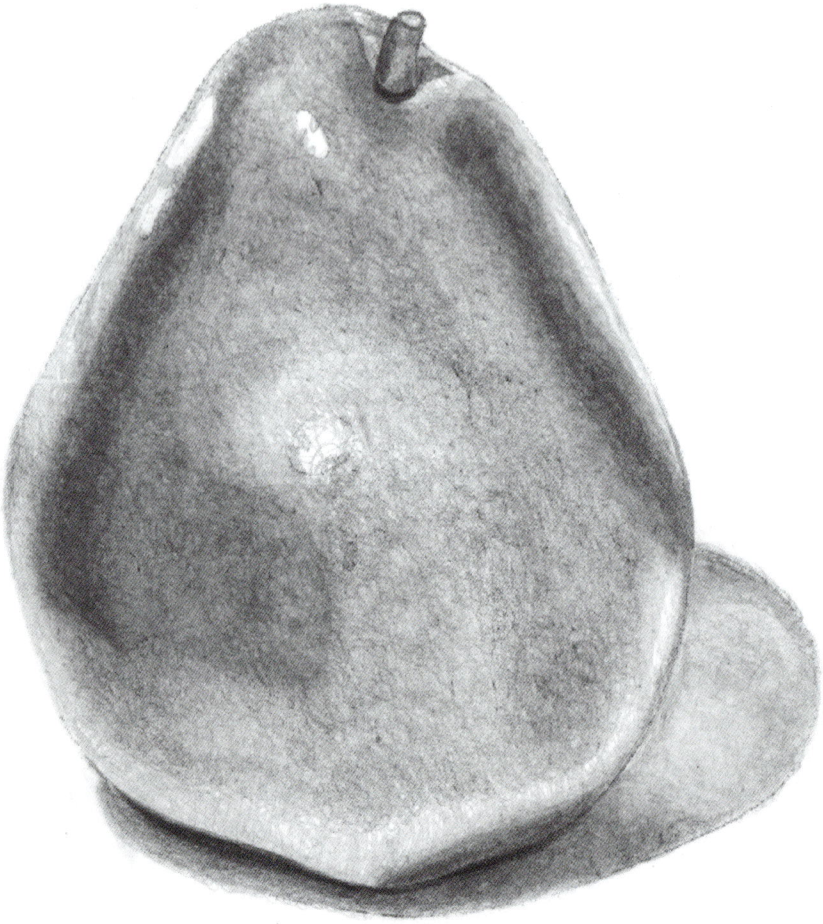

Use a 2H pencil where the light reflects from the table to the bottom areas of the fruit.

Use a larger eraser to clean up any smudges in the areas around your drawing.

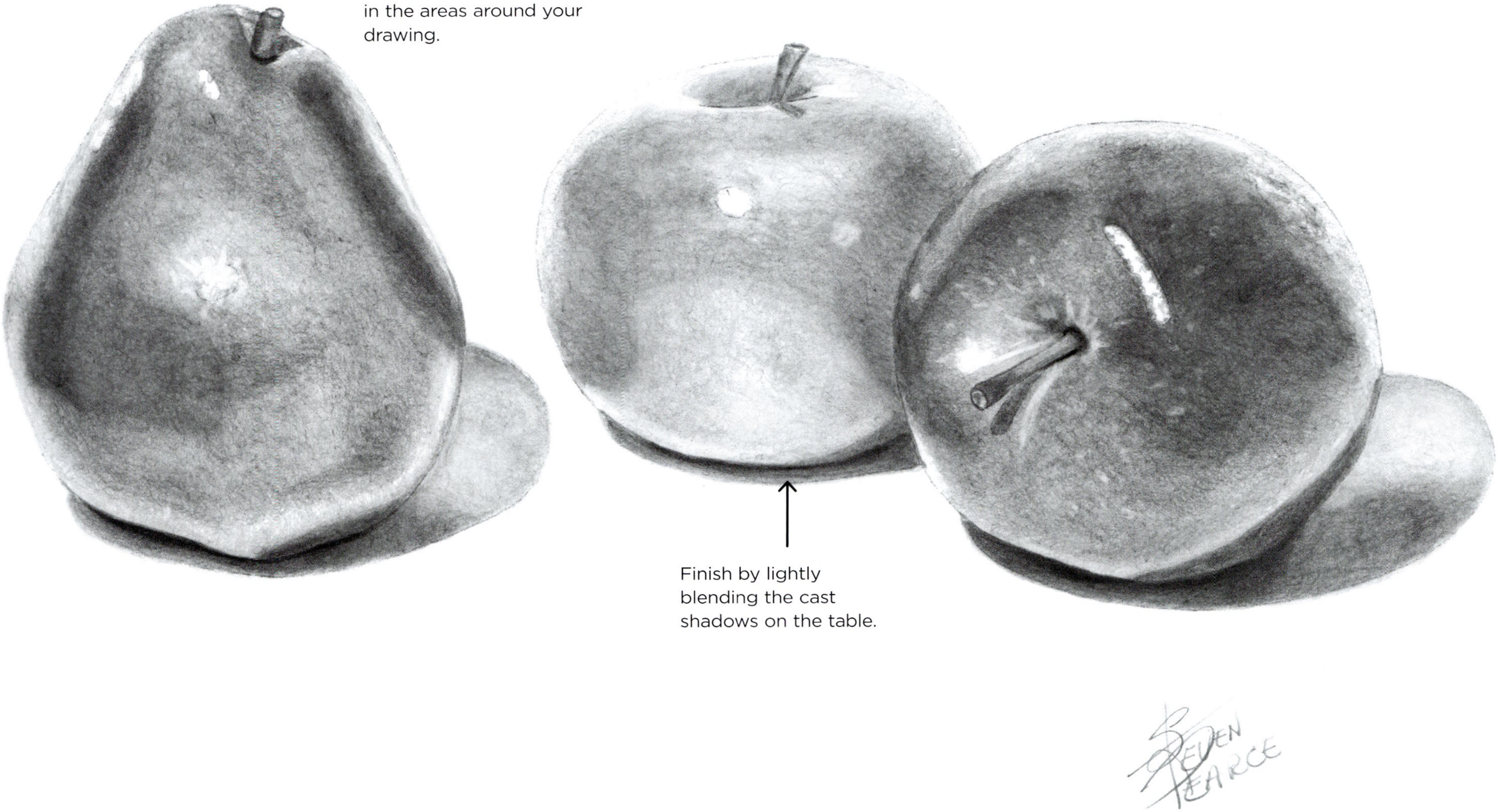

Use a kneaded eraser to lift out some of the lighter areas on the fruit. You can also sharpen a stick eraser to a point using a utility knife to bring out the spots and other fine details.

Finish by lightly blending the cast shadows on the table.

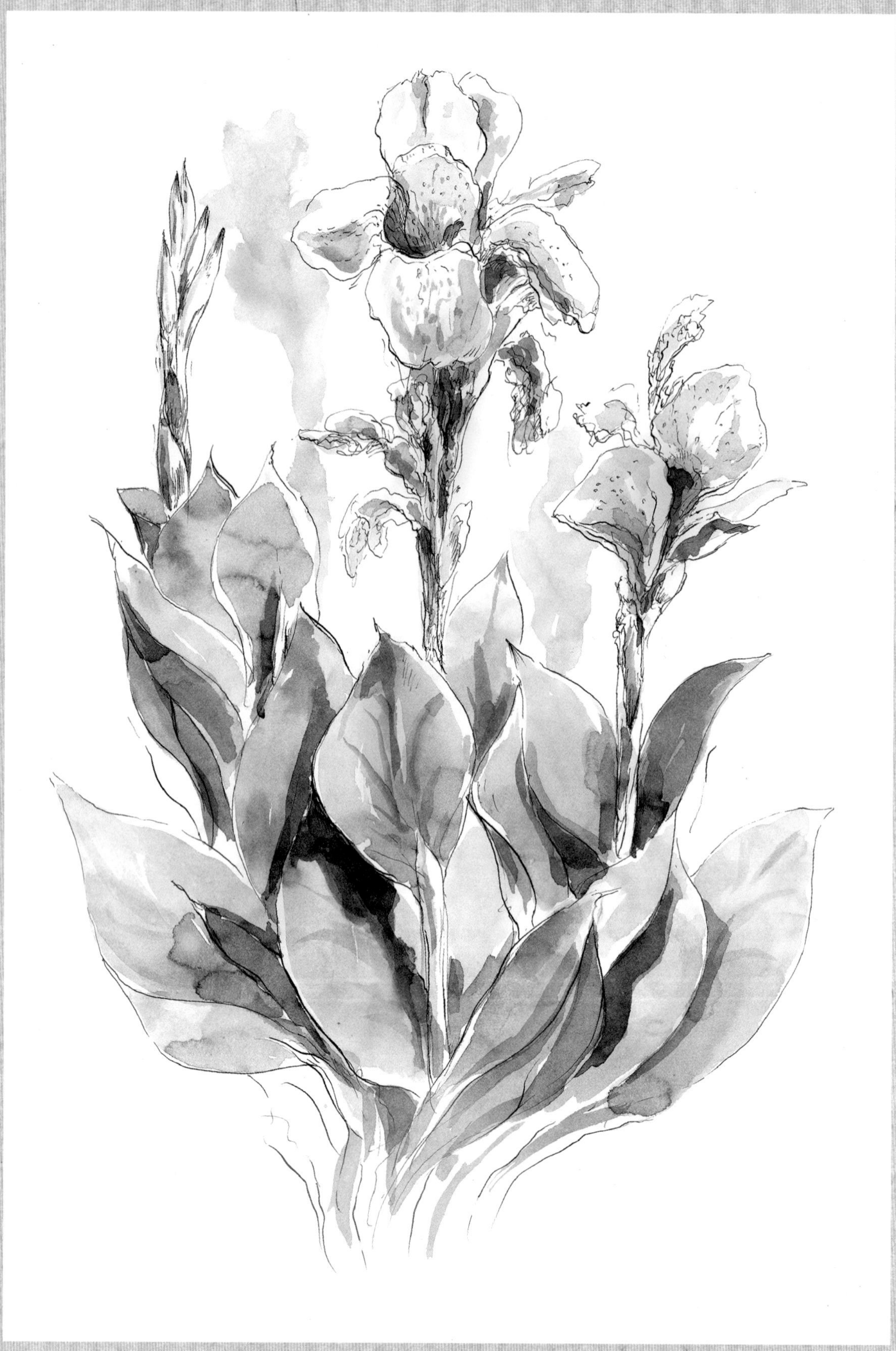

INK LINE & TONE APPLICATION

This chapter will discuss techniques and tips that make the entire ink drawing experience a more pleasurable one—for both the beginning student and the seasoned professional artist. Drawing with ink does not have to be the dreadful experience that some believe it to be. With a few adjustments to the viscosity of the ink—and practice with a variety of pen nibs—ink can become as comfortable a drawing tool as graphite. Ink can create a bold statement of the highest contrast; yet it can just as easily generate the lightest, most delicate washes possible in a variety of gradations. Again, as always, practice in this medium is the key to consistent, successful drawings.

Ink

Aside from carving in stone, ink is probably the most permanent of art media. Permanent India ink lasts as long as the paper on which it is drawn. This permanence can be intimidating for artists of any skill level; however, it does not need to be.

Ink has been used as a communication medium for thousands of years, and its versatility in print and the world of art makes it a medium that any artist should attempt to be comfortable with. It takes patience and practice to work successfully with ink, but the results are well worth the effort.

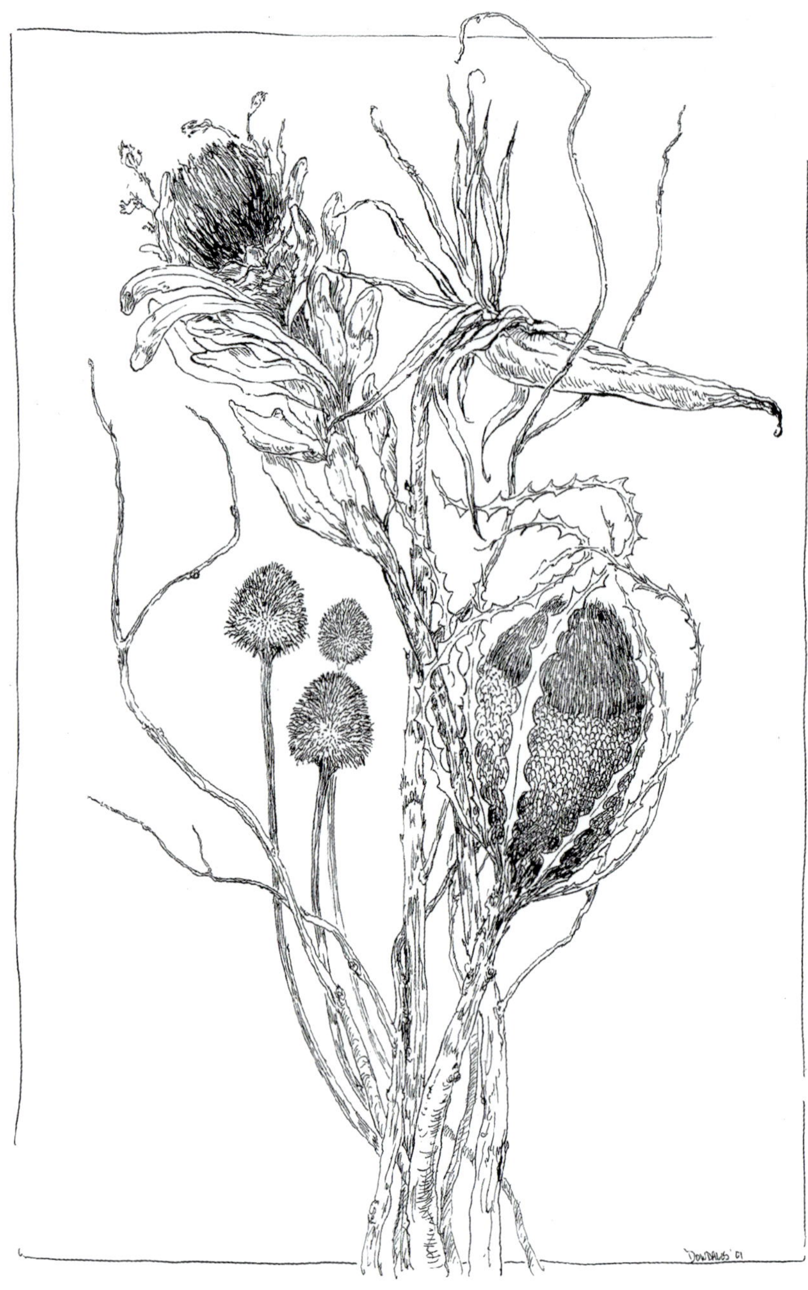

Organic subjects like this collection of exotic dried flowers are ideal for the beginning student's introduction to ink line drawing. Hard edges and straight lines can be avoided and replaced with long, flowing organic lines that offer the opportunity to gain confidence with the medium.

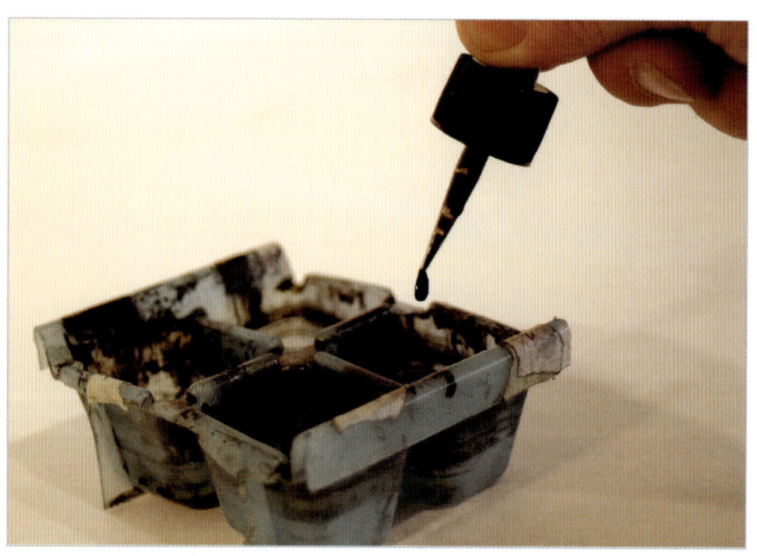

A common misconception about ink is that it is too heavy and black and difficult to draw with. Try diluting black India ink with a ratio of approximately 3 or 4 parts ink to 1 to 2 parts water. Part of an ice cube tray works well as an ink reservoir when using a diluted mixture, as the depth of the well allows most of the pen nib to be submerged into the ink.

Adding water to ink directly out of the bottle gives it more flow, but won't dilute it enough to affect its velvety black appearance.

The smaller the pen nib, the finer the line will be. To achieve very light lines for gesture drawings, simply add more water to the mixture. Try using a larger nib, such as a B3, to sketch in gestural preliminary drawings; rounded nibs tend to flow across the paper, as opposed to fine-point nibs, which can be "scratchy" in a quick sketch. Save finer points for detail line work toward the end of the drawing.

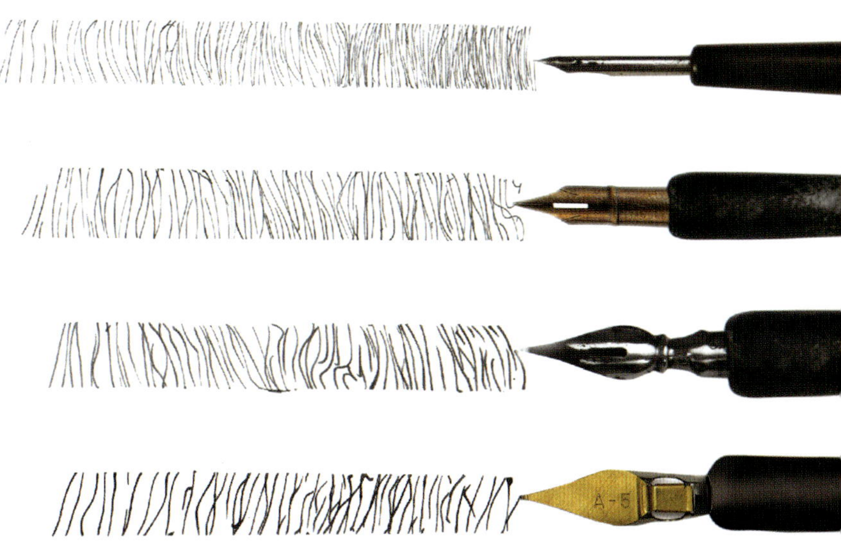

Even a small selection of nib sizes and types can produce a variety of lines and mark-making.

Appreciation for the Past

There isn't much of a difference between the type of pen nibs that are used today and the classic nib and holder used in centuries past—from illuminated manuscripts of the Middle Ages and the Renaissance to Rembrandt, Goya, Van Gogh, and the Golden Age of Illustration. It is important to introduce these artists and make their work relevant to students so that they may appreciate the skills, understand the potential, and reinterpret the usage of this timeless medium for a modern era.

Ink Line Mark-Making

It's important to understand the different types, sizes, and uses of a variety of ink nibs and points, which can create a multitude of marks on paper. Using a variety of different line weights and line textures will make any drawing more interesting and compelling. In this student piece, notice the detail of line-weight variety and mark-making employed.

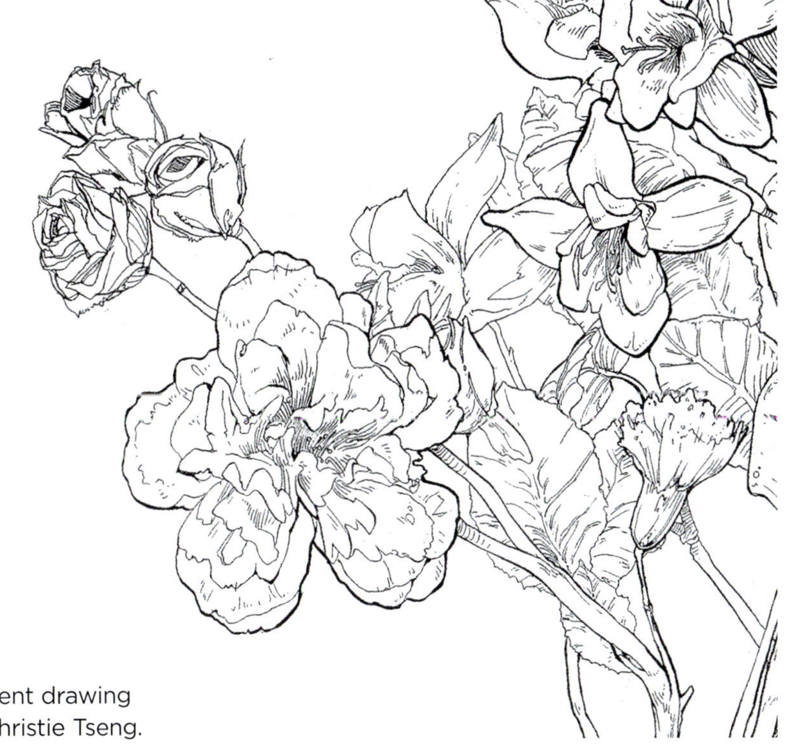

Student drawing by Christie Tseng.

Creating Tone with Dots

One way to create tonal variation in ink drawing is with a technique called "stippling." To stipple means to create tone out of an accumulation of dots created with the point of a pen. To create a true dot, the pen nib should be held completely perpendicular to the paper, depositing the ink as a point without dragging it into a line.

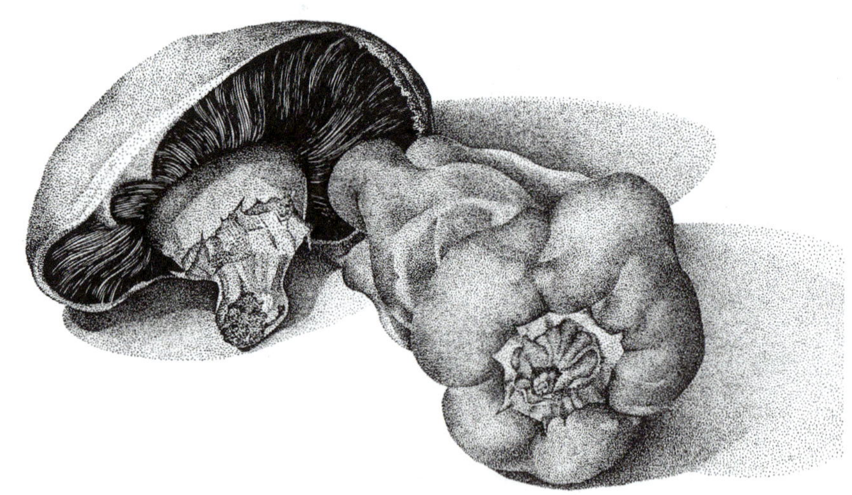

Above is an ink stipple value scale. A variety of values can be accomplished by adding more dots of ink placed closer together or by changing the size of the nib to create larger, darker dots.

Creating Tone with Line

Creating tone with ink can also be accomplished with line, or linear mark-making. The line can be hatched (one direction), crosshatched (multiple directions), or scribbled to create tone.

Creating a value scale with linear marks is a vital way to understand how to add techniques to an artist's "toolbox" and create interesting and complex drawings.

This type of tonal application can be employed for a variety of subjects, including still lifes, portraits, and architecture. The combination of crisp, clean ink marks with a variety of subtle-to-strong application techniques makes this linear mark-making a versatile way in which to build a successful value drawing.

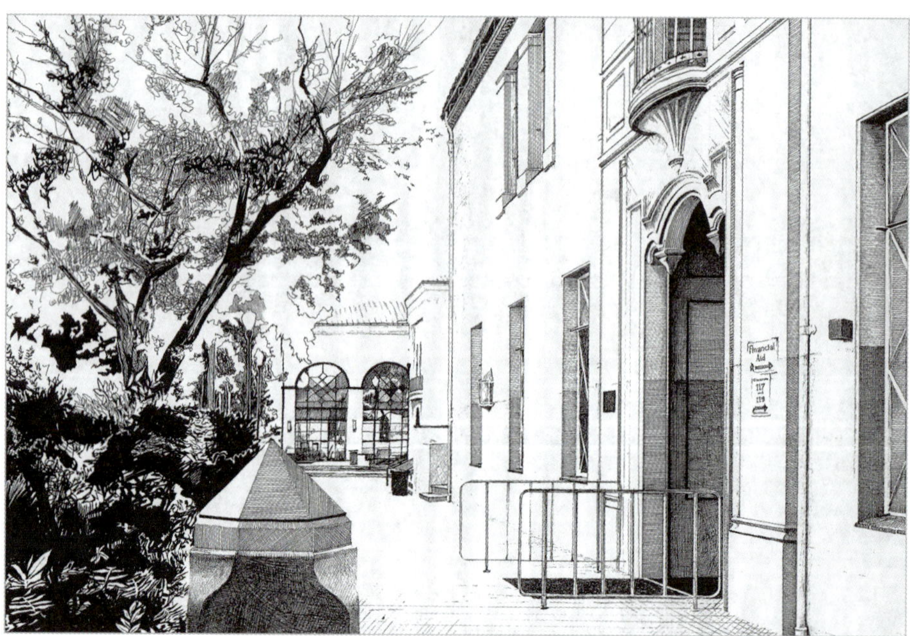

This student's architectural drawing incorporates line and value with ink nibs and brush. Time: 12–15 hours.

Create a line value scale using hatching and crosshatching with various ink nib sizes for value development from light to dark.

Creating Tone with Washes

Another way to create tone with ink is to dilute the ink in various shades of gray, from very light (lots of water) to very dark (less water), and apply the resulting washes with a brush.

The types of brushes most often used for this purpose are very soft and absorbent natural-hair brushes, such as squirrel or beaver. (The hair for these brushes is humanely harvested, and the brushes are inexpensive.)

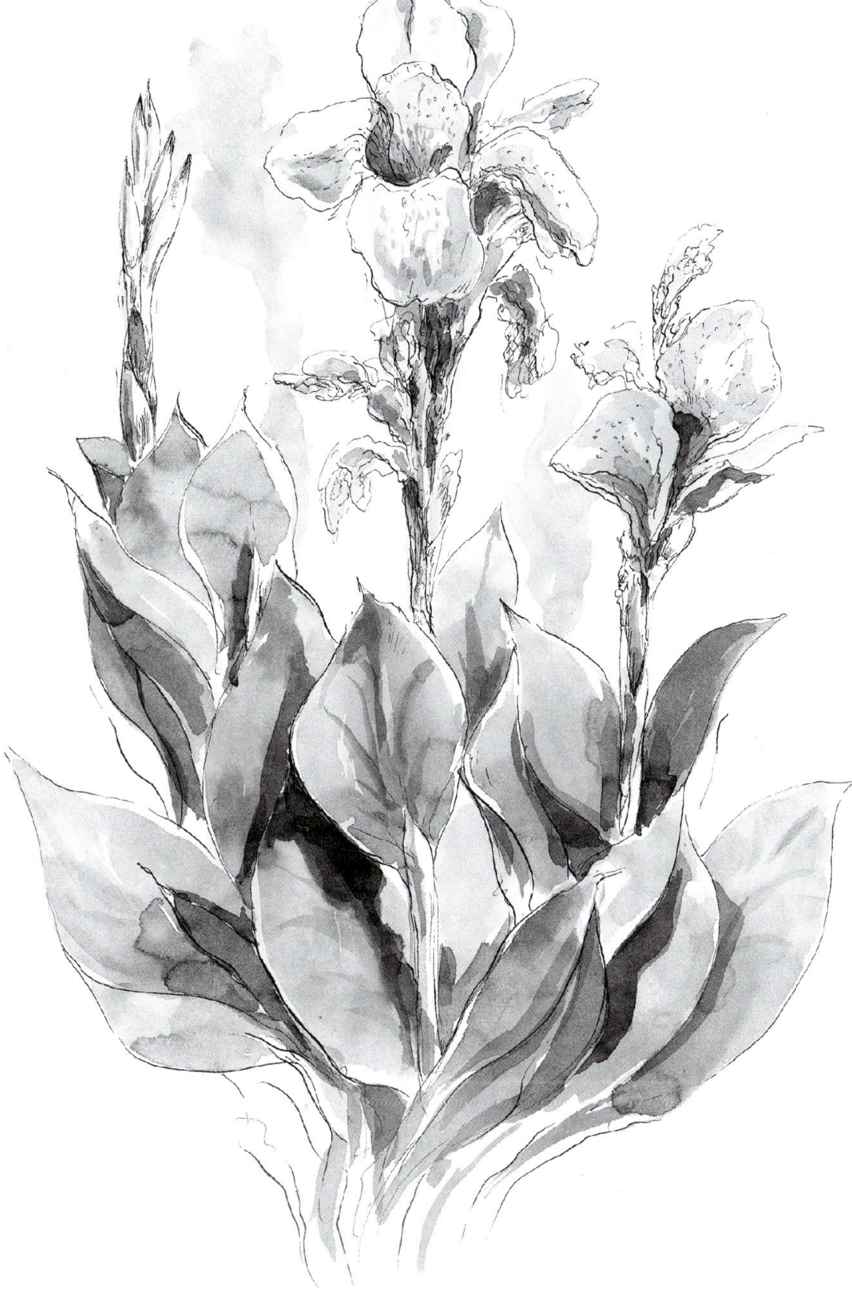

An example of four washes used in an ink line drawing. Time: 1 hour.

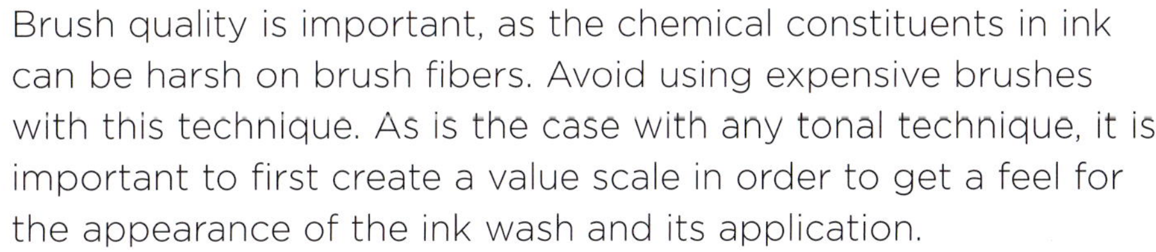

Brush quality is important, as the chemical constituents in ink can be harsh on brush fibers. Avoid using expensive brushes with this technique. As is the case with any tonal technique, it is important to first create a value scale in order to get a feel for the appearance of the ink wash and its application.

Experiment with the water/ink ratio until you achieve four distinct values from light to dark. With four washes, plus the white of the paper and the straight black ink from the bottle, you will effectively have six different values to work with.

YOUR HOMEWORK

In this homework exercise, you'll have the opportunity to practice all the elements that we discussed in this chapter. Gather two to three different types of flowers—real or artificial—and bundle them in a vase or hang them on a wall with fishing line. Use a single light source for illumination.

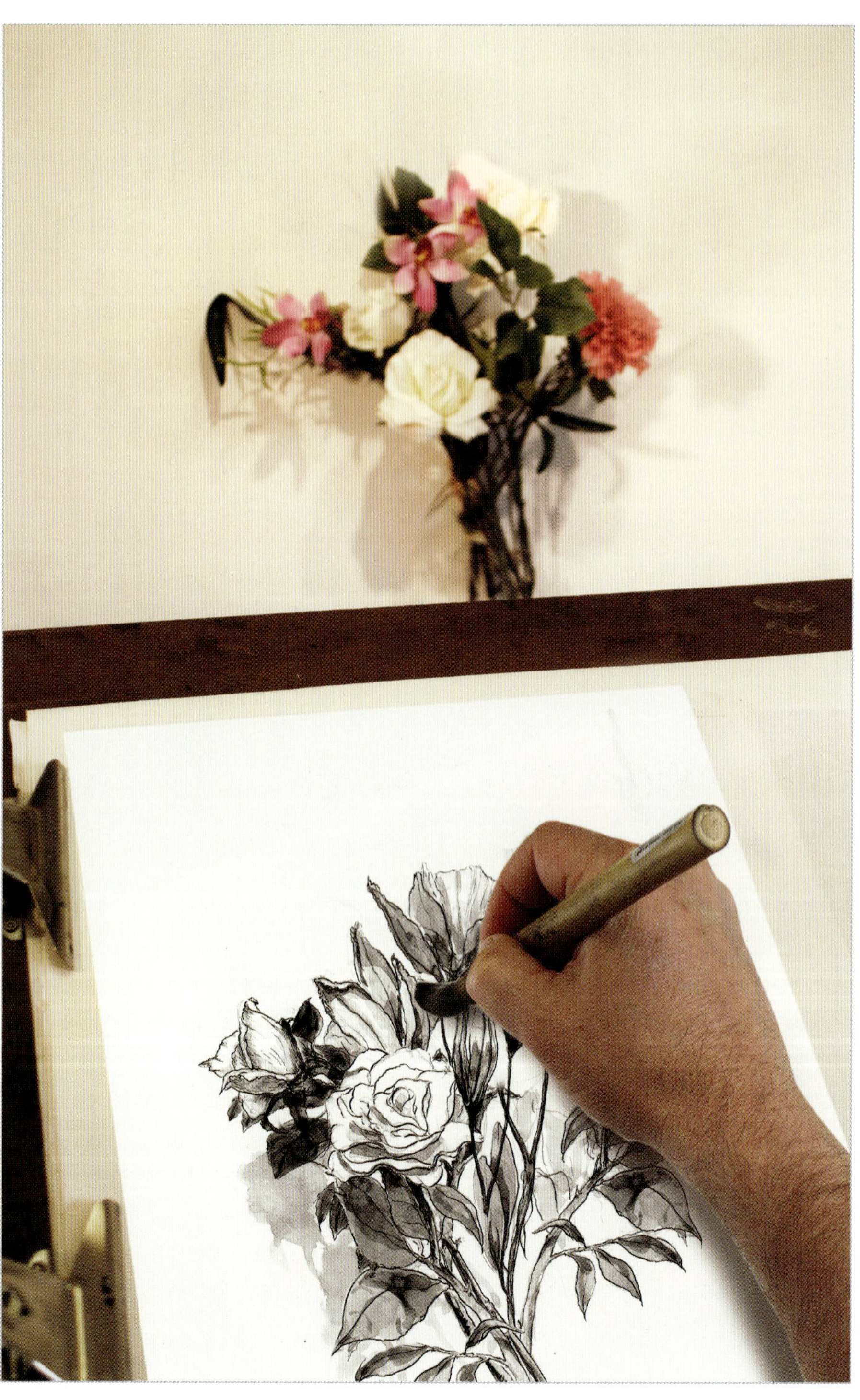

Create a light gesture sketch, followed by a contour line drawing. Add a tonal wash application of four distinct values, from very light to very dark, with a brush. This exercise should take 90 minutes to 2 hours to complete.

EXERCISES FOR PRACTICE

Giulio Campagnola first used stippling, or pointillism, in his engravings during the 16th century. Pointillism was recognized as a distinct technique during the 18th century, when Post-Impressionist painter Georges-Pierre Seurat popularized it.

Stippling involves applying black dots to a white surface to create a pattern that determines values' tones and thus represents form. Dots can be used to represent textures through variations in light and temperature. With less intense dots, the shape of an object is made clearer.

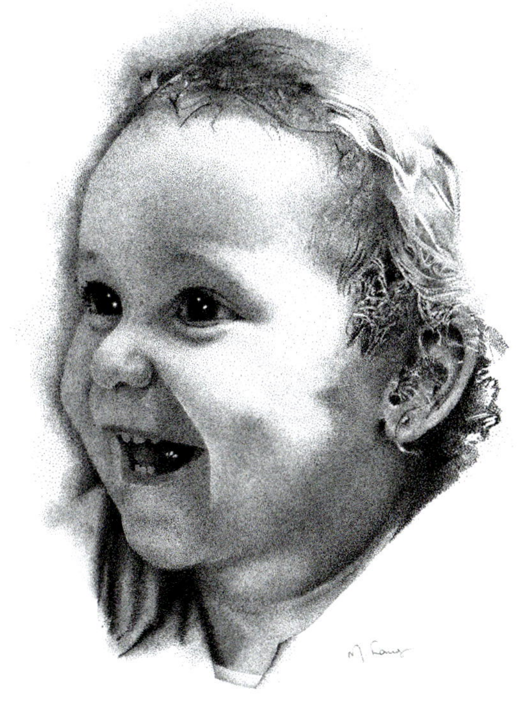

How to Work with Stippling

For your first exercise, create a grayscale drawing to use as a reference. Use a pencil to sketch it out, and then add dots with a pen. It might help you to use two reference photos: one with many variations in lighting and one with fewer. View the reference photo on a light table, and map out the grays with a soft pencil, such as a 2B. Place your reference photo near your drawing, and notice how the light falls on the object(s) in the photo. If we assume that the white paper is the high key (light tones with little contrast) and the black pen is the low key (darker tones that offer a great deal of contrast), then the dots' closeness will be used to form a medium-gray color.

Start by drawing a pattern of gray, and then add more and more dots to create the darker areas. The idea is to fill the entire surface of the paper to create the shape of the object. Avoid placing dots too fast and without control. Stippling requires a great deal of concentration and discipline.

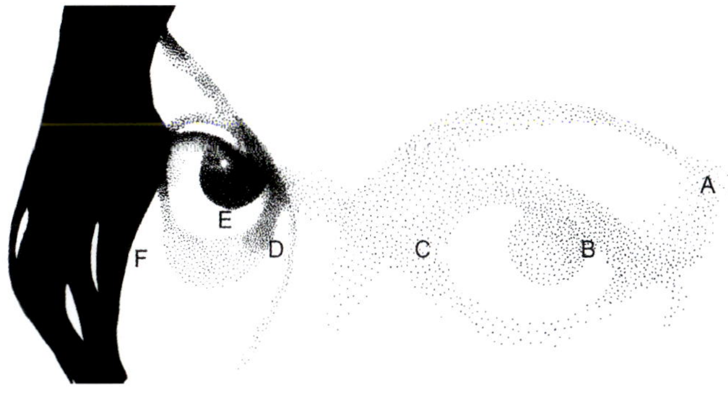

A. Scatter dots to create texture.

B. Group dots that determine the boundaries of a form.

C. Evenly distribute dots to avoid errors and to help viewers see the form of an object or person.

D. Adding more dots allows you to intensify the shadow of an object.

E. Create a counterpoint.

F. Use hard edges and create completely black areas by filling in with dots to emphasize adjacent light areas.

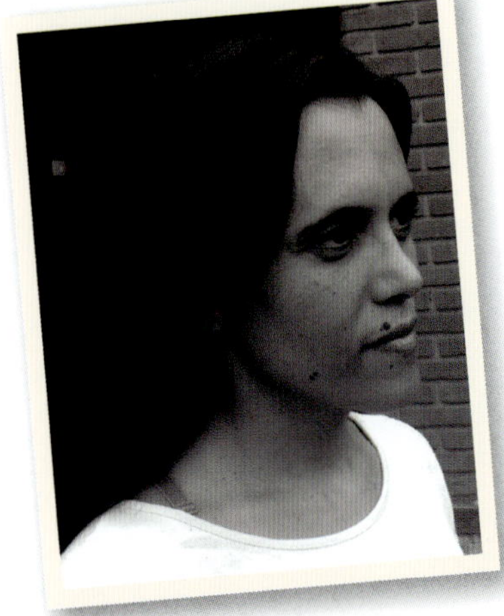

A Portrait of a Woman

This reference photo presents the subject from a three-quarter angle. She stands in a relaxed position, and she is naturally lit.

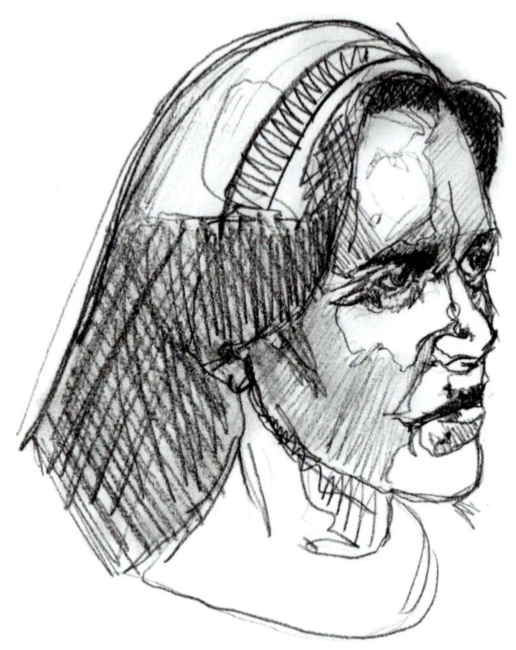

STEP 1 Sketching the piece first helps you isolate the light sources on the model's face. A light table can make the sketch more accurate.

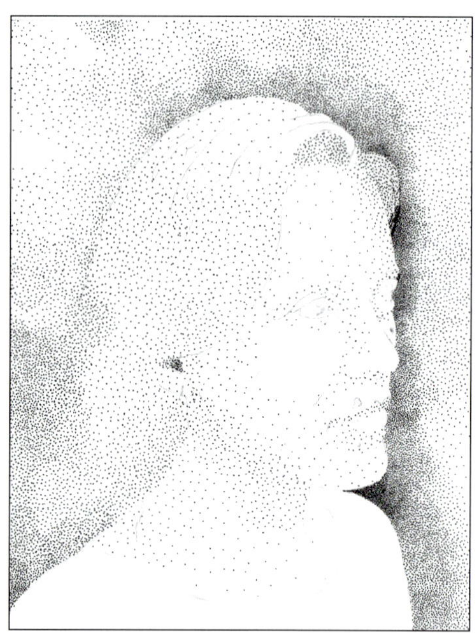

STEP 2 First, the dots are distributed all over. Study the gray values in the photo as well as its background, determining which spots are dark and light, and notice the negative space. Once the light source has been determined, add more dots to choose a counterpoint in the image, which is the center of the face in this case. You can reduce the light's intensity by placing the dots closer together in darker areas.

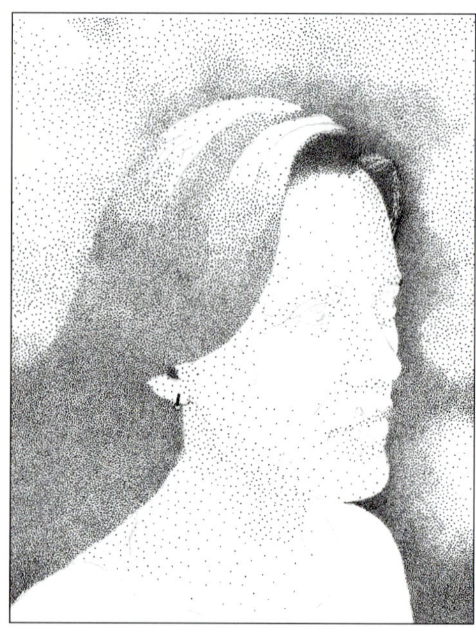

STEP 3 Once you have chosen a counterpoint, draw the dots closer together in the background. The background should be darkened to highlight the woman's face. Her hair is black, and it can be merged with the background. Draw the hair, and determine the light values in it.

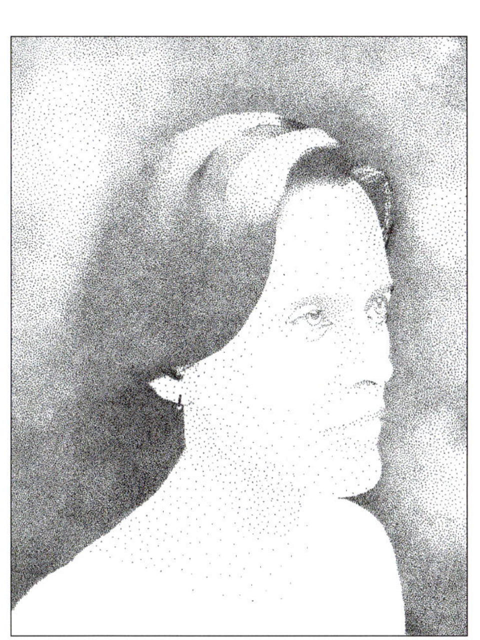

STEP 4 Add more dots in the background and hair, and increase the light intensity in the model's face. Then start building details like the eyes, nose, and mouth.

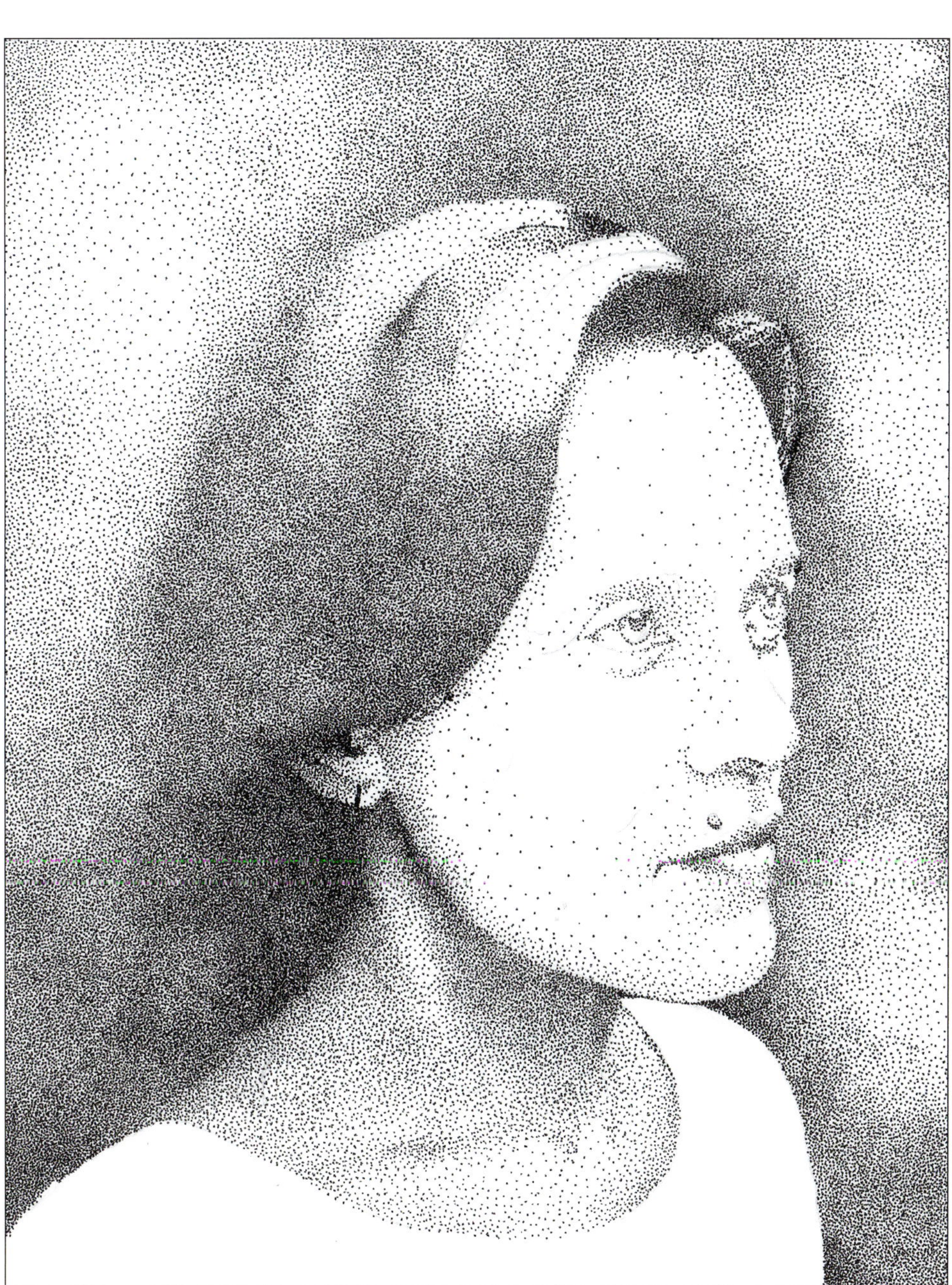

STEP 5 To form a counterpoint to the light areas on the subject's face, more dots can be added to her chest, making her face the primary focus. The chest should be lighter than the background and not as detailed as the face.

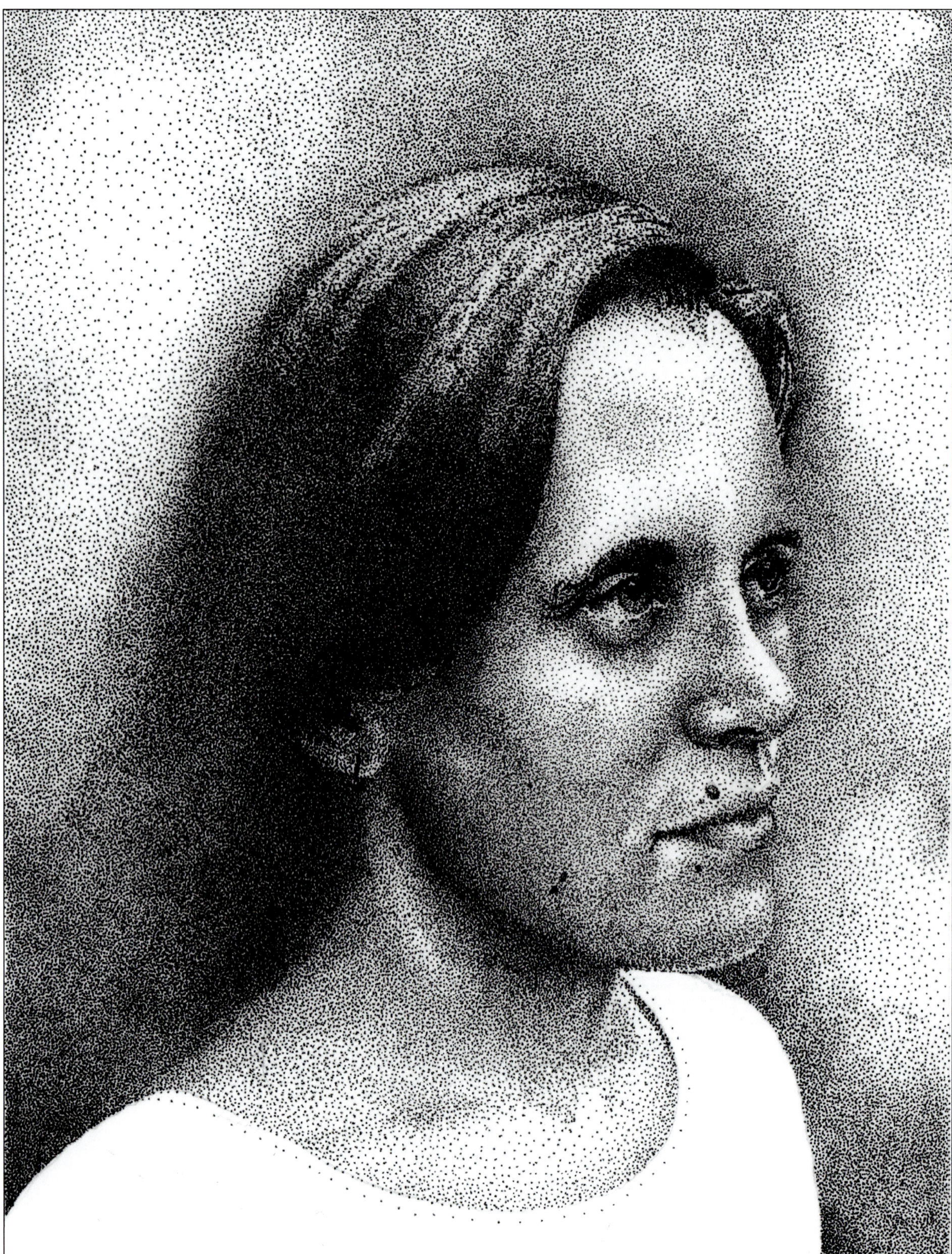

STEP 6 Now draw the details on the face, making the eyes the main focus and the hair their counterpoint. The hair should be less detailed than the eyes so it doesn't draw attention away from the face. Create the hair as a gray mass without drawing each strand of hair. There's no need to add details to the hair. The viewer will know what it is, and the focus should stay on the woman's face. To isolate the three key elements in the artwork (the subject's eyes, the top of her head, and her hair), build a "frame" that will draw focus to the woman's eyes. Add light below the eyes and to her jaw and neck, and give the hair more weight as a counterpoint to the light values in the face.

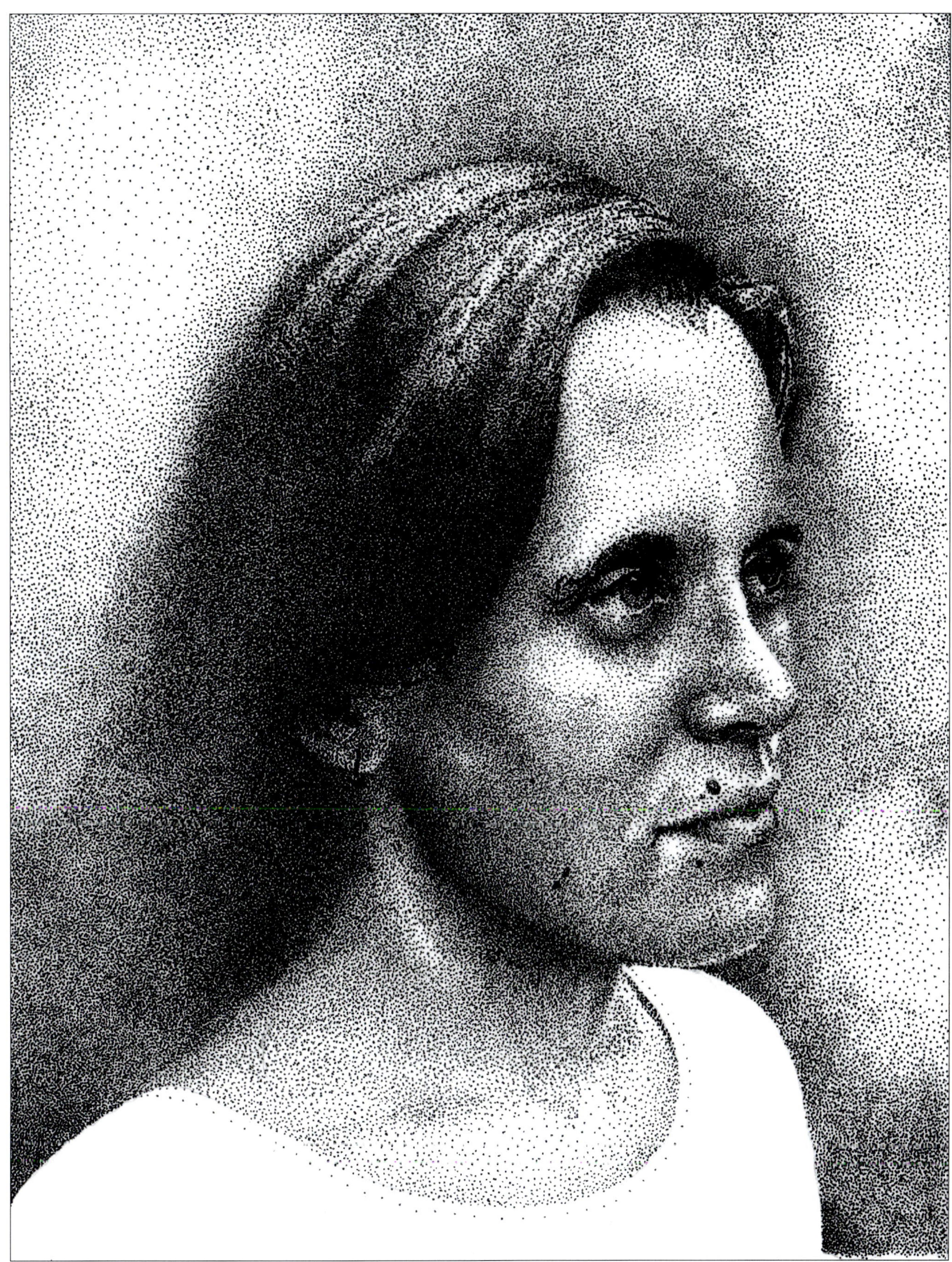

STEP 7 In the final drawing, you see the diagonal line going from the bottom left to the top right, dividing the weight of the drawing. The hair is on one side and the face is on the other, and the light values in the forehead direct the viewer's eyes. The negative space of the subject's shirt creates a balance between the upper and lower halves of the drawing.

Still Life

This piece provides an excellent opportunity for studying the light and texture in various objects. First do just a quick sketch of all of the objects. The idea here is to play with the different textures in the scene.

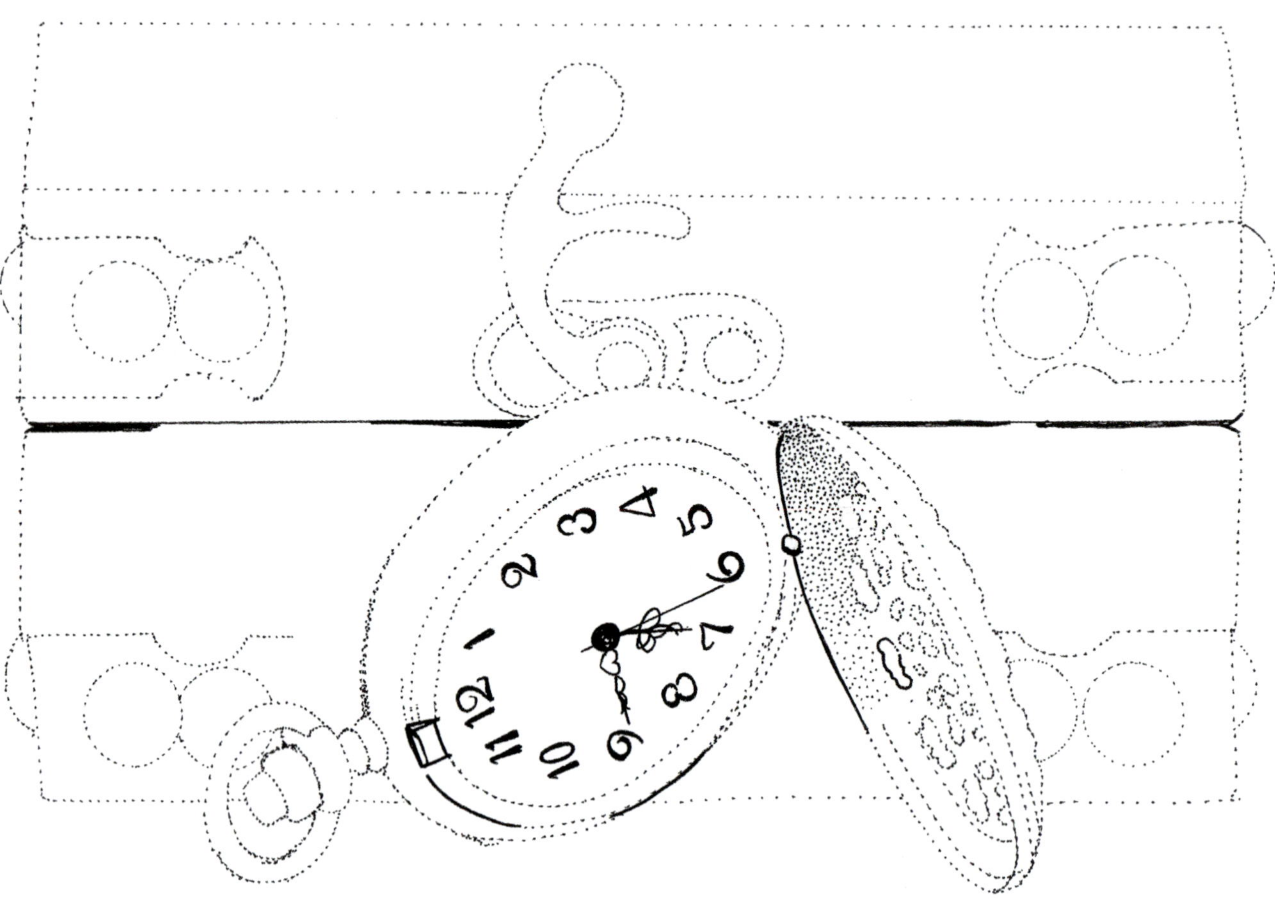

STEP 1 Using a light table, outline the objects with dots. Mark the direction of the light and where its shadow lays. Adding numbers to the pocket watch makes it the focus of the piece.

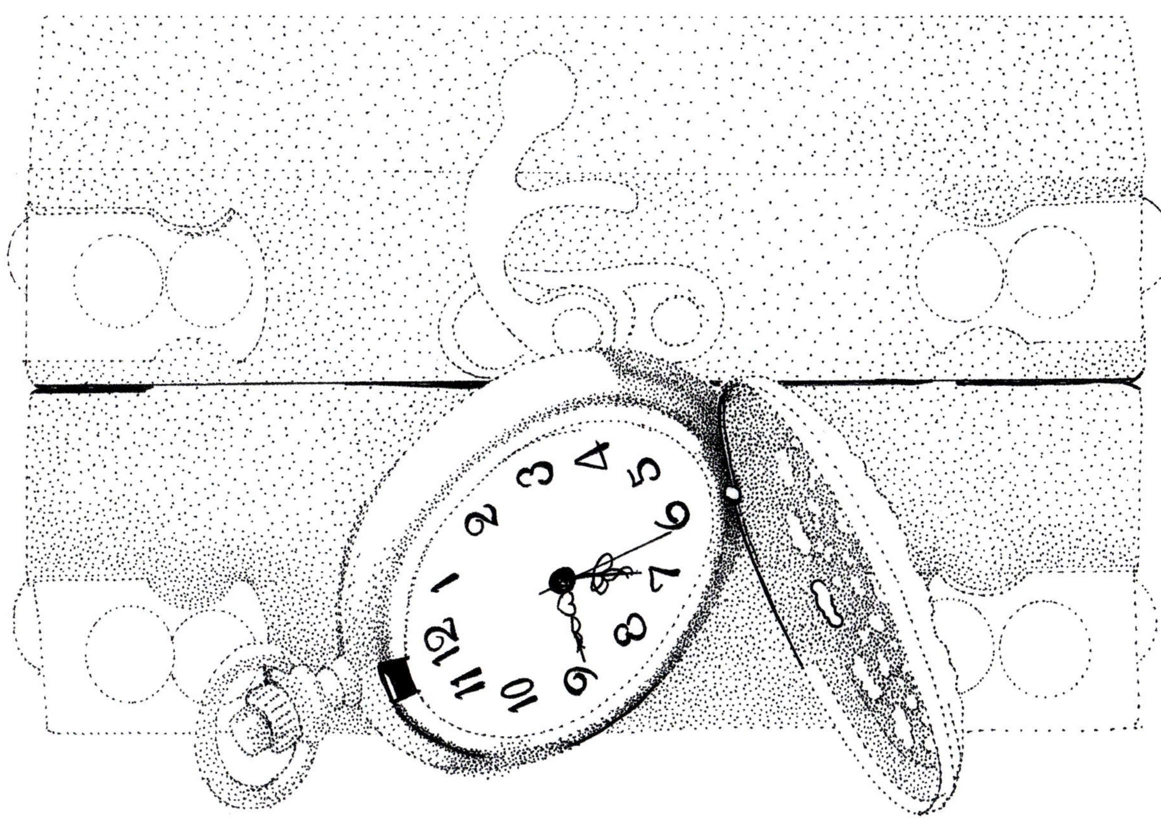

STEP 2 Begin distributing dots throughout all of the objects without drawing the background. Notice the pocket watch's light values and metallic texture.

STEP 3 Now work the pocket watch into the foreground and distribute the dots to add volume and texture. The open cover serves as the light's counterpoint and creates balance and shadows in the pocket watch.

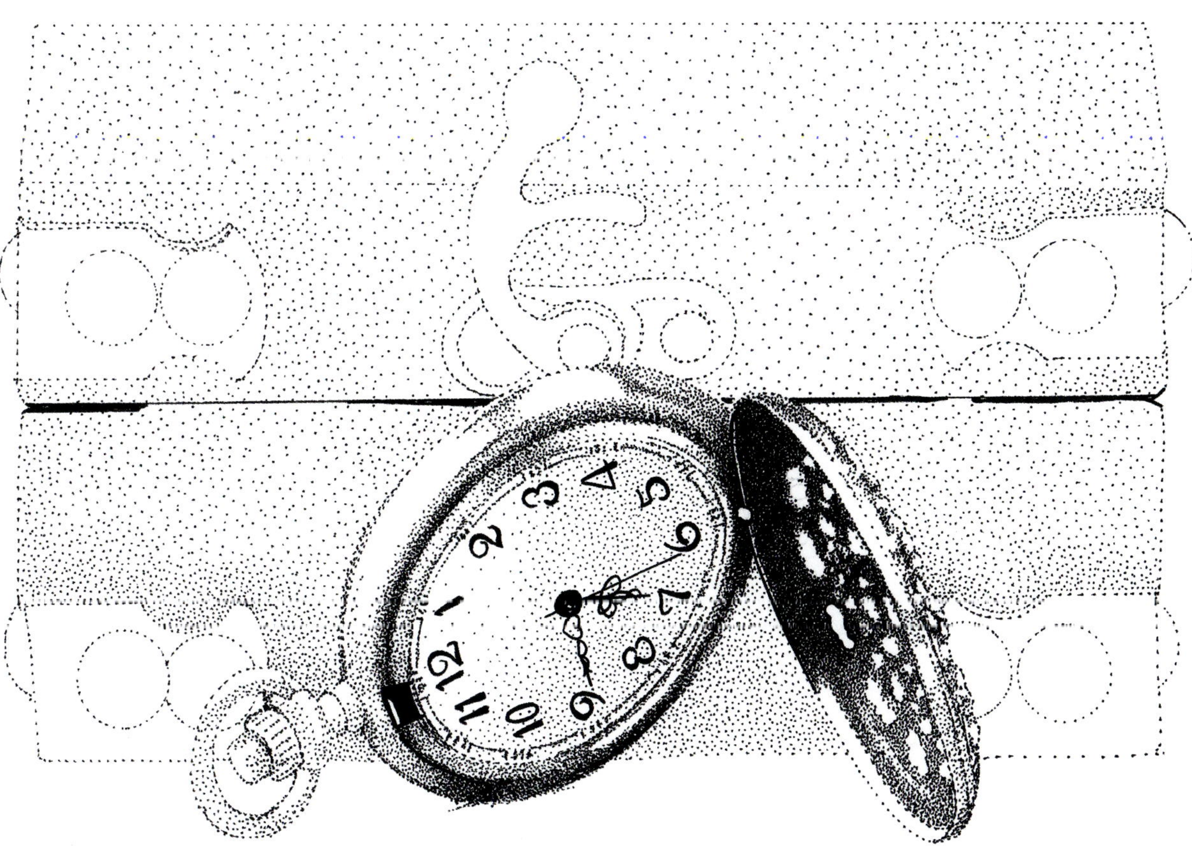

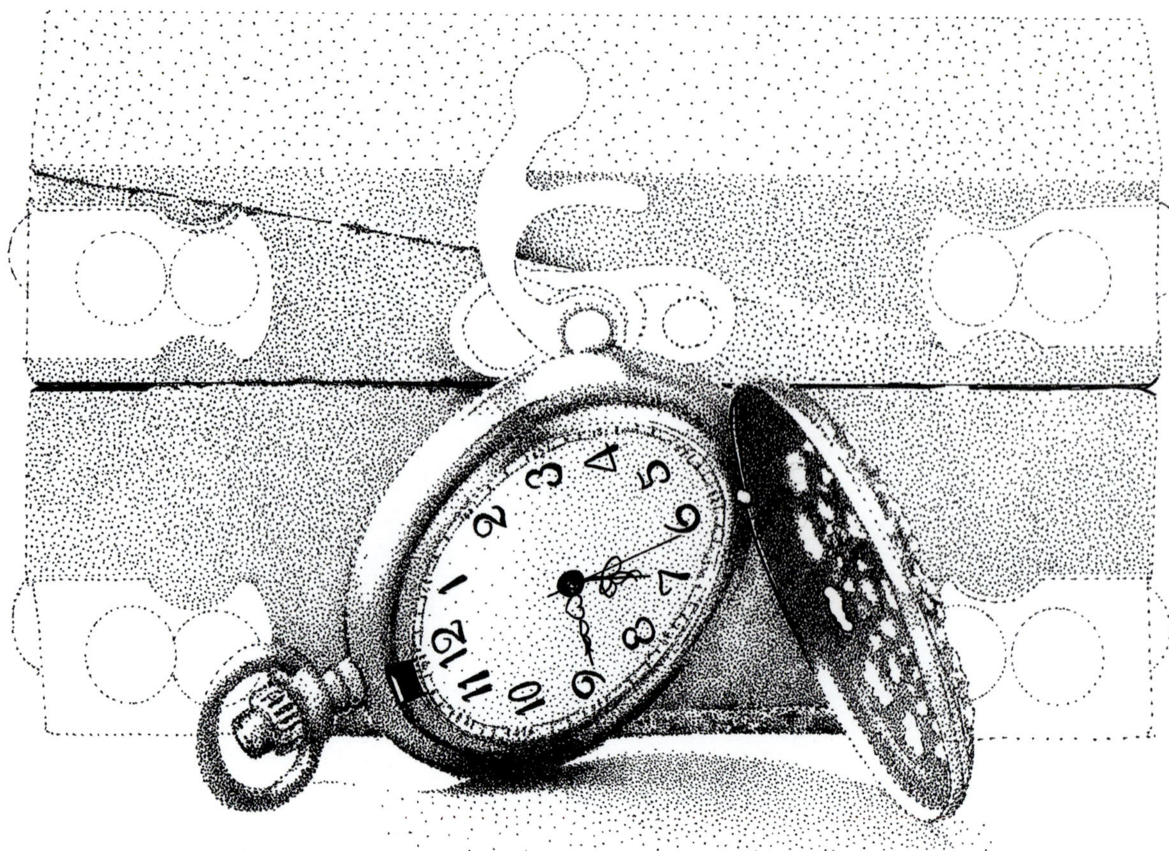

STEP 4 Now turn your attention to the small chest, distributing dots throughout. The pocket watch should remain the focus of the piece, so work to create a balance between it and the chest.

STEP 5 Starting in the middle of the chest, work in its texture and light absorption values. Then add the same texture to the upper portion of the chest.

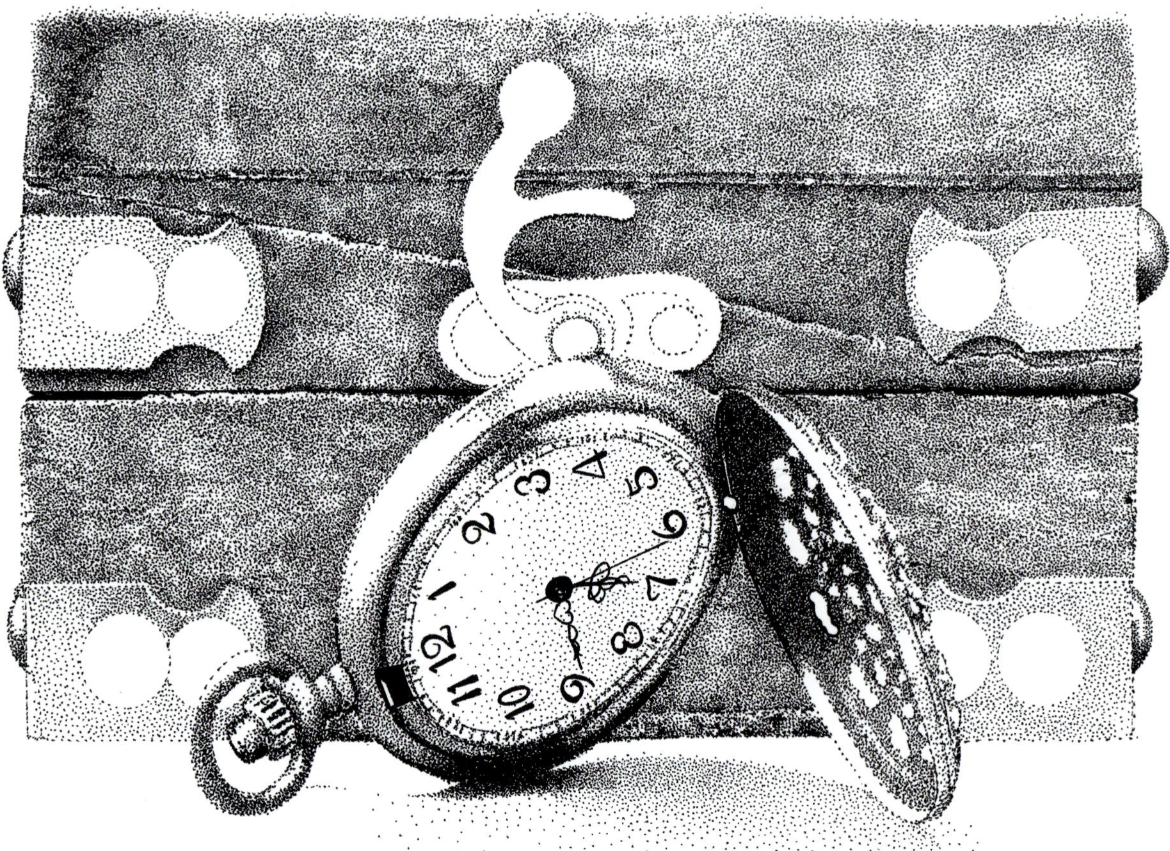

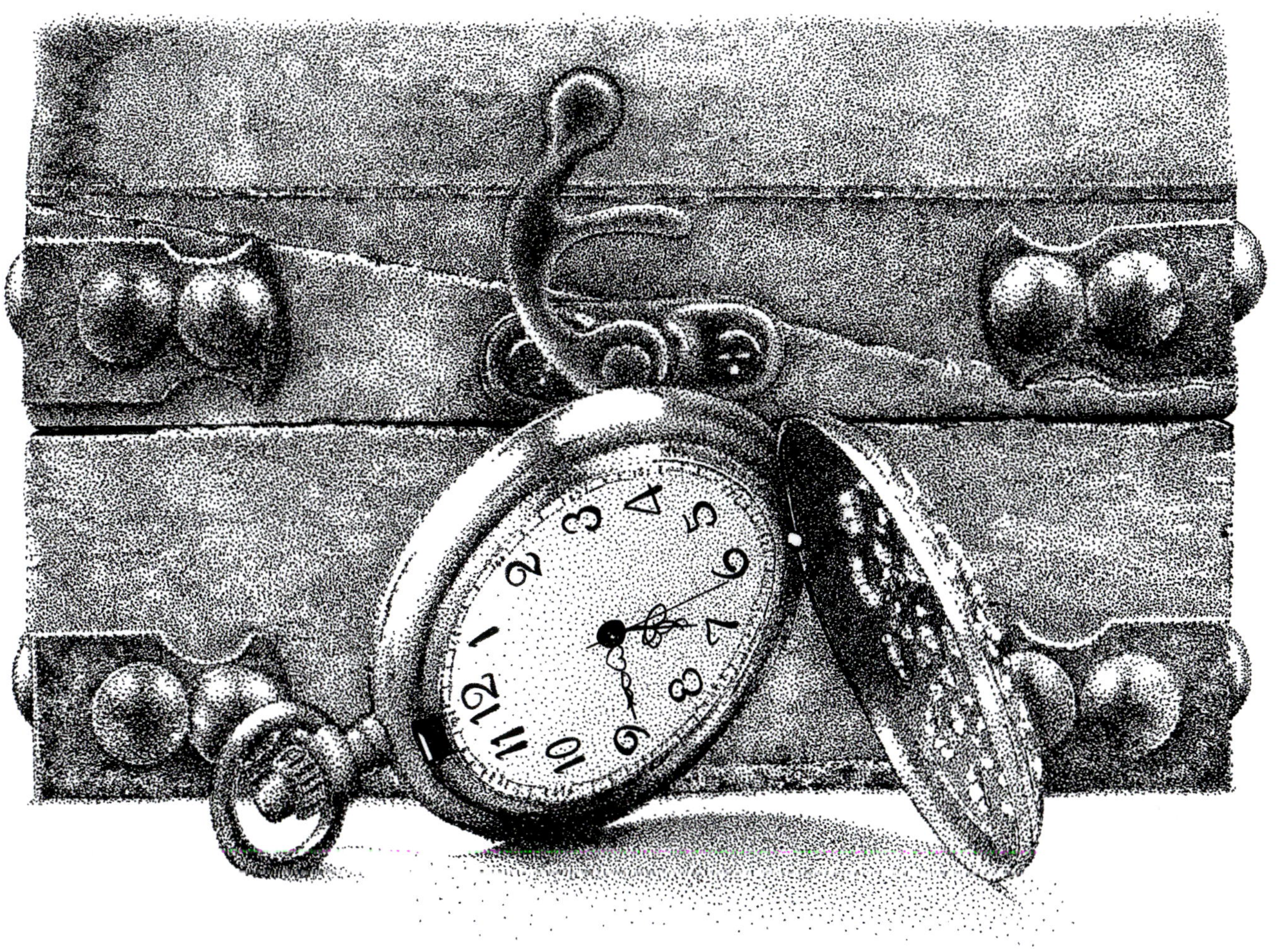

STEP 6 Two layers of dots are added to the chest: a shaded layer and a textured layer.

Stippling doesn't allow for mistakes, so review each step before moving on to the next. Always work from light to dark; this makes it easier to control light values.

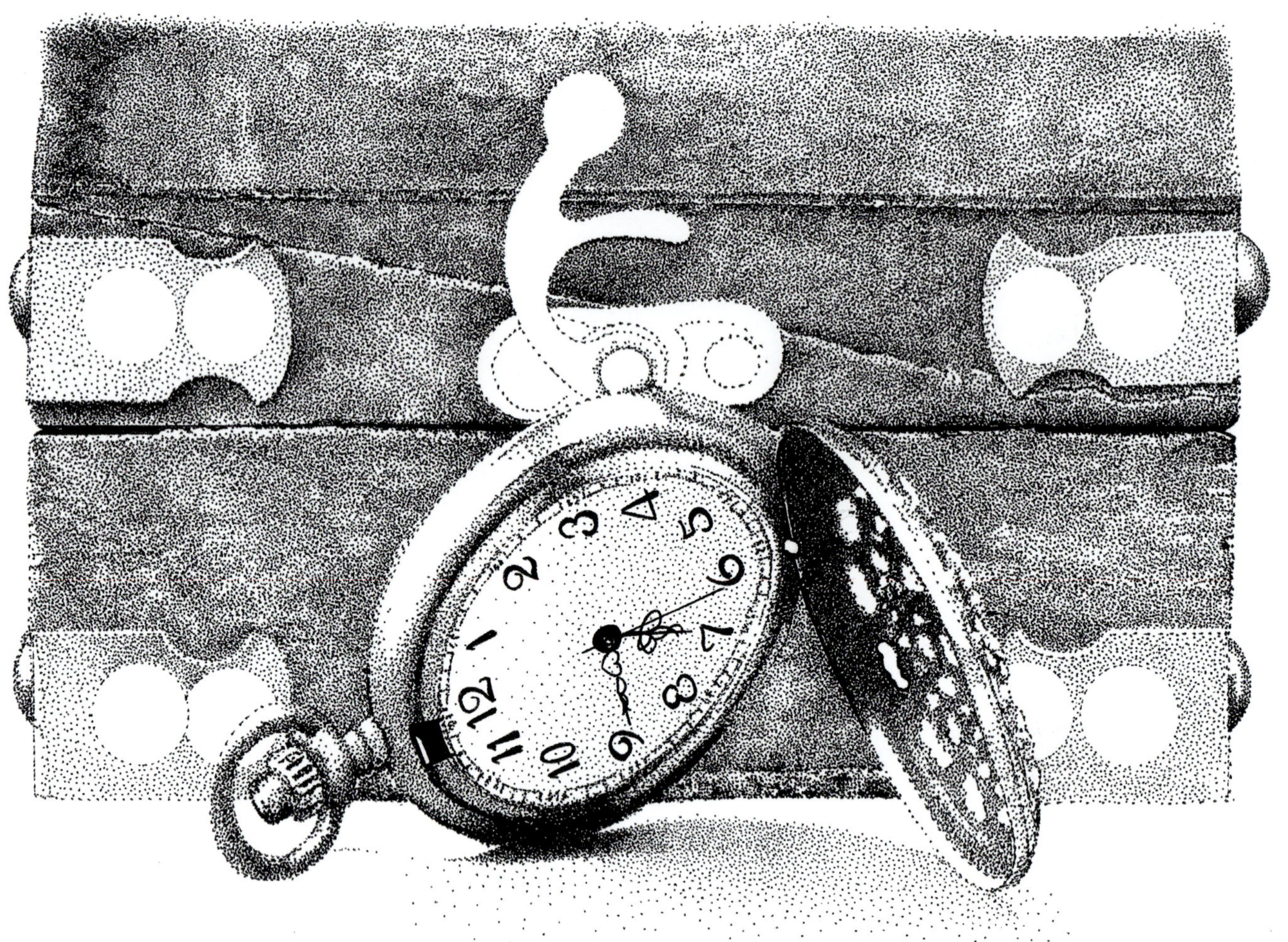

STEP 7 The top of the chest doesn't need the same texture, and its lighting can be more diffused. The focus should remain on the clock; the chest needs fewer details.

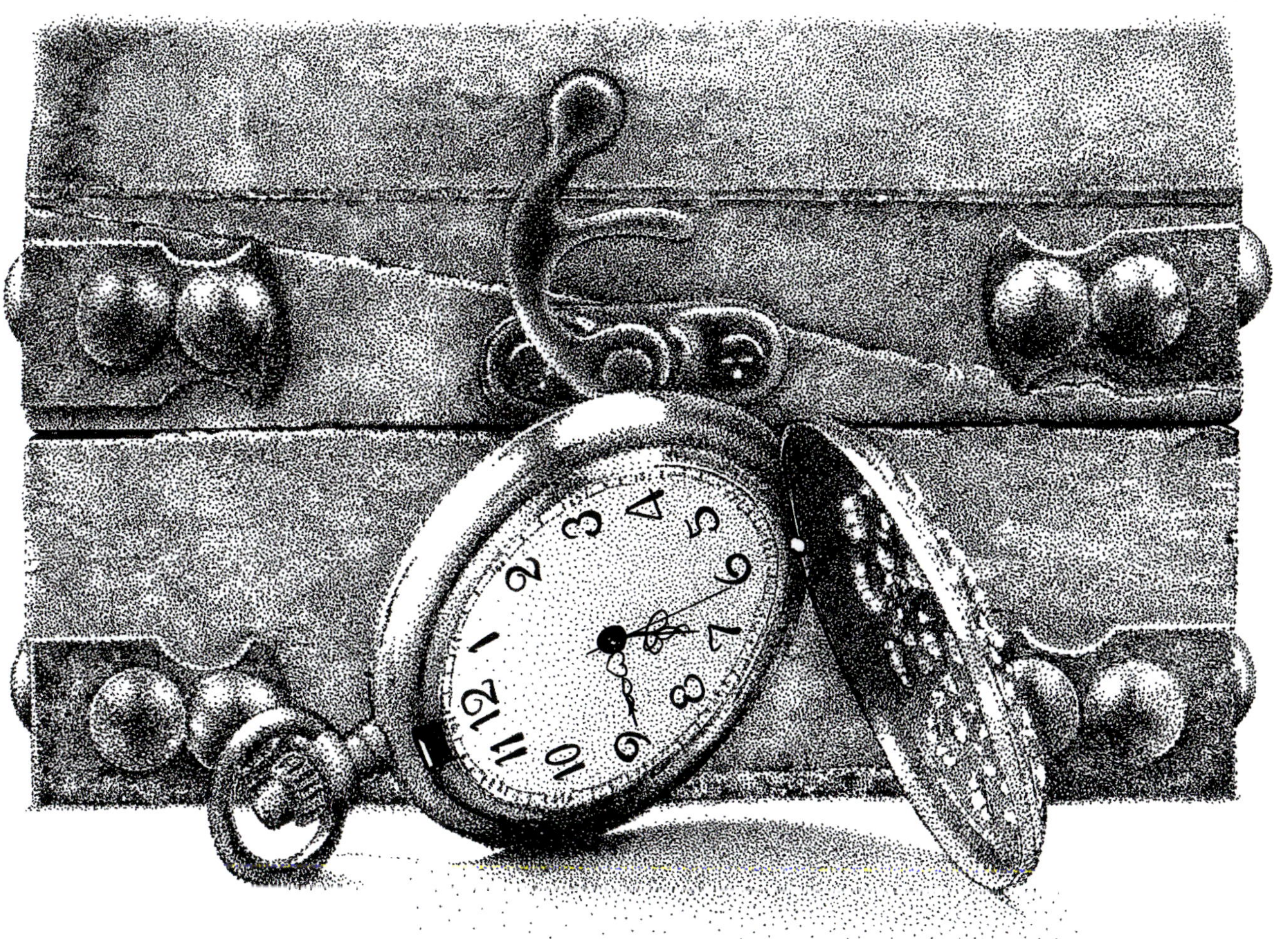

STEP 8 Add dots to work in the chest's metal parts without drawing many details; just read the texture. More shadows are added to the clock and the surface beneath it to finish the piece.

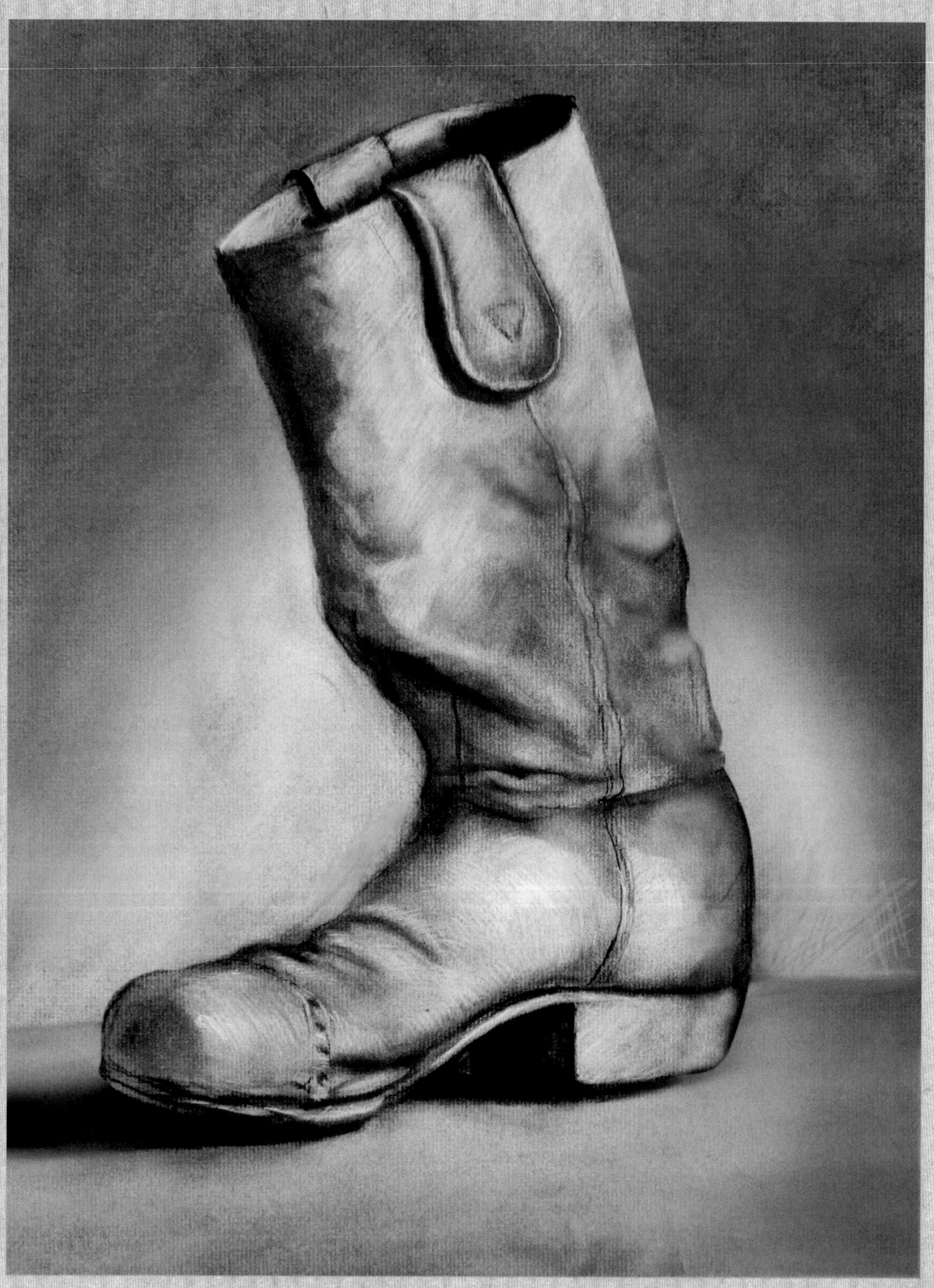

CHARCOAL

Charcoal is one of the most versatile drawing media available, capable of rich, velvety darks, easily achieved midtones, and subtle shading differences. It is an easy medium to learn, albeit messy—and there are ways to control that characteristic. A full range of tonal values can be developed much faster and easier with charcoal than with graphite. We have already discussed the term *chiaroscuro*, which describes the appearance of strong, high-contrast lighting on the subject matter. Charcoal is the ideal medium for creating a high-contrast, dramatic drawing that epitomizes the meaning of chiaroscuro.

Cast Drawing

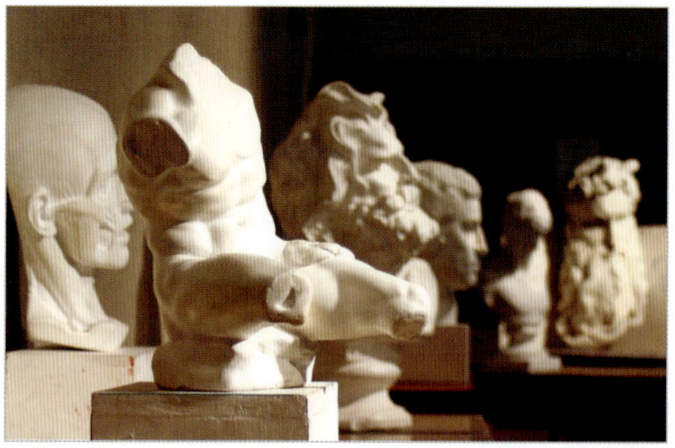

In these first few techniques we will focus on creating chiaroscuro effects on white or off-white subjects, as this is the easiest and most direct way to view the play of light across a form.

A tonal drawing from cast sculpture is a great introduction to using charcoal to indicate the tonal range across a fully lit form. Cast sculptures can be found and purchased online, as well as from local statuary stores. Set the statue up in a semi-darkened room with a single strong light source. Light cast from a 45-degree angle is usually more dramatic than direct lighting from above.

Remembering that all good drawings start with an overall gesture sketch, begin by considering composition, placement on the page, size, etc. Small thumbnail sketches at the outset are a very valuable tool for composing and cropping the subject (A).

Once the gesture drawing is lightly sketched in, refine the drawing for accuracy with a chopstick, checking the proportion, creating an overall linear envelope around the form to understand perspective angles, and lining up structures horizontally and vertically. This initial sketch can be developed with vine or willow charcoal and then strengthened and refined with charcoal pencil. You may find it helpful to work on tracing paper, as you develop your skills, so that you can experiment with changes before committing them to your final piece.

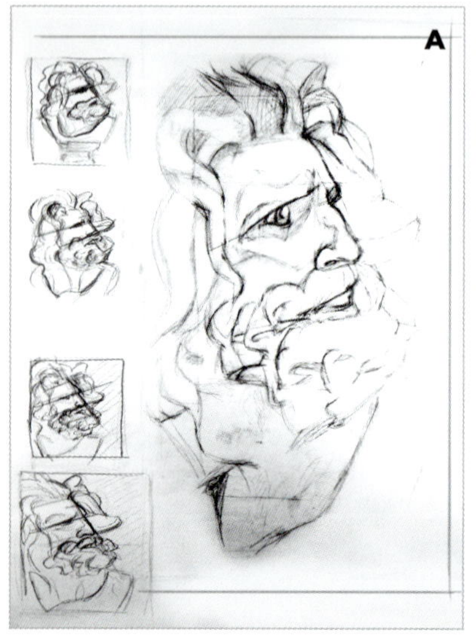

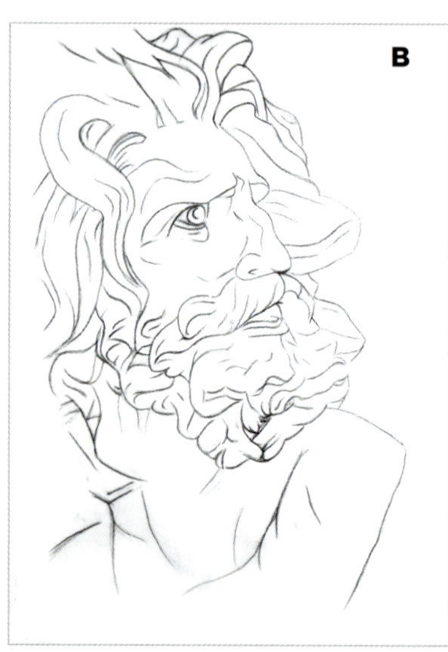

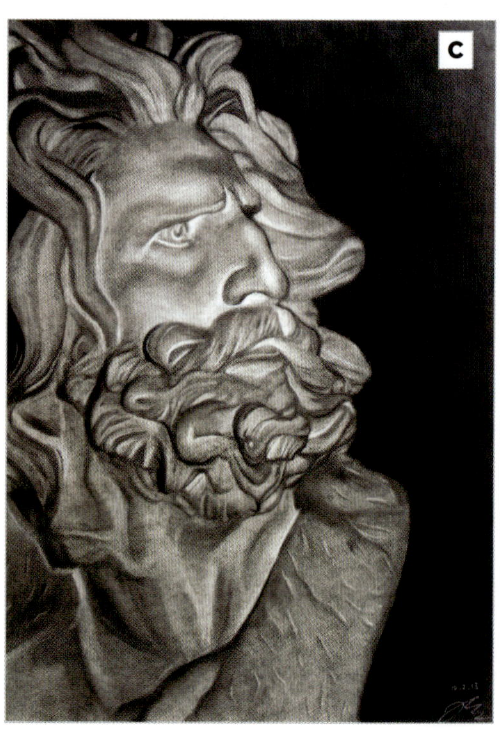

Once the sketch is refined on tracing paper, it can be transferred to a suitable drawing surface by rubbing charcoal over the back of the sketch and tracing the contour lines to transfer the line drawing to the drawing paper (B). (For transferring review, see page 16). After transferring a clean sketch to drawing paper, it is ready for tonal development (C).

Demonstration: Cast Torso

The subject of this charcoal tonal development and technique demonstration is a cast reproduction of the Belvedere torso—a famous fragment of a human torso from the first century BC in Greece—from the Vatican museum in Rome.

Chiaroscuro depends on an understanding of direct light, transitional light to shade, core shadow, reflected light, and cast shadow. This is the lighting phenomenon that you see on the subject. Next let's discuss the actual application of charcoal to create this lighting situation accurately.

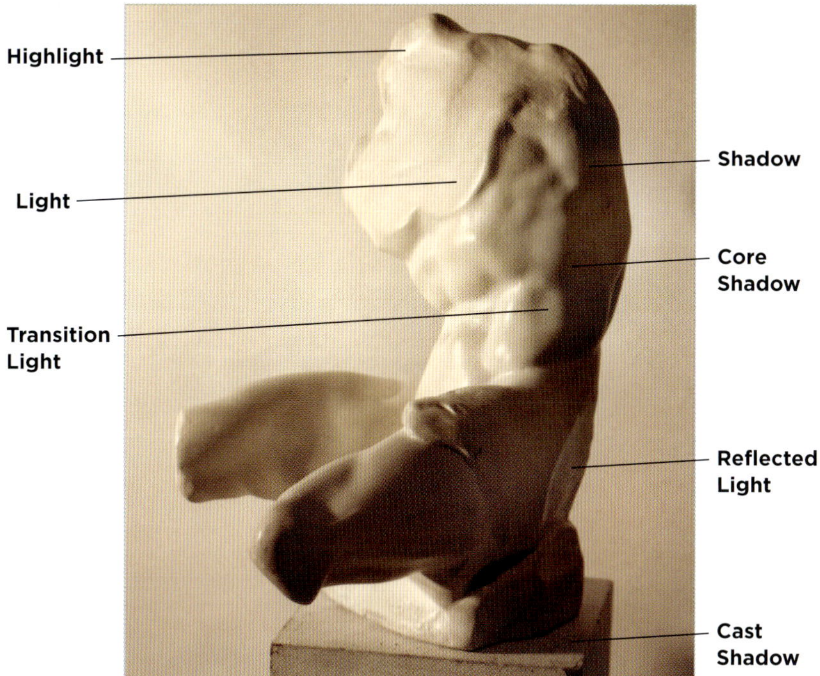

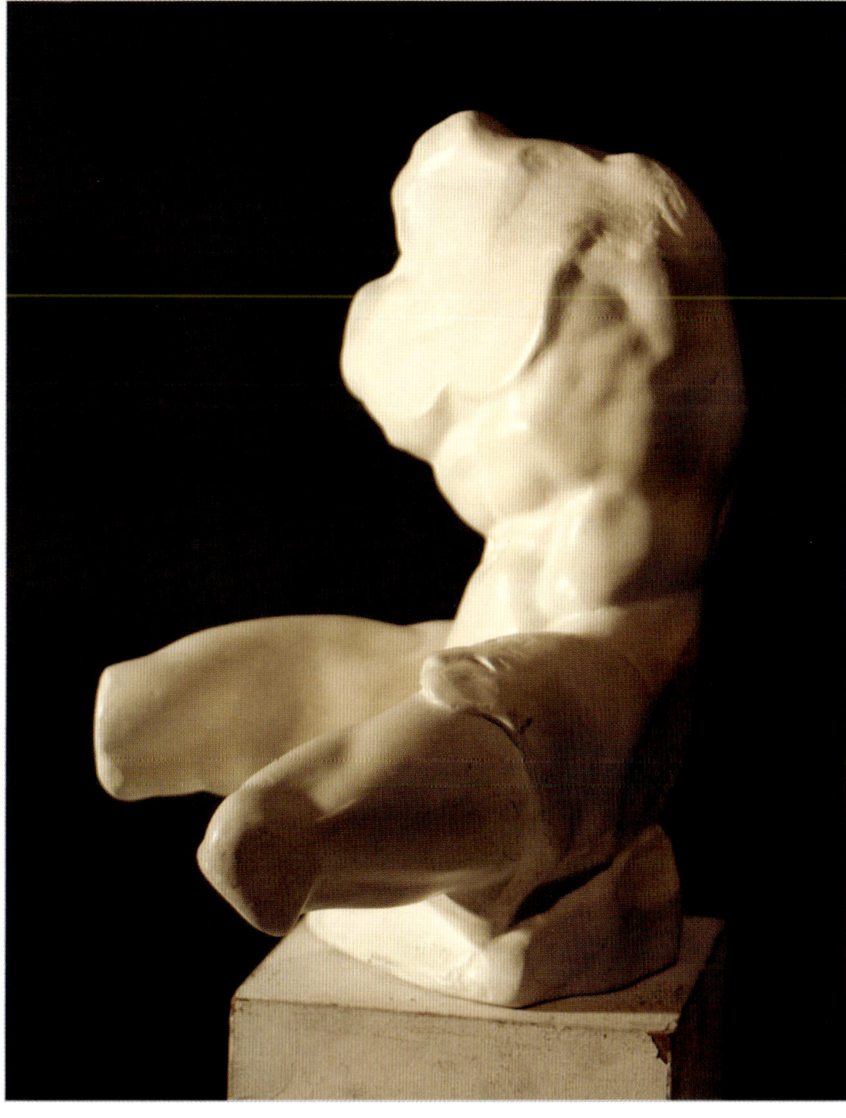

This is the same lighting situation as above, with the exception of a dark background. This arrangement is more dramatic, and dark-value backgrounds are fairly easy to develop with charcoal, compared to most other drawing media.

Tonal Contrast

How we perceive the actual values of a subject depends on the contrasting relationship of values that are adjacent to it. The dark background for this cast statue creates more contrast between the subject and the background, as well as a low-key and dramatic lighting situation. Tonality is a relative situation, based on the effects of lighting and adjacent values. When you compare the statues on page 143, you can see the relative differences in the appearance of the values, especially in the shaded areas—particularly the core shadows, which appear darker in the statue with the lighter background.

Use a variety of charcoal to create this scale from very light to rich, velvety black. From left to right: vine charcoal, compressed charcoal, and charcoal pencil, all blended with a chamois or tissue.

Tonal Techniques with Charcoal

Start with a value scale like the one above, using all the charcoal materials you plan to use in your drawing. In almost every tonal charcoal drawing, use the same tools (see above), usually in the same order, for the best results. It's important to remember that using lighter to darker tools—and generalized techniques before details—is a key to success.

The best way to fully understand the strengths and weaknesses of each material is to experiment. There are no set rules with these materials. You can use all of them, or leave some out completely. Most people work best when they have all these tools at their disposal, along with a logical progression in which to use them.

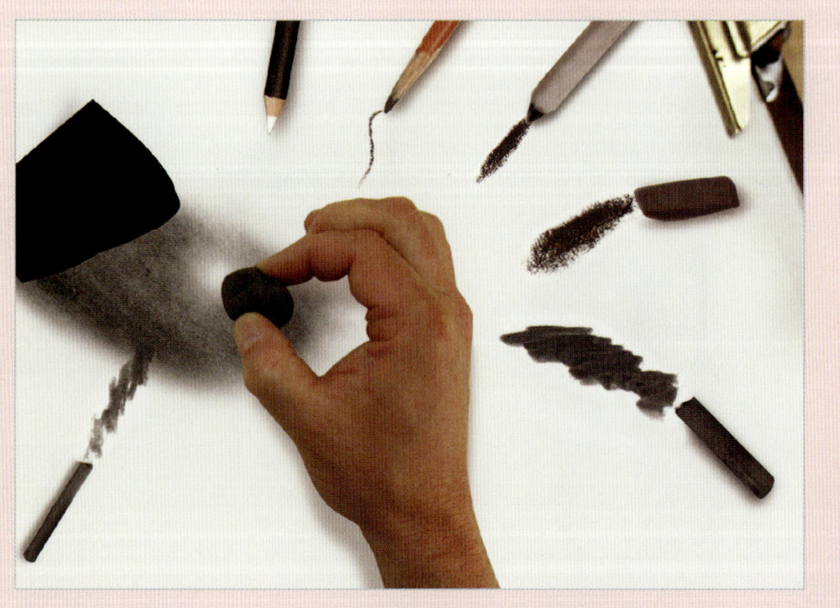

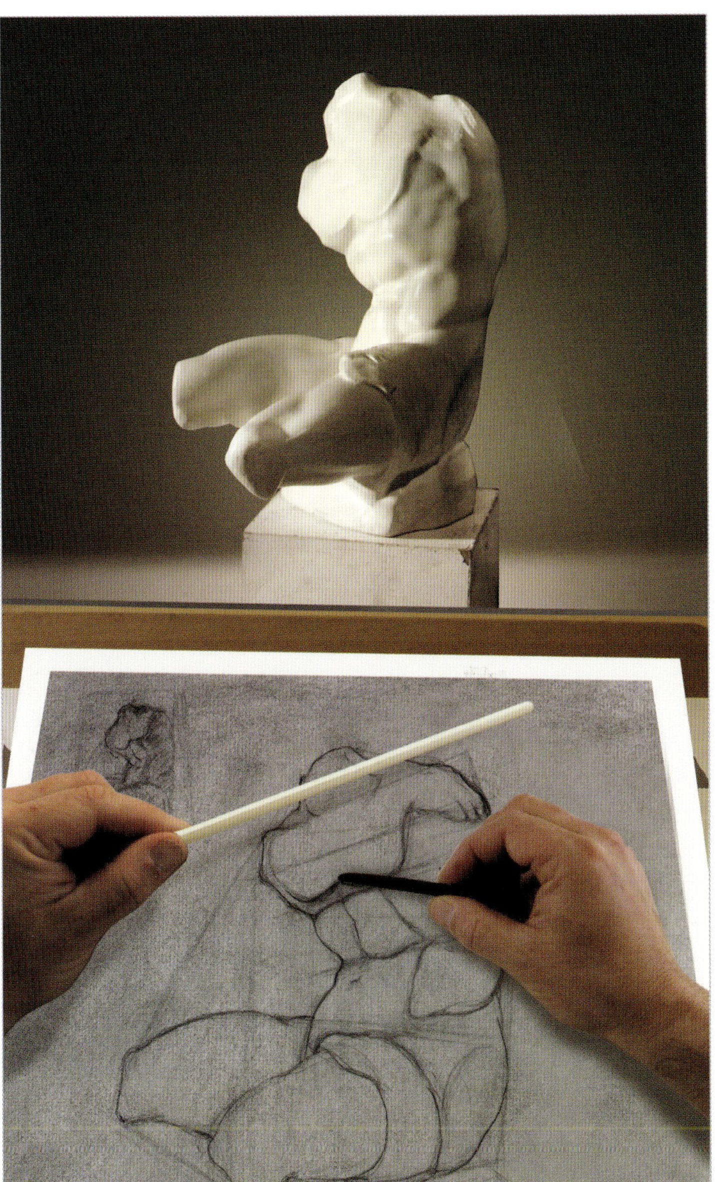

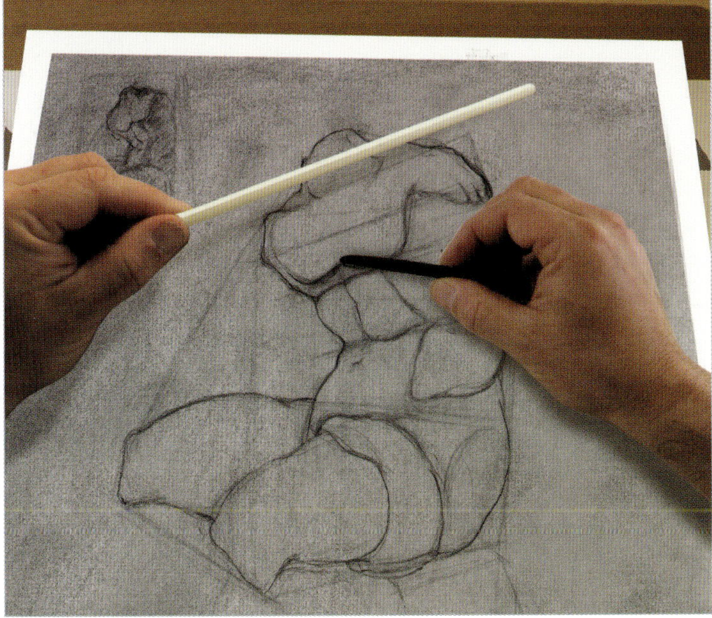

STEP 1 Tone the surface of white charcoal paper with vine or willow charcoal, stroking across the paper with the side of the charcoal. Then rub softly with a chamois or tissue. After sketching a small thumbnail in the upper corner, create an overall gesture sketch with a stick of vine charcoal, which is light, soft, and easily changeable. Use a chopstick for linear angles, horizontal and vertical alignments, and relative proportions within the torso.

STEP 2 When you're satisfied with the sketch, go over it lightly with a hard or medium charcoal pencil. This step is important, as the soft vine sketch lines can disappear quickly as you begin to develop the tonal range.

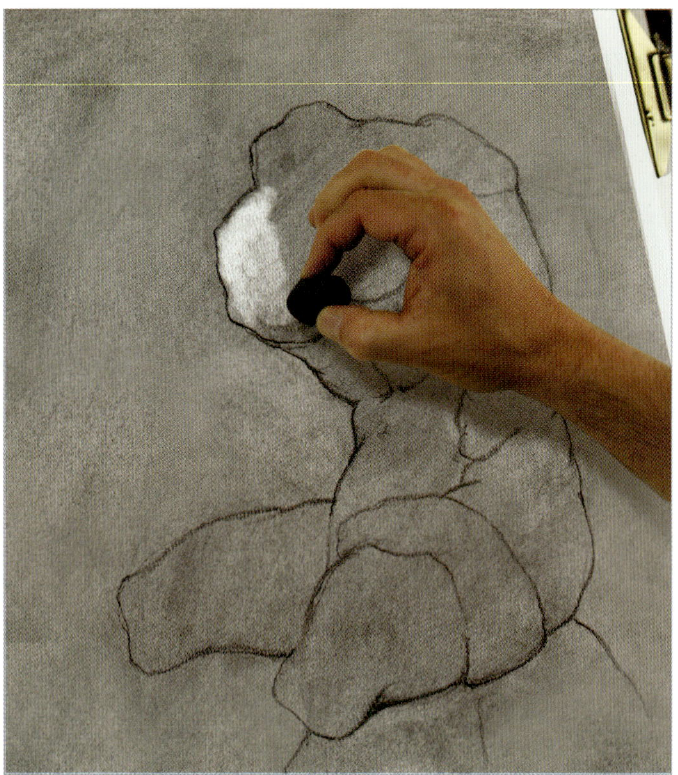

STEP 3 Next begin to pull out the generalized lighting on the form with a kneaded eraser. Don't attempt to achieve too much detail at this stage; it will likely disappear and need to be redone toward the end of the tonal process.

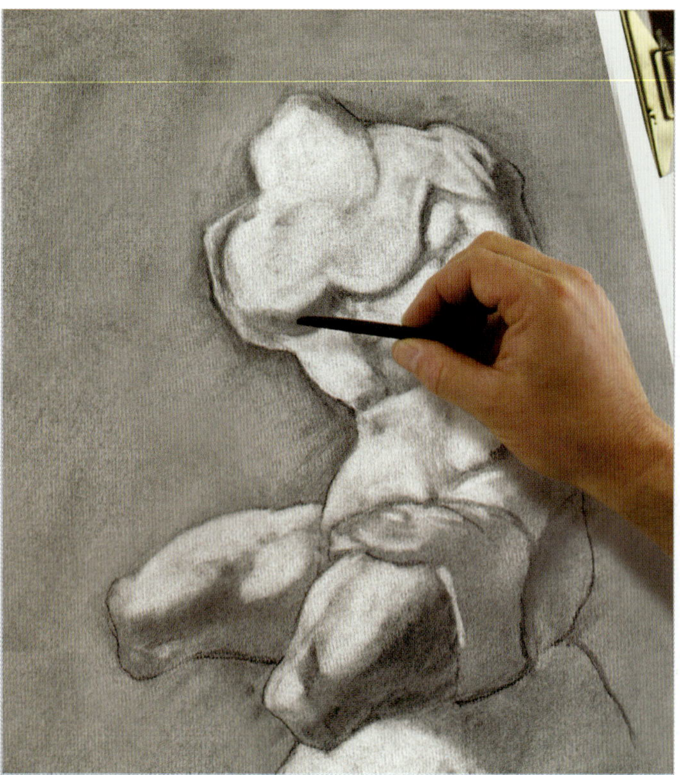

STEP 4 After pulling out the generalized lights, add in the overall shadows—the third value—with vine or willow charcoal.

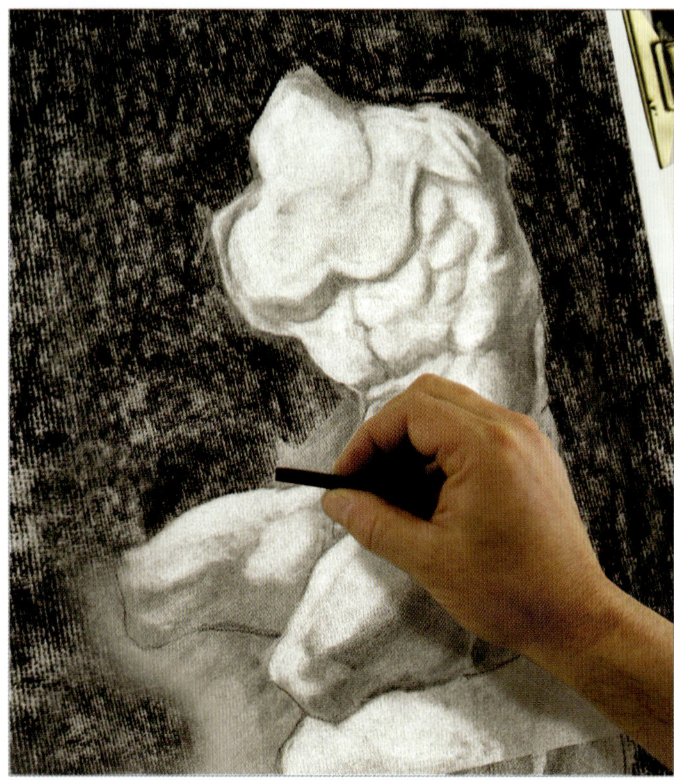

STEP 5 About mid-way through the tonal application process, it's a good idea to block in the background value, especially if it is a dark background. This makes it easier to judge the values within the subject. Try using a stick of compressed charcoal for this purpose, as it is darker and more permanent than either vine or willow charcoal.

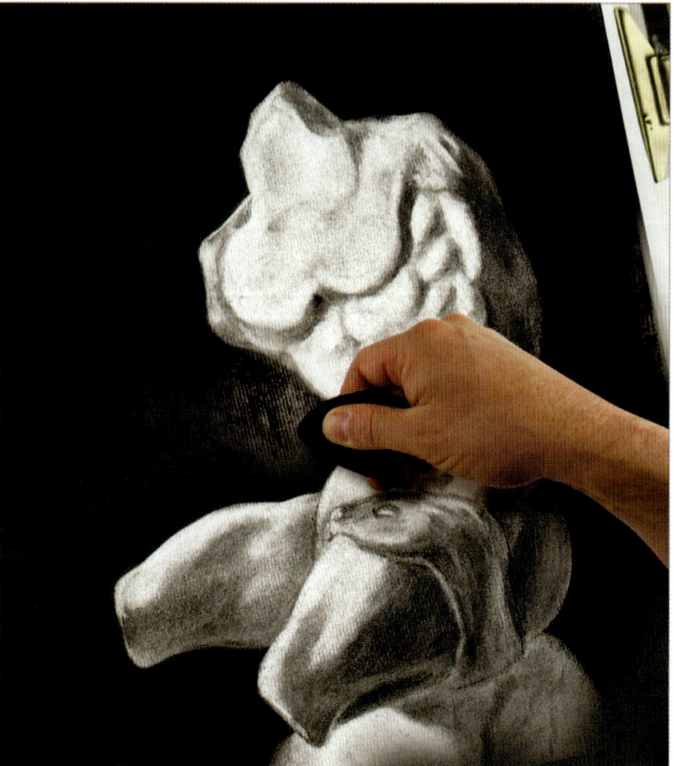

STEP 6 Use a chamois to rub the charcoal into the paper for soft and even tone. Compressed charcoal provides a velvety, rich black. At this point, apply a light spray of workable fixative over the entire surface to help adhere the compressed charcoal to the paper.

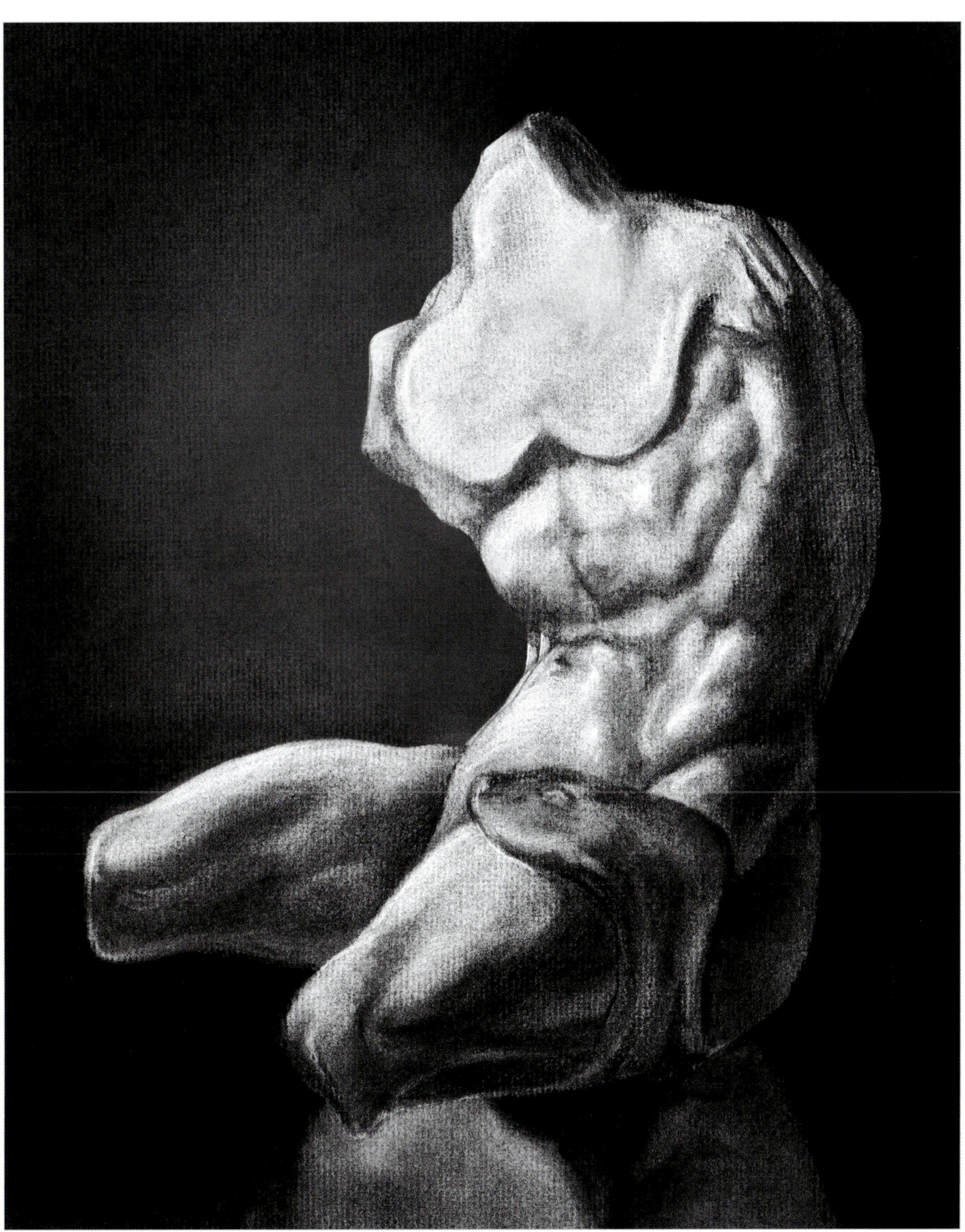

STEP 7 Apply the finishing touches. Clean up and refine the edges with a kneaded eraser. Then use charcoal pencils (soft grade), to create dark core shadows and cast shadows on the form. You can use a stump or tortillon to smooth the darker surfaces. Finally, use a white charcoal pencil sparingly to accent the lights and create highlights. It is best not to blend whites, as it tends to muddy them; use the whites conservatively, and leave them alone.

Additional Subject Matter

Still Lifes

In the still life composition below left, the shapes of objects are fairly simple, but the arrangement is complex. By this stage in your drawing education, you should be ready to take on more challenging compositions. Give it a try!

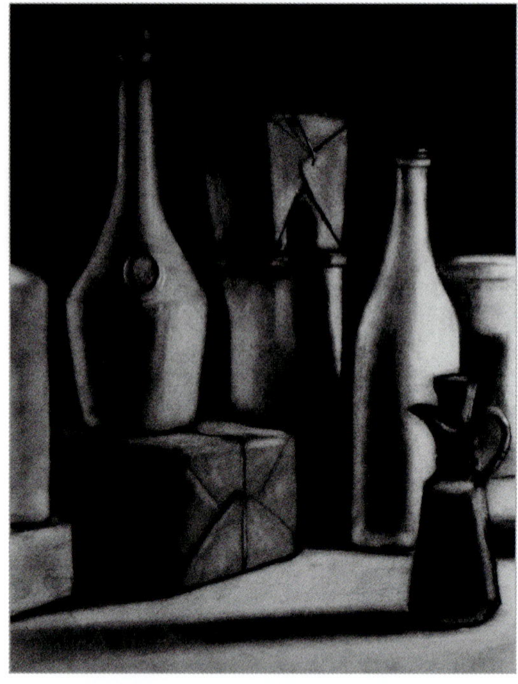

As you progress, you'll be able to approach more complex subject matter, with more value and texture contrasts.

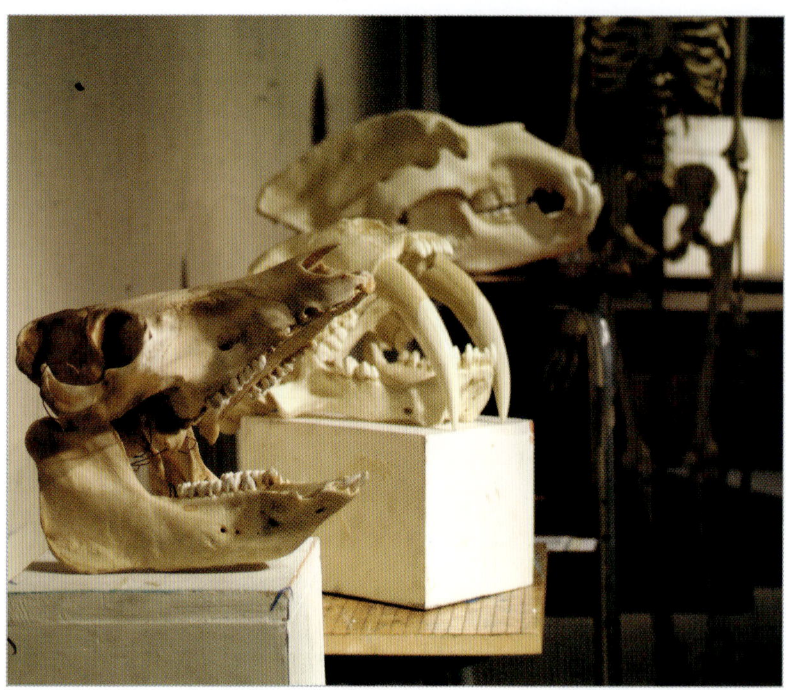

Animal skulls—real or cast in plastic—are also good subjects for drawing white or light-colored objects, and they have a bit more texture and complex structure than cast statues.

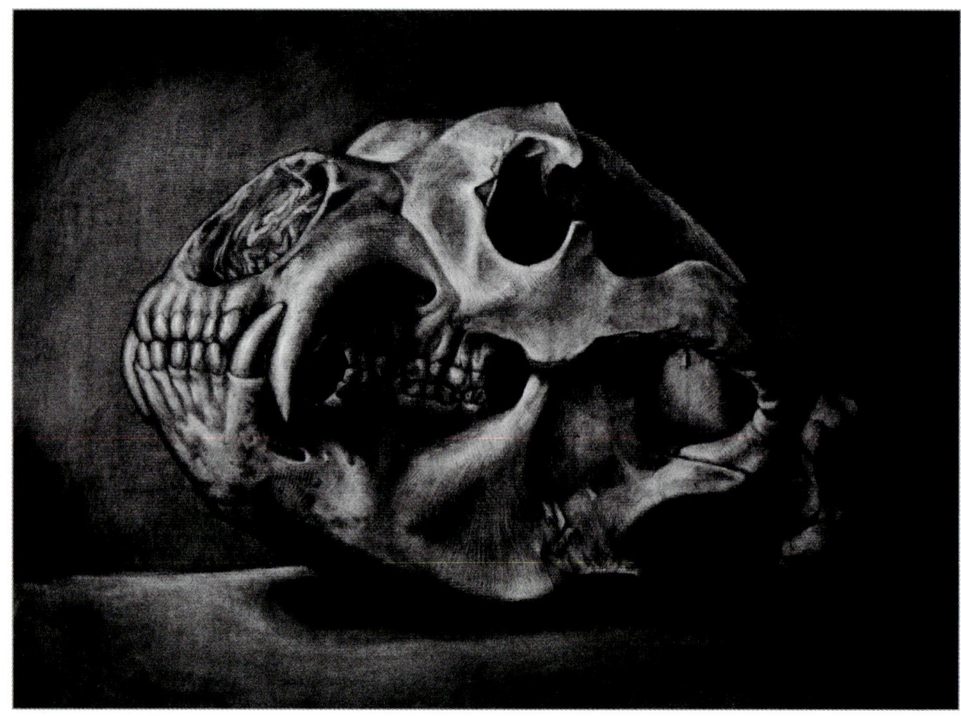

Student tonal drawing by Yea Jin Shin. Notice how the artist used crosshatching very effectively, with both charcoal pencil and white charcoal pencil. Time: 4–5 hours.

Figure Drawing and Charcoal

The speed at which the artist can attain a full value range makes charcoal a natural medium to use for figure drawing. Charcoal can be used for 1- to 2-minute gesture drawings, as well as intermediate poses of 20 to 40 minutes and, of course, for tonal drawings of longer duration. When used on toned paper, the addition of white charcoal for lights and highlights can be expedient as well as dramatic.

This is a 1-minute student gesture drawing in vine charcoal.

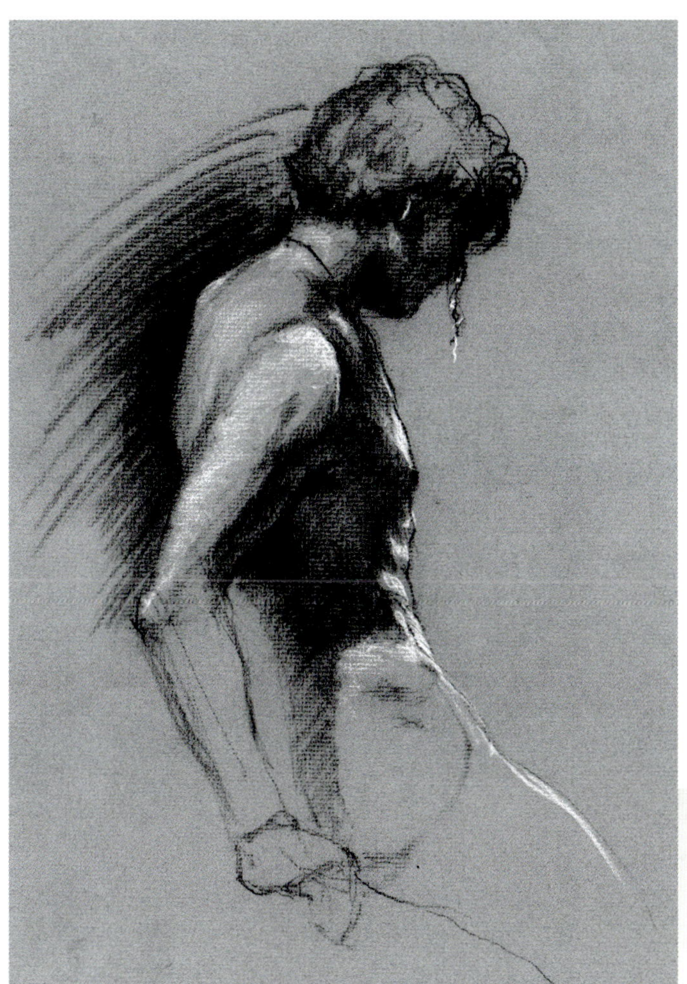

Here is a quick study in black and white charcoal pencil on toned paper. On this middle-value paper, the paper tone becomes the middle value for the softer shadows and reflected light on the figure. The use of white pencil is limited, as it can too easily dominate the value structure.

Charcoal has been used for centuries by artists wishing to portray the human body with dramatic form, mass, volume, and effective tonality. Student charcoal drawing by De Tran.

Conté Crayon

Conté crayons were invented near the end of the eighteenth century in France, and they continue to be used today—especially for drawing the human figure. Their warm, rich tones of sanguine, terra cotta, sienna, and black lend a unique tonal quality to a drawing that few other mediums can. Though waxier than charcoal, with a claylike feel, Conté crayons can be used like charcoal. This medium has hard edges that can be used to draw fine, semi-permanent lines, and it also has superior blending capabilities. Conté crayons come in sets containing several different shades of red and brown, as well as gray, black, and white. They are a very versatile and tactile tonal drawing medium that every serious drawing student should try.

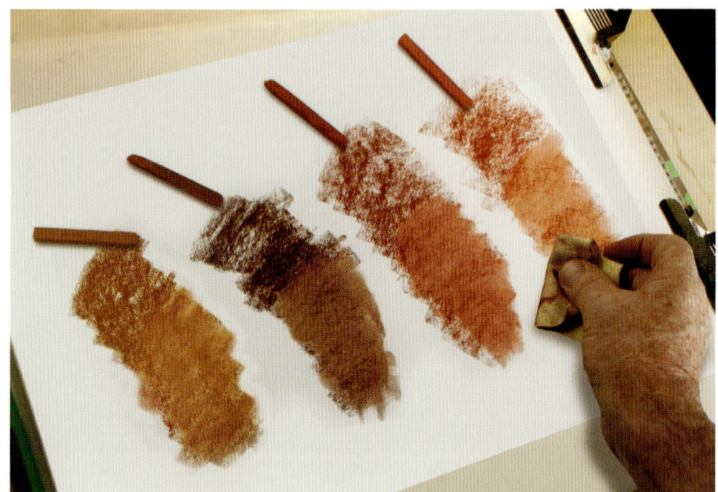

Conté crayons typically come in a variety of earth tones historically related to the color of the soil in different parts of France. They contain a waxy binder that gives them a silky, smooth application and appearance. This range includes a very dark brown (bistre), as well as a very light, reddish orange (sanguine).

Copying the Masters

A great way to improve your drawing technique, with any medium, is to copy a Master drawing, working in the style of the Master artist. Working with the same tools and in the same style and line quality as the Master artist, you will learn to bring that type of quality, and perhaps spontaneity, to your own work. Conté crayon and charcoal are excellent media for replicating the type of tonality and line work used by the Masters.

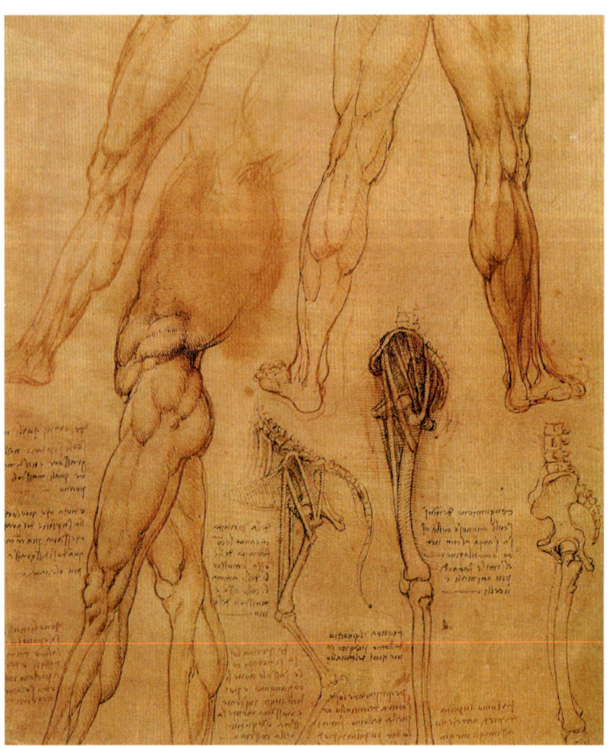

Masters' reproduction drawings are a great way to be introduced to the techniques of the chosen artist. This is a reproduction of a page of anatomical drawings from Leonardo da Vinci's sketchbook on anatomy.

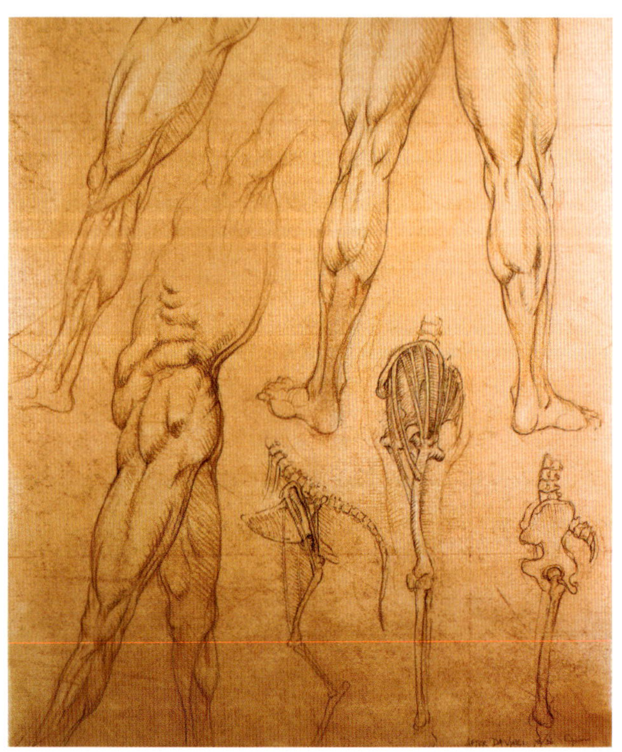

This is an interpretation of da Vinci's work in sanguine Conté crayon and Conté pencil for detail. Conté crayons had not been invented yet in da Vinci's time; he and other Renaissance Masters used various earth-based chalks and earth-toned inks.

For Master reproductions, try using the grid method that was introduced on pages 114–116). If the size of the original reproduction is approximately 8″ x 10″, have students scale up and double the size. This makes the composition large enough to attain good line quality when drawing from the arm and shoulder, yet small enough to fit on standard 18″ x 24″ paper.

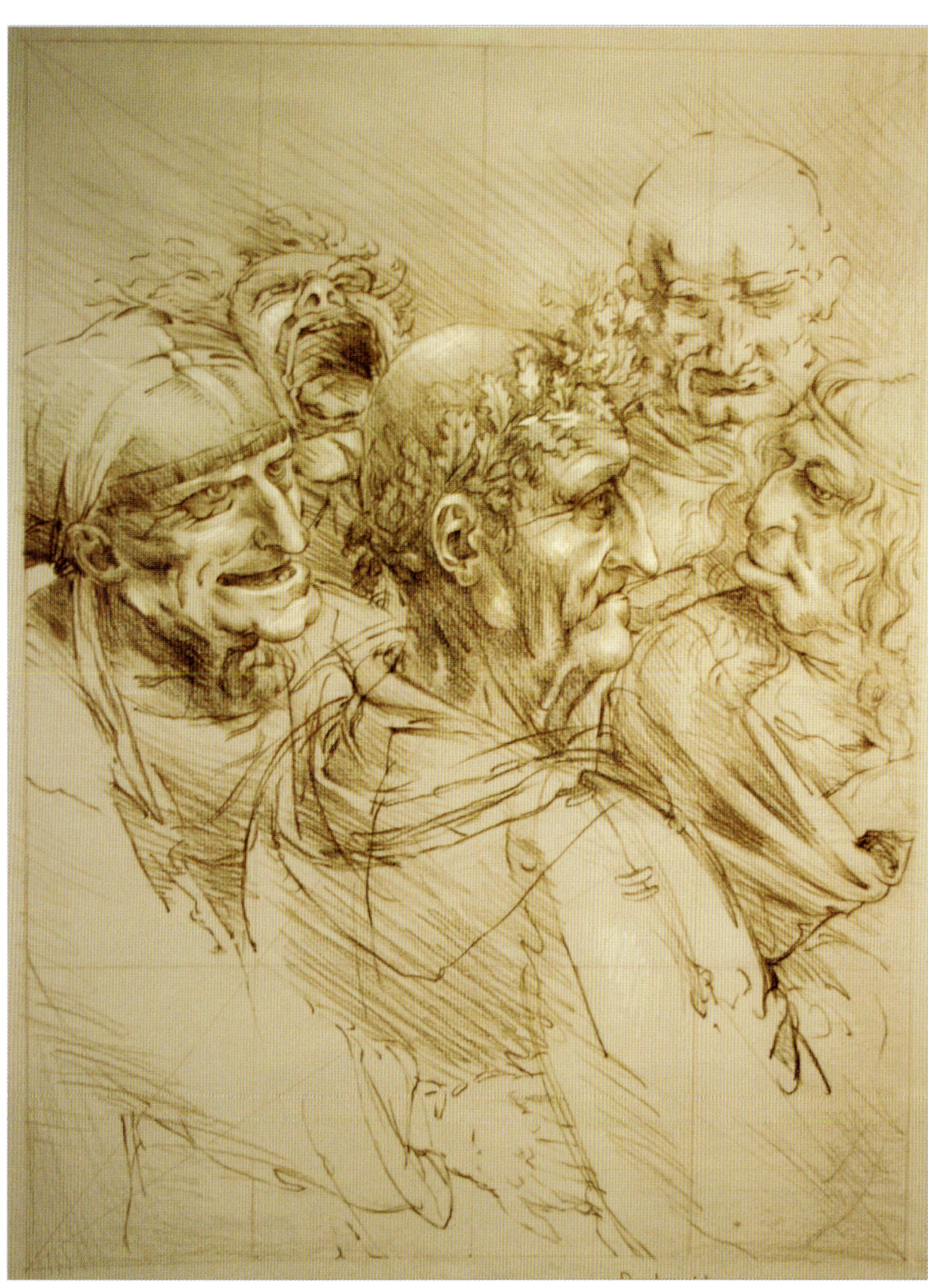

This is a reinterpretation of the *Sketch of Five Characters* by Leonardo da Vinci. The student artist used bistre Conté crayon on cream-colored charcoal paper; the artist did not need to tone the paper with a chamois at the beginning of the drawing, as she intended to use hatching for value—just as da Vinci did in his original sketch. Student drawing by Pauline Huang. Time: 3-4 hours.

YOUR HOMEWORK

Your homework for this chapter is to create a tonal drawing of an old shoe or boot, preferably white (or painted white) for maximum value contrast within the form. Use the torso demonstration at the beginning of this chapter as a guide for the tonal development process.

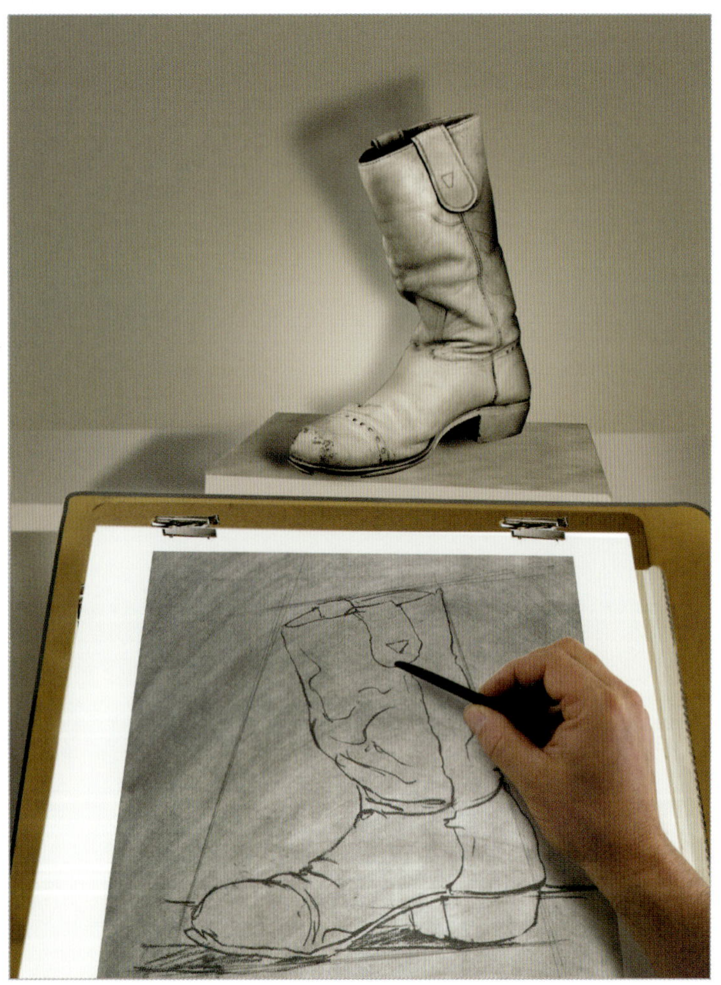

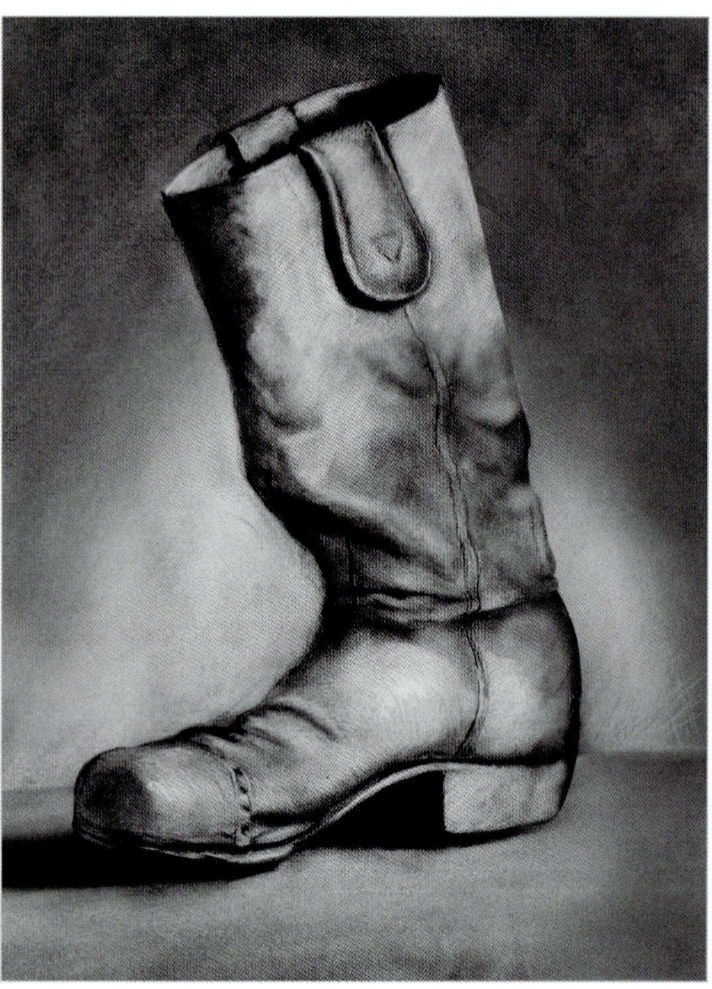

A helpful recipe for achieving value balance in a composition is: a gallon of gray, a pint of black, and a tablespoon of white. This balanced light-logic recipe can be successfully applied to any lighting situation and adjusted for different values in the same ratios (e.g., a gallon of white, a pint of gray, a tablespoon of black).

EXERCISES FOR PRACTICE

In this book-and-coffee still life, the flow of parallel lines through the composition adds interest and movement to an otherwise simple scene.

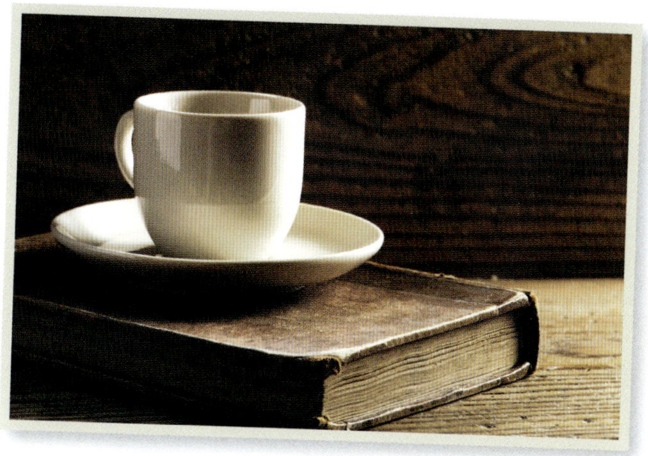

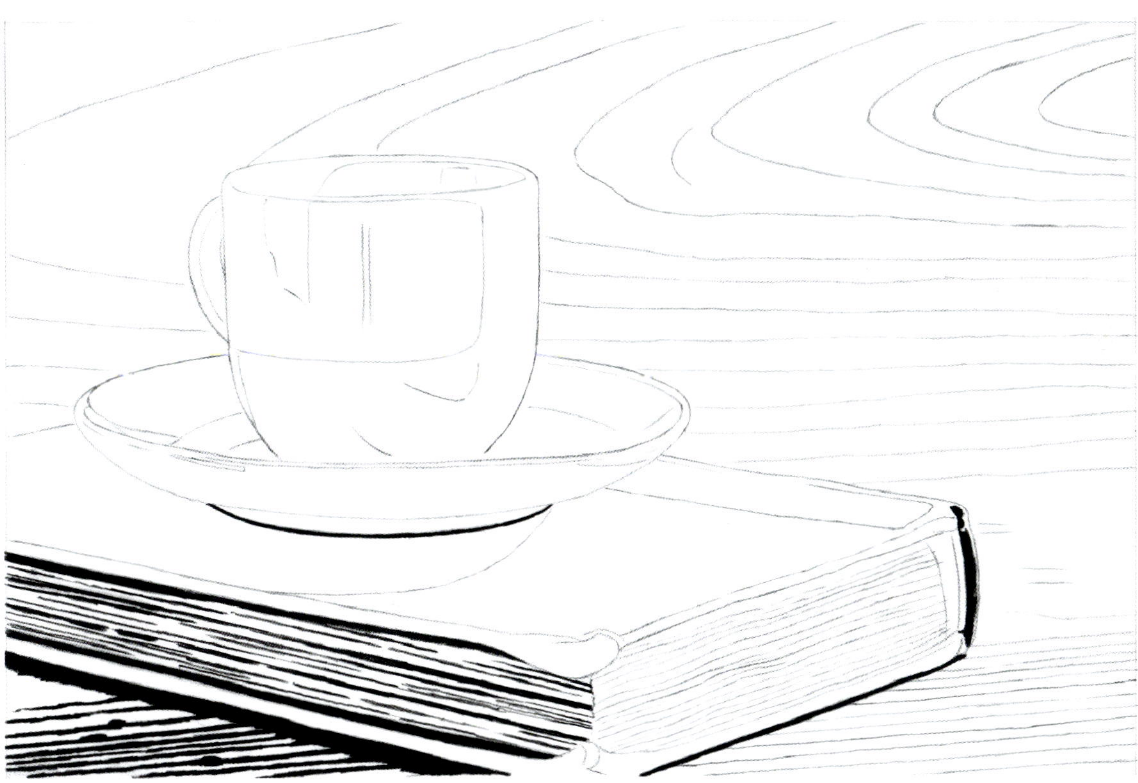

STEP 1 Use a 4B to establish the darkest values on the shaded side of the book and the bottom of the saucer. Also use the 4B to draw in some of the page edges on the shadow side of the book, which will subtly show through later after placing a shadow here. In the cast shadow of the book, use the 4B to create irregular thick lines to represent the deep, weathered wood grain. Also add several dots for holes on the tabletop. At this point, save the background for a later stage, and think about how dark you wish to make it.

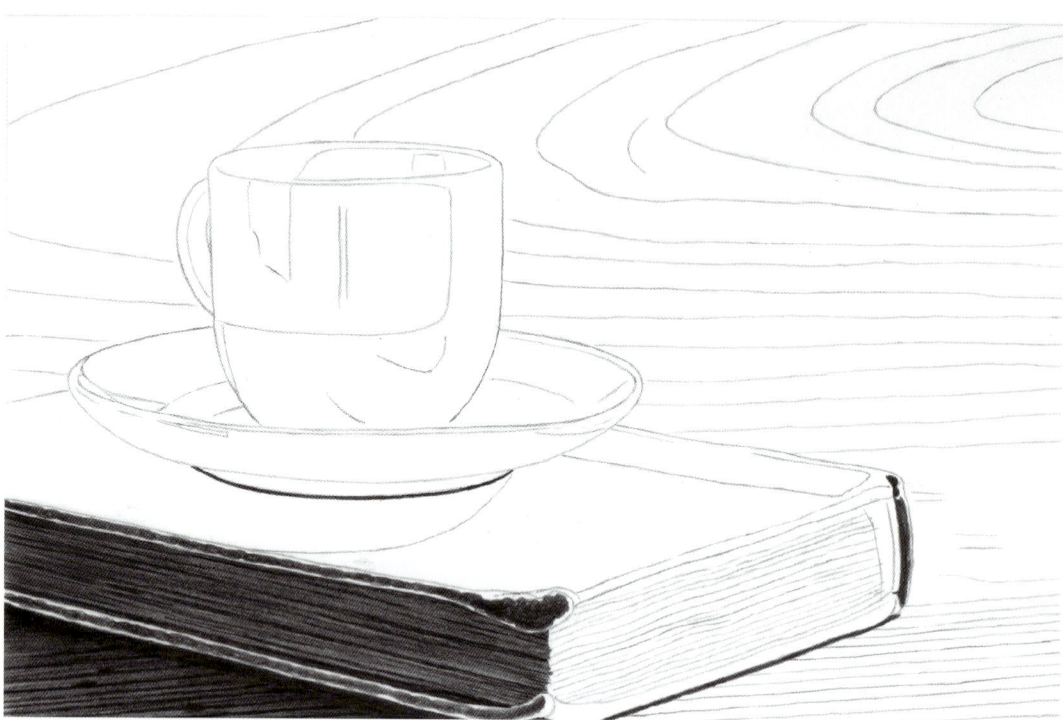

STEP 2 Continuing with the 4B, shade the dark side of the shadowed edge of the book, leaving a white area on each edge of the book cover. To shade in the pages on the shadow side and the shadowed area of the table, use the 2B and draw long strokes parallel to the earlier darker strokes.

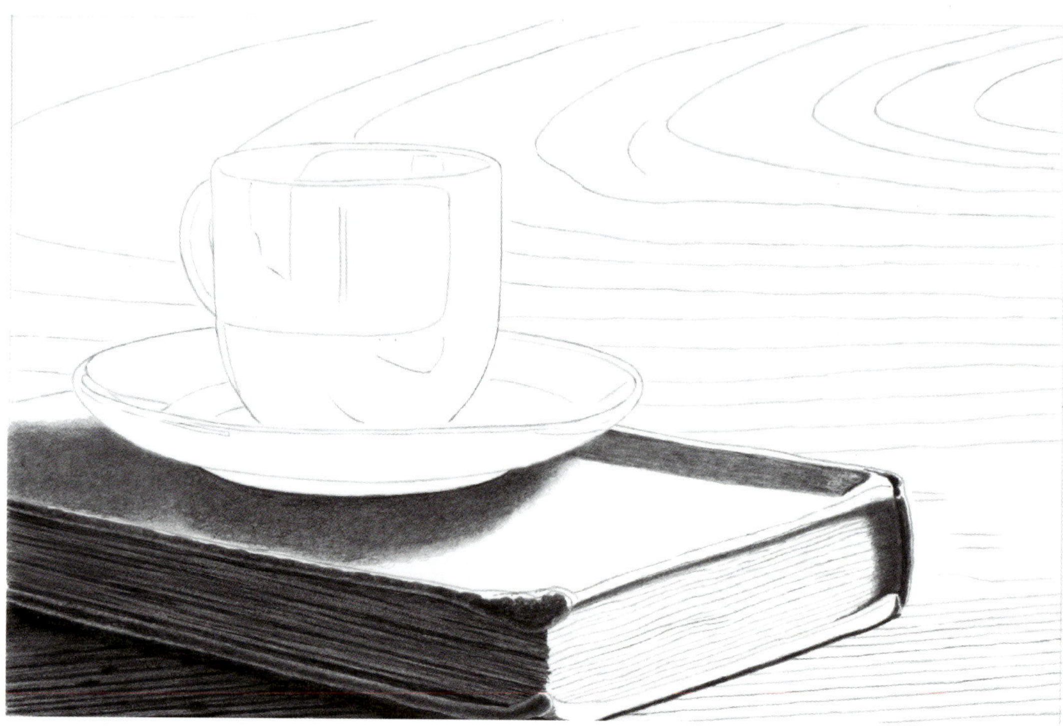

STEP 3 Create the shadows under and around the cup with a 2B using a circular scribbling motion, which will match the texture on the book cover. Use the 2B over the white edges of the book cover on the shadowed side, allowing the darker strokes made earlier to show through. Then draw the small shadow cast by the book spine. Add more strokes along the pages, and then use the 2B for the dark strip on the cover. Resist the urge to blend right away in a drawing that has a lot of texture—you may or may not need any after viewing the finished product.

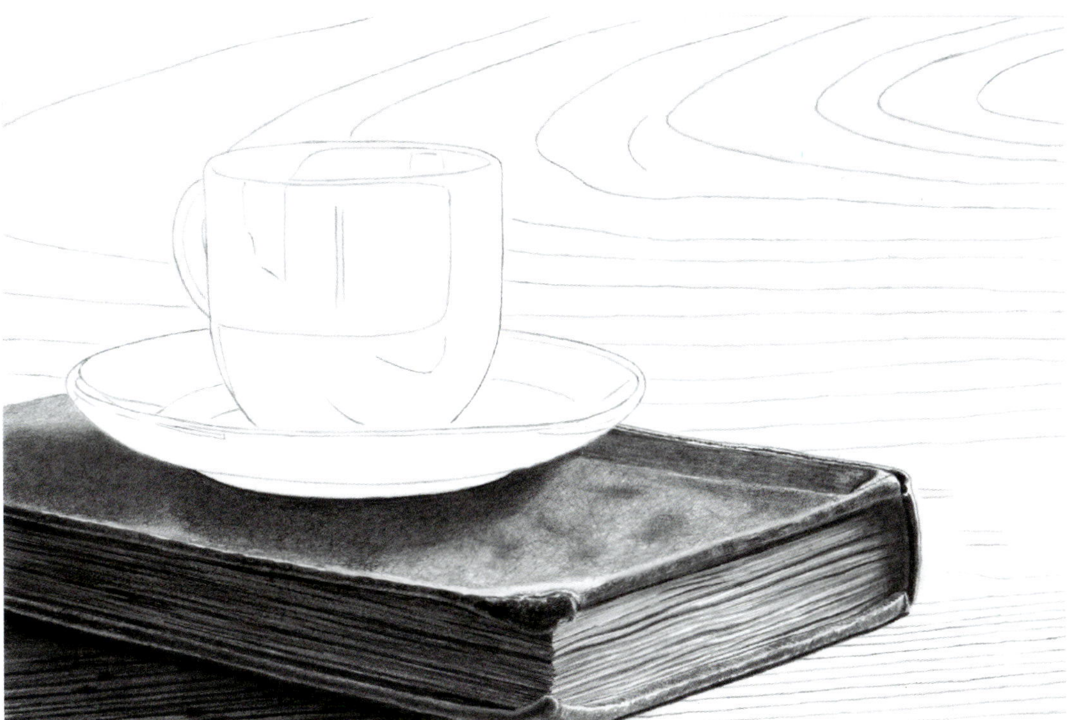

STEP 4 Scribble with a 2B on the remaining edges and front of the book cover, leaving thin, highlighted areas on the edges. Include darker patches as well. Use a 2B for the darker shadows and an HB for the lighter shadows that are created by the pages on the non-shadowed side of the book. There is no need to draw every edge of paper; the viewer's eye will do the work.

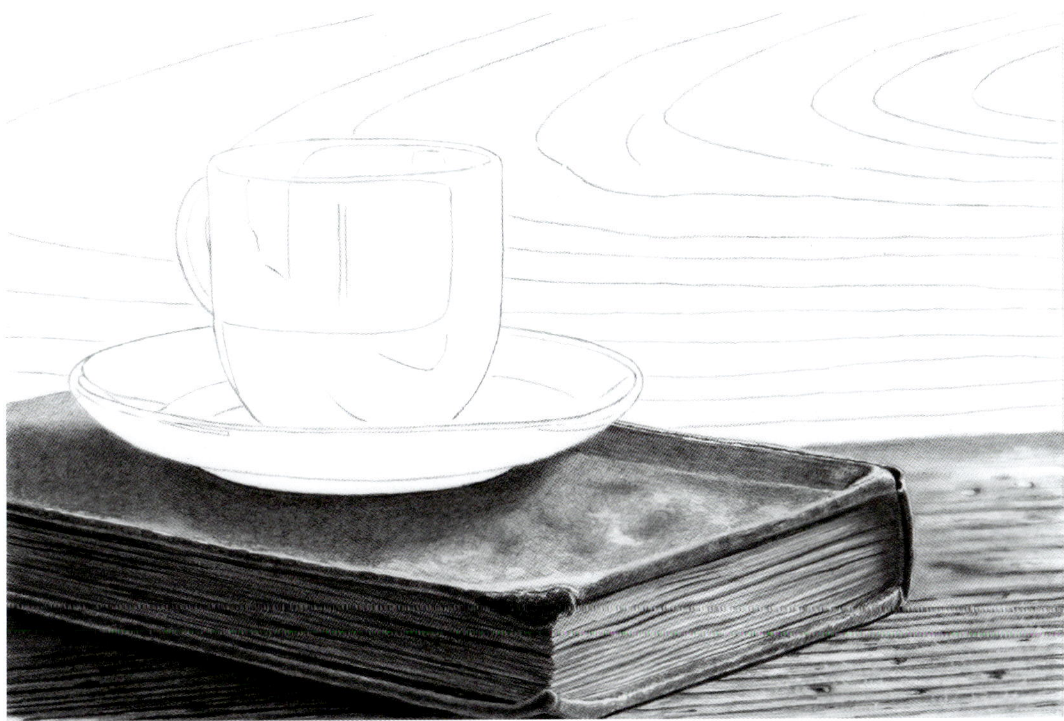

STEP 5 Finishing the non-shadowed side of the tabletop, use a 2B and an HB to draw thicker wood grain and add the imperfections. Between the wood grain, lightly shade with the HB and blend with a tortillon. The table blurs toward the background as it moves out of focus, so use a tortillon dipped in graphite to create this texture. Create the lighter areas and imperfections of the wood grain with a sharpened pencil eraser. Use it to bring out some of the lighter areas on the surface of the book cover.

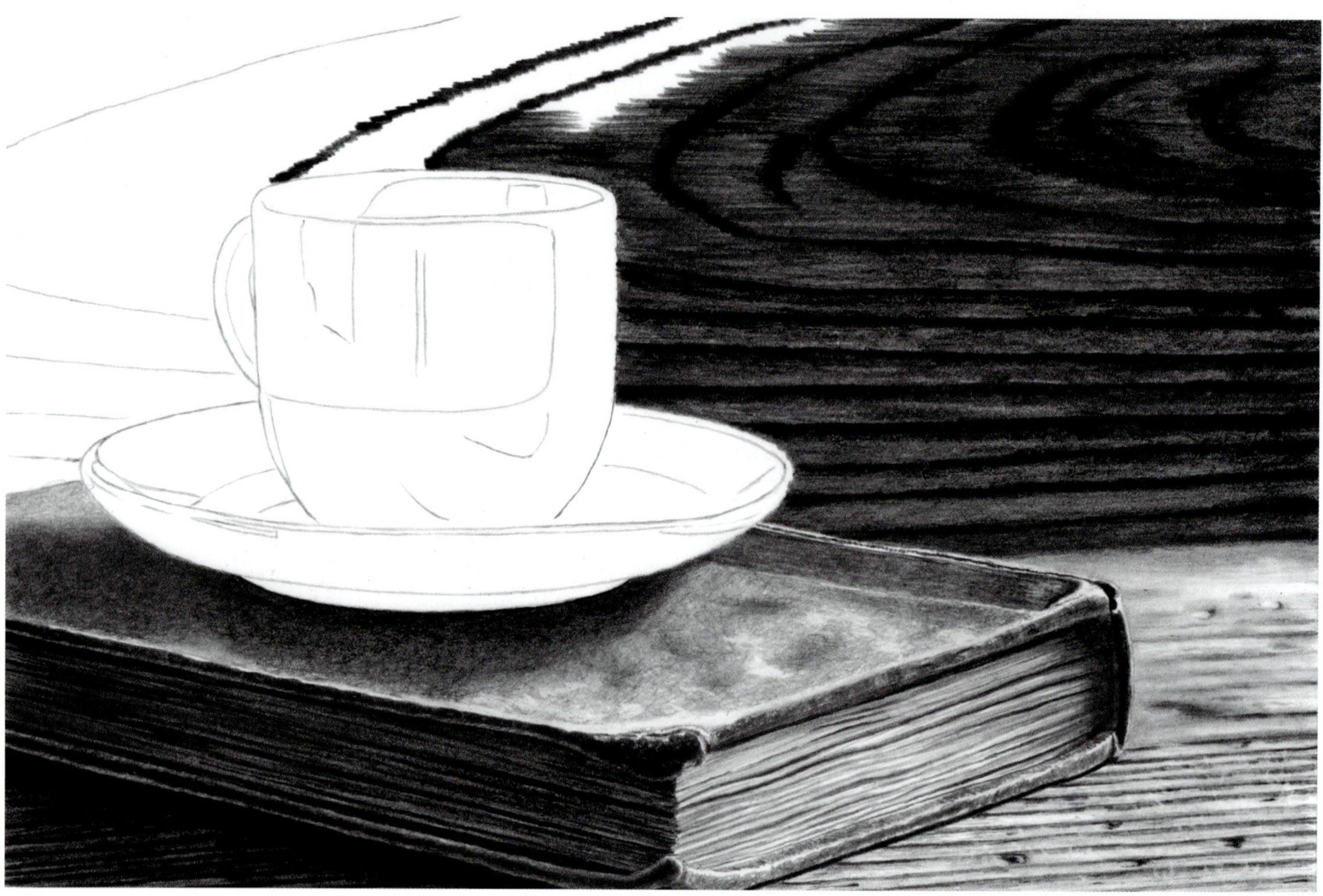

STEP 6 Work on the background wood before the cup. Use a 6B for the dark wood grain. Make it thick, and don't worry about getting it perfect. Then go over the entire background with a 4B using horizontal stokes, making sure they are visible. Notice that one side of the thick wood grain is shadowed, which gives it a raised, weathered look. Use the 6B on these areas.

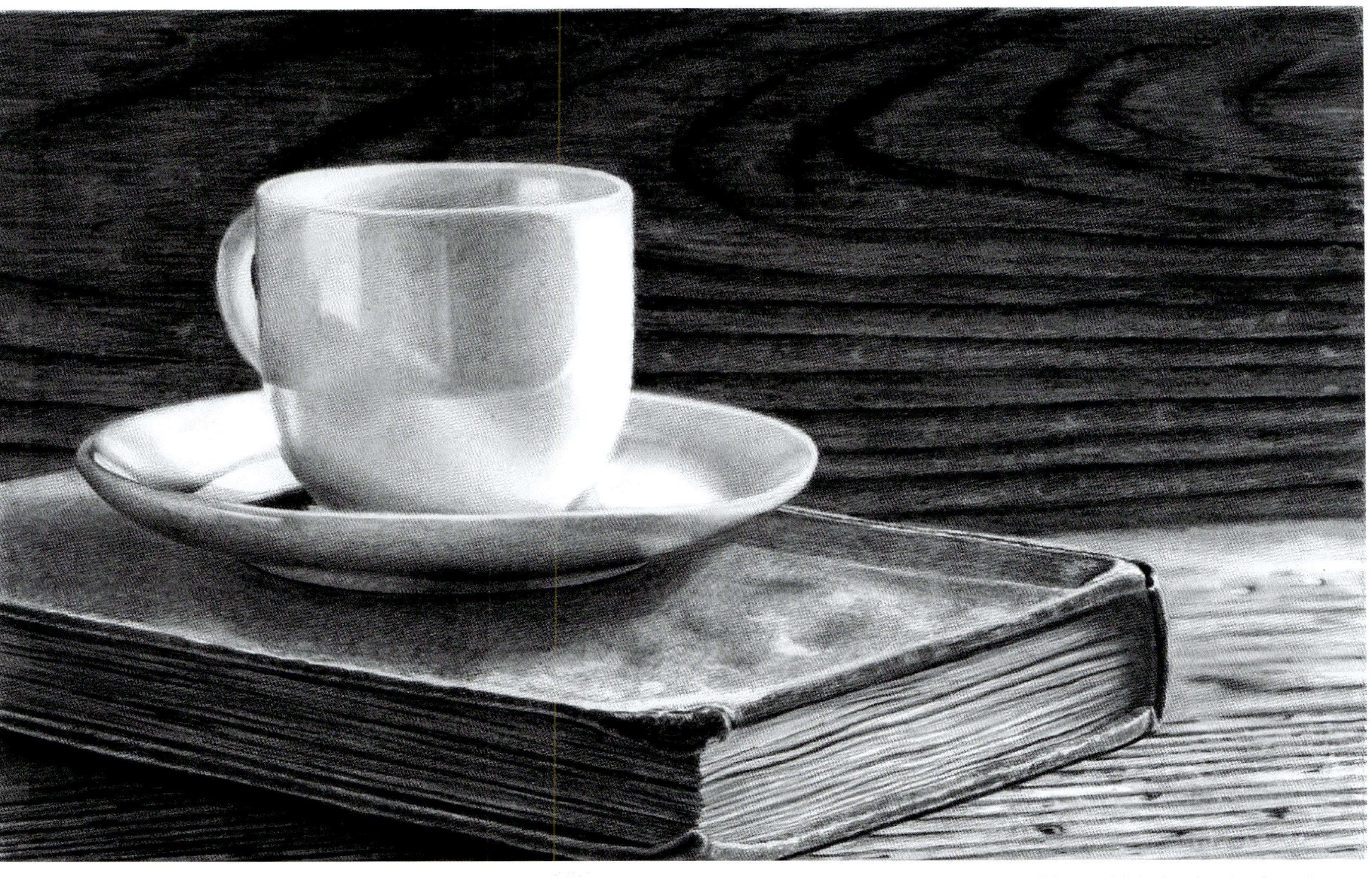

STEP 7 Use 2B, HB, and F pencils to shade the various shadows on the cup, and then use both a tortillon and a tissue to blend. Finish the drawing by using a kneaded eraser to pull out some graphite to create the imperfections on the background.

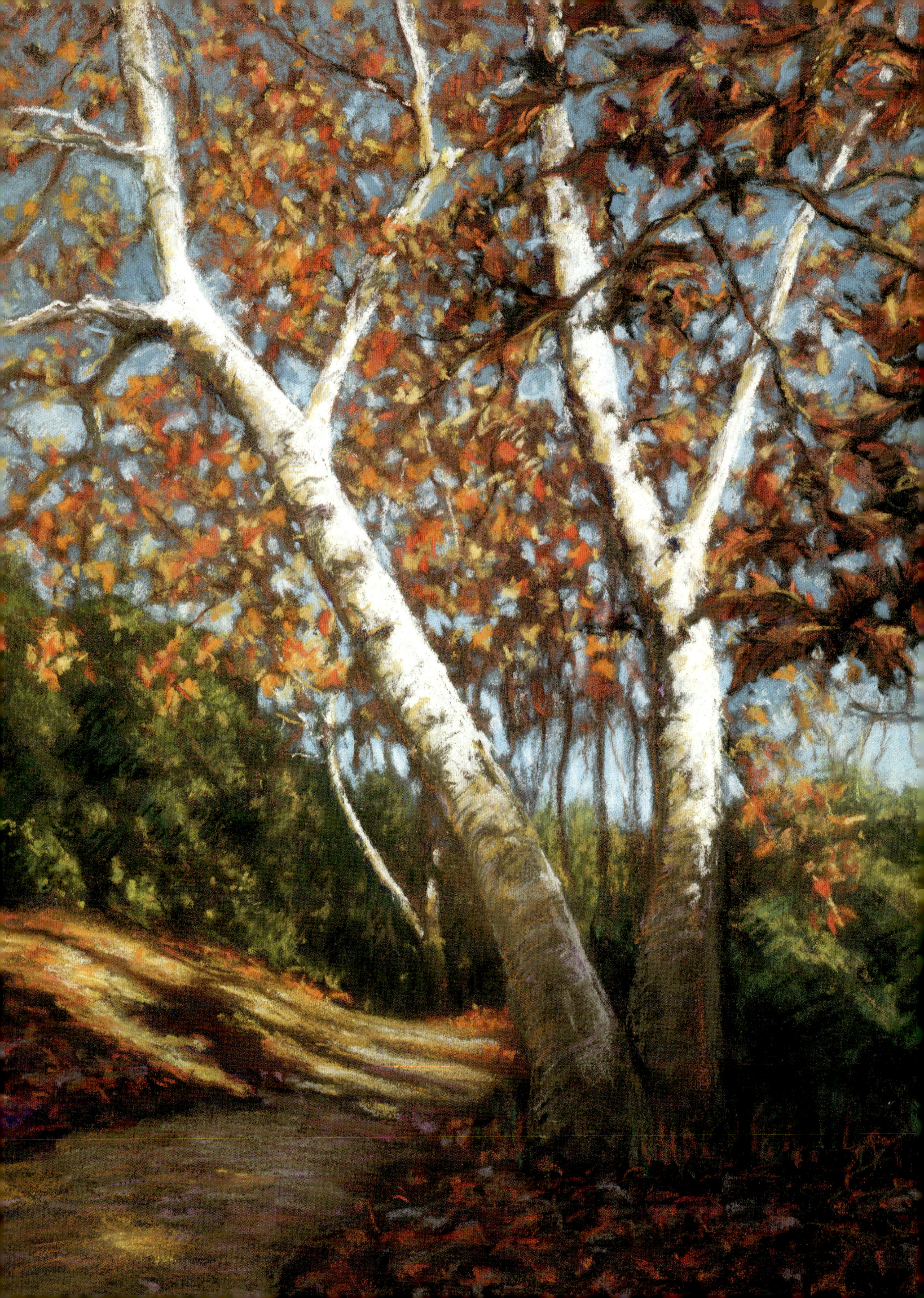

COLOR

This chapter deals with two different drawing media: colored pencil and pastel. This chapter is not meant to be a color theory or painting class, but rather a simple introduction to the beauty and pleasure that color can bring, as well as an introductory lesson in color application with drawing media. As we learned in the previous chapter, value can add drama to a drawing, and in the last chapter, we'll see how perspective is the mathematics of drawing. But in this chapter, we'll explore how color is the magic in drawing.

Colored Pencil

Colored pencil is a versatile drawing medium that can emulate watercolor, oil, or pastel effects. It can also be used successfully on its own or in conjunction with other dry media for high contrast, intense color, and value application.

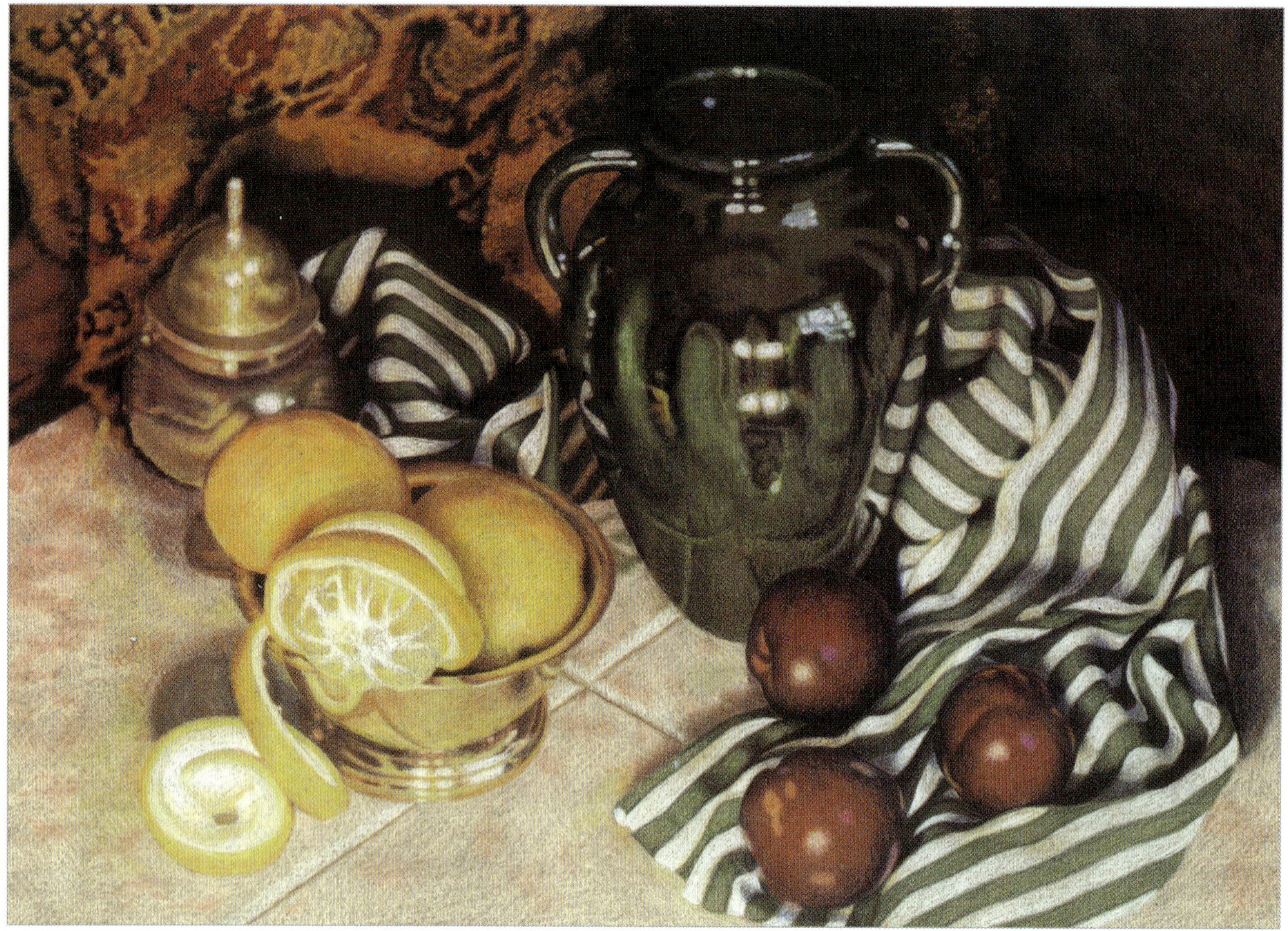

Student colored pencil drawing. Time: 12–15 hours.

The best and easiest way to develop high-contrast, high-chromatic drawings in colored pencil is to use gray marker as an initial value underpainting, with glazes of transparent and opaque colored pencil layered on top—a technique known as *grisaille*. Similarly, gray marker on gray toned paper acts as a monochromatic underpainting upon which transparent glazes of colored pencil can be applied, without a heavy buildup of wax—a key ingredient in most colored pencils. Too much waxy buildup on paper will limit the artist in the number of colors and layers that can be successfully used, which can be problematic when trying to build up color and value simultaneously with only colored pencil. By applying a marker underpainting, the value is already there, soaked into the paper without any changes in paper surface. At the end of the process, the brightest and lightest colors can be applied as strongly as desired with a technique called "burnishing," which involves laying down heavier pressure with the opaque light colors.

Color Basics

Colored pencils are transparent by nature, so instead of "mixing" colors as you would for painting, you layer colors on top of one another to create blends. Knowing a little about basic color theory can help you tremendously in drawing with colored pencils. The primary colors (red, yellow, and blue) are the three basic colors that can't be created by mixing other colors; all other colors are derived from these three. Secondary colors (orange, green, and purple) are each a combination of two primaries, and tertiary colors (red-orange, red-purple, yellow-orange, yellow-green, blue-green, and blue-purple) are a combination of a primary color and a secondary color.

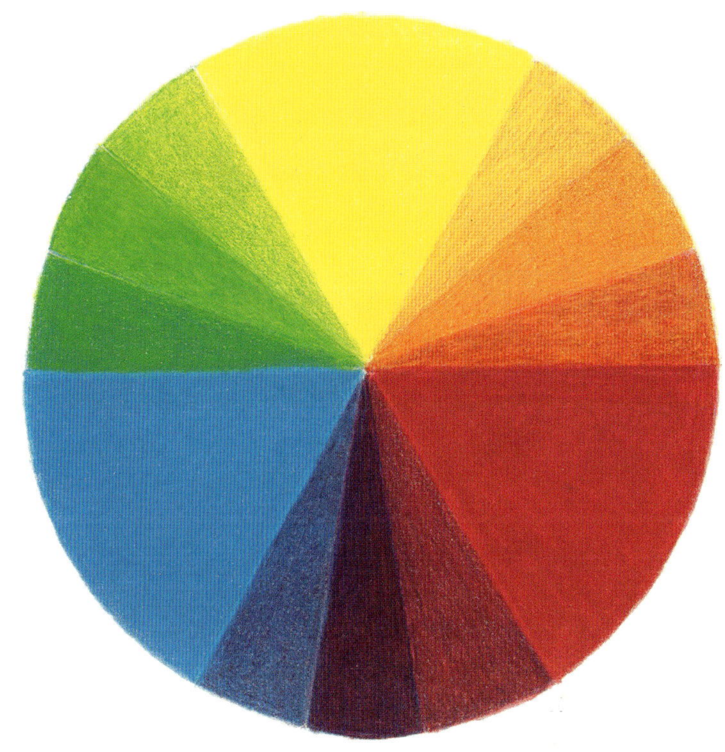

COLOR WHEEL A color wheel is a useful reference tool for understanding color relationships. Knowing where each color lies on the color wheel makes it easy to understand how colors relate to and react with one another.

Complementary Colors

Complementary colors are any two colors directly across from each other on the color wheel (such as red and green, orange and blue, or yellow and purple). You can actually see combinations of complementary colors in nature—for instance, if you look at white clouds in a blue sky, you'll notice a hint of orange in the clouds.

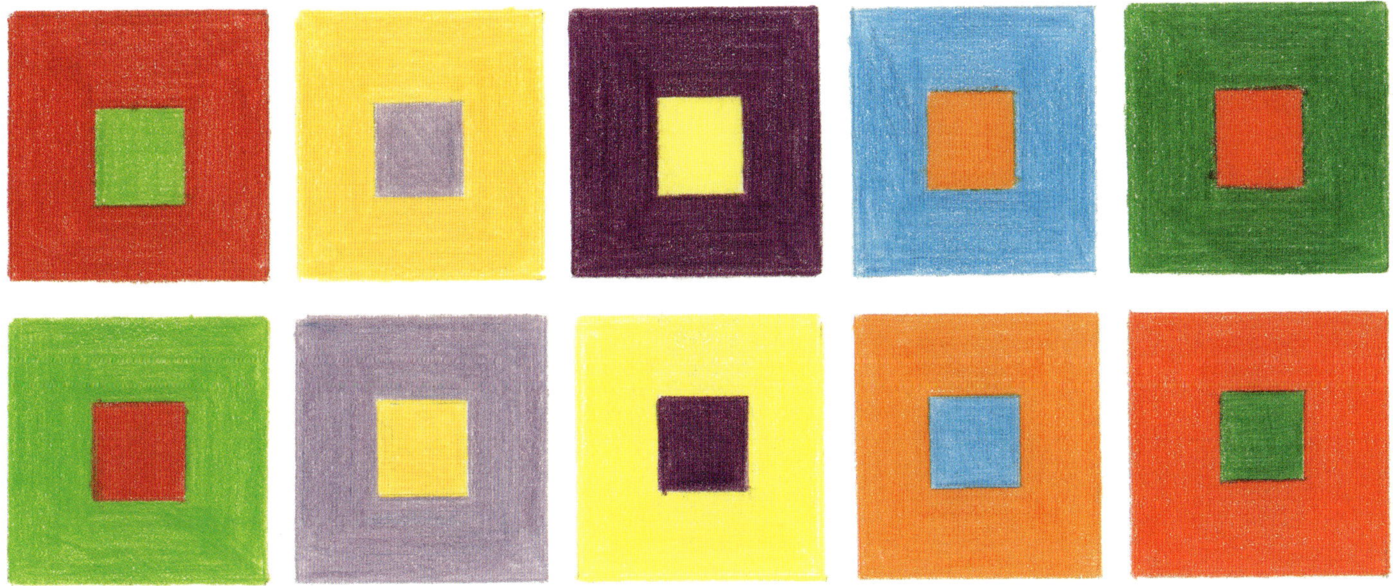

USING COMPLEMENTS When placed next to each other, complementary colors create lively, exciting contrasts. Using a complementary color in the background will cause your subject to seemingly "pop" off the paper. For example, you could place bright orange poppies against a blue sky or draw red berries amid green leaves.

Colored Pencil Techniques

Colored pencil is an amazingly satisfying medium to work with because it's so easily manipulated and controlled. The way you sharpen your pencil, the way you hold it, and the amount of pressure you apply all affect the strokes you create. With colored pencils, you can create everything from soft blends to brilliant highlights to realistic textures. Once you get the basics down, you'll be able to decide which techniques capture your subject's unique qualities. There are as many techniques in the art of colored pencil as there are effects—and the more you practice and experiment, the more potential you will see in the images that inspire you.

Pressure

Colored pencil is not like paint: You can't just add more color to the tip when you want it to be darker. Because of this, your main tool is the amount of pressure you use to apply the color. It is always best to start light so that you maintain the tooth of the paper for as long as possible. Eventually, you will develop the innate ability to change the pressure on the pencil in response to the desired effect.

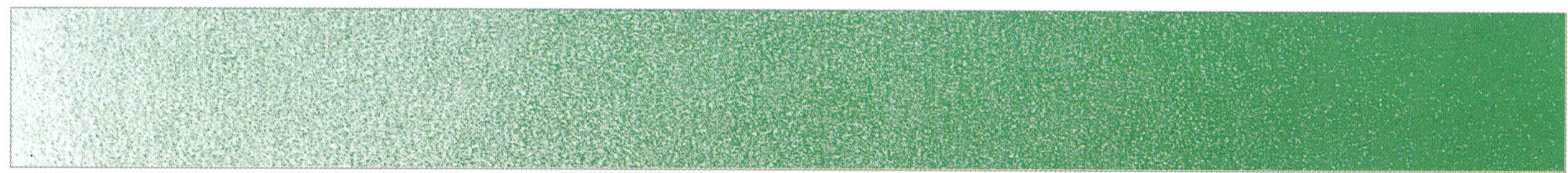

LIGHT PRESSURE Here color was applied by just whispering a sharp pencil over the paper's surface. With light pressure, the color is almost transparent.

MEDIUM PRESSURE This middle range creates a good foundation for layering. This is also the pressure you might want to use when signing your drawings.

HEAVY PRESSURE Really pushing down on the pencil flattens the paper's texture, making the color appear almost solid.

Strokes

The direction, width, and texture of each line you draw will contribute to the effects you create. Practice making different types of strokes. You may have a natural tendency toward one or two strokes in particular, but any stroke can help convey texture and emotion in your work.

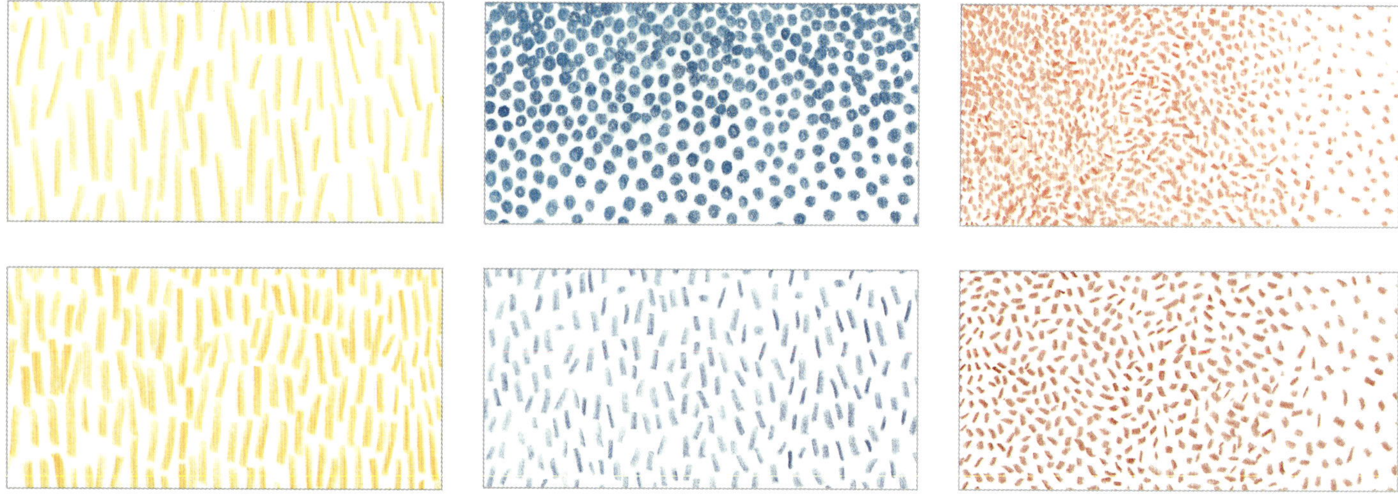

STROKES AND TEXTURE You can imitate a number of different textures by creating patterns of dots and dashes on the paper. To create dense, even dots, twist the point of your pencil on the paper.

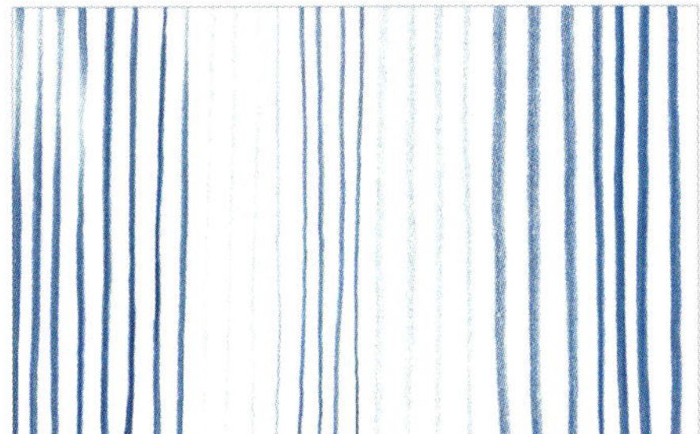

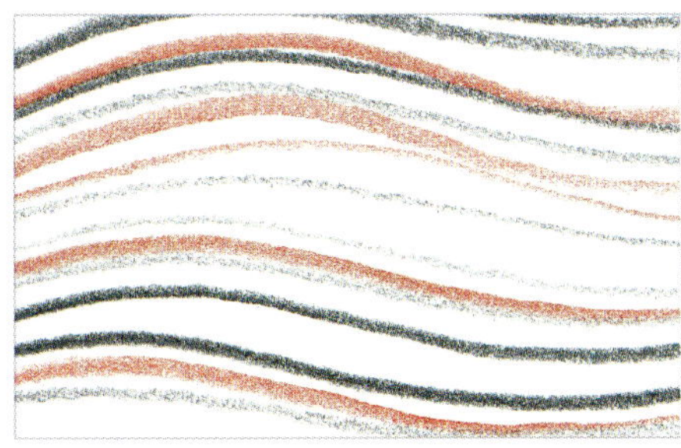

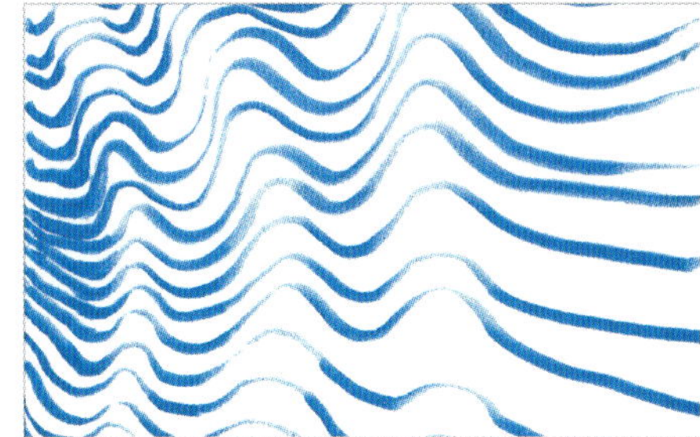

STROKES AND MOVEMENT While a group of straight lines can suggest direction (above left), a group of slightly curved lines (above right) conveys a sense of motion more clearly. Try combining a variety of strokes to create a more turbulent, busy design. These exercises can give you an idea of how lines and strokes can be expressive as well as descriptive.

VARIED LINE Vary the width and weight of the lines you create to make them more textured and interesting. These calligraphic lines can create a feeling of dimension in your drawing.

Types of Strokes

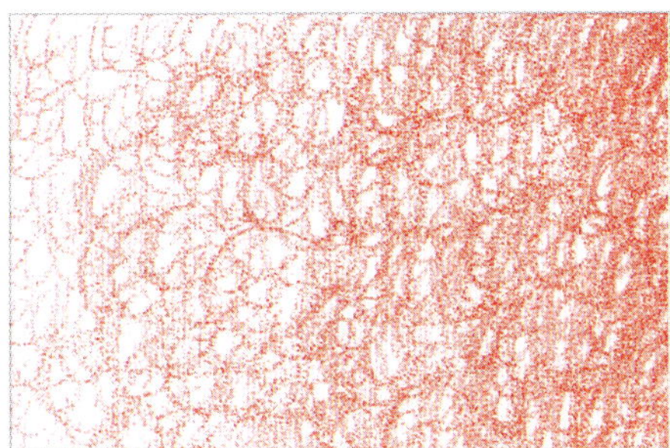

CIRCULAR Move your pencil in a circular motion, either in a random manner as shown here or in patterned rows. For denser coverage, as shown on the right side of the example, overlap the circles. You can also vary the pressure throughout for a more random appearance.

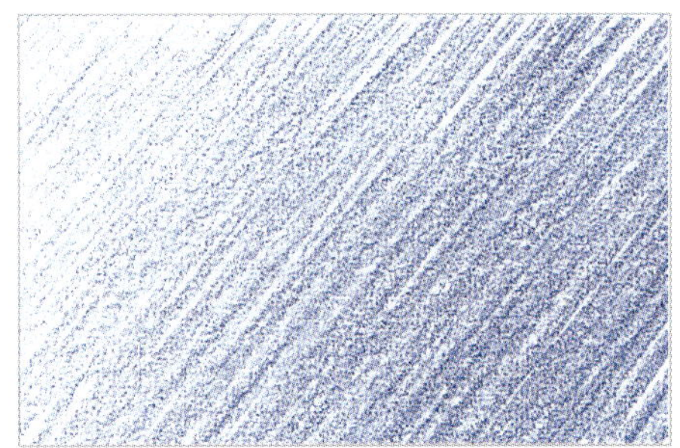

LINEAR Work in a linear fashion, depending on your preference: vertically, horizontally, or diagonally. Your strokes can be short and choppy or long and even, depending on the texture desired.

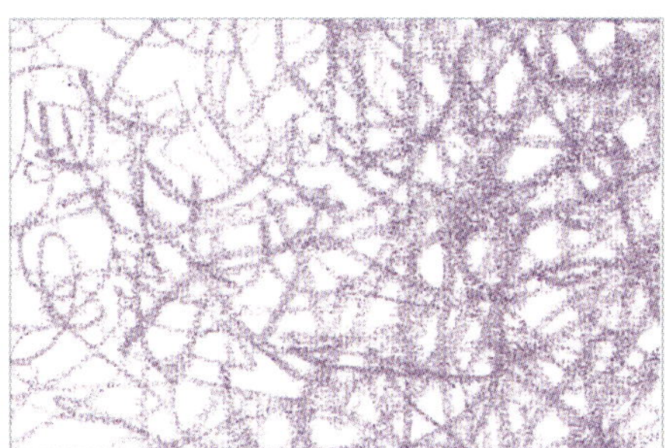

SCUMBLING Create this effect by scribbling your pencil over the surface of the paper in a random manner, creating an organic mass of color. Changing the pressure and the amount of time you linger over the same area can increase or decrease the value of the color.

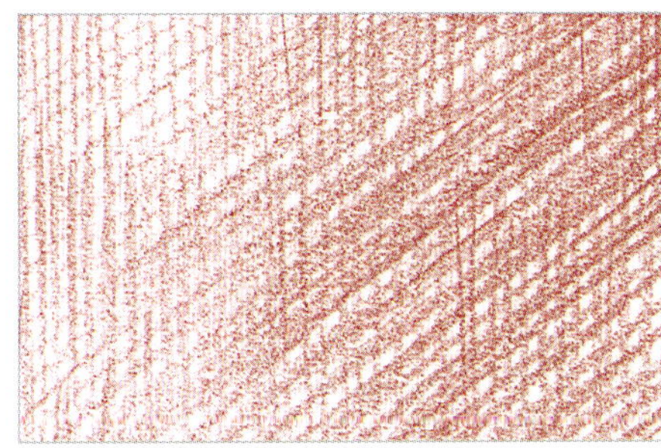

HATCHING This term refers to creating a series of roughly parallel lines. The closer the lines are together, the denser and darker the color. *Crosshatching* is laying one set of hatched lines over another but in a different direction. You can use both of these strokes to fill in an almost solid area of color or to simply to create texture.

SMOOTH No matter what your favorite stroke is, strive to control the pencil and apply a smooth, even layer of color. I tend to use small circles, as shown in this example. Note that the color is so smooth you can't tell how it was applied.

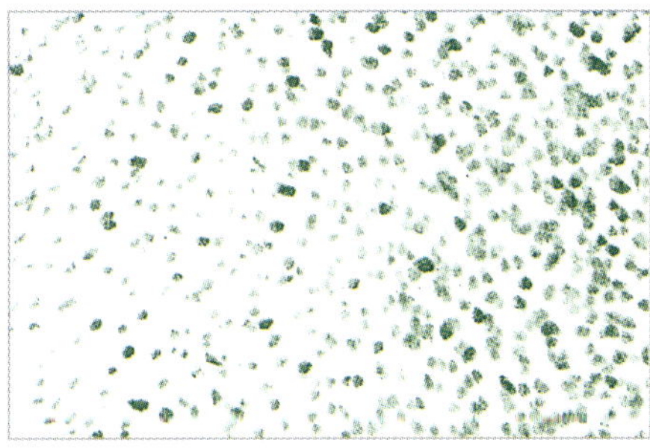

STIPPLING This is a more mechanical way of applying color, but it creates a very strong texture. Simply sharpen your pencil and create small dots all over the area. Make the dots closer together for denser coverage.

Layering & Blending

Painters mix their colors on a palette before applying them to the canvas. With colored pencil, all color mixing and blending occurs directly on the paper. By layering, you can either build up color or create new hues. To deepen a color, layer more of the same over it; to dull it, use its complement. You can also blend colors by burnishing with a light pencil or using a colorless blender.

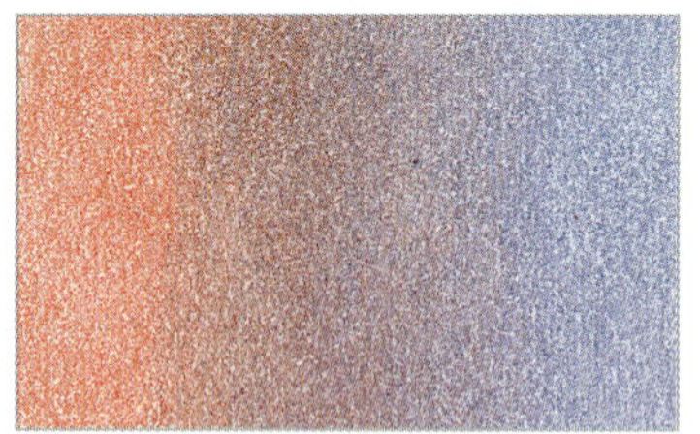

LAYERING The simplest approach to blending colors together is to layer one color directly over the other. This can be done with as many colors as you think necessary to achieve the color or value desired. The keys to this technique are to use light pressure, work with a sharp pencil point, and apply each layer smoothly.

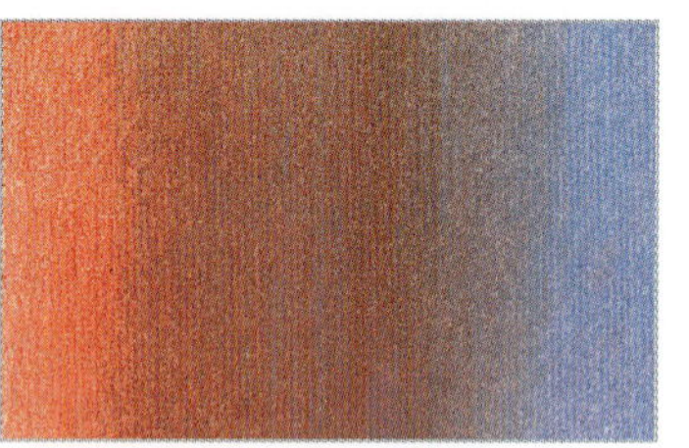

BURNISHING WITH A COLORLESS BLENDER Burnishing requires heavy pressure to meld two or more colors together for a shiny, smooth look. Using a colorless blender darkens the colors, whereas using a white or light pencil lightens the colors and gives them a hazy appearance.

BURNISHING LIGHT OVER DARK You can also burnish using light or white pencils. To create an orange hue, apply a layer of red and then burnish over it with yellow. Always remember to place the darker color first; if you place a dark color over a lighter color, the dark color will overpower and no real blending will occur.

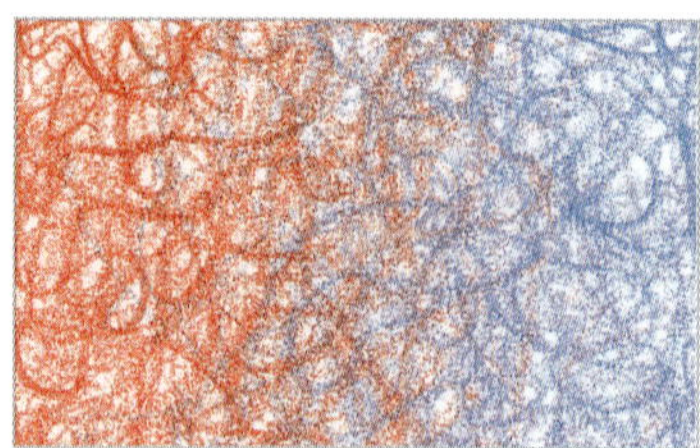

OPTICAL MIXING In this method, the viewer's eye sees two colors placed next to each other as blended. Scumble, hatch, stipple, or use circular strokes to apply the color, allowing the individual pencil marks to look like tiny pieces of thread. When viewed together, the lines form a tapestry of color that the eye interprets as a solid mass.

Creating Form

Value is the term used to describe the relative lightness or darkness of a color (or of black). By adding a range of values to your subjects, you create the illusion of depth and form. Color can confuse the eye when it comes to value, so a helpful tool can be a black-and-white copy of your reference photo (if you're using one). This will take color out of the equation and leave only the shades of gray that define each form.

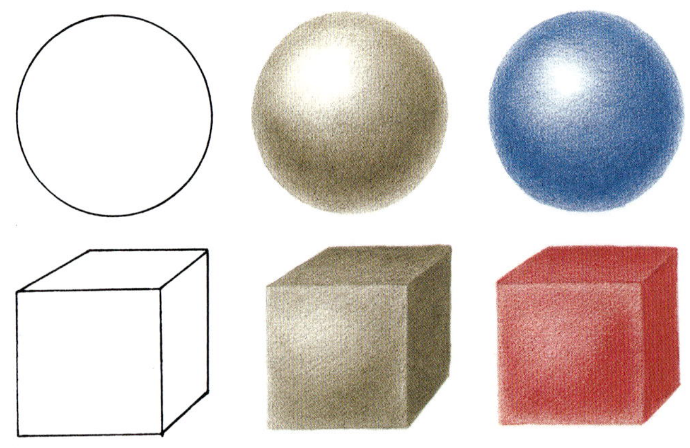

Creating Form with Value In this example, you can see that the gray objects seem just as three-dimensional as the colored objects. This shows that value is more important than color when it comes to creating convincing, lifelike subjects. To practice before you begin the projects, first draw the basic shape. Then, starting on the shadowed side, begin building up value, leaving the paper white in the areas where the light hits the object directly. Continue adding values to create the form of the object. As the object gets farther away from the light, the values become darker, so place the darkest values on the side directly opposite the light.

VALUE SCALE Another helpful tool for understanding value is a scale showing the progression from white (the lightest value) to black (the darkest value). Most colored pencil brands offer a variety of grays, distinguished with a name of either "warm" or "cool" and a percentage to indicate the concentration of color, such as "cool gray 20%." (Lower percentages are lighter.)

Color Psychology

Colors are often referred to in terms of temperature, which can be understood by thinking of the color wheel divided into two halves: The colors on the red side are warm, and the colors on the blue side are cool. So colors with red or yellow in them appear warmer, and colors with more green or blue in them appear cooler. For instance, if a normally cool color (like green) has more yellow added to it, it will appear warmer; and if a warm color (like red) has a little more blue, it will seem cooler. Another important point to remember about color temperature is that warm colors appear to come forward and cool colors appear to recede; this knowledge is valuable when creating the illusion of depth in a scene.

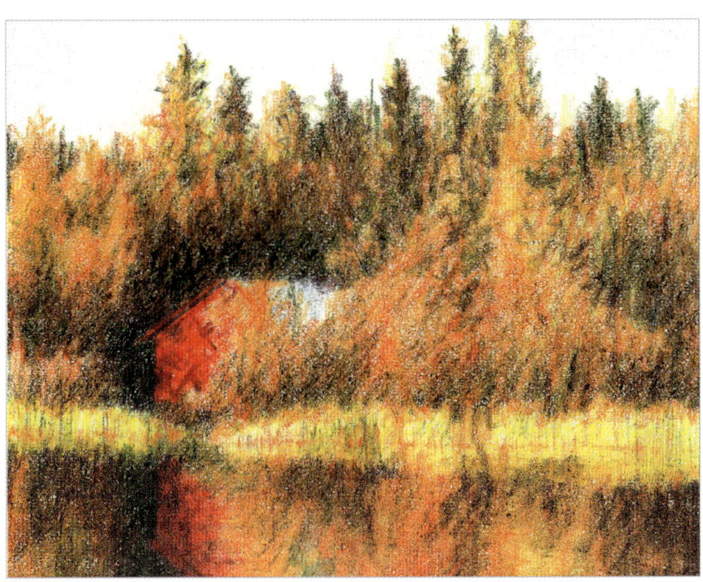

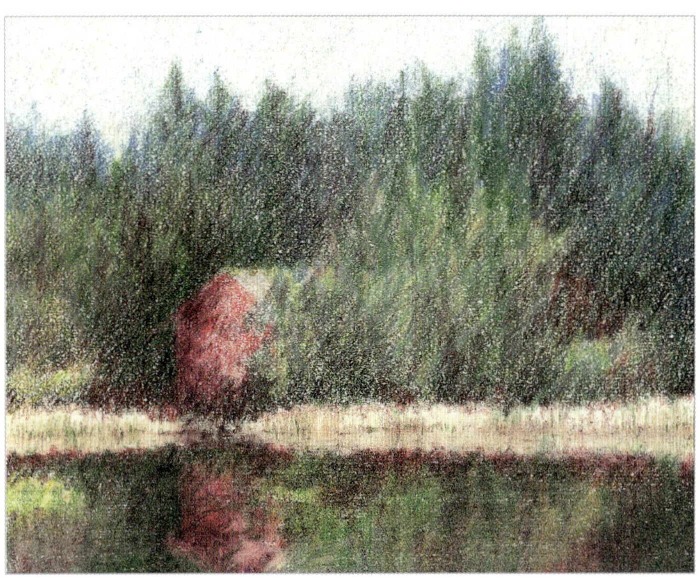

WARM VERSUS COOL Here the same scene is drawn with two different palettes: one warm (left) and one cool (right). Notice that the mood is strikingly different in each scene. This is because color arouses certain feelings; for example, warm colors generally convey energy and excitement, whereas cooler colors usually indicate peace and calm.

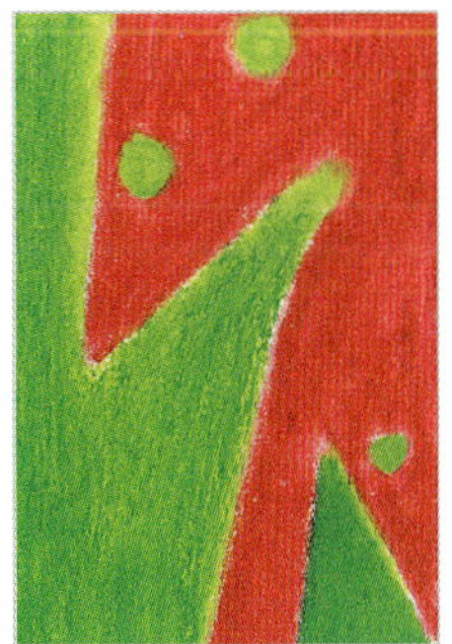

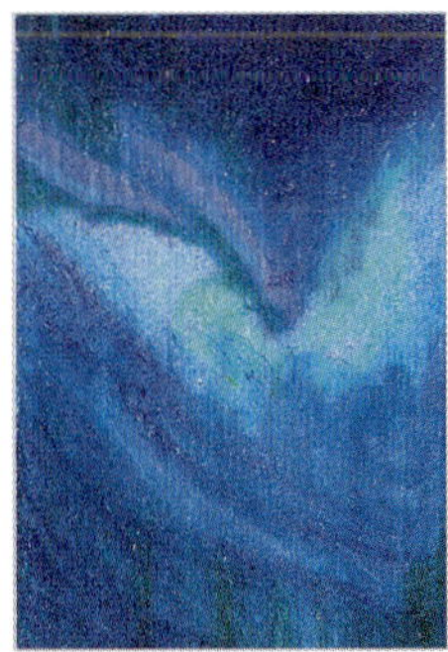

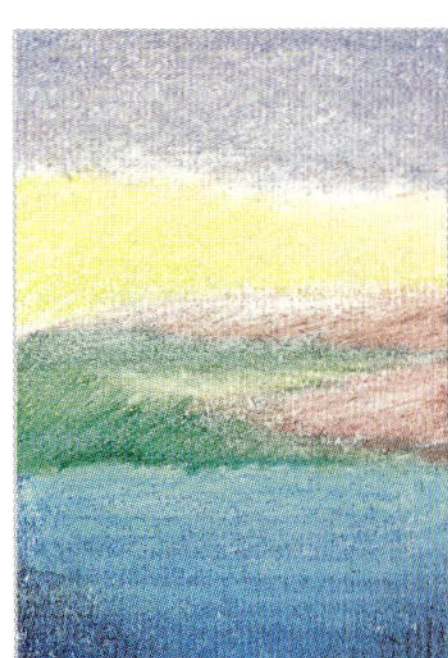

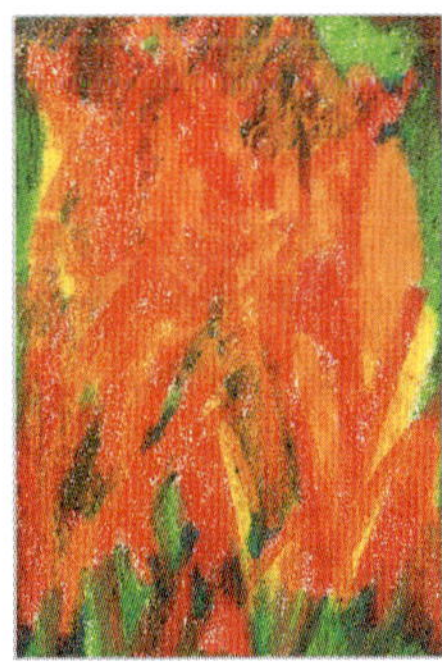

COLOR MOOD The examples here further illustrate how color can be used to create mood (left to right): Complements create a sense of tension; cool hues evoke a sense of mystery; light, cool colors provide a feeling of tranquility; and warm colors can create a sense of danger.

Tints, Shades, and Tones

Colors can be *tinted* with white to make them lighter, *shaded* with black to make them darker, or *toned* with gray to make them more muted. Here each color was applied using graduated pressure—light, then heavy, then light. Black was applied at the top and white at the bottom to tint and tone the colors, respectively. To tint a color without muting it, apply the white first and then the color.

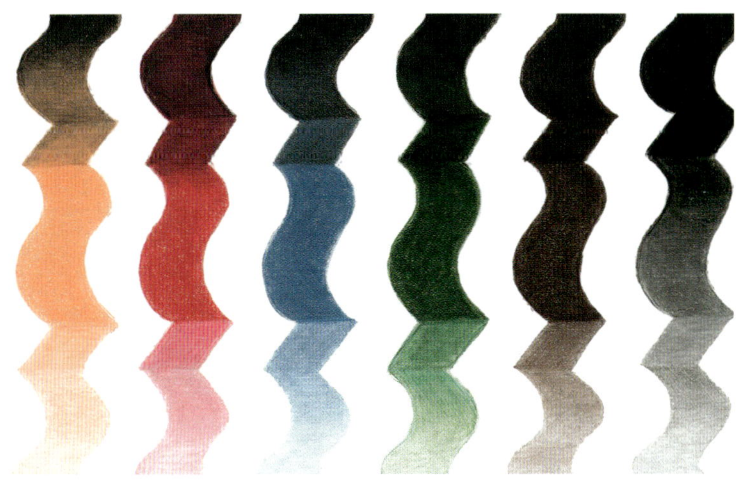

Working from Photographs

Working from photographs is almost always inferior to working from life, but they are a necessary, practical alternative whenever there are complex arrangements with living subject matter or when referencing outside subjects. The negative aspect of working with photographs is that key information can get lost in deep shadow. Additionally, light and bright colors can be "blown out," due to the insensitivity of a camera to low or bright lighting. Unlike a camera, our eyes can easily adjust to see light in dark shadows and interpret the accurate colors in any lighting situation. When working from a photograph, a thorough knowledge of the perspective structure of symmetrical objects can be very helpful. To paraphrase a noted plein-air painter, "Draw what you know, not what you see (or don't see)."

Mixed-Media Colored Pencil Demonstration

In this first demonstration of a still life of oyster shells, concentrate on the marker value application, which is really the foundation of most of the colored pencil drawings in this chapter. We'll take a closer look at colored pencil techniques in the second and third demonstrations in this chapter. Work on gray paper. As a rule, avoid white paper because it takes much longer to achieve color buildup and requires lots of extra practice and skill.

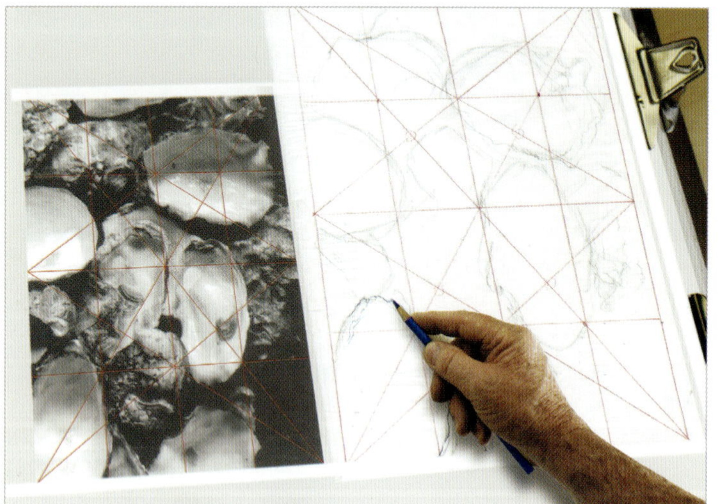

STEP 1 First place a grid on the grayscale photocopy of the reference photo and a slightly larger grid on the paper for the initial gesture sketch. After quickly and lightly blocking in the forms, refine each of the generalized subjects with stronger line.

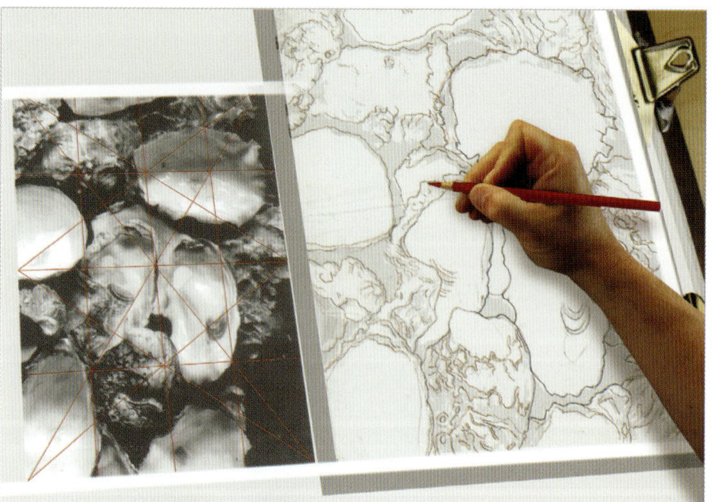

STEP 2 Place a second layer of tracing paper over the initial gesture drawing and create a clean contour line layer for the transfer. To transfer the drawing to art paper, rub brown pastel over the back of the drawing and smooth it with a tissue. Then turn the drawing right-side up, tape it to the art paper, and redraw the contour lines. Try using a different color of pencil to trace the contour lines so it is easy to see what has been transferred.

For working with a value range of markers, purchase a limited number of markers, for example 20%, 40%, 60%, 80%, and black (or 30%, 50%, 70%, and 90%). It isn't necessary to use 10 different markers to achieve a good range of values on gray paper.

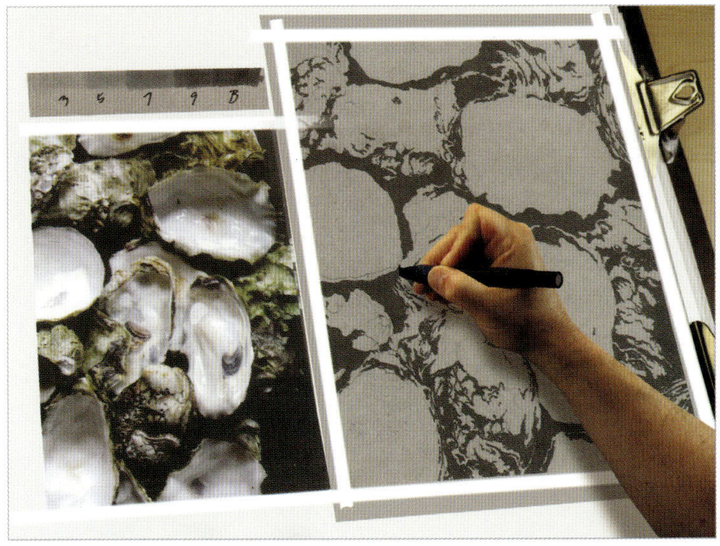

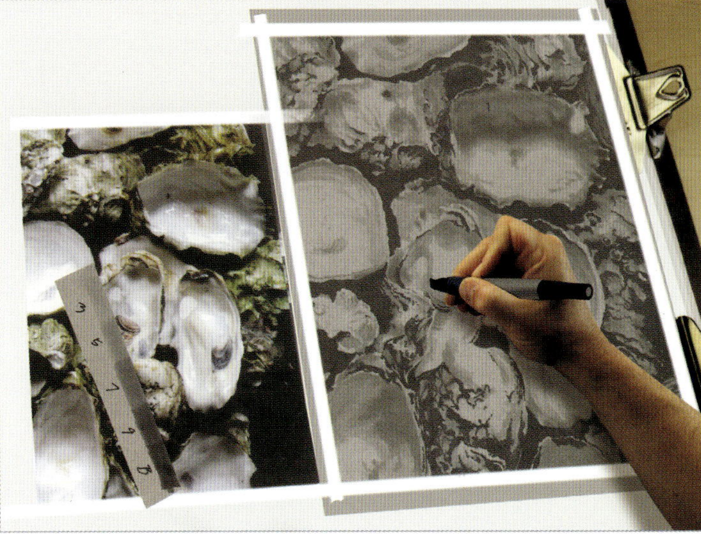

STEP 3 Now you're ready to develop a grayscale underpainting with gray markers (including 30%, 50%, 70%, 90%, and black). Normally, it's best to start with the lightest marker first and follow the scale up to the darkest value; however, start with black marker here, because the area between the shells is very dark. This is a good way to define the different shells. Switch to the color reference, which better illustrates the variety of values.

STEP 4 With the dark background established, work from the lightest to the darkest values, with the paper being the lightest of the gray tones. Use a value scale, labeled "3" through "B" for black, which represents the percentage of the marker ink. Work in small circular strokes, which blend into the paper well.

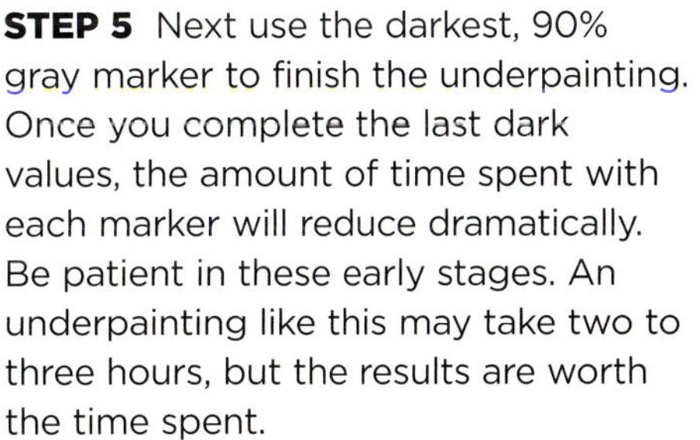

STEP 5 Next use the darkest, 90% gray marker to finish the underpainting. Once you complete the last dark values, the amount of time spent with each marker will reduce dramatically. Be patient in these early stages. An underpainting like this may take two to three hours, but the results are worth the time spent.

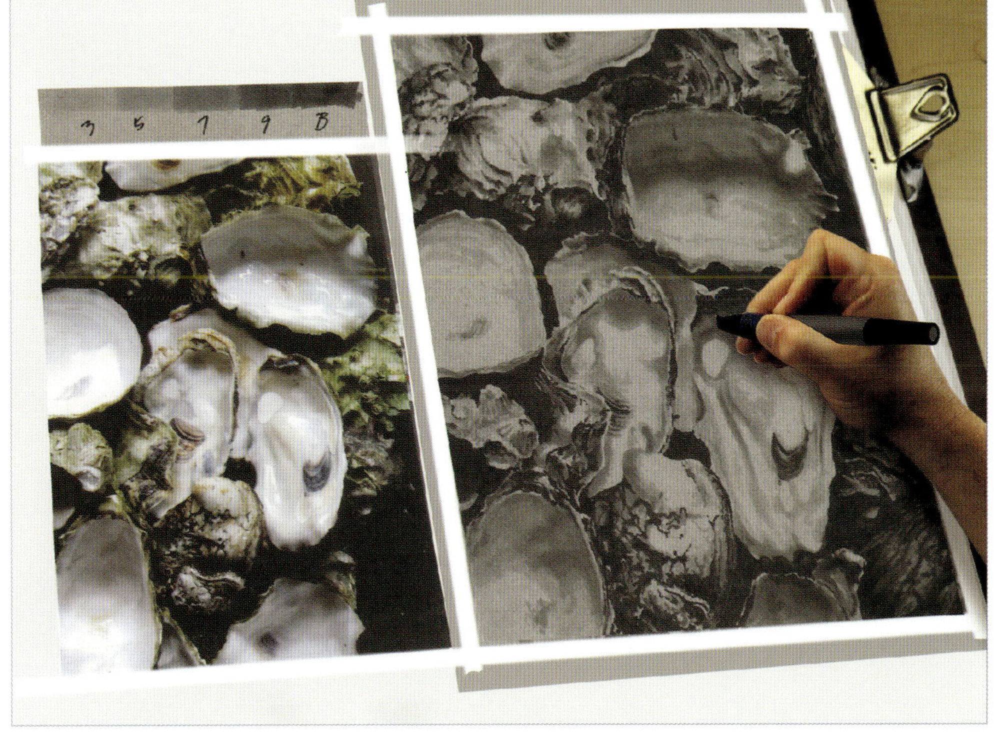

Working from light to dark with markers is easier and more logical, as you can always go darker, but it's impossible to go lighter. Basically, you are building up any value that is the same as your paper value or darker. Colors or values that are lighter than the paper can be accomplished with colored pencil.

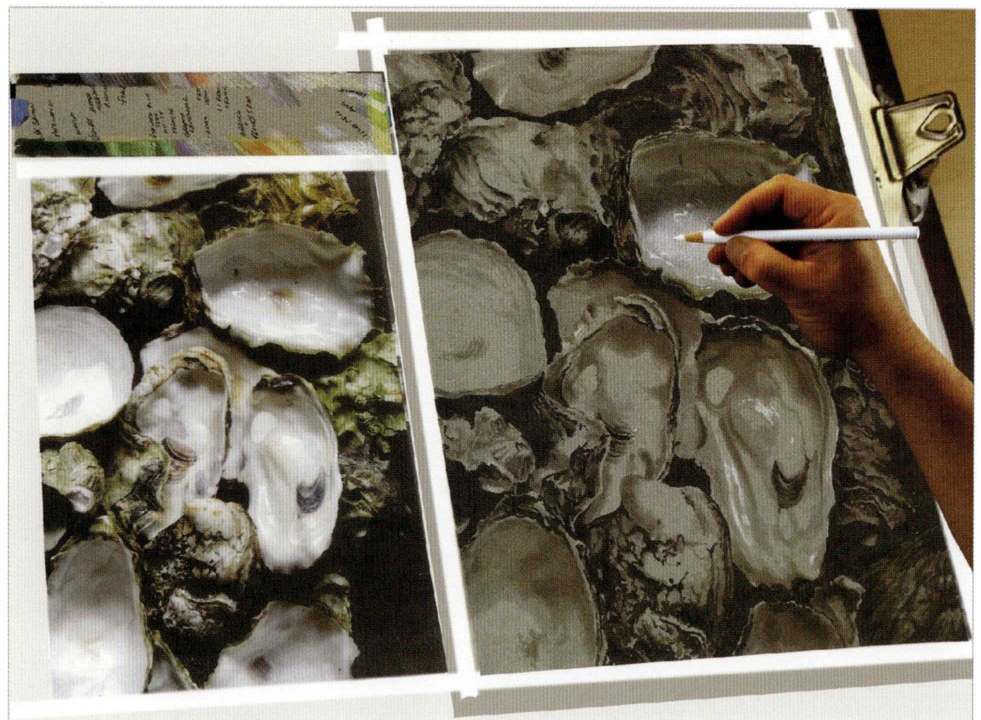

STEP 6 With the underpainting finished, start the colored pencil application. If there are strong highlights, draw them first, so you don't have to worry about whether there will be enough paper surface at the end to accept them. Eventually, every inch of the drawing will be in colored pencil, with no visible marker on the surface of the finished artwork. However, the value applications, especially the darkest values, make their presence known in a substantial way.

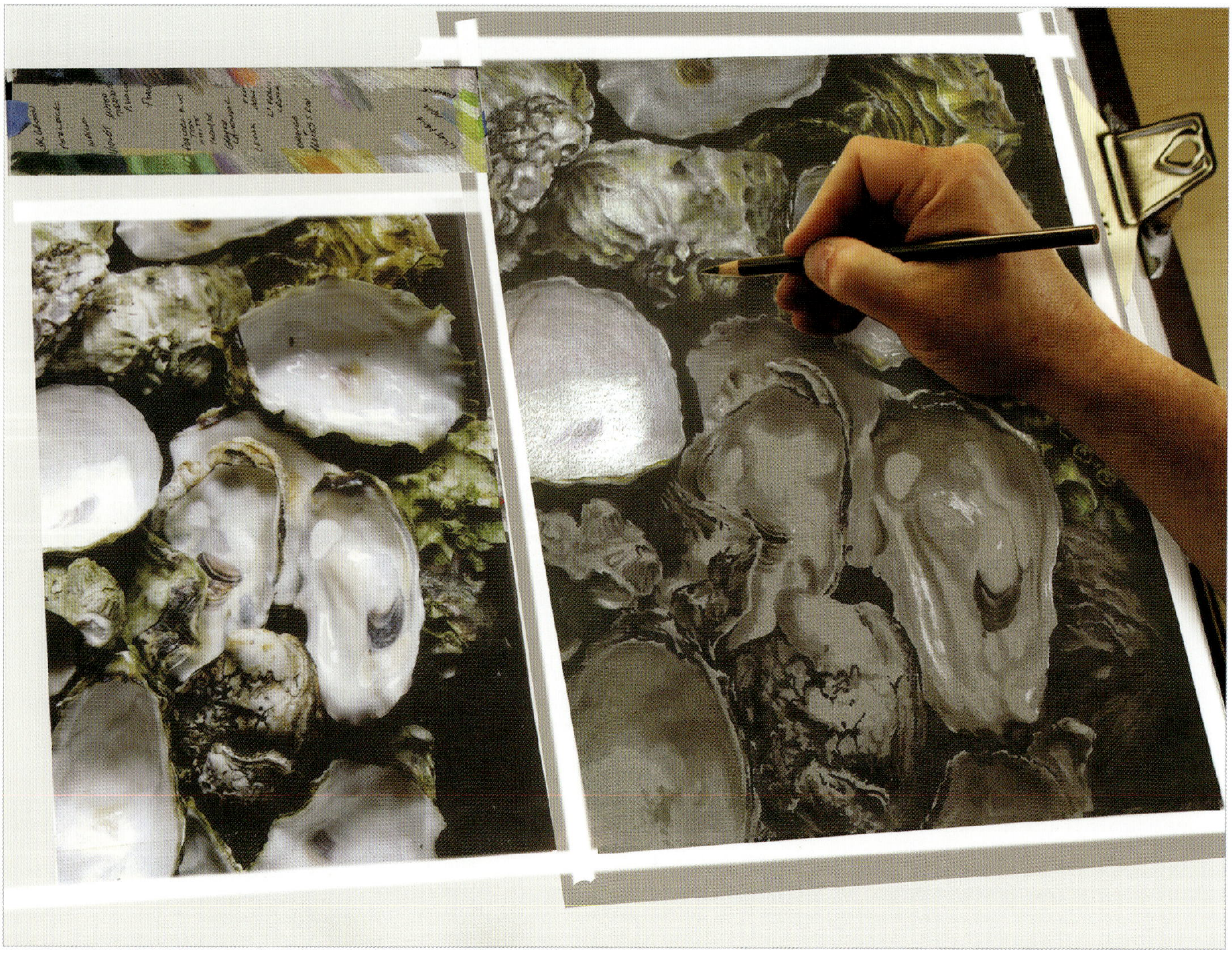

STEP 7 As you progress through the color development process, start with the light or middle colored pencils first and work up to the darkest colors to make sure that there will be enough paper texture for the lightest and brightest colors.

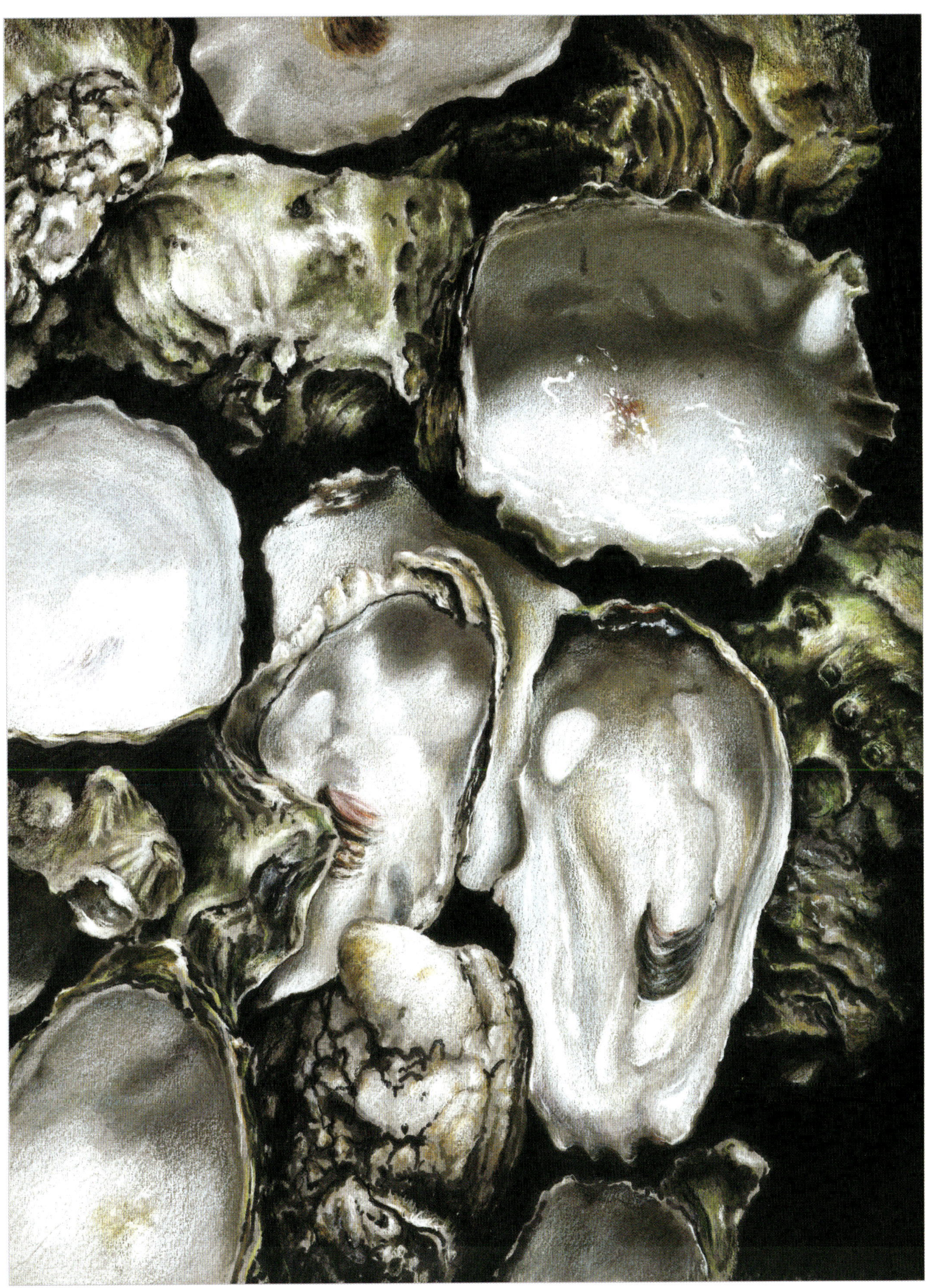

The final colored pencil drawing. Time: 8 hours.

Color Application

This second demonstration focuses on colored pencil application techniques, which can be used with or without marker and on white paper or a toned surface. Work on gray or neutral-toned art paper to get the most out of the brighter colors. You may also find that it is more difficult to develop dark values on white paper. Start the color build-up process from light to dark, leaving plenty of paper surface left at the end for the strongest, lightest, and brightest colors. There are always exceptions to any rule, but this method is usually the most successful.

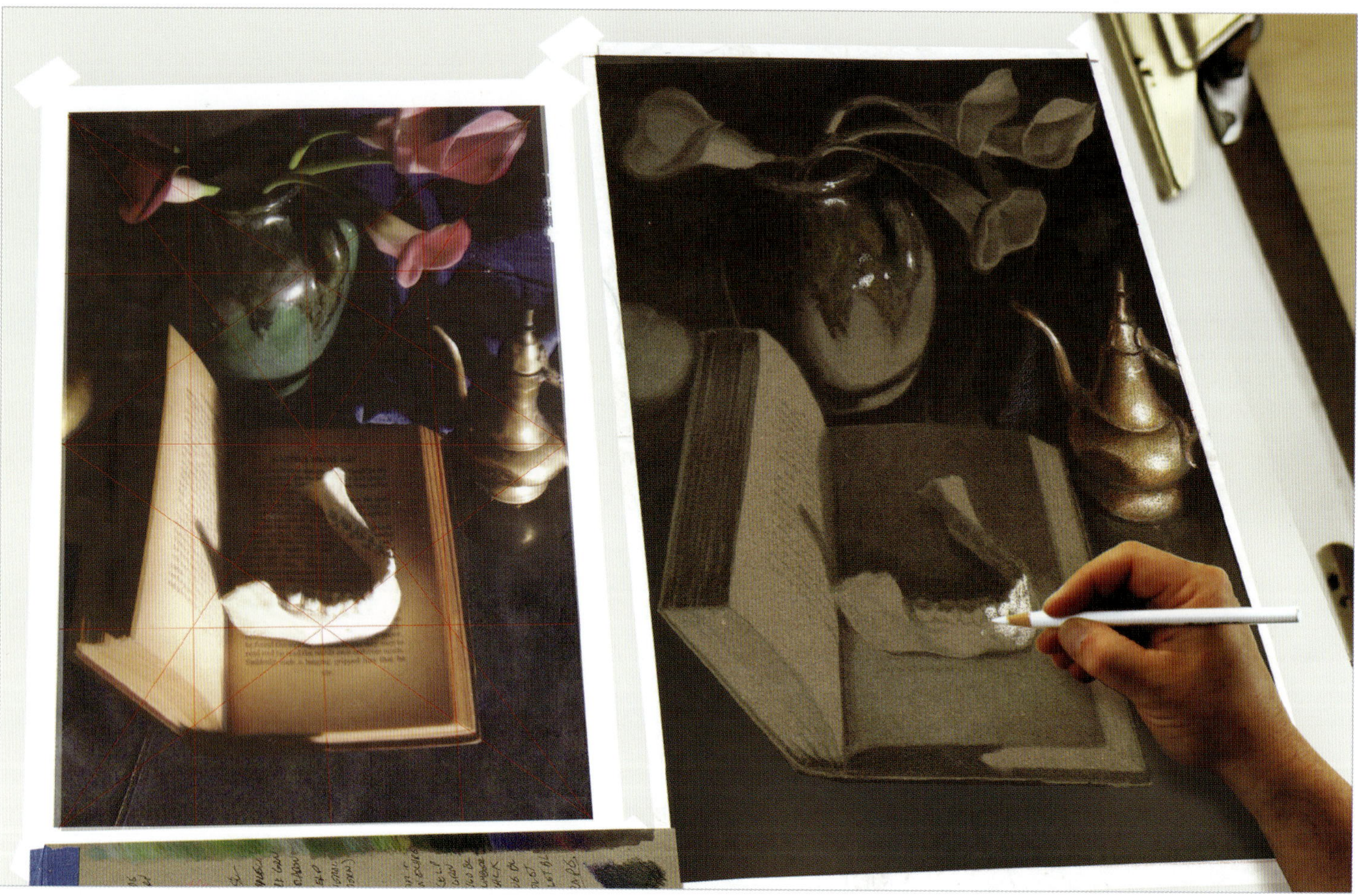

STEP 1 After sketching and transferring the drawing and creating a marker underpainting, begin applying color, working from light to dark.

There is no singular "best" technique for applying colored pencil to paper. Sometimes you may want to use hatching and crosshatching. For smooth surfaces or a gradient, use circular strokes. To cover large areas, use sandpaper to soften the tip of the pencil before applying. For maximum color application without heavy pressure, keep the point very sharp.

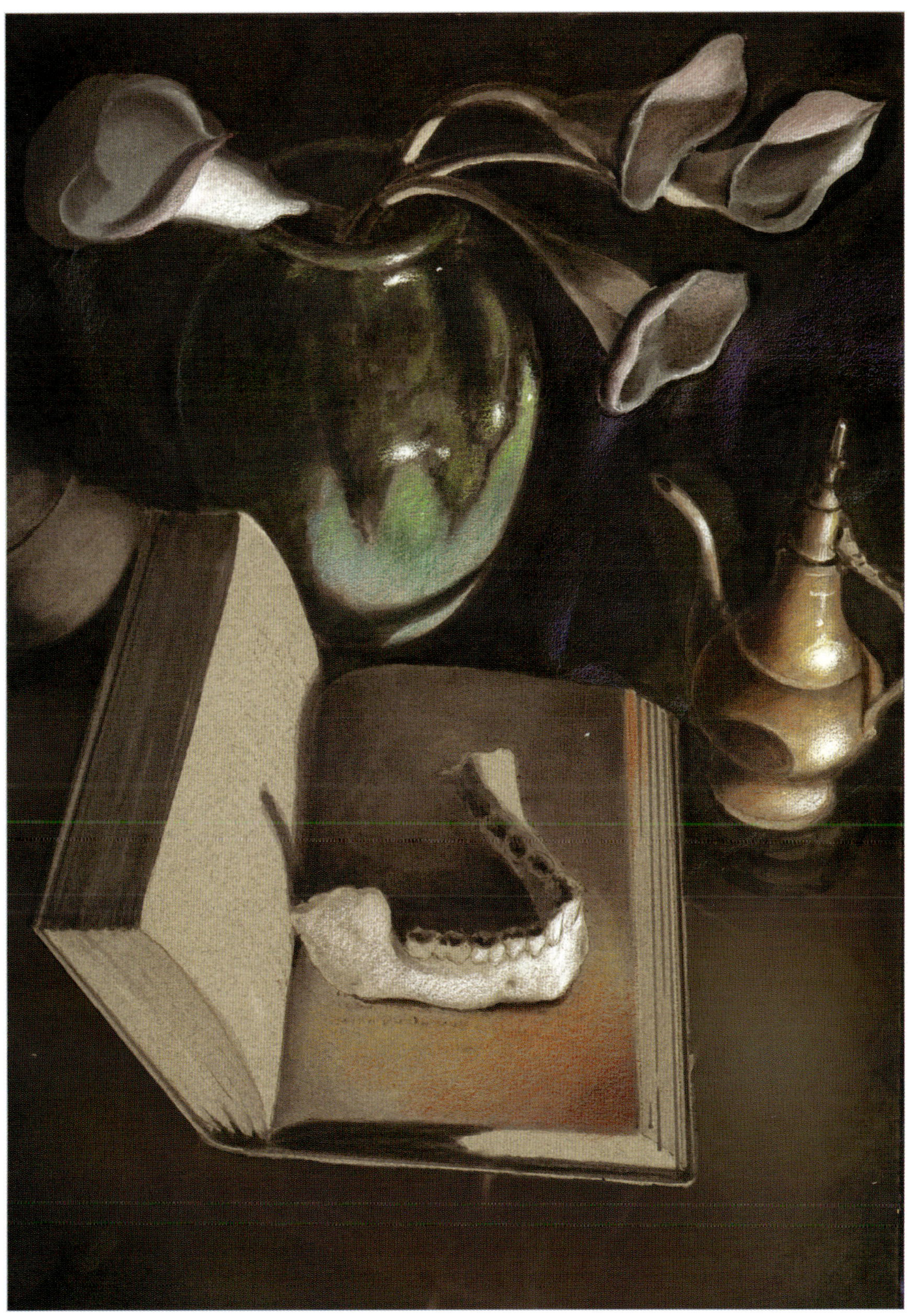

STEP 2 Lay on initial glazes of color in most still lifes from light to dark, planning to return to each object later for refinement and contrast.

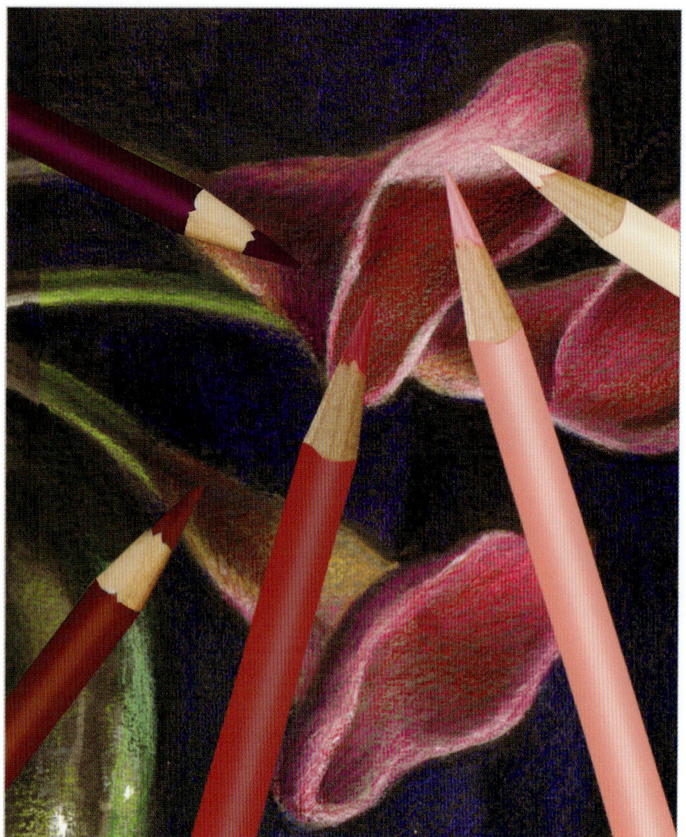

FLOWERS DETAIL Develop the flowers with a light layering of cream, pink, and red, in that order. Don't use heavy applications; each layer is softly developed into the last with light circular, rotating strokes. You want soft gradations of color and value. For the shadows, use combinations of Tuscan red and black grape pencils.

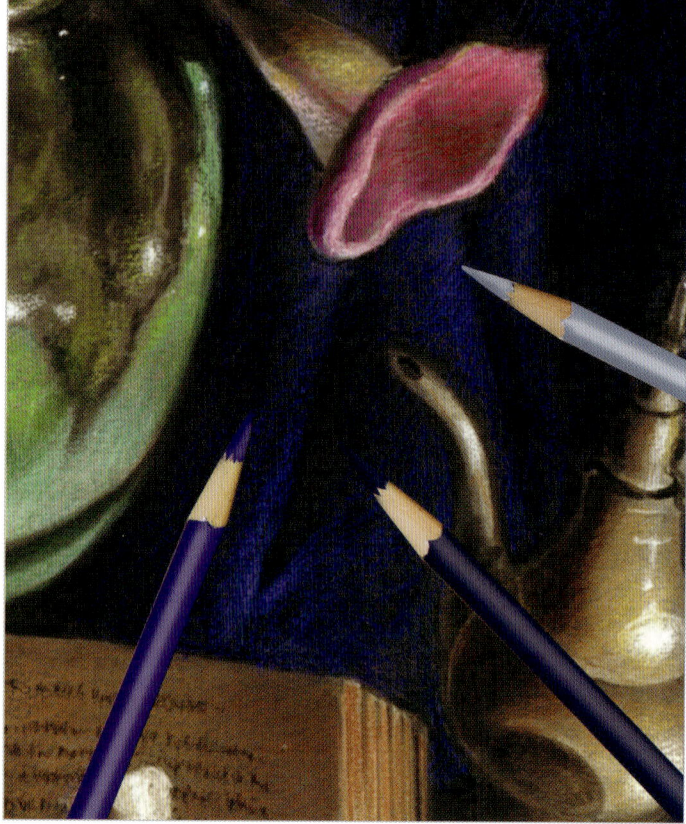

DRAPE DETAIL To render the background drape, start with the middle color, blue violet. Then use indigo blue for the deepest shadows. Finish with a light cerulean blue, using very soft pressure, because you only need a small amount of highlight on the dark cloth. It's easy to correct overdone highlights by softly applying a middle color to tone it back down.

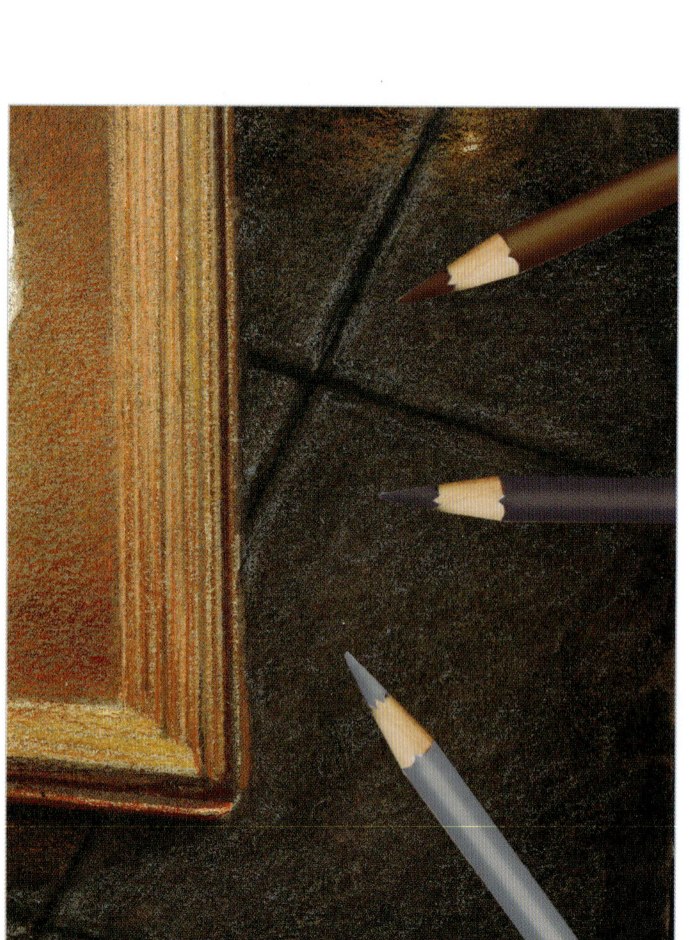

TILE DETAIL Develop the tile with light circular strokes of color, starting with muted turquoise and following with espresso and dark umber. To render the brass pot reflection, use the same colors originally used on the brass pot, but with much less pressure and a glaze of espresso over the reflection.

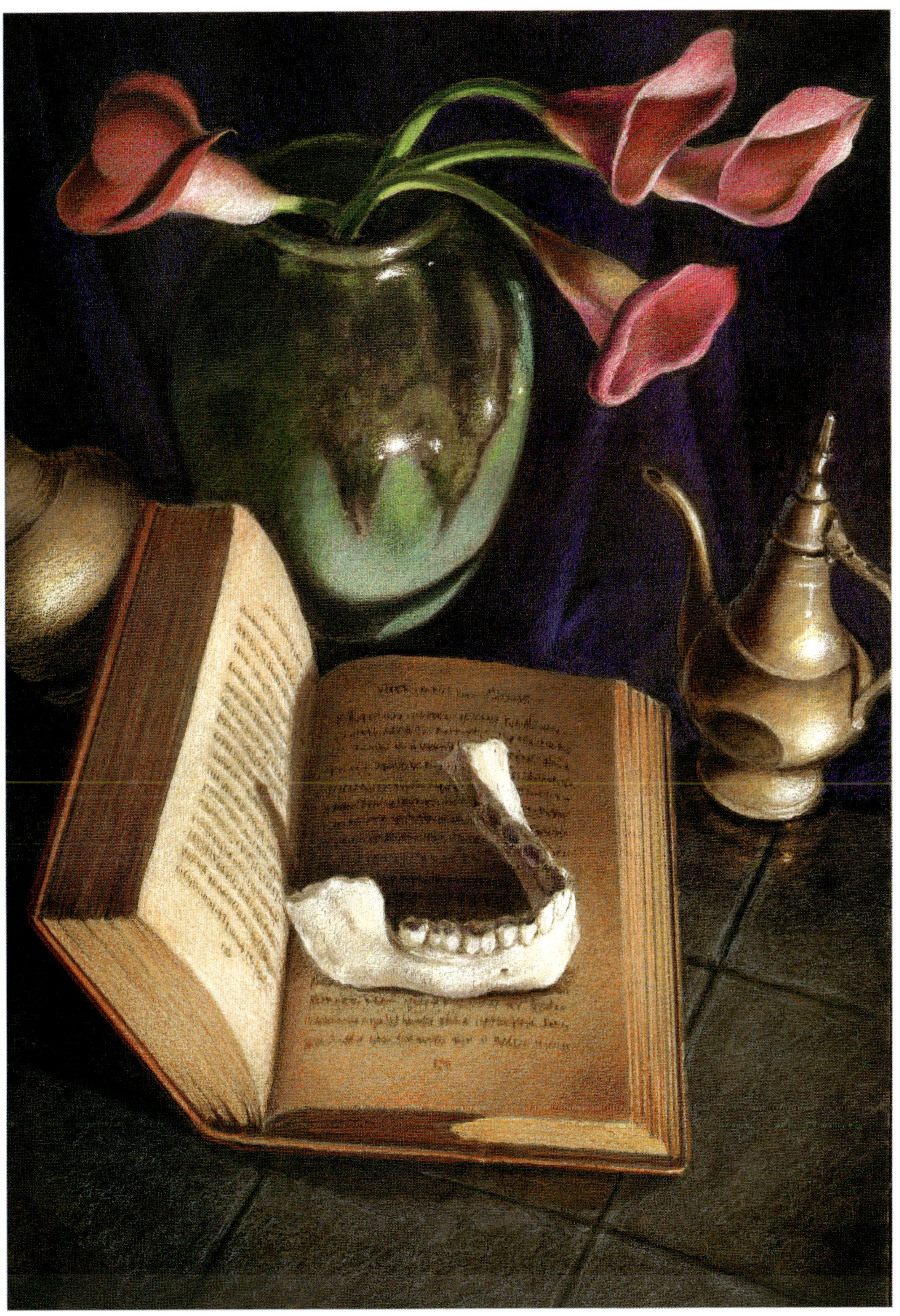

STEP 3 I develop the rest of the drawing with layers of color. (See the details on page 172.)

Burnishing the Brightest Colors

In this seashell demonstration, focus on the finishing burnished highlights. In a drawing such as this, save plenty of paper surface for the brightest colors. Use a felt-gray Canson paper—the smoother of the two sides—which still affords plenty of necessary texture.

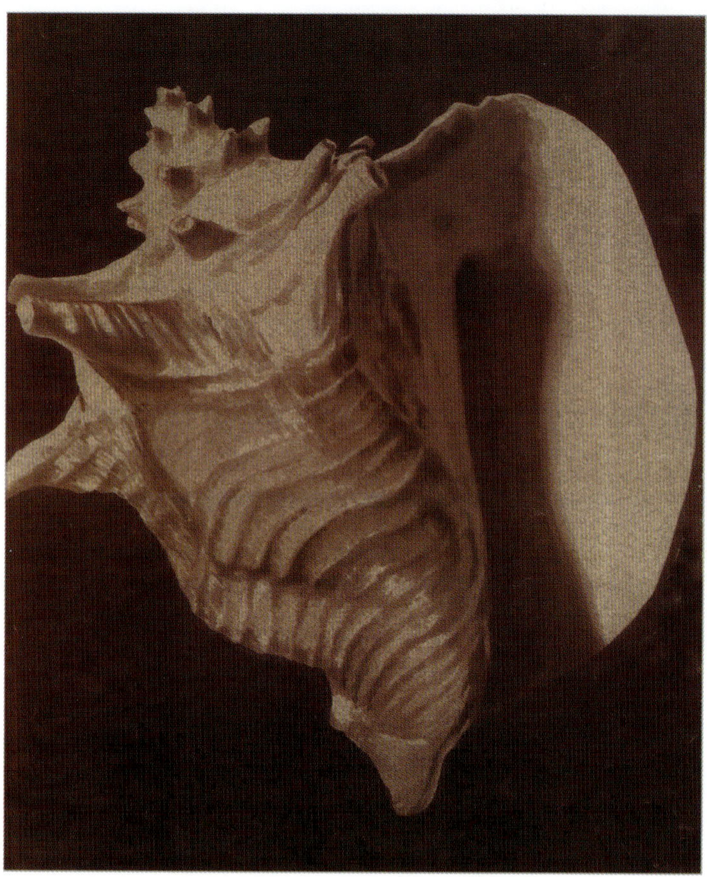

◀ The initial value underpainting took 60 to 90 minutes to complete.

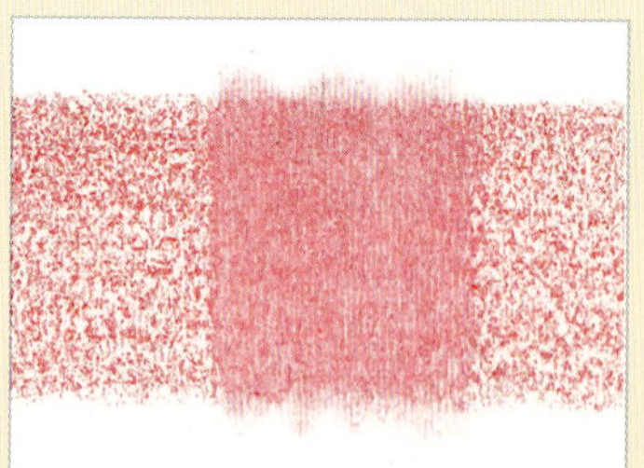

Burnishing

Colored pencil catches in the tooth of the paper; therefore the layers can appear rough. For a smooth, shiny effect, burnish the layer by stroking over it with a colorless blender, a white colored pencil (to lighten), or another color (to shift the hue) using heavy pressure. Burnishing pushes the color into the tooth and distributes the pigment for smooth coverage.

It is always a good idea to create a value/color scale before starting an extended drawing. This will help solve any glazing or layering problems before the process starts. A student created the colored pencil value chart at right. Notice that she even added marker values for comparison.

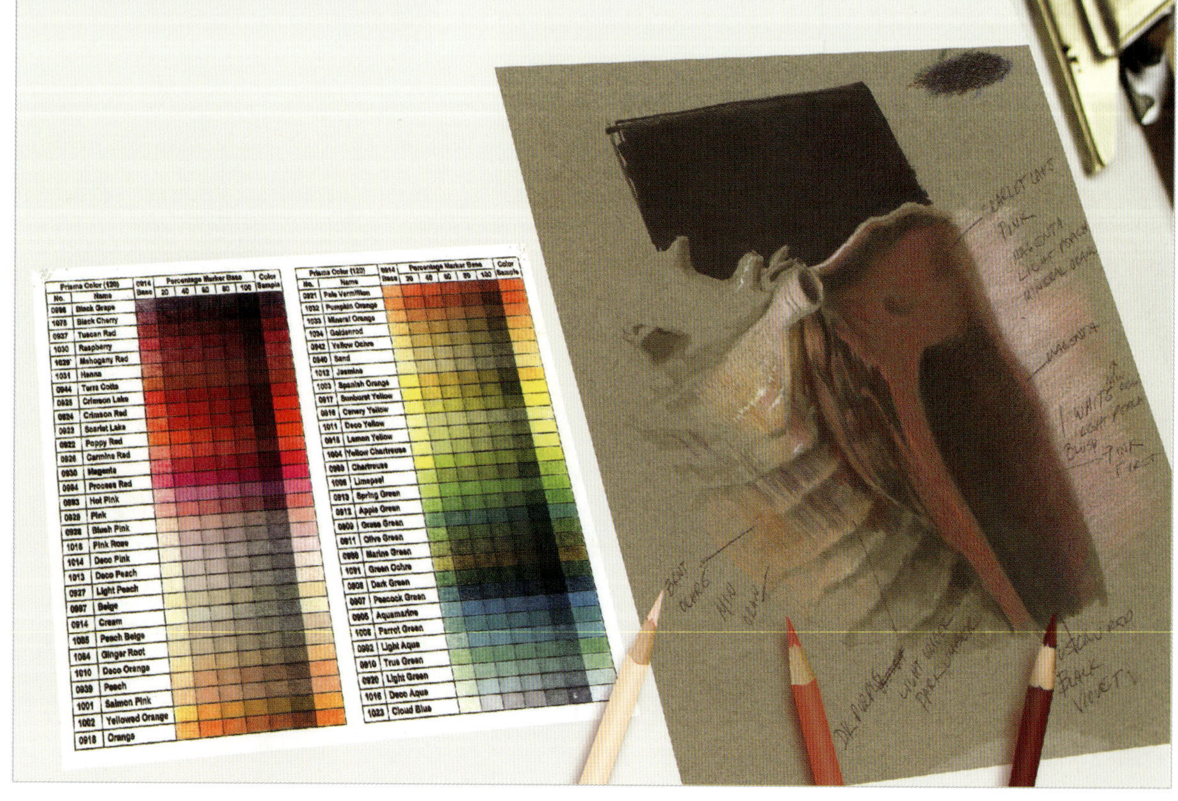

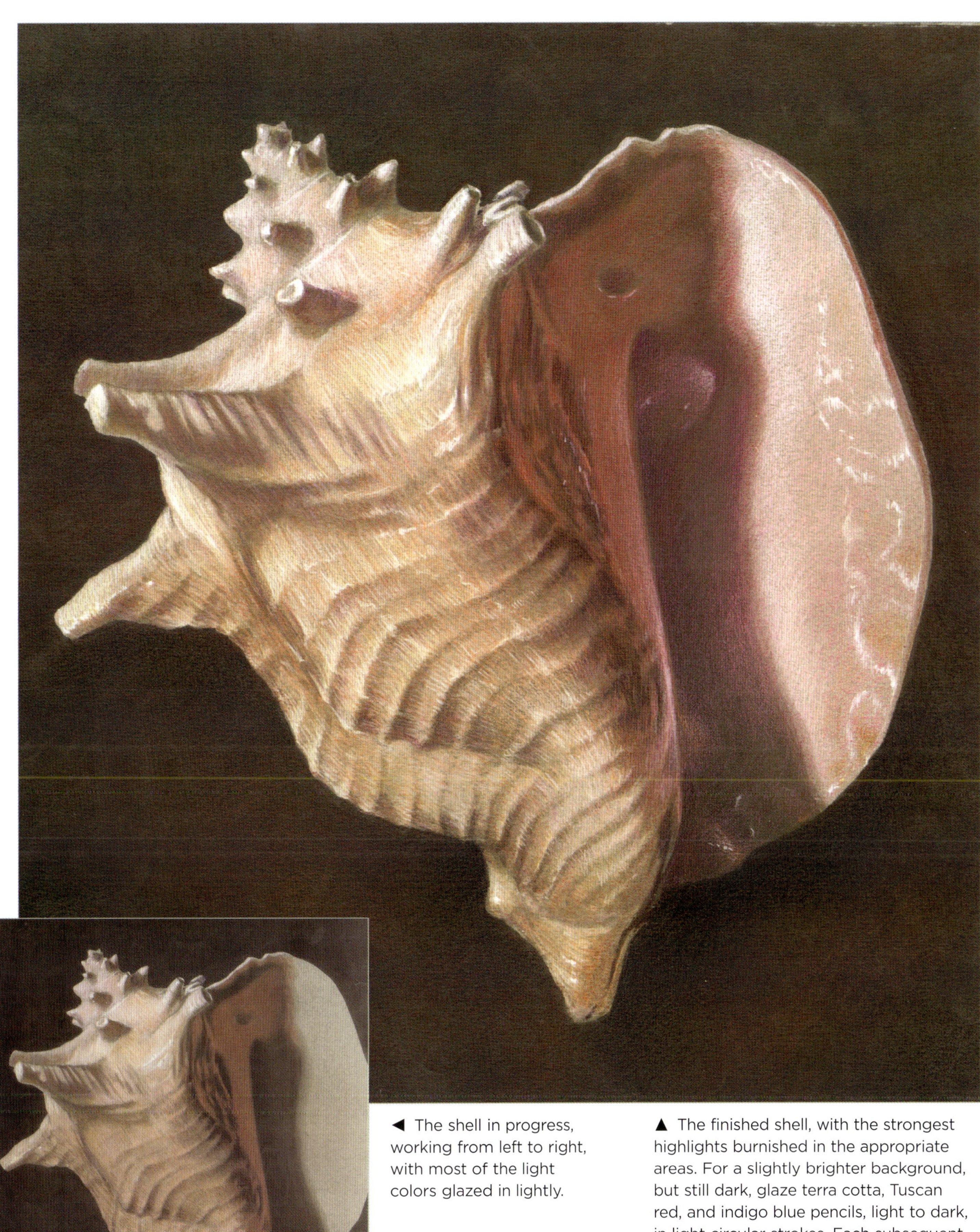

◀ The shell in progress, working from left to right, with most of the light colors glazed in lightly.

▲ The finished shell, with the strongest highlights burnished in the appropriate areas. For a slightly brighter background, but still dark, glaze terra cotta, Tuscan red, and indigo blue pencils, light to dark, in light circular strokes. Each subsequent color subtly affects the previous layer. Time: 6 hours.

Monochromatic Artwork in Colored Pencil

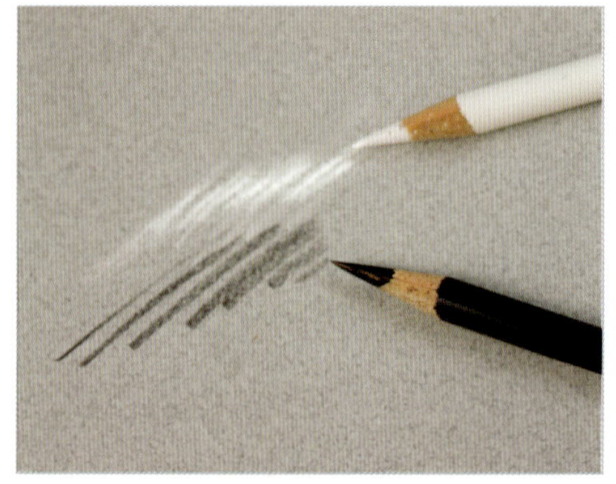

When not working from a color reference or subject, black, white, and neutral colored pencils can be a great way to produce high-contrast, dramatic drawings.

Black colored pencil on a more textured white art paper, such as Bristol vellum or stipple paper (also known as coquille paper) is an effective, expedient way to build up a wide range of values without the need to layer different grades of graphite pencil. The rich, black, matte appearance of the black colored pencil is also a plus.

Conversely, white colored pencil on black illustration board or art paper can be as dramatic and beautiful as any typical drawing. The amount of pressure used with the pencils, as well as the textured surface of the paper, is a key factor, as is the sensitivity of the artist to the effects of light on the forms.

A combination of black and white colored pencils on gray-toned paper is also a logical and effective way to build up dark and light values efficiently and quickly, with the neutral paper acting as the middle value.

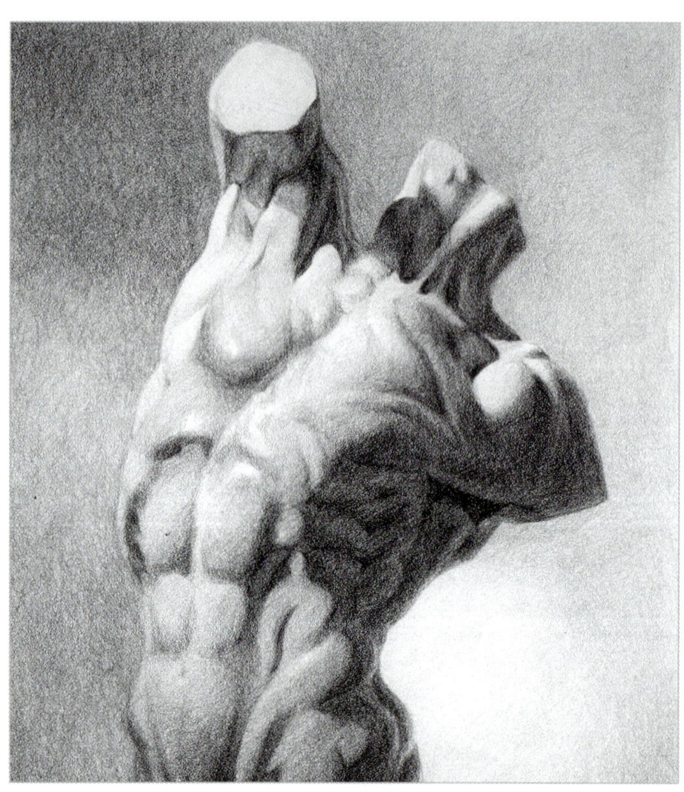

This torso was rendered with black colored pencil on white stipple board. The textured and pebble-like surface lends itself to creating a good range of values with black colored pencil, using a variety of pressure-sensitive strokes. Student drawing by Jason Slavin.
Time: 6–8 hours.

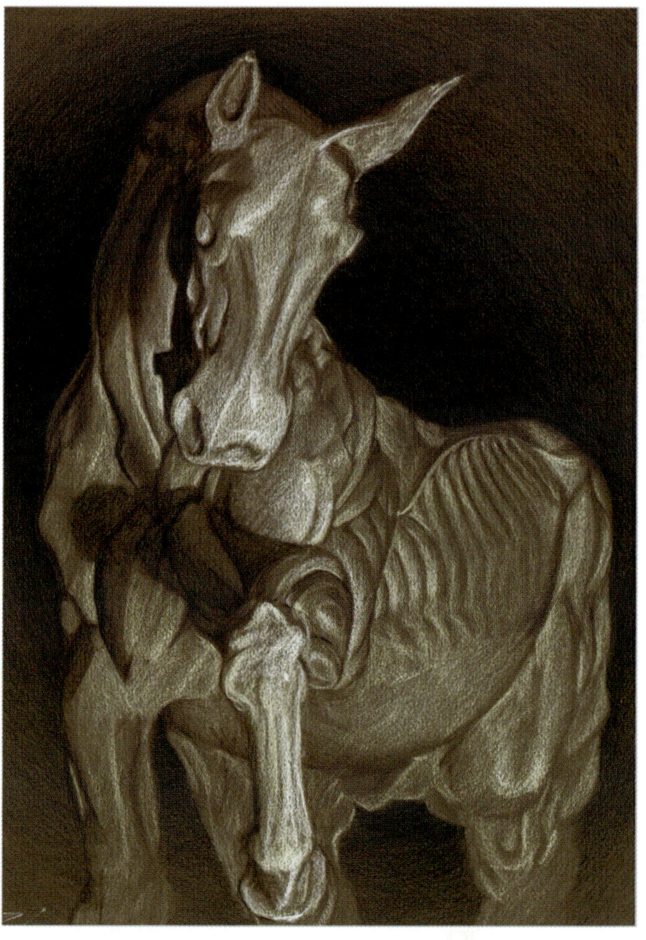

For this dramatic tonal drawing on dark Canson paper, black and white pencils were supplemented by subtle additions (as desired) of cream and dark umber pencils, which act as a subtle bridge for the white and black colored pencils, respectively. Student drawing by Huy Huynh.
Time: 6–8 hours.

YOUR HOMEWORK

This homework project can be created using an actual still life or a color photograph of your choice.

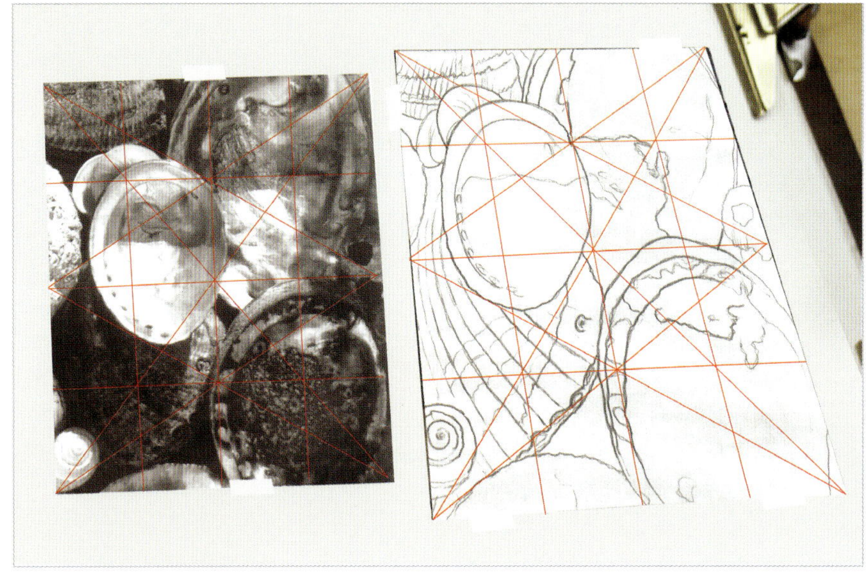

Choose a still life to render in colored pencil; find subject matter that you prefer, but look for strong color and value choices in your subject.

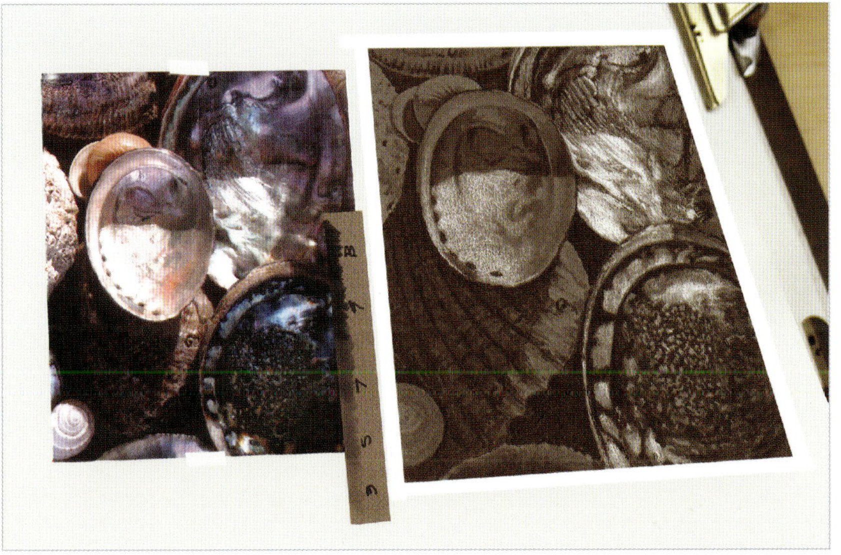

If you're working from a photo, try using the grid method to transfer a line drawing to art paper. Add marker value, with ranges of 20% to 80% and black, or 30% to 90% and black. Use a value scale for value development and a color-swatch scale for color development.

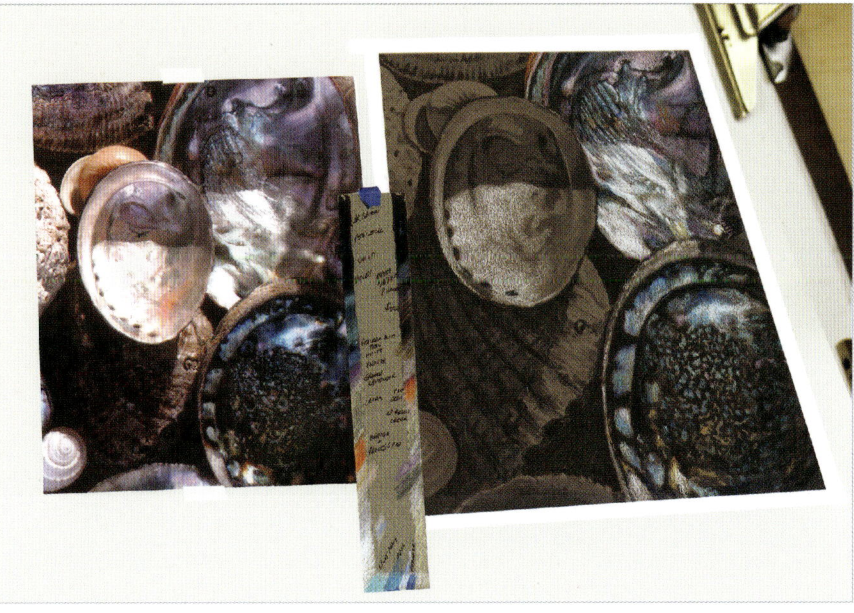

Try to work in the size range of 14″ x 17″ to 16″ x 20″ for your final drawing.

EXERCISES FOR PRACTICE

Complementary colors are two colors that are opposite each other on the color wheel. (See "Color Basics," page 161.) While we may not understand why these color combinations work so well, we instinctively know that they do. In this project, we'll use red and green, and you'll learn how to accentuate and then subdue the vivid colors with several layers of blending and burnishing.

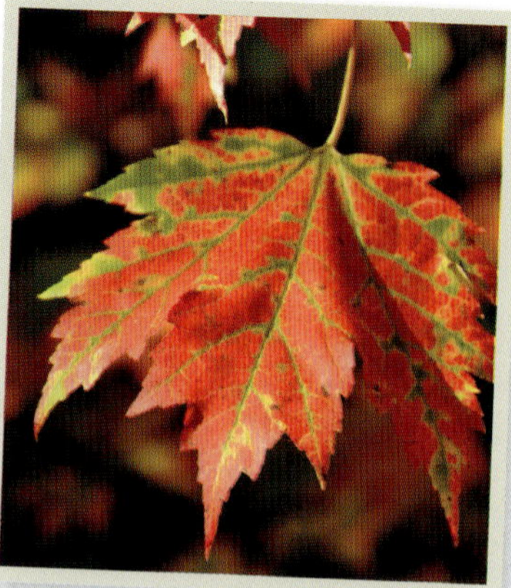

Autumn leaves near the peak of their splendor in the Northeast.

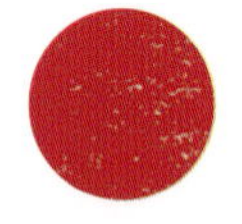

crimson red

Kelly green

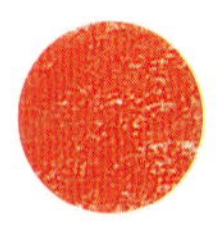

poppy red

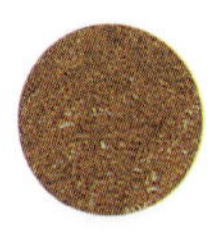

sienna brown

sunburst yellow

Tuscan red

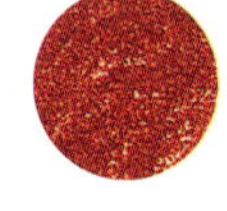

terra cotta

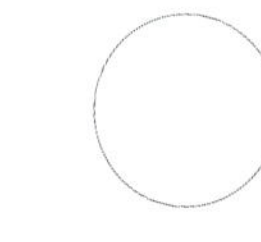

white

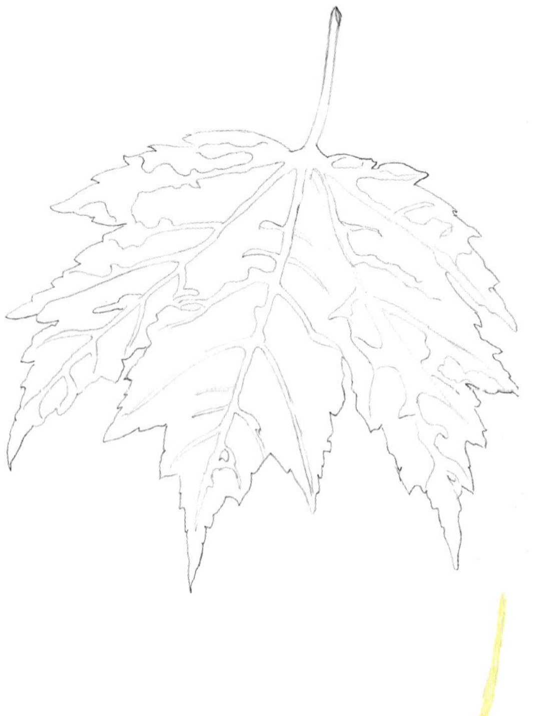

STEP 1 Sketch an outline of the bottom leaf with an H graphite pencil. You will later erase these lines as you work on each section so the graphite doesn't show through the colored pencil.

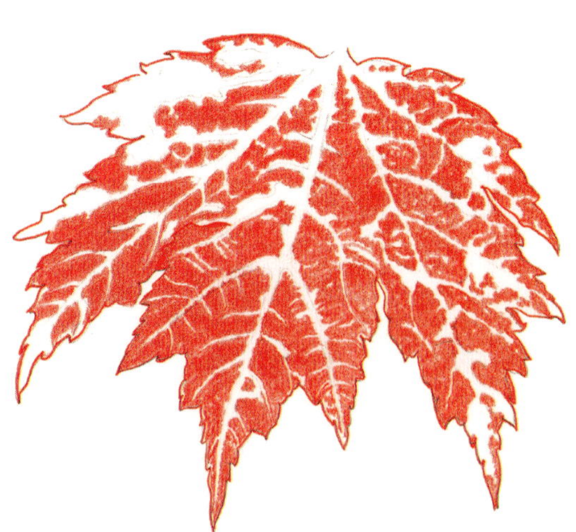

STEP 2 Outline the exterior of the leaf with crimson red. Then use circular strokes and light pressure to fill in the red sections. Leave space for the veins and the areas of yellow and green, which you'll develop in the next steps.

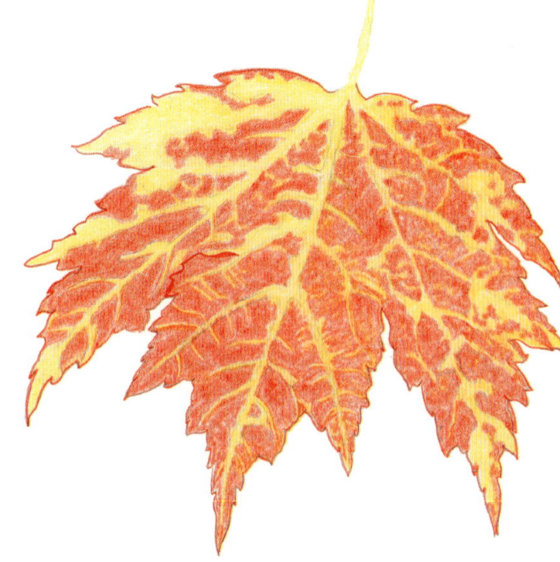

STEP 3 Fill in all of the uncolored areas, including the stem, with sunburst yellow. Use small circular strokes and medium pressure throughout.

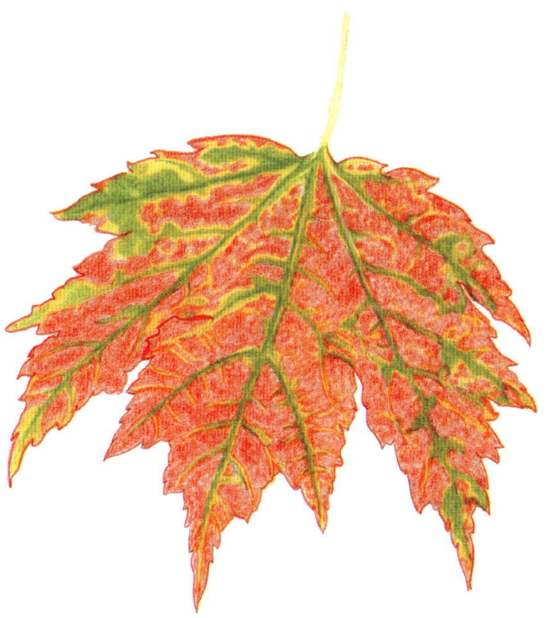

STEP 4 With firm pressure, apply Kelly green over the sunburst yellow in areas that need to be green. This is the last of the three main colors you need to establish; now you can begin developing color intensity. To brighten the yellows and greens, burnish with sunburst yellow using heavy pressure and a blunt point, covering the yellow and green areas.

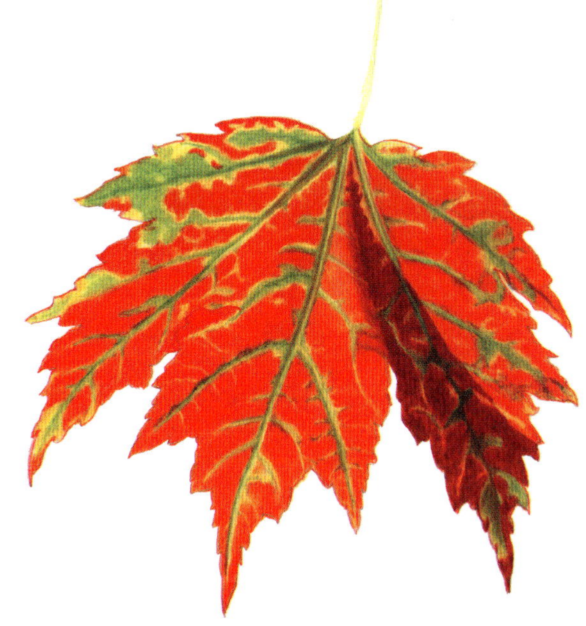

STEP 5 Enhance the reds with another layer of crimson red and a layer of poppy red. Then burnish the entire leaf with sunburst yellow. Line the darkest vein edges with sienna brown. For the dark shadow, apply Tuscan red. Use sunburst yellow and Kelly green to intensify the yellows and greens over the shadowed section. Also begin to burnish the sunlit sections with white.

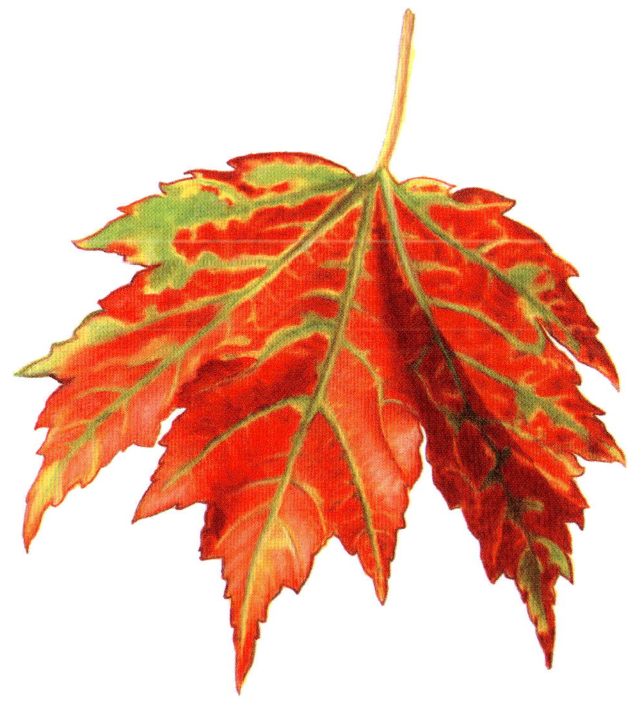

STEP 6 Using Tuscan red with firm pressure, intensify all of the dark red areas. Use Kelly green to darken and define the greens. Burnish the remaining sunlit sections with white, blending the colors together and pressing hard to bring out the highlights. Blend and burnish to restore the reds and yellows where needed. Then outline the leaf with a sharp Tuscan red. Color the stem with sunburst yellow, add terra cotta down the right side, and then burnish with white. Draw a thin line of terra cotta down the left side of the stem for definition. Finish by erasing all smudges and spraying with workable fixative.

Many beginning artists wrongly assume that heavier coats of a particular color will create a deep shadow. Instead, use darker colors to create shadows and contrasts. The best pencils for doing this include dark umber, Tuscan red, black grape, cool gray 70% and 90%, and black. Keep your strokes small and use a light touch to build density. If you overdo it or accidentally create dark marks, use a sharp white pencil to "erase" them.

When drawing subjects that are transparent like this fishbowl, you are actually rendering the reflections on its surface. Clear glass and water have little or no color of their own, so the colors you see and use are reflected from the objects around them. This example uses mostly grays and blues, but all the colors in the rainbow are possible options. Just draw what you see and be open to using all the colors you observe.

black

cool gray 30%

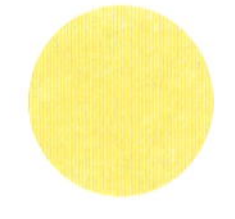

Deco yellow

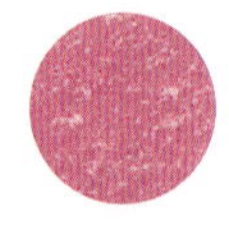

lavender

light cerulean blue

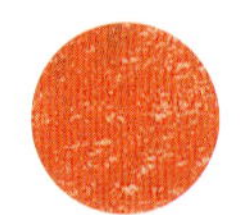

pale vermilion

scarlet lake

slate gray

warm gray 50%

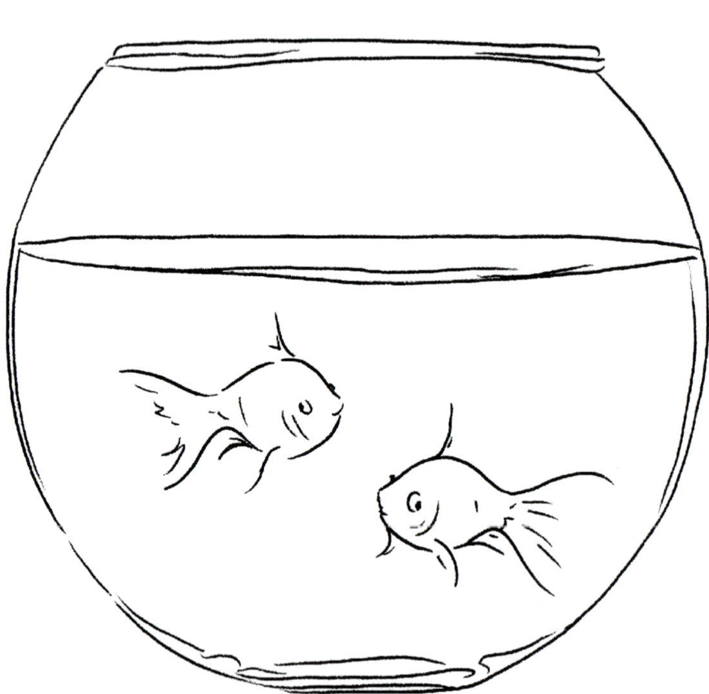

STEP 1 Use very light lines to transfer the basic outline onto drawing paper.

STEP 2 Use cool gray 30% to outline the shape of the fishbowl and shade areas of the goldfish. Then add darker outlines to the bowl using warm gray 50%. Bring in some light cerulean blue for the water. Next add slate gray to the bottom of the bowl and along the surface of the water.

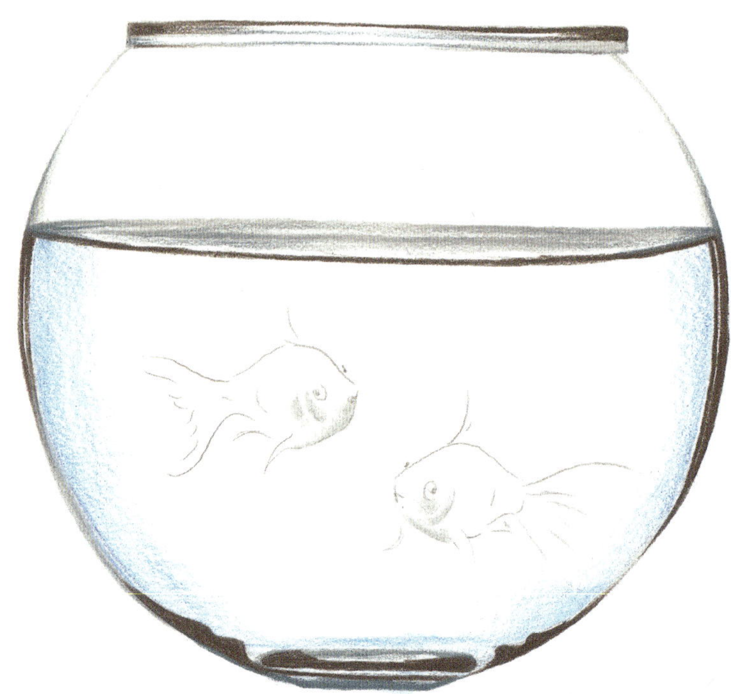

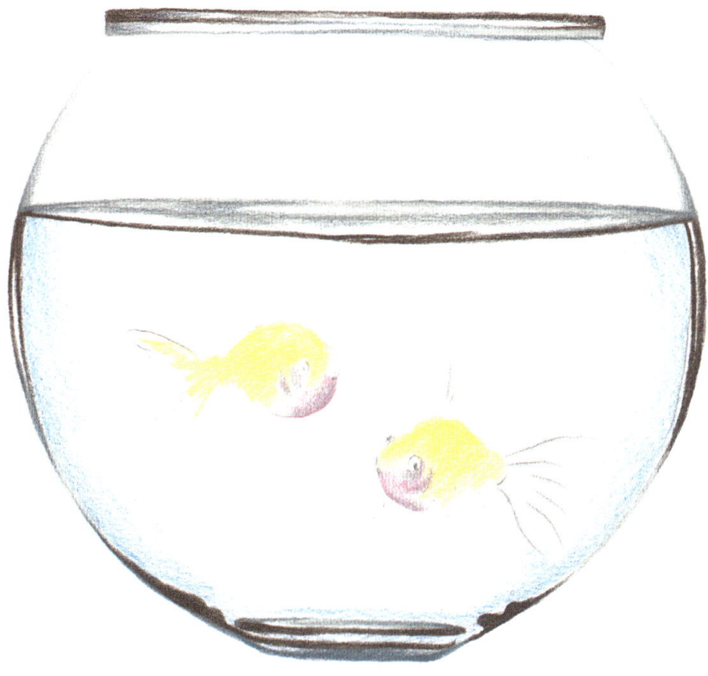

STEP 3 Lighten the outlines of the fish with an eraser; then fill them in with Deco yellow. Apply lavender over the gray areas on the fish.

STEP 4 Cover the majority of both fish with pale vermilion, leaving some of the lavender showing through. Then use black to fill in the pupils and create the gill on the fish on the right.

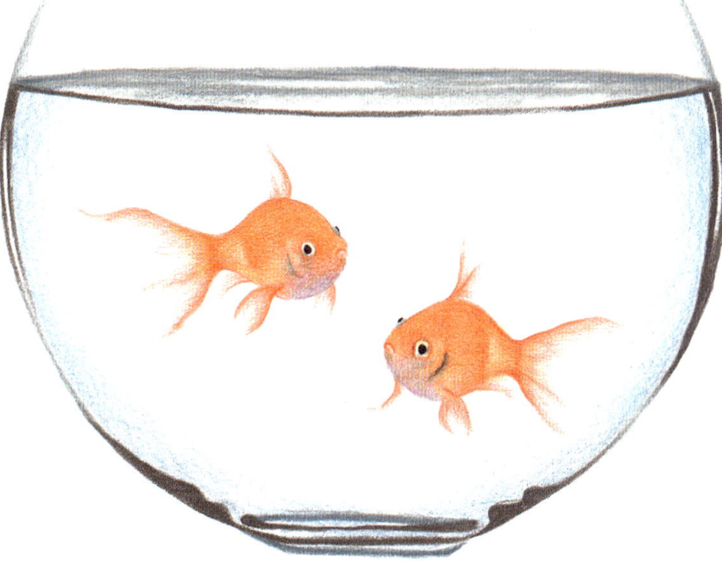

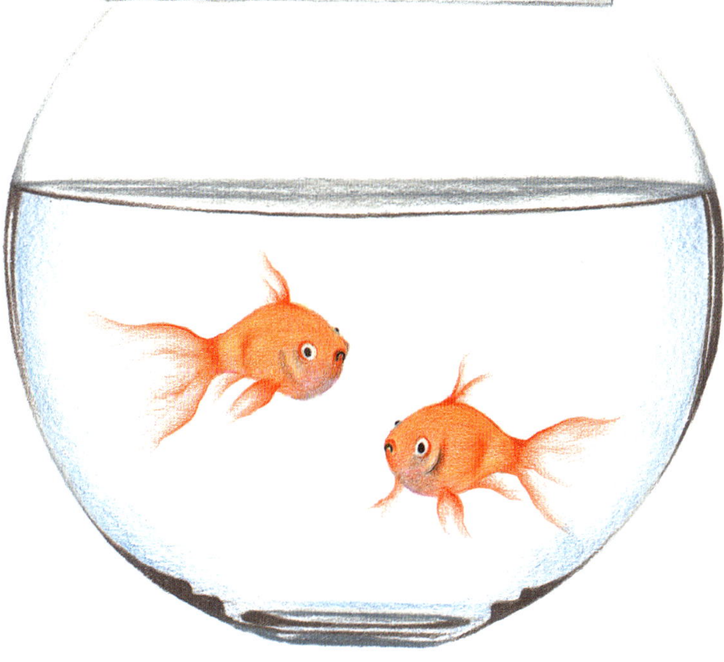

STEP 5 Create the mouths with black. Then accent the fish with scarlet lake and erase any remaining pencil lines.

This project is just plain fun! It is a great opportunity to use a multitude of different colors in one drawing. You are not limited to the colors chosen, so feel free to experiment and explore your own color palette. In order to make your pencil barrels round, you need a light side and an opposite shadow side. For the shadow side you'll simply apply your color with heavier pressure than on the light side. Another option for creating more complex shadows is to choose a slightly darker color and apply it to the shadow side of the pencil barrel; then place your final color over it for a deeper layered effect.

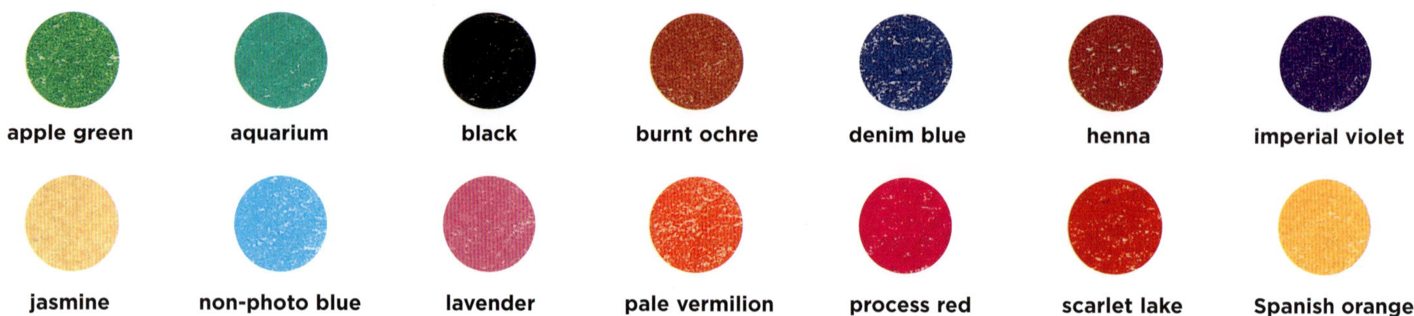

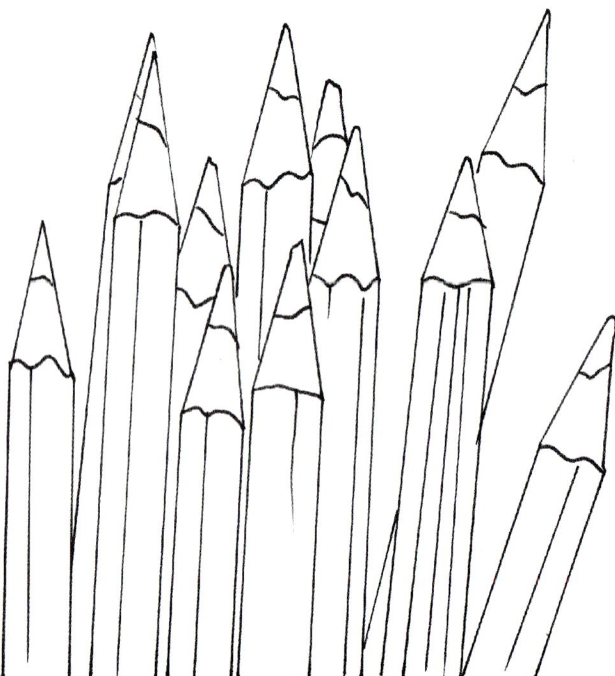

STEP 1 Lightly transfer the basic line drawing onto a sheet of smooth, acid-free drawing paper. It may help you to use a small ruler to keep your lines straight for this project.

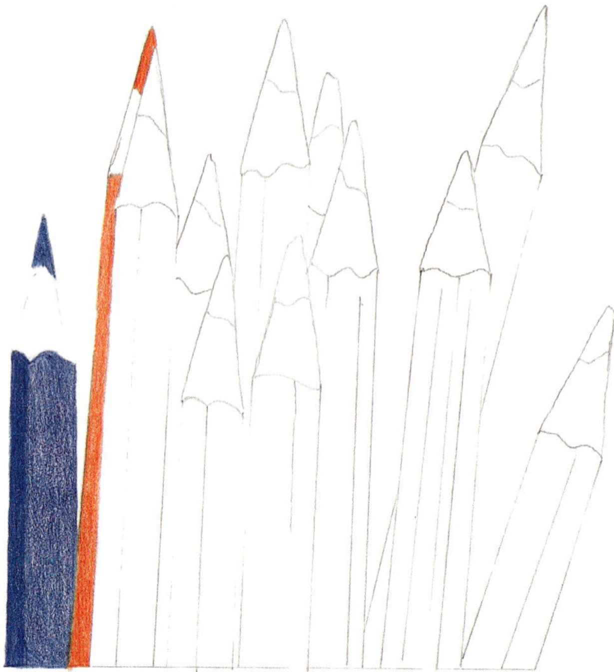

STEP 2 Use denim blue and pale vermilion to fill in the first two pencils. Apply heavier pressure on the left side of the barrels and lighter pressure on the right to indicate roundness.

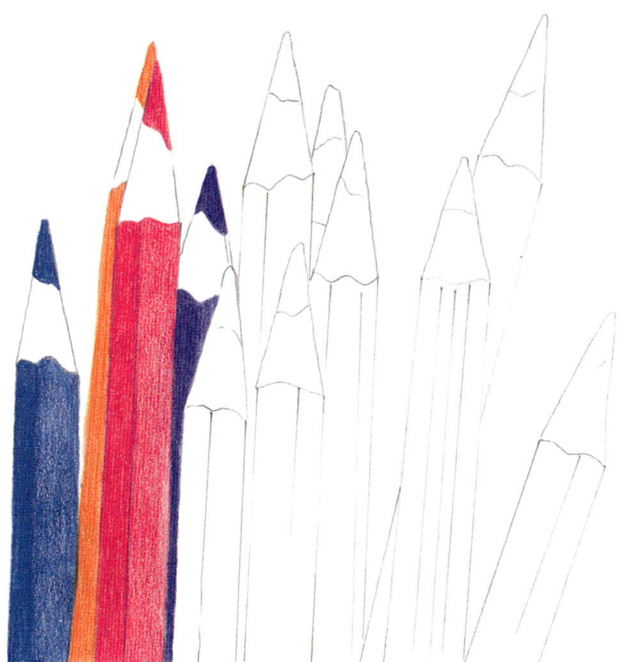

STEP 3 Use the same shading technique from step 2 for the next two pencils, this time using process red and imperial violet.

STEP 4 Use Spanish orange and apple green for the next set, remembering to keep my pressure varied.

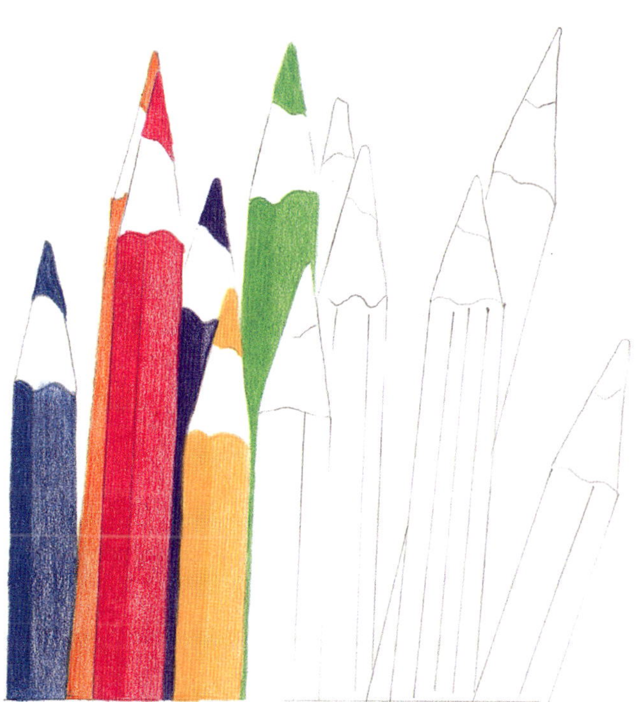

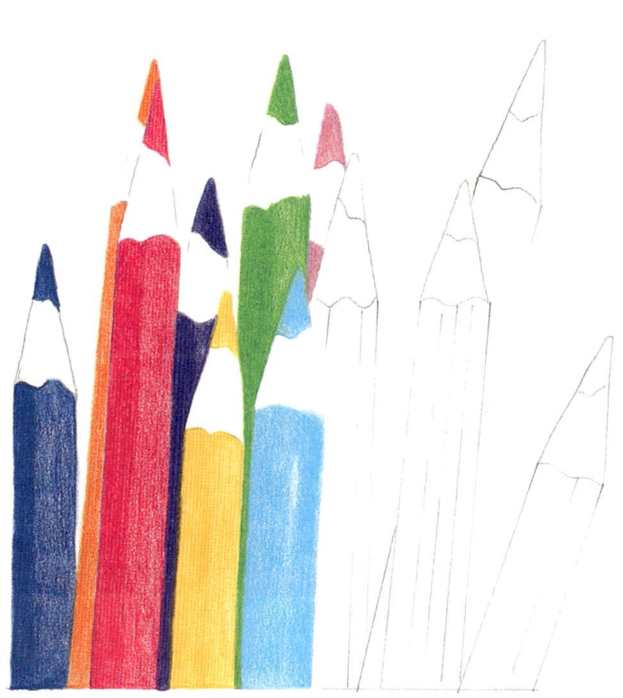

STEP 5 Fill in the next two with non-photo blue and lavender.

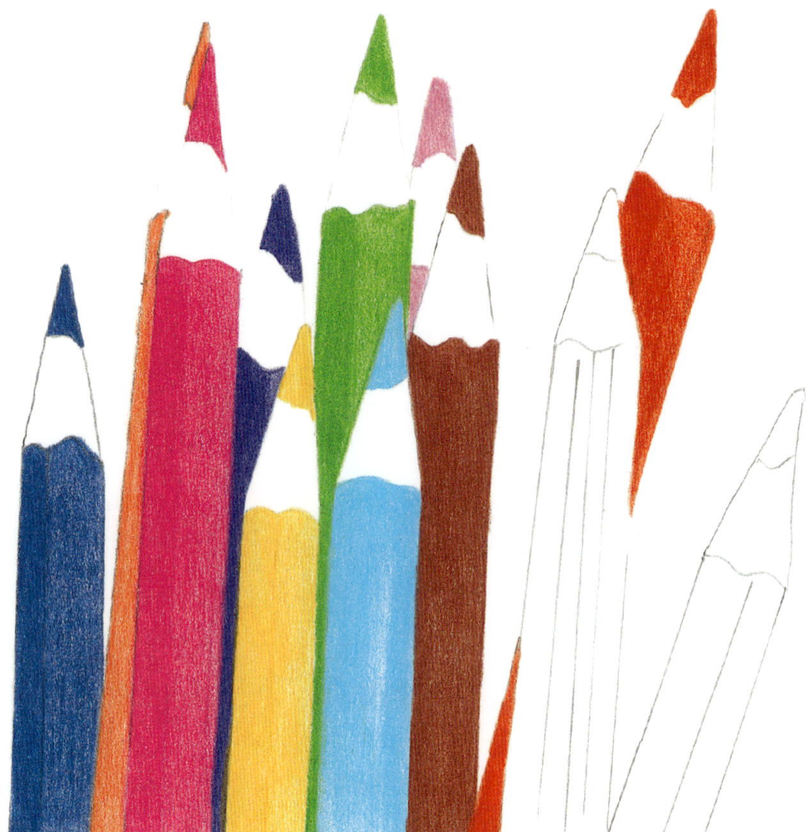

STEP 6 Now add the henna and scarlet lake pencils.

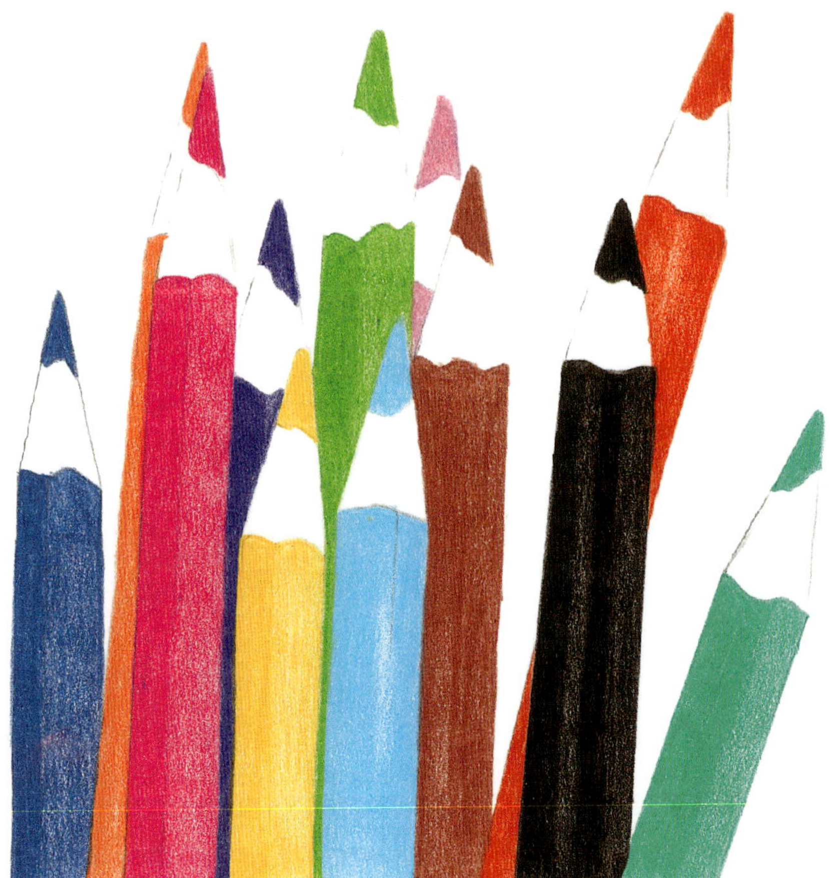

STEP 7 Using black and aquamarine, complete the line of pencils.

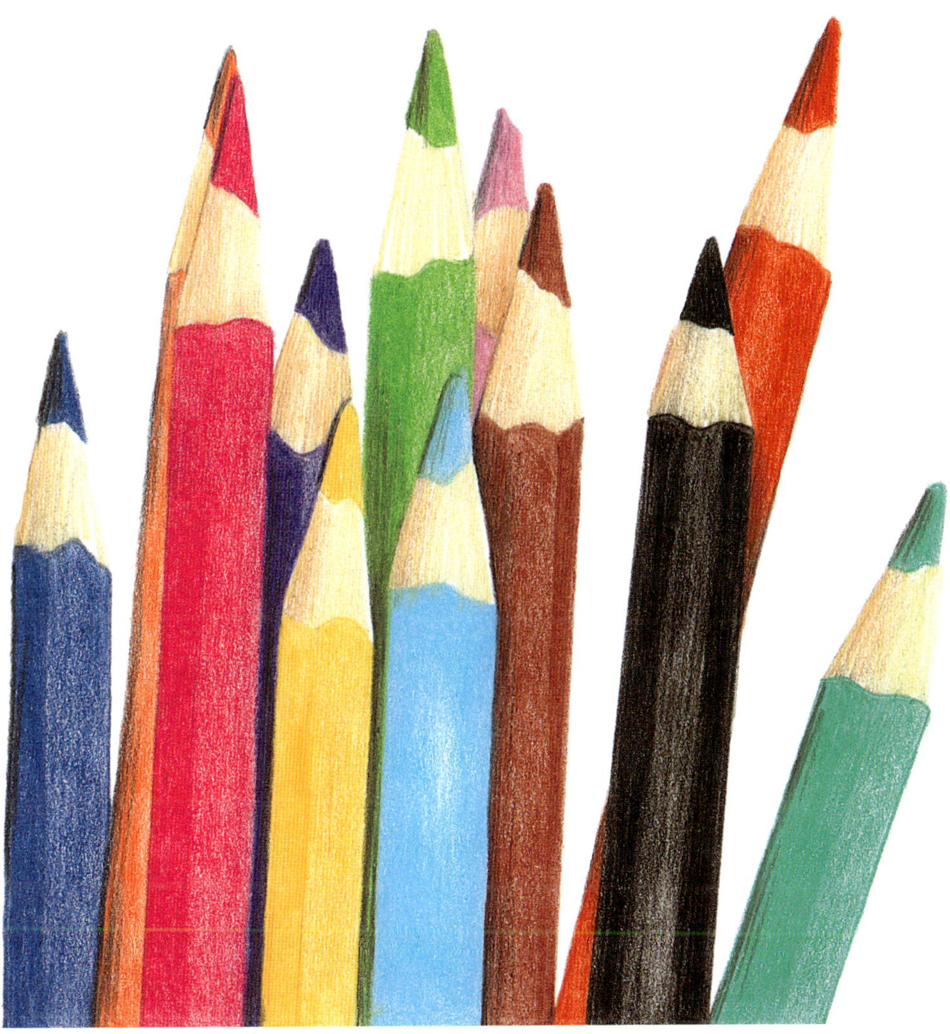

STEP 8 In the final step, place an even layer of jasmine on the sharpened end of each pencil to indicate the wood. Add burnt ochre on the left side of this area to create the shadow side and to make the wood appear round. Then add black to shadow the barrels of the pencils in the back row.

Pastel

Pastel lends itself very well to bold strokes of color, as well as subtle blends in value, color, and edge variety. Pastel is the softer side of color drawing media, with little to none of the hard, waxy binders that give colored pencils their hardness and permanence. Pastels range from just a bit softer than colored pencil to soft and buttery, easily crumbling to the touch. This section discusses techniques using both pastel sticks and pastel pencils.

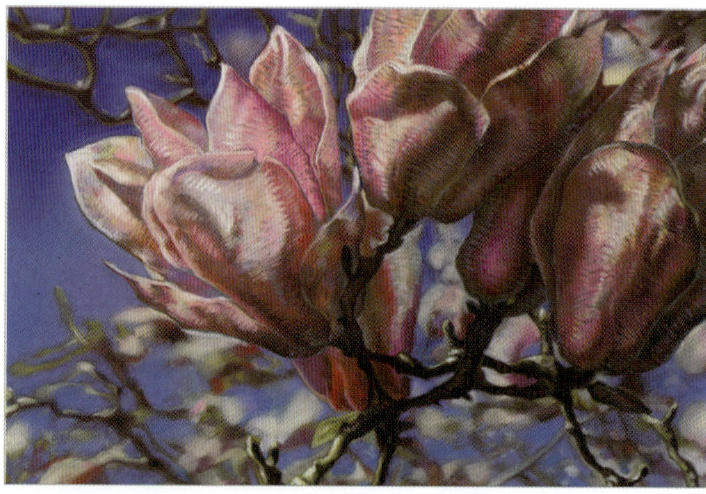

Student pastel drawing by Yea Jin Shin. Time: 6–8 hours.

Similar to colored pencils, when working with pastel, it's best to use toned or colored paper, from a 50% value to darker, for dramatic, bright colors. Work on sanded pastel board, which, though expensive, can make a big difference in the success of the project. With pastel and its relative softness, the more texture the paper has, the better.

Pastel Techniques

The way you hold and manipulate the pastel stick or pencil will directly affect the resulting stroke. Some grips will give you more control than others, making them better for detail work; some will allow you to apply more pigment to the support to create broad coverage. The pressure you exert will affect the intensity of the color and the weight of the line you create. Experiment with each of the grips described below to discover which are most comfortable and effective for you.

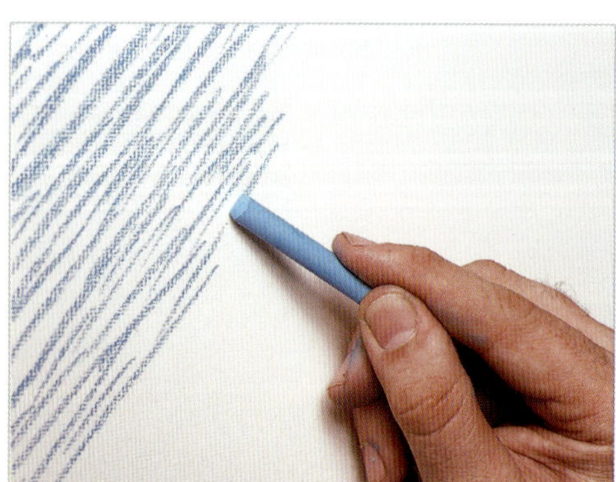

LINEAR STROKES To create linear strokes, grip the pastel stick toward the back end, and use your thumb and index finger to control the strokes. This grip is ideal for creating fine lines and details; however, it offers less control than the other grips.

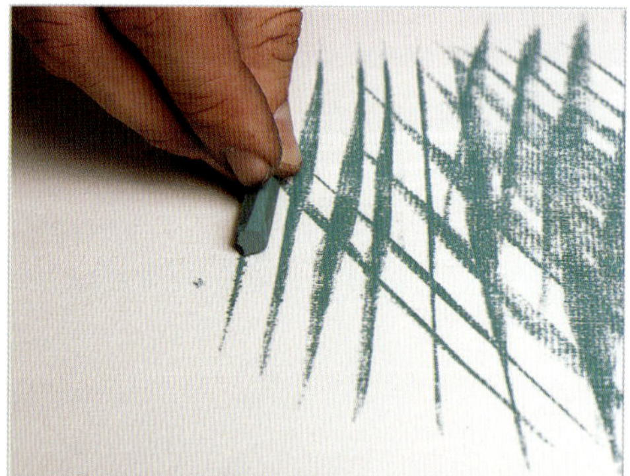

BROAD STROKES Place the pastel flat on the paper and slide it back and forth to create broad linear strokes. This grip is also useful to create a "wash"; use the length of the pastel to cover large areas and create backgrounds quickly.

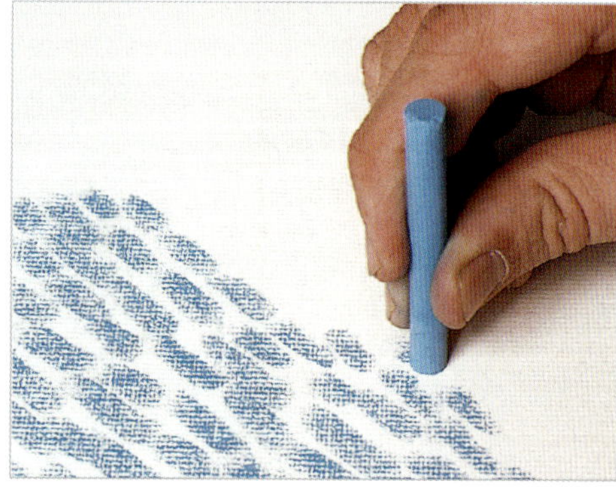

ROUND STROKES Turn the pastel stick on its end and grip it toward the front to create short, rounded strokes. This grip is perfect for creating texture quickly in large areas.

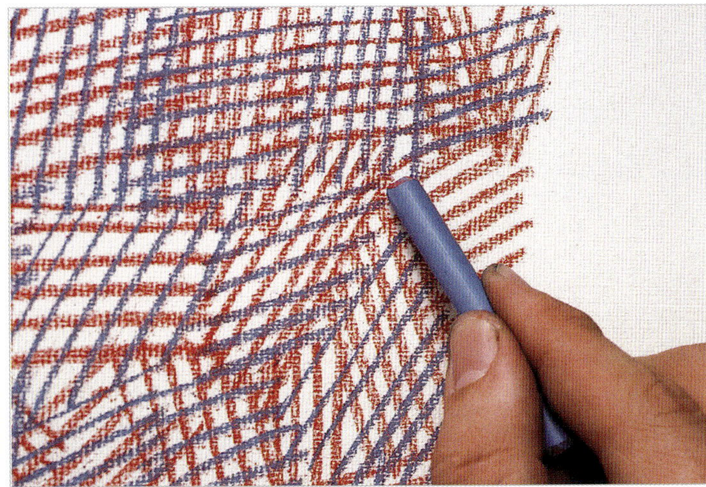

CROSSHATCHING *Hatched* strokes are a series of parallel lines; *crosshatched* strokes are simply hatched lines layered over one another, but in opposite directions. You can crosshatch strokes of the same color to create texture or use several different colors to create an interesting blend.

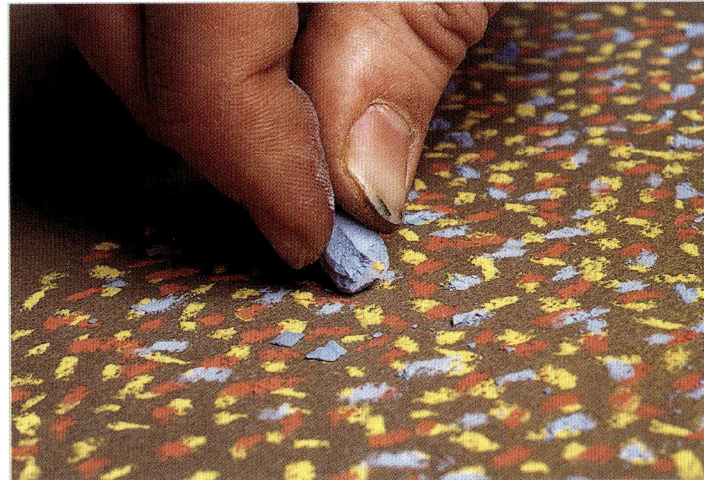

POINTILLISM Another way to build up color for backgrounds or other large areas of color is to use a series of dots, a technique called "pointillism." This technique creates a rougher, more textured blend. When viewed from a distance, the dots appear to merge, creating one color.

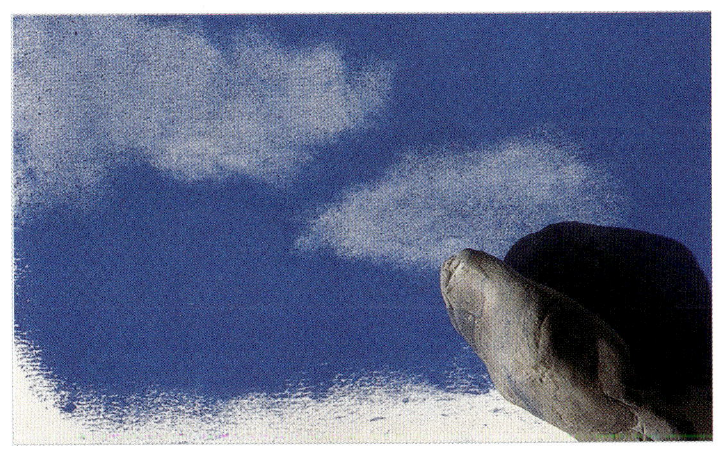

REMOVING PIGMENT When you need to remove color from a given area, use a kneaded eraser to pick up the pigment. The more pressure you apply, the more pigment will be removed. Keep stretching and kneading the eraser to expose clean, new surfaces.

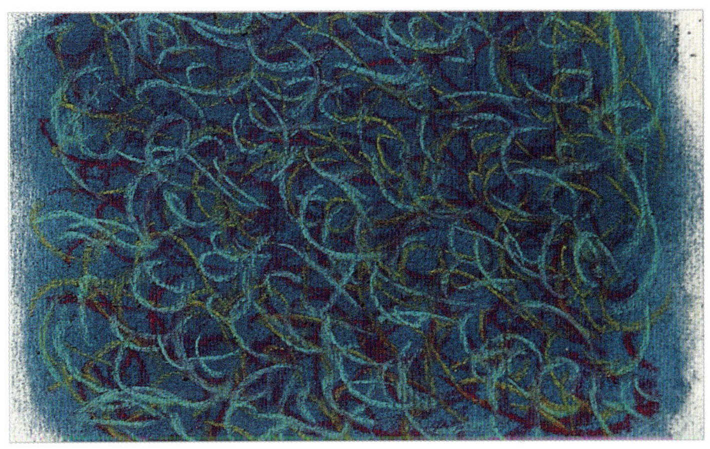

CREATING PATTERNS To create textures or patterns when rendering fabric or clothing, first lay down a solid layer of color using the side of the pastel stick or pencil. Then use the point of a pastel pencil to draw a pattern, using several different colors if you wish.

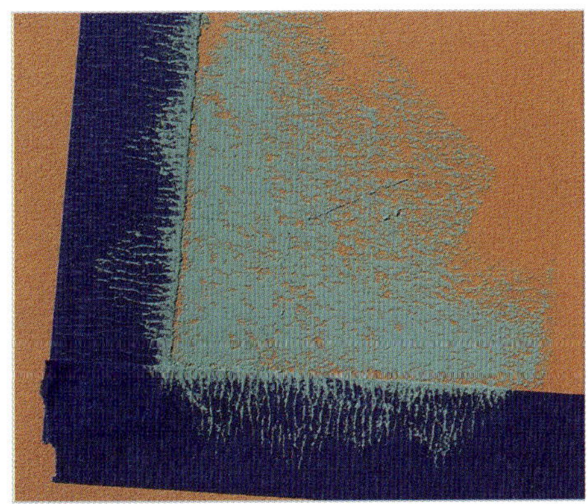

USING TAPE You can create straight, even edges by using house painter's tape. Just apply it to your support, and

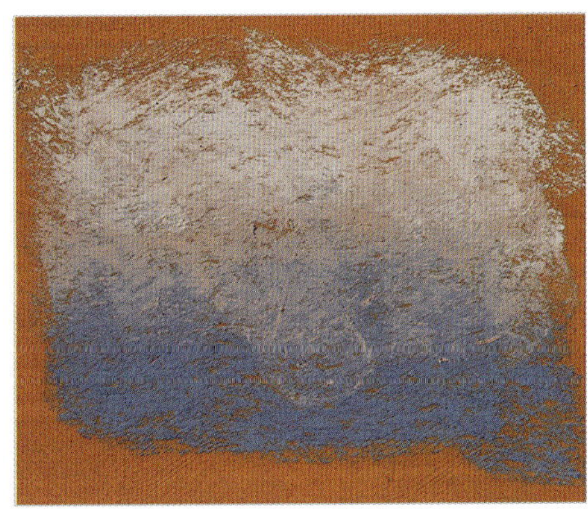

GRADATING Creating a smooth, even gradation on textured ground can be a little tricky. Add the colors one at a

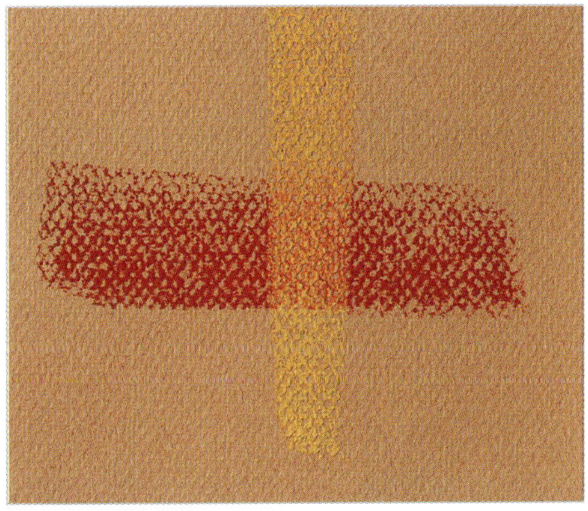

GLAZING Create a "glaze" just as you might with watercolor by layering one color over another. Use the length of

Blending Pastels

There are a number of ways to blend pastel, and the method you use depends on the effect you want to achieve and the size of the area you're blending. Smooth, even blends are easy to achieve with a brush, a rag, or even your fingers. You can also use your finger or a paper blending stump to soften fine lines and details. Still another method is to place two or more colors next to each other on the support and allow the eye to visually blend them together.

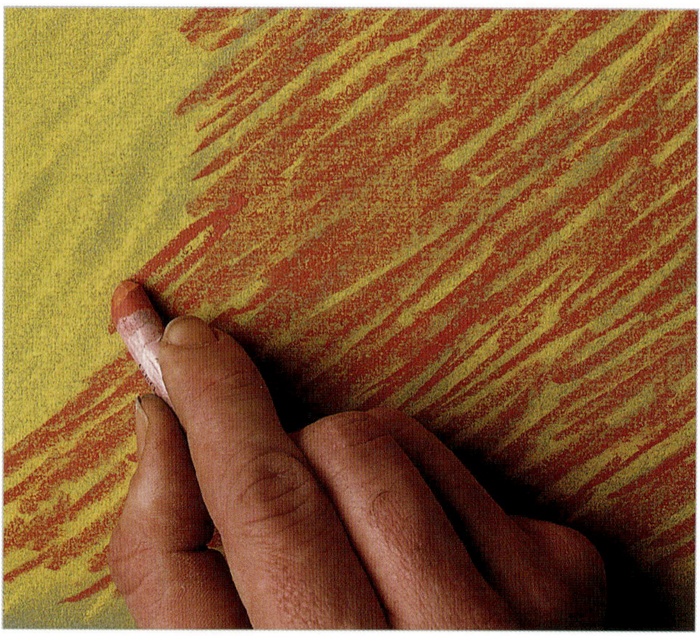

UNBLENDED STROKES In this example, magenta is layered loosely over a yellow background. The strokes are not blended together, and yet from a distance the color appears orange—a mix of the two colors.

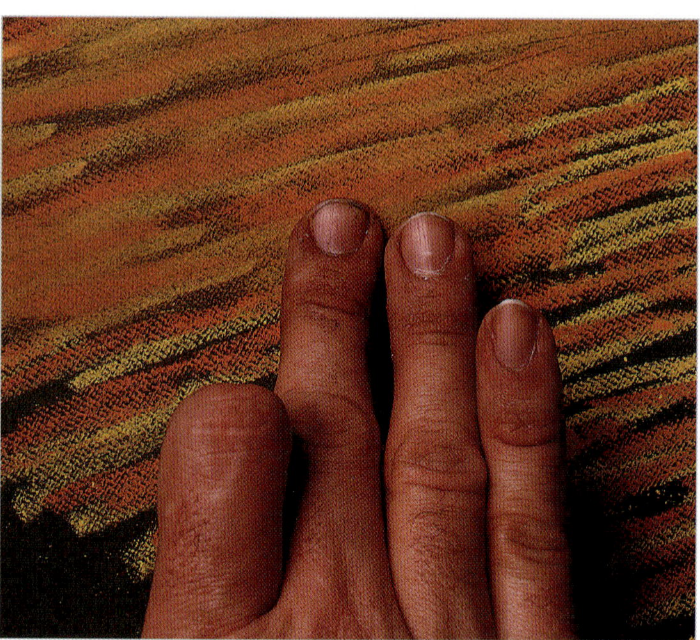

BLENDING WITH FINGERS Using your fingers or the side of your hand to blend gives you the softest blend and the most control, but be sure to wipe your hands after each stroke so you don't muddy your work. Or use rubber gloves to keep your hands clean.

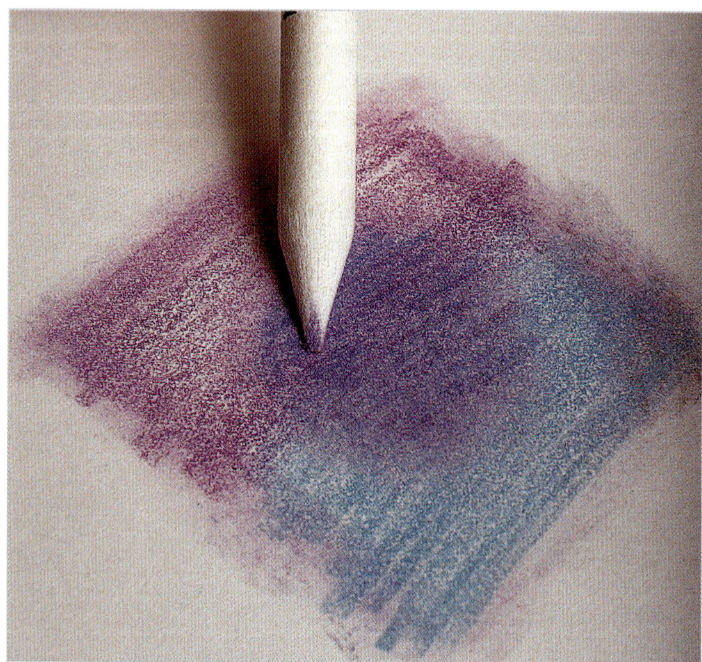

BLENDING WITH A TORTILLON For blending small areas, some artists use a paper blending stump, or tortillon. Use the point to soften details and to reach areas that require precise attention.

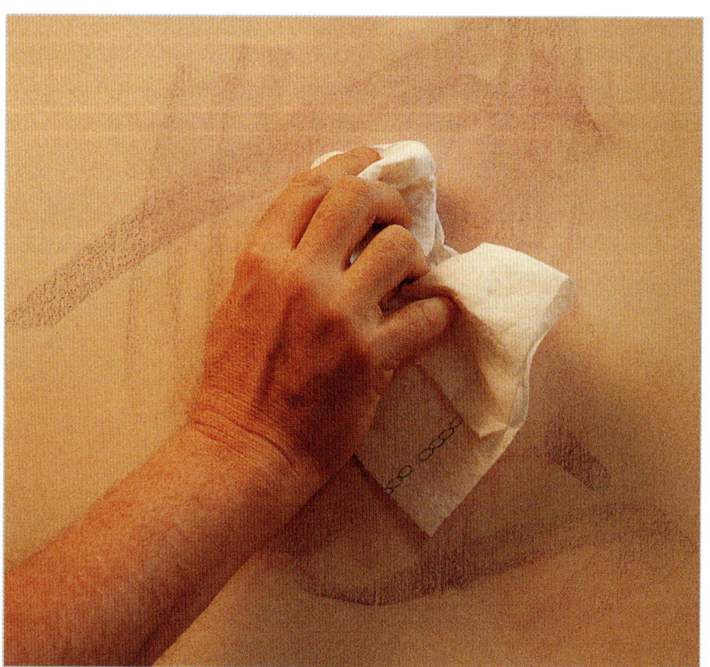

USING A CLOTH For a large background, it is sometimes helpful to use a cloth or a paper towel to blend the colors. To lighten an area, remove the powdery excess pastel by wiping it off with a soft paper towel.

Masking

The dusty nature of pastel makes it difficult to create clean, hard edges; but employing a simple masking technique is a great way to produce sharp edges. To mask, use a piece of paper or tape to create a straight edge, or create a clean-edged shape with a special mask you make yourself. Of course, you would use tape only to save the white of the paper; never apply it to a support that already has pigment on it.

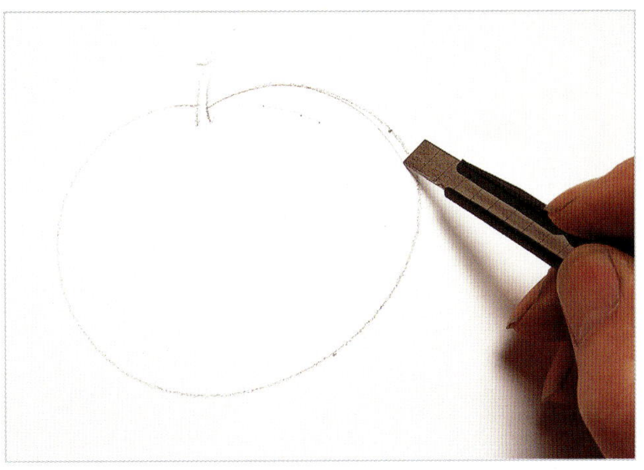

CUTTING THE SHAPE Begin by drawing the shape on a piece of tracing paper and cutting it out.

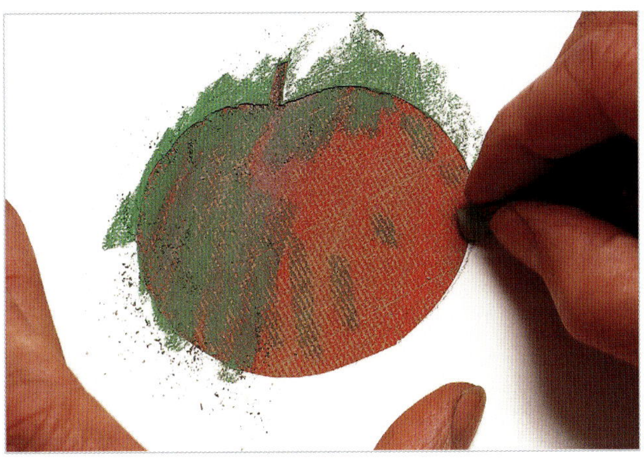

APPLYING THE COLOR After painting the background, place the mask on top and apply color.

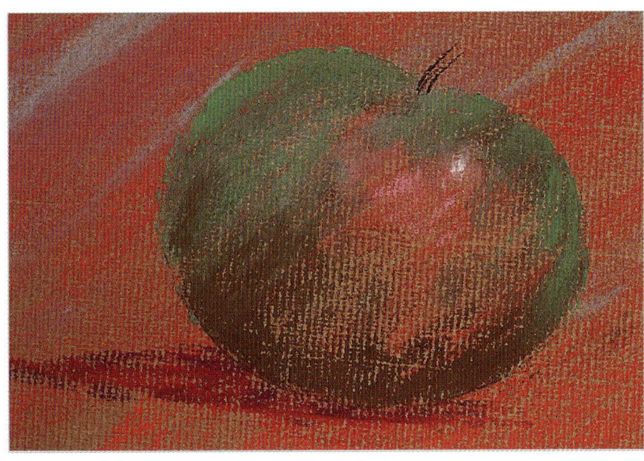

REMOVING THE MASK Carefully peel away the mask to reveal the crisp shape underneath.

Using a Combination of Techniques

These techniques are useful in and of themselves, but you won't truly understand the effects you can achieve until you apply them to an actual subject. Here you can see how the same subject is rendered using three different methods; notice the different look of each.

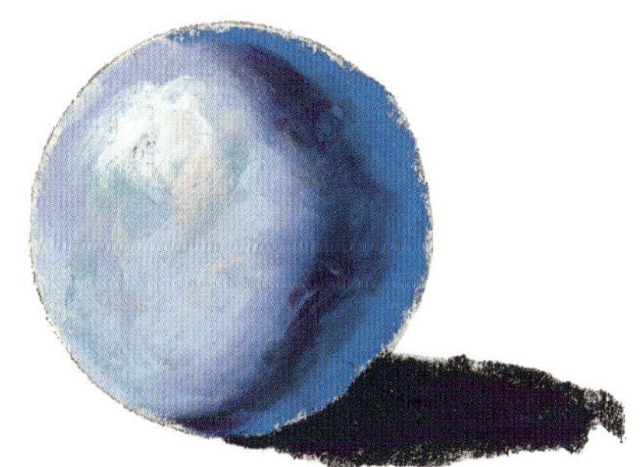

BLENDING Here the colors are applied

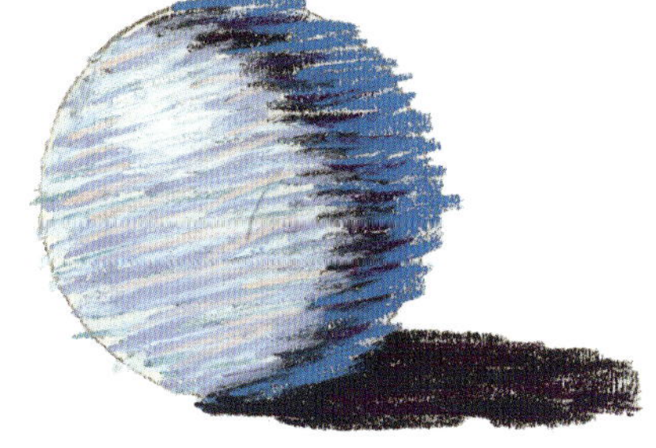

LINEAR STROKES Linear strokes are

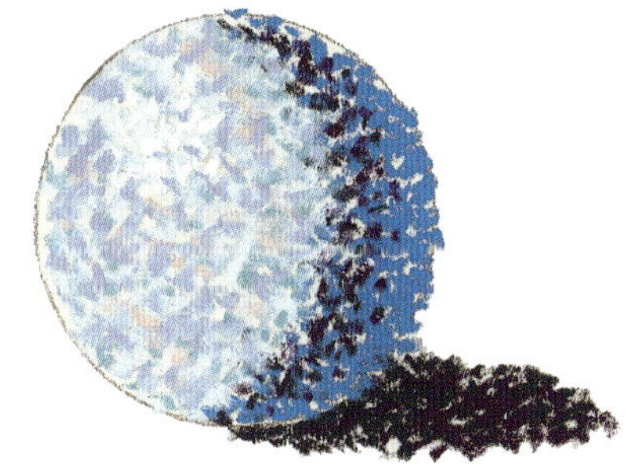

POINTILLISM Pointillism is used to

Pastel Pencil Demonstration

This demonstration uses a reference photo taken at the Huntington Museum and Gardens in San Marino, California. Similar to colored pencil application, after an initial block-in of dark values/colors, start with middle values and work up to darker colors, saving the lightest and brightest colors for the end. Other than the initial underpainting, only blend with strokes of the tip or the side of the pencil, one color against or over another.

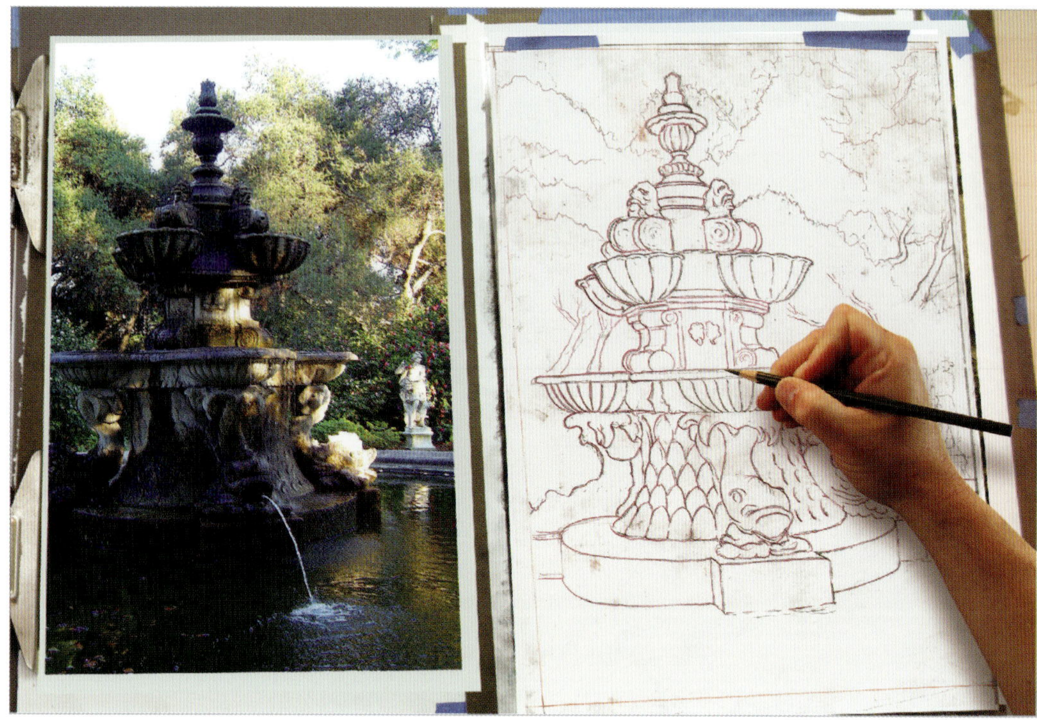

STEP 1 Transfer the drawing onto a sheet of dark green, sanded pastel paper. To transfer, rub a dark pastel stick on the back of the drawing, tape it upright onto the pastel paper, and redraw the image.

STEP 2 In the initial pastel application, use a large stick of soft pastel to create the dark shadow areas in the trees and on the fountain. Use large strokes of dark blue and black for the fountain and dark green in the trees.

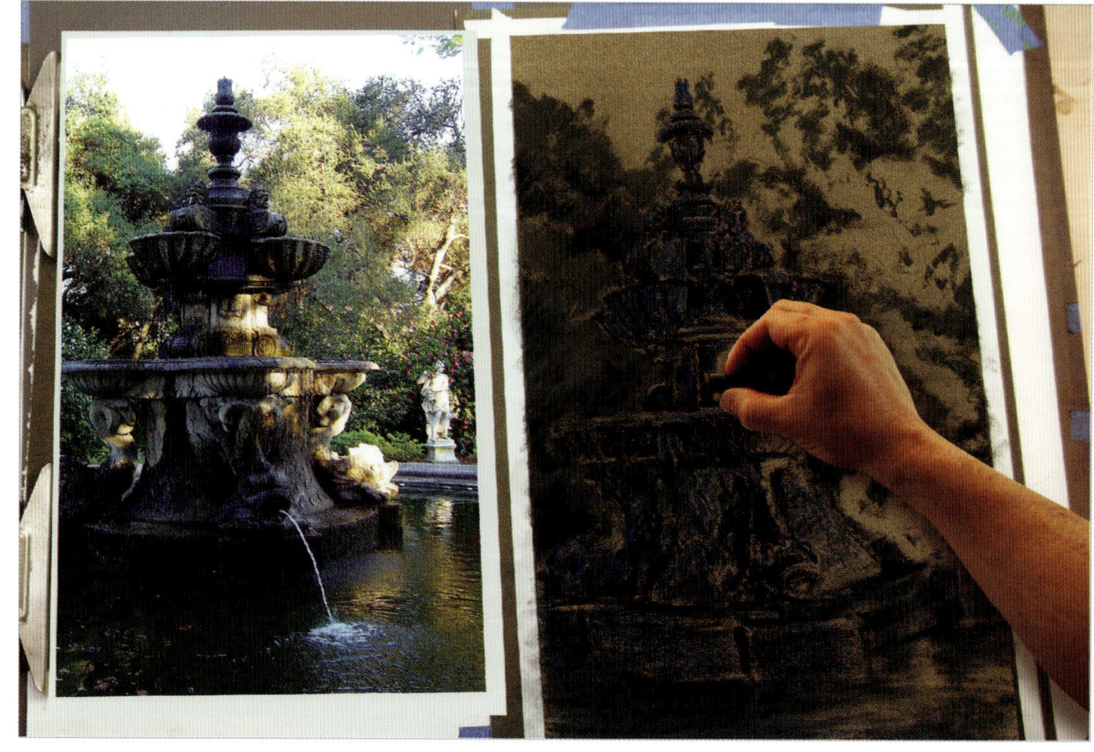

When using pastels, avoid blending as much as possible, except for the very first layer of dark value, which is worked into the surface of the paper as much as possible. Protect it with a coat of workable fixative that prepares it for the layers and glazes of pure color to follow.

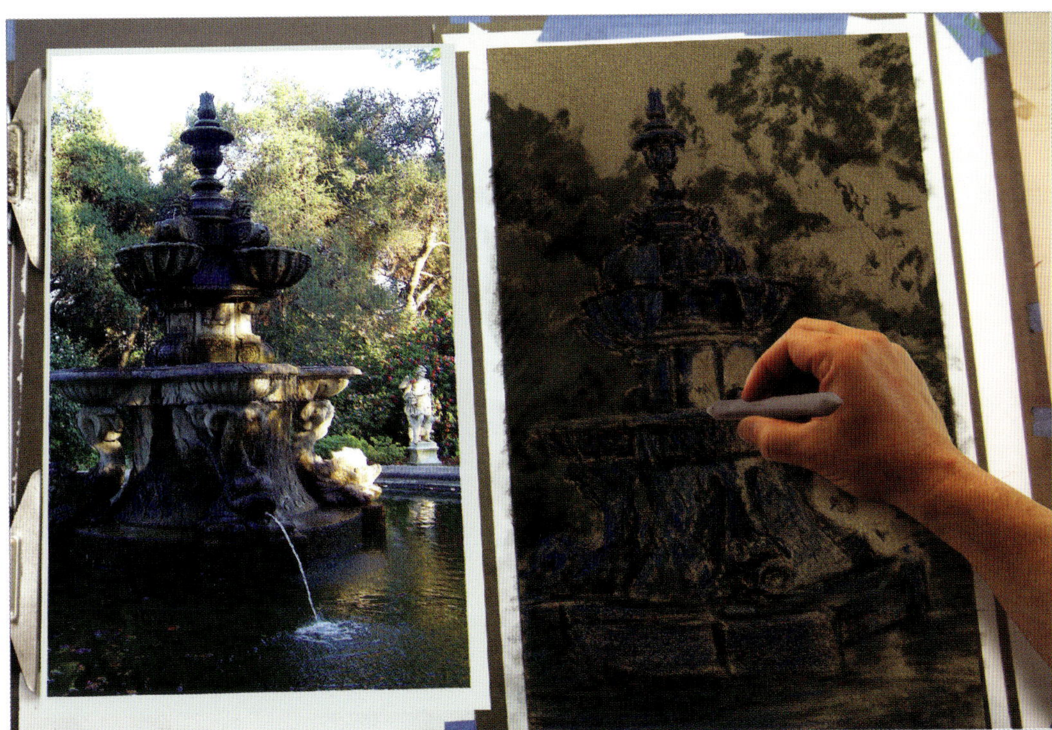

STEP 3 Use a clean stump to blend and work these dark colors into the surface of the paper. Then spray several light coats of workable fixative over the surface to really adhere the dark colors into the paper. You want successive layers of lighter and brighter colors to stay clean and avoid muddy blending from the undercolor.

STEP 4 Generally work from top to bottom in order to avoid smearing any of the color. Try keeping a piece of paper under your hand while working. Build up initial layers of color in the trees and sky with strokes of color from pastel pencils. The only blending of color from this point on will come from pencil strokes, not from a finger or stump.

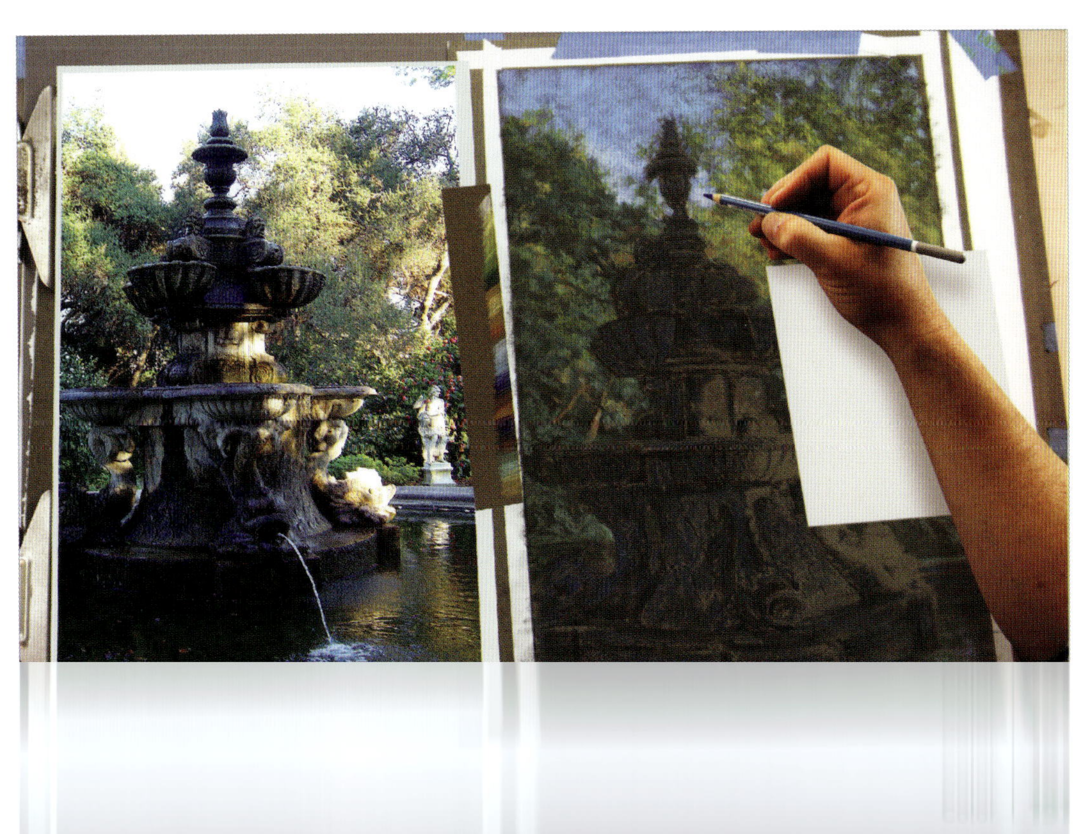

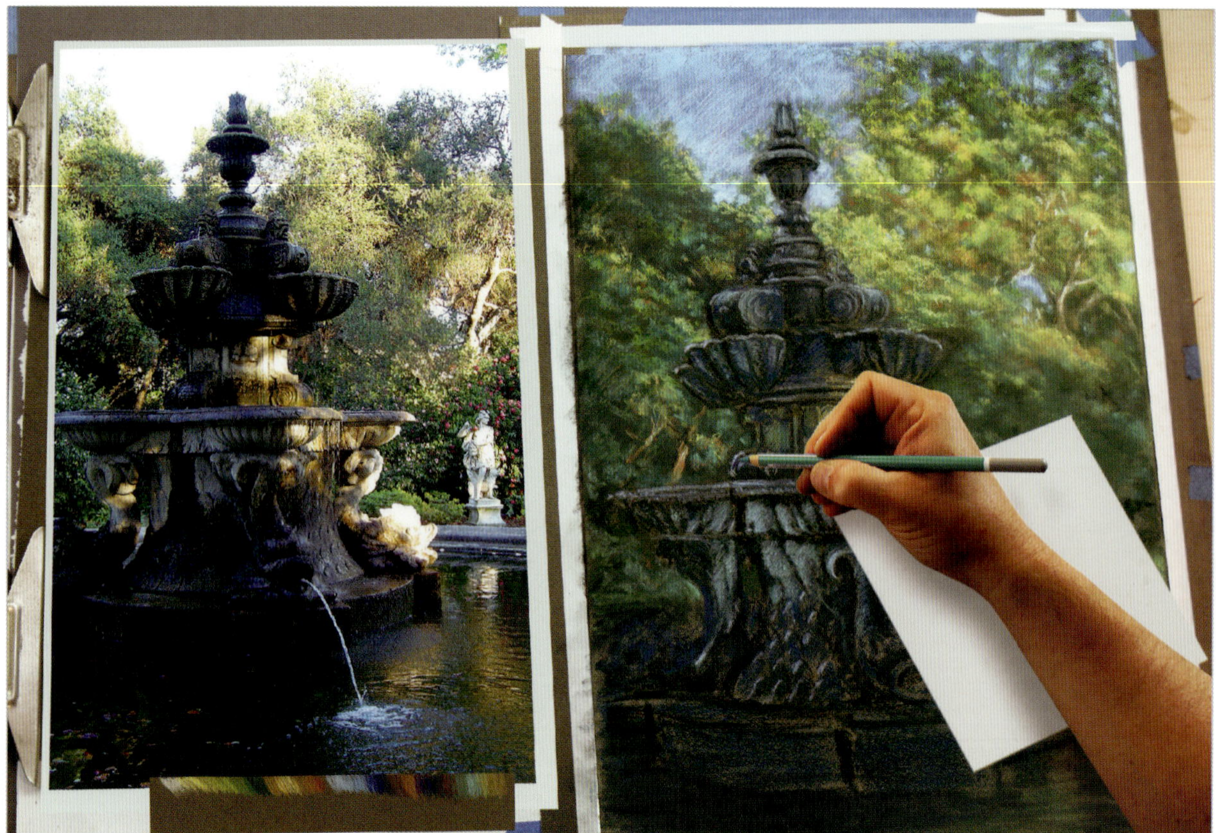

STEP 5 Working down the drawing, add brighter colors to the shadowed areas of the fountain. Use 6 to 8 different colors of greens, blues, and browns in these shadows alone!

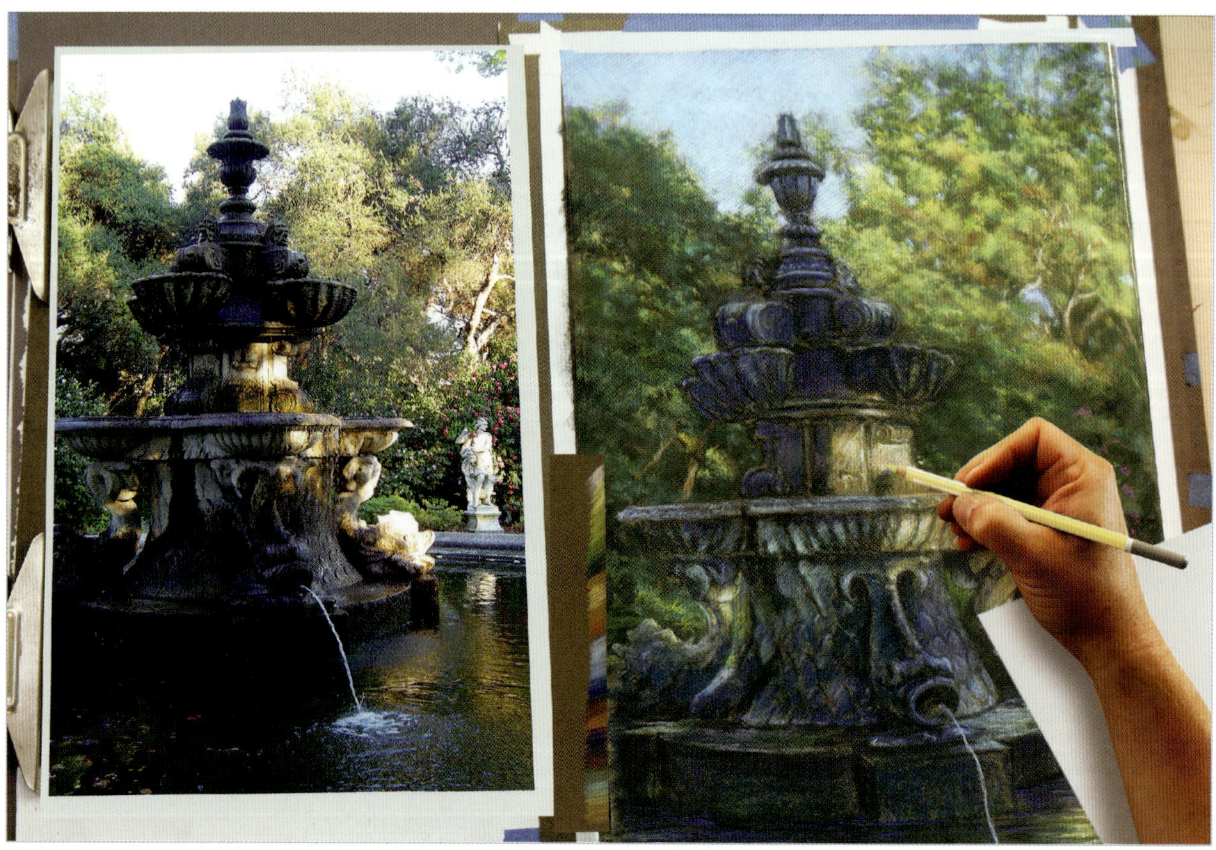

STEP 6 After establishing the values of most of the shadows on the fountain, you can more clearly judge how bright, or how subtle, the sunlight should be.

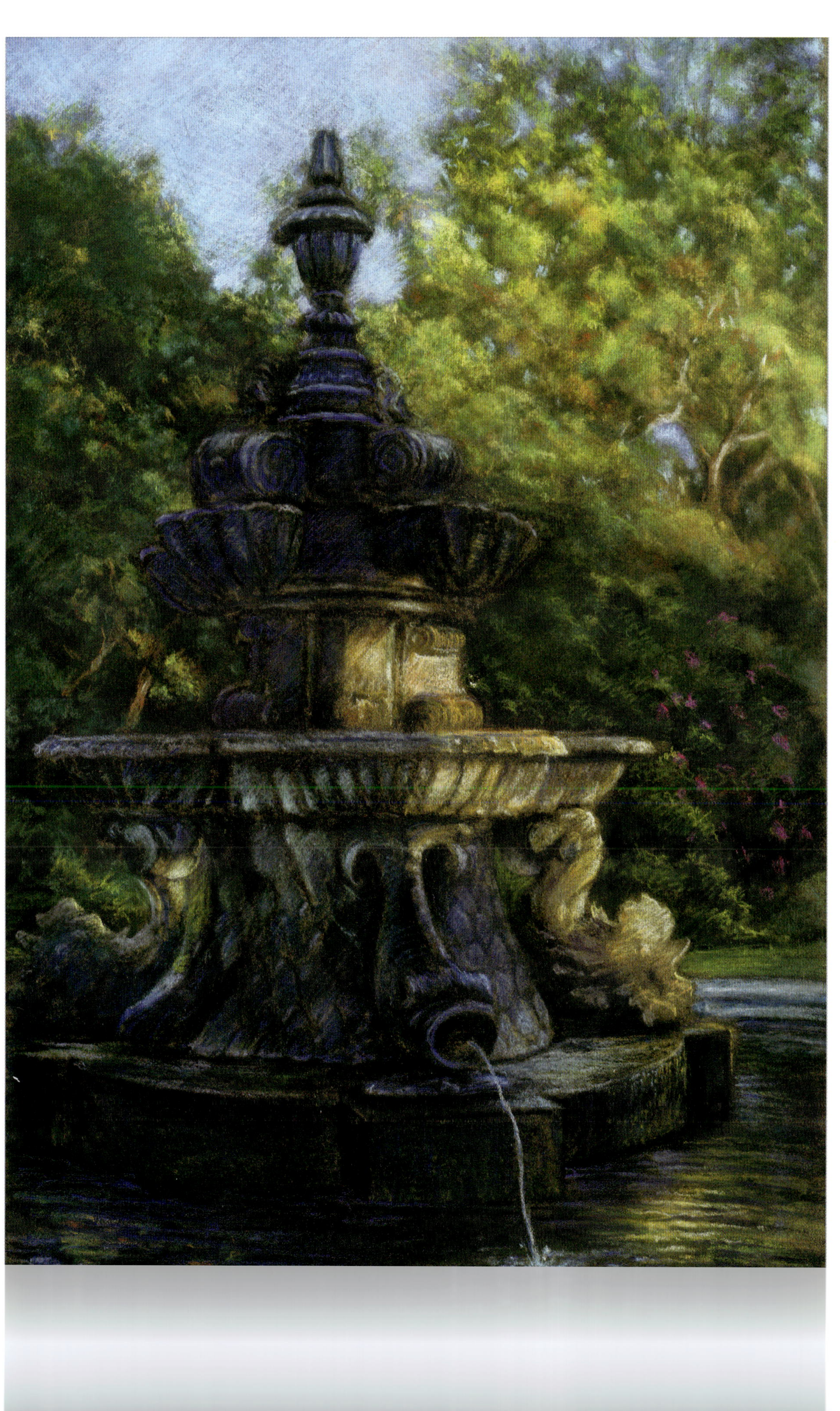

The final pastel drawing.
Time: 8 hours.

Pastel Stick Demonstration

This idyllic autumn scene is influenced by the work of California Impressionists, both contemporary and past artists, and students should enjoy this joyful, artistic impulse to colorfully and creatively capture the color in the world around them. Even though this demonstration is not a true "plein-air" work created outdoors, it should have that same spontaneous feel.

By nature, pastel sticks do not have the detailed and precise application capabilities of pencils. They are best for laying in large, bold areas of color, using the side of the stick. For more direct application, you can use the tip of the stick, making pastel sticks relatively versatile.

STEP 1 After using a grid to create the line drawing, transfer it onto medium-gray, sanded pastel paper. Drag a stick of red pastel lightly across the paper's rough surface for tone and apply several coats of workable fixative to adhere the color. On top of the red background, add dark colors of blue violet and black to shadow areas.

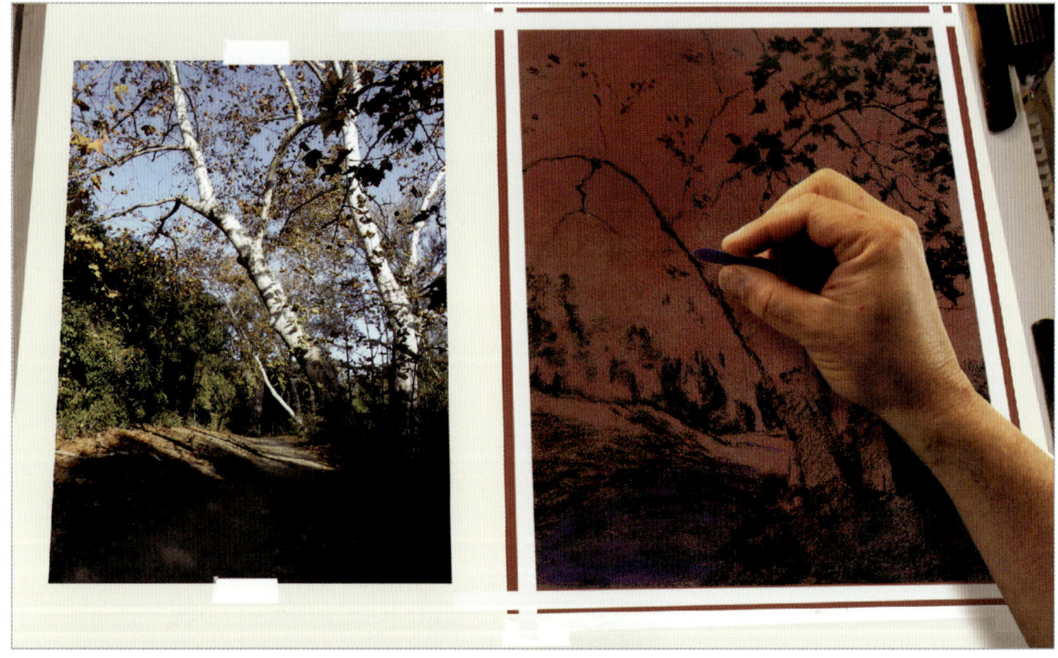

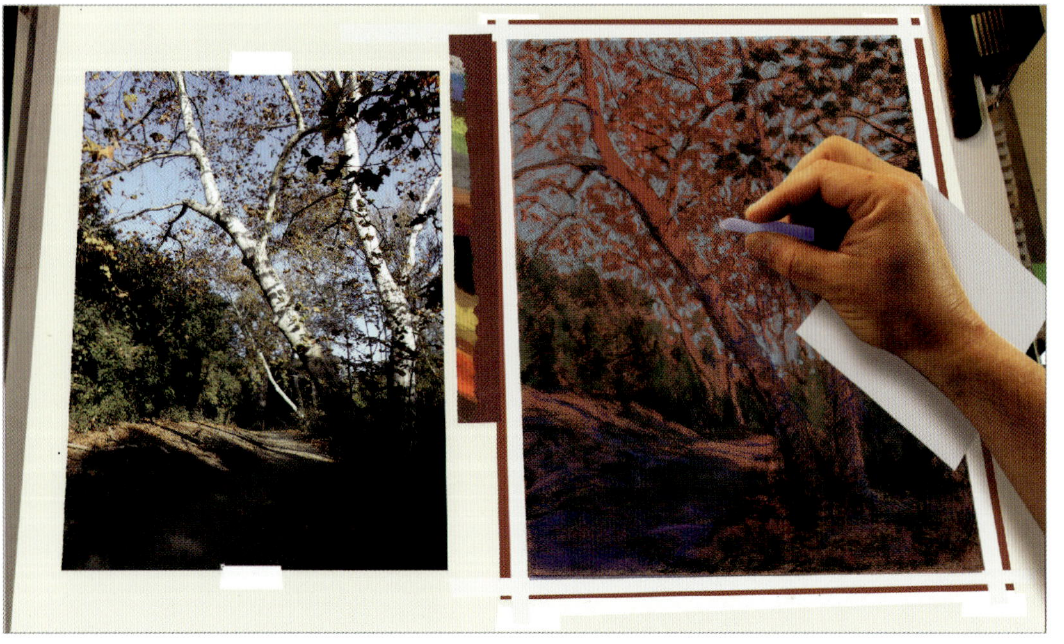

STEP 2 Blend the dark colors into the paper with a large stump and apply several more light coats of workable fixative to seal them into the paper surface. Establishing the value and color of the sky is an important element in any landscape drawing or painting, as a daytime sky is usually the brightest value. You will eventually use three different blue pastels in the sky, from lightest near the horizon to a middle-value at the top.

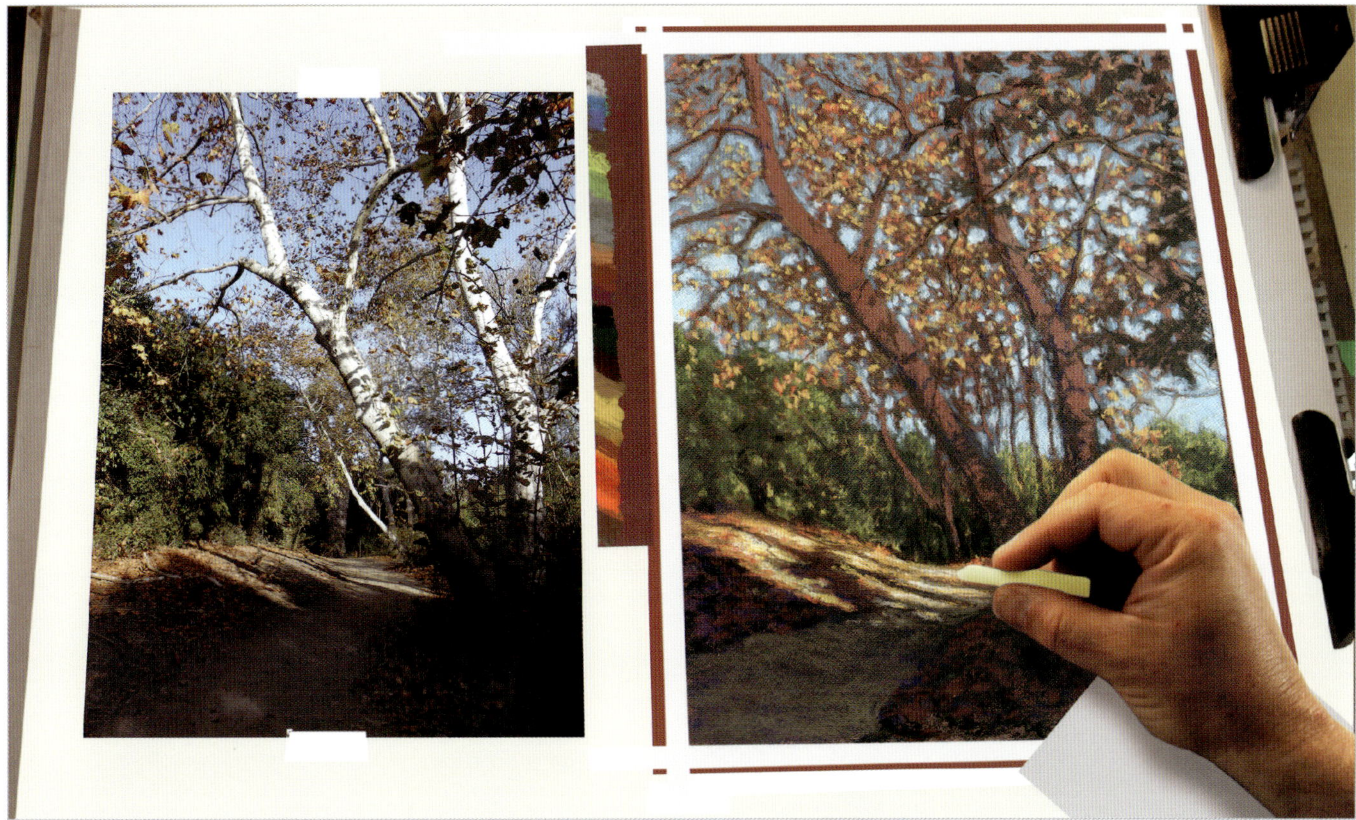

STEP 3 Once the sky and background trees are blocked in, start to develop the sunlit areas on the path and around the two foreground trees. The process for pastel color application is different than with colored pencil. In this case, start with the darkest color in any particular area and work up to the lightest colors at the end. Here finish the sunlit area with bright cream.

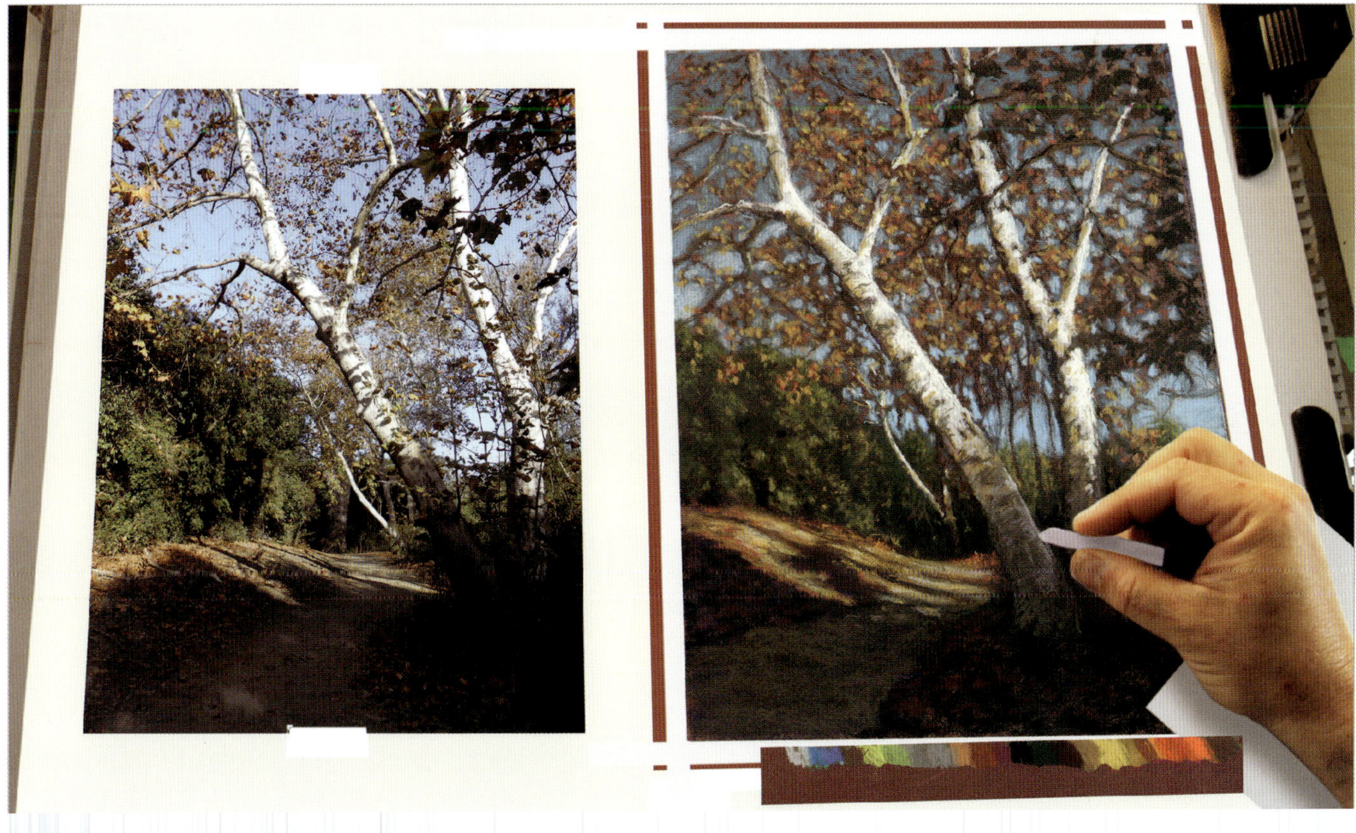

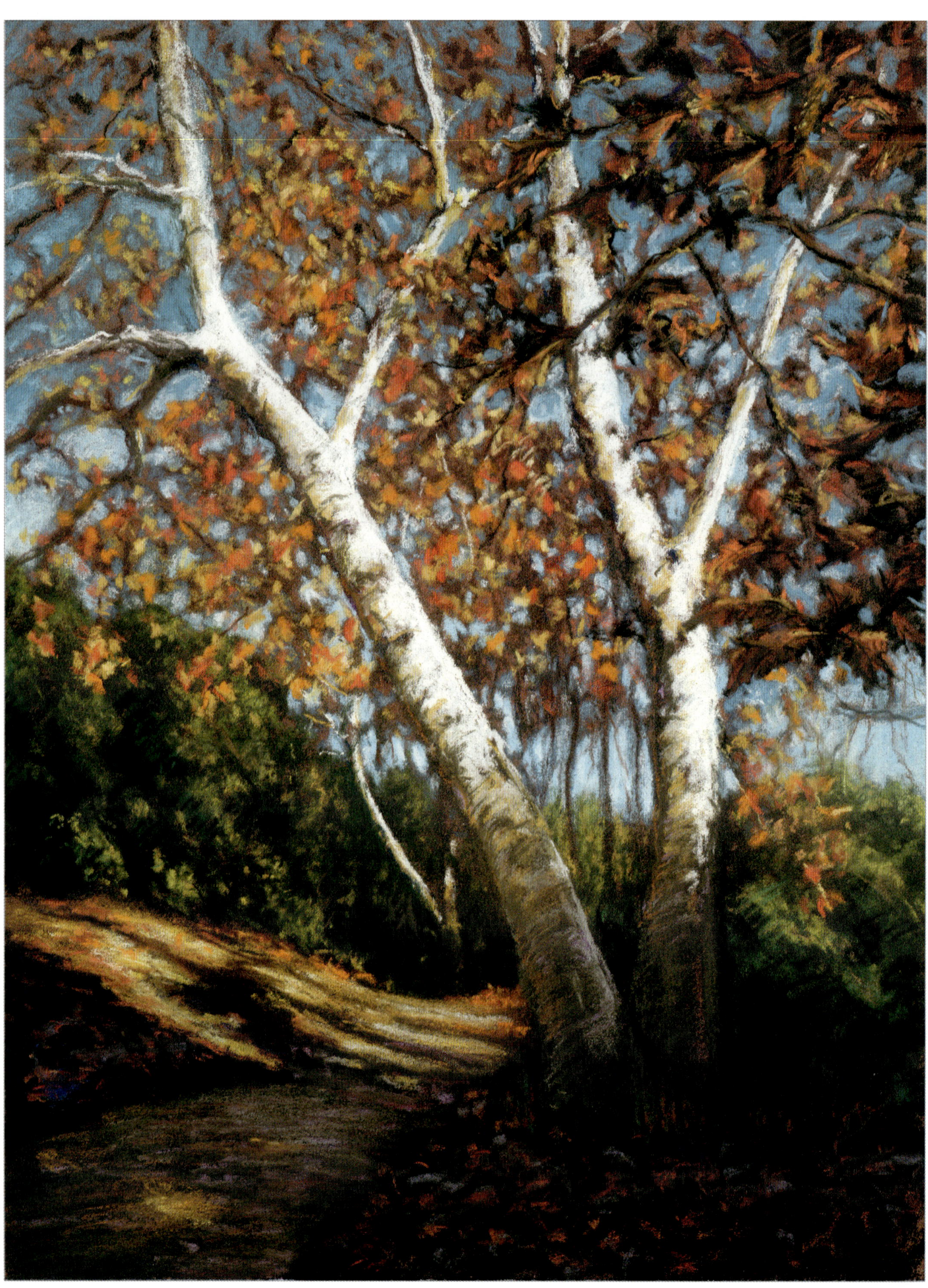

The finished pastel drawing, "El Dorado." Time: 8 hours.

YOUR HOMEWORK

Using any landscape or floral photograph, create a contour drawing, and transfer the drawing to quality toned art paper—preferably one designed specifically for pastel. Then experiment with the techniques demonstrated in this chapter for pastel sticks and pencils. Work in the size range of 14" x 17" to 16" x 20" for your final drawing.

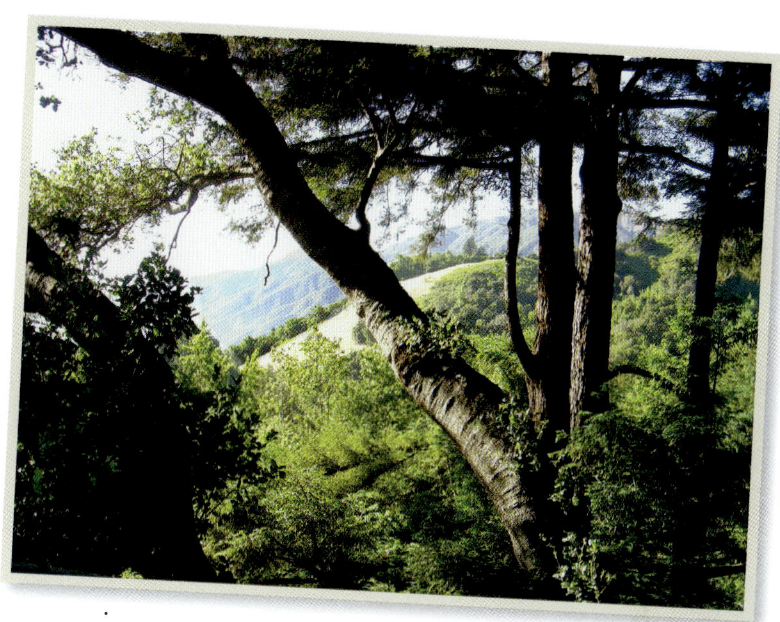

Photo reference and pastel drawing by student Huy Huynh. Time: 8 hours.

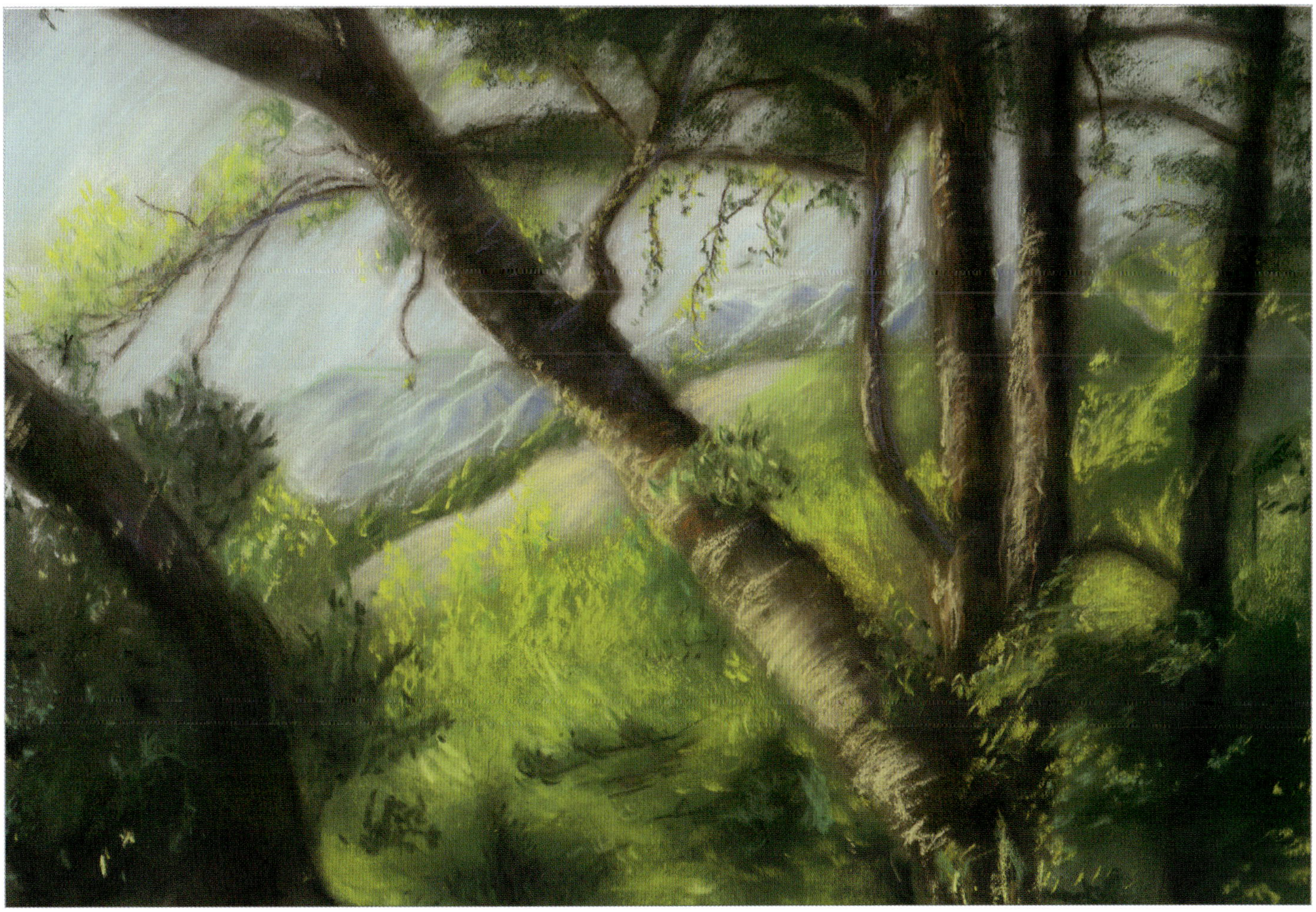

EXERCISES FOR PRACTICE

Painting animals is like painting anything else—you simply need to see shapes of color and put them in the correct place on paper. But when painting animals, you also want to capture the unique qualities of your subject, such as the animal's skin or hair texture and its features and body type. Consult books or magazines for appealing photographs, or take pictures of your pet. Look for subtle types of movement, like the twist of the body or the direction of a gaze.

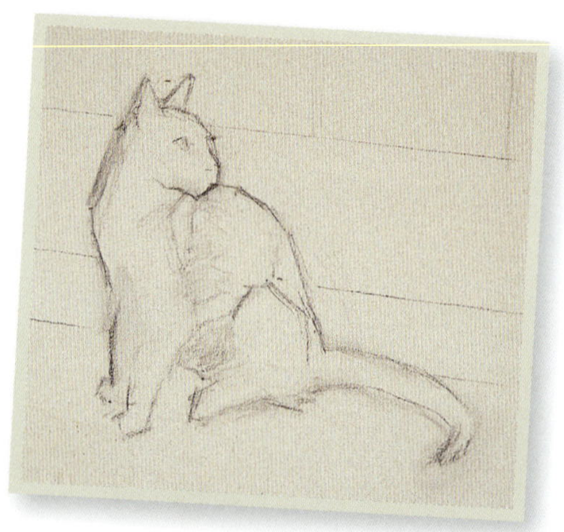

THE SKETCH The design of this painting is simple: The cat is silhouetted against the light of a patio door. Begin by drawing the main shapes, roughing in the outlines and sketching the lines of the glass and wood door. This pose shows movement even though the cat is sitting still.

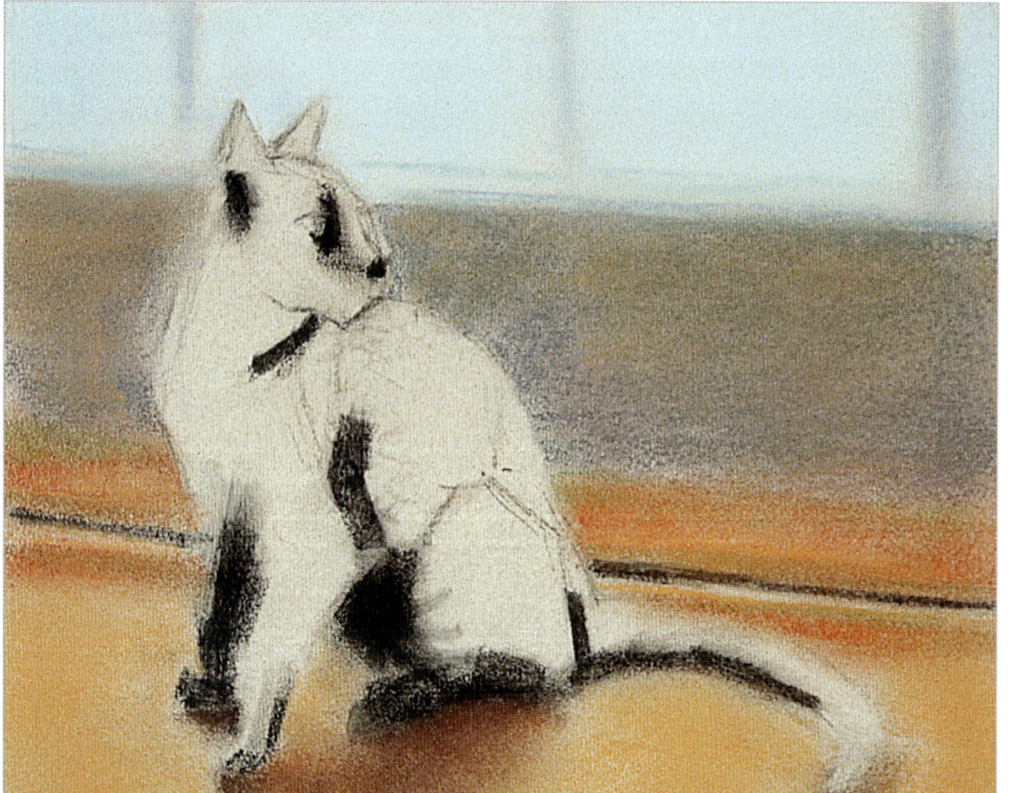

STEP 1 First establish the light area of the window with cobalt blue; then mix black with denatured alcohol, and paint the darks in the fur with a brush. In order to blend the softness of the cat's fur into the surroundings, paint the background first. Render the wall with blue-gray and gold ochre, blending them with your hand. Then use burnt sienna and chrome green for the molding. The basic tone of the floor is gold ochre. Next block in the shadow of the cat on the floor with light English red, carmine brown, and burnt sienna.

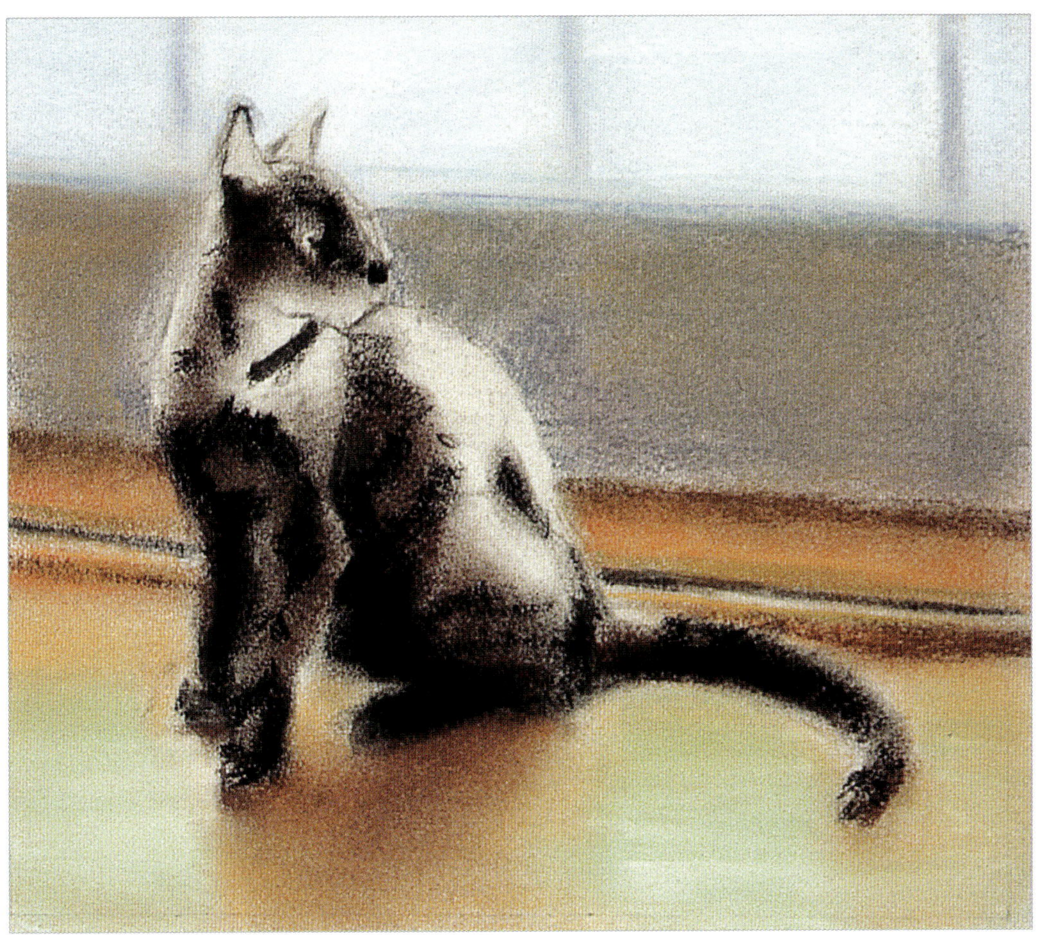

STEP 2 Lighten the floor with phthalo green, red-violet deep, and phthalo blue to show the reflected light from the door. Lighten the value on the window with permanent rose and use carmine for the dark of the molding. Next use a well-blended mix of carmine brown and bistre for the lighter colors in the fur and black for the deepest shadows in the fur.

STEP 3 Next use raw sienna to paint the shadows in the lighter areas of fur, making unblended strokes that follow the direction of the fur growth. For the eye, paint the pupil black; then draw around it with chrome green grayed with scarlet (its complement), touching lightly with my finger. Next use caput mortuum red for the warm color in the ear, and use gold ochre and yellow ochre for the highlighted fur.

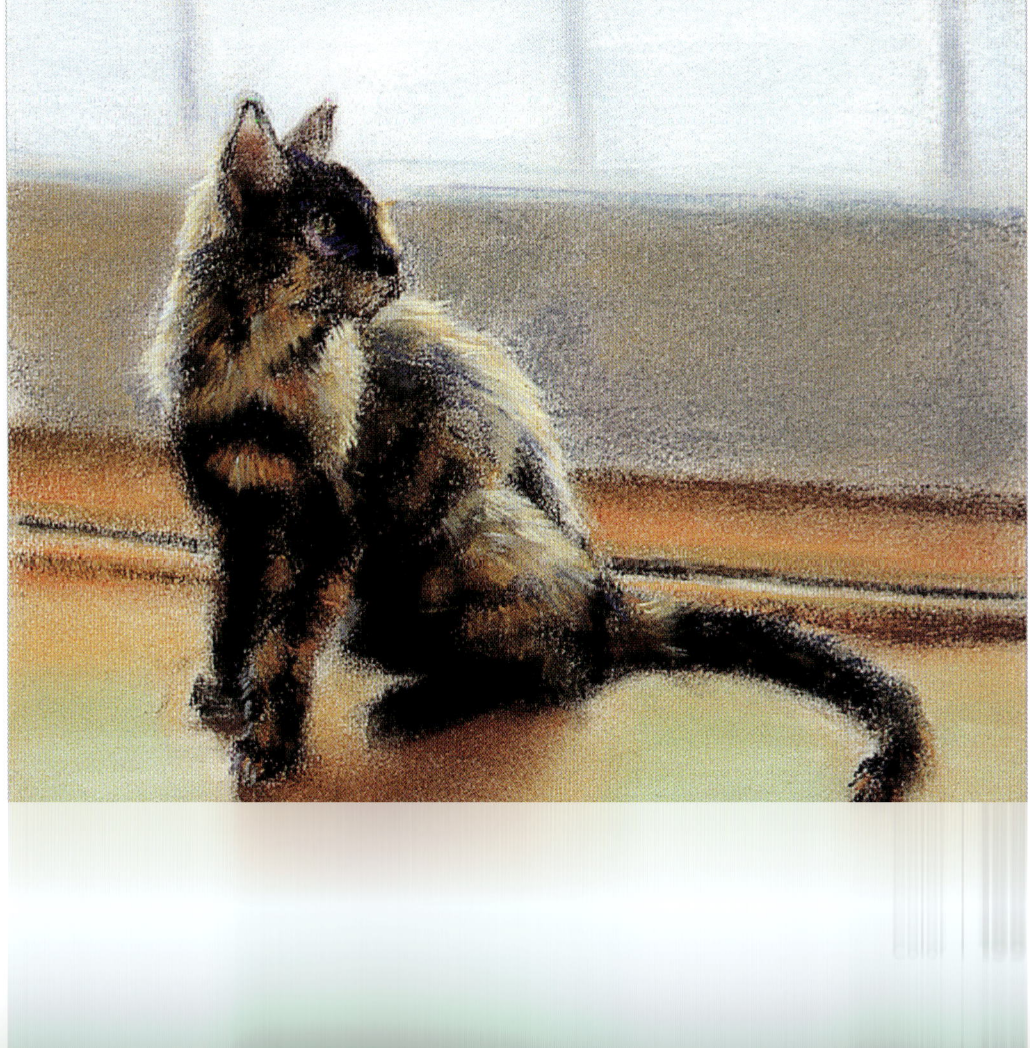

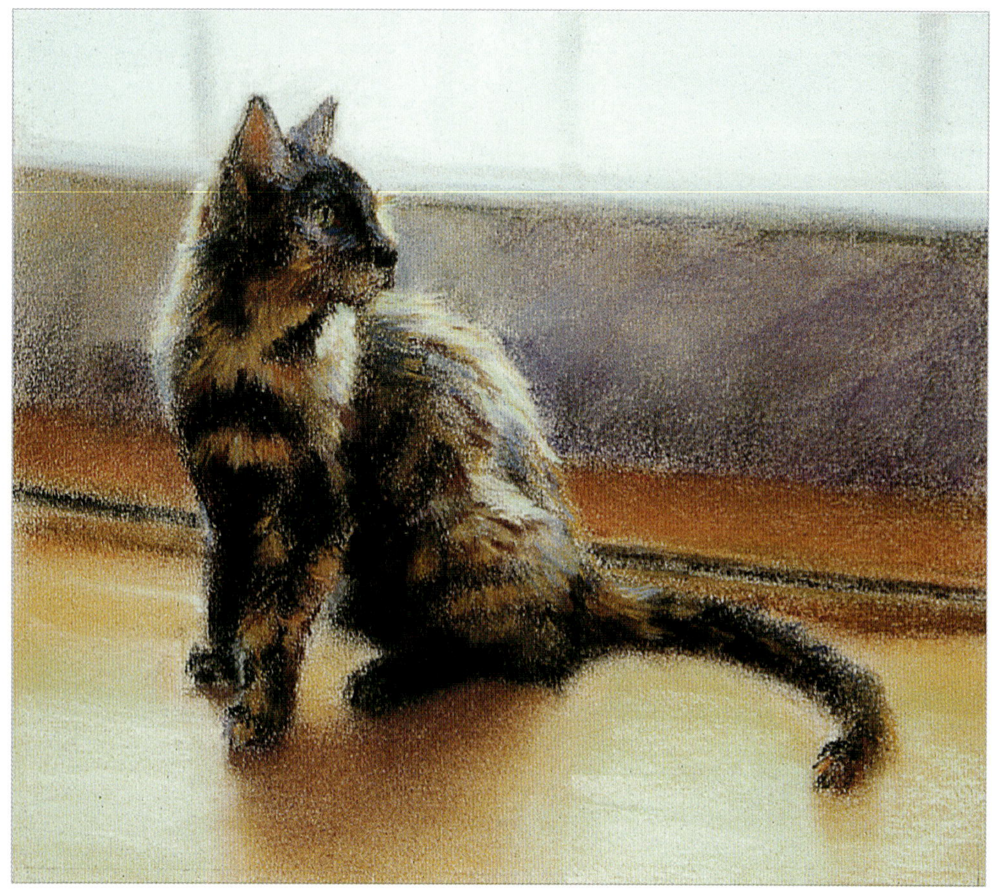

STEP 4 Lighten the window with viridian green and darken the wall with purple and blue-gray. Then add vermilion and olive green to the molding. For the dark accents in the shadowed fur, add unblended strokes of carmine brown and bistre. Next add more detail with English red. Indicate the reflected light on the muzzle with cobalt blue and use scarlet for the light shining through the ear. Then add a little crimson to add depth to the corner of the eye.

STEP 5 Shorten the muzzle, using Mars violet to paint the background into the nose a bit to define its shape. Then go over the dark patches of fur with black, particularly in the tail. Use light English red and cobalt blue for details in the light areas, and add thin strokes of cobalt blue that trail off into the background to create the illusion of backlit fur. Then paint into the edge of the tail with the floor color (gold ochre and phthalo green).

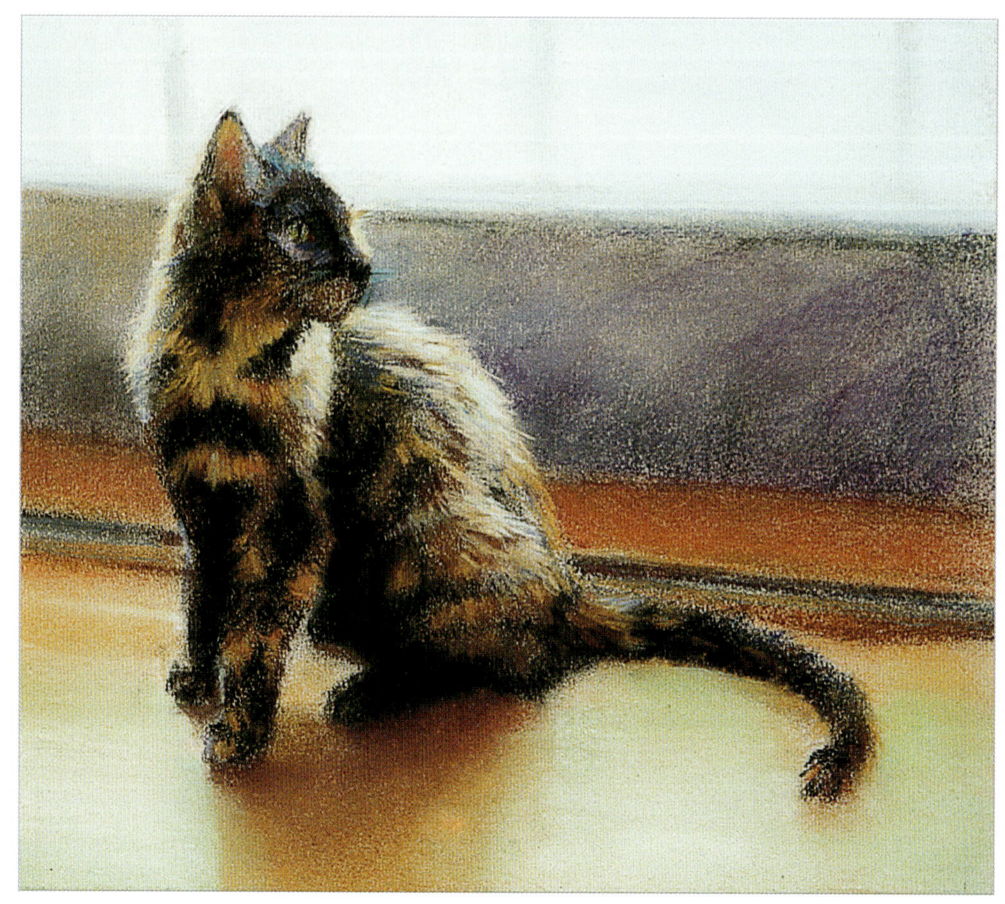

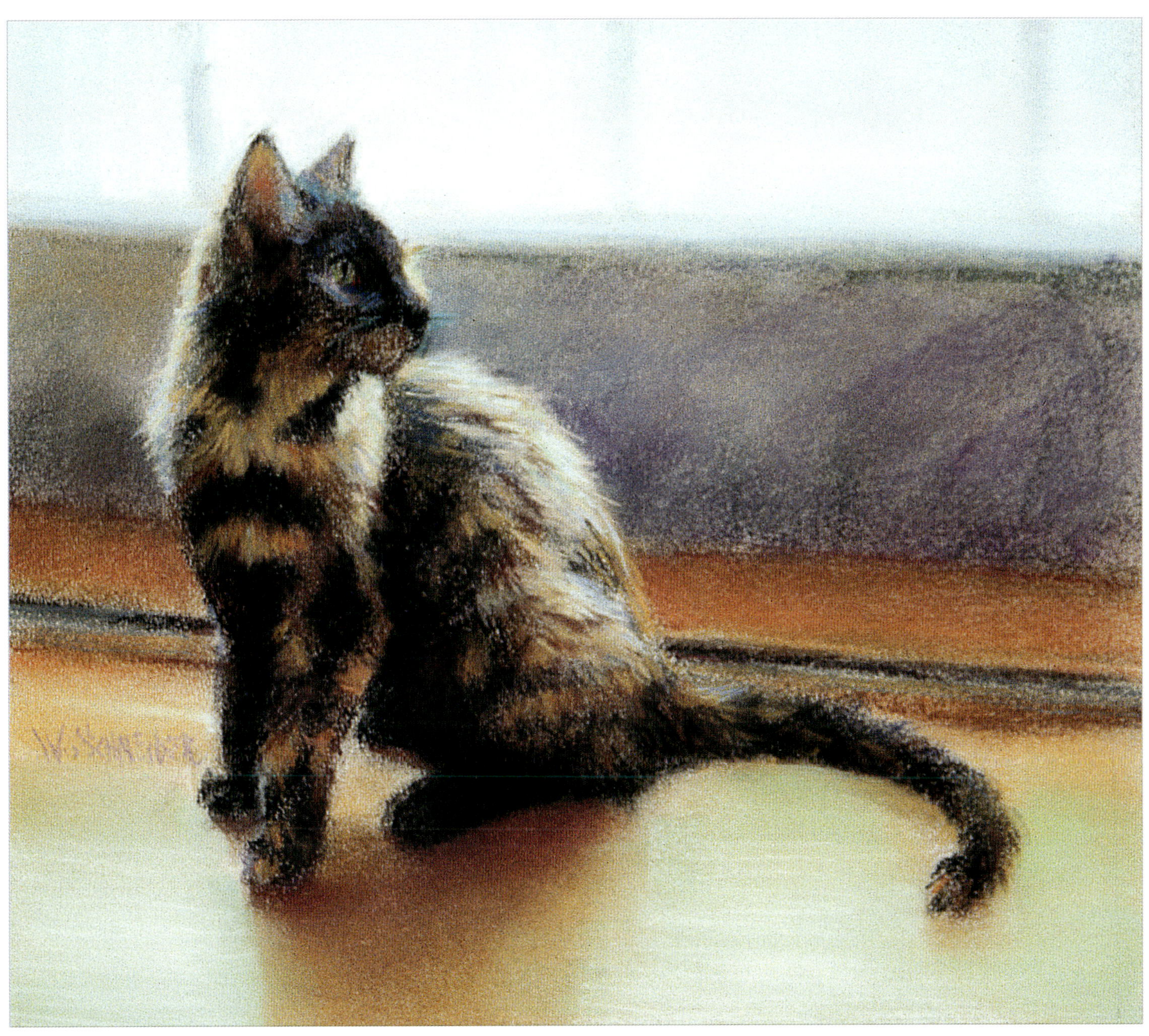

STEP 6 To complete the painting, lighten the window with white to create more contrast and make it appear as if the light were shining through it. Then add a little phthalo blue to the sunlit areas of the floor, and highlight the fur with yellow ochre and phthalo blue.

Flowers are timeless and attractive subjects for a painting a variety of shapes, colors, and textures. Rendering a floral bouquet gives you the chance to combine various types of flowers and foliage. Although it's probably more convenient to paint from photos, It's best to paint floral bouquets from life. That way, you can play around with different arrangements before settling on the one you like best. When setting up a bouquet, try to create a well-balanced color scheme; this painting features flowers with complementary colors: purple lilacs and yellow roses.

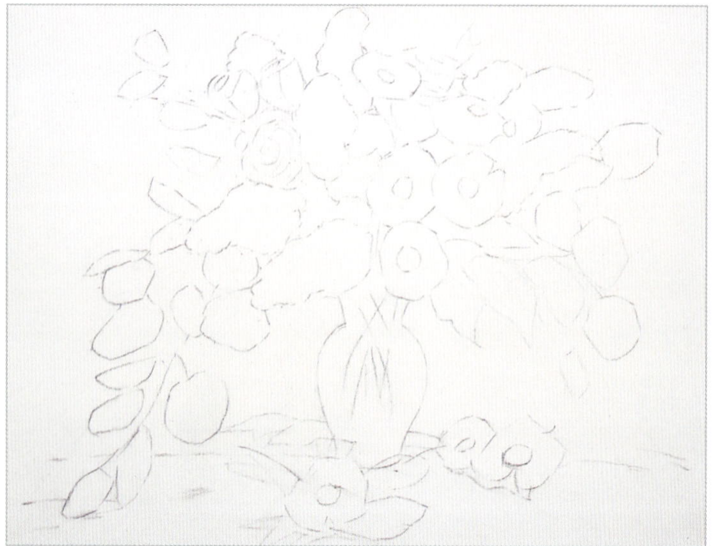

STEP 1 For this piece, choose a piece of white sanded pastel paper that will allow me to see my detailed drawing more clearly. First create a careful line drawing of the basic shapes with a light gray pastel pencil. Concentrate on the largest flower shapes and think of the daisies as concave disks, facing some toward the light and placing others in shadow.

STEP 2 Use a lilac hard pastel for the middle tones of the lilacs and a hyacinth violet hard pastel for the darks. Then block in the roses with a light ochre hard pastel, using medium pressure. Use fern green for the eucalyptus leaves in the light and palm green for those in shadow. Place the shadows on the daisies with warm light gray, but leave the white of the paper showing for the light areas. The centers of the daisies are the same light ochre used for the roses.

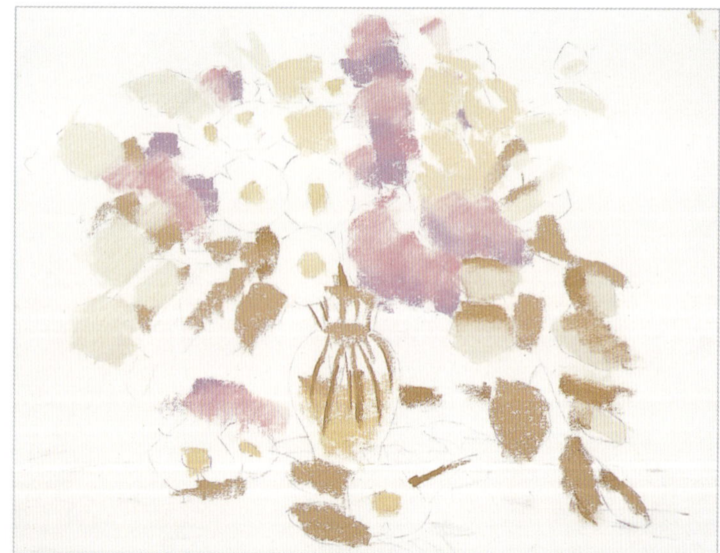

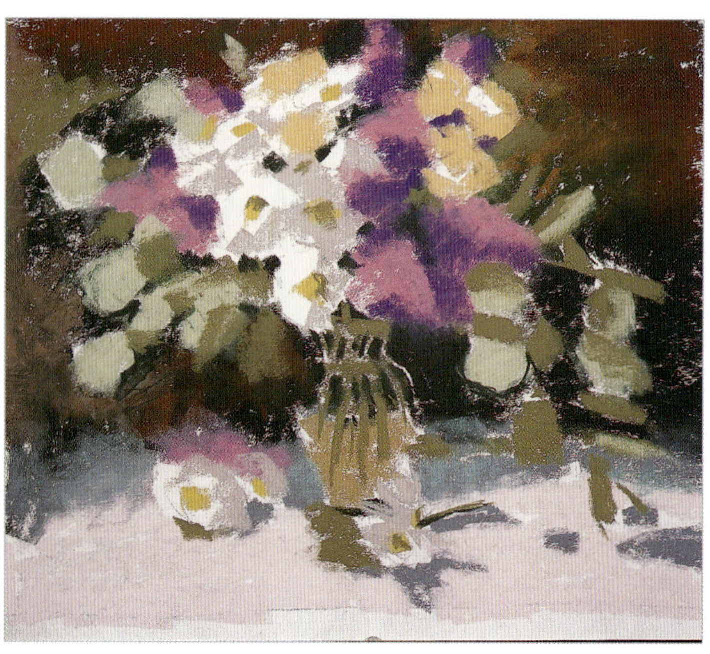

STEP 3 Next block in the background with spruce blue, burnt umber, cold medium gray, and palm green. Then rough in the foreground with shell pink. Use neutral gray green inside the vase and palm green for the stems in the vase. Let some paper show through around the edge of the vase where the glass is the thickest, letting the white paper act as the highlight.

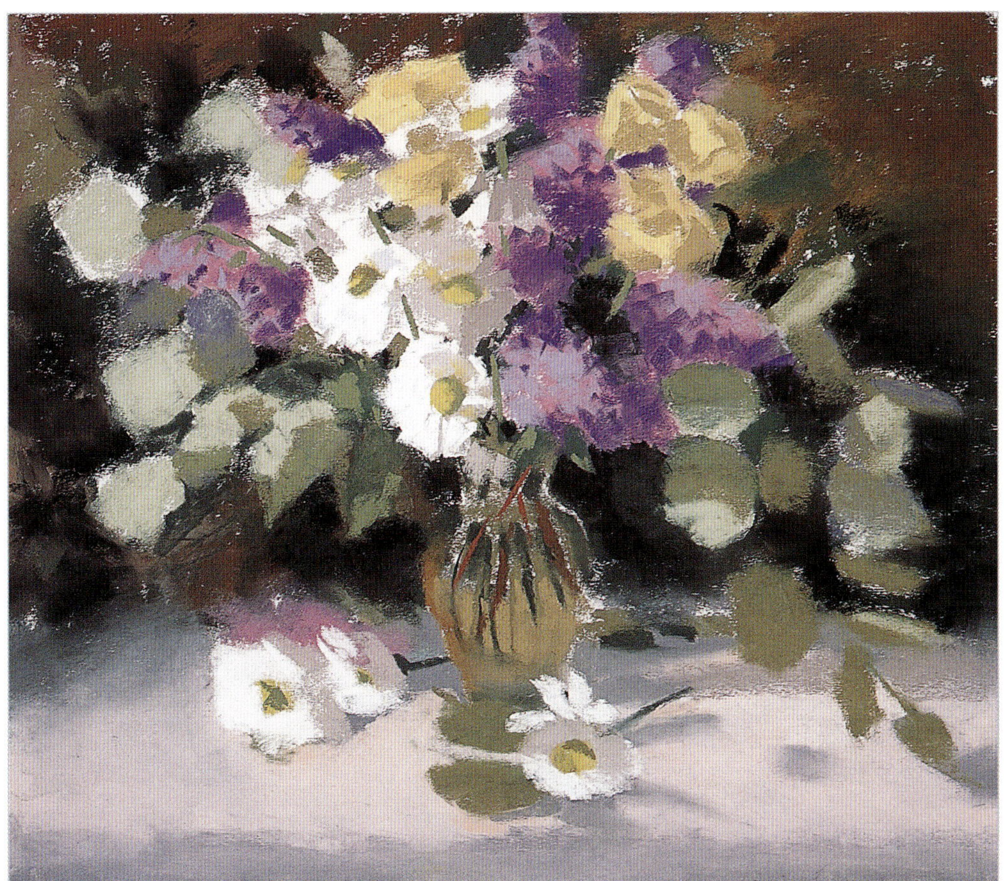

STEP 4 Next use spruce blue to draw the contours around the leaf shapes and "cut" into the lighter values to define them. Create some texture in the lilacs by using the square end of a blue-violet hard pastel to render the petals. Then add a layer of light blue in the same manner. Create shadows in the roses with gray phthalo blue-green, and add the edge of the table with cold medium gray. Then create some stems throughout the arrangement with palm green, adding more in the vase with rust.

STEP 5 Blend in some Van Dyke brown on the right side of the vase to soften it and add some black to the background. Continue to refine the shapes of the leaves, and add some more leaves with light blue and light gray-green. Then focus on the daisies; try to capture each flower without using too much detail, keeping strokes loose. Add peach to the shadowed sides of the daisies, and then add a little white to the light sides, beginning to cover the paper.

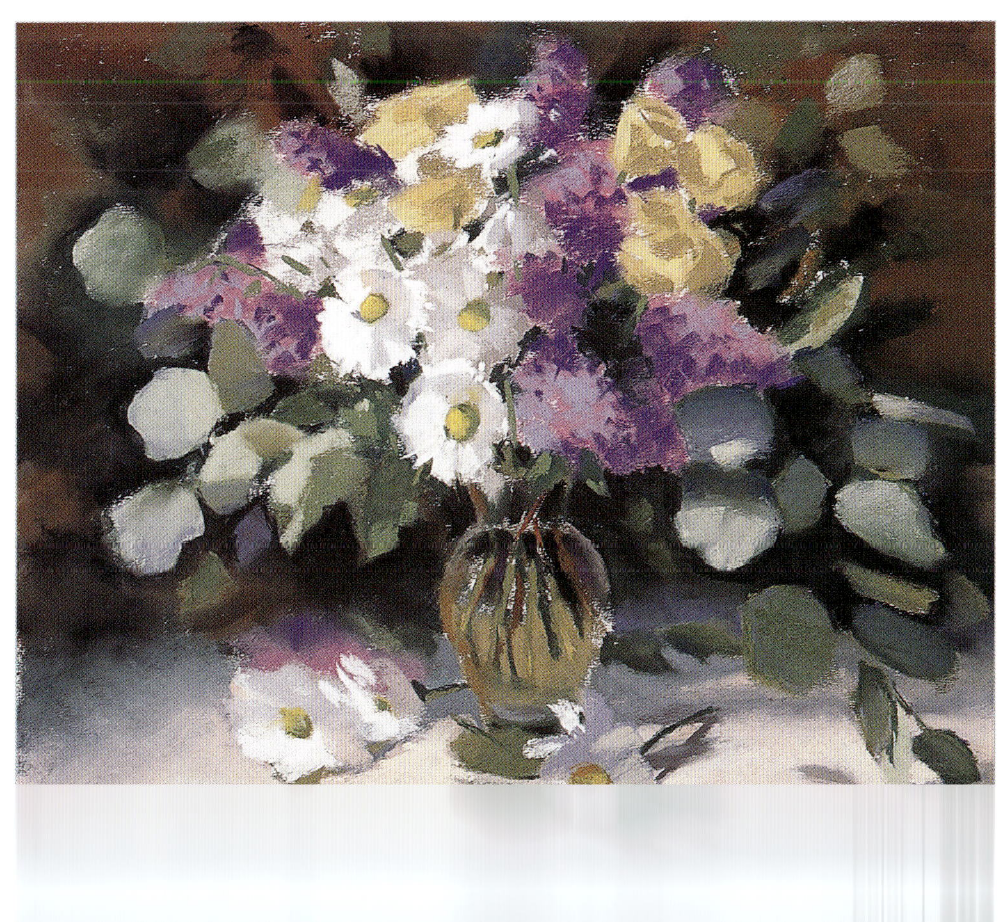

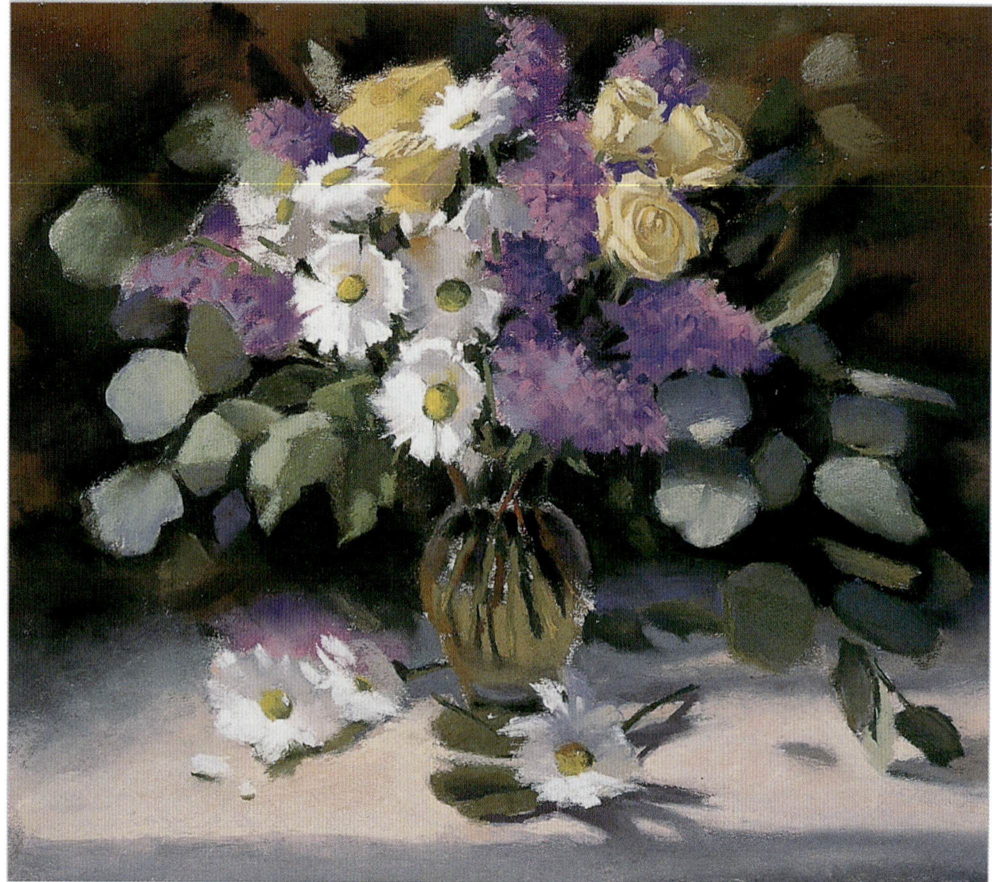

STEP 6 Each flower has a light side, a shadowed side, a core shadow, and reflected light. In some instances this is more obvious than in others. To define the roses, use yellow ochre light to cut into the shapes, and use light gray-green to depict the reflected light on them. Then start to give the lilacs more texture, using the same colors as before but pressing harder and using a variety of strokes to shape them.

STEP 7 Next add warm ochre to the inside of the roses and continue to define the leaves and flower shapes. Add more texture to the lilacs, making the lilac on the table a little more solid by creating a dramatic contrast between the light and shadow.

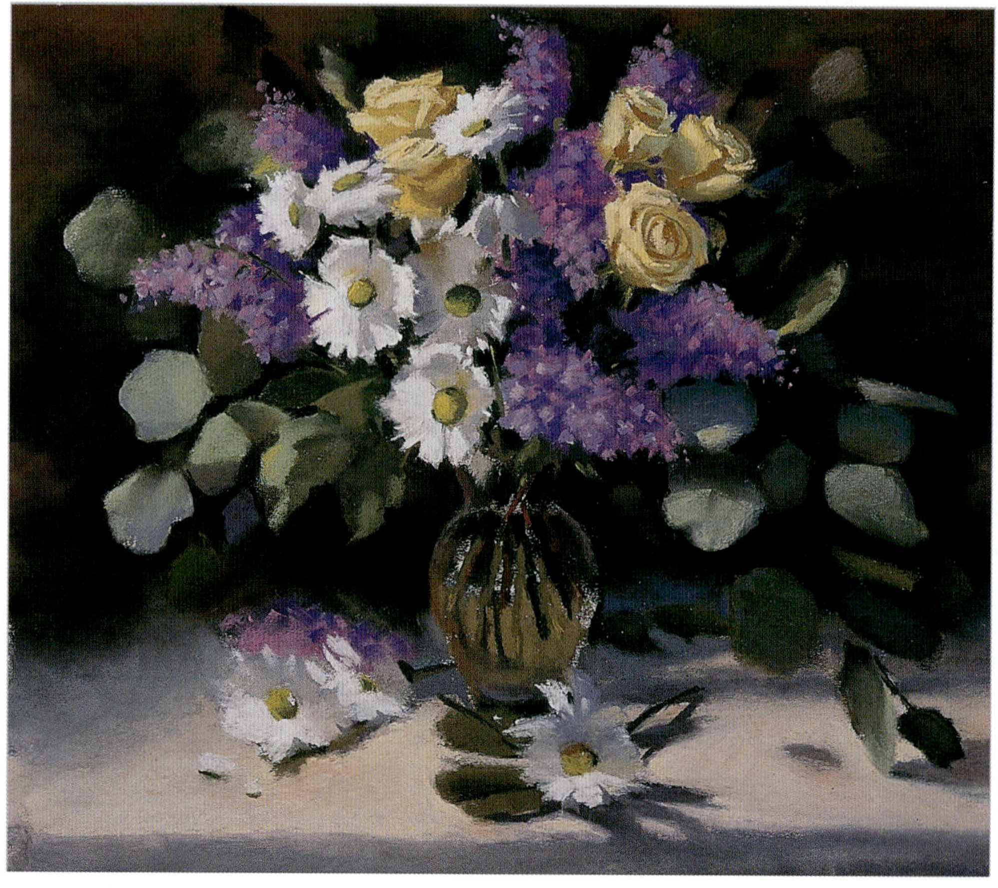

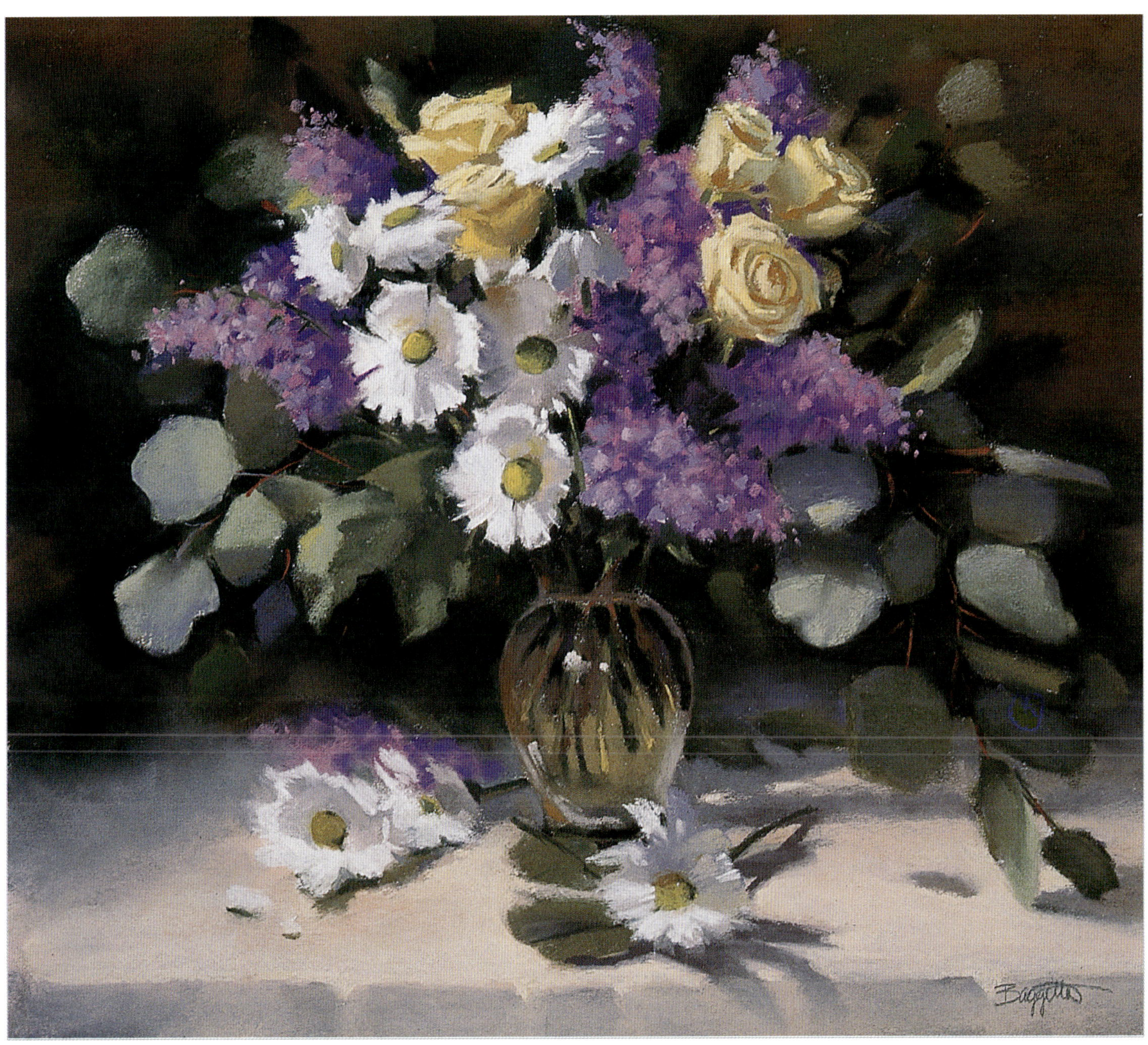

STEP 8 In this final stage, add some wispy branches on the eucalyptus with a sharpened rust pastel. Also add Van Dyke brown and cool gray to the vase, blending it smoothly with my finger.

This wooded road, laced with shadow, provides an excellent opportunity to study the contrast between cool shadow and warm light. The project also allows the artist to capture and interpret light using impressionistic techniques.

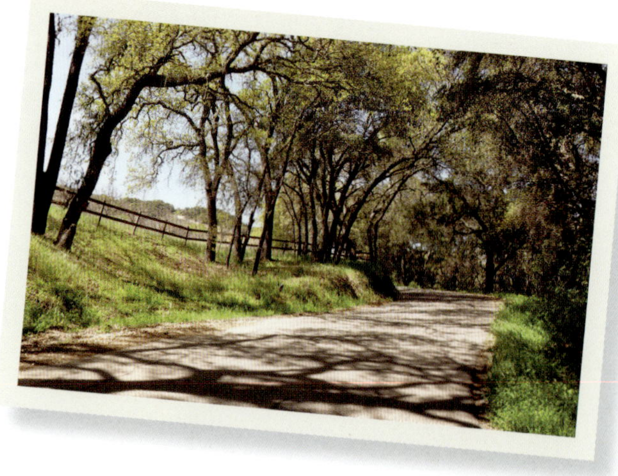

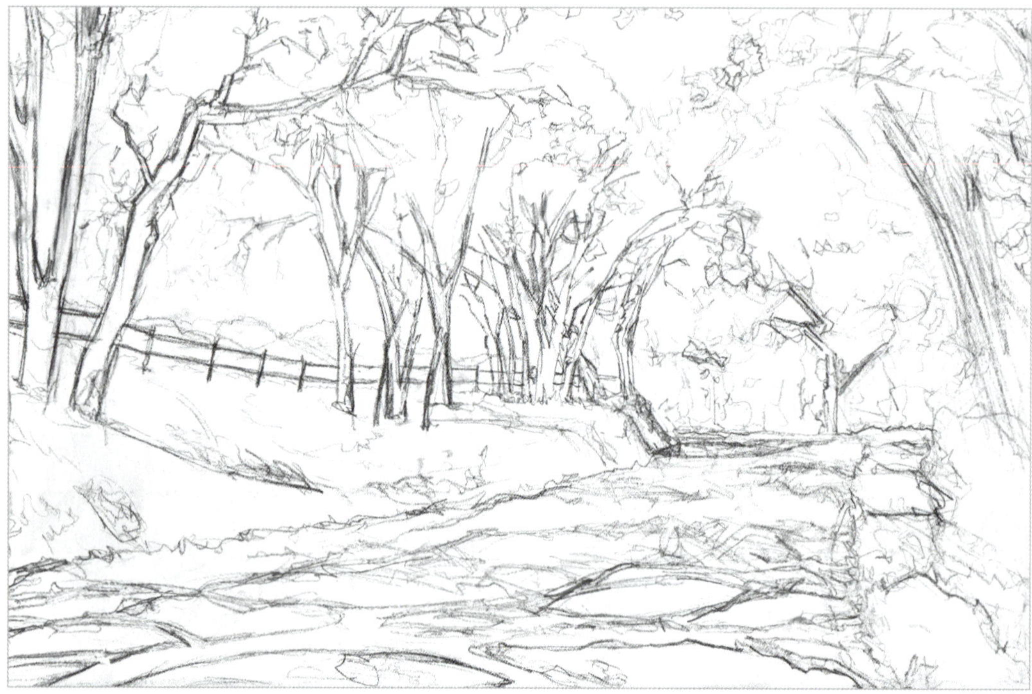

STEP 1 First, establish an expressive and gestural drawing. To achieve this, begin by separating the major shapes of light and dark, figure, and ground. Variation in line weight is extremely important at this point.

STEP 2 Next, paint a transparent layer over the drawing, using matte medium and ultramarine blue acrylic paint. This process seals the drawing, tones the image, and unifies the colors. Ultramarine blue is a good color to use for landscapes as a base.

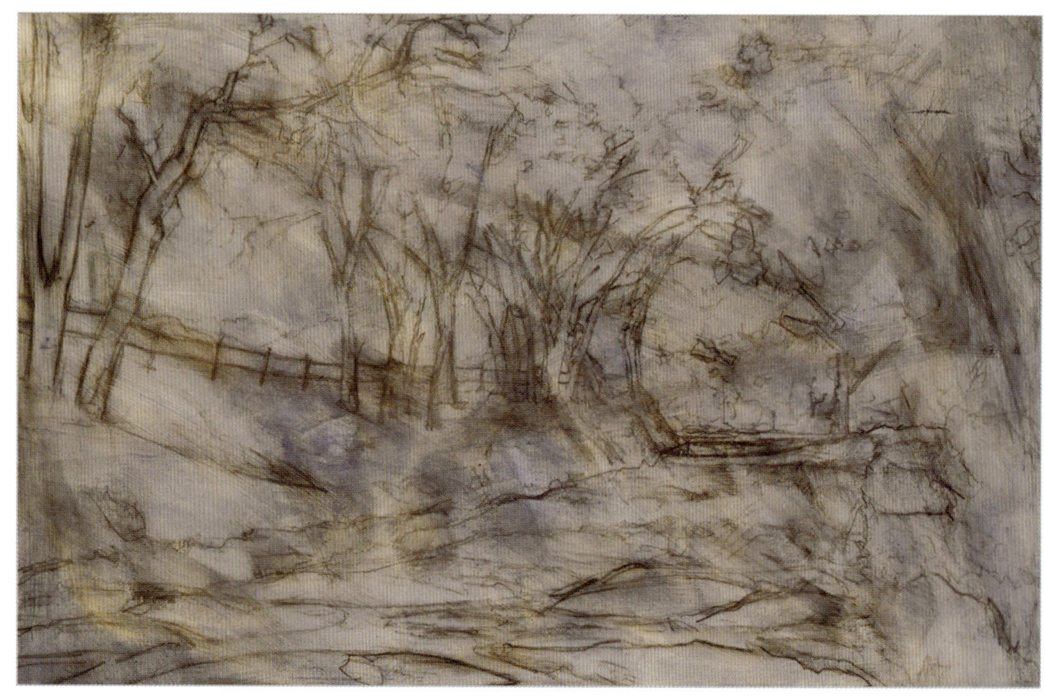

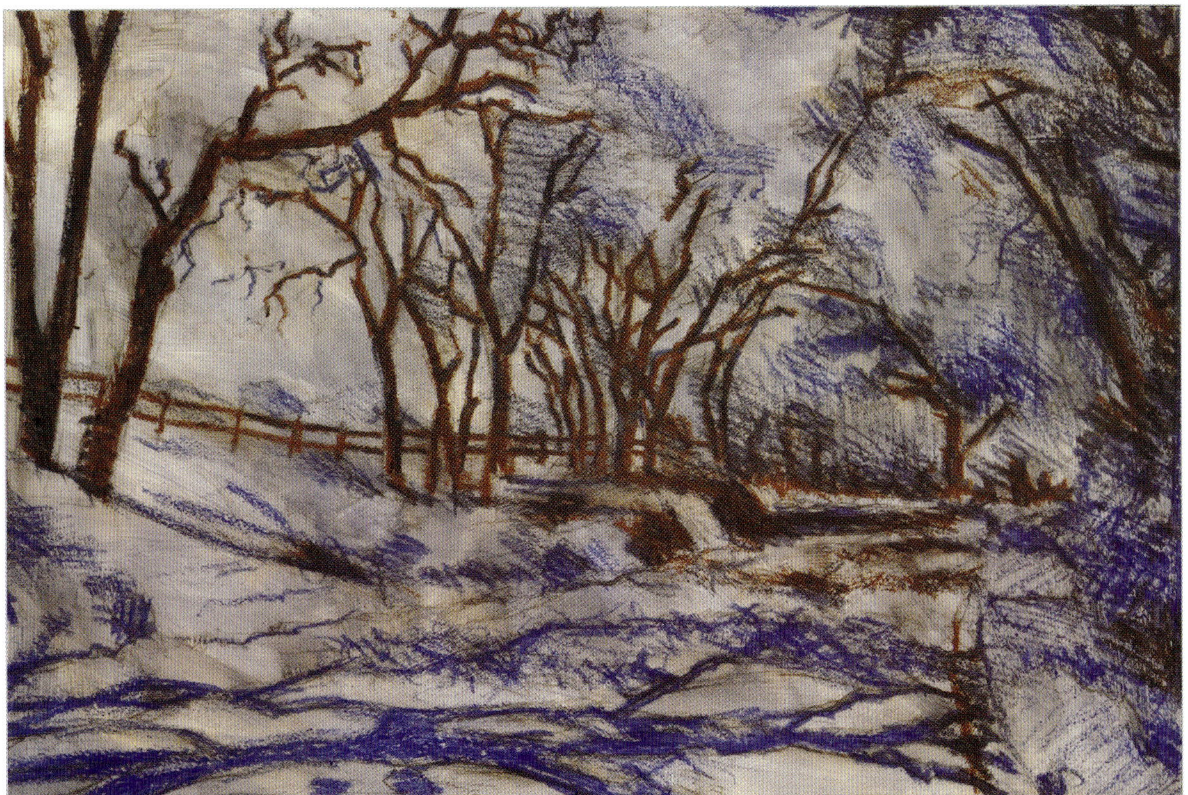

STEP 3 Draw in the darkest darks with Van Dyke brown. Begin to separate the shadow shapes using ultramarine blue. Then layer ultramarine blue on top of the Van Dyke brown to create a darker color. Use a variety of marks, crosshatching, and gestural movements, always maintaining variation in line weight. At this point, the only oil pastel used on the foreground shadow shapes is ultramarine blue. Keep the shadows cool—that way, when later blocking in the light sections, they will be warm.

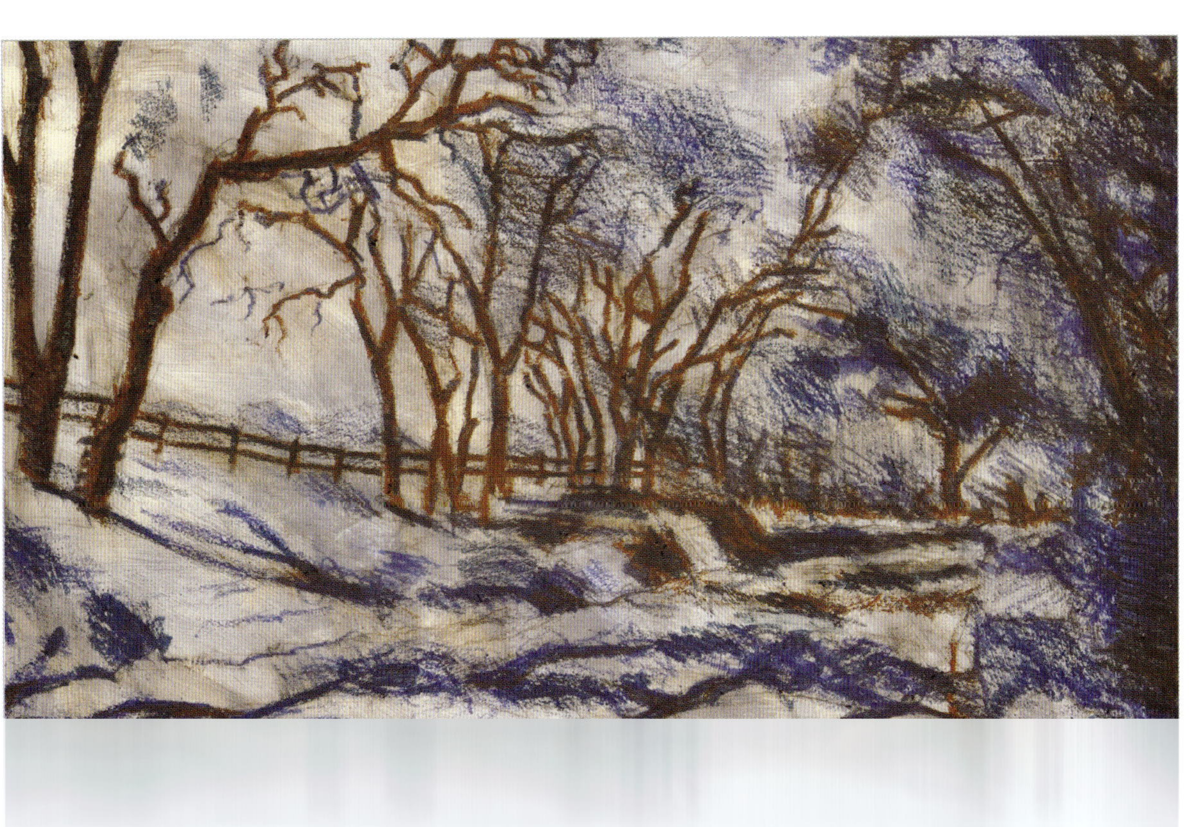

STEP 4 With Prussian blue, keep working the darks and shadow shapes. As needed, go back in with Van Dyke brown to correct and darken. Continue working the overall shadow shapes in the trees and on the ground, correcting the drawing as needed.

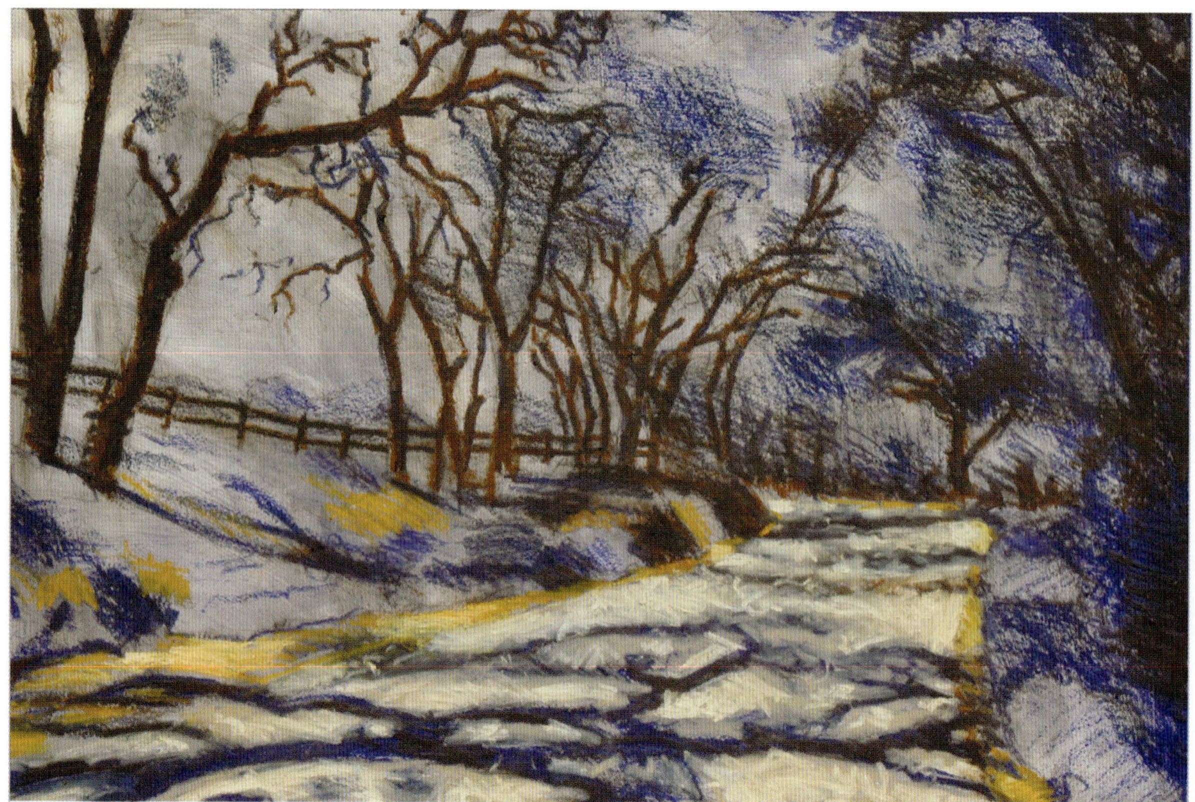

STEP 5 Using gray, begin to block in the light sections of the road. Then layer with white to brighten the lightest lights in the street. If necessary, blend slightly and remove excess oil pastel with your finger. After finishing the white in the road, begin working on the shoulder of the road. Here use yellow ochre as a base, adding white over that.

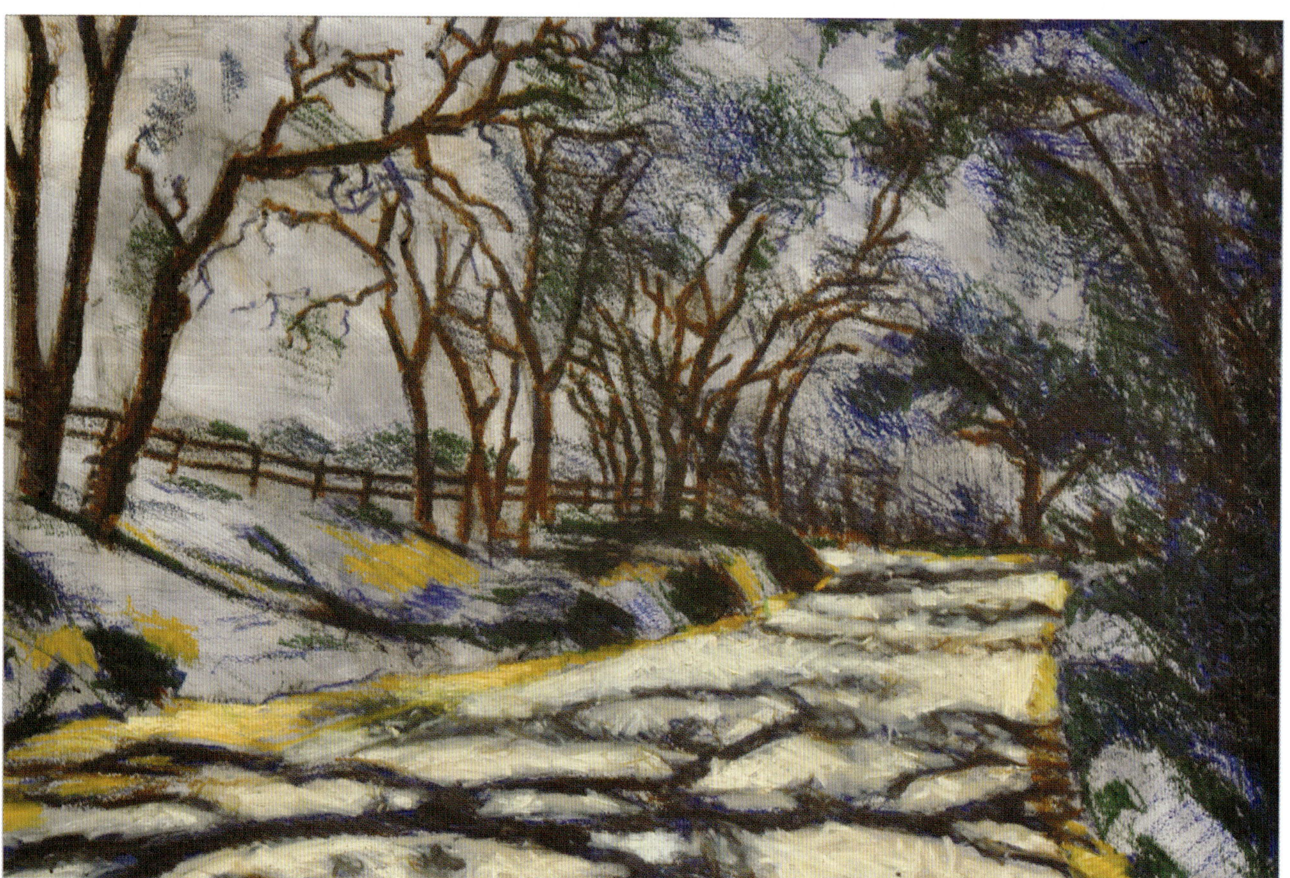

STEP 6 In this step, adjust the foreground branch shadows, making them a bit darker with Van Dyke brown. Then, using deep green, layer the darks in the trees, ground, mountains, and everywhere as needed. Continue to employ crosshatching and variation in line weight by alternately pushing harder, then softer, when making marks.

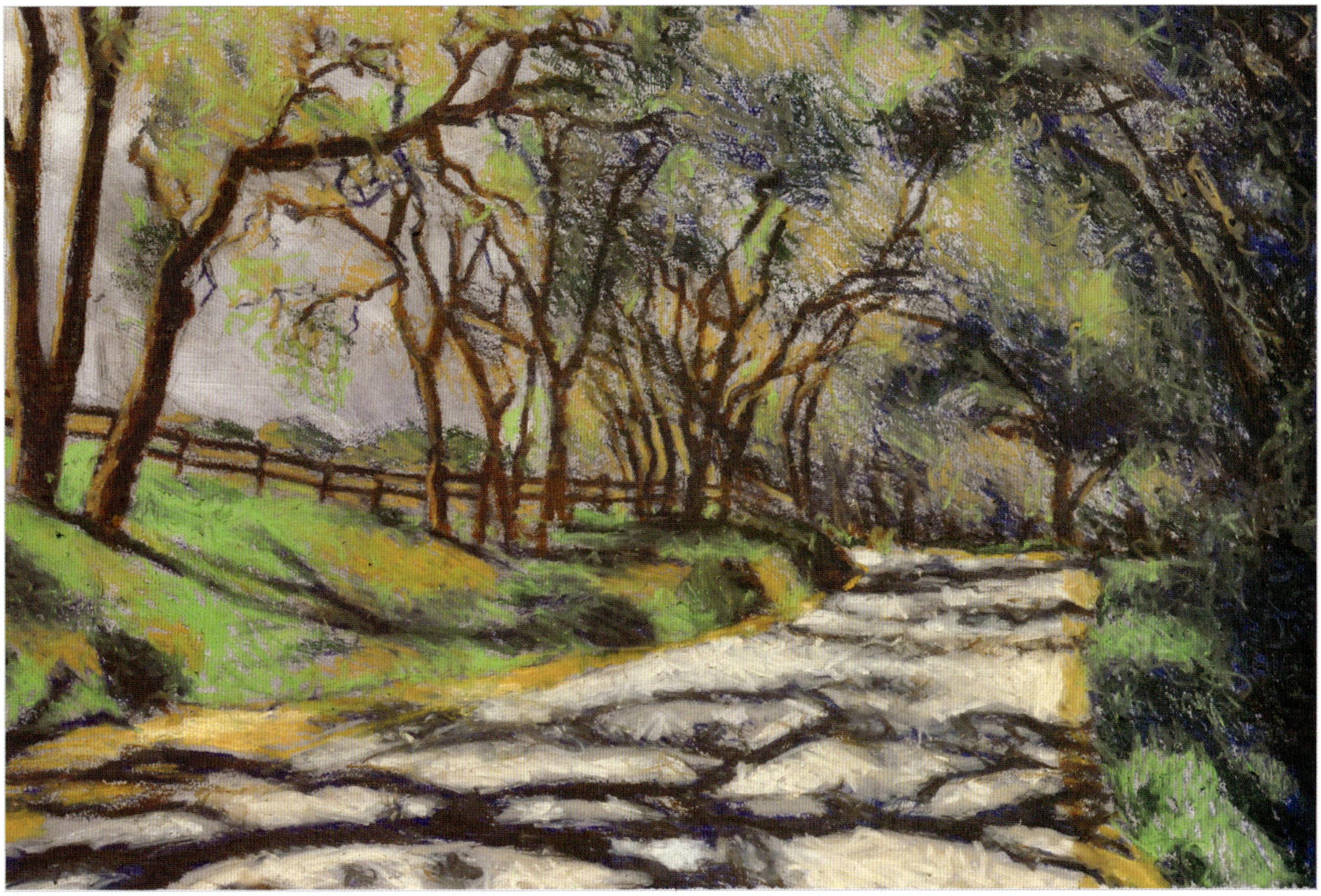

STEP 7 Next add olive brown throughout the piece and start to work your way toward the lights. This creates a transition between tones and is used for the dead branches and dry grass. Then add yellow green in the grass, layering it to saturate the color. Finally, move into the trees using a gestural stroke that mimics trees and branches.

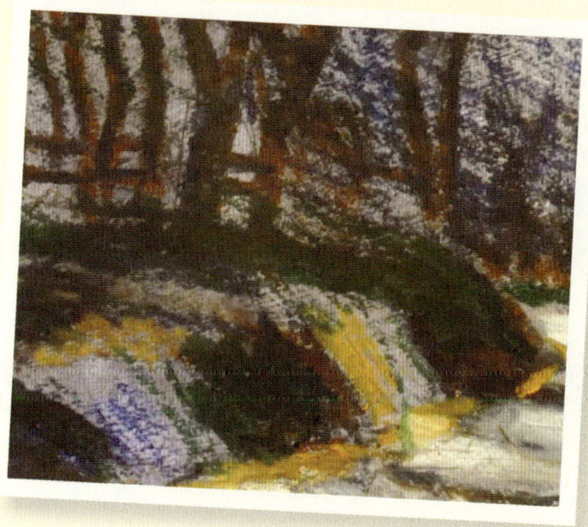

Layer the green and blend, using pressure. This creates an even tone. Make sure to keep your

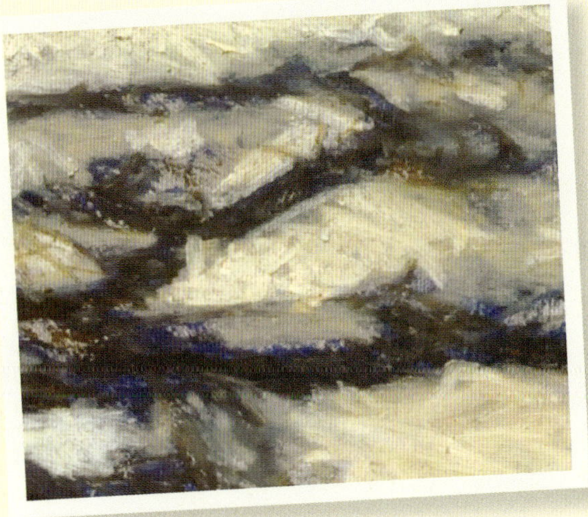

Notice the texture created by oil pastel. Use this to your advantage to increase the contrast of the

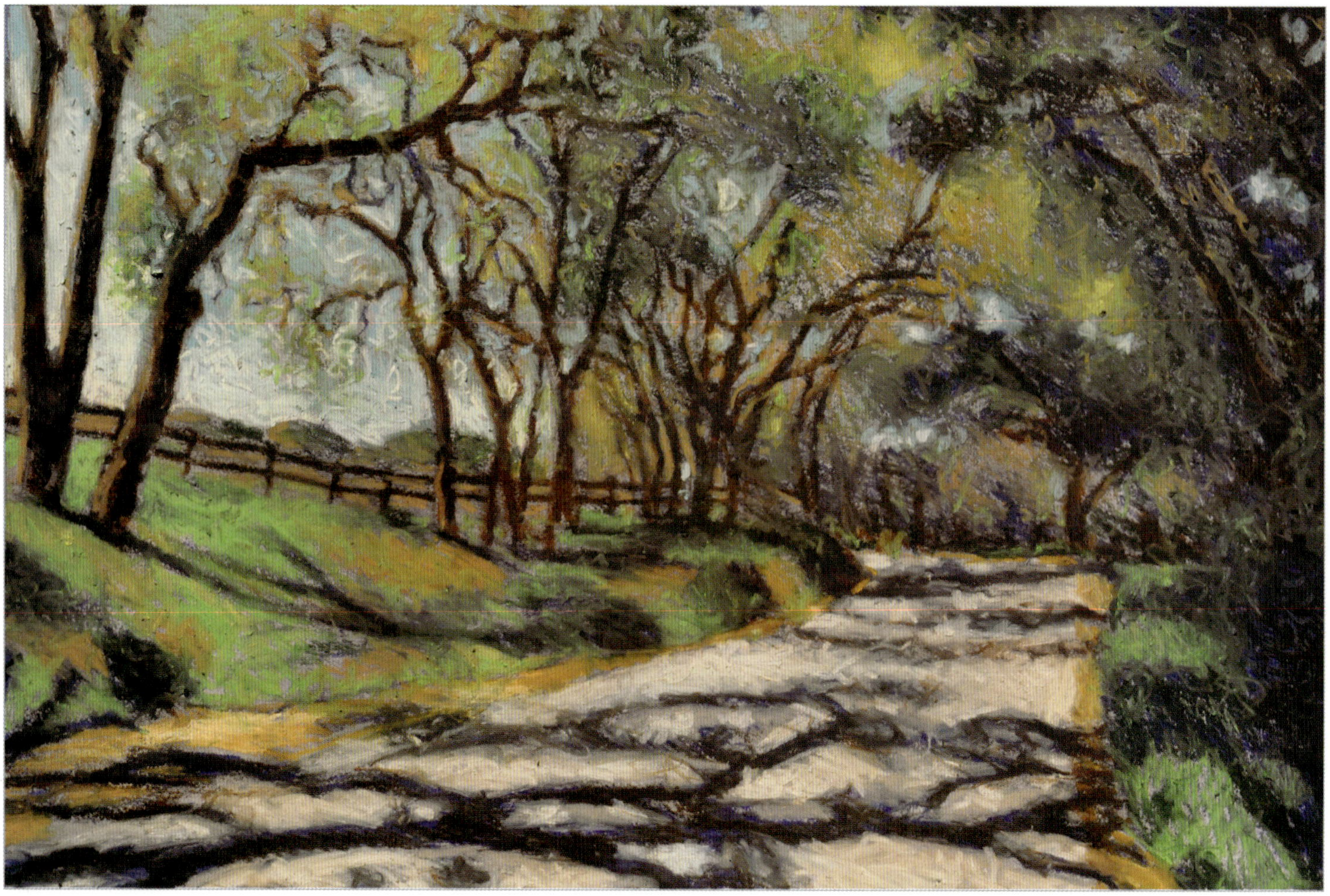

STEP 8 Continue working the trees with green gray, yellow ochre, and lemon yellow. Then follow the light pattern and scratch away mistakes. At this point, press hard to layer the oil pastel. Next, using a palette knife, begin to scrape away the oil pastel in the sky shapes in the trees. Then use pale blue to block in the sky shapes. It is important to remember that the blue is darker at the top of the image and gets lighter as it approaches the horizon line. To accomplish this, apply white at the horizon line and transition to the pale blue. Then correct the sky shapes using yellow green.

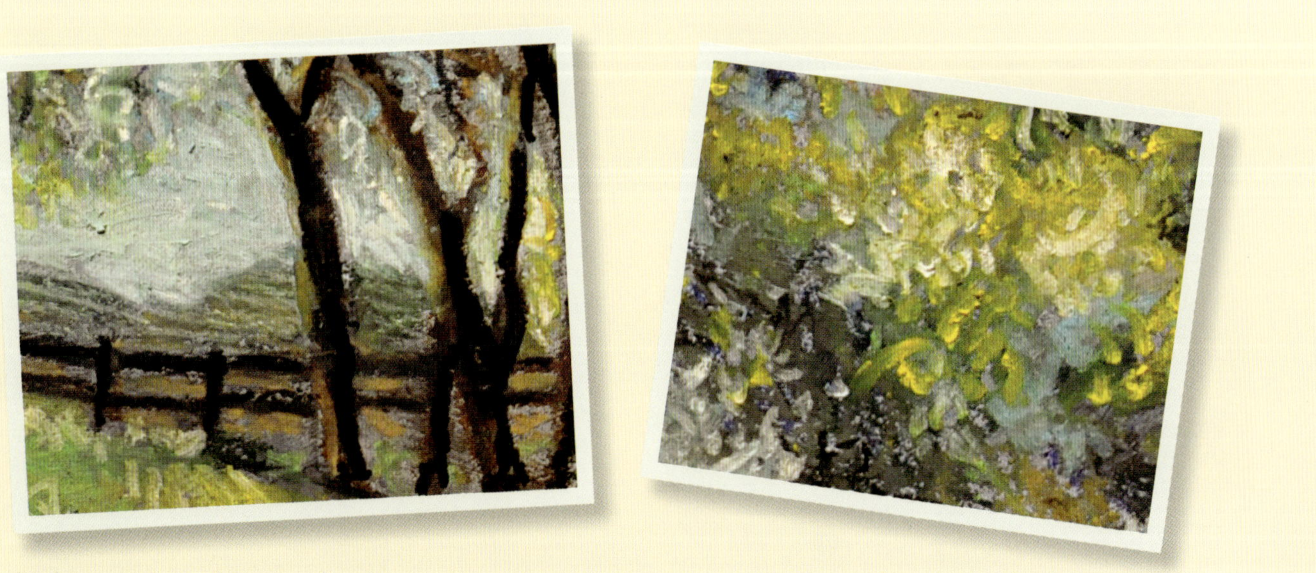

It's important to give your drawing an atmospheric perspective and a sense of space. Notice how a simple layer of white does the trick in the detail shown above left. Influenced by Impressionism, the marks of color creates the light in the detail shown above right. These marks are similar to stippling—a practice of using dots in color or tonal application.

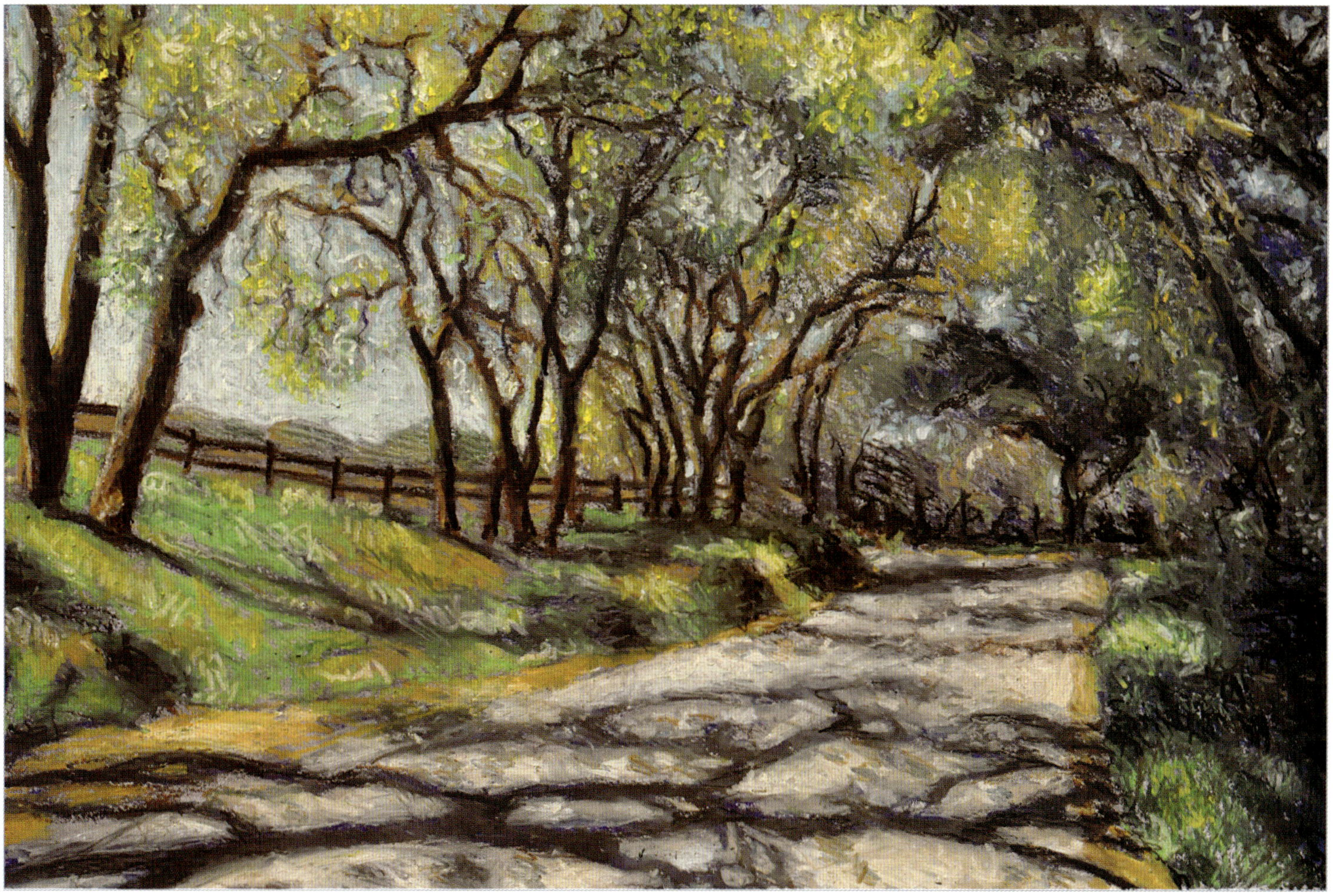

STEP 9 For the final step, use white and lightly go over the background hills for more atmospheric perspective. Then, with the palette knife, scrape away oil pastel to increase the lights with yellow, yellow ochre, pale blue, and white. Make these marks by jabbing and pushing to create stippling, dots of light. Then clean up the tree darks with Prussian blue. Soften and work the shadow shapes in the grass to make them more irregular. With Prussian blue and Van Dyke brown, soften the dappled light on the road. Use your finger to blend and soften edges, then use white to increase lights. Finally, use black to solidify the darkest darks.

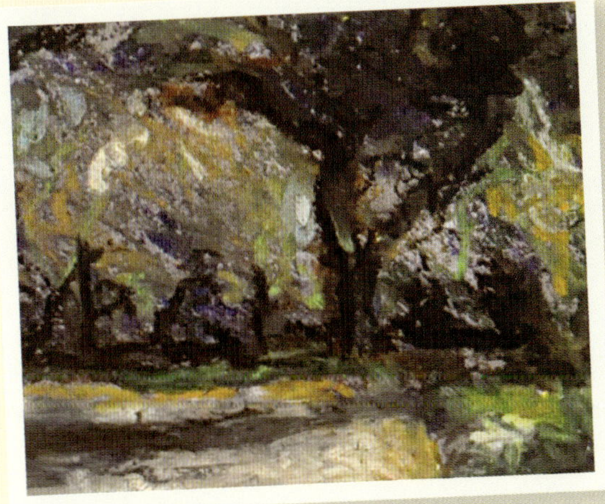

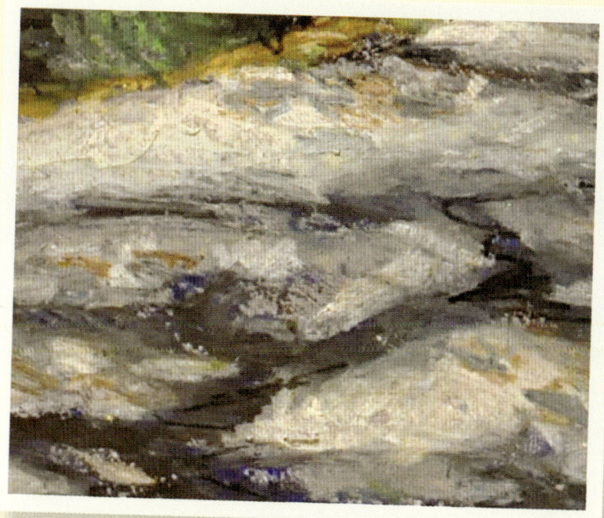

To capitalize on the beauty of line and variation in line weight, push the depths of the shadows with black. It's good to have variation in your line, combining hard and soft edges. This can

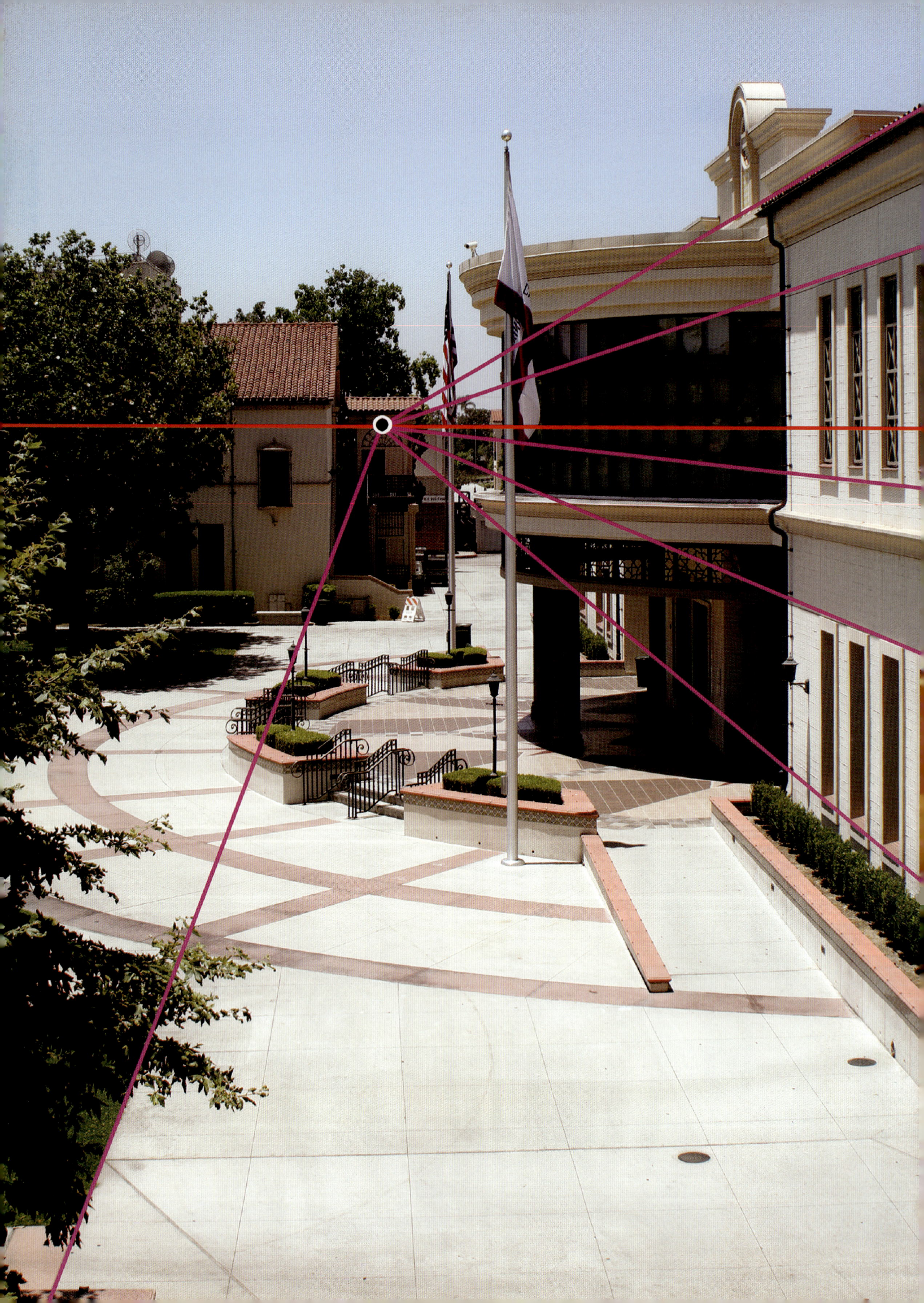

LINEAR PERSPECTIVE

Previously we have discussed the picture plane, eye level, "table-top" perspective, and perspective terminology, giving us a basic understanding of one- and two-point perspective. In this final chapter, we will go into more depth on perspective as it relates to observation and drawing architecture—both interior and exterior. Understanding perspective theory—and how to apply it—will help you create strong, accurate spatial drawings.

Principles of Perspective

For centuries prior to the Renaissance, artists struggled to portray the world around them with an accurate depiction of spatial dimensions, usually with little or no success. Just before the Renaissance, several artists (among them, Andrea Mantegna and Tommaso Masaccio) discovered clues to solving the mystery of where lines and edges converge in a depiction of deep spatial dimension. The main discovery was the vanishing point and the theory behind it, which states that lines and planes converge to a point or points on the artist's eye level, based on the artist's viewpoint.

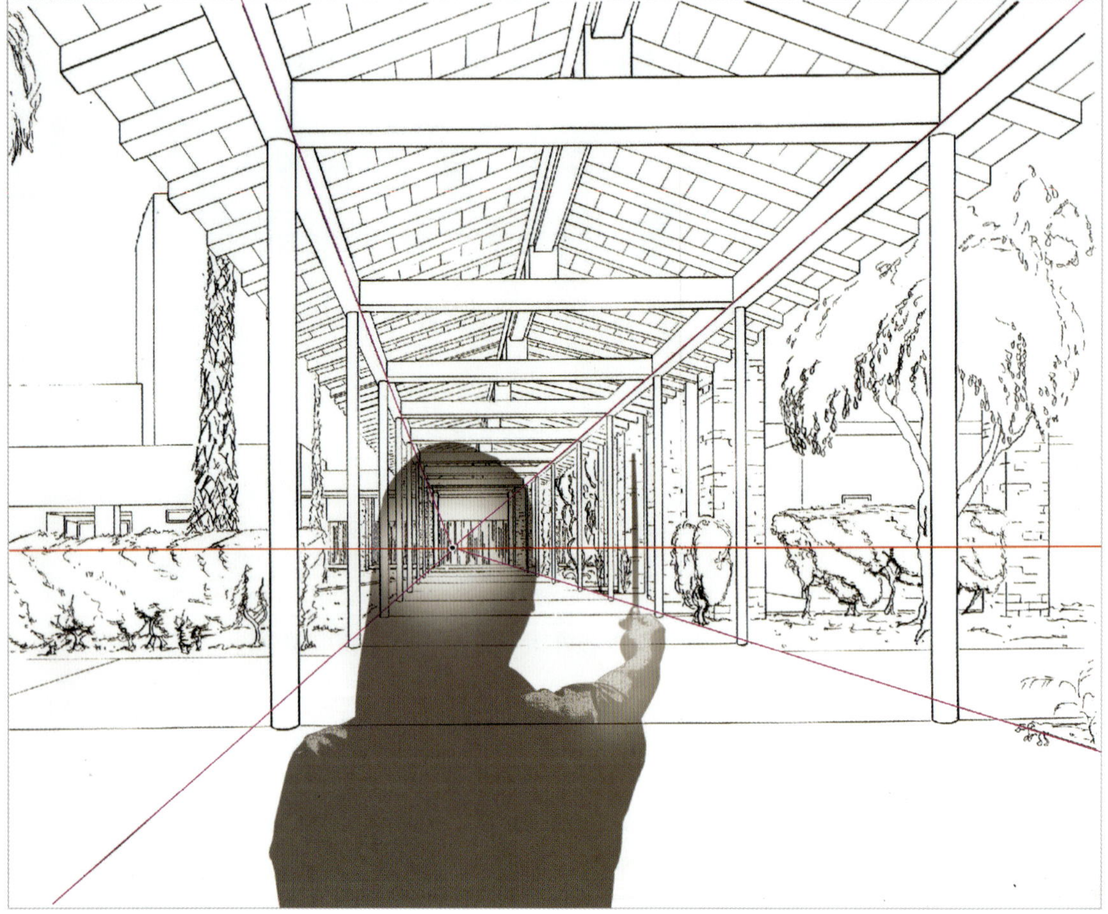

To truly understand the logic of perspective, you need to start with eye level. Eye level and the horizon line are one and the same. Eye level is the viewer's perspective—the way things appear at the viewer's level of observation. If the viewer changes his or her height by climbing up a staircase or sitting on the floor, the perspective view changes as well. Eye level is always horizontal, never at an angle. *Note: Eye level/ horizon line is portrayed as a horizontal red line here and in all further illustrated examples.*

There are a few other consistent principles inherent in all perspective situations:

Convergence is the appearance of parallel lines, planes, or edges coming together toward a common point as they retreat from the viewer.

Size diminishment means objects or structures of the same size appear to get proportionally smaller as they retreat in space from the viewer.

Foreshortening means the sides, tops, and bottoms of objects seem to become narrower and flatter as they move away from the viewer.

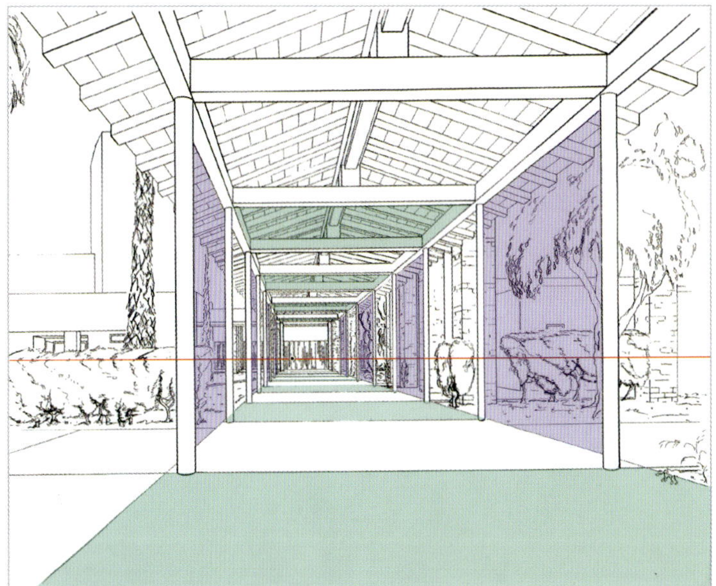

Foreshortening As planes of the same size move away from the viewer, they become narrower and flatten as they recede.

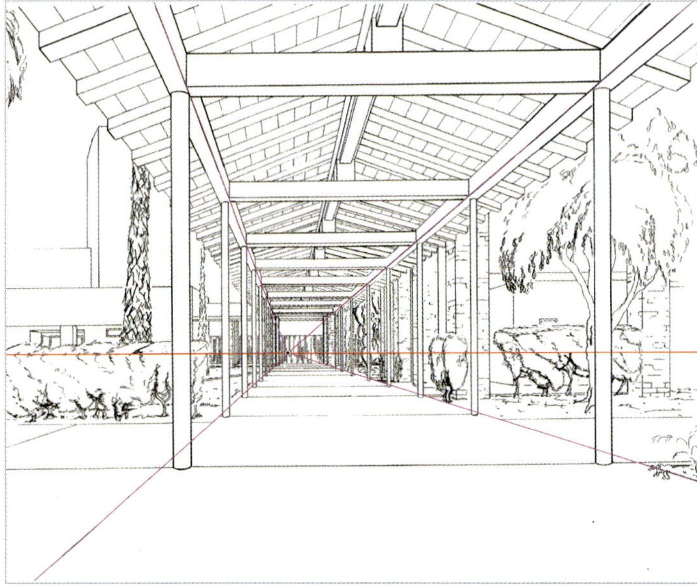

Vanishing Points Lines or planes recede into in the distance to a mutual point(s). Vanishing points are always on the horizon line (eye level).

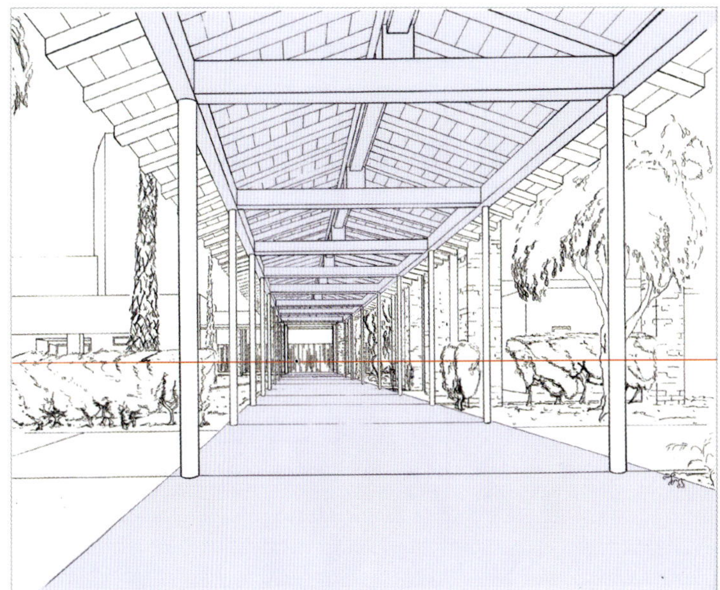

Convergence Lines or planes that are parallel to each other appear to converge, or come together, as they move away from the viewer.

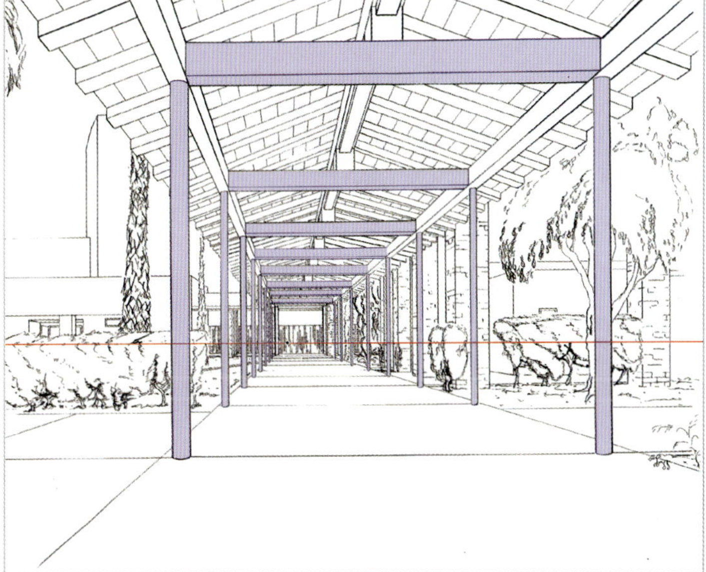

Size Diminishment The posts and beams diminish in scale proportionally, as there is equal distance between each set.

Understanding the key relationship between eye level, also called the horizon line, and the vanishing point is crucial. Vanishing points are always on eye level. Later in this chapter we will discuss different types of convergence points, but true vanishing points are always on the horizon line. Vanishing points may not always be directly in front of the viewer, as is the case in a two-point perspective situation. Even so, always know that the angled edges of parallel and perpendicular planes (walls) are converging on perspective vanishing points that are always on the viewer's eye level.

Eye Level

Understanding where eye level falls is a key component to drawing in perspective. When observing and drawing an architectural subject, always know initially where true eye level falls. The example below is of a very low eye level; the artist is sitting and drawing from the ground. Even if you're not sure exactly where the vanishing points are located, you can assume that they are on eye level.

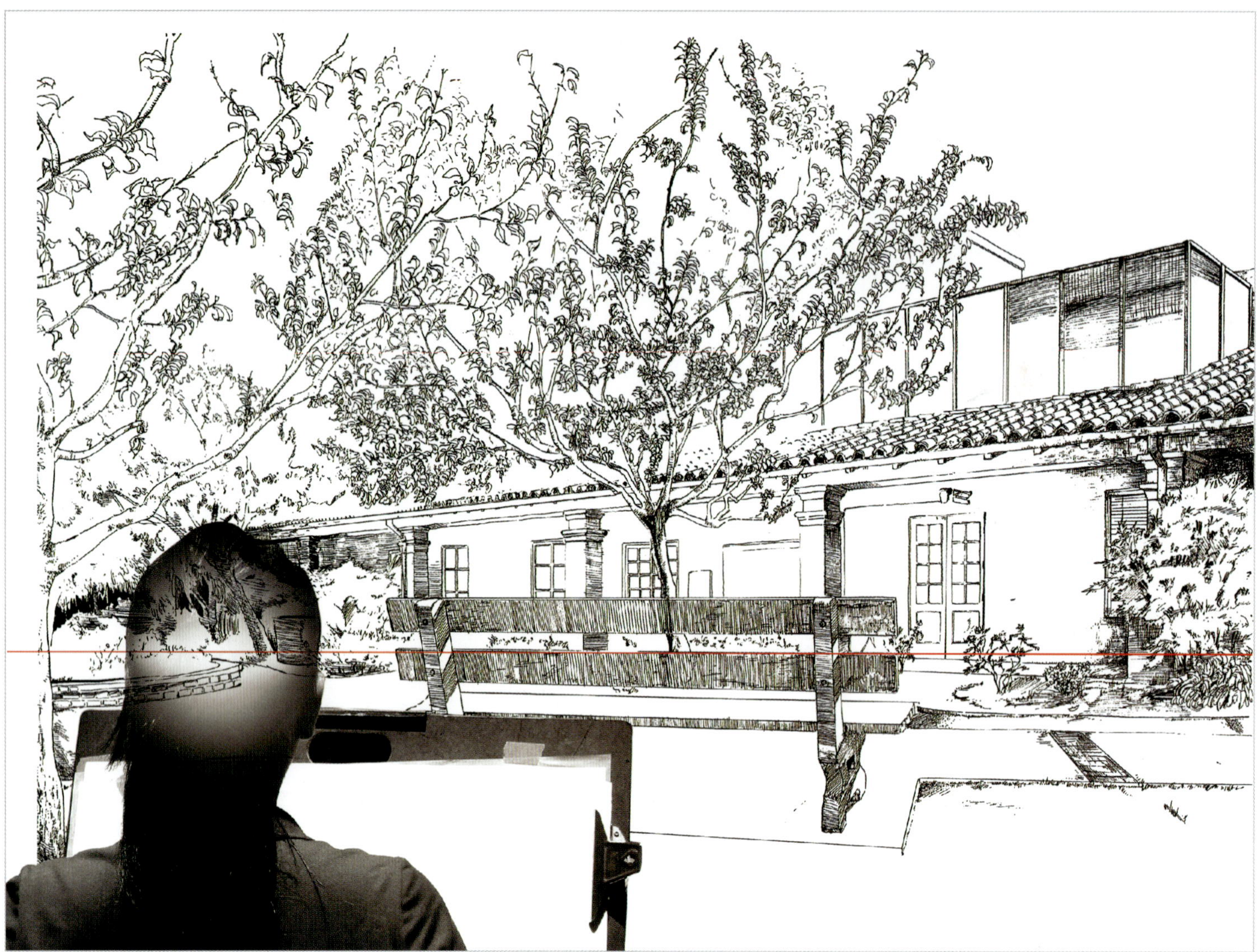

When the eye level is elevated, as demonstrated above, notice what happens to the angles on the rooflines, windows, and sidewalks. Once an artist understands the importance of eye level location, it's easy to spot inaccuracy in a drawing. Remember not to confuse line of vision with eye level. You can move your eyes up and down to see objects, but the true eye level stays constant.

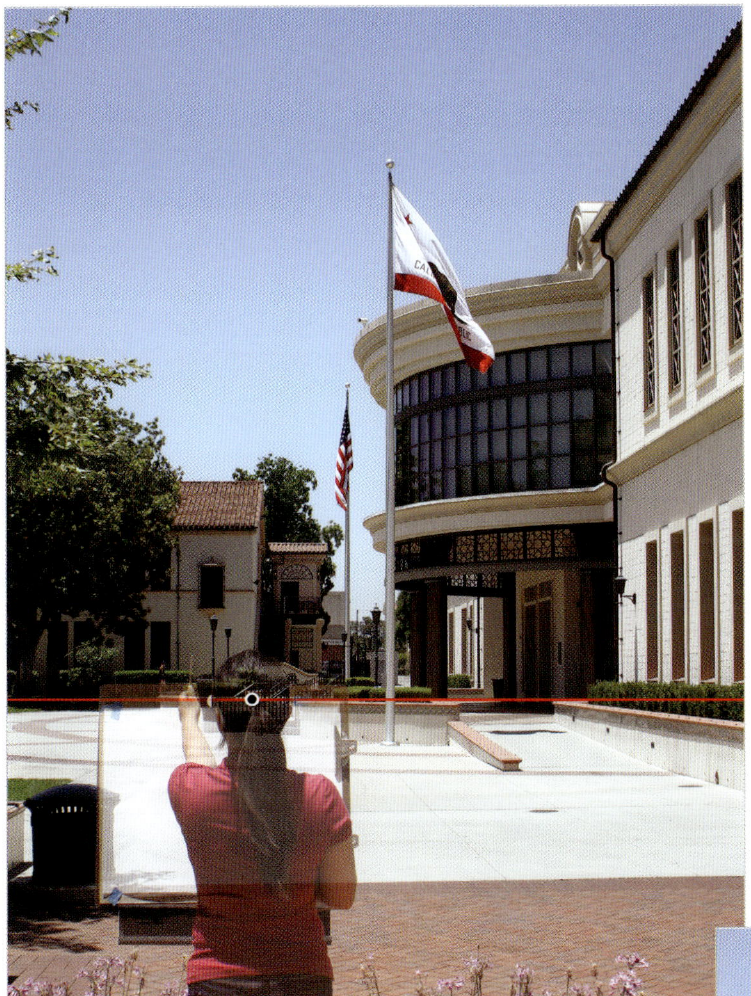

Illustrated here is a normal eye level for most people. The sidewalks widen dramatically as they advance toward the viewer. The tops of doors and windows converge down toward the vanishing point on eye level; the higher the windows and rooflines, the more acute the angles become.

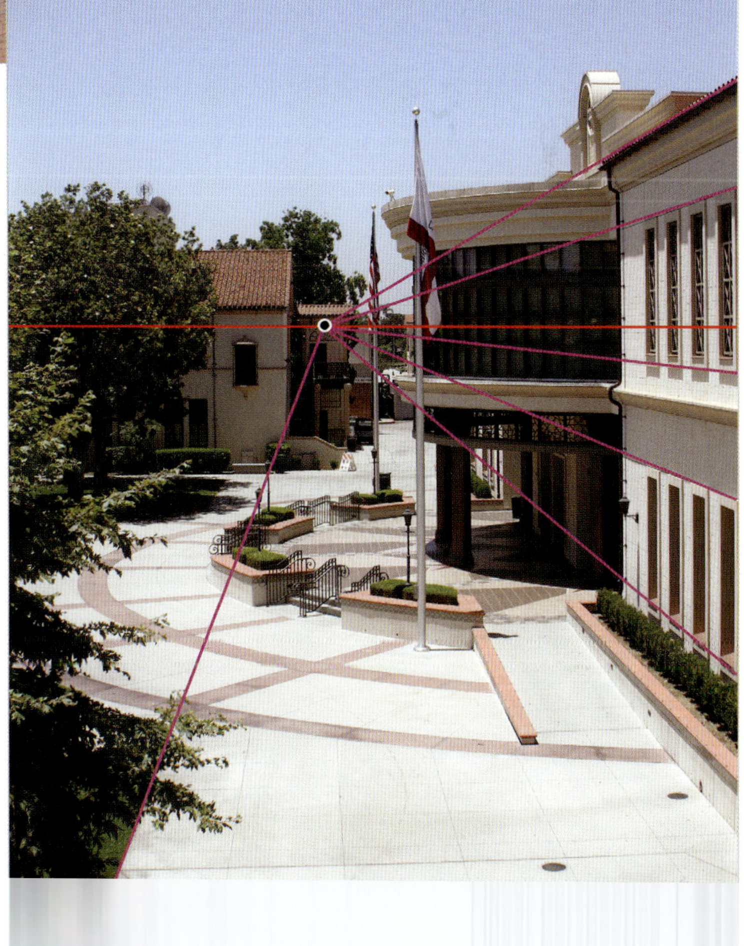

Here is the same view from several floors up. The eye level has changed and so has the perspective view. The sidewalk edges closest to the viewer are narrower and less foreshortened. Most of the window tops and bottoms on the building to the right are below eye level, so their edges converge up to the vanishing point on eye level.

The Picture Plane

As discussed on page 38, the picture plane is an imaginary sheet of glass between the viewer and the subject. It is meant to represent your drawing board, and the viewer's line of vision should extend through it at a right angle. The picture plane, in theory, is facing exactly what you are drawing, which encompasses roughly a 60° circle around the viewer, which is called the cone of vision. If you find yourself turning your head to see what is on one side within that zone, you are basically turning your picture plane and your cone of vision, and there will be distortion in your drawing.

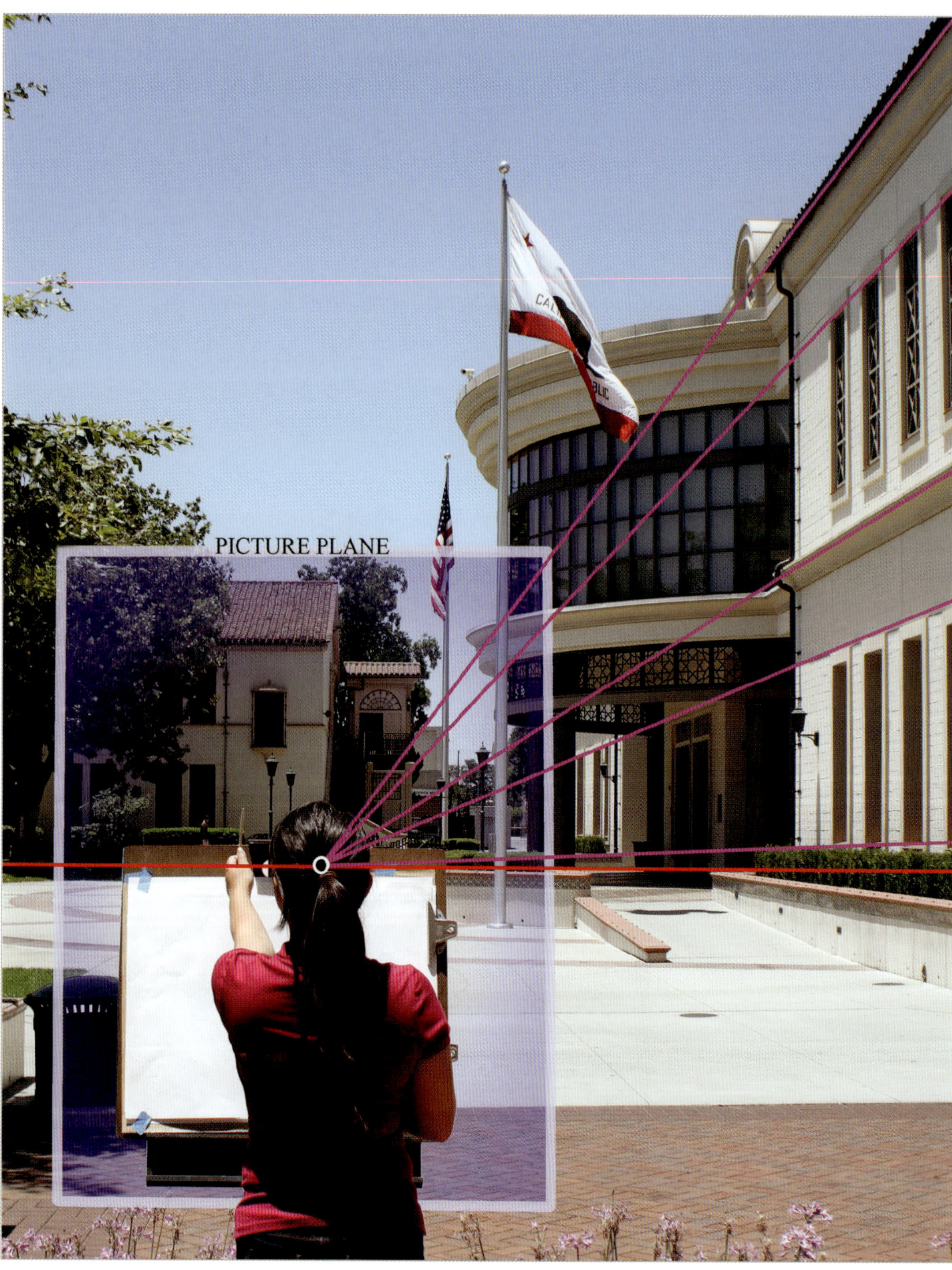

This is a one-point perspective situation. The back wall, or plane, of the far building is parallel to the picture plane. The vanishing point is directly in front of the viewer. The one-point perspective is apparent on the building to the right, which is perpendicular to the far building that is parallel to the picture plane. The tops and bottoms of this far building are horizontal, parallel to eye level.

One-Point & Two-Point Perspectives

If the wall or plane in the background of your view is parallel to the picture plane, or if the building that you are drawing is perpendicular to the picture plane, it is a one-point perspective situation. In this situation, the edges of the walls are parallel and vertical to the picture plane, and the top and bottom edges of the floor and roofing are horizontal.

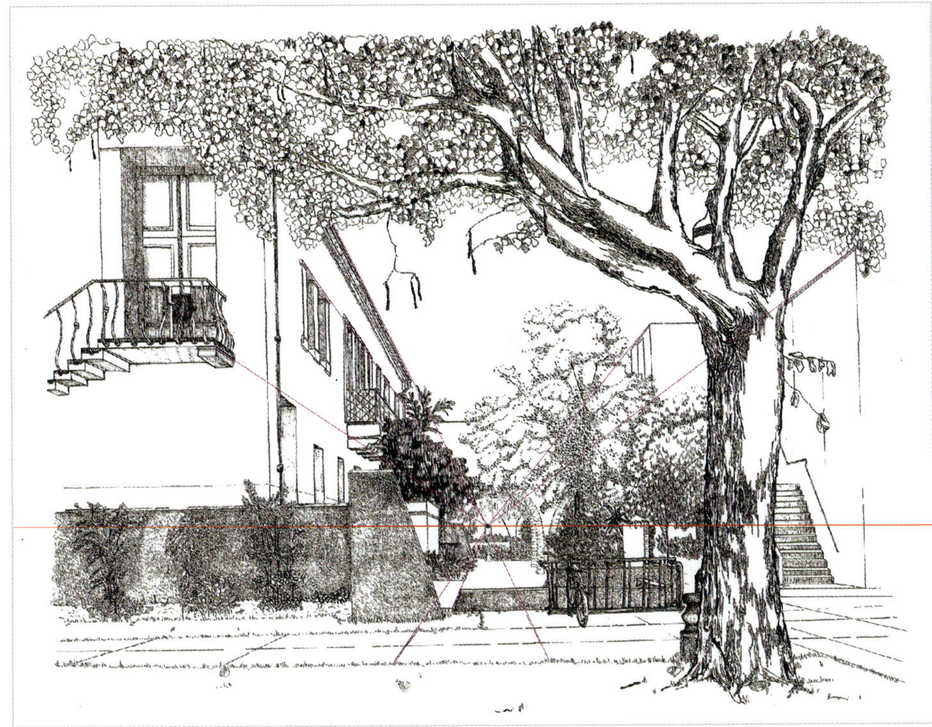

Here is a classic one-point situation, with the back wall and arched opening parallel to the picture plane and the walls on both sides perpendicular to the back wall. Student perspective drawing by Jane James. Time: 8–10 hours.

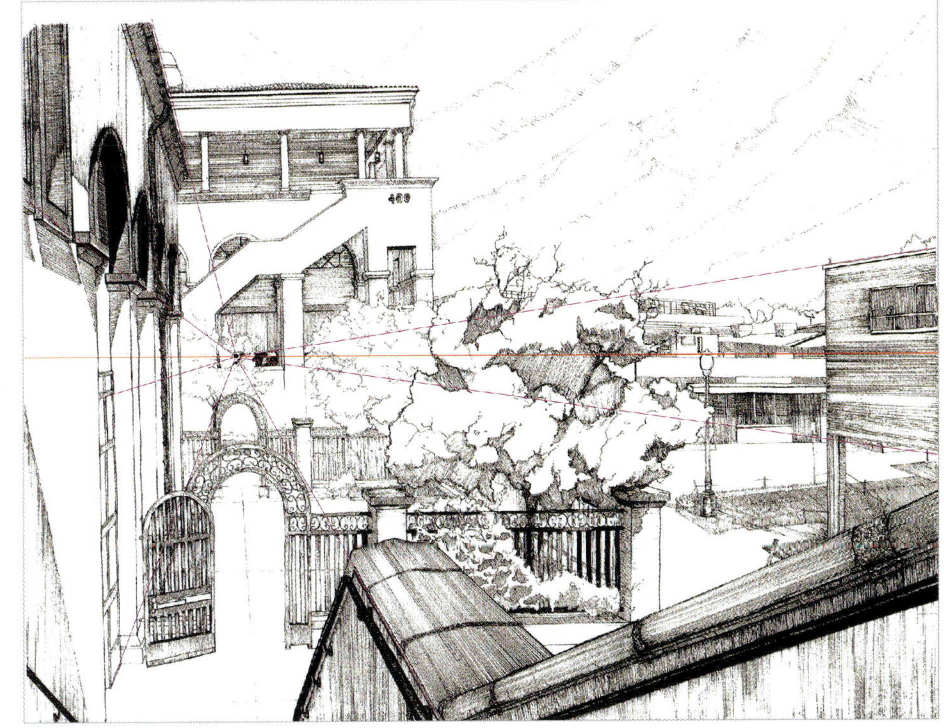

This is also a one-point drawing, but the eye level is very elevated; the artist is sitting on a staircase somewhere around the second floor. To understand and portray this perspective, the artist must focus on a point directly in front of him or her on true eye level; otherwise, the drawing will not be accurate.

In two-point perspective, neither wall of a building is parallel or perpendicular to the picture plane. Lines, planes, and edges on each side converge to common vanishing points on their perspective sides. The only edges that are horizontal within this view are lines or edges that coincide with the horizon line. In order to accurately portray the correct proportions of a building in two-point perspective, it may be that one or both vanishing points for the building are located beyond the limit of the paper.

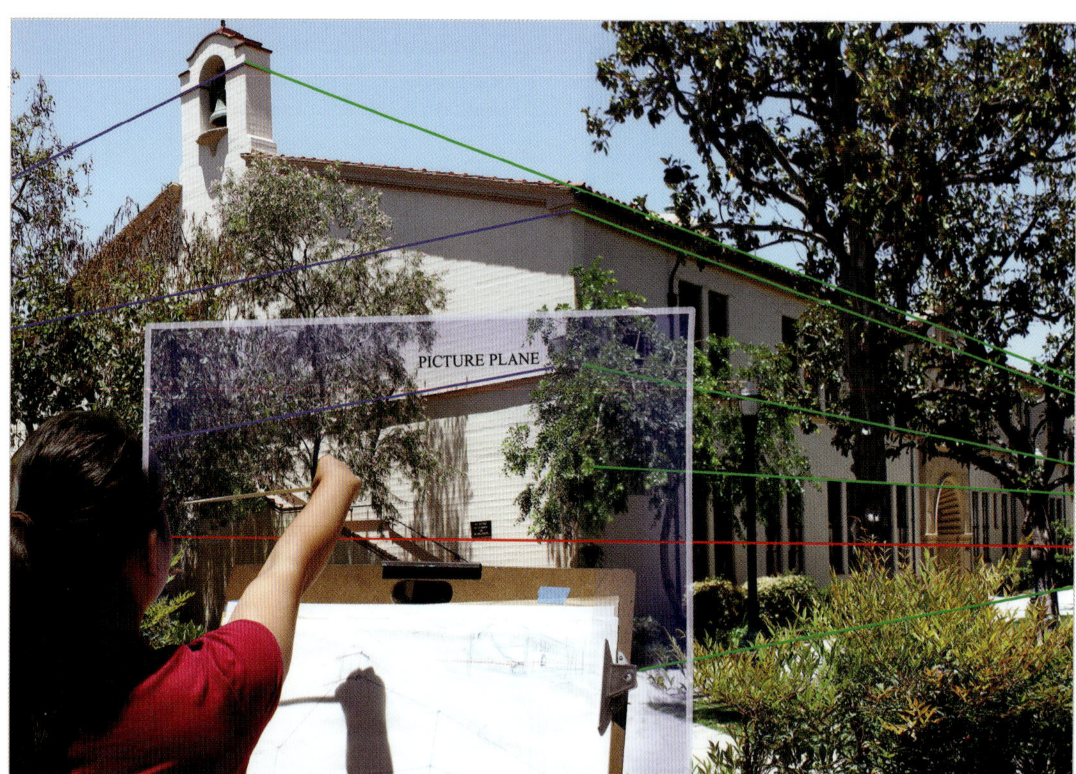

The main difference between one- and two-point perspective is that, in a two-point view, none of the planes (or walls) of the building are parallel to the picture plane. Think of this building as a large box that is tilted away from the picture plane. The edges of the walls on the right (green lines) converge to a vanishing point on the same side on eye level. The edges of the walls on the left (blue lines) converge to a vanishing point on the left side, also on eye level.

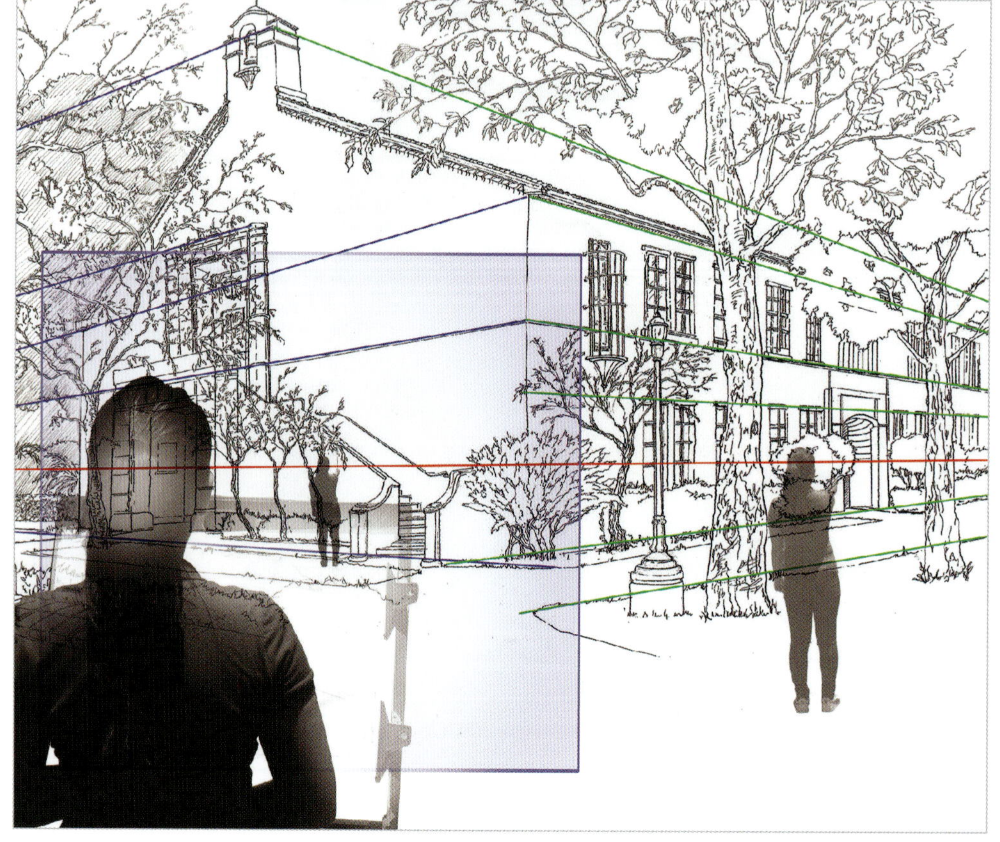

Here is what the line drawing of the building would look like to the artist looking through the picture plane. Notice the angles of the receding lines as they move away from horizontal (eye level). As the lines rise away from each other, there is a gradual change in the angles, culminating in the steepest angle at the top-most point of the building. Notice also that eye level is the same for all three people depicted in the image. The figures become proportionally smaller as they move further from the picture plane, but on a flat surface like this, their eye levels stay the same.

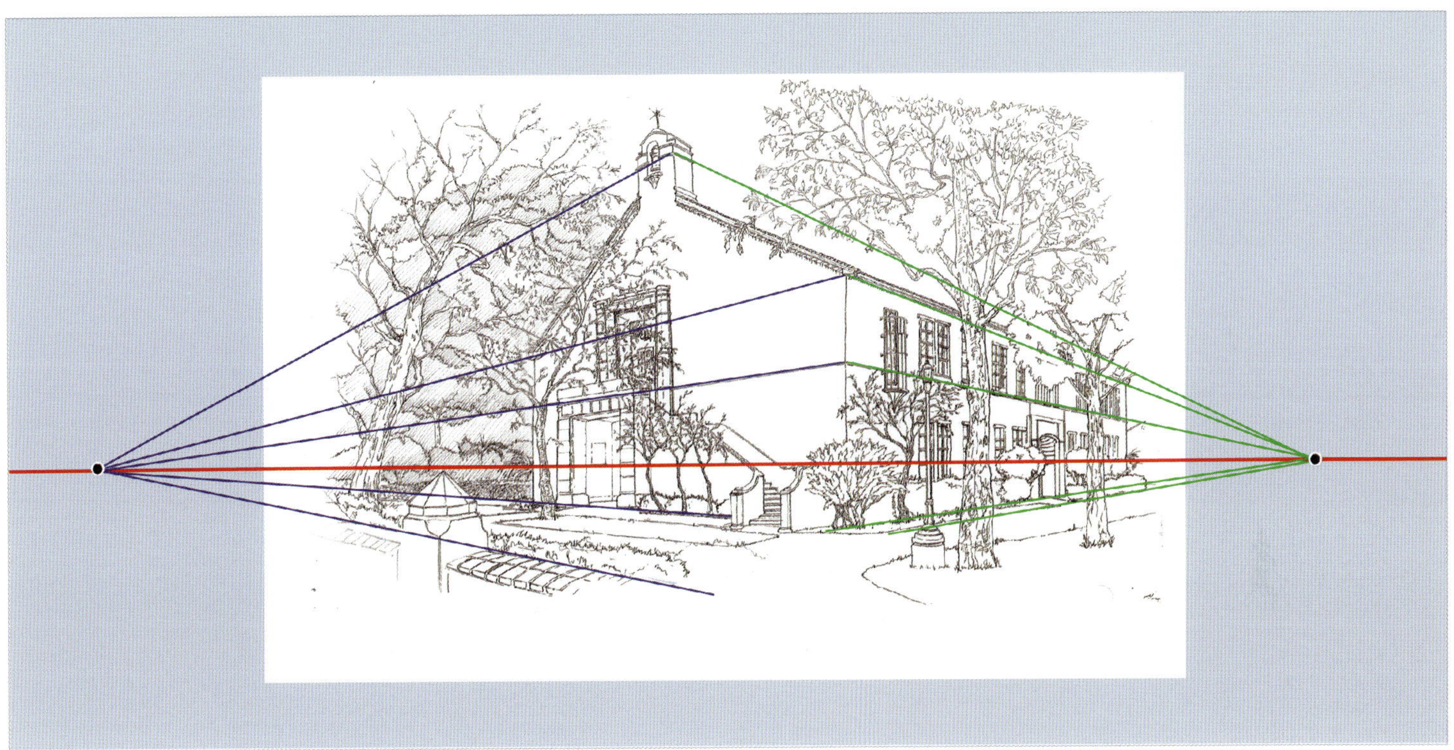

This illustration demonstrates where the vanishing points actually are for this two-point perspective drawing. In most two-point drawings, vanishing points fall off the page if they are drawn accurately.

Vanishing Point Exceptions

There are a few exceptions to the rule that vanishing points are always on the horizon line. These exceptions include lines that create inclined planes, such as staircases, rooflines, wheelchair ramps, etc. We'll call these convergence points *trace points* in order to separate them from true vanishing points.

Another exception to the rule is points of convergence for three-point perspective architecture, which we will not discuss in this chapter. The points of convergence for three-point perspective are known as vertical vanishing points. However, for our purposes in this chapter, one can reasonably expect vanishing points to always be at eye level.

Drawing Interior Perspectives

Drawing an interior perspective can be described simply as drawing the inside of a box, rather than the outside; all the same principles still pertain, with a few subtle differences.

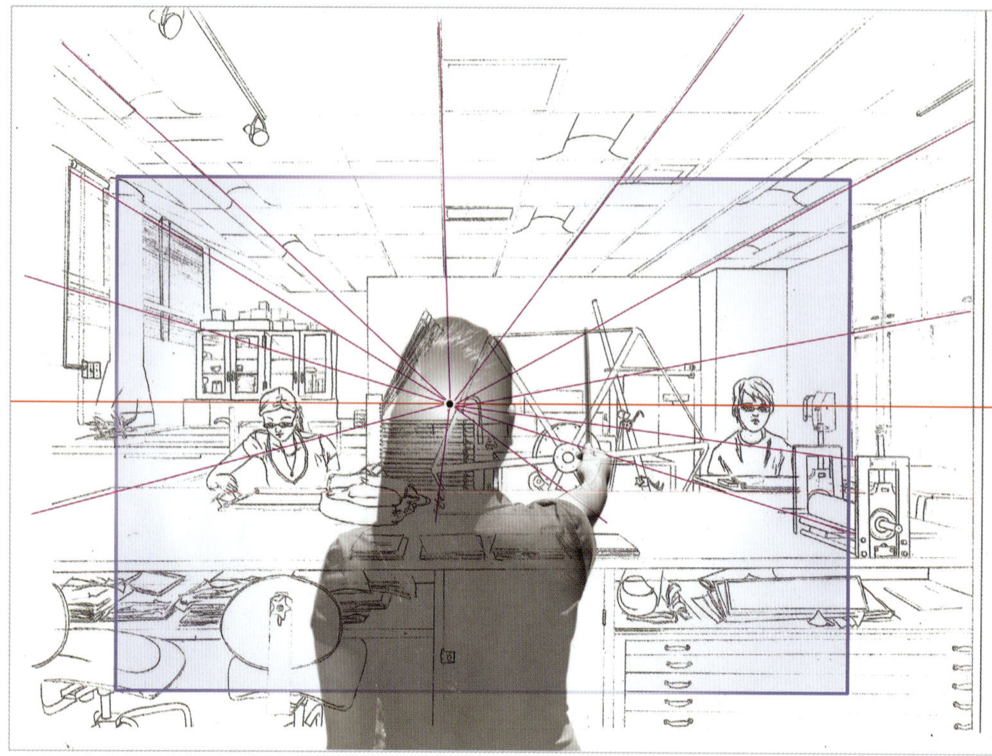

A one-point interior: Remember that the picture plane is parallel to the back wall facing the artist, and we can see that all of the lines on the perpendicular walls converge directly to one vanishing point on eye level. Student perspective drawing by Stephanie De Roo. Time: 4–5 hours.

First establish whether the view is a one-point or two-point perspective situation. If the back wall facing you is parallel to the picture plane, it is a one-point perspective. If none of the walls within your view are parallel to the picture plane, it is a two-point perspective. Always remember to find the eye level right away; if it is a one-point perspective, the vanishing point for the perpendicular walls will be directly in front of you.

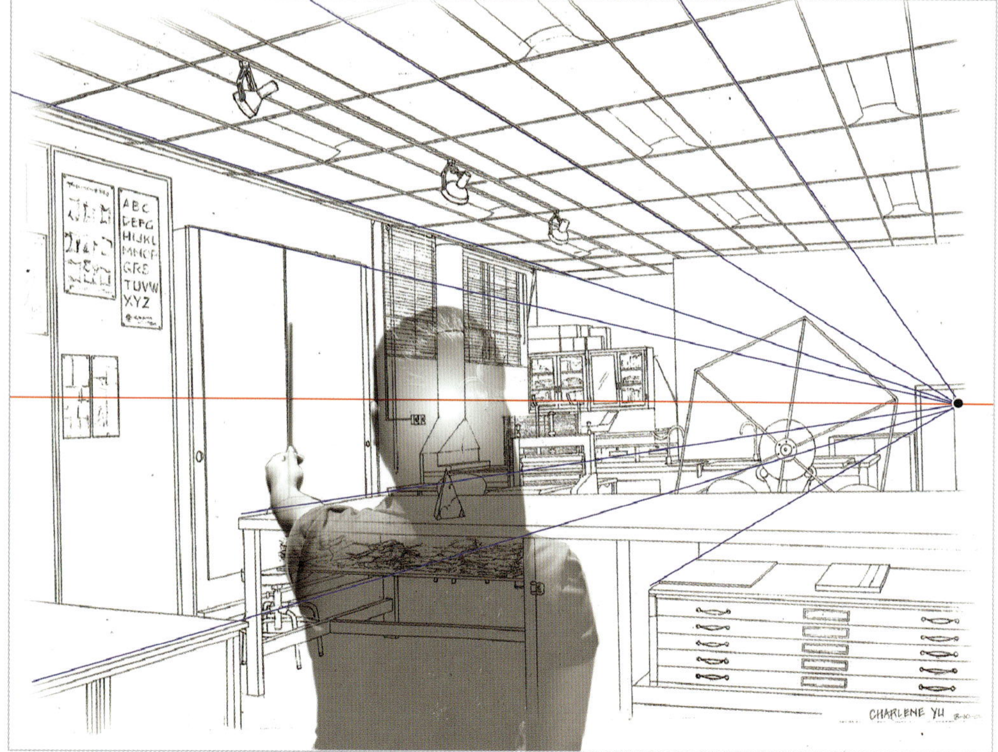

A two-point interior: The picture plane (and the artist) have turned away from the back wall; the picture plane is now parallel to the corner of the room, and the artist's line of vision is directed at the corner of the room. The blue lines on the left wall, as well as any structural edges on or parallel to that wall, all converge to a common vanishing point on the right side of the drawing. Student perspective drawing by Charlene Yu.

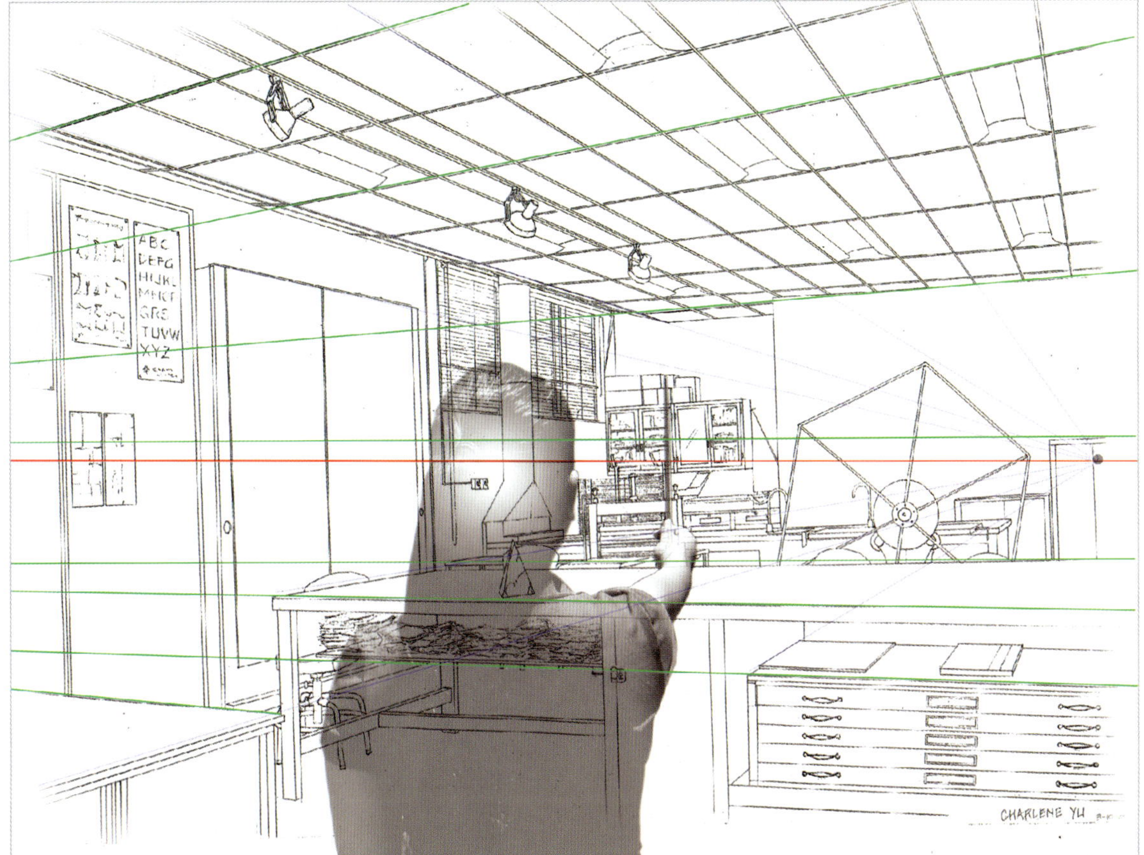

The right-side wall and all structures parallel to it are represented as green lines that converge to a common vanishing point to the left side of the drawing. Again, look at the angles presented by the lines above and below eye level as they move away from horizontal. Student perspective drawing by Charlene Yu.

In the two-point perspective demonstrated above, you can see that the vanishing point for the left wall is within the picture plane, but the vanishing point for the right wall is well outside of the picture plane. In a two-point perspective drawing, it's a good idea to expect that neither vanishing point will be on the paper; but it's always a nice surprise when one of them is.

Two-Point Perspective Construction Demonstration

Creating a perspective drawing from observation is a logical process that involves understanding the picture plane and how it is used, transferring accurate sight-size measurements of the subject to the drawing, and being able to accurately see and draw angles in perspective—even if there are no vanishing points within the drawing.

Remember the all-important rule when sight-size measuring. Your arm must always be straight when measuring for consistent proportional measurements. Follow along with the demonstrated steps as you work on your own drawing.

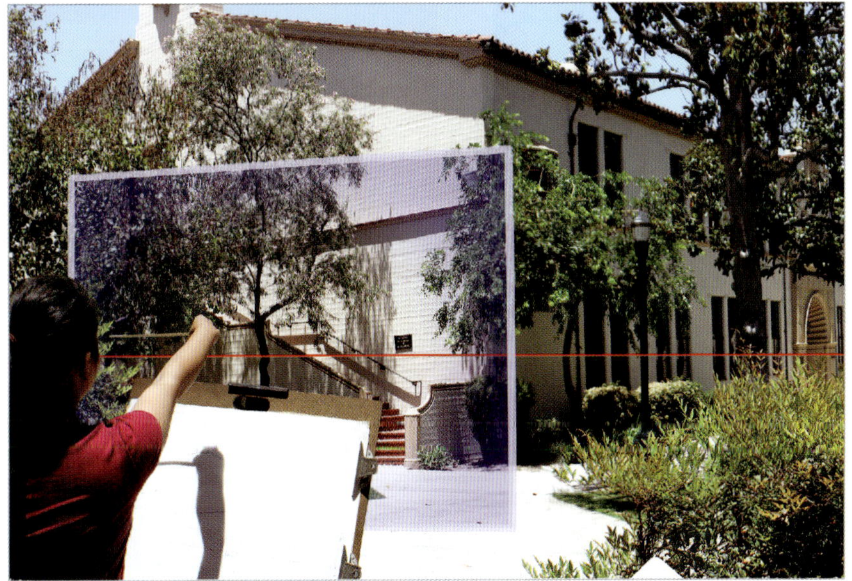

USING A CHOPSTICK for angles and exact measurements, we will make extensive use of the picture plane and follow a logical, step-by-step

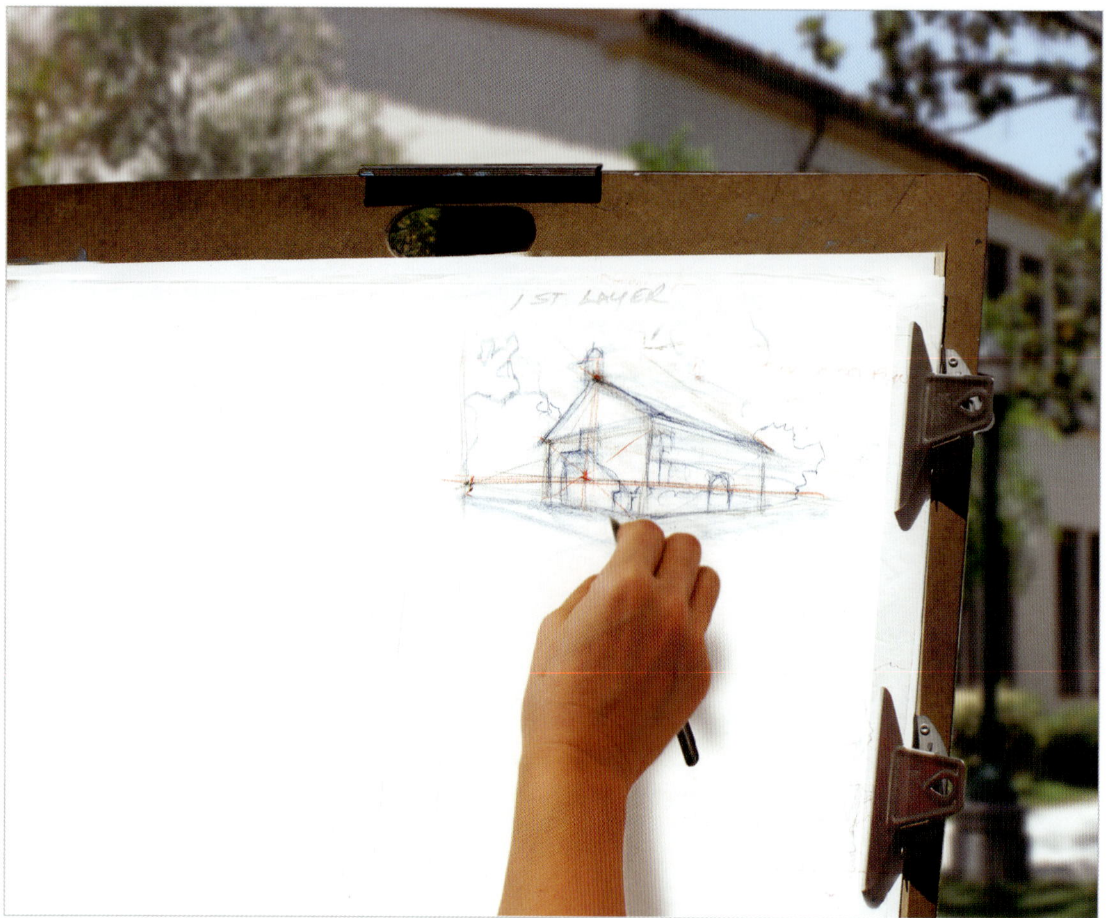

STEP 1 Start with a thumbnail sketch. This is a helpful reference throughout the drawing process, and it provides the artist with more knowledge of the subject before beginning the main drawing. Try using a red pencil for eye level, both on the thumbnail sketch and the main drawing. Thumbnail sketches should always be done freehand, without rulers or measuring, in about 15 minutes.

STEP 2 Once eye level is identified, determine its placement on the paper. (It's usually about a quarter of the way up from the bottom of the page, as there is more architecture above eye level than below it.) Use actual sight-size measuring, meaning the actual size you measure with a chopstick on the building is the same measurement you put on the paper. Start with a measurement on the corner of the building closest to you; measure from eye level up to the top corner of the building (purple arrow) and then from eye level down to the bottom corner. Apply the exact measurement of the front corner of the building from eye level to the roofline to the drawing. Sight-size measuring is a very easy and logical way to obtain accurate measurements and angles for this type of drawing.

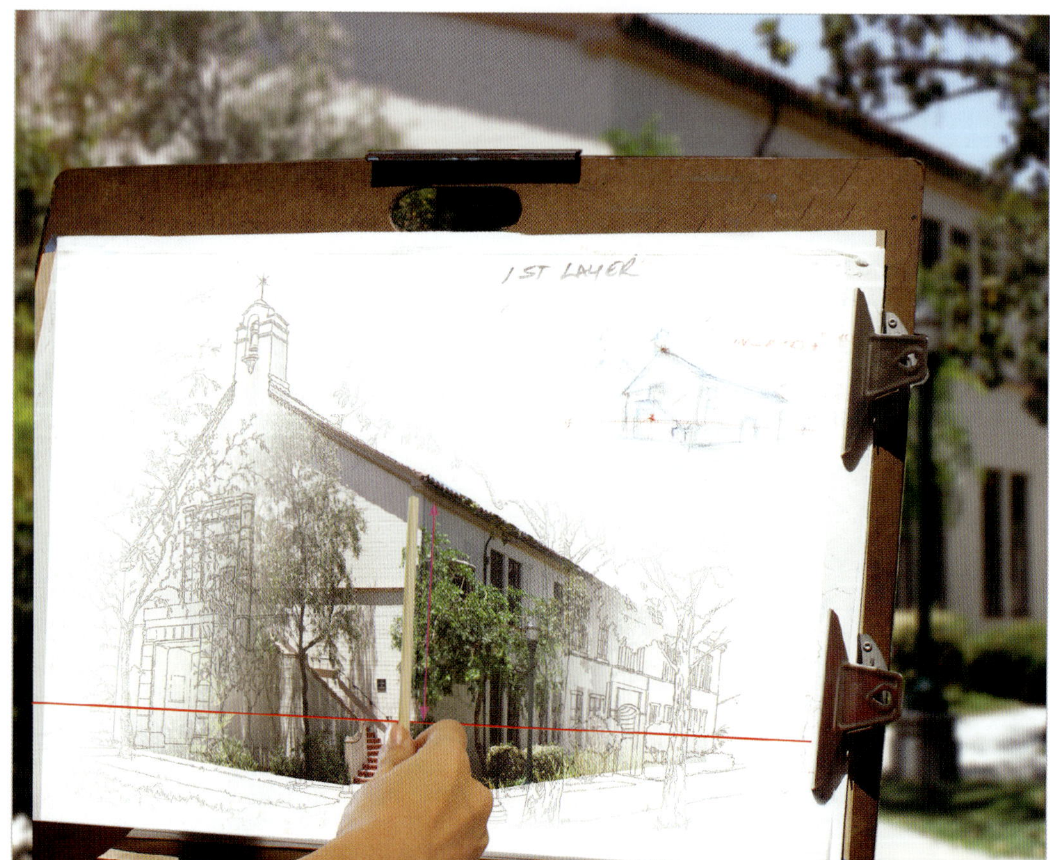

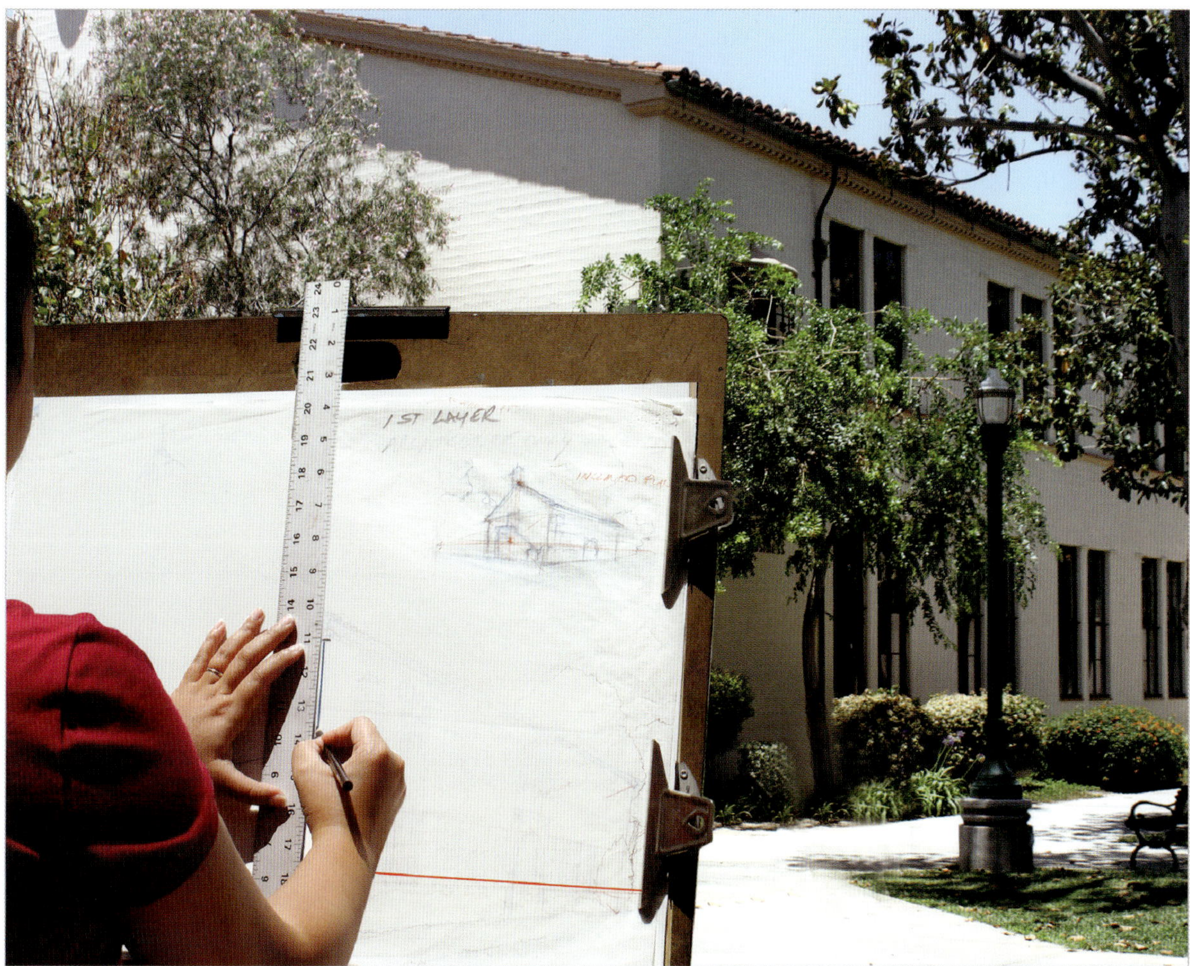

STEP 3 Use a chopstick to quickly check measurements and mark your paper, and use a ruler to achieve accurate sketched lines.

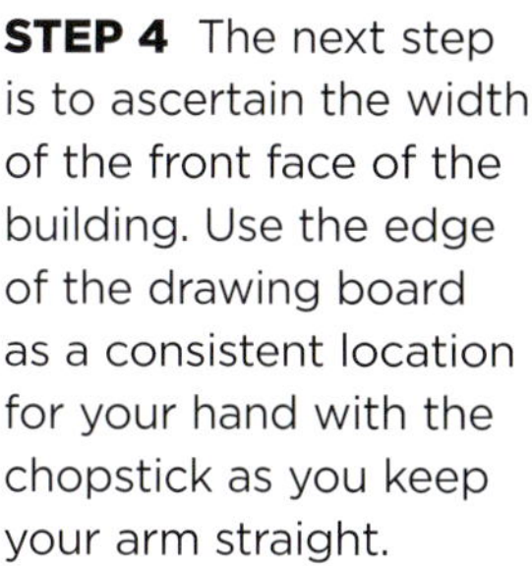

STEP 4 The next step is to ascertain the width of the front face of the building. Use the edge of the drawing board as a consistent location for your hand with the chopstick as you keep your arm straight.

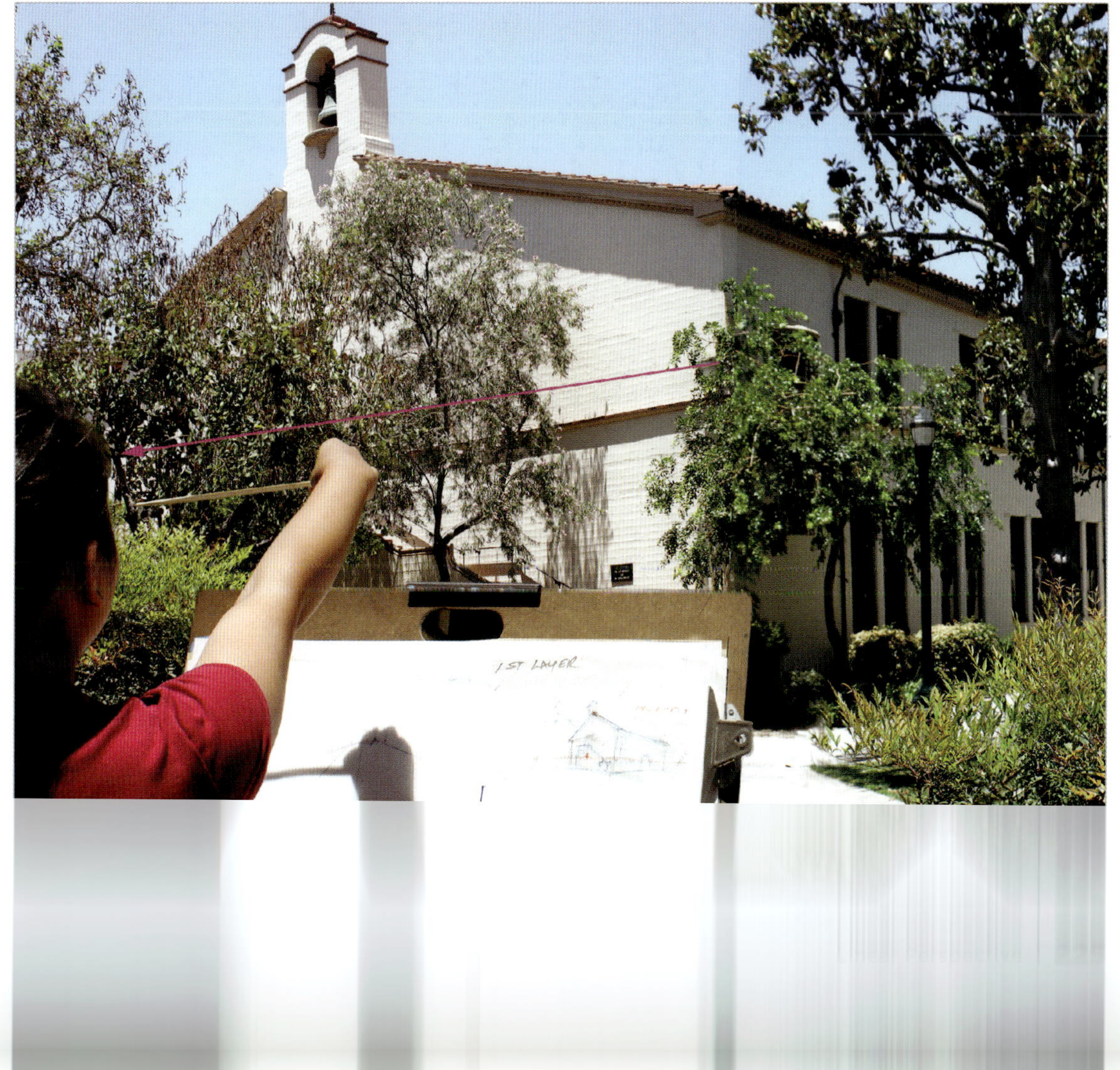

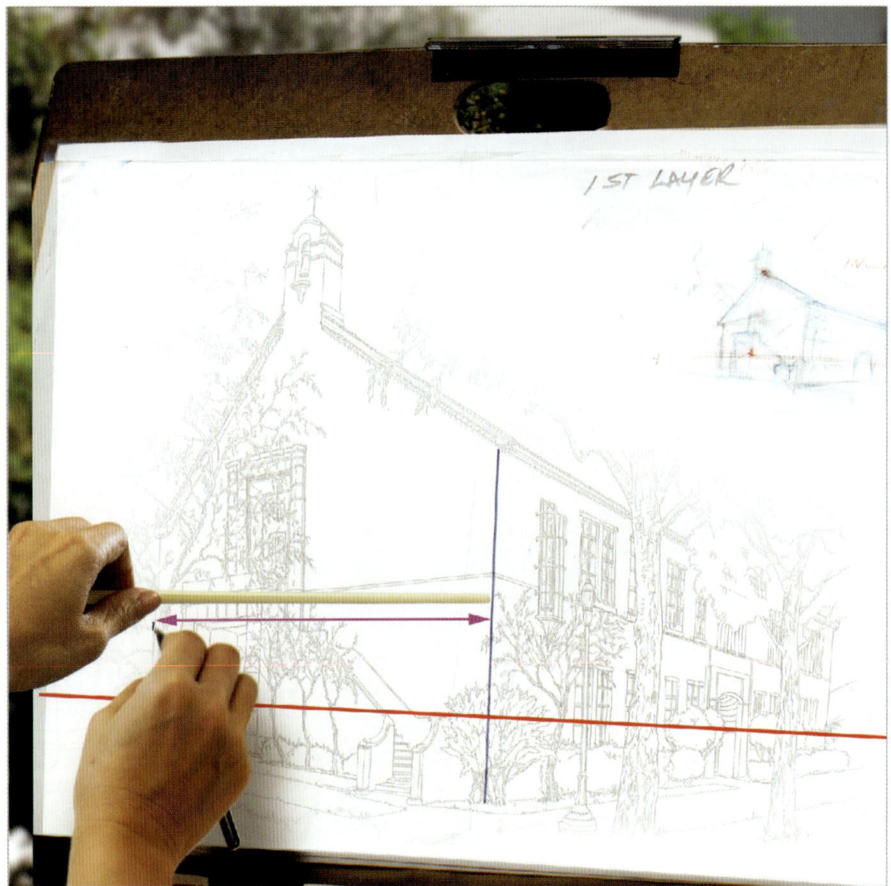

STEP 5 Apply the same measurement of the width of the front of the building to the drawing. Make a mark on the page where the location of the far corner of the building will be. When using the chopstick for angles and measurements, it is a good idea to use your nondrawing hand, as it is much easier to measure and make marks at the same time, without changing hands. Draw in the far corner, above and below eye level before moving on.

Note: The finished sketch is "ghosted" onto this image to more easily demonstrate the action.

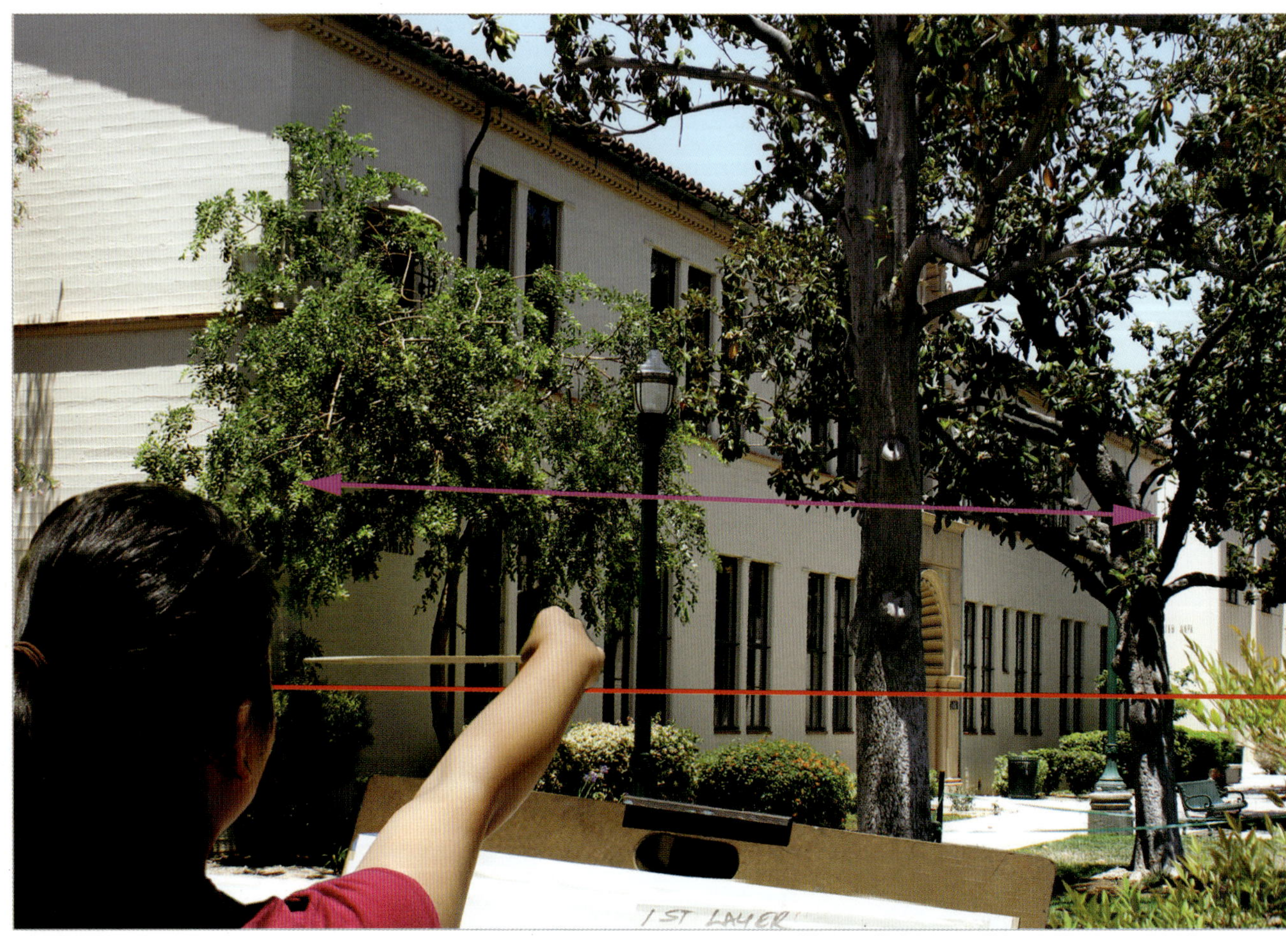

STEP 6 Now it's time to add the right side of the building. Start with the end of the chopstick on the nearest corner, which has already been drawn, and measure to the far end of the building.

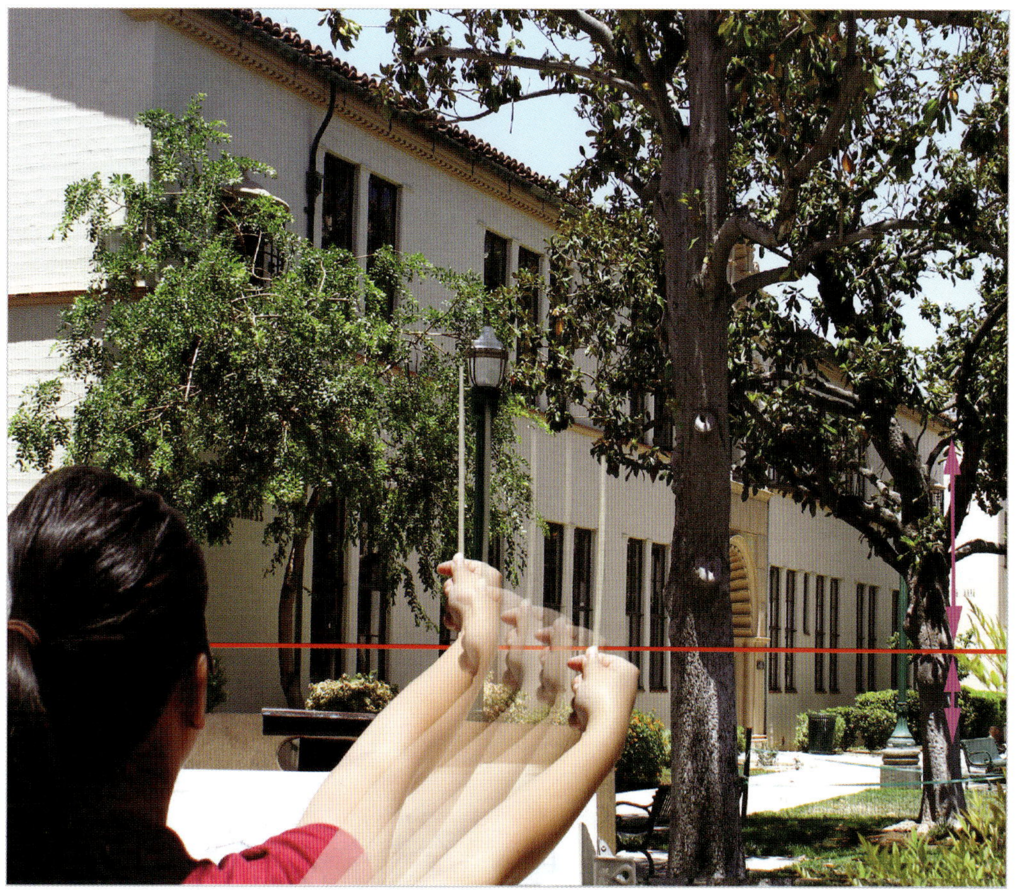

STEP 7 Establish the length of the building and mark your paper. Measure the height of the building's end above and then below eye level. Remember this step; if you only measure the entire height of the wall, including both above and below eye level, you can't be certain where to locate eye level on the line.

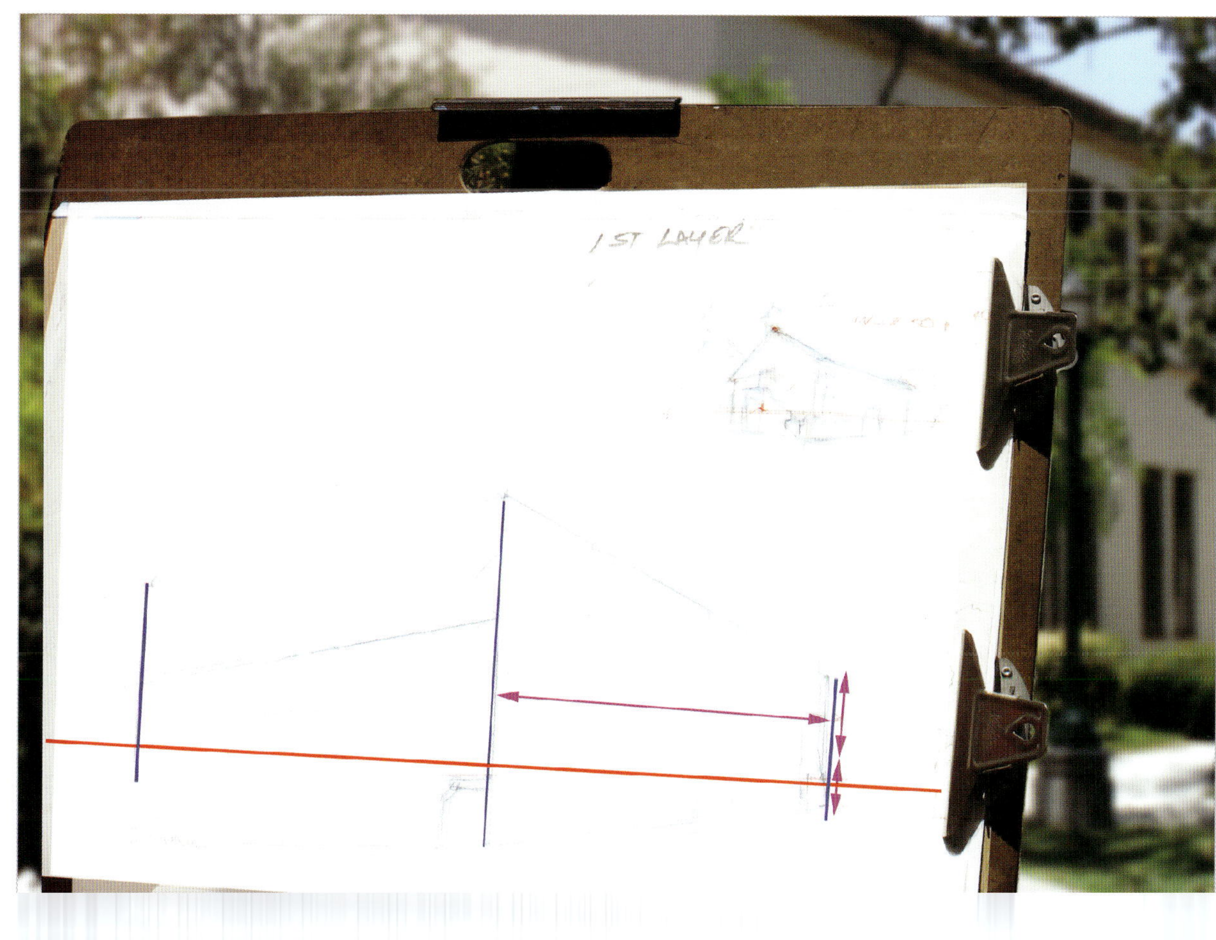

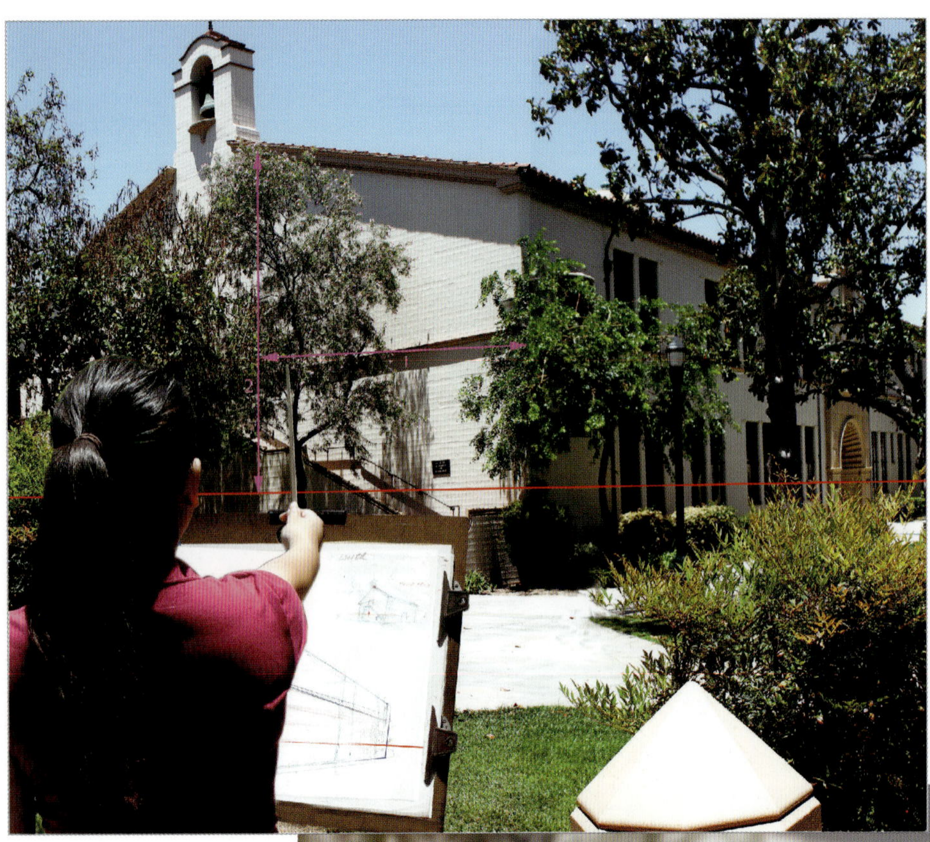

STEP 9 In order to ascertain the pitch of the roof, measure laterally from the nearest corner of the building to the vertical-axis location of the roof. You can then establish the height of the roof in that lateral location from eye level.

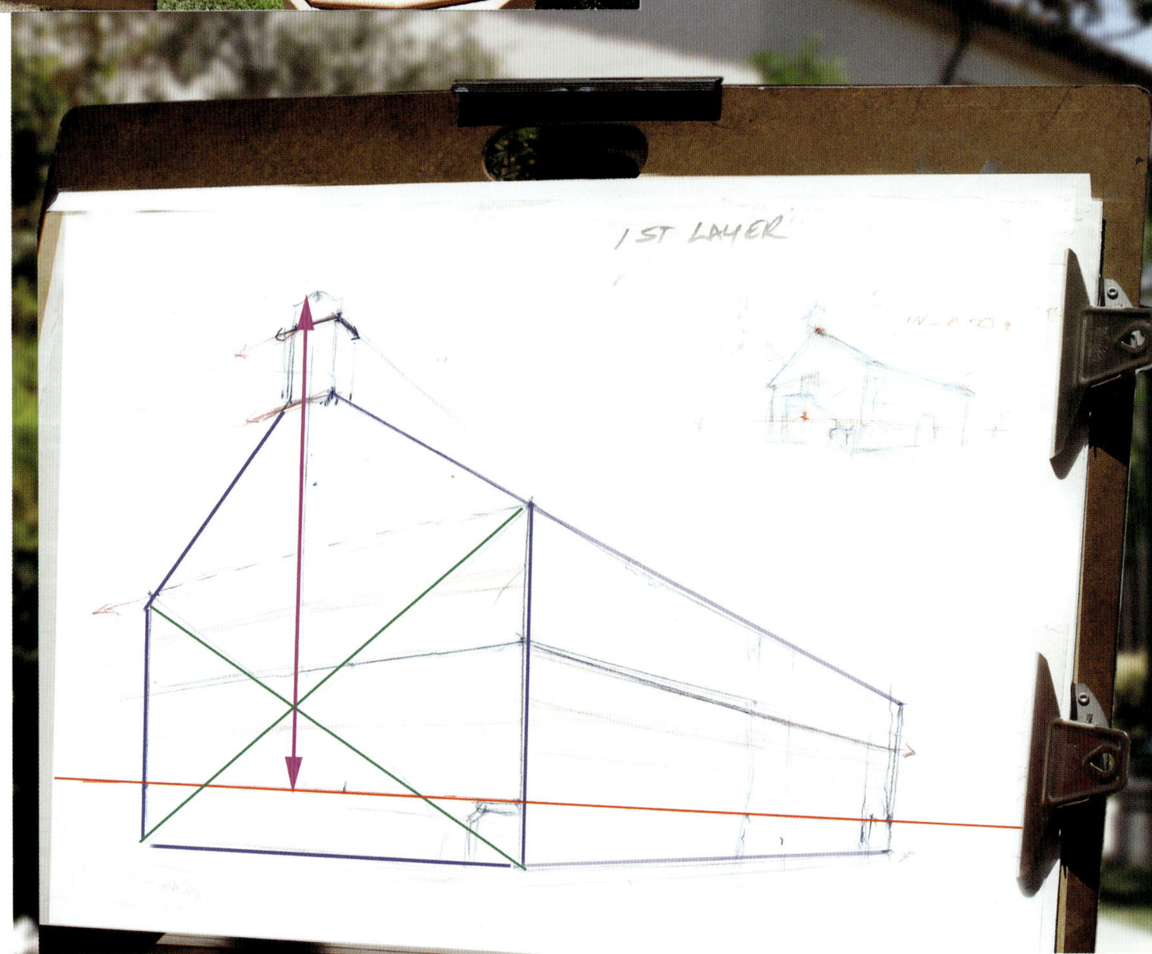

STEP 10 Once the rooflines are established, the bell tower can be constructed by finding the midline of the structure. Extend lines from each corner of the vertical edges that establish the height of the walls; those lines form an "X" (shown here in green), dividing the wall into perspective halves. The middle of the "X" is the location of the midline of the structure. At this point, a vertical measurement with the chopstick from eye level will locate the top of the building.

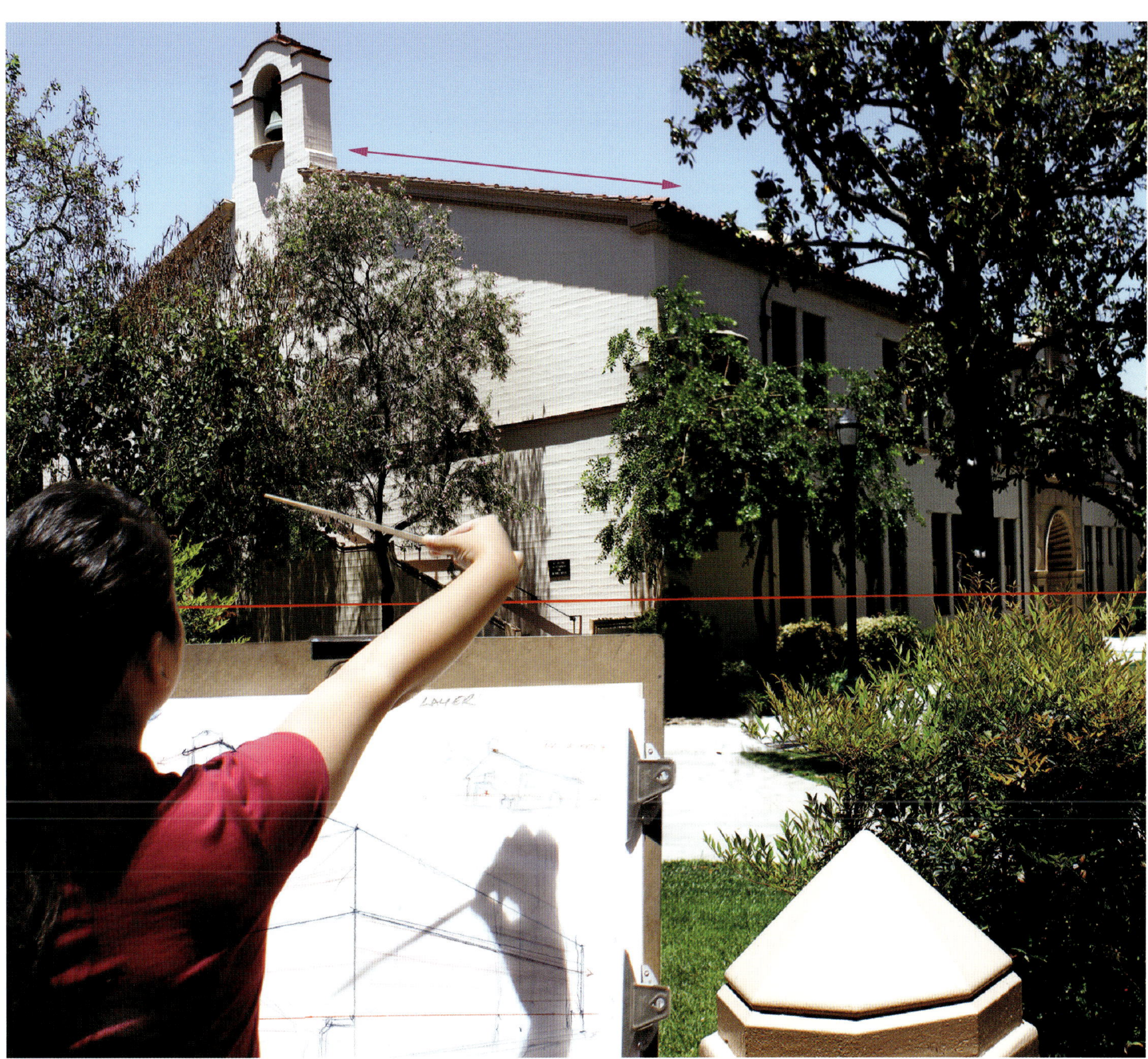

STEP 11 Check the roof angle with the chopstick.

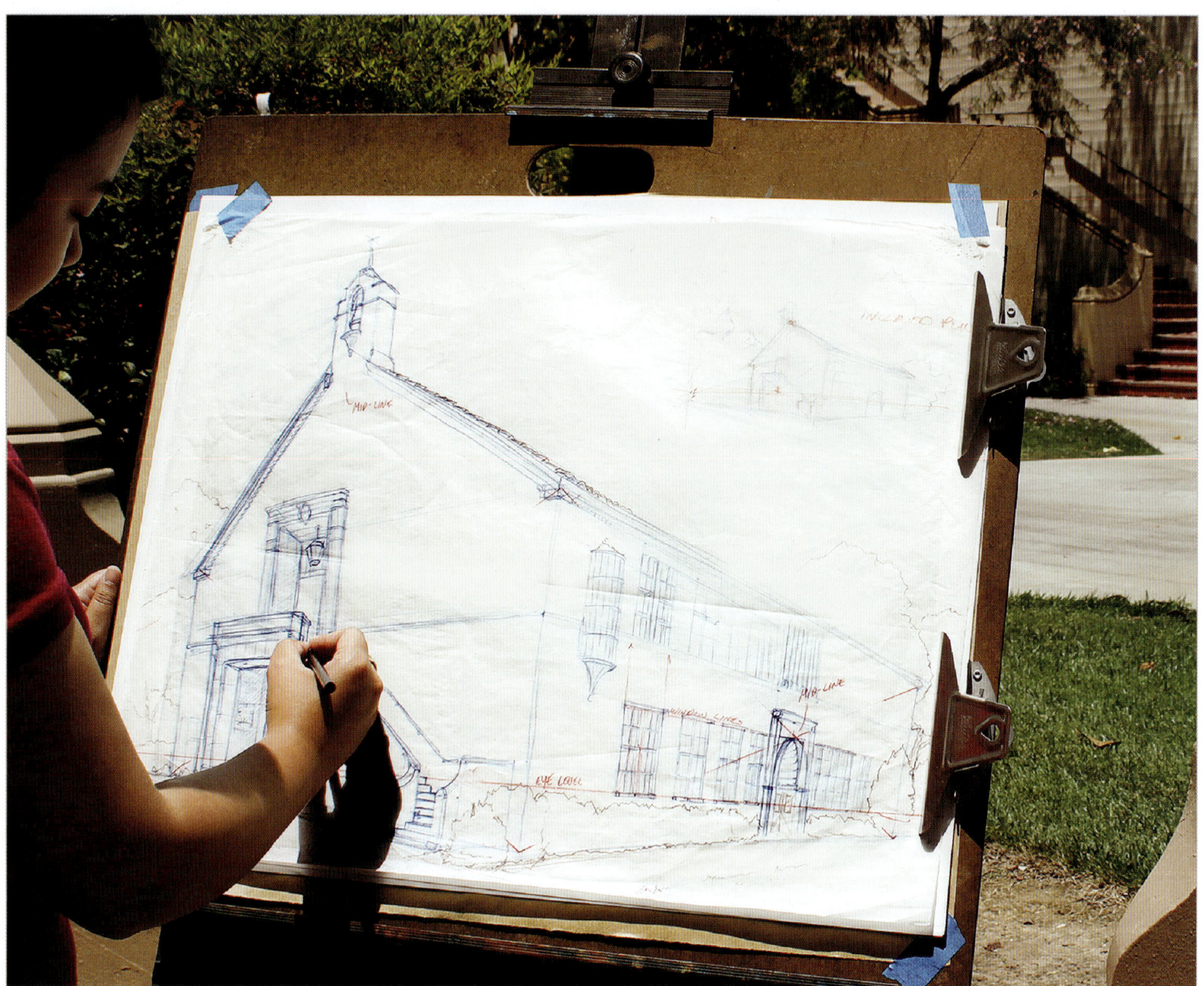

STEP 12 After all of the measurements are finished on the first layer, add a second layer of tracing paper to refine the freehand sketch, finishing the windows, doors, trees, sidewalks, and building details.

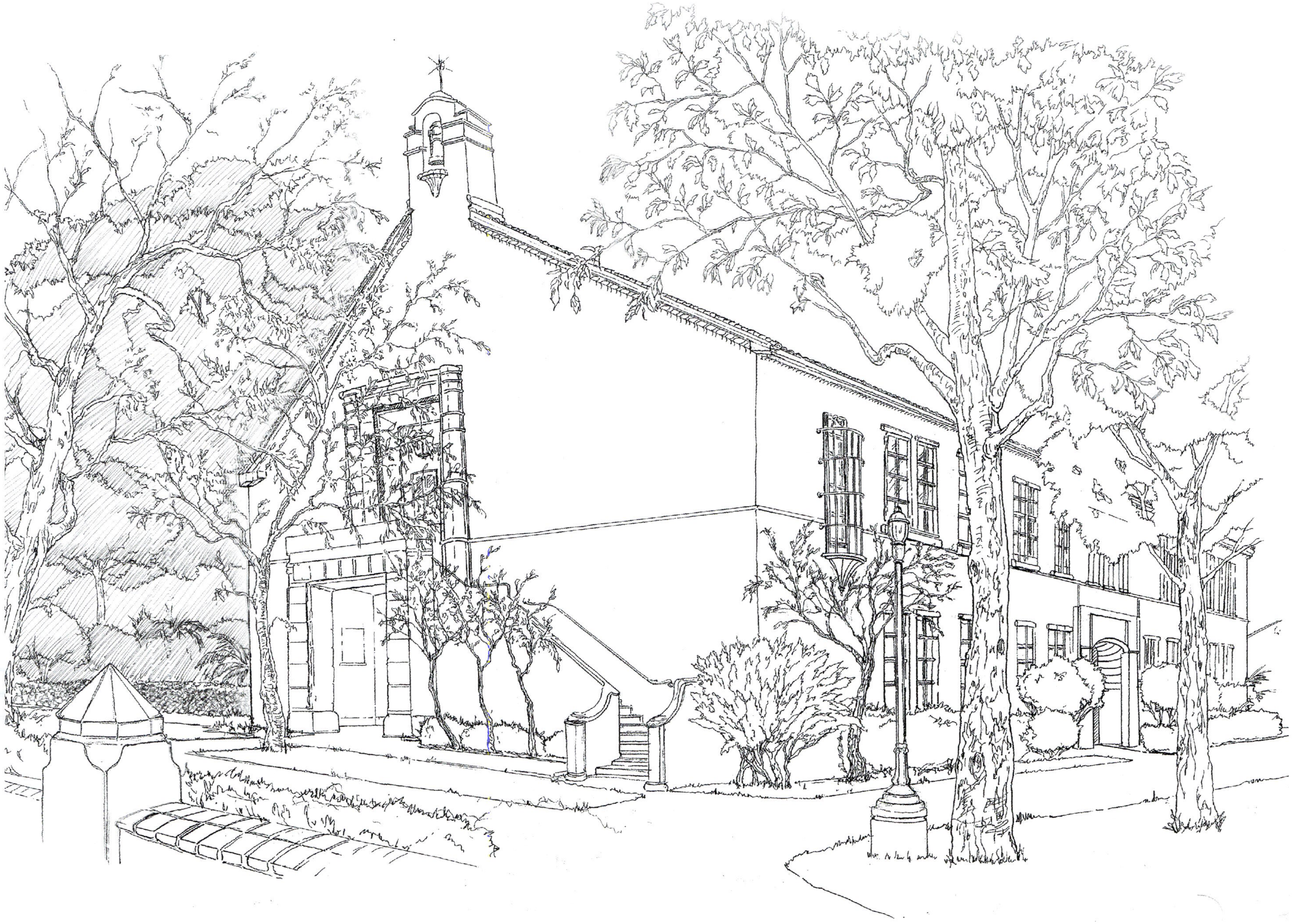

The final ink perspective drawing. Time: 6–8 hours.

Inclined Planes

Inclined planes are parallel-edged planes that are neither horizontal nor vertical to the picture plane, but rather, they are angled to it. Examples of inclined planes include staircases, elevated ramps, and angled rooftops.

These parallel-edged planes have their own point of convergence, called a trace point. These trace points rise either above or below eye level, depending on the direction that the inclined plane slants away from the picture plane. One of the rules that governs inclined planes is that parallel edges that incline away from a set of parallel and perpendicular planes (that are parallel to the picture plane) converge to a trace point that is directly vertical to the vanishing point on that side.

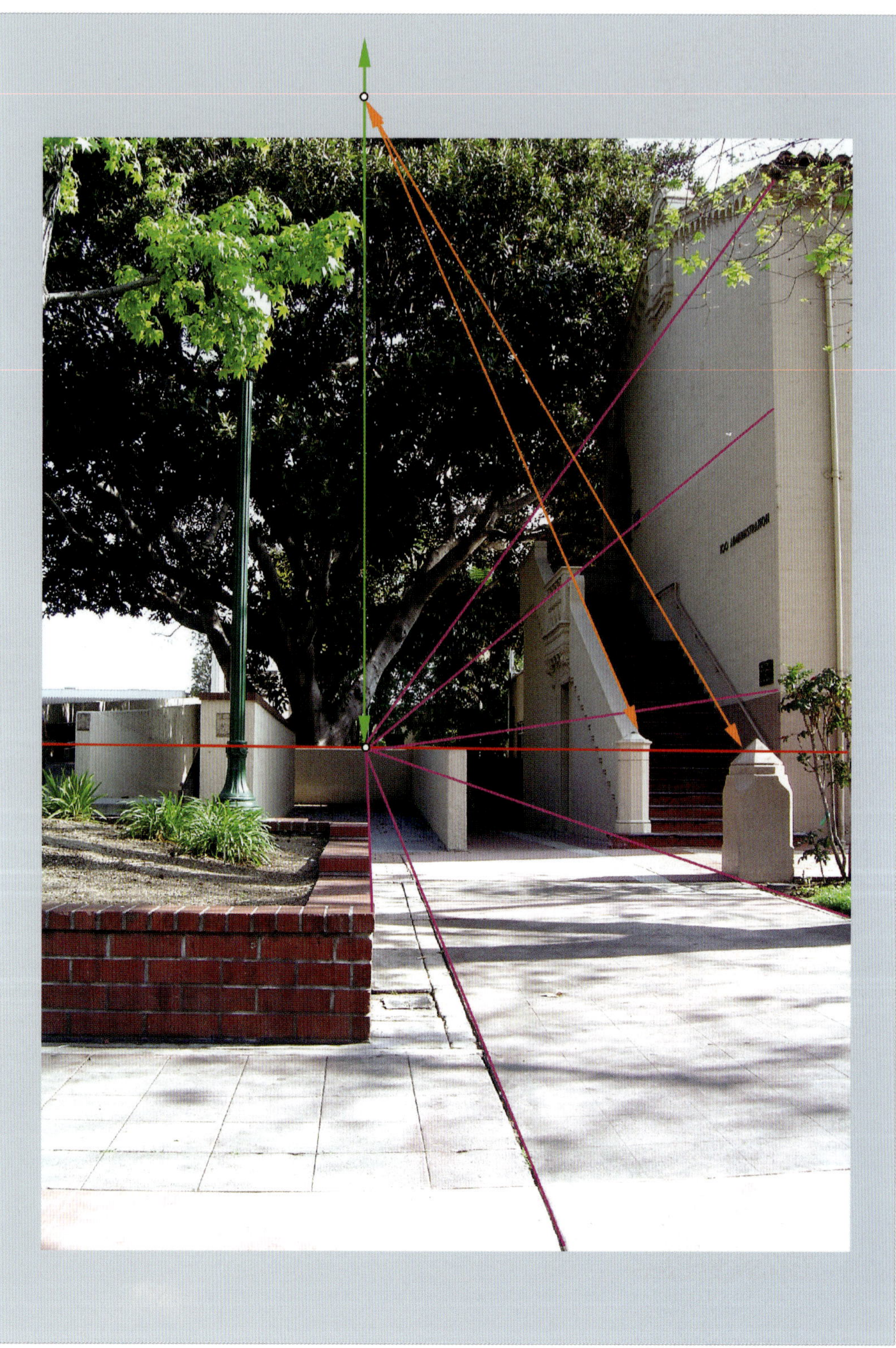

Inclined planes are angled structures, such as stairways and rooflines, that don't follow the same perspective rules as structural walls parallel to the picture plane. However, they do have their own set of rules and logic. One rule seen here is that the parallel edges of the inclined plane (in this case, a staircase) converge to a trace point directly above the vanishing point.

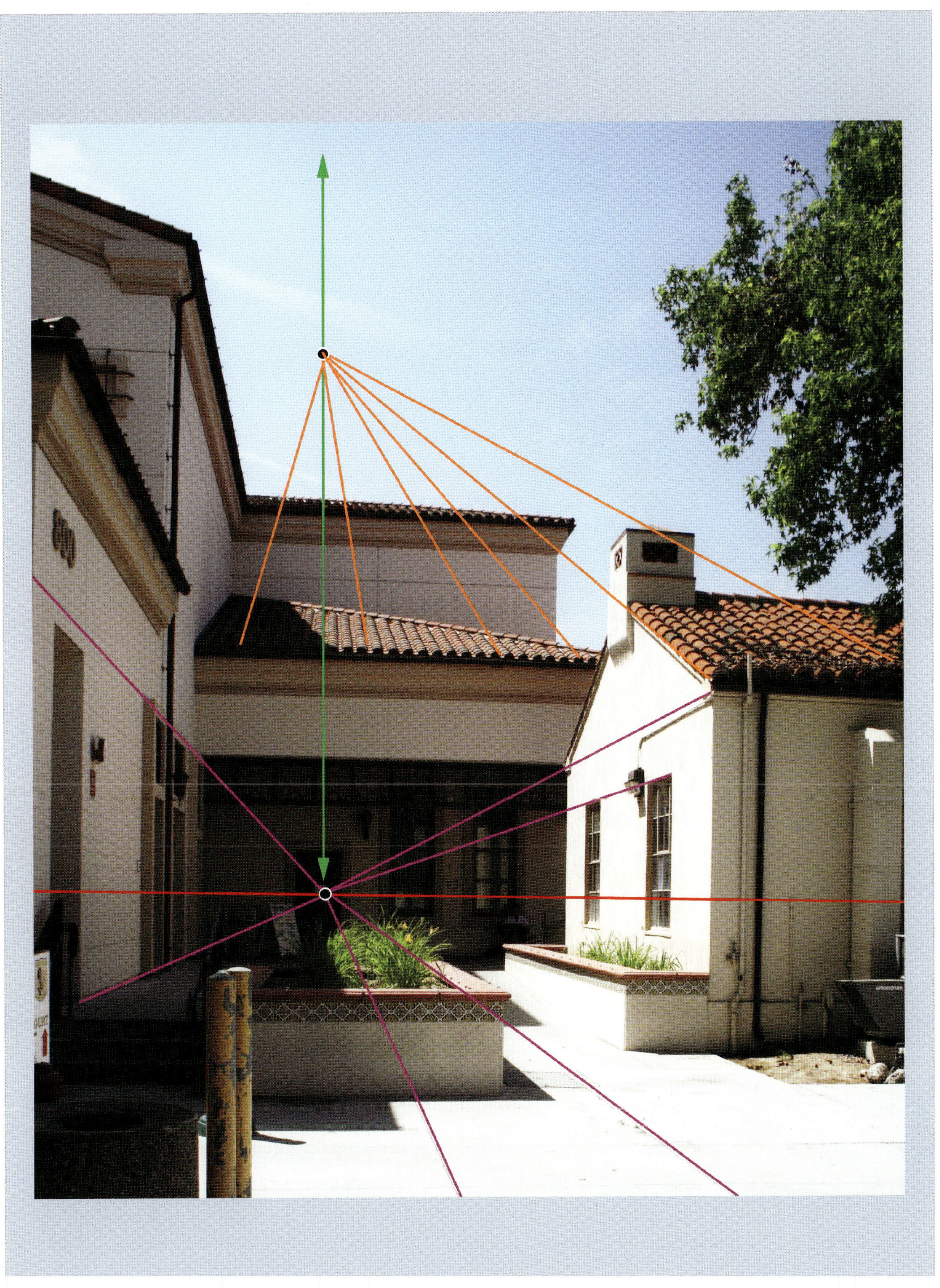

Aerial Perspective

The rules for this type of perspective were also discovered during the Renaissance (usually attributed to Leonardo da Vinci) and state that as objects move away from the viewer, they become softer and lighter in color and value. Da Vinci called this phenomenon the perspective of disappearance. We know now that as the distance of an object increases, more and more atmosphere comes between the viewer and the object, causing the distant object or structure to appear bluish in color.

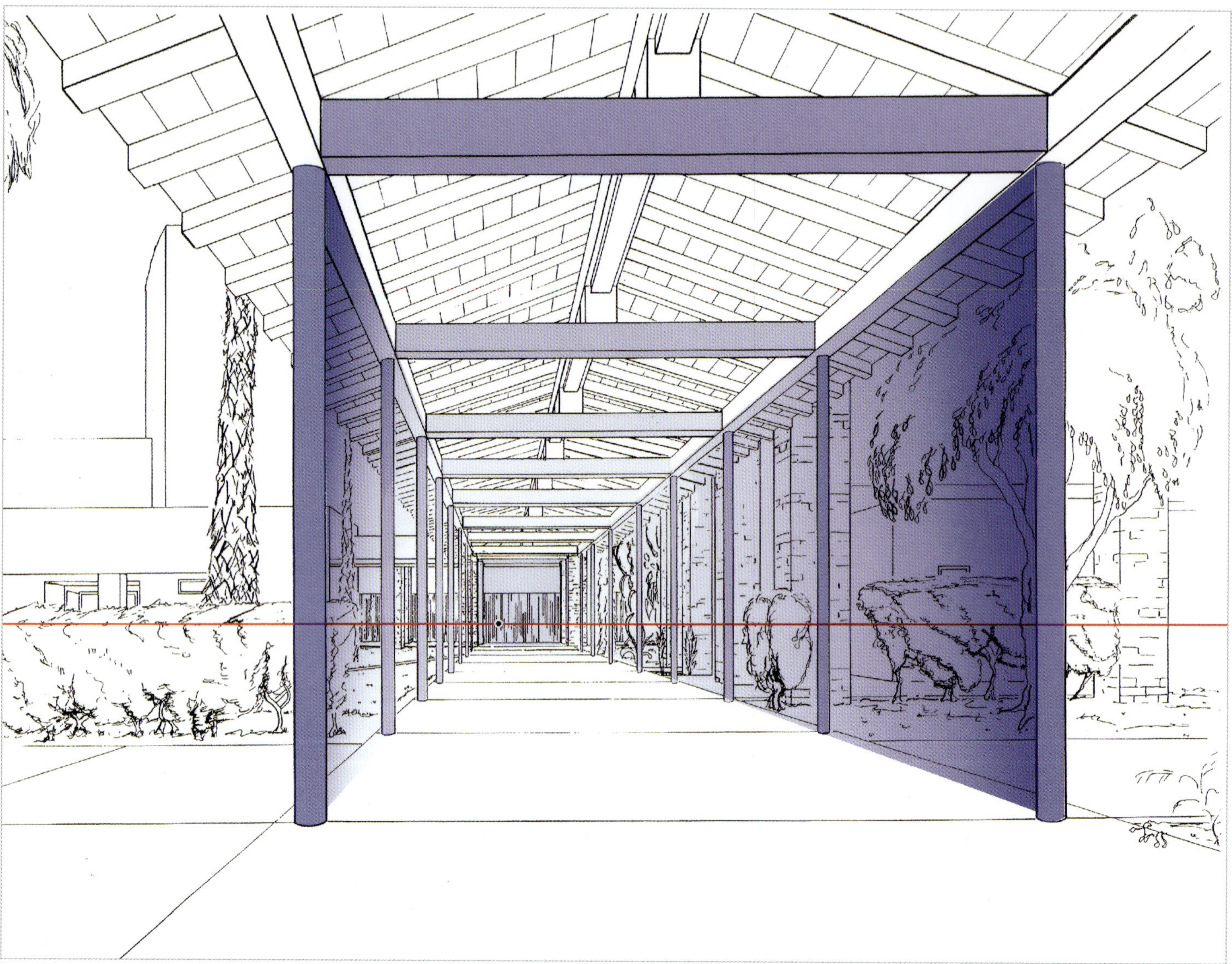

Aerial, or atmospheric, perspective occurs as objects that are the same in color and value become muted as they move away from the viewer. As the distance of an object increases, it becomes somewhat softer and less distinct because of the atmosphere that comes between it and the viewer; the greater the distance, the greater the reduction in contrast and detail. This explains why mountains in the distance appear bluish during daylight hours. An artist can suggest atmospheric perspective by varying the line weight from the back to the front, with lighter receding lines and darker approaching lines. This same theory works with value in tonal drawings, as well as changes in value and intensity in color drawing and painting.

YOUR HOMEWORK

Create a one- or two-point perspective drawing from observation anywhere in your home. The larger and more interesting the space the better, although I have seen some very good bathroom drawings!

Start with a small thumbnail sketch of the space, understanding from the outset where your eye level is within the room, if it will be a one-point perspective drawing, and where the vanishing point is.

Sketch lightly at first, using a pencil or chopstick for measuring and angles, and refine your final drawing with the surrounding details of the room, such as houseplants, bookcases, paintings and photographs, lamps, etc.

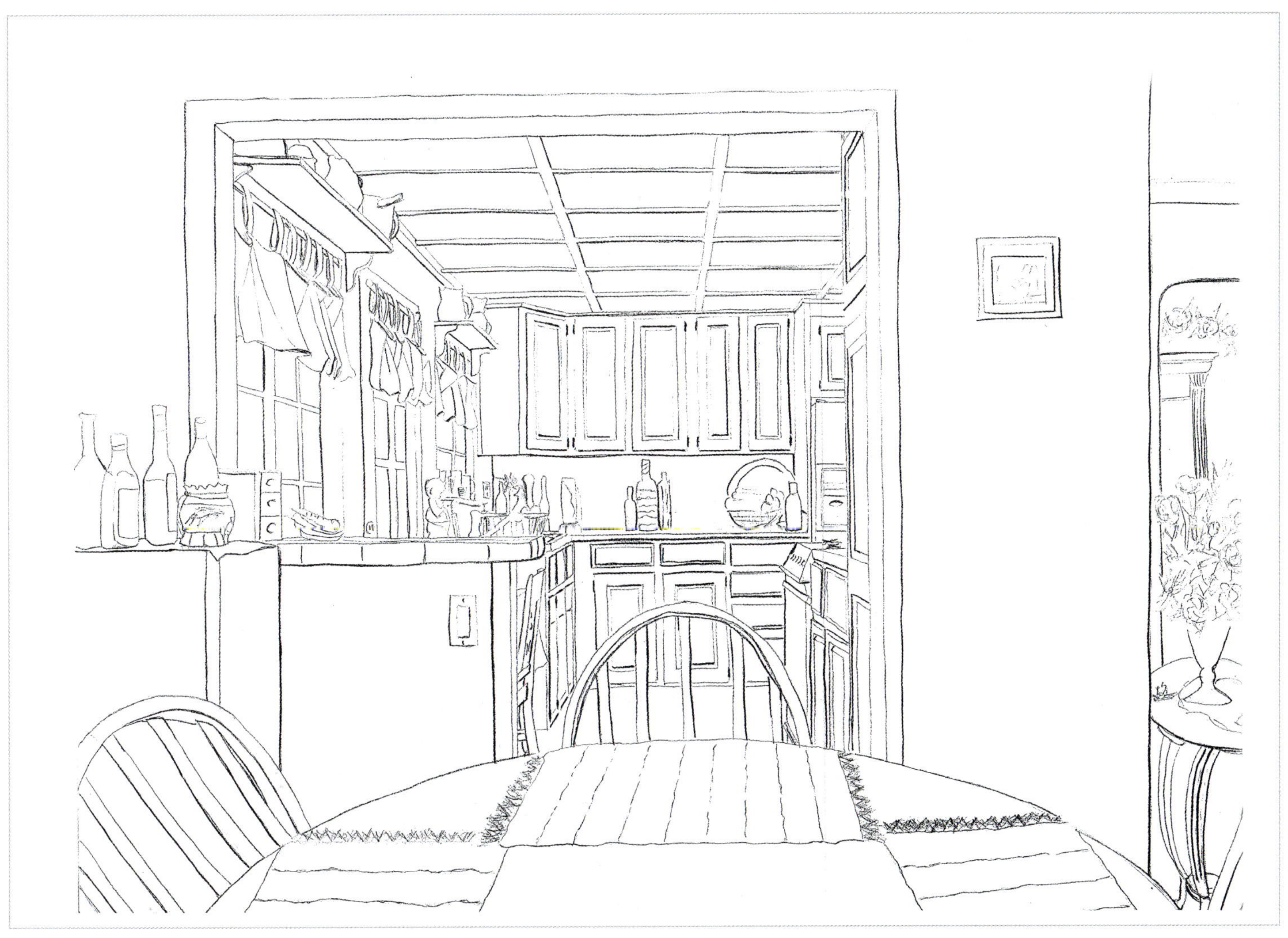

Employing Aerial Perspective and Shadows

In nature, impurities in the air (such as moisture and dust) block out some rays of sunlight, making objects in the distance appear less distinct than objects in the foreground. This phenomenon is referred to as "aerial perspective," and it creates the illusion of depth. This quiet scene takes advantage of aerial perspective, and foreground shadows give the drawing dimension.

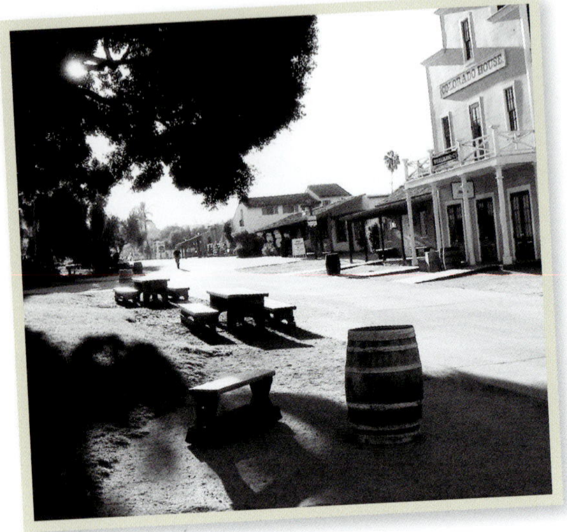

CHOOSING A SCENE This location is more interesting in the summer when long shadows come from the side, but this photo was shot in winter with the sun coming in from the south. The solution? Simply shift the direction of the shadows by modifying the composition to match the summer memory. Despite the limitations of the photo, you still can use it to reference when building an appealing composition.

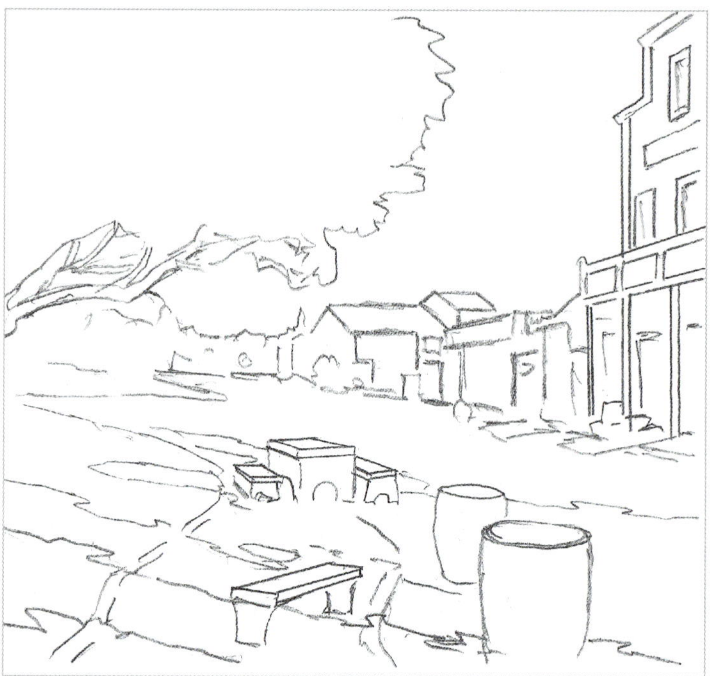

THUMBNAIL SKETCH Before starting the actual rendering, draw a thumbnail sketch. After blocking in the basic shapes, lay in the new, summer shadow areas. The intention is to lead the viewer's eye into the scene by establishing dark, contrasting shadows across the foreground. This thumbnail is now a value guide; the photo is only a reference for the shapes and details.

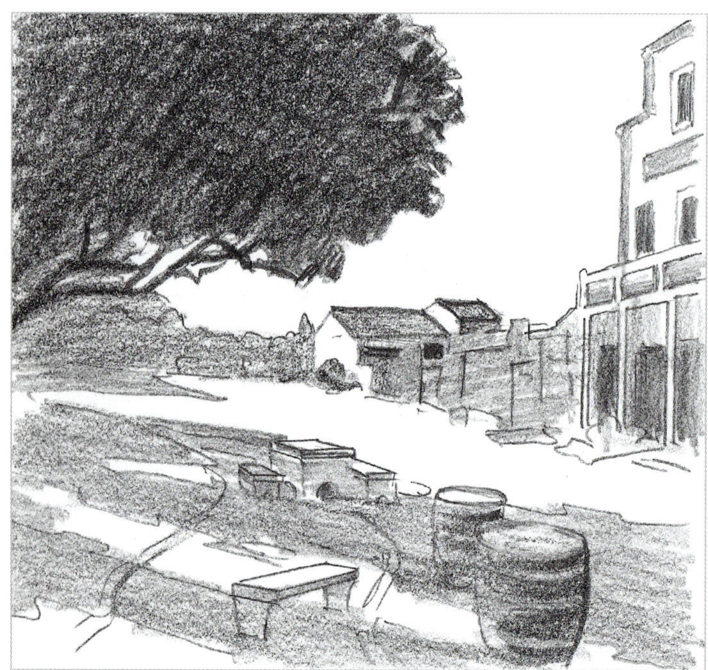

ROUGH VALUE STUDY Now shade in the three main values you intend to use: The tree is the darkest value, the shadows and background are middle values, and the rest is light. This is not a final, detailed value study—just a rough guide to recognize the light and dark families as you proceed toward the final rendering shown on page 239.

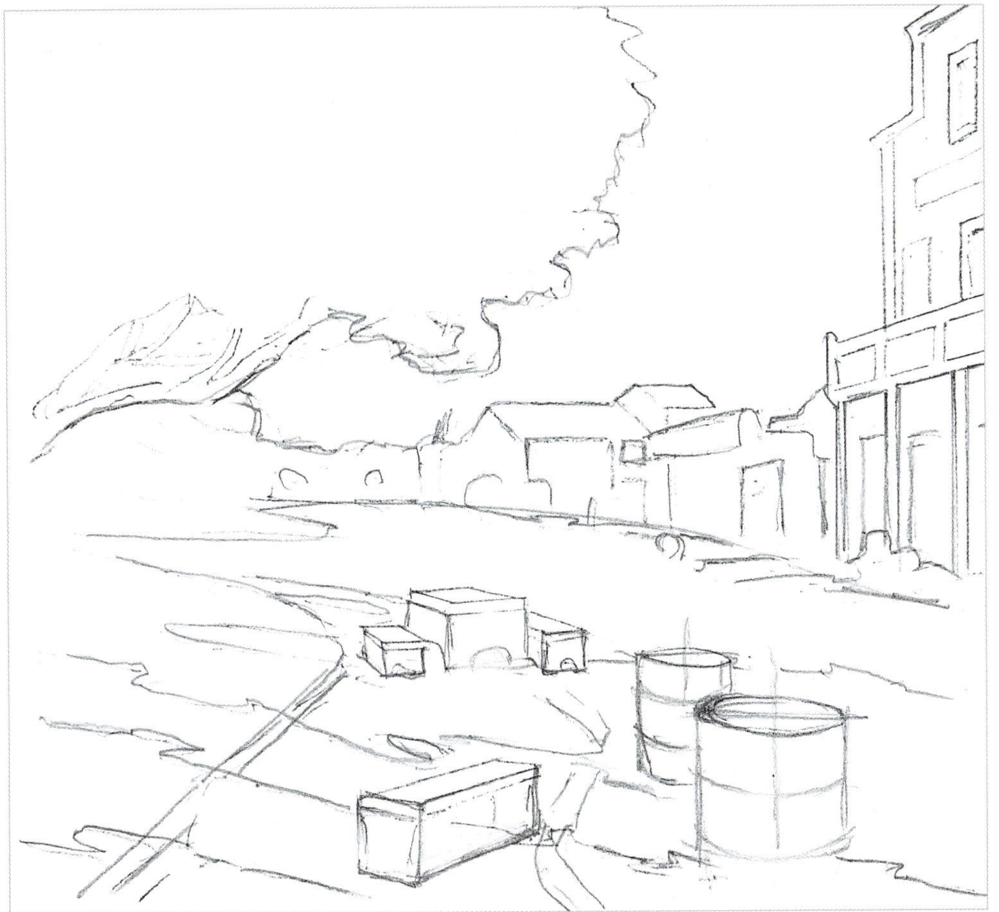

STEP 1 Using an HB pencil, lightly block in the general composition, paying special attention to the perspective on the benches, table, and barrels. These shapes, if drawn correctly, will give an indication of the artist's eye level, which is slightly above them.

STEP 2 Now further refine the shapes and begin to lay in darker values with underhand strokes. Don't get as dark as the value study yet to be sure that the shapes of the foreground shadows are placed correctly.

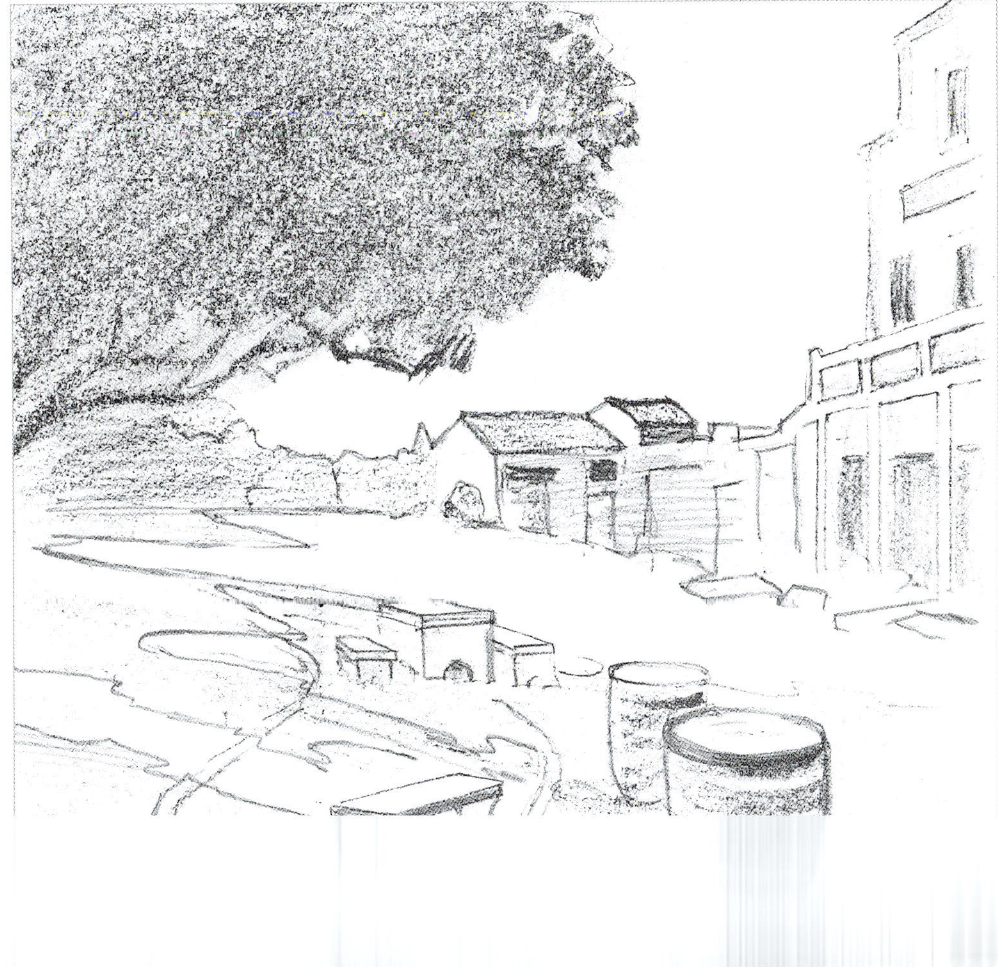

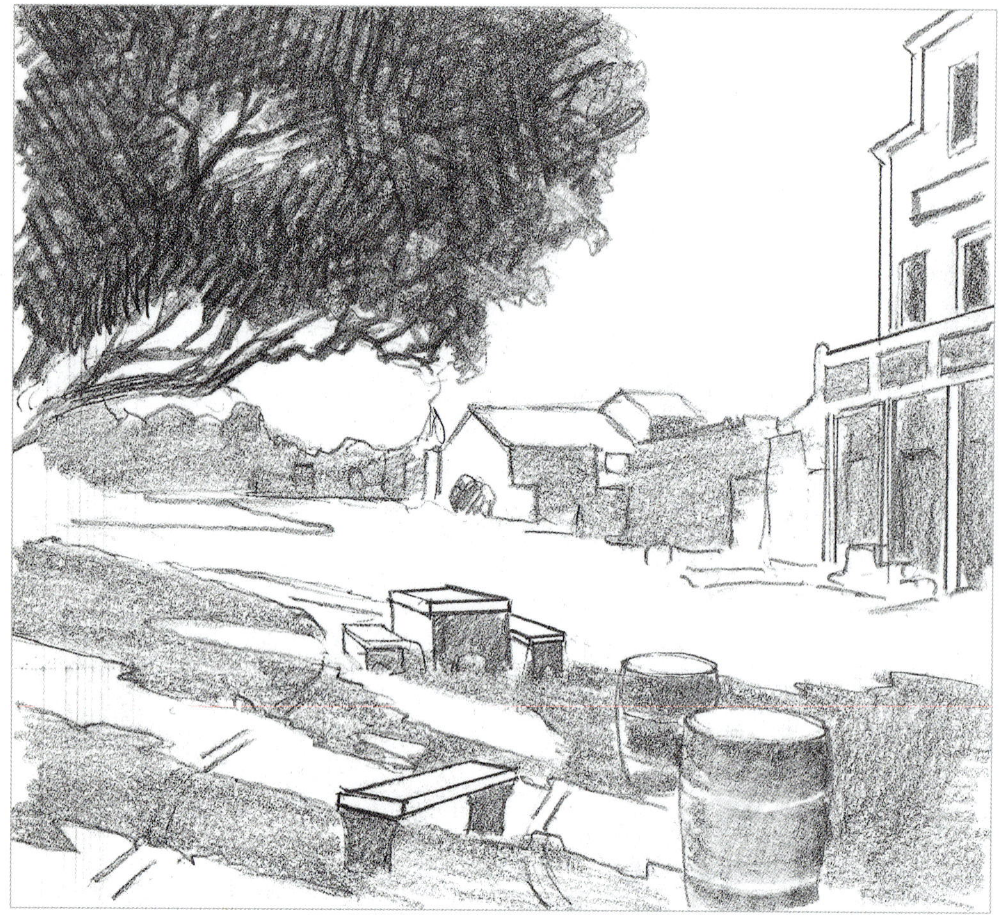

STEP 3 At this point, take out your softer 2B and 4B pencils and carefully refine the areas of value. Now the darkest shadows are about as dark as the value study, and now you can focus on adding textures while maintaining the correct values.

STEP 4 At this stage, begin to experiment with various textures, but do not completely finish any particular area. Add details such as palm trees in the background, the gradated sky, and the dark windows and doorways.

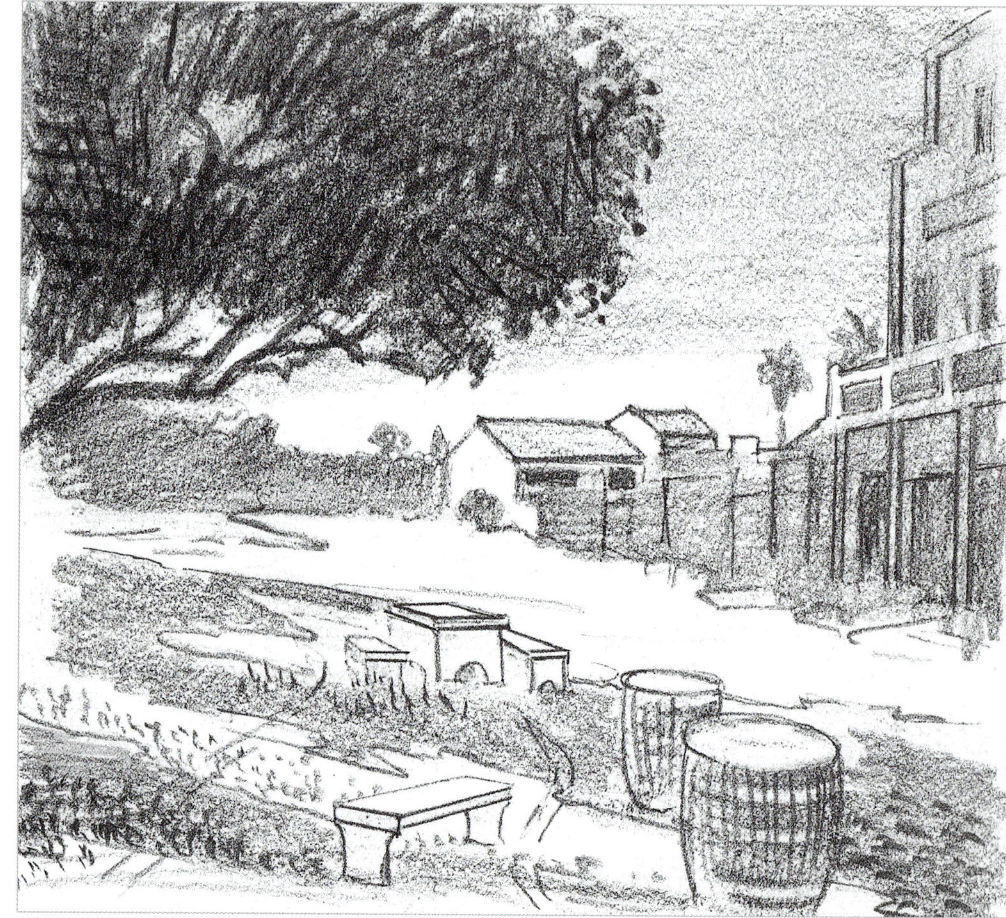

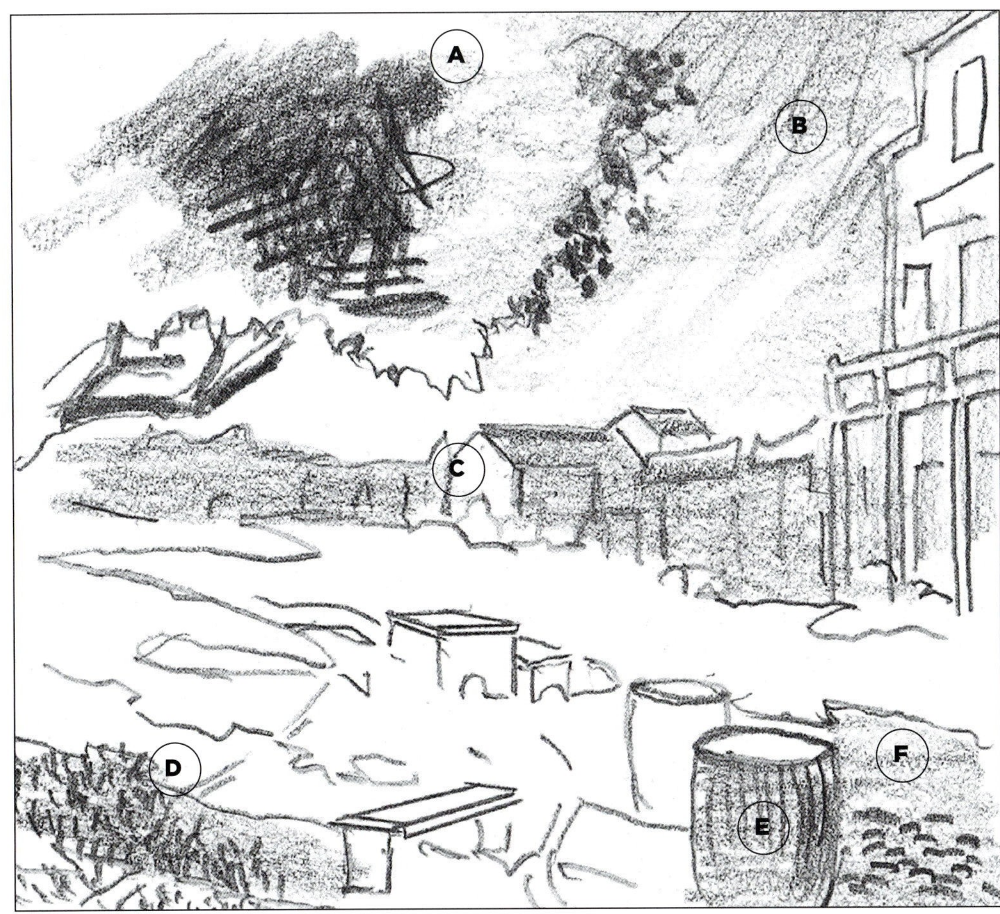

ADDING TEXTURES Use these strokes to finish the drawing: darken the tree with 4B and 6B pencils, combining sidestrokes and cross-hatching (A). For the sky, combine sidestrokes, linear strokes, and some erasing to lift out lighter streaks (B). For the background, use sidestrokes and an eraser (C). For the grassy area in the foreground, use sidestrokes and grassy strokes (D). Darken the barrel with sidestrokes and linear, vertical strokes (E). The dirt is—appropriately—dirt texture (F).

STEP 5 Complete the drawing by adding value and texture. The addition of larger figures in the middle ground and smaller figures in the background helps create depth. Note how to employ aerial perspective by giving the objects in the foreground the most detail. The darker foreground shadows add to the illusion of depth by contrasting the lighter middle ground and background.

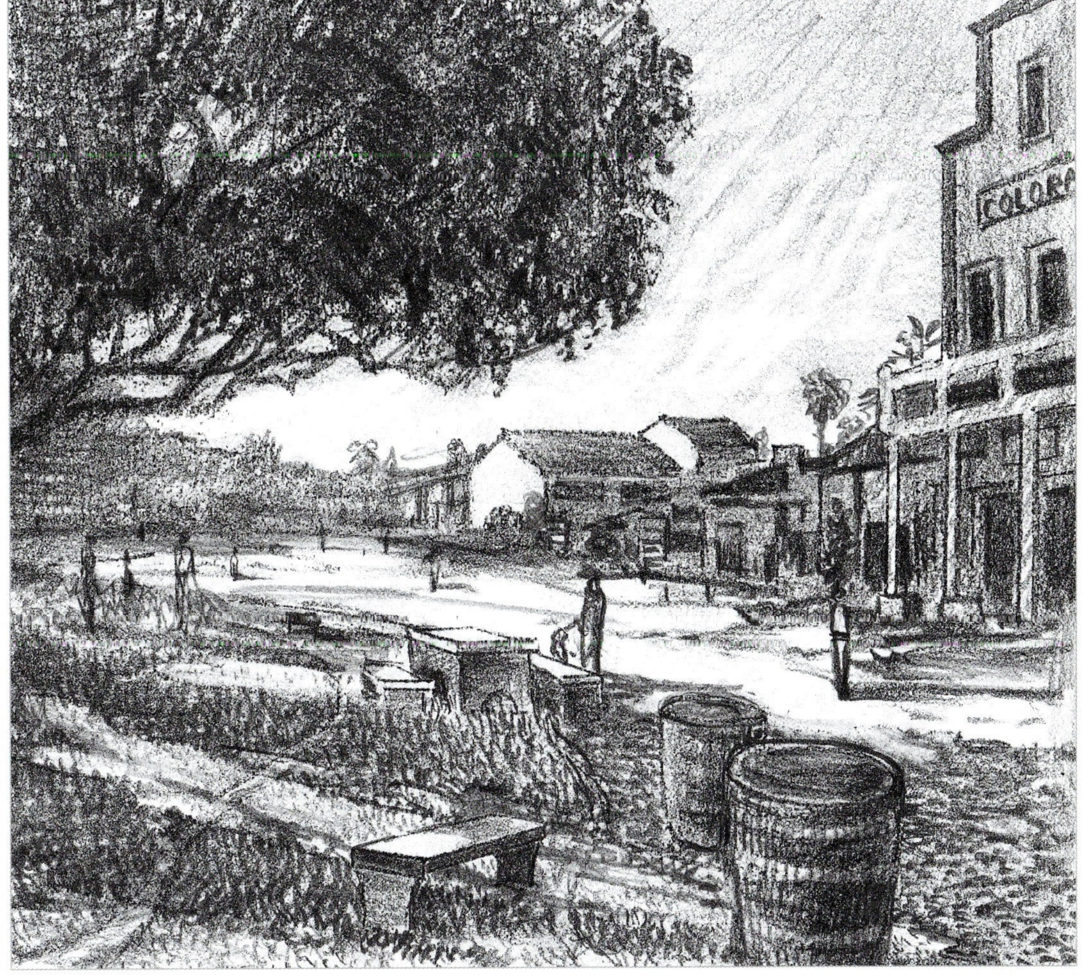

About the Author

JIM DOWDALLS

Jim Dowdalls is an accomplished medical illustrator, working with healthcare-industry clients for more than 25 years. His illustrations have won numerous awards from the Society of Illustrators and the Association of Medical Illustrators. He has created illustrations for some of the top pharmaceutical and medical product corporations, international advertising agencies, and periodicals in the United States and abroad. Jim is currently the Art Department Chair at Fullerton College in Fullerton, CA., where he teaches representational drawing, life drawing, and illustration. In addition, he is also an adjunct lecturer in the Medical Illustration program at Cal State Long Beach, his alma mater.

Other Contributors

STEVEN PEARCE

Like many artists, Steven Pearce got his start at a very early age. His mother was an accomplished oil painter, and his father was an oil painter, sculptor, and master jeweler. He enjoys experimenting with other media, including charcoal, colored pencil, oil, and acrylic. Steven loves drawing portraits, still life, wildlife, landscapes, and anything that represents well in graphite and charcoal.

CYNTHIA KNOX

Cynthia Knox is an award-winning artist who specializes in works of traditional realism. She is a Signature Member of the Colored Pencil Society of America, a juried member of the International Guild of Realism, a commissioned portrait artist, and an occasional art instructor.

EILEEN SORG

Eileen Sorg created her company, Two Dog Studio, in 2000 after graduating from the University of Washington with a B.S. in wildlife science., and now spends much of her time creating custom artwork for her many clients. Eileen is a signature member of the Colored Pencil Society of America and a juried member of the International Guild of Realism and the Society of Animal Artists in New York. Her work is represented in several regional galleries.

M. RAMOS

M. Ramos is a Brazilian artist who's worked with pointillism and stippling since 2000. He currently lives in São Paulo, Brazil, where he works in a studio and spends his time drawing, teaching art classes, and creating a webcomic called *Gem Café Racing War*. His works range from editorial and scientific illustrations to commissioned art and are featured in private collections in Brazil, the United States, and Europe.

MARLA BAGGETTA

A prolific painter and teacher, Marla's artwork and workshops are nationally sought after. Her work has been represented throughout the country for over 30 years. Contributing to many art publications such as Pastel Journal, she is a signature PSA member and an IAPS Master Circle Recipient.

WILLIAM SCHNEIDER

William A. Schneider's work has evolved since he finished his studies at the American Academy of Art. He is now a recognized member of Oil Painters of America, the Pastel Society of America, and The International Association of Pastel Societies. William's work is featured in many publications and galleries across the U.S.

NATHAN ROHLANDER

Nathan Rohlander's bright, vibrant paintings have been featured in the pages of Esquire and Shuz magazines, on the cover of Coast magazine, in Super Bowl commercials, in numerous television shows, and even in MTV videos. Having graduated with honors and a fine arts degree from the Art Center College of Design in Pasadena, California, Nathan is currently working toward a master of fine arts at California State University, Long Beach.

KEN GOLDMAN

Ken Goldman is a popular instructor at the Athenaeum School of the Arts in La Jolla, California, where he teaches portraiture, artistic anatomy, and landscape painting classes. He received his training in New York at the Art Students League, National Academy of Design, and New York Studio School. Ken's artwork is now featured in the permanent collections of several major museums.